WEB DESIGN
IN A NUTSHELL

A Desktop Quick Reference

WEB DESIGN
IN A NUTSHELL

A Desktop Quick Reference

Second Edition

Jennifer Niederst

O'REILLY®

Beijing • Cambridge • Farnham • Köln • Paris • Sebastopol • Taipei • Tokyo

Web Design in a Nutshell, Second Edition

by Jennifer Niederst

Copyright © 2001, 1999 O'Reilly & Associates, Inc. All rights reserved.
Printed in the United States of America.

Published by O'Reilly & Associates, Inc., 101 Morris Street, Sebastopol, CA 95472.

Editors: Lorrie LeJeune and Richard Koman

Production Editor: Emily Quill

Cover Designer: Edie Freedman

Printing History:

> January 1999:   First Edition.
>
> September 2001:   Second Edition.

ISBN: 0-596-00196-7

[C]

Table of Contents

Part IV: Multimedia and Interactivity

Part V: Advanced Technologies

Part VI: Appendixes

Preface

In the beginning, the Web was simple. When I first encountered it in early 1993 (working for O'Reilly's Global Network Navigator), there was only one browser for viewing web pages, and it ran exclusively on the Unix platform. There were only about a dozen tags that did anything interesting. Designing a web page was a relatively simple task.

It didn't stay simple for long. With the explosion of the Web came an avalanche of new technologies, proprietary tags, and acronyms. Even for someone who is immersed in the terminology and environment on a professional basis, it can be truly overwhelming. You just can't keep all this stuff in your head anymore.

Since leaving O'Reilly's Cambridge, MA offices for a freelance career, I never feel more alone than when I get stuck—whether it's because I don't know what audio format to use for a project, or I just can't remember what tag uses that MARGINWIDTH attribute. And I'm not ashamed to admit that I've been reduced to tears after battling a table that mysteriously refused to behave, despite my meticulous and earnest efforts.

It's at times like these that I wish I could walk down the hall and get advice from an expert co-worker. Without that luxury at my home office, I do the best I can with the volumes of web design information available online (on the Internet, no one knows you have red, puffy eyes). Unfortunately, finding the answer to a specific question is a time-consuming and sometimes equally frustrating process in itself. Deadlines often can't accommodate a two-hour scavenger hunt.

I wrote *Web Design in a Nutshell* because it was the book I needed—one place to go to find quick answers to my questions. Apparently, lots of other folks needed it too, as it went on to be a best-seller and found a permanent home on the desks of web designers around the globe.

The difficult thing about writing about the Web is that it's a moving target, constantly changing and evolving. A lot has happened with the Web since I wrote the first edition in 1998. We've seen new technologies emerge and others fade away. The raging browser wars have quieted and the industry is inching towards standards compliance. Countless software versions have come and gone.

This new edition has been thoroughly reviewed and revamped to reflect the new web design environment. All HTML chapters have been updated to reflect the 4.01 specification, and the browser support information now reflects Microsoft Internet Explorer 6 (in beta as of this writing) and Netscape 6. In keeping with current trends, there is a new emphasis on creating web pages according to standards—using HTML for structure and Cascading Style Sheets for all style information. Although traditional nonstandard web tricks are still included for the sake of thoroughness, they are presented in a more cautionary tone.

In addition to the buff and shine on existing chapters, I've added a number of new chapters on important topics, including: printing pages from the Web (Chapter 5), making web pages accessible to users with disabilities (Chapter 6), Flash and Shockwave (Chapter 26), multimedia presentations with SMIL (Chapter 27), XHTML (Chapter 31), and designing for the wireless web with WML (Chapter 32). I'm pleased to say that this edition is a significant improvement over the last.

Contents

This book focuses on the front-end aspects of web design: HTML authoring, graphics production, and media development. It is not a resource for programming, scripting, or server functions; however, whenever possible, I have tried to provide enough background information on these topics to give designers a level of familiarity with the terminology and technologies. The content in this book is appropriate for all levels of expertise—from professionals who need to look up a particular detail, to beginners who may require full explanations of new concepts and individual tags.

The book is divided into six parts, each covering a general subject area.

Part I, *The Web Environment*

Part I introduces some broad concepts about the way the Web works, which should orient designers to the peculiarities of the medium. It ends with an introduction to the server and basic Unix concepts.

Chapter 1, *Designing for a Variety of Browsers*, looks at how differing browser capabilities affect design decisions.

Chapter 2, *Designing for a Variety of Displays*, discusses varying monitor resolutions and accessibility issues and their effects on the design process.

Chapter 3, *Web Design Principles for Print Designers*, introduces how the Web deals with color, graphics, and fonts. This is particularly useful for those accustomed to print; however, it is also essential background information for any new web designer.

Chapter 4, *A Beginner's Guide to the Server*, provides a primer on basic server functions, system commands, uploading files, and file types.

Chapter 5, *Printing from the Web*, shows you how to control the way your pages look when they're printed.

Chapter 6, *Accessibility*, covers ways in which you can make your pages accessible to users with hearing, sight, cognitive, or motor skills impairments.

Chapter 7, *Internationalization*, addresses key issues for internationalization, including character sets and new language features in HTML 4 and CSS2.

Part II, *Authoring*

Part II focuses on HTML tags and their use. Most chapters begin with a listing of available tags with short descriptions (for easy access), followed by more detailed explanations and practical advice for their use.

Chapter 8, *HTML Overview*, gives a detailed introduction to HTML syntax, including how to specify color and special characters.

Chapter 9, *Structural HTML Tags*, lists the tags used to establish an HTML document and structure its contents, including settings that control or pertain to the whole document.

Chapter 10, *Formatting Text*, lists all tags related to the formatting of text elements in an HTML document.

Chapter 11, *Creating Links*, lists HTML tags related to linking one document to another, including imagemaps.

Chapter 12, *Adding Images and Other Page Elements*, focuses on the tags used for placing objects such as images, rules, or multimedia objects on a web page.

Chapter 13, *Tables*, provides everything you'd ever want to know about tables, including a list of table-related HTML tags, troubleshooting tips, and templates for popular table structures.

Chapter 14, *Frames*, covers the structure and creation of framed documents, including explanations of frame-related HTML tags, as well as tips and tricks.

Chapter 15, *Forms*, lists all tags related to form creation and provides an introduction to working with CGI scripts.

Chapter 16, *Specifying Color in HTML*, covers the two methods for specifying colors in web documents: RGB values and color name.

Chapter 17, *Cascading Style Sheets*, describes how to use CSS to control presentation of HTML documents, including detailed explanations of available selectors, properties, and values. It also introduces CSS Level 2 features and provides tips for style sheet use.

Chapter 18, *Server Side Includes*, provides an overview of Server Side Includes, including their capabilities and listings of the available elements and variables.

Part III, *Graphics*

The chapters in Part III provide background information on web graphics file formats as well as overviews of available tools and practical tips for graphic production and optimization.

Chapter 19, *GIF Format*, describes the popular GIF format and provides tricks for working with transparency and minimizing file sizes.

Chapter 20, *JPEG Format*, describes the JPEG format and provides tips on minimizing file sizes.

Chapter 21, *PNG Format*, shows you when and how to use this powerful graphic file format.

Chapter 22, *Designing Graphics with the Web Palette*, discusses the tools and techniques used in creating graphics with colors from the Web Palette.

Chapter 23, *Animated GIFs*, looks at the creation and optimization of those flashing, bouncing, and wiggling animated GIFs.

Part IV, *Multimedia and Interactivity*

The chapters in Part IV focus on the animation, audio, and interactive capabilities of the Web.

Chapter 24, *Audio on the Web*, provides an overview of tools and file formats for creating nonstreaming and streaming audio on the Web.

Chapter 25, *Video on the Web*, provides an overview of basic technology and concepts for creating nonstreaming and streaming video on the Web.

Chapter 26, *Flash and Shockwave*, looks at Macromedia's Flash and Director Shockwave formats.

Chapter 27, *Introduction to SMIL*, provides an introduction to how SMIL works and the elements used to control the timing and display of multimedia presentations.

Part V, *Advanced Technologies*

Part V provides overviews of key technologies that allow implementation of advanced features in web sites.

Chapter 28, *Introduction to JavaScript*, provides a general introduction to JavaScript as well as a number of templates for creating popular effects such as event handlers, browser-detection, and status-bar messages.

Chapter 29, *Introduction to DHTML*, provides a basic overview of Dynamic HTML and related concepts.

Chapter 30, *Introduction to XML*, briefly introduces XML (Extensible Markup Language) and explains why it is significant.

Chapter 31, *XHTML*, reviews the differences and similarities between HTML 4.0 and XHTML.

Chapter 32, *WAP and WML*, begins with a brief introduction to WAP and application development. The second half of the chapter focuses on WML and how it works, including a summary of the elements and attributes in the current WML specification.

Part VI, *Appendixes*

Part VI provides lots of useful look-up tables for HTML tags and CSS elements.

Appendix A, *HTML Elements*, lists all HTML tags as listed in the HTML 4.0 specification of April 1998. This list also serves as an index to finding full tag explanations throughout the book.

Appendix B, *List of Attributes*, lists all attributes and their respective tags and values.

Appendix C, *Deprecated Tags*, lists all tags that have been "deprecated" (discouraged from use) by the HTML 4.0 specification.

Appendix D, *Proprietary Tags*, lists tags that work only with Netscape Navigator or Internet Explorer.

Appendix E, *CSS Support Chart*, lists all CSS properties and the browsers that support them.

Appendix F, *Character Entities*, lists all characters not found in the normal alphanumeric character set. The first part of this appendix presents the standard HTML character entities. The second part presents newly added entities in the HTML 4.0 specification that are not as well supported

The Glossary defines many of the terms used in the book.

Conventions Used in This Book

The following typographical conventions are used in this book:

`Constant width`
 is used to indicate HTML tags, code examples, and keyboard commands.

`Constant width italic`
 is used to indicate replaceable text in code.

Italic
 is used to indicate variables, filenames, directory names, URLs, and glossary terms.

This icon designates a note, which is an important aside to its nearby text.

This icon designates a warning relating to the nearby text.

Request for Comments

Please address comments and questions concerning this book to the publisher:

O'Reilly & Associates, Inc.
101 Morris Street
Sebastopol, CA 95472
(800) 998-9938 (in the United States or Canada)
(707) 829-0515 (international/local)
(707) 829-0104 (fax)

There is a web page for this book, which lists errata and additional information. You can access this page at:

http://www.oreilly.com/catalog/wdnut2/

To comment or ask technical questions about this book, send email to:

bookquestions@oreilly.com

For more information about books, conferences, software, Resource Centers, and the O'Reilly Network, see the O'Reilly web site at:

http://www.oreilly.com

Acknowledgments

A small army of people were instrumental in the writing of this book. First, I'd like to thank my editor, Lorrie LeJeune, for her support and for keeping this project pleasant despite its breakneck schedule. I also greatly appreciate the time and attention of executive editor Paula Ferguson, who really knows how to whip a book into shape. Thanks also to Richard Koman, the editor of the first edition, which provided a solid foundation for this current edition.

Thanks to Bill Peña for writing chapters on JavaScript and DHTML (despite his many other duties at O'Reilly).

This edition was greatly improved by the thoughtful comments of a bevy of technical reviewers: Lane Becker (for his thorough cover-to-cover treatment), Ian Graham (and his uncanny knowledge of HTML and XML), Eric Meyer (Mr. CSS), Greg Roelofs (King of PNG), Timothy Plumer, Jr. (Adobe Acrobat), Lisa Coen (Flash and Shockwave), Josh Beggs (audio), Derek Story and Steve McCannell (video), and Bob Eckstein (WAP and WML).

Thanks also go to Ron Woodall, creator of the HTML Compendium, which provided the basis for the browser support charts in the first edition. I encourage you to check out the Compendium's site (*http://www.htmlcompendium.org*) for a complete list of tags and attributes, both current and obsolete, with detailed descriptions and browser support information.

Thanks to the following people who provided various forms of assistance, information, and tools I required to get my job done: Paul Anderson (Builder.com); Andrew King (Webreference.com); Kevin Lynch (Macromedia); and Doug Meisner and Timothy Plumer, Jr. (Adobe Systems, Inc.).

I also want to recognize the efforts of O'Reilly's great production team. Leanne Soylemez worked as the developmental editor; Emily Quill handled production; Anne-Marie Vaduva graciously provided tools support; and Rob Romano and Jessamyn Read updated the figures. I'd also like to thank Tim O'Reilly for his careful crafting of the "In a Nutshell" series and for giving me the green light on this book back in 1998.

Finally, I'd like to thank my Mom, Dad, and brother Liam for their unending support and the inspiration they each provide. And last, but not least, warm thanks go to my new husband, Jeff Robbins, for keeping life interesting and love-filled.

PART I

The Web Environment

CHAPTER 1

Designing for a Variety of Browsers

Most web authors agree that the biggest challenge (and headache!) in web design is dealing with the variety of browsers and platforms. While the majority of HTML elements are reliably rendered in most browsers, each browser has its own quirks when it comes to implementation of HTML and scripting elements.

Features and capabilities improve with each new major browser release, but that doesn't mean the older versions just go away. The general public tends not to keep up with the latest and greatest—many are content with what they are given, and others may be using the computers of a company or institution that chooses a browser for them. The varying functionality of browsers has a strong impact on how you author your site, that is, which web technologies you can safely use to make your site work.

How do you design web pages that are aesthetically and technically intriguing without alienating those in your audience with older browsers? Does a page that is designed to be functional on all browsers necessarily need to be boring? Is it possible to please everyone? And if not, where do you draw the line? How many past versions do you need to cater to with your designs?

There is no absolute rule here. While it's important to make your content accessible to the greatest number of users, experimentation and the real-world implementation of emerging technologies is equally important to keep the medium pushing forward. The key to making appropriate design decisions lies in understanding your audience and considering how your site is going to be used.

This chapter provides background information, statistics, and current wisdom from professional web designers that may help you make some of these decisions. It begins with an introduction to the most common browsers in use today, their usage statistics, and supported features. After describing the browser landscape, it discusses various design strategies for coping with browser difference and, finally, what's being done in the industry to set things straight again.

Browsers

Before you can develop a strategy for addressing various browser capabilities, it is useful to have a general knowledge of the browsers that are out there. While web browsing clients are increasingly being built into small-display devices such as PDAs, telephones, and even car dashboards, this chapter focuses on the traditional graphical computer-based browsers that developers generally keep in mind. The particular needs of handheld devices are discussed further in Chapter 32.

The "Big Two"

The browser market is dominated by two major browsers: Microsoft Internet Explorer and Netscape Navigator. As of this writing, Internet Explorer is in Version 5.5 for Windows (5.0 for Macintosh) and the Navigator browser is one component of Netscape 6 (they did not release a Version 5). Together, the "Big Two," including their collective past versions, account for over 95% of browser use today.

Since 1994, these two contenders have battled it out for market dominance. Their early struggle to be cooler than the next guy has resulted in a collection of proprietary HTML tags and incompatible implementations of new technologies (JavaScript, Cascading Style Sheets, and most notoriously Dynamic HTML). On the positive side, the competition between Netscape and Microsoft has also led to the rapid advancement of the medium as a whole.

Netscape publishes information for developers at *http://developer.netscape.com*. Information about the Netscape 6 release can be found at *http://home.netscape.com/browsers/6/index.html*.

For information on designing for Internet Explorer, visit Microsoft's Internet Explorer Developer Center (part of its MSDN Online developer's network) at *http://msdn.microsoft.com/ie/default.asp*. Additional information is available on the Microsoft product pages at *http://www.microsoft.com/windows/ie/* (for Windows) and *http://www.microsoft.com/mac/products/ie/* (for Macintosh).

 Although Netscape's browsing component is still officially called Navigator, Netscape seems to be downplaying "Navigator" and promoting its latest product release simply as Netscape 6. Because this is the title that has stuck with the industry, this book refers to "Netscape 6," but uses "Navigator" for previous releases.

Other Browsers

Most web authors base their designs on the functionality of Navigator and Internet Explorer on Windows systems, since they claim the lion's share of the market; however, there are a number of other browsers you may choose to take into consideration.

Internet Explorer on the Macintosh

For better or worse, Internet Explorer releases for the Macintosh platform have varied in functionality from their Windows counterparts. Web usage statistics indicate that Mac users account for just 2–3% of global web traffic, but if your site has Mac-targeted content, keep the following browser differences in mind.

IE 5.0 for the Mac (the current version as of this writing) was the first browser on any platform to be almost fully standards-compliant, thanks to its specially developed Tasman rendering engine (see "The Importance of Standards" later in this chapter). In general, you can treat Mac IE5.0 like Windows IE5.5 or Netscape 6.

The Macintosh version of IE4.0 lacks significant functionality found in its Windows sibling. This Mac version has no embedded font support, no support for CSS filters and transitions (such as drop shadow effects), and a very problematic DHTML implementation. Some of these issues were addressed in Version 4.5 (the first Mac version that significantly deviated from the Windows version). As a general guideline, treat Mac IE4.0 and 4.5 like Navigator 3.0.

America Online

America Online subscribers use a variety of Internet Explorer browsers, ranging from Version 2 to 5.5 (the most current as of this writing). The browser version number is not necessarily tied to the AOL release, as noted in this excerpt from AOL's developer site:

> Beginning with Windows AOL 3.0 (32-bit), the AOL client does not have a browser embedded, but instead uses the Internet Explorer browser the user already has installed within their system. On the Mac and 16-bit Windows clients, the AOL client contains various versions of Internet Explorer embedded directly within the client, and independent of the version of Internet Explorer installed outside AOL in the system. Therefore, browser compatibility is mostly independent of any specific AOL version.

As of this writing, approximately 80% of AOL users view the Web on Windows machines using Internet Explorer 5.0 or higher. While this is encouraging news, the reality is that Internet Explorer's functionality is limited somewhat when used in conjunction with the AOL client. This is due to the way the specific AOL clients interact with the browser and AOL's reliance on proxy servers and image compression techniques. Many web designers have been horrified to see their site design (which works perfectly in all the major browsers) once it's been run through the AOL system.

Fortunately, AOL publishes a site specifically for web developers who want their sites to be accessible and attractive to AOL users. Of particular use is the browser chart, which provides a specific listing of each of its browsers (by release and platform), the technologies and features supported, and a breakdown in percentage of users for each browser. It also provides a style guide for optimizing web pages for its newly released AOLTV set-top browsing device.

AOL's web developer site can be found at *http://webmaster.info.aol.com.*

WebTV

WebTV was the first to bring web surfing to the living room with a set-top box, an ordinary television, and a remote control (an optional keyboard is also available). WebTV uses its own specialized browser for viewing web pages.

The WebTV browser supports HTML 3.2 (plus a few 4.0 tags and handful of WebTV proprietary tags), graphics, tables, frames (with some problematic behavior), forms, cookies, JavaScript 1.2, a subset of the CSS1 Style Sheets specification, a wide variety of audio and video formats, and Flash 3. The browser does not support Java, PDF files, or streaming Flash formats.

Because WebTV displays web pages on televisions, it introduces new concerns regarding color and screen size.

WebTV publishes a developers' resource where you can find specific information regarding developing sites for WebTV (*http://developer.webtv.net*). It includes information on HTML and various web technology support.

You may also choose to download their free tool called WebTV Viewer (available for both Windows and Mac, although the Windows version is more up to date as of this writing). WebTV Viewer shows how your web page will look and perform on WebTV, right from the comfort of your own computer. For information on WebTV Viewer, go to *http://developer.webtv.net/design/tools/viewer/Default.htm*.

Opera

Opera, in Version 5.0 as of this writing, is a lean and mean little browser created by Opera Software in Oslo, Norway. It is currently available for Windows and Linux platforms, although the Opera 5 for Mac beta version was released in mid-2001. Opera is free if you don't mind ad banners as part of the interface. To register the browser and get rid of the ads, the price is $39.

Opera boasts extremely quick download times and a small minimum disk requirement (around 2 MB, compared to IE's 24 MB download). Opera is respected for its exact compliance with HTML standards. Sloppy tagging that gets by the larger browsers (such as missing closing tags, improper nesting, etc.) does not render correctly in Opera.

Opera 5.0 supports Java, HTML 4.01, Cascading Style Sheets (CSS1 and the vast majority of CSS2), JavaScript, and DHTML. While it does accept plug-ins, the word on the street is that they are somewhat difficult to install.

The general public is not likely to flock to Opera, and it never so much as blips in the browser statistic charts; however, many designers continue to test their sites in Opera to make sure their code is clean.

For more information about Opera, see *http://www.opera.com*.

Lynx

Last, but not least, is Lynx, a freely distributed, text-only browser that offers fast, no-nonsense access to the Web. It stands proud as the lowest common denominator standard against which web pages can be tested for basic functionality. Lynx may be a simple browser, but it is not stuck in the past. Lynx is constantly being improved and updated to include support for tables, forms, even JavaScript. People do use Lynx, so don't be surprised if a client demands a Lynx-compliant site design. Lynx is also important to users with disabilities who browse with Lynx and a speech or braille device.

The Extremely Lynx page is a good starting point for finding developer information for Lynx. You can find it at *http://www.crl.com/~subir/lynx.html*.

For information on designing Lynx-friendly pages, see *http://www.crl.com/~subir/lynx/author_tips.html*.

Browser Usage Statistics

Knowing which browsers are out there is just part of the battle. What really matters is how many people are actually using them. Browser usage is constantly shifting, so it is important to keep up with the latest trends.

Whether you use a free general statistics listing or your own server logs, knowing what browsers are most used can be helpful in deciding which technologies to adopt and where to draw the line for backwards compatibility. For instance, if you find that for some reason 45% of visitors to your site are still using Version 3 browsers, you might not want to switch your site over to style sheets just yet.

Browser Usage Resources

There are several methods for tracking browser usage: log analysis tools which you run on your own server, free general statistics listings, and professional statistics services.

Server log analysis

The most meaningful statistics are those culled from your own site's usage. There are software tools designed just for this purpose, all of which work basically the same way.

When a browser accesses files from a server, it leaves a record of that transaction on the server, including a little data about itself: specifically, its version and the platform it is running on. This information is known as the *user agent string*, and it is used by analysis software to generate statistics about the browser usage for a site. A typical user agent string might look like this:

```
Mozilla/4.0 (compatible; MSIE 5.5; Windows 98)
```

There are dozens of log analysis tools available at a wide variety of costs. Many are listed in the Yahoo! Directory under Business and Economy → Business to Business → Communications and Networking → Internet and World Wide Web → Software → World Wide Web → Log Analysis Tools.

You may also choose to sign up with a service such as The Counter (see *http://www.thecounter.com*) that puts a counter on your web page and provides usage stats on the page for free (in exchange for ad placement on your page). Other companies, such as SuperStats from MyComputer.com (*http://www.superstats.com*) provide remote analysis of your server for a monthly fee.

The Mozilla Legacy

The "Mozilla" identifier at the beginning of a typical user agent string is an interesting artifact from the earliest days of the browser wars. Netscape first released its browser under the codename Mozilla. Mozilla, for its time, was a fairly turbo-powered browser, so webmasters began targeting their content to it specifically.

When competing browsers (most significantly, Microsoft Internet Explorer) began featuring similar capabilities, they didn't want to be left out of the targeting action, so they put "Mozilla" in their user agent identification as well. Eventually, everyone was doing it, so the only way to truly identify the browser version was to include it in parentheses (such as MSIE 5.5 in the previous example).

Targeted statistics consulting

If you want fairly accurate browser usage statistics, but your own site isn't up and running yet, you may hire the services of a user trends consultant to analyze similar site usage. One such company is StatMarket (*http://www.statmarket.com*). They offer statistics on a subscriber basis and can customize the statistics reports to match the needs of individual businesses.

General statistics listings

If you are interested in a general breakdown of overall browser usage, there are a number of web sites that provide listings for free. They also offer usage statistics on other useful criteria such as screen resolution and various web technologies.

The Counter (*http://www.thecounter.com/stats/*) bases its global statistics on millions of visitors using hundreds of thousands of web sites registered with their service. This is an easy (and free) way to get a good general overview of browser usage.

BrowserWatch (*http://browserwatch.internet.com*) bases its statistics on visitors to its own pages and the Internet.com family of sites, which they admit skews the data towards developers, journalists, and other technically inclined visitors. BrowserWatch provides statistics that are meticulously broken down by version, sub-version, and sub-sub-version for each particular browser. They also provide useful news articles about the latest trends in browsers.

Current Browser Usage Trends

As of this writing, the current trend in browser usage is the dominance of Internet Explorer due to its integration with the Windows operating system. In mid-1997, Netscape Navigator enjoyed a comfortable 70–80% of overall browser usage (according to statistic sites such as those listed above); by 1998, that share was down to 50%. Currently, the various versions of Internet Explorer claim over 80% of browser usage, with some estimates even higher.

Browser statistics change much faster than book publishing schedules, so the statistics presented below are not necessarily meaningful. If you are completely unfamiliar with the typical browser breakdowns, however, these statistics from BrowserWatch (based on visits to Internet.com) should give you an idea of who's using what—as of this writing of course. These were the numbers presented on May 1, 2001:

Microsoft Internet Explorer 5.x	77.63%
Microsoft Internet Explorer 4.x	9.53%
Netscape Navigator 4.x	8.33%
Netscape Compatible	2.74%
Unknown User Agents	0.59%
Mozilla 5.x	0.30%
Opera x.x	0.25%
Netscape 3.x	0.22%
Microsoft Internet Explorer 3.x	0.21%
Microsoft Internet Explorer 2.x	0.20%

Again, the most meaningful browser usage statistics are those gathered from your own site.

Browser Features

Once you've determined the browsers of choice for the majority of your audience, you can make better decisions regarding which HTML tags and web technologies are safe to incorporate into your design. Likewise, you can determine how much of your audience you risk alienating by relying on certain features such as Java or DHTML.

Every HTML tag in Part II of this book is accompanied by a chart indicating which browsers support it. Exceptional attribute support (or lack thereof) is noted in the descriptions following each tag.

Table 1-1 provides a general listing of popular browsers and the web features and technologies they support. Bear in mind that although a browser may claim to support a given technology, there may be slight exceptions or irregularities in its support.

This table uses the following key:

✓   Supported

✗   Not supported

P   Partially supported

M   Mostly supported

Table 1-1: Browser Support

Browser	HTML 3.2	HTML 4.01	Animated GIFs (GIF89a)	Tables	Frames	Plug-ins	Java	JavaScript	Style Sheets (CSS1)	Style Sheets (CSS2)	DHTML	XML
Windows												
MSIE 5.5	✓	✓	✓	✓	✓	✓	✓	✓	✓	✓	✓	✓
MSIE 5.0	✓	✓	✓	✓	✓	✓	✓	✓	✓	✓	✓	✓
MSIE 4.0	✓	P	✓	✓	✓	✓	✓	✓	✓	P	✓	—
MSIE 3.0	✓	✗	✓	✓	✓	✓	✓	✓	✓	✗	✗	✗
MSIE 2.0	✗	✗	✗	✓	✗	✗	✗	✗	✗	✗	✗	✗
MSIE 1.0	✗	✗	✗	✓	✗	✗	✗	✗	✗	✗	✗	✗
Netscape 6.0	✓	✓	✓	✓	✓	✓	✓	✓	✓	✓	✓	✓
Navigator 4.7	✓	P	✓	✓	✓	✓	✓	✓	✓	P	✓	✗
Navigator 4.5	✓	P	✓	✓	✓	✓	✓	✓	✓	P	✓	✗
Navigator 3.0	✓	✗	✓	✓	✓	✓	✓	✓	✗	✗	✗	✗
Navigator 2.0	✓	✗	✓	✓	✓	✓	✓	P	✗	✗	✗	✗
Navigator 1.0	✗	✗	✗	✓	✗	✗	✗	✗	✗	✗	✗	✗
AOL 3.0 (Win95)	✓	✗	✓	✓	✓	✓	✓	✓	✗	✗	✗	✗
AOL 3.0 (Win3.0)	✓	✗	✓	✓	✓	✓	✗	✓	✗	✗	✗	✗
Opera 5.0	✓	✓	✓	✓	✓	✓	✓	✓	✓	✓	✓	?
Opera 4.02	✓	✓	✓	✓	✓	P	✓	✓	✓	P	no	✓
Opera 3.0	M	✗	✓	✓	✓	✗	✗	✓	✗	✗	✗	✗
Lynx	✓	✗	no	✓	✓	✗	✗	✗	✗	✗	✗	✗
Macintosh												
MSIE 5.0	✓	✓	✓	✓	✓	✓	✓	✓	✓	✓	✓	P
MSIE 4.0	✓	P	✓	✓	✓	✓	✓	✓	P	✗	✓	✗
MSIE 3.0	✓	✗	✓	✓	✓	✓	✓	✓	✗	✗	✗	✗
MSIE 2.1	✗	✗	✗	✓	✓	✓	✗	✗	✗	✗	✗	✗
Netscape 6.0	✓	✓	✓	✓	✓	✓	✓	✓	✓	✓	✓	✓
Navigator 4.74	✓	P	✓	✓	✓	✓	✓	✓	✓	P	✓	✗
Navigator 4.5	✓	P	✓	✓	✓	✓	✓	✓	✓	P	✓	✗
Navigator 4.06	✓	P	✓	✓	✓	✓	✓	✓	P	✗	✓	✗
Navigator 3.0	✓	✗	✓	✓	✓	✓	✓	✓	✗	✗	✗	✗
Navigator 2.0	✗	✗	✓	✓	✓	✓	✗	P	✗	✗	✗	✗
Navigator 1.0	✗	✗	✗	✓	✗	✗	✗	✗	✗	✗	✗	✗
AOL 3.0	✓	✗	✓	✓	✓	✓	✗	✗	✗	✗	✗	✗
AOL 2.7	✗	✗	✗	✗	✗	✗	✗	✗	✗	✗	✗	✗
iCab	✓	P	✓	✓	✓	✗	P	✗	P	P	P	✗

Table 1-1: Browser Support (continued)

Browser	HTML 3.2	HTML 4.01	Animated GIFs (GIF89a)	Tables	Frames	Plug-ins	Java	JavaScript	Style Sheets (CSS1)	Style Sheets (CSS2)	DHTML	XML
Unix												
MSIE 5.0	✓	✓	✓	✓	✓	✓	✓	✓	✓	✓	✓	✓
MSIE 4.01	✓	P	✓	✓	✓	✓	✓	✓	P	✗	✓	✗
Netscape 6.0	✓	✓	✓	✓	✓	✓	✓	✓	✓	✓	✓	✓
Navigator 4.6	✓	P	✓	✓	✓	✓	✓	✓	✓	P	✓	✗
Navigator 4.06	✓	P	✓	✓	✓	✓	✓	✓	P	✗	✓	✗
Navigator 3.0	✓	✗	✓	✓	✓	✓	✓	✓	✗	✗	✗	✗
Navigator 2.0	✗	✗	✓	✓	✓	✓	✗	P	✗	✗	✗	✗
Navigator 1.1	✗	✗	✗	✓	✗	✗	✗	✗	✗	✗	✗	✗
Lynx	✗	✗	✗	✓	✓	✗	✗	✗	✗	✗	✗	✗
Set-Top												
WebTV	✓	✗	✓	✓	✓	P	✗	✓	✓	P	✗	✗
AOL TV	✓	✗	✓	✓	✓	P*	✗	✓	✗	✗	✗	✗

* Quicktime 2.5 and Flash 3 only.

Design Strategies

Faced with the dilemma of varying browser capabilities, web designers have developed a variety of design approaches, some more extreme than others. The "correct" way to handle a particular site, of course, depends on its use and audience, but this section should provide a peek into the different positions in the ongoing debate over where to draw the line.

Lowest Common Denominator Design

One way to make sure your pages are accessible to everyone is to stick with the safest HTML standard (such as HTML 3.2) and shun any extras. That way your pages are sure to work on all browsers, including Lynx and Version 2.0 of the popular browsers.

A minority of web developers take the position that the current embellishments to HTML (Java, JavaScript, DHTML, and plug-in technologies like Flash) are unnecessary to successful communication over the Web. Designers who design for the lowest common denominator may choose not to use any of these technologies in their designs. This approach reflects the conservative extreme of the range of web design strategies.

Current Version Design

Another minority, at the other end of the spectrum, are the web developers who design *only* for the most current version of popular browsers (as of this writing,

Netscape 6.0 and Internet Explorer 5.5), with little concern for site performance for other users. The statement "Tell them to upgrade—it's *free!*" has often been used in defense of this design tactic. Beyond this, there are even designers who design for only the most current version of one *particular* browser or platform. This may be perfectly appropriate for intranet design in organizations that have standardized on a particular version of a single browser, but in general, it's unrealistic.

This approach has the obvious disadvantage of alienating a significant percentage of the audience. If the functionality of a site depends on a specific trick—for example, if you can't get off the front page without DHTML support—then your site has problems communicating. On the positive side, these designers tend to be the ones who forge new territories and put new technologies to the test. Creating exciting sites that depend on cutting-edge features does create an incentive for users to keep themselves up-to-date. Unfortunately, in many cases, upgrading is out of the control of the end user.

Splitting the Difference

Far more commonly, designers take a more balanced approach to web site creation. Designing web pages that "degrade gracefully" is the buzz phrase in web design circles. This design incorporates cutting-edge web technologies, such as DHTML or JavaScript, but implements them in such a way that the pages are still fully functional on older browsers.

One strategy is to design pages that take advantage of technology supported in the previous version of major browsers. As of this writing, that would be the Version 4.0 browsers. So, tables, frames, and much of JavaScript are fine, but DHTML effects may still be a problem.

The trick is to code your page such that it degrades well for older or more simple browsers. Simply being careful about always adding alternative text for images with the ALT attribute will make a web page more functional for Lynx users. When tables are used, they can be constructed so they read logically when scanned by a text-only browser.

Once working pages are developed using Version 4.0 technologies (while keeping an eye on performance on older browsers), the site can be embellished using the latest techniques and tricks. For instance, it is possible to create a page that looks just fine for all browsers but also takes advantage of Cascading Style Sheets for those browsers that can use them. It doesn't hurt the other browsers; the up-to-date users just get something extra. The same goes for DHTML tricks. They're fine as long as they're not used to carry the crucial message or functionality of the site. Think of these things as icing on the cake.

By being mindful of how well elements degrade, you can construct pages that wow 'em on the current browsers but don't drive users away if they're using an earlier version.

Something for Everyone

An approach that is common (albeit more labor-intensive) among professional web developers is to create multiple versions of a site aimed at different levels of users. One site might incorporate DHTML tricks and JavaScript events. Another could be a solid HTML 3.2–compliant site with images and attractive page layouts, but without the bells and whistles. You could create a text-only version to serve the folks using Lynx, nonvisual browsers, and browsers on handheld electronic devices. If you were feeling ambitious, you could provide an all-Flash version of your site for those who are interested. In most cases, two carefully planned versions are plenty: one that takes advantage of the full functionality of the latest graphical browser and another stripped-down version that serves everyone else.

Some sites allow their users to decide which version they'd like to see. It's not uncommon to arrive at a site and be asked to choose between a souped-up version or a text-only version, or to choose frames/no-frames or Flash/no Flash. This puts the control in the hands of the viewer.

A more sophisticated approach is to automatically serve up an appropriate version of the page for the browser that is making the request. JavaScript is capable of performing actions based on the browser being used (see Chapter 28). Pages can also be assembled on the fly for a particular browser using Server Side Includes (see Chapter 18). Hotwired's WebMonkey site is a great example of this method in action, plus they share their secrets, so check it out at *http://www.webmonkey.com.*

Of course, this approach takes a bit more time and technical know-how, but it has its rewards.

Take Advantage of Tools

Whether you are designing with particular browsers in mind or with the goal of reaching the widest browser audience possible, the good news is that there are tools that can help you. The latest web authoring tools, such as Macromedia Dreamweaver and Adobe GoLive, have functions that ensure that your code will work with your preferred browsers. They give you a good head start toward creating HTML properly for your intended audience.

Dreamweaver 4.0 has a "Check Target Browser" feature that checks your HTML (but, unfortunately, not scripts) against a list of browser profiles to see if any tags or attributes are unsupported and then generates a report with its findings. Go to Macromedia's site (*http://www.macromedia.com*) to download browser profile updates as new browsers are released. To take some of the guesswork out of browser support for scripting, Dreamweaver allows you to set a target browser, to which it responds by limiting the behaviors you can select to just those supported in that browser. There are also built-in functions for doing browser detection.

Similarly, Adobe GoLive lets you define a set of browsers you want to support and automatically lets you know if it finds HTML tags or attributes that are not supported. Select the set of browsers you want to support using the Browser Sets option under the Source category in the Preferences dialog box. In fact, GoLive has a Web Database feature that lists all the HTML tags and their browser-support information. You can also select a target browser when adding scripts to your page and use the Browser Switch icon to detect the browser version and serve the appropriate script.

Knowing Your Audience

As with most design challenges, making appropriate decisions regarding which browsers to support and which new technologies to adopt largely depends on knowing your audience. Before designing a new site, be sure to spend plenty of time up front researching the likely platforms, browsers, technical savvy, and connection speeds of the users you are targeting. If you are redesigning an existing site, spend time with the server logs to analyze past site usage.

There are no browser-support guidelines that can anticipate every design situation; however, the following scenarios should start you thinking:

- If you are designing a scientific or academic site, you should probably pay extra attention to how your site functions in Lynx (or other graphics-free browsing environments), because Lynx is more commonly used on academic and scientific networks than by the Web community at large. In addition, since the academy tends to be more Unix-oriented, Netscape figures more prominently than Internet Explorer because it is better supported.

- If your site is aimed at a consumer audience—for instance, a site that sells educational toys to a primarily parent audience—don't ignore your site's performance and presentation in the AOL browsers or older browser versions.

- If you are designing for a controlled environment, such as a corporate intranet or, even better, a web-based kiosk, you've got it made! Knowing exactly what browser and platform your viewers are using means you can take full advantage of the bells and whistles (and even proprietary features) appropriate to that browser. If you are designing a standalone kiosk, you may even have the luxury of loading the fonts you want to use. Just be sure your design won't crash the browser since there won't be anyone there to restart it for you immediately. In these situations, the "current version design" strategy discussed earlier in this chapter is entirely appropriate (just don't get spoiled)!

- If your site is *about* the technology being used, such as SVG graphics or Beatnik audio, you have every right to expect users to use the appropriate browser or plug-in to catch up with your content. (But it might be nice to at least provide some screenshots or other alternative content to let the others know what they're missing!)

- If you are designing a government site, you are required by law under Section 508 to make your pages accessible to all browsing devices. For more information, see Chapter 6.

For most multipurpose web sites, stick with the safer "splitting the difference" approach to design, or if you have the resources, create multiple versions and serve them appropriately.

Test, Test, Test!

The final word in the dilemma of designing for a variety of browsers is *test*! Always test your site on as many browsers, browser versions, and platform configurations as you can get your hands on.

Professional web design firms run their sites through a vigorous quality assurance phase before going "live." They generally keep a bank of computers of varying platforms and processing powers that run as many versions of browsers (including Lynx) as possible.

If you do not have the resources to keep a similar setup on your own, make the site available on a private test site and take a look at it on your friends' computers. You might view it under corporate conditions (a fast Windows machine with a 6.0 browser and a T1 connection), then visit a friend at home to see the same site on AOL with a 28.8 modem. (If nothing else, this is a good excuse to get away from your computer and visit your friends!)

Although your pages will certainly look different in different environments, the idea is to make sure that nothing is outright broken and your content is being communicated clearly.

The Importance of Standards

The Internet was built on standards. When a need for functionality was identified (email attachments, for example) a person or group proposed a system to make it work. After a discussion phase, the proposal was made public in the form of a Request for Comments (RFC). The RFC process is overseen by the Internet Engineering Task Force (IETF), an international community of network designers, operators, vendors, and researchers concerned with the evolution of the Internet (see *http://www.ietf.org* for more information). Once the kinks were worked out, other developers adopted the method and a standard was born.

The Web, with its early explosion of excitement and opportunism, skipped over this traditional standards process. Although the World Wide Web Consortium (W3C), a group of industry experts and professionals who guide the evolution of the Web) began working on HTML standards in 1994, the browser software companies didn't wait for them.

Once Netscape Navigator popped up on the scene with its set of proprietary tags, they set in motion the process by which we've inherited the browser chaos outlined in this chapter. The problem only got worse as web design grew beyond simple HTML to encompass richer web technologies such as Cascading Style Sheets and DHTML. Not only does developing for a multitude of incompatible browsers cause headaches, but redundant development time also costs a lot of money.

It didn't take long for the development community to say, "Enough is enough!" and demand that the browser creators slow down and abide by the web standards set forth by the W3C. The champion of this effort is the Web Standards Project (WaSP). WaSP is a collective of web developers who are pushing hard for action.

Their first goal, of course, is to get all browsers to support the same standards for HTML and other web technologies. In an ideal world, there would be one way to code a page for a particular effect, and it would work exactly the same way on 100% of the browsers, regardless of platform. Although Netscape 6 and Internet

Explorer 5 (Mac) and Internet Explorer 5.5 (Windows) boast standards compliance, there are still a few bugs to work out. It will also take some years for older browser versions to fade away. But the current trend is encouraging.

WaSP also works hard to educate web developers on the need to observe standards. The end goal is total observance of standards, which means that web content and style information should be kept separate: the content in a structured HTML or XML document, and the instructions for how it is displayed contained in a style sheet. This becomes especially pertinent as we see more alternative browsing clients (such as wireless handheld devices with tiny screens) hitting the scenes. As long as web designers continue to use <font> and other hacks to the HTML concept, the standards effort is diluted and web content is not fully accessible.

The third community WaSP takes on is the developers of web authoring tools. Currently, the code generated by WYSIWYG authoring tools is far from standard (note the abundance of <font> tags and cheats for creating indents). It is essential that the available tools make it simple for developers to create web pages properly—using standard HTML for structure and style sheets for presentation.

Every web designer should be well versed in the importance of standards. For a thorough (albeit strongly opinionated) introduction, visit the Web Standards Project site at *http://www.webstandards.org*. To study the specifics, go right to the source, the World Wide Web Consortium's site at *http://www.w3.org*.

CHAPTER 2

Designing for a Variety of Displays

One of the most vexing aspects of web design is knowing that your page is at the mercy of the software and hardware configuration of each individual user. A page that looks great on your machine may look radically different, or perhaps even ghastly, when viewed on another user's setup. This is partly due to the browser's functionality (as discussed in Chapter 1) and the individual user's preferences (font size, colors, etc.), but the display device itself also plays a large part in the success of the page's design.

This chapter looks at the ways in which design decisions are influenced by the wide range of displays and viewing conditions. The variation in display is a function of the monitor's size (or, more accurately, its resolution), color capabilities, and user's personal preferences. However, it is important to keep in mind that the diversity does not end there. Some users may be watching your web page on TV. Still others may be viewing it in the palm of their hand on a PDA (personal digital assistant) or cell phone. Sight-impaired users may be listening to your page, not viewing it.

Dealing with Unknown Monitor Resolutions

Browser windows can be resized to any dimension, limited only by the maximum size of the monitor. Designing for an unknown amount of browser real estate is a challenge unique to web design and one that is particularly troublesome for designers who are accustomed to the printed page.

In discussion forums frequented by web design professionals, no topic is more often addressed (nor hotly debated) than the question of which monitor resolution to design for. As with most web design issues, there is no "right" way to design for the Web, and your decisions should always be guided by your knowledge of your target audience and the purpose of your site. Still, it is helpful to understand the environment and to know how others are maneuvering within it.

This section looks at the range of monitor resolutions and presents the current wisdom on making appropriate design decisions.

Standard Monitor Sizes and Resolutions

The first step in determining the likely size of your web page is to look at the maximum amount of space provided by the computer monitor. Computer monitors come in a variety of standard sizes, typically indicated in inches. Some typical monitor sizes are 15", 17", 19", 20", and 21".

The more meaningful measurement, however, is *monitor resolution*—the total number of pixels available on the screen. The higher the resolution, the more detail can be rendered on the screen. When you know the available number of pixels, you can design your graphics (also measured in pixels) and page elements accordingly. Table 2-1 presents a list of some standard monitor resolutions supported by Windows and Macintosh platforms. This is not a complete listing, merely the most commonly occurring configurations.

Table 2-1: Common monitor resolutions for personal computers

Windows	Macintosh
640×480	512×384
800×600	640×480
1024×768	800×600
1280×1024	832×624
1600×1200	1024×768
	1152×870
	1280×960
	1280×1024
	1600×1200

Resolution is related to but not necessarily determined by monitor size. Depending on the video card driving it, a single monitor can display a number of different resolutions. For instance, a 17" monitor can display 640×480 pixels, 800×600 pixels, or even higher.

It is important to keep in mind that the higher the resolution on a given monitor, the more pixels are packed into the available screen space. The result is smaller pixels, which will make your images and page elements appear smaller as well. If you create graphics and pages on a monitor with a relatively high resolution, say 1280×1024, be prepared for everything to look a lot bigger on standard 17" monitors running at 640×480.

For this reason, web measurements are made in pixels, not inches. Something that appears to be an inch wide on your system may look smaller or larger to other users. When you design in pixels, you know how elements measure in proportion to each other. Chapter 3 further discusses resolution as it applies to graphics.

"Live" Space in the Browser Window

Knowing the size of the monitor is just the beginning. The operating system and the browser itself occupy a fair amount of this space. The amount of space that is actually available within the browser window (referred to in this chapter as the browser window's "live" space) is dependent on the computer's operating system, the browser being used, and the individual user's preference settings.

Figure 2-1 measures the parts of the major browsers (menus, status bar, etc.) on both Windows and Macintosh platforms. Knowing these exact measurements may be useful when designing a pop-up window for which you can control the display of each part; you'll know just how large to size the window to fit your content. (The code for creating pop-up windows is provided in Chapter 28.)

Knowing how much space the system and browsers take up should tell us how much space is left over for content. Table 2-2 lists the amount of live space that is available at standard monitor resolutions. Measurements were taken with the browser maximized to fill the monitor and with all possible browser tools such as buttons, location bars, and scrollbars visible (except for Navigator's "My Sidebar" and IE's Explorer panel). In a way, this can be considered a worst case scenario for available space (with the browser maximized).

Table 2-2: Minimum live space at various monitor resolutions

| | *Minimum Live Space* | | | |
Browser	*640× 480*	*800× 600*	*1024× 768*	*1280× 1024*
Windows				
Internet Explorer 5+	620×303	780×423	1004×591	1260×847
Netscape 6	618×301	778×421	1002×589	1258×845
Netscape 4.7	620×286	780×406	1004×574	1260×830
Macintosh				
Internet Explorer 5	591×309	751×429	975×597	1231×853
Internet Explorer 4.5	592×316	752×436	976×604	1232×860
Netscape 6	607×322	767×442	991×610	1247×866
Netscape 4.7	613×307	773×427	997×595	1253×851

Bear in mind that these are theoretical extremes, and actual browser window dimensions will vary. Users may have some of the buttons showing, but not all of them. Scrollbars turn on and off automatically, so they are difficult to anticipate. Users with high monitor resolutions (1024 pixels wide and higher) do not necessarily open their browser windows to fill the whole area, but may keep several narrow windows open at the same time.

Fixed Versus Flexible Web Page Design

Closely related to the issue of varying monitor resolutions is the question of whether web pages should be designed to be flexible (resizing and adapting to various window sizes) or fixed at a particular size (giving the designer more control of the page's dimensions). There are very strong opinions on both sides, and there are good reasons for and against each approach, naturally.

You may find that you choose a fixed structure for some sites and allow others to be flexible, or you may have strong convictions that one or the other approach is the only way to go. Either way, it is useful to be familiar with the whole picture and the current opinions of professional web designers. This section attempts to present a balanced overview of the possibilities and the pitfalls.

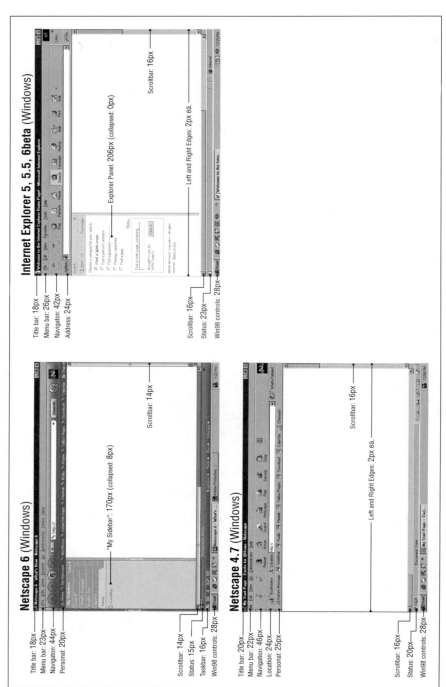

Figure 2-1: Browser and system measurements

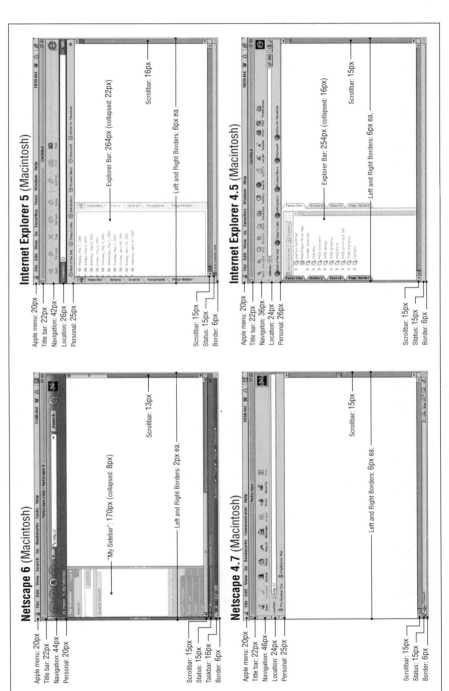

Netscape 6 (Macintosh)

Apple menu: 20px
Title bar: 22px
Navigation: 44px
Personal: 20px

"My Sidebar": 170px (collapsed: 8px)

Scrollbar: 13px

Left and Right Borders: 2px ea.

Scrollbar: 15px
Status: 15px
Taskbar: 16px
Border: 6px

Internet Explorer 5 (Macintosh)

Apple menu: 20px
Title bar: 22px
Navigation: 42px
Location: 26px
Personal: 25px

Explorer Bar: 264px (collapsed: 22px)

Scrollbar: 16px

Left and Right Borders: 6px ea.

Scrollbar: 15px
Status: 15px
Border: 6px

Netscape 4.7 (Macintosh)

Apple menu: 20px
Title bar: 22px
Navigation: 46px
Location: 24px
Personal: 25px

Scrollbar: 15px

Left and Right Borders: 6px ea.

Scrollbar: 15px
Status: 15px
Border: 6px

Internet Explorer 4.5 (Macintosh)

Apple menu: 20px
Title bar: 22px
Navigation: 36px
Location: 24px
Personal: 26px

Explorer Bar: 254px (collapsed: 16px)

Scrollbar: 15px

Left and Right Borders: 6px ea.

Scrollbar: 15px
Status: 15px
Border: 6px

Figure 2-1: Browser and system measurements (continued)

Flexible Design

Web pages are flexible by default. The text and elements in a straightforward HTML file flow into the browser window, filling all available space, regardless of the monitor size. When the browser window is resized, the elements reflow to adapt to the new dimensions. This is the inherent nature of the Web. Designers who are initially traumatized by the unpredictability of where page elements land usually just learn to let go of some control over the page.

Many designers make a conscious decision to construct pages so they can adapt to stretching and shrinking browser windows. This approach comes with advantages and disadvantages.

Advantages

The advantages of a flexible design include the following:

- The reality is that web pages *are* displayed on a variety of monitor resolutions and conditions; keeping the page flexible allows it to be "customized" for every display.

- Designing flexible pages is in keeping with the spirit and the nature of the medium. A "good" web page design by these standards is one that is functional to the greatest number of users.

- The whole window is filled, without the potentially awkward empty space left over by many fixed-width designs.

- You don't need to worry about choosing a target monitor resolution.

Disadvantages

Keep in mind, though, the following potential pitfalls of a flexible design:

- On large monitors, the text line length can get out of hand when the text fills the width of the browser. Long lines of text are particularly uncomfortable to read on a screen, so allowing the text to stretch to the full width of the window or frame risks poor reading conditions for some users.

- Elements float around on large monitors, making the design less coherent and potentially more difficult to use. Likewise, on very small monitors, elements can get cramped.

- The results of flexible design are unpredictable, and users will have varying experiences of your page.

Creating flexible pages

As noted previously, simple HTML files are flexible by default, so you don't need to do anything special to ensure flexibility. However, you can format your page layout and content using relative measurements so that elements resize in proportion to one another.

Tables and frames can be used to give the page a flexible structure. Tables are often used to create columns of text and to divide the page into logical sections.

By using relative (percentage) measurements for tables and cells, the table resizes with the browser window; however, the columns and elements remain proportional to one another. For instance, two columns with widths of 25% and 75% always retain those proportions, regardless of the table size. Sizing tables is discussed in Chapter 13.

Frames can also be used to add structure to a flexible design. They, too, can be specified with percentage values or to automatically fill any remaining space in the window. For instance, two frames with widths of 25% and 75% always retain those proportions, regardless of the size of the window in which they are displayed. The contents within each frame flow to fill the frame. Frames are discussed in Chapter 14.

The size of the content (text size, margins, images, etc.) can be set to relative sizes using Cascading Style Sheets. For instance, style sheets allow designers to specify measurements in *ems*, a unit used in printing to refer to the width of one capital letter "M". On the Web, an em translates to the font size; in other words, an em unit in 12-point text will be 12 points square. Using em measurements for text height, line length, leading, etc. ensures that page elements will scale proportionally with the user's chosen text preference. See Chapter 17 for more information on using style sheets.

Fixed Design

If you want more control over the layout of a page, you may opt to design a web page with a fixed width that stays the same for all users, regardless of monitor resolution or browser window size. This approach to web design is based on design principles learned in print, such as constant grid, relationship of page elements, and comfortable line lengths.

Advantages

These are the advantages of fixed design:

- The basic layout of the page remains the same regardless of monitor size. This may be a priority for companies interested in presenting a consistent corporate image for every visitor.

- Fixed-width pages and columns provide better control over line lengths. Tables can be used to prevent line lengths from becoming too long when the page is viewed on a large monitor.

Disadvantages

Consider also these disadvantages:

- If the available browser window is smaller than the grid for the page, parts of the page will not be visible and may require horizontal scrolling to be viewed. Horizontal scrolling is nearly universally considered to be a hindrance to ease of use, so it should be avoided. (One solution is to choose a page size that serves the most people, as discussed later in this section.)

- It is still difficult to control type size in browsers (see Chapter 3 for more information), so elements may shift unpredictably if the browser type is larger or smaller than the type used in the design process.

- Trying to exert absolute control over the display of a web page is bucking the medium. The Web is not like print; it has its own peculiarities and strengths. Advocates of the flexible design strategy will tell you that fixed web page designs are out of place on the Web.

Creating fixed pages

Fixed web page designs are created by putting all the contents of the page in a structural table with absolute measurements specified in pixels. Other tricks, such as sized transparent graphics or Netscape's proprietary `<spacer>` tag, may also be used to maintain consistent element placement or to hold specific amounts of white space on the page. Cascading Style Sheets also provide ways to set dimensions and placement of web page elements in specific pixel increments.

Some visual HTML authoring tools make it easy to create fixed-width designs. Most notably, Adobe GoLive (*http://www.adobe.com/products/golive/main.html*) has an option for laying out your page on a grid as though it were a page-layout program. GoLive then automatically generates the corresponding (and often complicated) table.

Pop-up windows

Some web sites take advantage of the ultimate in fixed web page design by automatically popping up a new window sized precisely for displaying the contents of the page. The advantage is that all viewers, regardless of their monitor size, see the page in a browser window with the proper dimensions (unless the window is set to a size larger than the monitor resolution). It gives the designer even more control over the presentation of the page.

This trick is achieved using JavaScript to launch a window with specific pixel dimensions, so the obvious disadvantage is that it will not work for users without JavaScript-enabled browsers. Furthermore, many users have a strong adverse reaction to having new windows spontaneously opened for them. It takes control of the presentation—and the entire desktop—away from the end user, which is unacceptable to many web designers. It can also be disorienting for users with disabilities. Many users have learned to automatically close pop-up windows before the content even has time to load in the window, rendering them ineffective. Finally, because users may have different font settings, text might wrap or be cut off in unpredictable ways. See Chapter 28 for a window-opening code example.

Combination Pages

Of course, web pages need not be all-fixed or all-flexible. It is certainly possible to create pages that are a combination of the two.

One common technique is to create a fixed page layout using a table, but then to center the table on the page so it is more balanced when displayed on large monitors (avoiding the "blank right screen" effect). The drawback to this technique is that when a table is centered, it can no longer be precisely placed over a background image. Some sites use color in the background image to reinforce the columns in a fixed page design, but unfortunately, the background image remains in the same place even when the table is allowed to recenter itself on the screen. (One possible solution is to center the background image using Cascading Style Sheets, but that trick is not universally supported.)

Another approach is to use a table or frameset that consists of a combination of absolute- and relative-sized column or frame measurements. With this method, when the window is resized, one column or frame remains the same width while the rest resize and reflow to fill the new available space. These techniques are outlined in Chapters 13 and 14.

Choosing a Page Size

Obviously, if you decide to design a fixed web page, you need to make a decision regarding which screen size you want it to fit. Common sense dictates that the page should be accessible (and display properly) to the greatest possible number of people. The idea is to find the most common monitor resolution and design pages that safely fill its live space.

640 × 480 versus 800 × 600

Although finding the most common monitor resolution sounds fairly simple, there remains some controversy over which resolution is the safest. Over the past few years, the number of users with 800×600 monitors or higher has grown substantially, leading many designers to believe that it is perfectly safe to create web pages that fill the 800×600 monitor live space. Other designers disagree, maintaining that 640×480 monitor users should still be taken into consideration.

The statistics

According to TheCounter (*http://www.thecounter.com*), the breakdown of users browsing the Web with various monitor resolutions in April 2001 is as follows:

640 × 480	6%
800 × 600	51%
1024 × 768	35%
1152 × 864	1%
1280 × 1024	3%
1600 × 1200	0%
unknown	1%

Of course, this is only an approximation based on traffic to a limited set of web sites. The only worthwhile statistics are those culled from your own server logs. You can install software to check browser resolution yourself, or sign up for tracking services such as TheCounter (free in exchange for ad placement) or for-pay services such as SuperStats (*http://www.superstats.com*) or StatMarket (*http://www.statmarket.com*).

The conventional wisdom

Because approximately 92% of users view web pages at resolutions of 800×600 or higher, professional web designers tend to consider 800×600 to be the standard web page size, as of this writing. More and more commercial web sites are being designed to these specifications. (Very few designers create pages for 1024×768 resolutions or higher.)

However, the low-end 640×480 monitor users are not being written off entirely. Even the small percentage of users with 640×480 monitors translates to millions of viewers.

Again, knowledge of your audience can help you make your design decision. For instance, if you are designing an online resource for graphic designers, you can be certain they will be using 800×600 pixel monitors or higher. An 800-pixel page width is also fairly safe for sites targeting other professional groups because office hardware is more likely to be upgraded regularly. However, if you are designing an educational site to be viewed in schools that may not have the budget for state-of-the-art hardware, the lowest-common-denominator 640×480 is a safer bet. The same goes for sites that are likely to be viewed in households, libraries, or other institutions where older hardware setups are still in use.

Remember that it is possible to use HTML and Cascading Style Sheets to design flexible pages that will resize to fit any window size. You don't need to choose one size or another.

If you are designing a site especially for WebTV (with its particularly small window size) or some other display device, you should follow the appropriate guidelines for those devices. And, as always, test your designs in as many monitor configurations as you can get your hands on to see how your page holds up under diverse conditions.

Designing "Above the Fold"

Newspaper editors have always designed the front page with the most important elements "above the fold," that is, visible when the paper is folded and sitting in the rack.

Likewise, the first screenful of a web site's homepage is the most important real estate of the whole site, regardless of whether the page is fixed or flexible. It is here that the user makes the decision to continue exploring the site or to hit the "Back" button and move along. Web designers have adopted the term "above the fold" to apply to the contents that fit in that important first screen. My personal experience shows that users tend not to scroll beyond the first page, even when the vertical scrollbar is visible. Thus, the first screen bears the entire burden of enticing users to stay at your site.

As discussed throughout this chapter, a "screenful" can be quite different depending on the resolution of the monitor. To play it absolutely safe, consider the space available for the lowest common denominator 640×480 monitor— approximately 600×300 pixels. That's not a lot of space!

Some elements you should consider placing above the fold include:

- The name of the site.

- Your primary marketing message.

- Some indication of what the site is about. For instance, if it is a shopping site, you might place the credit card logos or shopping cart in the top corner to instantly communicate that "shopping happens here."

- Navigation to other parts of the site. If the entire navigation device (such as a list of links down the left edge of the page) doesn't fit, at least get it started in the first screen; hopefully users will scroll to see the remainder. If it is out of sight completely, it is that much more likely to be missed.

- Any other information that is crucial for visitors to the site, such as a toll-free number or special promotion.

- Banner advertising. Advertisers may require that their ads appear at the top of the page.

Monitor Color Issues

Monitors also differ in the number of colors they are able to display, if they display colors at all. This is another aspect of the final display that may influence design decisions. Monitors typically display 24-bit color (approximately 17 million colors, also known as the "true color space"), 16-bit color (approximately 65,000 colors), or 8-bit color (256 colors). When colors taken from the "true" 24-bit color space are rendered in browsers on 8-bit monitors, many of the colors have to be approximated, and a speckled pattern (called *dithering*) may occur.

However, there is a set of 216 colors, made up from the cross-section of the Windows and Macintosh system palettes, that will not dither on Windows and Mac 8-bit displays. This set of colors is known as the *web palette*, among other names. Many designers choose to design web graphics and HTML elements using colors from this palette so the pages look the same for all users. The web palette is discussed thoroughly in Chapters 3, 15, and 22.

If you are concerned about users with grayscale or black and white displays, be sure to design graphics with good contrast. When colors are converted to grayscale values (or dithered with black and white pixels), only the brightness of the colors matters. Imagine setting purple text on a teal background; although the colors are of contrasting hues, they are close enough in overall brightness that the text will be illegible when the colors are displayed on a grayscale monitor.

Monitors also vary in the brightness of their displays, known as the *gamma* value. PC monitors tend to be much darker than Macintosh monitors, so colors that are deep and rich when created on a Mac may look black when displayed on a Windows machine. Likewise, graphics created in Windows may look washed out when viewed on a Mac. Gamma is discussed further in Chapter 3.

Alternative Displays

The Web isn't just for personal computers anymore! Web browsers are increasingly making their way into our living rooms, briefcases, and cars, in the form of WebTV, handheld PDA devices, cellular phones, and dashboard devices. These extra-small displays introduce new design concerns.

WebTV

WebTV, a device that turns an ordinary television and phone line into a web browser, hit the market in 1996 and is experiencing a slow but steady growth in market share. As of this writing, it is barely a blip on the radar screen of overall browser usage, but because numbers are increasing, some developers are taking its special requirements into consideration. Some sites are being developed specifically for WebTV.

WebTV uses a television rather than a monitor as a display device. The live space in the WebTV browser is a scant 544×378 pixels. The browser permits vertical paging down, but not horizontal scrolling, so wider graphics are partially obscured and inaccessible, or resized to fit. Principles for designing legible television graphics apply, such as the use of light text on dark backgrounds rather than vice versa and the avoidance of any elements less than 2 pixels in width. These and other guidelines are provided on WebTV's special developer site at *http:// developer.webtv.net*.

Of particular interest is WebTV Viewer, which shows you how your web page will look on WebTV, right from the comfort of your computer. It is available for free for both Windows and Mac (although the Windows version is more up-to-date as of this writing). For information on WebTV Viewer, go to *http://developer.webtv. net/design/tools/viewer/Default.htm*.

Hand-held Devices

The increased popularity and usefulness of the Web combined with the growing reliance on hand-held communications devices (such as palm-top computers, PDAs, and cellular telephones) has resulted in web browsers squeezing into the coziest of spaces. Typically, wireless devices are used to view applications designed especially for them (see Chapter 32), not the graphically-rich web sites that we are accustomed to on our computer browsers. Therefore, it is generally not necessary to worry about how your site will fare on a microbrowser.

The typical mobile phone with Internet capabilities has a display area that is between 95 and 120 pixels wide and 50 to 65 pixels high. Newer phones and PDAs may have larger screens (approximately 300 by 100 pixels). A more meaningful measurement than pixel size is the amount of text that can fit on the screen. In general, mobile browsers can display only three to six lines of text at a time with 12 to 20 characters per line.

The majority of mobile devices (particularly in North America) have only black and white LCD displays. However, in Japan, mobile devices with 8-bit color displays are growing in popularity.

CHAPTER 3

Web Design Principles
for Print Designers

If you are accustomed to designing for print, the Web introduces a number of new concepts and new ways of doing things. Part of what makes web design unique is that the pages are displayed on a computer monitor, not paper, requiring familiarity with new color models. In addition, you need to work within the unique environment of the web browser. The HTML markup language brings its own limitations to the mix.

This chapter discusses some basic web design concepts, which may be new for print designers or for anyone who is just getting started in web design. It provides necessary background information about the web environment, including how browsers deal with color, graphics, and typography, so that you can make design decisions that are appropriate to the medium.

The Web Is Not Like Print

Designing pages for the Web is fundamentally different from designing a printed page. The single most difficult challenge in making the transition from print to web design is that on the Web, you cannot control absolutely the way your page looks to the end user. The way the page displays is a function of the browser it is viewed on and the user's preference settings, as shown in Figure 3-1. By its nature, the Web forces designers to give up control over the very things designers are traditionally responsible for controlling, such as page size, alignment, fonts, and colors. The experience is a shock until you get used to it. Becoming a good web designer requires a solid understanding of the web environment in order to anticipate and plan for these shifting variables.

Designing for the Unknown

When you design a web page, you are creating a page that will be viewed under a vast range of unknown conditions. There are a number of factors that will directly impact the design and functionality of a web page.

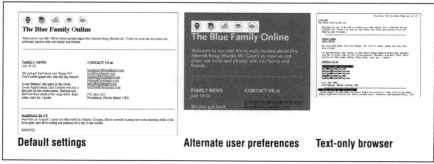

Default settings   **Alternate user preferences**   **Text-only browser**

Figure 3-1: The same HTML page viewed on different browsers and with different user preferences

Unknown browsers

As discussed in Chapter 1, there are hundreds of browser versions in use today. The same page source may look and function differently depending on the browser rendering it.

Unknown platform

The user's operating system also impacts how a web page looks and functions. Some technologies are better supported on Windows than on a Macintosh or Unix system. The platform also affects basic display elements, such as fonts, colors, and form elements.

Unknown user preferences

Every browser is built with the opportunity for users to set the default appearance of the pages they view. The user's settings will override yours, and there's not much you can do about it. Not only can users adjust the fonts and colors, but they may also opt to turn off basic functionality, such as image display, JavaScript, and Java support.

Unknown window size

In print, one of the first things you establish about a project is its trim size (the size of the printed page). On the Web, there is no way to know the size of the "page" since browser windows can fill a variety of monitor resolutions or be resized to any random dimension. This is discussed in Chapter 2.

Unknown connection speed

Most likely, the people viewing your pages access the Internet at a wide range of speeds: from high speed T1, cable, and DSL connections all the way down to pokey 28.8-kilobaud modems. Unless you are designing specifically for broadband applications, assume the worst when it comes to connection speeds. The golden rule of web design is to keep your files as small as possible. On the Web, graphics should measure just a few kilobytes (K). For commercial sites, pages with files totalling more than 50K or 60K are considered bloated (although it seems miniscule compared to file sizes typically used in desktop publishing for print).

Unknown colors

When you are publishing materials that will be viewed on computer monitors, you need to deal with the varying ways computers and browsers handle color. This is discussed later in this chapter.

Unknown fonts

It may come as a shock to learn that you cannot really specify fonts on web pages. The way text appears is a result of browser settings, platform, and user preferences. Typography on the Web is discussed later in this chapter.

To sum it up bluntly, there's no way to know exactly how your page will look or function for the end user. This is a tough pill to swallow for most print designers.

Surviving the Unknown

The best advice for conquering this new medium is to *let go* of some of the control you are accustomed to having over the page. Elements shift around, text resizes, and pages look different to different people. That's the way it works. Don't expect to design a page in Quark and have it reproduced precisely in a web browser or you're bucking the medium. Good web design is judged by a different set of criteria. On the Web, what's important is how a page works and that it is accessible to everyone. As a web designer, you will learn to design structures and impose a set of rules rather than fuss with absolute alignment. After a while, you will develop a feel for designing around the "unknowns" on the Web.

For an excellent explanation of the unique characteristics of web design and the new responsibilities it places on designers, read *The Art and Science of Web Design* by Jeffrey Veen (New Riders, 2001). And for a thoughtful essay on how to work with the medium, not against it, see "The Dao of Web Design" by John Allsopp, published on A List Apart (*http://www.alistapart.com/stories/dao/dao_1.html*).

Typography on the Web

HTML was created with the intent of putting ultimate control of the presentation in the hands of the end user. This principle makes its most resounding impact when it comes to typography. Take a look at your browser's preferences and you will find that you (and every other surfer) are able to specify the fonts and sizes that you prefer for online viewing.

For anyone accustomed to designing for other media, this loss of font control is cause for major frustration. From the time they discovered the Web, designers (and their corporate clients) have been pushing for ways to control typography in order to produce attractive and predictable web sites.

Great strides have been made in this effort since the early days of the Web and HTML 1.0; however, as of this writing, the font issue is still unfolding. This section discusses possible strategies and technologies (along with their advantages and disadvantages) for designing type in web documents.

You Have Two Fonts

About the only thing you can be sure of when you're designing web pages with basic HTML is that you have two fonts to work with: a proportional font and a fixed-width font. The problem is that you don't know specifically which fonts these are or at what size they will be displayed.

Proportional font

A *proportional font* (called "Variable Width Font" in Netscape Navigator) is one that allots different amounts of space to each character, based on its design. For instance, in a proportional font, a capital "W" takes up more horizontal space on the line than a lowercase "i". Times, Helvetica, and Arial are proportional fonts.

Web browsers use a proportional font for the majority of text in the web page, including body text, headings, lists, blockquotes, etc. In general, proportional fonts are easier to read for large bodies of text.

Because the majority of users do not take the time to change the default font in their browser preferences, you can make a *very* broad assumption that most of the text on your page will be displayed in 10- or 12-point Times (Navigator default) or Helvetica (the default in Microsoft Internet Explorer). Remember, this is only a very general guideline.

Fixed-width font

Fixed-width fonts (also known as "constant-width" or "monospace" fonts) are designed to allot the same amount of horizontal space to all characters in the font. A capital "W" takes up no more or less space than a lowercase "i". Examples of fixed-width fonts are Courier and Monaco.

Web browsers use fixed-width font to render type within the following HTML tags:

`<pre>`	Preformatted text
`<tt>`	Typewriter text
`<code>`	Code
`<kbd>`	Keyboard entry
`<samp>`	Sample text
`<xmp>`	Example text

Again, because most people do not change the default font settings in their browser preferences, you can make a reasonable guess that text marked with the above HTML tags will be displayed in some variation of Courier.

Text in Graphics

Designers quickly learned that the sure-fire way to have absolute control over font display is to set the text in a graphic. It is common to see headlines, subheads, and call-outs rendered as GIF files. Some web pages are made up exclusively of graphics that contain all the text for the page.

Advantages of GIF text

The advantage to using graphics instead of HTML text is fairly obvious—control!

- You can specify text font, size, leading, letter spacing, color, and alignment—all attributes that are problematic in HTML alone.

- Everyone with a graphical browser will see your page the same way.

Disadvantages of GIF text

As enticing as this technique may seem, it has many serious drawbacks. Many professional sites have adopted a "no text in graphics" rule. Keep the following disadvantages in mind when deciding whether to use graphics for your text.

- Graphics take longer to download than text. Graphics are likely to be many orders of magnitude larger than HTML text with the same content, and will result in slower downloads.

- Content is lost on nongraphical browsers. People who cannot (or have chosen not to) view graphics will see no content. Alternative text (using the `alt` attribute) in place of graphics helps, but this is a limited solution and not always reliable.

- Information in graphics cannot be indexed, searched, or copied and pasted. In effect, by putting text in a graphic, you are removing useful pieces of information from your document. Again, the `alt` attribute helps here.

Why Specifying Type Is Problematic

Cascading Style Sheets and the nonstandard `<font>` tag give web designers an added level of control over typography by enabling the specification of fonts and sizes. Although it is a step in the right direction, using these tags by no means guarantees that your readers will see the page exactly the way you've designed it.

Specifying fonts and sizes for use on web pages is made difficult by the fact that browsers are limited to displaying fonts that are already installed on the user's local hard drive. So, even though you've specified text to be displayed in the Georgia font, if users do not have Georgia installed on their machines, they will see the text in whatever their default font happens to be. Fortunately, HTML allows you to specify backup fonts if your first choice is not found (this technique is described in the "Specifying Fonts with <font>" section of Chapter 10).

Platforms also handle type size display in different ways. Using style sheets and the `<font>` tag is more like *recommending* fonts and sizes than actually specifying them.

Type size

Traditionally, type size is specified in points (there are approximately 72 points per inch), but unfortunately, point sizes do not translate well between platforms. In part, this is because their operating systems drive monitors at different resolutions. Typically, Windows uses 96ppi for screen resolution and the Mac OS uses 72ppi, but multiscan monitors allow higher resolutions.

On a Mac, a font is displayed at roughly the same size at which it would appear in print (e.g., 12pt Times on screen looks like 12pt Times on paper). Microsoft, however, threw out that convention and chose to display point sizes larger to make it easier to read on a monitor. As a result, 12pt type on a Windows machine is closer to 16pt type in print. To get 12pt print-size type on Windows, you need to specify a point size of 9 (but then Mac users will see that text at a nearly illegible 6.75pt type).

Selecting fonts for web pages

Each platform has its own set of standard fonts (and font file formats), making it difficult to specify any one font that will be found universally. Although there are many commercial fonts available for both Mac and PC, you can't assume that your audience will have them. The majority of users are likely to be content with the collection of fonts that are installed with their systems. Table 3-1 lists the fonts that are installed with various platforms.

Table 3-1: Fonts installed on Windows, Macintosh, and Unix platforms

Microsoft Windows (3.1x, 95, 98, NT, 2000, ME):
Arial (Bold, Italic)
Courier New (Bold, Italic, Bold Italic)
Times New Roman (Bold, Italic, Bold Italic)
Symbol
Wingdings
Lucida Sans Unicode (NT 3.x and higher only)
Marlett (95 and 2000 only)

Unix/Xfree bitmap fonts:
charter
clean
courier
fixed
helvetica
lucida
lucidabright
lucidatypewriter
new century schoolbook
symbol
terminal
times
utopia

Macintosh (System 7 and higher):
Chicago
Courier
Geneva
Helvetica
Monaco
New York
Palatino
Symbol
Times

Macintosh System 8 and higher, add:
Apple Chancery
Hoefler Text
Hoefler Text Ornaments
Skia

Macintosh System 8.5 and higher, add:
Capitals
Charcoal
Gadget
Sand
Techno
Textile

Macintosh OS X comes with all of the above and dozens of other "classic, modern, and fun" fonts

Microsoft Internet Explorer installs some fonts on users' systems as well. You can be certain that folks surfing the Web with IE will have the fonts listed in Table 3-2.

Table 3-2: Fonts installed with Internet Explorer

Internet Explorer (3 and 4):	Internet Explorer (4.5 and 5):
Arial Black	Andale Mono
Comic Sans (Bold)	Arial
Impact	Arial Black
Verdana (Bold, Italic, Bold Italic)	Comic Sans
Webdings	Courier New
	Georgia
	Impact
	Times New Roman
	Trebuchet MS
	Verdana
	Webdings
	Wingdings

Core fonts for the Web from Microsoft

The problem with reading text on web pages is that many fonts (most notably the ubiquitous Times) are difficult to read at small sizes. The serifs that aid readability in print are actually a hindrance when rendered with a limited number of black and white pixels.

Responding to the need for fonts that are easy to read on the screen, Microsoft has created a collection of TrueType fonts (for both Windows and Mac) that have been specially designed to be optimized for on-screen viewing. They distribute them for free with the hope that they might grow to be standard and "safe" fonts to specify in web documents. The Microsoft web fonts currently include:

Andale Mono (formerly Monotype.com)
Arial
Comic Sans
Courier New
Georgia
Impact
Times New Roman
Trebuchet MS
Verdana
Webdings (Windows only)

These fonts have generous character spacing, large x-heights, and open, rounded features that make them better for online reading. Georgia and Verdana were designed by esteemed type designer Matthew Carter, with hinting provided by Vincent Connare (who also designed Comic Sans and Trebuchet MS).

The complete set of TrueType core fonts for the Web is available for free via download at *http://www.microsoft.com/typography/fontpack/default.htm*.

Embedded Fonts

Both Navigator and Internet Explorer support technologies for embedding fonts in a web page, enabling your viewers to see your page exactly as you have designed it. Because the font travels with the HTML file, it is not necessary for the user to have the font installed on the client end in order for specified fonts to display. A few years ago, there was a fair amount of excitement about embedded fonts, but the interest has since waned and we are now left with two poorly supported and incompatible standards. In fact, Netscape opted to no longer support embedded fonts in its Version 6 release.

Not surprisingly, Netscape and Microsoft have lined up with competing technologies. Netscape, partnering with Bitstream (a font design company), created TrueDoc Dynamic fonts. Microsoft and Adobe worked together to develop Embedded OpenType.

Both technologies work basically the same way: a special font embedding tool is used to compress the type into a downloadable font file. This font file is referenced by the HTML document using the `<link>` tag. To use the font, just call it by name using Cascading Style Sheets or the `<font>` tag in the document. Users with browsers that support embedded font technology see your special fonts; otherwise, text is rendered in the browser's default font.

TrueDoc Technology ("Dynamic Fonts")

TrueDoc technology was developed by Bitstream in 1994, and in 1996, Netscape included "Dynamic Font" support in the Navigator 4.0 browser. Dynamic fonts are saved in the Portable Font Resource (*.pfr*) format. To create them, it is recommended that you use WebFont Wizard from Bitstream (available for both Windows and Mac; see Bitstream's web site at *http://www.truedoc.com*).

Browser support for TrueDoc is slightly better than its competitor but is still problematic. Dynamic fonts can be viewed on Navigator 4.x for Windows, Mac, and Unix, and Internet Explorer 4+ for Windows only. Internet Explorer users must download an ActiveX control for the WebFont Player in order to view Dynamic Fonts. Although dynamic fonts can be viewed on IE5.5, they cannot be printed. Netscape 6 has dropped embedded font support on all platforms, so TrueDoc works only on Netscape Version 4.x.

For more information on TrueDoc technology, see Bitstream's web site.

OpenType (for Internet Explorer)

OpenType technology was developed by Microsoft and Adobe. It uses the Embedded OpenType (*.eot*) file format, which can be created with Microsoft's WEFT (Web Embedding Font Tool). WEFT is freely available, but it works only on Windows systems. Embedded OpenType is currently supported only on Internet Explorer Versions 4 and higher running on Windows machines. Macintosh users are out of luck both creating and viewing OpenType on the Web.

For more information on Embedded OpenType, including options for downloading WEFT, see Microsoft's "Typography on the Web" page at *http://www. microsoft.com/typography/web/default.htm*.

Color on the Web

The Web requires designers to think about color in new ways. In part, it means understanding color in a more technical manner—the appearance of a page can benefit greatly if a designer knows what's going on "under the hood." The peculiarities of working with color in web design are functions of the following simple principles:

Monitors

> Web pages are displayed on computer monitors, therefore they follow the basic rules of how computers and monitors handle color.

Browsers

> Because browsers have built-in resources for rendering color when running on systems with limited color display capacity, they can alter the appearance of the colors in your pages.

HTML

> Colors on a web page that are not part of a graphic (for example, background and text colors) need to be properly identified in the HTML tags of the document. This topic is covered in more detail in Chapter 16.

Color on Computer Monitors

Color on monitors is made of light, so traditional systems for specifying color for print (CMYK, Pantone swatches, etc.) do not apply. Monitors differ in the number of colors they can display at a time. On the high end, 24-bit monitors are capable of displaying nearly 17 million colors. 16-bit monitors can display over 65 thousand colors. On the low end, 8-bit monitors are able to display only 256 colors at a time.

RGB color

Computer monitors display colors by combining red, green, and blue light. This color system is known as RGB color.

RGB color is a 24-bit system, with eight bits of data devoted to each of three color channels. Eight bits of data can describe 256 colors. With 256 possible colors in each of the three channels, the total possible number of colors is calculated by multiplying $256 \times 256 \times 256$ for a total of 16,777,216. That's more than enough colors to provide stunning representations of artwork and photography. 24-bit color is often referred to as the *true color space*.

Although all colors on computer monitors are made up of combinations of red, green, and blue light, there are actually a number of numerical systems for identifying colors, including RGB (red, green, and blue values), Lab (lightness, a channel, and b channel), and HSB (hue, saturation, brightness).

For purposes of web design, colors are referred to by their numerical RGB values, on a scale from 0 to 255. For instance, the RGB values for a particular dark orange color are R:198, G:83, B:52.

Palettes

Colors from the true color space can be approximated reasonably well on 16-bit monitors (see sidebar "Color Issues on 16-bit Displays" later in this chapter). 8-bit monitors make use of a *color palette*, a set 256 colors, to determine which colors to display at any one time.

For system-level operations, computers use a specific set of 256 colors called the *system palette*. Macs and PCs use slightly different sets of 256 colors in their system palettes. But specific applications may use their own palettes; for instance, browsers have a built-in palette, known as the *web palette*, which gets called into use only when the browser is used on an 8-bit monitor.

Gamma

Gamma refers to the overall brightness of a computer monitor's display. In more technical terms, it is a numerical adjustment for the nonlinear relationship of voltage to light intensity—but feel free to think of it as brightness. The default gamma setting varies from platform to platform. Images and pages created on a Macintosh generally look a lot darker when viewed on a Windows or Unix/Linux system. Images created on Windows machine generally look washed out when seen on a Mac. The higher the gamma value, the darker the display. Table 3-3 shows the standard gamma settings for the major platforms.

Table 3-3: Common default gamma settings

Platform	Gamma
Macintosh	1.8
PC	2.2
Unix	2.3-2.5

Because the vast majority of users are viewing the Web from the Windows environment, gamma differences are of particular concern to developers who are designing pages and graphics on a Macintosh. However, if you are designing under Windows and anticipate a large percentage of Mac traffic to your site (such as a site for graphic designers), be sure to test your pages under Macintosh gamma conditions.

Several popular web graphics tools come with utilities for simulating or adjusting gamma levels:

Adobe Photoshop Gamma Control Panel
> **For the Mac.** Adobe Photoshop comes with a Gamma control panel that affects the gamma setting for the whole monitor. To use it:
>
> 1. Choose Apple → Control Panels → Gamma to open the Gamma control panel. (If it is not there, drag it from the Photoshop → Goodies → Calibration folder into the System Folder → Control Panels folder.)
>
> 2. Turn the panel on using the switch in the lower-left corner.
>
> 3. Type a gamma value of 2.2 to simulate Windows gamma in the Monitor Setup dialog box. You should see the effect of the gamma change immediately. Click OK.

For Windows. Photoshop offers gamma control only within the Photoshop window (it does not affect the monitor globally, as on the Macintosh). To use it:

1. Choose File → Color Settings → Monitor Setup.

2. Type a gamma value in the Monitor Setup dialog box. Click OK.

3. You can preview the effects of the gamma setting by clicking Preview in the Calibrate dialog box.

Adobe ImageReady Gamma Simulator

ImageReady (bundled with Photoshop 5.5 and integrated with 6.0) has a function that allows you to preview how your graphic will appear with the gamma setting of an alternate operating system. It also allows you to adjust the gamma value (brightness) of the image to make the image look acceptable for both platforms.

To preview the image, choose View → Windows Gamma/Mac Gamma. The image brightness will adjust to simulate the gamma setting of the specified platform. Choosing it again restores the image to its previous gamma value.

To automatically adjust the gamma in ImageReady:

1. Choose Image → Adjust → Gamma.

2. Select Macintosh-to-Windows to adjust for Windows displays, or select Windows-to-Macintosh to adjust for Mac displays.

3. Click OK.

You can also apply a manual gamma adjustment by moving the Gamma slider or entering a value between 0.1 and 9.99 in the text box.

Macromedia Fireworks Gamma Preview

Macromedia Fireworks allows you to adjust the display mode of the image to preview how it will look under the gamma conditions of another platform.

On the Macintosh, select View → Windows Gamma to simulate how the graphic will look when viewed on Windows machines. In Windows, select View → Mac Gamma to view how your graphic will look on a Mac.

These adjustments affect only how the image appears on your monitor; it does not in any way affect the actual brightness of the image. If you find that your image is too dark or too light under the alternative gamma settings, you will need to make manual adjustments to fix it.

Color in Browsers (The Web Palette)

An interesting problem arises when colors from the full 24-bit color space need to be displayed on an 8-bit display. Rather than relying on the computer's system palette, browsers reduce and remap colors to their own built-in palette. This is a benefit to web designers because it guarantees that images will look more or less the same on all 8-bit systems. If images were mapped to the various system palettes, they would look quite different on different platforms. (Note that if the browser is running on a 24-bit display, the palette does not come into effect and all colors will be displayed accurately.)

This *web palette* consists of the 216 colors shared by the Macintosh and Windows system palettes; therefore, colors chosen from the web palette render accurately on Mac or Windows displays. The web palette was optimized for Macs and Windows; Unix machines use a different color model for their system palette, so "web-safe" colors may shift or dither when viewed on Unix systems.

The web palette is also known as the Netscape Palette, Netscape 216, Browser-Safe Palette, Web-Safe Palette, Non-dithering Palette, and the 6×6×6 cube. The web palette is displayed at *http://www.learningwebdesign.com/webpalette.html*.

Shifting and dithering

When a browser running on an 8-bit monitor encounters a color, it does its best to approximate it using colors from the web palette. This can happen in two ways: *shifting* and *dithering*.

Sometimes colors are simply replaced by, or *shift* to, the nearest available web palette color. This is common in colors specified in the HTML document, such as background or table colors, although colors can shift in images as well. Color shifting can result in large discrepancies between how a color (as defined by its RGB values) is rendered on a 24-bit display versus an 8-bit display.

Browsers may also approximate a color by *dithering*, mixing pixels of similar colors available in the palette, resulting in a random dot pattern. This is common in images, although Internet Explorer may dither background colors as well. For photographic images, the effects of dithering usually are not detrimental (and in some cases may be beneficial). However, in areas of flat color (such as in a logo or line-art illustration), the speckle pattern is usually undesirable.

Color Issues on 16-Bit Displays

As of this writing, approximately half of all users view the Web on 16-bit monitors capable of displaying over 65,000 colors. While this is plenty of colors, they are unfortunately not the same colors found in the 24-bit true color space. This means that the RGB colors you specify in HTML or select in a graphics program (even "web-safe" colors) are always approximated on 16-bit displays, resulting in subtle shifting or dithering.

This effect is most noticeable when trying to match a graphic exactly to a background tile or color specified in HTML. Despite the fact that the foreground and background elements may have numerically identical RGB values, the "seam" may still be slightly visible on 16-bit displays. The only way to prevent this mismatch is to make the edges of the graphic transparent instead of a solid color, allowing the background color to show through.

For an in-depth yet understandable explanation of how 16-bit displays handle color at the mathematical level, I highly recommend reading "Death of the Websafe Color Palette?" by David Lehn and Hadley Stern on Webmonkey (*http://hotwired.lycos.com/webmonkey/00/37/index2a.html*).

The web palette in numbers

An important way to look at the web palette is by its numerical values. The web palette recognizes six shades of red, six shades of green, and six shades of blue, resulting in 216 possible color values (6×6×6 = 216). This is sometimes referred to as the 6×6×6 color cube. Figure 3-2 shows the cubic nature of this palette.

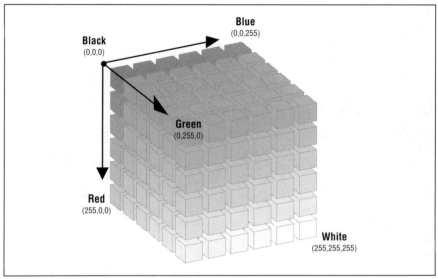

Figure 3-2: The 6×6×6 color cube of the web palette

There are three systems used for defining RGB values. Which one you use depends on the requirements of your software:

Decimal

Most image editing software displays the RGB value of a color in decimal values, ranging from 0 to 255. A color's decimal RGB value might be 51-51-255, meaning the red value is 51, the green value is 51, and the blue value is 255. Note that these numbers specify one of 256 possible values for each channel; they are not percentage values. Web-safe colors are multiples of 51.

Hexadecimal

HTML and many programming languages require that RGB numbers be specified in the hexadecimal numbering system. Hexadecimal is a base-16 system that requires only six characters to describe an RGB color. The hexadecimal equivalent of 51-51-255 is 3333FF. See Chapter 14 for more a thorough explanation.

Percentage

A few older programs for the Macintosh use the Apple Color Picker to specify colors in percentages, not absolute RGB decimal values. Web-safe color values are in increments of 20%. The percentage value equivalent of 51-51-255 is 20%-20%-100%.

Table 3-4 shows the decimal, hexadecimal, and percentage values for each of the six component values in the web palette.

Table 3-4: Numerical values for web palette colors

Decimal	Hexadecimal	Percentage
0 (darkest)	00	0%
51	33	20%
102	66	40%
153	99	60%
204	CC	80%
255 (lightest)	FF	100%

Designing with the Web Palette

While the web palette can lead to unpredictable and undesirable effects such as dithering or color shifting on 8-bit monitors, you can also use it to your advantage. Because you know *exactly* which colors will render accurately on Macs and Windows machines, you can use these colors exclusively when designing your graphics and HTML pages. It requires a little extra effort and means sacrificing color selection, but the advantage is that you'll be able to predict what the pages will look like for all users. Using web-safe colors in graphics production is discussed in Chapter 22.

If you choose to add color to the background and text on your web pages, chances are you'll need to do some experimenting with color to get the combinations just right. There are a number of tools and options for selecting web-safe colors and incorporating them into your designs.

Web authoring tools

Many WYSIWYG (What You See Is What You Get) web authoring tools (including Macromedia's Dreamweaver, Adobe GoLive, and Microsoft FrontPage), allow you to choose from swatches of web-safe colors when applying color to text and backgrounds. You can see the results of your choices immediately in the application window or when you preview in a browser. These tools automatically generate all the necessary HTML code for you.

Photoshop swatches

If you do not have a web authoring application, you can experiment with colors in a Photoshop file by loading the web-safe colors into the Swatches palette (see Chapter 22 for instructions on creating a web palette CLUT file). Using the eyedropper tool, you can then be sure that the colors you select for backgrounds and text are web-safe. You need to note the RGB values for your final color selections and convert them to their hexadecimal equivalents for insertion into the HTML color attribute tags in your document.

System Colors in Web Pages

If an 8-bit display allows 256 colors, and there are 216 colors in the browser's web palette, you may be wondering what happens to the other 40 colors. Normally, the browser allows colors from the user's system palette to fill in the extra 40 color slots. These extra colors can go a long way in smoothing out colors that can't be recreated accurately using web palette colors alone. This is particularly true for grayscale images, which are difficult to reproduce using only the four web-safe gray tones in the web palette.

There is a bug in Navigator 4.0 on the Macintosh that prevents system colors from seeping in, resulting in inferior image quality on 8-bit monitors. But chances are this problem affects few users, so it's nothing to worry about.

Graphics on the Web

Print designers need to adapt their graphics production skills for the Web to take into account the peculiarities of graphics that are distributed over a network and displayed on computer monitors.

Graphics File Formats

As of this writing, nearly all the graphics that you see on the Web are in one of two formats: GIF and JPEG. A third worthy contender, the PNG file, is struggling for browser support and attention. What follows is a very brief introduction to each of these online graphic formats. More detailed descriptions are provided in the chapters dedicated to each format.

The ubiquitous GIF

The GIF (Graphic Interchange Format) file format is the traditional darling of the Web. It was the first file format to be supported by web browsers, and it continues to be the format for the vast majority of graphics on the Web today.

GIFs are indexed color files with a maximum 8-bit palette capacity, which means that a GIF can contain a maximum of 256 pixel colors. Because they compress color information by rows of pixels, GIF files are most appropriate for graphics that contain areas of flat color.

See Chapter 19 for complete information on the GIF file format.

The handy JPEG

The second most popular graphics format on the Web today is the JPEG (Joint Photographic Experts Group) format. JPEGs contain 24-bit color information—that's millions of colors, as opposed to GIF's 256. They use what is called a "lossy" compression scheme, which means that some image information is thrown out in the compression process, but in most cases, the degradation of the image is not detrimental or even noticeable.

Photographic images, or any image with subtle gradations of color, are best saved as JPEG files because they offer better image quality packed into a smaller file. JPEGs, however, are not a good solution for flat, graphical images, because they tend to mottle colors, and the resulting file will generally be a lot larger than the same image saved as a GIF.

See Chapter 20 for complete information on the JPEG file format.

The lurking PNG

There is a third graphic format vying for usage on the Web—PNG (Portable Network Graphic), which, despite some very attractive features, has been slow to catch on.

PNGs can support 8-bit indexed color, 16-bit grayscale, or 24-bit true color images with a "lossless" compression scheme, which means higher image quality and, in some cases, file sizes even smaller than their GIF counterparts. Not only that, but PNG files also have some nifty features such as built-in gamma control and variable transparency levels (which means you can have a background pattern show through a soft drop-shadow).

See Chapter 21 for complete information on the PNG file format

Image Resolution

Simply put, all graphics on the Web need to be low-resolution: 72ppi (pixels per inch). Since web graphics are always displayed on low-resolution computer screens, higher resolution files are unnecessary.

Working at such a low resolution can be quite an adjustment for a designer accustomed to handling the 300dpi images appropriate for print. Most notably, the image quality is lower because there is not as much image information in a given space. This tends to make the image look more grainy or pixelated, and unfortunately, that's just the nature of images on the Web.

Measuring Resolution

Because web graphics exist solely on the screen, it is technically correct to measure their resolution in pixels per inch (ppi). Another resolution measurement, dpi (dots per inch), refers to the resolution of a printed image, dependent on the resolution of the printing device.

In practice, the terms dpi and ppi are used interchangeably. It is generally accepted practice to refer to web graphic resolution in terms of dpi.

Image size

When a graphic is displayed on a web page, the pixels in the image map one-to-one with the display resolution of the monitor. When the resolution is higher, the pixel size is smaller. Therefore, a graphic that appears to be about one inch square on your 72ppi monitor may actually appear to be quite a bit smaller on a monitor with a resolution closer to 100. (See Figure 3-3.)

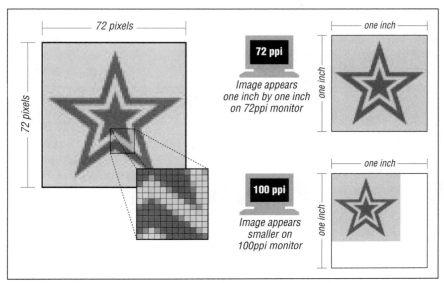

Figure 3-3: The size of an image is dependent on monitor resolution

Good-bye inches, hello pixels

Because the actual dimensions of a graphic are dependent on the resolution of the monitor, the whole notion of "inches" becomes irrelevant in the web environment. The only meaningful unit of measurement is the pixel.

It is general practice to create images at 72ppi (it puts you in the ballpark for screen presentation), but to pay attention only to the overall pixel dimensions. You can disregard inches entirely in the web graphics production process. After a while, thinking in pixels comes quite naturally. What's important is the size of the graphic relevant to other graphics on that page and to the overall size of the browser window.

For instance, some users still have monitors with resolutions of 640×480 pixels. To guarantee that my banner graphic fits in the screen in its entirety, I would make it no more than 600 pixels wide (taking into account that some pixels will be used on the left and right for the window and the scrollbar). The size of the remaining buttons and images on my page are measured in pixels relative to my 600-pixel-wide banner. For more information on designing for standard monitor resolutions, see Chapter 2.

Be Aware of File Size

It goes without saying that graphics have made the Web what it is today; however, as a web designer, you should know that many users have a love/hate relationship with graphics on the Web. Remember that graphics increase the time it takes a web page to move across the network; large graphics mean substantial download times, which can try the user's patience, particularly a user dialing in on a standard modem connection.

Here is the single most important guideline a web designer can follow: *Keep the file sizes of your graphics as small as possible!* The nature of publishing over a network creates a new responsibility for designers to be sensitive to the issue of download times. Fortunately, new web graphics tools, such as Macromedia Fireworks and Adobe Photoshop 5.5 and higher (including ImageReady), make it easy to make adjustments to the image while keeping an eye on the resulting file size.

Detailed strategies for minimizing graphic file size for each file format appear in the graphics chapters in Part III of this book.

Web Graphics Production Tips

The following is a collection of tips for maintaining quality in web graphics.

Work in RGB mode

When you are creating graphics for the Web, it is important to work in the RGB color mode. CMYK mode, while common to the print world, is incorrect for web graphics. When creating a GIF file, do your designing and editing in RGB mode and convert it to Indexed Color as the final step before saving. It's a good idea to hang onto an RGB original for later changes. To make this process easier, web graphics tools such as Photoshop 5.5 and higher, ImageReady, and Fireworks have separate export functions that create the final graphics while retaining the RGB original. JPEG graphics should simply be saved in RGB mode.

If you need to make adjustments to an existing GIF, you should convert it back to RGB mode before editing. When an image is in indexed color mode, the colors are restricted to those in its defined Color Table, and no new colors can be added. This prevents the color blends and adjustments that occur when image elements are transformed (resized, rotated, etc.) or when adding anti-aliased text. When the image is in indexed color mode, any text you add will automatically have aliased (stair-stepped) edges. (If you only need to crop the GIF or make other changes that don't require the addition of new pixel colors, it is okay to work directly in indexed color mode.)

The typical steps that should be taken when editing an existing GIF are:

1. Open the GIF in the image editing tool.
2. Change it to RGB color mode (in Photoshop, select Image → Mode → RGB Color).
3. Edit the image as necessary.
4. Change it back to indexed color mode, setting the desired palette and bit-depth.
5. Save or export to GIF format.

Resizing tips

The following tips pertain to resizing web graphics:

- **Convert to RGB before resizing.** As mentioned earlier, in order to resize an image, Photoshop (or any bitmap image editing tool) needs to create new transitions between areas of color in the image. Indexed color images (such as GIFs) are limited to the colors in the image's color table, which does not give Photoshop enough colors to create convincing "in-between" colors for these transitions.

- **Don't resize larger.** As a general rule, it is a bad idea to increase the dimensions of a low-resolution image (such as 72ppi images typically used on the Web). Image editing tools cannot add image information to the file—they can only stretch out what's already there. This results in a pixelated and blotchy image.

- **Resize smaller in increments.** Images can be made slightly smaller without much degradation in image quality; however, drastic resizing (making a snapshot-sized image postage-stamp size) usually results in an unacceptably blurry image. When acquiring an image (whether by scanning or from a CD-ROM), it is best to choose an image that is slightly larger than final size. That way, you don't need to make it larger, and you won't have to scale it down too much. If you must make a very large image very small, try doing it in a number of steps, fixing quality at each stage.

  Be sure to keep a clean copy of the original image in case you make something too small. Starting over is better than enlarging the image or resizing repeatedly.

Use anti-aliased text

In general, to create professional-looking graphics for the Web, you should use anti-aliased text. *Anti-aliasing* is the slight blur used on curved edges to make smoother transitions between colors. Aliased edges, by contrast, are blocky and stair-stepped. Figure 3-4 shows the effect of aliasing (left) and anti-aliasing (right).

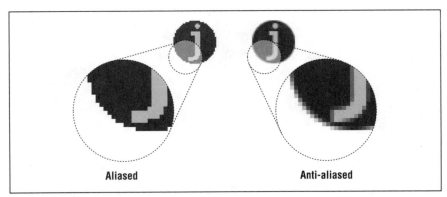

Figure 3-4: Aliased and anti-aliased edges

The exception to this guideline is very small text (10 to 12 points or smaller, depending on the font design), for which anti-aliased edges blur the characters to the point of illegibility. Text at small sizes may fare much better when anti-aliasing is turned off or set to "None."

The trade-off for better-looking graphics is file size—anti-aliasing adds to the number of colors in the image and may result in a slightly larger file size. In this case, the improved quality is usually worth a couple of extra bytes.

For Further Reading

If you feel you need more of a primer on making the transition to web design, check out my other book, *Learning Web Design* (O'Reilly, 2001), which is specifically for beginners. You can get more information about it at *http://www. learningwebdesign.com* or on O'Reilly's web site at *http://www.oreilly.com/catalog/ learnweb/*.

For more information on basic design principles as they apply to the Web, see Lynda Weinman's very popular book, *Designing Web Graphics, Third Edition* (New Riders, 2000).

One of the best online resources for designers is Joe Gillespie's site, Web Page Design for Designers (*http://www.wpdfd.com*). It is packed with very detailed explanations of how type and graphics work on the Web.

CHAPTER 4

A Beginner's Guide to the Server

Even if you focus primarily on what's commonly referred to as "front-end" web development—HTML documents and web graphics—the server and the way it is configured may impact the way you work. In most cases, there is no way to avoid making firsthand contact with the server, even if it's just to upload files.

For this reason, all web designers should have a basic level of familiarity with servers and what they do. At the very least, this will enable you to communicate more clearly with your server administrator. If you have permission for greater access to the server, it could mean taking care of certain tasks yourself without needing to wait for assistance.

This chapter provides an introduction to server terminology and functions, pathnames, and file (MIME) types. It also discusses uploading files and setting permissions, which designers often need to do.

Servers 101

A *server* is any computer running software that enables it to answer requests for documents and other data. The programs that request and display documents (such as a browser) are called *clients*. The terms "server-side" and "client-side," in regard to specific functions like imagemaps, refer to which machine is doing the processing. Client-side functions happen on the user's machine; server-side functions occur on the remote machine.

Web servers answer requests from browsers (the client program), retrieve the specified file (or execute a CGI script), and return the document or script results. Web browsers and servers communicate via the Hypertext Transfer Protocol (HTTP).

Popular Server Software

Any computer can be a server as long as it is running server software. Today, there are many server packages available, but the overwhelming leaders are Apache and Microsoft Internet Information Server (IIS).

Apache

> The majority of servers today (approximately 60%) run Apache. Its popularity is due to the fact that it is powerful and full-featured, and it has always been available for free. It runs primarily on the Unix platform but is being released to run on other platforms, including Windows NT/2000 and Mac OS X.
>
> The core installation of Apache has limited functionality, but it can be expanded and customized easily by the addition of *modules*. Apache calls on each module to perform a dedicated task, such as user authentication or database queries. You can pick up a copy of the Apache server and its documentation from the Apache home page at *http://www.apache.org*.

Internet Information Server (IIS)

> This is Microsoft's server package, which is also available without charge. IIS runs on the Windows NT platform (in fact, it comes bundled with Windows NT 4.0 and 2000). IIS has developed into a powerful and stable server option that is somewhat easier to set up and maintain than its Unix competitor. It has many advanced server features, including ASP (Active Server Pages) for server-side scripting. As of this writing, approximately 20% of sites run on IIS servers.

For more information on popular servers, check out the articles and resources at ServerWatch (*http://www.serverwatch.com*). If you are interested in up-to-date statistics on browser usage, see the server survey at Netcraft (*http://www.netcraft.com/survey/*).

The particular brand of server does not impact the majority of things the designer does, such as making graphics or developing basic HTML files. It certainly influences more advanced web site building techniques, such as Server Side Includes (discussed in Chapter 18), adding MIME types (discussed later in this chapter), and database-driven web pages. Be certain to coordinate with your server administrator if you are using your server in ways beyond simple HTML and graphic files storage.

Basic Server Functions

As a web designer, it is important that you have some level of familiarity with the following elements of the web server.

Root directory

When a browser requests a document, the server locates the document, starting with the server's root directory. This is the directory that has been configured to contain all documents intended to be shared via the Web. The root directory does not necessarily appear in the URL that points to the document, so it is important to know what your root directory is when uploading your files.

For example, if the root directory on *littlechair.com* is */users/httpd/www/* and a browser makes a request for *http://www.littlechair.com/super/cool.html*, the server actually retrieves */users/httpd/www/super/cool.html*. This, of course, is invisible to the user.

Index files

A slash (/) at the end of a URL indicates that the URL is pointing to a directory, not a file. If no specific document is identified, most servers display the contents of a default file (or index file). The index file is generally named *index.html*, but on some servers it may be named *welcome.html* or *default.html*. This is another small variation you will need to confirm with your server administrator.

If configured poorly, some servers may display the contents of the directory if an index file is not found, leaving files vulnerable to snooping. For this reason, it is a good idea always to name some page (usually the main page) in each directory *index.html* (or another specified name). One advantage is that it makes URLs to the index page of each directory more tidy (e.g., *www.littlechair.com* rather than *www.littlechair.com/homepage.html*).

HTTP response header

Once the server locates the file, it sends the contents of that file back to the browser, preceded by some *HTTP response headers*. The headers provide the browser with information about the arriving file, including its media type (also known as "content type" or "MIME type"). Usually, the server determines the format from the file's suffix; for example, a file with the suffix *.gif* is taken to be an image file.

The browser reads the header information and determines how to handle the file, either displaying it in the window or launching the appropriate helper application or plug-in. MIME types are discussed further at the end of this chapter.

Server-Side Programming

Web pages and sites have gotten much more interactive since the early days of simple HTML document sharing. Now web sites serve as portals of two-way information sharing, e-commerce, search engines, and dynamically generated content. This functionality relies on programs and scripts that are processed on the server. There are a number of options for server-side programming, of which CGI, ASP, PHP, and Java servlets/JSP are the most common.

CGI (Common Gateway Interface)

Instead of pointing to an HTML file, a URL may request that a CGI program be run. CGI stands for Common Gateway Interface, and it's what allows the web server to communicate with other programs (CGI scripts) that are running on the server. CGI scripts are commonly written in the Perl, C, or C++ language.

CGI scripts are the traditional method for performing a wide variety of functions such as searching, server-side imagemap handling, and gaming; however, their most common usage is form processing (information entered by the user through entry fields in the document). A typical CGI script is examined in Chapter 15. As other more powerful options for interfacing with databases become available (such as ASP, PHP, and Java servlets), traditional CGI programming is getting less attention.

Most server administrators follow the convention of keeping CGI scripts in a special directory named *cgi-bin* (short for CGI-binaries). Keeping them in one directory makes it easier to manage and secure the server. When a CGI script is requested by the browser, the server runs the script and returns the dynamic content it produces to the browser.

ASP (Active Server Pages)

ASP (Active Server Pages) is a programming environment for Microsoft's Internet Information Server (IIS). It is primarily used to interface with data on the server in order to create dynamically generated web pages. It can also be configured to process form information.

Often, you'll come across a web document that ends in the *.asp* suffix (as opposed to *.html*). This indicates that it is a text file that contains HTML and scripting (usually written in VBScript) that is configured to interact with ASP on the server.

For more information on ASP, see Microsoft Developer Network's page entitled "ASP from A to Z" at *http://msdn.microsoft.com/workshop/server/asp/aspatoz.asp*. Another good resource is ASP 101 (*http://www.asp101.com*).

PHP

PHP is another tool that allows you to create dynamically generated web pages (similar to ASP). PHP is a project of the Apache Software Foundation, so it is open source and freely available. PHP works with a variety of web servers, but it is most commonly used with Apache.

PHP code, which is similar to Perl or ASP, is embedded into the HTML document using special PHP tags. PHP's advantage over CGI scripting is that it is very easy to include short bits of PHP code directly in a web page, to process form data or extract information from a database, for example.

For more information on PHP, go to *http://www.php.net*, the official PHP web site.

Java Servlets and JSP

Although Java is known for its small applications (known as "applets") for the Web, it is a complete and complex programming language that is more typically used for developing large, enterprise-scale applications. With a Java-enabled web server, a programmer can write Java servlets that produce dynamic web content.

JavaServer Pages (JSP) is a related technology that is similar to ASP. JSP code is embedded directly in web pages; it provides a simple way for web authors to access the functionality of complex servlets that are running on the web server.

For more information on Java servlets and JSP, see *http://java.sun.com/products/servlet/* and *http://java.sun.com/products/jsp/*.

Unix Directory Structures

Because the Web was spawned from the Unix environment, it follows many of the same conventions. Directory structure and pathname syntax are prime examples. It is important for all web designers to have an understanding of how directory structures are indicated on the Unix platform since pathnames are used in hyper-links and pointers to images and other resources.

Directories ("places" to store files) are organized into a hierarchical structure that fans out like an upside-down tree. The topmost directory is known as the *root* and is written as a forward slash (/). The root can contain several directories, each of which can contain subdirectories; each of these can contain more subdirectories, and so on. A subdirectory is said to be the "child" of the directory that holds it (its "parent"). Figure 4-1 shows a system with five directories under the root. The directory *users* has two subdirectories, *jen* and *richard*. Within *jen* are two more subdirectories, *work* and *pers*, and within *pers* is the file *art.html*.

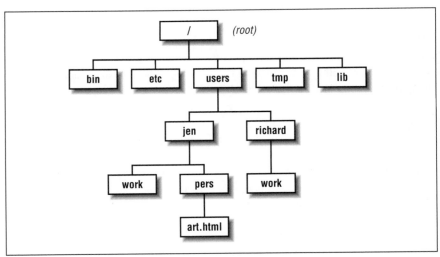

Figure 4-1: Example of a directory hierarchy

A *pathname* is the notation used to point to a particular file or directory; it tells you the path of directories you must travel to get to where you want to go. There are two types of pathnames: *absolute* and *relative*.

Absolute Pathnames

An *absolute pathname* always starts from the root directory, which is indicated by a slash (/). So, for example, the pathname for the *pers* directory is */users/jen/pers*, as shown in Figure 4-2. The first slash indicates that we are starting at the root and is necessary for indicating that a pathname is absolute.

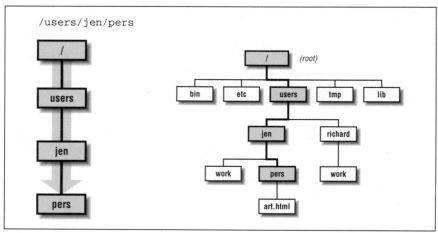

Figure 4-2: Visual representation of the path /users/jen/pers

Relative Pathnames

A relative pathname points to a file or directory relative to your current working directory. When building a web site on a single server, relative pathnames are commonly used within URLs to refer to files in other directories on the server.

Unless you specify an absolute name (starting with a slash), the server assumes you are using a relative pathname. Starting in your current location (your working directory), you can trace your way up and down the directory hierarchy. This is best explained with an example.

If I am currently working in the directory *jen* and I want to refer to the file *art.html*, the relative pathname is *pers/art.html*, because the file *art.html* is in the directory *pers*, which is in the current directory, *jen*. This is illustrated in Figure 4-3.

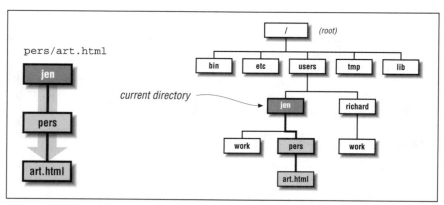

Figure 4-3: The path pers/art.html relative to the jen directory

Going back up the hierarchy is a bit trickier. You go up a level by using the shorthand .. for the parent directory. Again, let's use an example based on Figure 4-1.

If I am currently in the *jen* directory, and I want to refer to the directory *richard/work*, the pathname is *../richard/work*. The two dots at the beginning of the path take us back up one level to the to the *users* directory, and from there we find the directory called *richard* and the subdirectory called *work*, as shown in Figure 4-4.

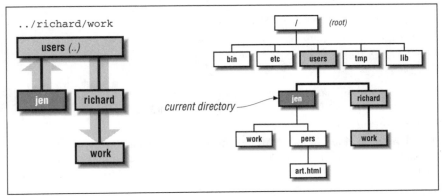

Figure 4-4: The path ../richard/work, relative to the jen directory

If I am currently in my *pers* directory and I want to refer to Richard's *work* directory, I need to go up two levels, so the pathname would be *../../richard/work*, as shown in Figure 4-5.

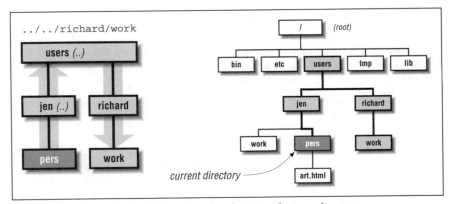

Figure 4-5: The path ../../richard/work, relative to the pers directory

Note that the absolute path */users/richard/work* accomplishes the same thing. The decision whether to use an absolute versus a relative pathname generally comes down to which is easiest from where you are.

Using relative pathnames in HTML

When pointing to another web page or resource (like an image) on your own server, it is common to use a relative URL, one that points to the new resource relative to the current document. Relative URLs follow the syntax for pathnames described above. For example, a hypertext link to *art.html* from another document in the *pers* directory would look like this:

```
<A HREF="art.html">
```

The URL for the link could also be written starting from the root directory:

```
<A HREF="/users/jen/pers/art.html">
```

Image tags also use pathnames to point to the graphic file to be displayed. For instance, this image tag in the *art.html* document:

```
<IMG SRC="../../daisy.gif">
```

points to a graphic named *daisy.gif* located in the jen directory. Two "../"s indicate that the graphic file resides in a directory two levels higher than the current document (*art.html*).

If you plan on doing your HTML coding by hand, pathname syntax will come naturally after a little practice. If you are using a WYSIWYG authoring tool (such as Macromedia Dreamweaver, Adobe GoLive, or Microsoft FrontPage), you have the luxury of letting the tool construct the relative URL pathnames for you. Some even have site management tools that automatically adjust the pathnames if documents get moved.

File Naming Conventions

In order for your files to traverse the network successfully, you must name them in accordance with established file naming conventions:

* Avoid character spaces in filenames. Although this is perfectly acceptable for local files on a Macintosh or Windows machine, character spaces are not recognized by other systems. It is common to use an underscore character to visually separate words within filenames, such as *andre_bio.html*.

* Avoid special characters, such as ?, %, #, /, :, etc., in filenames. It is best to limit filenames to letters, numbers, underscores (in place of character spaces), hyphens, and periods.

* Use proper suffixes. HTML documents require the suffix *.html* (or *.htm* if on a Windows server). GIF graphic files take the suffix *.gif*, and JPEGs should be named *.jpg* or *.jpeg*. If your files do not have the correct suffix, the browser may not recognize them as web-based files. Suffixes for a large number of common file types are listed later in this chapter.

* Filenames are case-sensitive. Consistently using all lowercase letters in filenames, while certainly not necessary, may make them easier to remember.

* Keep filenames as short as possible. They add to the size of the file (and they can be a nuisance to remember!).

Uploading Documents (FTP)

The most common transaction that a web designer will have with a web server is the uploading of HTML documents, graphics, and other media files. Files are transferred between computers over a network via a method called FTP (*File Transfer Protocol*).

If you are working in a telnet session on Unix, you can run the *ftp* program and transfer files with a hefty collection of command-line arguments (not covered in this book).

Fortunately, if you work on a Mac or PC, there are a number of FTP programs with graphical interfaces that spare you the experience of transferring files using the Unix command line. In fact, FTP functions are now built right into full-featured web authoring tools, such as GoLive, Dreamweaver, and FrontPage, among others. On the Mac, dedicated programs that allow "drag-and-drop" file transfer, such as Fetch and Interarchy (previously Anarchie), are quite popular. On the PC, there are numerous simple FTP programs, such as WS_FTP, AceFTP, and Transmit. These (and many others) are available for download at *http://www.shareware.com* (search for "ftp").

The Navigator and Internet Explorer browsers also function as FTP clients, offering the ability to both download and upload files with a drag-and-drop interface.

The FTP Process

Regardless of the tool you use, the basic principles and processes are the same. Before you begin, you must have an account with permission to upload files to the server. Check with the server administrator to be sure you have a login name and a password.

You don't necessarily need an account to upload and download files if the server is set up as an "anonymous" FTP site. However, due to obvious security implications, be sure that your personal directories are not configured to be accessible to all anonymous users.

1. **Launch the FTP program** of your choice and open a connection with your server. You'll need to enter the exact name of the server, your account name, and password.

2. **Locate the appropriate directory** into which you want to copy your files. You may also choose to create a new directory or delete existing files and directories on the remote server using the controls in your FTP program. (Note that some servers allow you to enter the complete pathname to the directory before logging in.)

3. **Specify the transfer mode.** The most important decision to make during uploading is specifying whether the data should be transferred in *binary* or *ASCII* mode.

   ASCII files are comprised of alphanumeric characters. Some FTP programs refer to ASCII files as "Text" files. HTML documents should be transferred as ASCII or text.

   Binary files are made up of compiled data (ones and zeros), such as executable programs, graphic images, movies, etc. Some programs refer to the binary mode as "raw data" or "Image." All graphics (*.gif*, *.jpeg*) and multimedia files should be transferred as "binary" or "Raw Data." Table 4-1 includes a listing of the transfer mode for a number of popular file types.

In Fetch (Mac), you may see a *MacBinary* option, which transfers the file with its resource fork (the bit of the file containing desktop icons and other Mac-specific data) intact. It should only be used when transferring from one Mac to another. This resource fork is appropriately stripped out of Mac-generated media files when transferred under the standard raw data mode.

Some FTP programs also provide an *Auto* option, which enables you to transfer whole directories containing files of both types. The program examines each file and determines whether it should be transferred as text or binary information. This function is not 100% reliable on all programs, so use it with caution until you are positive you are getting good results.

4. **Upload your files to the server.** Standard FTP uses the terminology "put" (uploading files from your computer to the server) and "get" (downloading files from the server to your computer), so these terms may be used in your FTP program as well. You can also upload multiple files at a time.

5. **Disconnect.** When you have completed the transfer, be sure to disconnect from the server. You may want to test the files you've uploaded on a browser first to make sure everything transferred successfully.

Setting Permissions

When you upload files to a web server, you need to be sure that the files' permissions are set so that everyone is able to read your files. *Permissions* control who can read, write (edit), or execute (if it is a program) the file, and they need to be established for the owner of the file, the file's group, and for "everyone." When you create or upload a file, you are automatically the owner, which may mean that only you can set the permissions.

Some FTP programs enable you to set the default upload permissions via a dialog box. Figure 4-6 shows Fetch 3.0.4's dialog box for doing this. For most web purposes, you want to grant yourself full permissions but restrict all other users to read-only. You may want to confirm that your server administrator agrees with these settings.

Figure 4-6: Standard permissions settings (using Fetch 3.0.4)

The server needs to be specially configured to recognize these permissions commands, so check with your administrator to see if you can use this easy method. He or she will give you instructions if any special permissions settings are necessary.

File (MIME) Types

Servers add a header to each document that tells the browser the type of file it is sending. The browser determines how to handle the file based on that information—whether to display the contents in the window, or to launch the appropriate plug-in or helper application.

The system for communicating media types closely resembles MIME (Multi-purpose Internet Mail Extension), which was originally developed for sending attachments in email. The server needs to be configured to recognize each MIME type in order to successfully communicate the media type to the browser.

If you want to deliver media beyond the standard HTML files and graphics (such as a Shockwave Flash movie or an audio file), you should contact your server administrator to be sure the server is configured to support that MIME type. Most common formats are built in to current versions of server software, but if the format isn't there already, the administrator can easily set it up if you provide the necessary information.

The exact syntax for configuring MIME types varies among server software; however, they all require the same basic information: type, subtype, and extension. Types are the most broad categories for files. They include text, image, audio, video, application, etc. Within each category are a number of subtypes. For instance, the file type image includes the subtypes gif, jpeg, etc. The extension refers to the file's suffix, which the server uses to determine the file type and subtype. Not all extensions are standardized.

Table 4-1 lists common media types by extension along with their MIME type/subtype information. The ASCII/Binary information is provided to aid in making upload decisions.

Of course, new technologies and file types are emerging every day, so keep in mind that it is the web designer's responsibility to make sure that for any new media type the appropriate information is communicated to the server administrator.

Table 4-1: MIME types and subtypes by extension

Extension	Type/Subtype	Description	ASCII/ Binary
.ai	application/ postscript	PostScript viewer	A
.aif, .aiff	audio/x-aiff	AIFF file	B
.aifc	audio/aifc	Compressed AIFF file	B
.au	audio/basic	μ-law sound file	B
.avi	video/avi or video/x-msvideo	AVI video file	B

Table 4-1: MIME types and subtypes by extension (continued)

Extension	Type/Subtype	Description	ASCII/ Binary
.bmp	image/x-MS-bmp	Microsoft BMP file	B
.dcr, .dir, .dxr	application/ x-director	Shockwave files	B
.doc, .dot	application/msword	Microsoft Word document	B
.eps	application/ postscript	Encapsulated PostScript	A
.exe	application/ x-msdownload	Self-extracting file or executable	B
.gif	image/gif	Graphic in GIF format	B
.gz, .gzip	application/ x-gzip	Compressed file, use gunzip (Unix decompressor)	B
.hqx	application/ mac-binhex40	Mac BinHex Archive	B
.htm	text/html	HTML document	A
.jpg, .jpeg, .jpe, .jfif, .pjpeg, .pjp	image/jpeg	Graphic in JPEG format	B
.mid	audio/midi or audio/x-midi	MIDI audio file	B
.mov	video/quicktime	QuickTime movie	B
.movie	video/x-sgi-movie	Silicon Graphics movie	B
.mpg, .mpe, .mpeg, .m1v, .mp2, .mp3, .mpa	video/mpeg	MPEG movie	B
.pbm	image/x-portable- bitmap	Portable bitmap image	B
.pcd	image/x-photo-cd	Kodak photo CD image	B
.pdf	application/pdf	Portable Document Format (Acrobat file)	B
.pic	image/x-pict	PICT image file	B
.pl	application/ x-perl	Perl source file	A
.png	image/x-png	Graphic in PNG format	B
.ppt, .pot	application/ powerpoint	PowerPoint file	B
.ps	application/ postscript	PostScript file	A
.qt	video/quicktime	QuickTime movie	B
.ra, .ram	audio/ x-pn-realaudio	RealAudio file (and metafile)	B
.rtx	text/richtext	Rich Text Format (Microsoft Word)	A
.rtf	application/rtf	Rich Text Format (MSWord)	A
.sea	application/ x-sea	Self-extracting Archive (Stuffit file)	B
.sit	application/ x-sit	Stuffit Archive	B

Table 4-1: MIME types and subtypes by extension (continued)

Extension	Type/Subtype	Description	ASCII/ Binary
.snd	audio/basic	Digitized sound file	B
.swf	application/ x-shockwave-flash	Shockwave Flash file	B
.tar	application/ x-tar	Compressed file	B
.tif, .tiff	image/tiff	TIFF image (requires external viewer)	B
.txt	text/plain	ASCII text file	A
.wav	audio/s-wav	Waveform audio file	B
.wrl, .wrz	x-world/x-vrml	VRML 3D file (requires VRML viewer)	B
.xll, .xls	application/ vnd.ms-excel	Microsoft Excel File	B
.zip	application/ x-zip-compressed	Compressed file (decompress using WinZip or Stuffit on Mac)	B

Servers

CHAPTER 5

Printing from the Web

The Web is undeniably an amazing resource for information, but it's not the most comfortable nor portable of reading environments. For this reason, many people print web pages to read away from their desks or to file for later use. The ability to print the contents of the window has been built into browsers from the beginning. Over the years, we've seen some advancement for controlling printouts, both from the browser application itself as well as in authoring languages such as Cascading Style Sheets. In addition, the Web has proven to be an effective delivery device for printed documents in the form of PDF (Portable Document Format) files.

Browser Print Mechanisms

All graphical browsers have basic print and page setup controls that interface with the printer the same as any other application. In the Page Setup dialog box, users can generally select whether the page should print in portrait (vertical) or landscape (horizontal) format and specify how many copies to print.

Internet Explorer goes beyond the simple print button by giving user more fine-tuned controls for printouts. Its Print Preview feature (introduced in Version 4.5 on the Mac and in 5.5 for Windows) shows how the web page will look when it's printed out. Within the Print Preview dialog box, users can select whether they want to add headers and footers with the URL and other page information, whether images print, and whether background and text colors should be preserved. The page shrinks to fit the print area by default, but users can opt to have it crop at the edge or print in tiles.

Internet Explorer Versions 4 and 5.0 (for Windows) use the Page Setup dialog box for setting page size, orientation, headers/footers, and margins, but there is no preview function. Background and text colors can be preserved by clicking the appropriate box under "Printing" in the advanced Internet Options dialog box.

Netscape Navigator offers similar printer controls for Windows users. Starting with Version 4.7, the Page Setup dialog box offers control over headers, footers, margins, and orientation. There is also a Print Preview option available. Unfortunately, these advanced options are not available for Navigator on the Macintosh.

Although browsers offer built-in print features, you can't depend on users to use them or even to know that they are available. Fortunately, in most cases, browsers released since 1998 do a reasonably good job of printing web pages by default. They generally try to shrink the contents to fit the print area, and they may also be sophisticated enough to preserve background and text colors (for printing light text on a dark background). But if you want to be absolutely sure your pages print in a predictable way, there are a few extra measures you may choose to take.

Printer-Friendly HTML Pages

One way to ensure that your users can get a good copy of your content to-go is to link to a separate "printer-friendly" HTML document especially for printing. In general, printer-friendly pages are stripped-down versions containing just a single column of content with minimum HTML formatting. Figure 5-1 shows pages from two web developer resource sites and their corresponding printed pages.

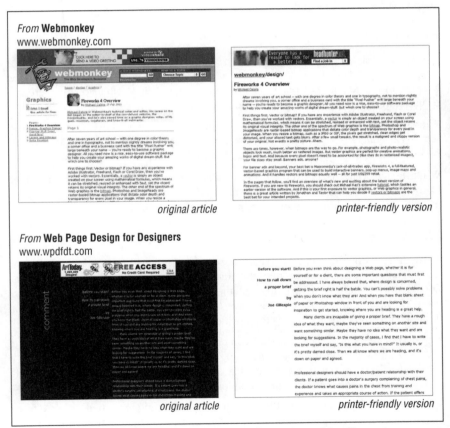

Figure 5-1: Two web pages and their corresponding printer-friendly versions

The following sections detail some steps you can take to design printer-friendly pages. Of course, if you anticipate that your audience will want to do a lot of printing from your site, you may choose to design your original pages according to the same printer-friendly guidelines.

Keep the Page Narrow

The most common problem with printing web pages is that the right edge can get cropped off. This happens when the page is fixed at a pixel width (using a table) or contains graphics such as a navigation bar that is wider than the printable area of the page.

So how wide is too wide? If you want to be absolutely sure that no content slips off the edge for anyone, keep the width of tables and graphics under 550 pixels. An even more conservative approach is to use HTML text only (with no tables fixing the page width) and only minimal graphics.

Browsers that shrink the page to fit the printable area can accommodate any page width, but you risk the contents becoming too tiny to be legible, so it's best to keep tables and images under 750 pixels wide.

Keep Text Visible

Another tip for keeping web pages fit to print is to use black (or dark) text on a white (or light) background. Some older browsers are known to print out dark backgrounds and the text black as well (even though it is white on the screen), resulting in a solid field of black on the paper.

While browsers are now more capable of printing colors as they are seen on the screen, in general, your printer-friendly version should be designed to look like a printed document, with dark type on a light background. It saves on toner as well!

While many home users print to color inkjet printers, people in offices are more likely to be printing on black-and-white laser printers. For this reason, printer-friendly pages shouldn't rely on color output for communication.

Think About Content

If you are taking the time to create a separate printer-friendly document, you should tailor the content of that document to be appropriate to the medium. Consider why the user is printing out the web page and how it is going to be used. Chances are, people just want the content of the page for later reading or filing. Following are some things to consider when assembling your page:

- If your readers are interested in content (such as an article), you can strip out anything extra on the page, including navigation, search boxes, etc. Whether you include ads may be more of a marketing mandate than a design decision, but in general, they should be left out too.

- The print document should have some way of identifying where it came from for future reference, including the site name and subsection labels when appropriate. It doesn't hurt to write out the URL if it is not clear, in case users don't have headers and footers turned on in their printouts.

- If your article is divided across several web pages, combine it into one printable document.

- On a printed page, hypertext links are useless, of course. Where the original article contains linked text, consider writing the complete URL for the link in parentheses after the linked word. That way, a reader can type in the URL to follow the link later.

- If your content pages are generated dynamically from a database, create a template specifically for printer-friendly versions. This prevents needing to make two HTML files for every page.

Cascading Style Sheets for Printouts

A more sophisticated way to control the way your page looks when it is printed is to take advantage of media-specific style sheets. This feature in the CSS2 specification allows a single document to be formatted on the fly depending on the device displaying or outputting it. When it's on the screen, it looks one way; when it prints out, its format changes to be read clearly on hard copy. That eliminates the need to create a separate printer-friendly version of every page on your site. See Chapter 17 for background information on how style sheets work.

The process involves creating two style sheets: one appropriate to screen display and one appropriate for print. Both style sheets are associated with the HTML document using the `media` attribute or the `@media` rule. When the browser sends the page to print, the appropriate style sheet is chosen for the job. A more detailed explanation follows.

The downside to using any feature from the CSS2 specification is poor browser support. As of this writing, the `media` attribute is supported on Internet Explorer 5.0 and higher on Windows and IE 4.5 and higher on the Macintosh (IE does not support the `@media` rule). Navigator began supporting media types in Version 6 for both platforms. Because of the spotty browser support, you can't rely on these techniques for 100% of your audience, but if you know that your users are up-to-date with their browser downloads (such as in an intranet environment), you can begin taking advantage of them immediately.

Creating the Style Sheets

In this simple example, I begin with a simple, yet properly tagged, HTML file that includes a navigational bar, a headline, and a few lines of text. (Structural tags have been omitted to save space, but they are implied.) I'll call this document *sample.html*.

```
<DIV class="navigation">
    <P><IMG src="navigation_bar.gif"></P>
</DIV>
<H1>Alternative Media Style Sheets</H1>
<P>With CSS2 you can create style sheets that are specific to a medium.
This enables on-the-fly formatting of the document.</P>
```

I now create a style sheet that specifies how I want my page to look on the screen. Just to be extreme, I've made my background black, my headline red and text gray. This style sheet is named *browser.css*.

```
BODY { background-color: black; }
H1 { color: red; font-family: impact; }
P { color: #999999; font-family: verdana; }
```

I also create a second style sheet that is better suited for a printout. I'd like all the text to be black on a white background. In addition, I don't want the navigation toolbar to appear, so I'll use the `display` selector to hide the `div` that contains the image. This style sheet is named *print.css*.

```
BODY { background-color: white;
       color: black;
       font-family: times; }
DIV.navigation { display: none;}
```

We're not done yet—we still need to link the style sheets to the HTML document. Figure 5-2 gives a sneak preview of the results of our media-targeted style sheets so you have an image of where this is going.

	Alternative Media Style Sheets
	With CSS2 you can create style sheets that are specific to a medium. This enables on-the-fly formatting of the document.
sample.html in the browser	*sample.html* printed out

Figure 5-2: Media-specific style sheets at work

Connecting the Style Sheets and HTML

There are four methods for associating the style sheets with the HTML document. Two use the `media` attribute within the `<link>` or `<style>` element to target the correct style sheet from within the HTML document. The other two use rules that are dependent on medium: `@import` and `@media`. The target medium can be one of ten different media types defined in the CSS2 specification. They are:

`all`
>Applies the styles to all media output (the default)

`screen`
>For monitors

`print`
>For printouts and print preview displays

`projection`
>For slideshow-like presentations

`braille, embossed`
>For tactile output

`aural`
>For speech-generating devices

tv

> For television displays (à la WebTV)

tty

> For fixed-width character displays

handheld

> For small palmtop devices

For now, of course, we are concerned with just the values screen and print. In all of the following methods, multiple media can be specified in comma-separated lists (for example: media="print,projection"). Any style that is set to all media will combine with other media-specific styles. Therefore, if you set a master style sheet to all and a second style sheet to print, the final printed output will reflect a combination of both style sheets.

Linking to media-dependent style sheets

The most familiar way to target the respective style sheets is to link to them from the HTML document using the <link> element in the <head> of the document. This is a standard method for referencing an external style sheet; however, in this case, the two links are differentiated by the values of their media attributes.

```
<HEAD>
<LINK rel="stylesheet" type="text/css"
    href="browser.css" media="screen">
<LINK rel="stylesheet" type="text/css"
    href="print.css" media="print">
</HEAD>
```

By specifying that *print.css* has a media of print, it is called into use only when the document is printed.

Using two embedded style sheets

A document may contain two embedded style sheets targeted at different media. The styles are differentiated using the media attribute in the <style> tag.

```
<HEAD>
<STYLE type="text/css" media="screen">
<!--
    BODY { background-color: black; }
    H1 { color: red; font-family: impact; }
    P { color: #333333; font-family: verdana; }
-->
</STYLE>
<STYLE type="text/css" media="print">
<!--
    BODY { background-color: white;
           color: black;
           font-family: times; }
    DIV.navigation { display: none; }
-->
</STYLE>
</HEAD>
```

@import rule

An external style sheet can be imported based on the display medium using the @import rule in a style sheet. Simply add the target medium value at the end of the rule as shown in this example:

```
<STYLE>
<!--
@import url(browser.css) screen;
@import url(print.css) print;
-->
</STYLE>
```

@media rule

The @media rule enables style instructions for a number of media to be placed within one style sheet. Each @media rule can be interpreted as, "If the final display is going to be this, use these style instructions." Unfortunately, it is not supported in Internet Explorer as of this writing. Using the same style sheet information from the original example, the code would look like this:

```
<STYLE>
<!--
@media screen {
    BODY { background-color: black; }
    H1 { color: red; font-family: impact; }
    P { color: #333333; font-family: verdana; }
}
@media print {
    BODY { background-color: white;
           color: black;
           font-family: times; }
    DIV.navigation { display: none; }
}
-->
</STYLE>
```

We've looked at a very simple example, but I hope it illustrates how powerful and versatile conditional style sheets can be. For complete information on using media types, read the official CSS2 specification at *http://www.w3.org/TR/REC-CSS2/media.html*.

Portable Document Format (PDF)

PDF (Portable Document Format) is a technology developed by Adobe for sharing electronic documents. The remarkable thing about PDF files is that they preserve the fonts, colors, formatting, and graphics of the original source document. Ideally, a PDF document looks exactly the way it was designed, regardless of the platform, hardware, and software environment of the end user. It can be viewed on the screen or printed out to a high-quality hard copy.

PDF existed before the Web, but the two make great partners—PDF is the ideal file format for sharing documents, and the Web provides a highly accessible network for distributing them. You can make any document into a PDF file and make it available from a web page. The advantage, of course, is that you have more control over fonts and layout, and the formatting is not limited by HTML.

Forms, documentation, and any other materials that rely on specific formatting are good candidates for PDF files. To use a classic example, the IRS makes tax forms available for download in PDF format so taxpayers can print them out at home without requesting them by mail or making a trip to the post office.

But PDF files are not totally static. They can contain links to online material and other PDF files. Adobe Acrobat 5 can even create interactive PDF forms which can be filled out, automatically updated, and submitted online. PDFs can also be dynamically generated based on user input.

With the control PDF offers over display, it's tempting to want to use it for all online material. It's important to understand that PDF is not a substitute for HTML, nor is it likely ever to be. But it is a powerful tool for sharing any sort of document electronically. It's like sending a piece of paper through the lines.

Viewing PDF Files

PDFs are viewed and printed via the freely available and widely distributed Acrobat Reader. Acrobat Reader is also available as a plug-in (called PDFViewer) or ActiveX control that is automatically installed with Internet Explorer and Netscape Navigator Versions 3.0 and higher on a variety of platforms including Windows, Mac, and Unix.

When a user clicks on a link to a PDF file from a web page, what happens depends on how the browser is configured. If the browser has the PDFViewer plug-in, the document displays right in the browser window; the plug-in adds a toolbar to the browser window for navigating through the PDF document. If the browser is configured to use Acrobat Reader as a helper application, the browser automatically launches the reader, and the PDF displays in the separate application window.

Without the Reader or plug-in, when a browser encounters a PDF file, it issues a prompt to install the plug-in, choose a helper application, or save the file to disk.

Creating PDF Files

The standard application for creating PDF files is Adobe Acrobat, which is in Version 5 as of this writing. This commercial product gives publishers the greatest control over PDF creation.

When Acrobat is installed on a computer, making PDFs is simple. From an Adobe application, just open the document and export it to the PDF format. In Microsoft Office (Windows only), there is a PDF Maker icon right on the toolbar. To create a PDF from a non-Adobe application, print it to a PostScript file (choose "File" instead of "Printer" in the Print dialog box). Then open the PostScript file in Acrobat Distiller (part of the Acrobat package) and save it as a PDF file. In both scenarios, a dialog box appears, in which you can specify a large number of quality and optimization settings.

Once the PDF file has been created, it can then be opened in Acrobat for further fine-tuning and advanced settings. See the Adobe web site (*http://www.adobe.com*) or the Acrobat documentation for more information on creating and fine-tuning PDF files.

The important thing to remember is that the PDF file needs to be optimized for web delivery, so be sure to check the "Optimized" box in whatever program you use to create your PDFs. Optimizing the PDF structures the document and the media it contains so that it can be delivered page by page. It also results in much smaller file sizes. When you save the PDF, be sure that you give it the proper *.pdf* suffix.

Alternatives to Acrobat

Acrobat is not your only option for converting your files to PDF. Because PDF is an open source technology, Adobe has opened the door to third-party developers who want to support the ability to create PDFs. These include shareware programs, Perl scripts, and even printer driver-based tools that fool your programs into thinking they are printing to a printer, when in fact they are creating a PDF file. A good place to look for PDF-related tools is PlanetPDF (*http://www.planetpdf.com*).

There are also online conversion services: you upload your file and it is converted for you for a small fee or subscription. Adobe has its own conversion service called Create Adobe PDF Online that charges a monthly fee, but your first three conversions are free. It is available at *http://cpdf.adobe.com*. Even better, check out Gohtm.com (*http://www.gohtm.com*), where they convert your documents to PDF for free!

These services may be a good alternative if you only need to create PDFs occasionally. If you plan to make PDFs part of your publishing process, Acrobat is a good investment because of the advanced features it offers.

HTML for Adding PDF Files to Web Pages

There are two basic ways of calling a PDF file from a web page: linking to the file (or a specific page within it) and embedding it in the page like an image.

Linking to a PDF file

Creating a link to a PDF file is the same as linking to any other document. Just include the file name in the URL as shown in this example:

```
<A HREF="documentation.pdf">Link to PDF file</A>
```

The PDF file resides on the server like any other media file. Most modern server software is preconfigured to recognize the PDF MIME type (type `application/pdf`, extension *.pdf*).

Linking to a specific page in a PDF file

It is possible to create a hypertext link to a specific page in a PDF document, allowing readers to jump just to the relevant information without waiting for the entire PDF document to download. It's a useful feature, but a number of criteria must be met in order for it to work:

- The server must support *byteserving*, a feature on web servers that allows them to deliver one page of the PDF file at a time. Byteserving is supported on the following servers: Microsoft Internet Information Server, Netscape Enterprise and Fastrack Servers, Apache, and Starnine Webster 3.0 (for Mac).

- The user's browser must be Netscape Navigator or Microsoft Internet Explorer Version 3.0 or higher.

- The user must have the Acrobat Plug-in or ActiveX control installed in the browser so that PDF files are displayed within the browser window.

Assuming all these elements are in place, it is easy to create the PDF and link to it. With the PDF document open in Acrobat, create a new destination at the page you want to link to and give it a logical name (e.g., *section3*). Add destinations with the Destinations palette (Window → Choose Destinations). Repeat for additional destinations. When you save the PDF file, be sure to check the Optimized checkbox. Optimizing the PDF file structures it page by page.

In the HTML document, make a link to the PDF file and the specific destination. The section name is separated from the file name by a hash symbol (#), as shown in this example:

```
<A HREF="article.pdf#section3">
```

For more information on page-serving PDF files, see the Adobe.com tutorial at *http://www.adobe.com/epaper/tips/acrlongpdf/main.html*. For more technical information about byteserving, see *http://www.adobe.com/support/techguides/acrobat/byteserve/byteservmain.html*.

Embedding a PDF file

A single-page PDF file can be embedded in a web page just like an image using the <img> tag:

```
<IMG SRC="directions.pdf" WIDTH="450" HEIGHT="400">
```

If a multipage PDF document is embedded in a web page, only the first page is displayed, without an Acrobat navigation toolbar. It is treated just like a static graphic. It is also advisable to list the file size of the file next to the link so users can make an informed decision whether to download it.

If the user clicks on the embedded PDF image, however, it launches the Acrobat Reader, where the multipage document is fully functional. This technique can be used to show a thumbnail of the PDF file before the file itself is opened.

Tips for Linking to PDF Files

As for any large media file, it is good web design etiquette to provide some indication of what users will get when they click on a link to a PDF file. The file format itself can be shown with a small PDF icon, by writing out the name of the file with its *.pdf* suffix, or by identifying the file type next to the link in parentheses, e.g., "link (PDF)".

As a courtesy to your users, consider also including a link to the Acrobat Reader download site. As of this writing, the URL is *http://www.adobe.com/products/ acrobat/readermain.html.*

For Further Reading

Gordon Kent's book *Internet Publishing with Acrobat* (Adobe Press), although somewhat out of date (it's based on Acrobat 3.0), is packed with succinct information about creating and using PDFs over the Web. It is also available for free in PDF format at *http://www.novagraphix.com/Internet_Publishing_with_Acrobat/.*

The Adobe site offers the best online resources for information on PDF. Be sure to check the following sections:

http://www.adobe.com/products/acrobat/main.html
   Adobe Acrobat Product Page

http://www.adobe.com/epaper/main.html
   ePaper Center

http://www.adobe.com/epaper/tips/main.html
   ePaper Center Tutorials

http://www.adobe.com/support/techguides/acrobat/main.html
   Acrobat Technical Guides

Once you are up and running, these sites have links and resources to keep you up to date with PDFs:

http://www.pdfzone.com
   PDF Zone

http://www.planetpdf.com
   PlanetPDF

Flash Printing

Another interface between the browser and printer comes from the folks at Macromedia. Flash 4.0 introduced a new feature to give developers control over printing Flash content. In the past, when a Flash movie was printed from a browser, the printout contained only the first frame (probably not the most useful frame) or nothing at all. To fix this, Flash Player (release 4.0.20 and higher) can print any content specified by the designer.

This feature can be used to print out a more meaningful frame from the movie, but why stop there? Since any content can be cued to print, the Flash movie can serve as an interactive interface to all sorts of documents. A banner ad can spit out a coupon that shoppers can take to the store. A small diagram could print pages of detailed specifications. You could also use Flash to design customized documents specifically for printing, such as greeting cards. Flash printing offers powerful possibilities for enhancing online interactivity with print components.

Users print Flash content via a context-sensitive menu accessed when clicking (option-click for Windows; control-click for Mac) on the Flash content, or by using a button designed into the Flash movie itself. The print function in the browser does not print the alternative Flash content.

The Flash print command triggers an ActionScript (the scripting language used in Flash) that detects the plug-in version; if it finds the compatible plug-in, it prints the specified Flash content. The content it prints is stored in a separate file in the Flash (SWF) format. This could be an image chosen from the current Flash movie, or any document created in Macromedia Flash, Freehand, Adobe Illustrator, or any program that supports Flash (SWF) files.

Again, this effect works only in Flash Player 4.0.20 or higher (4.0.20 has been shipping since December 16, 1999). In Flash 4.x, Flash printing works only within web browsers. The later 5.0 release works in a standalone Flash Player so printing functions can be added to CD-ROMs.

Because there is no print preview available for Flash content, it is recommended that you label your Flash print button very clearly with what happens if it is clicked. This is especially true if there is a large discrepancy between what you see on the screen and what will come out of the printer (like a banner ad that prints a 12-page brochure).

For more information on Flash printing, take advantage of these resources from Macromedia:

http://www.macromedia.com/support/flash/ts/documents/printing_from_browsers.htm
    The Flash Printing SDK contains information for creating printable Flash content. It includes a detailed and easy-to-follow set of instructions in PDF format.

http://www.macromedia.com/software/flash/open/webprinting/authoring.html
    The Flash 5 Print Authoring Kit contains more how-to information on creating Flash content for print.

CHAPTER 6

Accessibility

Responsible web design includes making pages accessible even to users with disabilities, such as hearing, sight, cognitive, or motor skills impairments. Millions of people have disabilities that affect their access to information on the Web.

Many disabled users take advantage of assistive technologies for web browsing, both for input and output. For instance, some people have disabilities that make it impossible to input information using a standard keyboard or mouse. Instead, they may use a speech input device or a simple pointer attached to a headset. Others have disabilities that hinder the way they get information from a page. Vision impaired users may use a text browser (such as Lynx) in conjunction with software that reads the contents of the screen aloud. Some use devices that translate the text into Braille for tactile reading.

For most sites, accessibility is proper web design etiquette; for government web sites, it is the law. Section 508 (effective June 25, 2001) mandates that all Federal agencies' electronic and information technology be accessible to people with disabilities. For more information, see *http://www.section508.gov.*

By promoting accessibility for those with disabilities, content becomes more available to all users, regardless of the device they use to access the Web. This includes any alternative to the standard desktop graphical browser, such as palmtop computers or automobile dashboard browsing systems. Even users who have graphics turned off in their browsers to speed up download times will benefit from basic accessibility measures.

The Web Accessibility Initiative (WAI)

The World Wide Web Consortium (W3C) has launched its Web Accessibility Initiative (WAI), which aims to make the Web universally accessible. The WAI ensures that web technologies such as HTML and CSS support accessibility and promotes education and research to see that the standards are understood and followed.

In addition to overseeing the development of web technologies, the WAI has created recommendation documents that address three key audiences. First, the *Web Content Accessibility Guidelines* recommendation provides rules and techniques for web designers and authors on how to create content that is as accessible as possible. This chapter focuses primarily on these efforts. The *Authoring Tool Accessibility Guidelines* speaks to software developers making web authoring tools. Tools should make it easy to create standards-compliant content, as well as being accessible themselves. And third, the *User Agent Accessibility Guidelines* are for developers of browsing devices, from standard desktop graphical browsers to specialized assistive technologies.

These documents, as well as useful news, tools, and resources, are available at the WAI site (*http://www.w3.org/WAI/*).

Web Content Accessibility Guidelines

In general, to make web content accessible to everyone, there is a greater reliance on text and document structure. That is not to say that sites need to be text-only and media-free in order to be accessible to everyone. The goal is to create sites that (as the WAI puts it) "transform gracefully" when accessed via alternative methods. Some simple examples include providing alternative text for images that can be read if the image can't be viewed, or providing a text transcript of an audio track if it can't be heard. It also requires the proper use of HTML markup for document structure and Cascading Style Sheets for presentation.

The *Web Content Accessibility Guidelines 1.0* document is a recommendation by the WAI for web designers and web content developers. It outlines the general principles of accessible design in the form of 14 guidelines. Each guideline is supported by a number of "checkpoints" that describe how the guideline applies. In addition, each point is given a priority rating: *Priority 1* means the guideline must be followed in all cases, *Priority 2* items should be addressed in order to make the material more accessible, and *Priority 3* means that the point may be addressed for the most thorough compliance with standards.

The Guidelines

Web Content Accessibility Guidelines 1.0 is a thorough and highly detailed document. What follows here is a summary of the guidelines to point you in the right direction. For the details, read the original document online at *http://www.w3.org/TR/WAI-WEBCONTENT/*.

Guideline 1: Provide equivalent alternatives to auditory and visual content.
> When providing text alternatives to images, video, and audio, be sure that the text has the same function and purpose as the media it is replacing. For example, if there is a graphic of an arrow that is used as a link to the top of the page, the alternative text should read "go to the top of the page," not "arrow." In addition, consider providing an auditory track (like a narrative explanation) for video media whose meaning is lost if it can't be seen.

Guideline 2: Don't rely on color alone.
> Make sure your site is usable in black and white and colors contrast sufficiently.

Guideline 3: Use markup and style sheets and do so properly.

Great strides have been made in HTML and CSS technology to aid in accessibility, but they are only successful if they are used consistently to separate style from content.

Guideline 4: Clarify natural language usage.

Identify the language of the document and mark up exceptions such as foreign words, abbreviations, and acronyms. This makes it easier for speech devices and other assistive technologies to interpret the content.

Guideline 5: Create tables that transform gracefully.

The WAI recommends that tables be used for tabular data only. In addition, taking advantage of the more descriptive HTML 4 table markup can help users with disabilities navigate through complex tables. It is also useful to provide a summary of the table's contents in the `<table>` tag.

Guideline 6: Ensure that pages featuring new technologies transform gracefully.

Make sure that your page still works and makes sense without style sheets, JavaScript, applets, or other objects added to the page.

Guideline 7: Ensure user control of time-sensitive changes.

Any scrolling, blinking, or otherwise moving object should be able to be paused or stopped. Audio should be able to be paused or turned off as well.

Guideline 8: Ensure direct accessibility of embedded user interfaces.

This means that if you create your own site interface using a Java applet or Flash, the interface should follow basic accessibility guidelines.

Guideline 9: Design for device-independence.

Keep in mind that users may be using a variety of input devices, such as a mouse, keyboard, voice, head wand, or other device. Take advantage of technologies that allow shortcuts to links and elements on the page.

Guideline 10: Use interim solutions.

The W3C is developing technologies that will be useful just while older browsers are catching up to the current HTML 4.0/CSS2 way of doing things. These interim solutions ensure that older browsers operate correctly.

Guideline 11: Use W3C technologies and guidelines.

This one seems like a given, but be sure to use the current technologies since they have been developed and reviewed thoughtfully to support accessibility.

Guideline 12: Provide context and orientation information.

Provide clear labels for frames, sections of the page, and any complex page structure that requires extra explanation. Keep in mind what it would be like to use your site if you couldn't see it.

Guideline 13: Provide clear navigation mechanisms.

Take measures to ensure your site is easy to navigate, including clearly identified links, a site map or index, and consistent navigation.

Guideline 14: Ensure documents are clear and simple.

Everyone benefits from web pages that are laid out clearly and use simple language.

The Techniques

WAI has also compiled a list of very practical applications of each of these principles in a document called *Techniques for Web Content Accessibility Guidelines 1.0*. It provides specific techniques that address each of the checkpoints outlined in the general guidelines document. It also acts as a gateway to a number of other resources that describe the specifics on how HTML, CSS, and other core technologies address accessibility.

The WAI Techniques document is too vast to summarize here, but the following list presents a few simple measures you can take to make your pages more accessible:

* Avoid using images for text and information.

* Provide alternative text for all images (via the `<img>` tag's `alt` or `longdesc` attribute). Make the alternative text rich and meaningful. Adding `alt` text should be standard procedure for all web page creation; in fact, in the new HTML 4.0 specification, the `alt` attribute is now a *required* part of the `<img>` tag. (See Chapter 9 for more information.)

* Add periods at the end of `alt` text so a speech device can locate the logical end of the phrase.

* When linking a graphic, provide a caption under it that also serves as a text link.

* Always provide text link alternatives for imagemaps.

* Offer a text-only version of the whole site from the home page.

* Provide transcripts or descriptions of audio clips to make that content accessible to those with hearing impairments.

* Provide alternative mechanisms for online forms, such as a text-based order form or a phone number for personal assistance.

* Avoid the `<blink>` tag, which is said to wreak havoc with Braille and speech displays.

* Be aware that misuse of HTML structural tags for presentation purposes (such as using the `<blockquote>` tag purely to achieve indents) hinders clear communication via a speech or Braille device.

* Avoid using pop-up windows as they can be disorienting to sight-impaired users.

If you would like to check how accessible your web page is, try running it through a validator, such as Bobby (*http://www.cast.org/bobby/*), that will scan your page and point out accessibility issues.

Accessibility in Web Technologies

Accessibility—addressing both the needs of the disabled and the growing usage of alternative and mobile browsing devices by the general public—has been a guiding force in the evolution of the technologies we use to create web content. Under the supervision of the WAI, both the HTML 4.0 and CSS2 specifications feature many methods for increasing access to web sites.

HTML 4.01 Features

The HTML 4.01 specification incorporates a number of new attributes and tags aimed specifically at making web documents available to a broader audience. This section lists only a broad summary of accessibility features in HTML 4.01. For a more detailed listing, see the WAI's *HTML Techniques for Web Content Accessibility Guidelines 1.0* at *http://www.w3.org/TR/WCAG10-HTML-TECHS/*. Or tackle the HTML 4.0 Specification yourself at *http://www.w3.org/TR/REC-html40/*. Accessibility features of the Specification include:

- Increased distinction between document structure and presentation. HTML 4.0 encourages the use of Cascading Style Sheets for stylistic information.

- Navigational aids such as access keys and tab index for keyboard-only access to page elements.

- A new client-side imagemap recommendation that integrates image and text links.

- Introduction of the `<abbr>` and `<acronym>` tags, which assist speech devices and other agents in the interpretation of abbreviations and acronyms.

- The ability to group table columns and rows logically and to provide captions, summaries, and long descriptions of table contents, thus making the table interpretation easier.

- The ability to group form controls and make long lists of choices easier to comprehend. Form elements are also accessible via tabbing and access keys.

- Improved mechanisms for providing alternative text. The `alt` attribute is now required in the `<img>` tag. The `longdesc` attribute has been introduced to provide a link to longer text explanations of images. The `title` attribute can be added to provide additional information to any element.

CSS2 Features

The latest Cascading Style Sheets recommendation, CSS Level 2 (or CSS2), also provides mechanisms for improved interpretation by nongraphical and nonvisual devices. The following is just a summary of features. For more information, read the WAI's review at *http://www.w3.org/TR/WCAG10-CSS-TECHS/* or look at the CSS2 Recommendation directly at *http://www.w3.org/TR/REC-CSS2/*. Improvements include:

- Mechanisms by which a user-created style sheet can override all the higher style sheets in the cascade, giving the end user ultimate control over display. The user can create a custom style sheet for displaying pages according to special needs.

- Positioning and alignment mechanisms that further separate content from presentation. These style sheet rules aim to eliminate the abuse of HTML tags in order to achieve special presentation effects. The HTML tags can be used for the logical structuring of the document, making them more easily interpreted by nonvisual agents.

- The ability to customize style sheets for a variety of media (including screen, Braille, aural, etc.) using the `media` attribute and `@media` rule. Unfortunately, alternative media are not well supported as of this writing, with the exception of targeting printed output (see Chapter 5).

- A set of controls for the audio rendering of web-delivered information.

- Improved navigation devices, such as the ability to add numbered markers throughout a document for orientation purposes.

- Specific support for downloadable fonts, eliminating the tendency to put text in graphics to improve the appearance of the page.

Accessibility in Tools

In addition to educating web developers, the WAI works with software and hardware developers to ensure accessibility in the tools used to create and utilize web content.

Content Creation

WAI works closely with web authoring tool developers to ensure that their tools make it easy for web content authors and designers to create accessible and standards-compliant code. In addition, it is necessary for these tools to be accessible themselves.

Web technology companies are keenly aware of the importance of accessibility on the Web, and they are also proud of their efforts to comply. The bigger players publish manifestos on their efforts to make their products and proprietary technology available to as wide an audience as possible.

http://www.microsoft.com/enable/
    Microsoft has been throwing its muscle at raising the standards of accessibility in the software industry since 1988 and is at the forefront of the accessibility initiative on the Web. Their site, *Microsoft Accessibility: Technology for Everyone*, contains background information, news, tools, product information, and many other resources related to their efforts.

http://www.macromedia.com/macromedia/accessibility/
    This overview of Macromedia's accessibility program provides information on how each of their products supports W3C accessibility guidelines. Macromedia has developed the Flash Accessibility Kit, which includes code and guidelines for improving the accessibility of Flash content, and the Dreamweaver Accessibility Extension, which allows authors to check the accessibility of the pages they create.

http://access.adobe.com
    This page summarizes Adobe's efforts to make the PDF format more accessible to users with disabilities. It provides highlights of accessibility features built into Acrobat 5.0, tools to help authors optimize PDF files for accessibility, and links to online conversion tools that turn PDF files into HTML or ASCII documents (so they can be read by assistive technologies).

Browsing Devices

The WAI also works to coordinate the efforts of developers of assistive technologies. Users with disabilities use a whole range of approaches for browsing. There is a useful list of alternative devices and assistive technologies on the WAI site at *http://www.w3.org/WAI/References/Browsing/*. It contains lists of browsers specifically designed for people with disabilities, screen readers that can read content from standard browsers, existing browsers with accessibility features, voice browsers that can interpret web content from a direct telephone connection, and a variety of other access methods. In addition to links and descriptions of each tool, some also feature demonstrations so you can get a feel for what it is like to browse pages with alternative methods.

CHAPTER 7

Internationalization

If the Web is to reach a truly worldwide audience, it needs to be able to support the display of all the languages of the world, with all their unique alphabets and symbols, directionality, and specialized punctuation. This poses a big challenge to HTML constructs as we know them. However, according to the W3C, "energetic efforts" are being made toward this complicated goal.

The W3C's efforts for internationalization (often referred to as "i18n"—an i, then 18 letters, then an n) address two primary issues. First is the handling of alternative character sets that take into account all the writing systems of the world; second is how to specify languages and their unique presentation requirements within an HTML document. Many solutions presented by internationalization experts in a document called RFC 2070 were incorporated into the current HTML 4.0, XML 1.0, and CSS2 specifications.

This chapter addresses key issues for internationalization, including character sets and new language features in HTML 4 and CSS2. Be aware that many of these features are not yet supported by browsers, even the most current.

Character Sets

The first challenge in internationalization is dealing with the staggering number of unique character shapes (called "glyphs") that occur in the writing systems of the world. This includes not only alphabets, but also all ideographs (characters that indicate a whole word or concept) for languages such as Chinese, Japanese, and Korean.

8-Bit Encoded Character Sets

Character encodings (or character sets) are organizations of characters—units of a written language system—in which each character is assigned a specific number. Each character may be associated with a number of different glyphs; for instance, the "close quote" character may be displayed using a " or » glyph, depending on the language. In addition, a single glyph may correspond to different characters, such as a comma serving as both the punctuation symbol for a pause in a sentence as well as a decimal indicator in some languages.

The number of characters available in a character set is limited by the bit-depth of its encoding. For example, 8 bits are capable of describing 256 unique characters, which is enough for most western languages.

HTML 2.0 and 3.2 are based on the 8-bit character set for western languages called Latin-1 (or ISO 8859-1). There are a number of other 8-bit encodings, including:

ISO 8859-5	Cyrillic
ISO 8859-6	Arabic
ISO 8859-7	Greek
ISO 8859-8	Hebrew
SHIFT_JIS	Japanese
EUC-JP	Japanese

16-Bit Encoded Character Sets

Sixteen bits of information are capable of representing 65,536 (2^{16}) different characters—enough to contain a large number of alphabets and ideographs. In 1991, the Unicode Consortium created a 16-bit encoded "super" character set called Unicode (practically identical to another standard called ISO 10646-1) which includes nearly every character from the world's writing systems. The combination of Unicode and ISO 10646 is called the Universal Character Set (UCS). Each character is assigned a unique two-octet code (2 groups of 8 bits, making 16 bits total). The first 256 slots are given to the ISO 8859-1 character set, so it is backwards compatible.

The HTML 4.01 specification officially adopts Unicode as its document character set. So regardless of the character encoding used when a document was created, it is converted to the document character set by the browser, which interprets characters with special meaning in HTML (such as < and >) and converts character entities (such as © for ©). In cases where a character entity points outside of the Latin-1 character set (e.g., ϖ for π), HTML 4.0 browsers use the Unicode character set to display the correct character.

This is the first step toward making the Web truly multilingual. The current refinements to character-set handling on the Web are documented in a working draft, the *Character Model for the World Wide Web 1.0*, published by the W3C (*http://www.w3.org/TR/charmod/*).

A Unicode Font

Bitstream has created a TrueType font called "Cyberbit" that contains a large percentage of the Unicode character set. It is available only via licensing to developers and is unfortunately no longer offered as a retail product. For more information about Cyberbit, contact Bitstream's developer products department at *oemsales@bitsream.com*.

Specifying Character Encoding

When a web client (a browser) and a server make a transaction, meta-information about the requested and returned document is communicated in the HTTP headers for the request and response. One of the most important bits of information specified is the content-type, which describes the type of data the server is sending. The charset parameter further specifies the character set used for a text document. A typical HTTP header looks like this:

```
Content-type: text/html; charset=ISO-8859-8
```

To deliberately set the character-encoding information in a document header, use the <meta> tag with its http-equiv attribute (which adds its values into the HTTP header). The meta tag that corresponds to the above header message looks like this:

```
<META http-equiv="Content-Type" content="text/html; charset=ISO-8859-8">
```

Note that the browser must support your chosen character set in order for the page to display properly.

Browsers that are capable of sending an accept-charset value can specify their preferred character encoding when requesting a document. The server can then serve the document with the appropriate encoding, if the preferred version is available.

The accept-charset attribute is already a part of the HTML 4.0 specification for form elements. With the accept-charset attribute, the document can specify which character sets the server can receive from the user in text input fields.

HTML 4.01 Language Features

Coordinating character sets is only the first part of the challenge. Even languages that share a character set may have different rules for hyphenation, spacing, quotation marks, punctuation, and so on. In addition to character shapes (glyphs), issues such as directionality (whether the text reads left-to-right or right-to-left) and cursive joining behavior have to be taken into account as well.

This prompted a need for a system of language identification. The W3C responded by incorporating into HTML the language tags put forth in the RFC 2070 standard on internationalization.

The lang Attribute

The lang attribute can be added within any tag to specify the language of the contained element. It can also be added within the <html> tag to specify a language for an entire document. The following example specifies the document's language as French:

```
<HTML LANG="fr">
```

It can also be used within text elements to switch to other languages within a document; for example, you can "turn on" Norwegian for just one element:

```
<BLOCKQUOTE lang="no">...</BLOCKQUOTE>
```

The value for the `lang` attribute is a language code (not the same as a country code). The current HTML and XML specifications support the two-letter country codes established in RFC 1766. These are listed in Table 7-1. However, there have been advancements in language identification to include three-letter codes, two-letter codes with country subcode (for example, fr-CA for French as used in Canada), and other descriptive subcodes as proposed in RFC 3066. Eventually, this revised system will be supported in future updates of HTML and XML specifications.

Table 7-1: Two-letter codes of language names

Code	Country	Code	Country	Code	Country
aa	Afar	fy	Frisian	lv	Latvian
ab	Abkhazian	ga	Irish	mg	Malagasy
af	Afrikaans	gd	Scots Gaelic	mi	Maori
am	Amharic	gl	Galician	mk	Macedonian
ar	Arabic	gn	Guarani	ml	Malayalam
as	Assamese	gu	Gujarati	mn	Mongolian
ay	Aymara	ha	Hausa	mo	Moldavian
az	Azerbaijani	he	Hebrew (formerly iw)	mr	Marathi
ba	Bashkir	hi	Hindi	ms	Malay
be	Byelorussian	hr	Croatian	mt	Maltese
bg	Bulgarian	hu	Hungarian	my	Burmese
bh	Bihari	hy	Armenian	na	Nauru
bi	Bislama	ia	Interlingua	ne	Nepali
bn	Bengali; Bangla	id	Indonesian (formerly in)	nl	Dutch
bo	Tibetan	ie	Interlingue	no	Norwegian
br	Breton	ik	Inupiak	oc	Occitan
ca	Catalan	is	Icelandic	om	(Afan) Oromo
co	Corsican	it	Italian	or	Oriya
cs	Czech	iu	Inuktitut	pa	Punjabi
cy	Welsh	ja	Japanese	pl	Polish
da	Danish	jw	Javanese	ps	Pashto, Pushto
de	German	ka	Georgian	pt	Portuguese
dz	Bhutani	kk	Kazakh	qu	Quechua
el	Greek	kl	Greenlandic	rm	Rhaeto-Romance
en	English	km	Cambodian	rn	Kirundi
eo	Esperanto	kn	Kannada	ro	Romanian
es	Spanish	ko	Korean	ru	Russian
et	Estonian	ks	Kashmiri	rm	Kinyarwanda
eu	Basque	ku	Kurdish	sa	Sanskrit
fa	Persian	ky	Kirghiz	sd	Sindhi
fi	Finnish	la	Latin	sg	Sangho
fj	Fiji	lm	Lingala	sh	Serbo-Croatian
fo	Faroese	lo	Laothian	si	Sinhalese
fr	French	lt	Lithuanian	sk	Slovak

Table 7-1: Two-letter codes of language names (continued)

Code	Country	Code	Country	Code	Country
sl	Slovenian	tg	Tajik	uk	Ukrainian
sm	Samoan	th	Thai	ur	Urdu
sn	Shona	ti	Tigrinya	uz	Uzbek
so	Somali	tk	Turkmen	vi	Vietnamese
sq	Albanian	tl	Tagalog	vo	Volapuk
sr	Serbian	tn	Setswana	wo	Wolof
ss	Siswati	to	Tonga	xh	Xhosa
st	Sesotho	tr	Turkish	yi	Yiddish (formerly ji)
su	Sundanese	ts	Tsonga	yo	Yoruba
sv	Swedish	tt	Tatar	za	Zhuang
sw	Swahili	tw	Twi	zh	Chinese
ta	Tamil	ug	Uighur	zu	Zulu
te	Telugu				

Directionality

An internationalized HTML standard needs to take into account that many languages read from right to left. Directionality is part of a character's encoding within Unicode.

The HTML 4.01 specification provides the new `dir` attribute for specifying the direction in which the text should be interpreted. It can be used in conjunction with the `lang` attribute and may be added within the tags of most elements. The accepted value for direction is either `ltr` for left-to-right or `rtl` for right-to-left. For example, the following code indicates that the paragraph is intended to be displayed in Arabic, reading from right to left:

```
<P LANG="ar" DIR="rtl">...</P>
```

There is also a new tag introduced in HTML 4.01 that deals specifically with documents that contain combinations of left- and right-reading text (bidirectional text, or Bidi for short). The `<bdo>` tag is used for "bidirectional override," in other words, to specify a span of text that should override the intrinsic direction (as inherited from Unicode) of the text it contains. The `<bdo>` tag takes the `dir` attribute as follows:

```
<BDO DIR="ltr">English phrase in an otherwise Hebrew text</BDO>...
```

The `<bdo>` element and `dir` attribute are currently not supported by browsers.

Cursive Joining Behavior

In some writing systems, the shape of a character varies depending on its position in the word. For instance, in Arabic, a character used at the beginning of a word looks completely different when it is used as the last character of a word. Generally, this joining behavior is handled within the software, but there are Unicode characters that give precise control over joining behavior. They have zero width and are placed between characters purely to specify whether the neighboring characters should join.

HTML 4.01 provides mnemonic character entities for both these characters, as shown in Table 7-2.

Table 7-2: Unicode characters for joining behavior

Mnemonic	Numeric	Name	Description
‌	‌	zero-width non-joiner	Prevents joining of characters that would otherwise be joined
‍	‍	zero-width joiner	Joins characters that would otherwise not be joined

Style Sheets Language Features

The first version of Cascading Style Sheets (CSS) did not include any mechanisms for dealing with anything but standard western, left-to-right languages.

CSS Level 2 introduces a few controls that specifically address multilingualism. For more information on these properties, see the CSS2 recommendation (*http://www. w3.org/TR/REC-CSS2/*).

Directionality
> The direction and unicode-bidi properties in CSS2 allow authors to specify text direction, similar to the <dir> and <bdo> tags in HTML.

Automatic list numbering
> Using the list-style-type property, it is possible to specify a variety of automatic numbering schemes, including some foreign languages such as Hebrew and Japanese.

Quotation marks
> The quotes property is used to specify quotation marks appropriate to the current language of the text.

Future levels of CSS will address advanced foreign language attributes such as vertical text and *ruby* text. Ruby text is a run of text that appears alongside another run of text (the base). It serves as an annotation or pronunciation guide, as in the case of phonetic Japanese characters that run above the pictorial kanji symbols to aid readers who do not understand the symbols. The current efforts to extend CSS for internationalization are published in the working draft *International Layout* (*http://www.w3.org/TR/i18n-format/*). It includes interesting proposals for page layout grids for accommodating vertical text, representing ruby text, and applying existing CSS2 properties to alternative text layouts.

For More Information

The following are good sources of information on the internationalization of the Web.

World Wide Web Consortium (W3C): Internationalization and Localization
> This site contains excellent technical information, as well as updates on activities surrounding the efforts to make the Web multilingual. See *http://www. w3c.org/International/*.

Babel

Babel is an Alis Technologies/Internet Society joint project to internationalize the Internet. See *http://babel.alis.com:8080*.

HTML Unleashed, by Rick Darnell, et al. (Sams.net Publishing, 1997)

This book contains an excellent and in-depth explanation of internationalization issues in Chapter 39, *Internationalizing HTML Character Set and Language Tags*. This chapter is available online at *http://www.webreference. com/dlab/books/html/39-0.html*.

International-
ization

PART II

Authoring

CHAPTER 8

HTML Overview

HTML (Hypertext Markup Language) is the language used to create web documents. It defines the syntax and placement of the elements that make up the structure of a web document. All web page elements are identified by special tags that give browsers instructions on how to display the content (the tags themselves do not display). Some HTML tags are used to create links to other documents, either locally or over a network such as the Internet.

This chapter provides a basic introduction to the background and general syntax of HTML, including document structure, tags, and their attributes. It also looks briefly at good HTML style and the pros and cons of using WYSIWYG authoring tools.

For a more in-depth study of HTML, I recommend *HTML and XHTML: The Definitive Guide*, by Chuck Musciano and Bill Kennedy (O'Reilly, 2000). Another excellent resource for HTML tag information is the HTML Compendium (created by Ron Woodall). The Compendium provides an alphabetical listing of every HTML tag and its attributes, with explanations and up-to-date browser support information for each. The browser support charts accompanying each tag in this book are based on the Compendium. The HTML Compendium can be found at *http://www.htmlcompendium.org*.

The HTML Standard

The HTML standard and all other Web-related standards are developed under the authority of the World Wide Web Consortium (W3C). Standards, specifications, and drafts of new proposals can be found at *http://www.w3.org*. The most recent standard for document markup is the HTML 4.01 specification.

The HTML standard traveled a long, difficult road to its current state of relative stability. Early on, competition between the major web browsers led to a mess of proprietary tags, HTML extensions, and practices that muddied the original intent of HTML in favor of more control over page display.

The W3C has pulled in the reins with the HTML 4.0 specification (which is further refined in the current 4.01 version). It incorporates many of the tags introduced by the popular browsers that improve web functionality. It also officially "deprecates" tags that are used in common practice but are not in keeping with the priorities of the markup language (such as keeping style information out of content).

Keeping Style Separate from Content

Before HTML there was SGML (Standard Generalized Markup Language), which established the system of describing documents in terms of their structure, independent of appearance. SGML is a vast set of rules for developing markup languages such as HTML, but it is so all-encompassing that HTML uses only a small subset of its capabilities.

Publishers began storing SGML versions of their documents so that they could be translated into a variety of end uses. For example, text that is tagged as a heading may be formatted one way if the end product is a printed book, but another way for a CD-ROM. The advantage is that a single source file can be used to create a variety of end products. The way it is interpreted and displayed (i.e., the way it looks) depends on the end use.

Because HTML is one application of an SGML tagging system, this principle of keeping style information separate from the structure of the document remains inherent to the HTML purpose. Over the past few years, this ideal has been compromised by the creation of HTML tags that contain explicit style instructions, such as the <font> tag.

Cascading Style Sheets promise to keep style information out of the content by storing all style instructions in a separate document (or a separate section of the source document). With this system in place, the W3C is more diligent than ever to clean up the HTML standard to make it work the way it was intended. For more information, see Chapter 17.

Three Flavors of HTML 4.01

While the W3C has definite ideas on how HTML should work, they are also aware that it is going to be a while before old browsers are phased out and web authors begin to mark up documents properly. For that reason, the HTML 4.01 specification actually encompasses three slightly different specification documents: one "strict," one "transitional," and one just for framed documents. These documents, called Document Type Definitions (or DTDs), define every tag, attribute, and entity along with the rules for their use. DTDs are written following the rules and conventions of SGML (Standard Generalized Markup Language).

The HTML 4.01 Strict DTD excludes all deprecated tags and attributes (those scheduled to be phased out). In an ideal world, all developers would mark up the structure of their documents according to the strict version of HTML, leaving all presentation to be handled by style sheets.

The HTML 4.01 Transitional DTD is less restrictive, and it includes many of the elements dedicated to appearance (such as the <font> tag and the align attribute) that are in common use today. Most developers today comply with the transitional specification because it allows more control over presentation while the industry waits for older browsers (those that don't support new features such as style sheets) to fade away.

The Frameset DTD is identical to the Transitional DTD, except that it allows for the `<frameset>` element to be used in place of the standard `<body>` element. Frames are discussed in Chapter 14.

The Web Standards Movement

After years of frustration coding for incompatible browsers, the web development community finally said, "Enough is enough!" and began putting pressure on the browser developers to change their ways. The charge was led in part by the Web Standards Project (WaSP, *http://www.webstandards.org*), an industry watchdog group that works diligently to convince the browser developers that it is in everyone's best interest to comply with the established web standards.

Fortunately, the browser developers listened, and things have settled considerably in the last three years. Microsoft Internet Explorer began nearly complete support for HTML 4.01 in Version 5.5 for Windows (5.0 for Mac). Netscape's 4.x releases support most of the tags in the HTML 4.0 specification, and its 6.0 release is fully compliant with HTML 4.01 (with very few exceptions). Other browsers, most notably Opera, have stuck to the specifications from the very beginning.

But WaSP doesn't stop with the browser developers. If there is to be a true set of web standards (including HTML, but also CSS, JavaScript, and the Document Object Model), everybody needs to abide by them. Web developers need to give up the convenience and habit of sloppy HTML code and follow the HTML 4.01 mandates to keep style separate from structure and content. Web authoring tool developers must make it easy to generate standards-compliant code with their tools. Furthermore, users must ditch their old non-standards-compliant browsers and upgrade to current versions. WaSP is diligent in its efforts, but there is still much work to be done before all these pieces fall seamlessly into place.

Web Standards in This Book

The intention of this book is to be highly mindful of and compliant with the standards effort. The tag information in the following chapters reflects the current HTML 4.01 Transitional Specification. However, it also represents HTML common practices and includes some tags that are not necessarily part of the standard. In all cases where a tag or attribute is proprietary (works with only one browser) or deprecated by the W3C, it is clearly labeled as such. In this way, I hope to paint a complete picture of HTML while endorsing the standard.

The Future of HTML

According to the W3C, HTML 4.01 is the end of the line for HTML as we know it. The next version of HTML is the XHTML Version 1.0 specification. XHTML is the same HTML specification as we know it today, but rewritten using the new-and-improved rules of XML (Extensible Markup Language). XHTML uses all the same HTML 4.01 tags, but it enforces a set of rules (such as closing all tags, putting attribute values in quotation marks, and keeping tags all lowercase) that make a document "well-formed." Well-formed XHTML will work in next-generation XML-based browsers, where HTML will not. Our current HTML coding standards are incredibly lax by comparison.

These topics are discussed further in Chapters 30 and 31.

HTML Tags

Elements in the HTML specification are indicated by tags. An HTML tag is made up of the element name followed by an optional list of attributes, all of which appears between angle brackets (<>). Nothing within the brackets is displayed in the browser. The tag name is generally an abbreviation of the element's name or the tag's function (this makes them fairly simple to learn). Attributes are properties that extend or refine the tag's function.

In the current specification, the name and attributes within a tag are not case sensitive. <BODY BGCOLOR=white> works the same as <body bgcolor=white>. However, values for particular attributes may be case sensitive, particularly URLs and filenames.

 Because tags are not case-sensitive in the HTML 4.01 specification, the tags in sample code throughout this book are written in all uppercase letters for improved readability. In future iterations of HTML (namely XHTML, discussed in Chapter 31), tags and attributes will be required to be all lowercase. While it is recommended that developers begin the good habit of coding in all lowercase immediately, this book follows the conventions for tag display established within the HTML 4.01 specification itself.

Containers

Most HTML elements or components are containers, meaning they have a *start tag* and an *end tag*. The text enclosed within the tags follows the tag's instructions. In the following example, the <I> container tags make the enclosed text italic:

    The weather is <I>gorgeous</I> today.

Result: The weather is *gorgeous* today.

The end tag contains the same name as the start tag, but it is preceded by a slash (/). You can think of it as an "off" switch for the tag.

For some tags, the end tag is optional and the browser determines when the tag ends by context. This practice is most common with the <p> (paragraph) tag. Most browsers automatically end a paragraph when they encounter a new start tag (although Navigator 4.x has some problems with autoclosing), so many web authors take advantage of the shortcut. Not all tags allow this, however, and not all browsers are forgiving, so when in doubt include the end tag. This is especially

---

important when using Cascading Style Sheets (discussed in Chapter 17) with your document. The new XHTML standard also requires that all tags be closed.

In the HTML charts that appear in this book, container tags are indicated with the syntax < >...</ >. If the end tag is optional, it's noted in the tag's explanation.

Empty ("Standalone") Tags

A few tags do not have end tags because they are used to place standalone elements in the document or on the page. The image tag (<img>) is such a tag; it simply plops a graphic into the flow of the page. Other standalone tags include the linebreak (<br>), horizontal rule (<hr>), and tags that provide information about a document and don't affect its displayed content, such as the <meta> and <base> tags. Table 8-1 lists all the tags in the HTML 4.01 specification that do not take end tags.

Table 8-1: Empty HTML tags

<area>	<frame>	<link>
<base>	<hr>	<meta>
<basefont>	<img>	<param>
 	<input>	
<col>	<isindex>	

Attributes

Attributes are added within a tag to extend or modify the tag's actions. Attributes always go in the start tag only (end tags never contain attributes). You can add multiple attributes within a single tag. Tag attributes, if any, go after the tag name, each separated by one or more spaces. Their order of appearance is not important.

Most attributes take *values*, which follow an equals sign (=) after the attribute's name. Most browsers cannot handle attribute values more than 1,024 characters in length. Values may be case-sensitive, particularly filenames or URLs.

The syntax for a container tag with attributes is as follows:

```
<ELEMENT ATTRIBUTE="value">Affected text</ELEMENT>
```

The following are examples of tags that contain attributes:

```
<IMG SRC="graphics/pixie.gif" WIDTH="45" HEIGHT="60">
<BODY BGCOLOR="#000000">...</BODY>
<FONT FACE="Trebuchet MS, Arial, Helvetica" SIZE="4">...</FONT>
```

The HTML 4.01 specification recommends that all attribute values be enclosed in quotation marks, but it acknowledges that in some cases, they may be omitted. If the value is a single word containing only letters (a-z or A-Z), digits (0-9), hyphens (-), periods (.), underscores (_), and colons (:), then it can be placed directly after the equals sign without quotation marks. If you are still unsure, using quotation marks consistently for all values works just fine and is definitely a good idea. In the XHTML specification, all attribute values must be enclosed in quotation marks in order to be well-formed.

Be careful not to leave out the closing quotation mark, or all the content from the opening quotation mark until the browser encounters a subsequent quotation mark will be interpreted as part of the value and won't display in the browser. This is a simple mistake that can cause hours of debugging frustration.

Nesting HTML Tags

HTML elements may be contained within other HTML elements. This is called *nesting*, and to do it properly, both the beginning and end tags of the enclosed tag must be completely contained within the beginning and end tags of the applied tag. In this example, a bold style (`<b>`) is applied to already italic text:

```
The weather is <B><I>gorgeous</I></B> today.
```

Result: The weather is *gorgeous* today.

Nested tags do not necessarily need to appear right next to each other. In this example, the bold text is nested within a longer link.

```
This links to <A HREF="document.html">a really <B>cool</B> page</A>.
```

Result: This links to a really **cool** page.

A common mistake is simply overlapping the tags. Nested tags must be contained entirely (both the start and end tags) within the outer set of tags. Although some browsers display content marked up this way, other browsers do not allow the violation, so it is important to nest tags correctly. The following example shows incorrect nesting of tags (the `<I>` tag should have been closed before the `<B>` tag):

```
INCORRECT: The weather is <B><I>gorgeous</B></I> today.
```

Information Browsers Ignore

Some information in an HTML document, including certain tags, is ignored when the document is viewed in a browser. These include:

Line breaks
Line returns in the HTML document are ignored. Text and elements wrap continuously until they encounter a `<p>` or `<br>` tag within the flow of the document text. Line breaks are displayed, however, when text is tagged as preformatted text (`<pre>`).

Tabs and multiple spaces
When a browser encounters a tab or more than one consecutive blank character space in an HTML document, it displays it as a single space. So, if the document contains:

```
far,            far              away
```

the browser displays:

far, far away

Extra spaces can be added within the flow of text by using the nonbreaking space character entity (` `). Multiple spaces are displayed, however, when text is tagged as preformatted text (`<pre>`).

Multiple <p> tags

A series of paragraph tags (`<p>`...`</p>` or `<p>` alone) with no intervening text is interpreted as redundant by all browsers and displays as though it were only a single paragraph break. Most browsers display multiple `<br>` tags as multiple line breaks.

Unrecognized tags

A browser simply ignores any tag it doesn't understand or that was incorrectly specified. Depending on the tag and the browser, this can have varied results. The browser displays nothing at all, or it may display the contents of the tag as though it were normal text.

Text in comments

Browsers do not display text between the special `<!--` and `-->` elements used to denote a *comment*. Here is a sample comment:

```
<!-- This is a comment -->
<!-- This is a
multiple line comment
that ends here. -->
```

There must be a space after the initial `<!--` and preceding the final `-->`, but you can put nearly anything inside the comment otherwise. You cannot nest comments. Microsoft Internet Explorer also supports its own proprietary way of indicating comments with `<comment>` ... `</comment>` tags. Comments are useful for leaving notes within a long HTML file, for example:

```
<!-- navigation table starts here -->
```

Document Structure

A typical HTML document is divided into two major portions: the **head** and the **body**. The **head** contains information about the document, such as its title and "meta" information describing the contents. The **body** contains the actual contents of the document (the part that is displayed in the browser window). The following example shows the tags that make up the standard skeletal structure of an HTML document. Document structure is discussed more thoroughly in Chapter 9.

```
<HTML>
  <HEAD>
    <TITLE>Document Title</TITLE>
  </HEAD>
  <BODY>
    Contents of Document
  </BODY>
</HTML>
```

HTML 4.01 specifies that the minimal HTML document should also include a line that identifies the HTML version using the `<!DOCTYPE>` declaration. This is discussed further in Chapter 9. It is also recommended that documents include an

`<address>` element that contains the name and contact information of the document's author, usually near the end of the document. This is slow to be adopted in common practice.

Tips on Good HTML Style

This section offers some guidelines for writing "good" HTML—code that will be supported by a wide variety of browsers, handled easily by applications expecting correct HTML, and extensible to emerging technologies built on the current HTML specification.

- **Follow HTML syntax as described by the current available W3C specification.**
  Writing HTML "correctly" may take extra effort, but it ensures that your document displays the way you intend it to on the greatest number of browsers. Browsers vary in how strictly they parse HTML. For instance, if you omit a closing `</table>` tag, some versions of Internet Explorer display the contents of the table just fine, while Netscape Navigator leaves that portion of your web page completely blank.

  The Opera browser is particularly stringent. Simple slips or shortcuts that slide right by Navigator or Internet Explorer may cause your whole web page to self-destruct. If you are careful in the way you write your HTML (minding your `<p>`s and `<q>`s!), you will have more success on more browsers.

- **Validate your HTML.** To be absolutely sure about how you're doing, you should run your HTML code through one of the many available online HTML validation services, such as the ones at the W3C (*http://validator.w3.org*), Net-Mechanic (*http://www.netmechanic.com*), Web Design Group (*http://www. htmlhelp.com*), and Doctor HTML (*http://www2.imagiware.com/RxHTML/*).

- **Follow code-writing conventions to make your HTML document easier to read.**
  Although not a true programming language, HTML documents bear some resemblance to programming code in that they are usually long ASCII documents littered with tags and commands. The overall impression can be chaotic, making it difficult to find the specific element you're looking for. There are a few techniques that can make your pages more legible:

  — Use comments to delineate sections of code so you can find them quickly.

  — Because browsers ignore line breaks, tabs, and extra spaces in the HTML document, they can be used to make your document easier to scan. Be aware, however, that these extra keystrokes add to the size of your document (because blank spaces are transmitted as ASCII just like all other characters), so don't go overboard.

  — And last, because HTML tags are not case-sensitive, you may choose to write tags in all capital letters to make them easier to find. However, this technique is discouraged now that the upcoming XHTML standard requires all tags and attributes to be lowercase.

- **Avoid adding extra or redundant tags.** Extra and redundant HTML tags add unnecessary bytes to the size of your HTML file, causing slightly longer download times. They also make the browser work harder to parse the file, further increasing display times. One example of redundant tagging is multiple and identical `<font>` tags within a sentence, a common side effect of making small edits with a WYSIWYG authoring tool.

- **Keep good HTML style in mind when naming your files.** Consider these guidelines:

  — Use the proper HTML document suffix *.html* (or *.htm* on a Windows server). Suffixes for a number of common file types can be found in Table 4-1.

  — Avoid spaces and special characters such as ?, %, #, etc. in filenames. It is best to limit filenames to letters, numbers, underscores (in place of spaces), hyphens, and periods.

  — Filenames are case-sensitive in HTML. Consistently using all lowercase letters in filenames, while certainly not necessary, may make them easier to remember.

 Line breaks and extra spaces can create unwanted white space in certain contexts. For instance, if you have a string of graphics that should abut seamlessly, adding a line break or a space between the `<img>` tags will introduce extra space between the graphics (even though, technically, it shouldn't). In addition, extra spaces within and between table cells (`<td>` tags) can add unwanted spaces in your table. This is discussed further in Chapter 13.

HTML Tools

HTML documents are simple ASCII text files, which means you can use any minimal text editor to write them. Fortunately, there are a number of tools that make the process of generating HTML documents more quick and efficient. They fall into two main categories: HTML editors and WYSIWYG (What-You-See-Is-What-You-Get) web authoring tools.

HTML Editors

HTML editors are text editing tools designed especially for writing HTML. They require that you know how to compose HTML by hand; however, they save time by providing shortcuts for repetitive tasks like setting up documents, tables, or simply applying styles to text.

There are scores of simple HTML editors available, and many of them are free. Just enter "HTML Editor" in the search field of Shareware.com (*http://www.shareware.com*) and wade through the results. For purposes of brevity, I'm going to cut to the chase.

Windows users should definitely check out HomeSite, a high-powered and inexpensive HTML editor from Allaire (recently merged with Macromedia). It features HTML shortcuts and templates, color-coded HTML syntax, an FTP function, HTML syntax checker, spell-checker, and multiple-file search-and-replace. In addition, it includes wizards for creating more complex elements (such as frames, JavaScript, and DHTML) and many other attractive features. For more information and to download a demo copy, see *http://www.allaire.com/products/HomeSite/*. Home-Site information is also accessible on the Macromedia site at *http://www.macromedia.com/software/*.

If you're working on a Macintosh, you want BBEdit, a commercial HTML editor from Bare Bones Software, Inc. It is overwhelmingly the editor of choice among Mac-based web developers. It includes features such as an array of HTML shortcut tools, color-coded HTML syntax, multiple-file search-and-replace, a built-in FTP function, support for 13 programming languages, a table builder, an HTML syntax checker, and a lot more. For more information and to download a demo version, see *http://www.bbedit.com*.

WYSIWYG Authoring Tools

WYSIWYG HTML editors have graphical interfaces that make writing HTML more like using a word processor or page layout program. So for instance, if you want to add an image, just drag it from the desktop onto the page; the authoring tool creates all the HTML coding needed to accomplish the effect on the screen. In addition to simple style and format shortcuts, many of these tools automate more complex tasks such as creating Cascading Style Sheets, adding JavaScript functionality, and generating time-based DHTML effects. Some can even tailor code to specific browsers.

In the beginning, the goal was to spare authors from ever having to touch an HTML tag in the same way that page layout programs protect designers from typing out PostScript. Today, the role of WYSIWYG authoring tools has shifted towards making document production and site management more efficient and automated while still providing access to the HTML source.

Pros and cons

Many professional HTML coders shun web authoring tools, preferring the "pure" experience of creating HTML documents by hand using only a full-featured HTML editor. Others appreciate being spared the grunt work of typing every HTML tag and find the WYSIWYG environment useful for viewing the page and making design decisions on the fly.

If you do choose to use a web authoring tool, don't expect it to excuse you from learning HTML altogether. In many cases, you will need to do some manual fine-tuning to the resulting HTML code. There are a few pros and cons to authoring tools that you should consider.

The pros include:

- They are good for beginners. They can even be useful for learning HTML because you can lay out the page the way you want and then view the resulting code.

- They are good for quick prototyping. Design ideas can be tried out on the fly.

- They provide a good head start for creating complex tables and other advanced functions, such as JavaScript and DHTML functions.

- They offer considerable time savings over writing code by hand.

But also keep in mind these cons:

- Some programs are infamous for not generating clean HTML documents. They add proprietary or redundant tags and often take circuitous routes to produce a desired effect.

- Some editors automatically change an HTML document when you open it in the program. They add their own tags and may strip out any tags they do not recognize.

- The code these programs generate may not conform to the latest HTML specifications.

- The built-in graphics-generating features do not offer much control over the quality or the file size of resulting graphics.

- They are expensive. The more powerful packages cost hundreds of dollars up front and additional costs to upgrade.

Some available web authoring tools

The following is an introduction to a handful of the tools that are popular as of this writing (versions are omitted because of the speed of updates). All are available for Mac and Windows systems.

Macromedia Dreamweaver
> As of this writing, Dreamweaver has emerged as the industry-standard HTML authoring tool, due the fact that it produces the cleanest code of any of its competitors. It does not generate proprietary code and it will not change any code that you add. It is one of the most full-featured authoring tools on the market. It has a fairly steep learning curve. For more information, see *http://www.macromedia.com*.

Adobe GoLive
> Another powerful and professional-level HTML editing tool, GoLive supports all the cutting-edge web technologies (JavaScript, ActiveX, WebObjects, style sheets, etc.). It also provides excellent site management tools. Its interface is more difficult to learn than other tools, but it seems to be worth the effort. For more information, see *http://www.golive.com*.

Microsoft FrontPage (Windows only)
> FrontPage is easy for beginners to learn and is popular with the business community. It offers wizards, themes, and tools that make web page creation easy for beginners. FrontPage 2000 won't mangle your code the way earlier versions did, which is good news, but it still produces code that many professional web authors consider to be unsatisfactory. Some FrontPage functions are closely integrated with Microsoft's Internet Information Server (IIS), so check with your hosting service for possible conflicts. For more information, see *http://www.microsoft.com/frontpage/*.

HTML Resources in This Book

In addition to the detailed descriptions of HTML tags and their use in the following eight chapters, there are several appendices at the end of the book that provide a quick reference for the entire set of HTML tags, sliced a number of different ways.

Appendix A, *HTML Elements*
> This is an alphabetical listing of all the currently available HTML tags mentioned in this book. It includes all the tags listed in the HTML 4.01 specification (including the complete list of attributes for each tag), tags in current use that are not specifically mentioned in the specification, and all browser-specific tags and attributes. It also provides chapter and page references so you can look up the detailed information for each tag quickly.

Appendix B, *List of Attributes*
> This is a listing of every available attribute as published by the HTML 4.01 specification. It indicates in which tags the attribute can be used, whether it is optional or required, and whether it has been deprecated by the HTML 4.01 specification.

Appendix C, *Deprecated Tags*
> This appendix lists all the tags and attributes that have been officially deprecated by the W3C in the HTML 4.01 specification. Deprecated tags are still supported by browsers for backward compatibility but are discouraged from use. Most attributes are deprecated in favor of style sheet controls. The table also lists recommended substitutes when noted by the W3C.

Appendix D, *Proprietary Tags*
> This appendix contains a list of tags supported only in Internet Explorer or Netscape Navigator.

Appendix E, *CSS Support Chart*
> This appendix lists all elements in the Cascading Style Sheets specification and notes how well Navigator and Internet Explorer support them.

Appendix F, *Character Entities*
> This is a chart of standard, proposed, and generally supported character entities for HTML. Character entities are introduced in Chapter 10.

CHAPTER 9

Structural HTML Tags

This chapter looks at the subset of HTML tags that is used primarily to give the document structure. It also discusses tags that are used for providing information about the document and those used for controlling its appearance or function on a global level.

Summary of Structural Tags

In this section, browser support for each tag is noted to the right of the tag name. Browsers that do not support the tag are grayed out. Tag usage is indicated below the tag name. Start and end tags are required unless otherwise noted. "Deprecated" means that the tag or attribute is currently supported but is due to be phased out of the HTML specification and is discouraged from use (usually in favor of similar style sheet controls). The attributes listed for each tag reflect those in common use. A more thorough listing of attributes for each tag, according to the HTML 4.01 specification, appears in Appendix A.

\<body\>   NN 2, 3, 4, 6   MSIE 2, 3, 4, 5, 5.5, 6   HTML 4.01   WebTV   Opera5

\<body\>...\</body\> *(start and end tags optional)*

Defines the beginning and the end of the document body. The body contains the content of the document (the part that is displayed in the browser window). Attributes to the \<body\> tag affect the entire document.

Attributes

alink="#*rrggbb*" *or* color name
> *Deprecated.* Sets the color of active links (i.e., the color while the mouse button is held down during a "click"). Color is specified in hexadecimal RGB values or by standard web color name. Chapter 16 explains these color specification methods.

background=*url*

Deprecated. Provides the URL to a graphic file to be used as a tiling graphic in the background of the document.

bgcolor="#*rrggbb*" or *color name*

Deprecated. Sets the color of the background for the document. Color is specified in hexadecimal RGB values or by standard web color name.

link="#*rrggbb*" or *color name*

Deprecated. Sets the default color for all the links in the document. Color is specified in hexadecimal RGB values or by standard web color name.

text="#*rrggbb*" or *color name*

Deprecated. Sets the default color for all the non-hyperlink and unstyled text in the document. Color is specified in hexadecimal RGB values or by standard web color name.

vlink="#*rrggbb*" or *color name*

Deprecated. Sets the color of the visited links (links that have already been followed) for the document. Color is specified in hexadecimal RGB values or by standard web color name.

Netscape Navigator 4.0+ only

marginwidth=*number*

Specifies the distance (in number of pixels) between the left and right browser edges and the text and graphics in the window.

marginheight=*number*

Specifies the distance (in number of pixels) between the top and bottom edges of the browser and the text or graphics in the window.

Internet Explorer only

bgproperties=fixed

When this attribute is set to fixed, the background image does not scroll with the document content.

leftmargin=*number*

Specifies the distance (in number of pixels) between the left browser edge and the beginning of the text and graphics in the window.

topmargin=*number*

Specifies the distance (in number of pixels) between the top edge of the browser and the top edge of the text or graphics in the window.

rightmargin=*number*

Specifies the distance (in number of pixels) between the right edge of the browser and the text or graphics in the window.

bottommargin=*number*

Specifies the distance (in number of pixels) between the bottom edge of the browser and the bottom edge of the text or graphics in the window.

<head>   NN 2, 3, 4, 6   MSIE 2, 3, 4, 5, 5.5, 6   HTML 4.01   WebTV   Opera5

<head>...</head> *(start and end tags optional)*

Defines the head (also called "header") portion of the document that contains information about the document. The <head> tag has no directly displayed content, but serves only as a container for the other header tags, such as <base>, <meta>, and <title>.

Attributes

profile=*URL*

> Provides the location of a predefined metadata profile that can be referenced by <meta> tags in the <head> of the document. This attribute is not yet implemented by browsers.

<html>   NN 2, 3, 4, 6   MSIE 2, 3, 4, 5, 5.5, 6   HTML 4.01   WebTV   Opera5

<html>...</html> *(start and end tags optional)*

Placed at the beginning and end of the document, this tag tells the browser that the entire document is composed in HTML.

Attributes

dir=ltr|rtl

> Indicates the direction the text should be rendered by the browser. The default is ltr (left-to-right), but some languages require rtl (right-to-left) rendering. The lang and dir attributes are part of the internationalization efforts incorporated into the HTML 4.01 specification. They can be added to almost any HTML element, but their use in the <html> tag is common for establishing the language for a whole document. For more information, see Chapter 7.

lang=*language code*

> Indicates the primary language of the document (see Chapter 7 for more information and language codes).

version="-//W3C//DTD HTML 4.01//EN"

> *Deprecated.* Specifies the version of HTML the document uses (the value above specifies 4.01). It has been deprecated in favor of the SGML <!DOCTYPE> declaration placed before the <html> tag.

<meta>   NN 2, 3, 4, 6   MSIE 2, 3, 4, 5, 5.5, 6   HTML 4.01   WebTV   Opera5

<meta> *(end tag forbidden)*

Provides additional information about the document. It should be placed within the <head> tags at the beginning of the document. It is commonly used for making documents searchable (by adding keywords) or to specify the character set for a document. They have been used for client-pull functions, but this function is discouraged. Meta tags are discussed at the end of this chapter.

Attributes

content=*text*
> *Required.* Specifies the value of the meta tag property and is always used in conjunction with name= or http-equiv=.

http-equiv=*text*
> The specified information is treated as though it were included in the HTTP header that the server sends ahead of the document. It is used in conjunction with the content attribute (in place of the name attribute).

name=*text*
> Specifies a name for the meta information property.

scheme=*text*
> Provides additional information for the interpretation of meta data. This is a new attribute introduced in HTML 4.0.

\<title\>   NN 2, 3, 4, 6   MSIE 2, 3, 4, 5, 5.5, 6   HTML 4.01   WebTV   Opera5

`<title>...</title>`

Required. Specifies the title of the document. The title generally appears in the top bar of the browser window. According to the HTML 4.01 specification, all documents must contain a meaningful <title> within the <head> of the document.

===

Setting Up an HTML Document

The standard skeletal structure of an HTML document according to the HTML 4.01 specification is as follows:

```
<!DOCTYPE HTML PUBLIC "-//W3C//DTD HTML 4.01//EN"
   "http://www.w3.org/TR/HTML4.01/strict.dtd">
<HTML>
  <HEAD>
    <TITLE>Document Title</TITLE>
  </HEAD>
  <BODY>
    Contents of Document...
  </BODY>
</HTML>
```

This document has three components: a document type declaration (<!DOCTYPE>), the header section (<head>), and the body of the document (<body>).

The HTML standard requires that the entire document appear within the <html> container, but most browsers can properly display the contents of the document even if these tags are omitted. All HTML documents are made up of two main structures, the *head* (also called the "header") and the *body*. The exception to this rule is when the document contains a *frameset* in place of the body. For more information about framesets, see Chapter 14.

The Document Type Declaration

In order to be valid (i.e., to conform precisely to the HTML standard), an HTML document needs to begin with a document type declaration that identifies the version of HTML that is used in the document. There are three distinct versions of HTML 4.01 (Strict, Transitional, and Frameset), each defined by a distinct document type definition (DTD). The DTD documents live on the W3C server at a stable URL.

The document's DTD is specified at the beginning of the document using the SGML declaration <!DOCTYPE> (document type). The remainder of the declaration contains two methods for pointing to DTD information: one a publicly recognized document, the other a specific URL in case the browsing device does not recognize the public identifier.

Strict

> If you are following the Strict version of HTML 4.01 (the version that omits all deprecated and browser-specific tags), use this document type definition:

```
<!DOCTYPE HTML PUBLIC "-//W3C//DTD HTML 4.01//EN"
   "http://www.w3.org/TR/HTML4.01/strict.dtd">
```

Transitional

> If your document includes deprecated tags, point to the Transitional DTD using this document type definition:

```
<!DOCTYPE HTML PUBLIC "-//W3C//DTD HTML 4.01 Transitional//EN"
   "http://www.w3.org/TR/HTML4.01/loose.dtd">
```

Frameset

> If your document uses frames, then identify the Frameset DTD. The Frameset DTD is the same as the Transitional version (it includes deprecated yet supported tags), with the addition of frame-specific tags.

```
<!DOCTYPE HTML PUBLIC "-//W3C//DTD HTML 4.01 Frameset//EN"
   "http://www.w3.org/TR/HTML4.01/frameset.dtd">
```

The Document Header

The header, delimited by the <head> tag, contains information that describes the HTML document. The head tag has no attributes of its own; it merely serves as a container for other tags that help define and manage the document's contents.

Titles

The most commonly used element within the header is the document title (within <title> tags, as shown in the example above), which provides a description of the page's contents. In HTML 4.01, this is a required element, which means that every HTML document must have a meaningful title in its header. The title is typically displayed in the top bar of the browser, outside the regular content window.

Titles should contain only ASCII characters (letters, numbers, and basic punctuation). Special characters (such as &) should be referred to by their character entities within the title, for example:

```
<TITLE>The Adventures of Peto &amp; Fleck</TITLE>
```

DOCTYPE and Standards-Compliant Browsers

Until recently, it was recommended that HTML documents begin with a DOCTYPE declaration, but it wasn't put to much practical use. That has changed, and now you can use DOCTYPE to make the latest browser versions live up to their full potential.

Netscape 6, Internet Explorer 6 (Windows), and Internet Explorer 5 (Mac) switch into a strict, standards-compliant mode when they detect a DOCTYPE specifying the Strict HTML 4.01 DTD. By placing this declaration at the beginning of your document, you can write your documents and style sheets according to the standards and have confidence that they will work the way they should in these latest browsers. This is a great way to get started using standards-compliant code right away.

If the DOCTYPE declaration is missing or set to Transitional, these browsers revert to their legacy behavior of allowing the nonstandard code, intricate hacks, and common workarounds that are common in current web authoring practices. This allows new browsers to display existing documents properly.

The title is what's displayed in a user's bookmarks or "hot list." Search engines rely heavily on document titles as well. For these reasons, it's important to provide thoughtful and descriptive titles for all your documents and avoid vague titles like "Welcome" or "My Page."

Other header elements

Other useful HTML elements are also placed within <head> tags of a document:

<base>
> This tag establishes the document's base location, which serves as a reference for all pathnames and links in the document. For more information, see Chapter 11.

<isindex>
> *Deprecated.* This tag was once used to add a simple search function to a page. It has been deprecated by HTML 4.01 in favor of form inputs.

<link>
> This tag defines the relationship between the current document and another document. Although it can signify relationships such as index, next, and previous, it is most often used today to link a document to an external style sheet (see Chapter 17).

<meta>
> "Meta" tags are used to provide information about a document, such as keywords or descriptions to aid search engines. It may also be used for client-pull functions. The <meta> tag is discussed later in this chapter.

```
<script>
```
JavaScript and VBScript code may be added to the document within its header using this tag.

```
<style>
```
Embedded style sheets must be added to the document header by placing the `<style>` element within the `<head>` container. For more information, see Chapter 17.

The Document Body

The document body, delimited by `<body>` tags, contains the contents of the document—the part that displays in the browser window.

The body of an HTML document might consist of just a few paragraphs of text, a single image, or a complex combination of text, images, tables, and multimedia objects. What you put on the page is up to you.

Global Settings with the <body> Tag

The `<body>` tag, originally designed to delimit the body of the document, has been extended to include controls for the backgrounds and text colors of a document. These settings are global, meaning they apply to the entire document. While these controls are currently well supported by major browsers, be aware that they have been deprecated by the HTML 4.01 specification and will eventually be phased out of use in favor of style sheet controls.

Colors

You can use the `<body>` tag to set colors for the document's background and text elements (see Table 9-1). Specified link colors apply to linked text and also to the border around linked graphics. (Chapter 15 shows how to specify color in HTML.)

Table 9-1: Attributes for specifying colors with the <body> tag

Page element	HTML tag	Description
Background color	`<BODY BGCOLOR="color">`	Sets the color for the background of the entire page.
Regular text	`<BODY TEXT="color">`	Sets the color for all the regular text in the document. The default color for text is black.
Links	`<BODY LINK="color">`	Sets the color for hyperlinks. The default color for links is blue.
Visited link	`<BODY VLINK="color">`	Sets the color for links that have already been clicked. The default color for visited links is purple.
Active link	`<BODY ALINK="color">`	Sets the color for a link while it is in the process of being clicked. The default color for an active link is red.

A single `<body>` tag can contain a number of specific attributes, as shown here:

```
<BODY BGCOLOR="color" TEXT="color" LINK="color" VLINK="color"
    ALINK="color">
```

Tiling Background Graphics

You've probably seen web pages that have a graphic image repeating behind the text. These are called *background tiles* or *tiling graphics*, and they are added to the document via the <body> tag using the background attribute and the URL of the graphic as follows:

```
<BODY BACKGROUND="background.gif">
```

Any web-based graphic file format (such as GIF or JPEG) can be used as a background tile (some new browsers even support animated GIFs in the background). Following are a few guidelines and tips regarding the use of background tiles:

- Use a graphic that won't interfere with the legibility of the text over it.

- Keep file sizes small. As usual for the web, it is important to keep the file size as small as possible for background graphics, which often lag behind the display of the rest of the page.

- Provide a background color specification in the <body> tag that will display while the background image downloads. In some cases, the background graphic may be the last element to display on the page while background colors display almost instantly. It is a nice trick to specify a background color that matches the overall intensity and hue of your background graphic, to at least set the mood while users wait for the background image to load. This is particularly useful if you've got light-colored text or graphics that will be unreadable or just ugly against the interim default gray browser background.

- If you want the color of the background image to match other graphics positioned inline in the web page, be sure that they are saved in the same graphic file formats. Because browsers interpret colors differently for JPEGs and GIFs, the file formats need to match in order for the colors to match seamlessly (GIF with GIF, JPEG with JPEG).

- Non-web-safe colors (colors not found in the web palette) are handled differently for background images than they are for foreground images when the page is displayed on an 8-bit monitor. This makes it very difficult to match inline images to the background seamlessly, even when the graphics use exactly the same color (or even when using the same graphic in both places).

To make matters worse, the way non-web-safe colors are handled differs from browser to browser. For instance, on the Mac, Navigator dithers the foreground graphic but shifts the background graphic to its nearest web palette value. In Internet Explorer, just the opposite happens: the background image dithers and the foreground image shifts. If you are trying to create a seamless effect, either make your foreground images transparent or stick diligently to the colors in the web palette.

The web palette is explained in the section "Color in Browsers—The Web Palette" in Chapter 3, and further in Chapter 22.

Adjusting Browser Margins

By default, browsers insert a margin of 10 to 12 pixels (depending on the browser and platform) between the edge of the browser window and the document's

---

contents. There is no method for changing these margins using tags from the HTML 4.01 specification alone (the W3C prefers style sheets adjusting margins); however, there are browser-specific attributes that can be added to the <body> tag that increase or decrease the margin width.

The drawback is that Internet Explorer and Netscape Navigator use different attributes to control margins. In addition, Netscape's tags only work with version 4.0 and higher. If you want to reach a broader audience, you can use frames for a similar effect (see "Frame Margins" in Chapter 14).

Internet Explorer uses the attributes leftmargin, rightmargin, topmargin, and bottommargin to specify pixel widths for the respective margins in the browser window. Navigator 4.0 and higher uses marginwidth (to adjust the left and right margins) and marginheight (for top and bottom margins).

For all these attributes, the value is a pixel measurement. The margin may be removed completely, allowing objects to sit flush against the window, by setting the attribute values to 0. Be aware that there is a bug in Navigator 4.x that inserts a 1-pixel border even when the margins are set to zero.

To set margins for both browsers, it is necessary to duplicate attributes. In the following example, the margins are turned off on the top and left edges using two sets of proprietary attributes:

```
<BODY MARGINWIDTH=0 MARGINHEIGHT=0 LEFTMARGIN=0 TOPMARGIN=0>
```

Using <meta> Tags

The <meta> tag has a wide variety of applications, but is primarily used to include information about a document, such as the creation date, author, or copyright information. The data included in a <meta> tag is useful for servers, web browsers, and search engines but is invisible to the reader. It must always be placed within the <head> of the document.

A document may have any number of <meta> tags. There are two types of <meta> tags, using either the name or http-equiv attribute. In each case, the content attribute is necessary to provide a value (or values) for the named information or function. The examples below show basic <meta> tag syntax. In the following sections, we will look at each type of meta tag and its uses.

```
<META HTTP-EQUIV="name" CONTENT="content">
<META NAME="name" CONTENT="content">
```

The http-equiv Attribute

Information provided by an http-equiv attribute is processed as though it had come from an HTTP response header. HTTP headers contain information the server passes to the browser just before it sends the HTML document. It contains MIME type information and other values that affect the action of the browser. Therefore, the http-equiv attribute provides information that will, depending on the tag description, affect the way the browser handles your document.

There are a large number of predefined http-equiv types available. This section will look at just a few of the most useful. For a complete listing, see the Dictionary of HTML META Tags at *http://vancouver-webpages.com/META/*.

Meta tags for client-pull

Client-pull refers to the ability of the browser (the client) to automatically request (pull) a new document from the server. The effect for the user is that the page displays, and after a period of time, automatically refreshes with new information or is replaced by an entirely new page. This technique can be used to automatically redirect readers to a new URL (for instance, if an old URL has been retired). Be aware, however, that the W3C strongly discourages the use of this method for automatic forwarding in favor of server-side redirects.

If you string documents with client-pull instructions and set very short time intervals, you can create a sort of slide show effect. Client-pull uses the `refresh` attribute value, first introduced by Netscape. It tells the browser to wait a specified number of seconds (indicated by an integer in the content attribute) and then load a new page. If no page is specified, the browser just reloads the current page. The following example instructs the browser to reload the page after 15 seconds (we can assume there's something fancy happening on the server side that puts updated information in the HTML document):

```
<META HTTP-EQUIV="refresh" CONTENT="15">
```

To reload a different file, provide the URL for the document within the content attribute as shown below:

```
<META HTTP-EQUIV="refresh" CONTENT="1; URL=http://doc2.html">
```

Note that there is only a single set of quotation marks around the value for `content`. Although URLs usually require their own quotation marks, these are omitted within the context of the `content` attribute.

To create a slide-show effect, add a `meta refresh` tag in the <head> of each document that points to the next HTML document in the sequence. You can set the time interval to as many seconds as you like; setting it to 0 will trigger the next page as soon as the current page has downloaded. Bear in mind, however, that the actual amount of time the page takes to refresh is dependent on complex factors of file size, server speed, and general web traffic.

In the following example, three files are coded to loop endlessly at five-second intervals.

Document *1.html* contains:

```
<META HTTP-EQUIV="refresh" CONTENT="5; URL=2.html">
```

Document *2.html* contains:

```
<META HTTP-EQUIV="refresh" CONTENT="5; URL=3.html">
```

Document *3.html* contains a tag which points back to *1.html*:

```
<META HTTP-EQUIV="refresh" CONTENT="5; URL=1.html">
```

Other uses

Here are some other uses of the `http-equiv` attribute:

expires

> Indicates the date and time after which the document should be considered expired. Web robots may use this information to delete expired documents

from a search engine index. The date and time format (as shown below) follows the date/time standard for HTTP headers (rather than the recommended date/time format for HTML*) since the `http-equiv` attribute is intended to mimic an HTTP header field.

```
<META HTTP-EQUIV="expires" CONTENT="Wed 12 Jun 2001 10:52:00 EST">
```

content-type

The content-type `text/html` is automatically added to the HTTP header for HTML documents. This attribute can be extended to include the character set for the document by specifying `"text/html; charset=character set identifier"`. This causes the browser to load the appropriate character set before displaying the page.

This is part of the HTML 4.01 measures to internationalize the Web. You can read more about identifying character sets in Chapter 7.

```
<META HTTP-EQUIV="content-type" CONTENT="text/html;
     charset=SHIFT_JIS">
```

content-language

This may be used to identify the language in which the document is written. Like the character set extension just mentioned, it is part of the ongoing effort to internationalize the Web. The browser can send a corresponding `Accept-Language` header, which causes the server to choose the document with the appropriate language specified in its `<meta>` tag.

For more information on internationalization and a listing of two-letter language codes, see Chapter 7.

This example tells the browser that the document's natural language is French:

```
<META HTTP-EQUIV="content-language" CONTENT="fr">
```

Inserting Meta-Information with the name Attribute

The `name` attribute is used to insert hidden information about the document that does not correspond to HTTP headers. For example:

```
<META NAME="author" CONTENT="Jennifer Niederst">
<META NAME="copyright" CONTENT="2001, O'Reilly & Associates">
```

You can make up your own `<meta>` names or use one of the names put forth by search engine and browser companies for standardized use. A few of the accepted and more useful `<meta>` names are discussed in the following sections.

Meta tags for search engines

The popular search engines Infoseek and AltaVista introduced several `<meta>` names that aid their search engines in finding pages. Note that not all search engines use meta data, but adding them to your document won't hurt. There is a blurry distinction between `name` and `http-equiv` in this case, so most of these meta names also work as `http-equiv` definitions.

---

* The date and time format for HTML values is described under the listing for `<del>` in Chapter 10.

description

This provides a brief, plain-language description of the contents of your web page, which is particularly useful if your document contains little text, is a frameset, or has extensive scripts at the top of the HTML document. Search engines that recognize the description may display it in the search results page. Some search engines use only the first 20 words of descriptions, so get to the point quickly.

```
<META NAME="description" CONTENT="Jennifer Niederst's resume
    and web design samples">
```

keywords

You can supplement the title and description of the document with a list of comma-separated keywords that would be useful in indexing your document.

```
<META name="keywords" content="designer, web design, training,
    interface design">
```

author

Identifies the author of the web page.

```
<META NAME="author" CONTENT="Jennifer Niederst">
```

copyright

Identifies the copyright information for the document.

```
<META NAME="copyright" CONTENT="2001, O'Reilly & Associates">
```

robots

This tag was created as an alternative to the *robots.txt* file, and both are used to prevent your page from being indexed by search engine "spiders." This tag is not as well supported as the *robots.txt* file, but some people like to include it anyway. The content attribute can take the following values: index (the default), noindex (prevents indexing), nofollow (prevents the search engine from following links on the page), and none (the same as setting "noindex, nofollow"). The advantage of using this attribute instead of the *robots.txt* file is that it can be applied on a page-by-page basis (whereas *robot.txt* applies to an entire site if it's located in the root directory).

```
<META NAME="robots" CONTENT="noindex, nofollow">
```

Other uses

Other uses of the name attribute include the following:

rating

This provides a method of rating the content of a web page to indicate its appropriateness for children. The four available ratings are general, mature, restricted, and 14 years.

```
<META NAME="rating" CONTENT="general">
```

generator *(or* formatter *for FrontPage)*

Many HTML authoring tools add an indication of the name and version of the creation tool. This is used by tools vendors to assess market penetration and has little or no value to individual users or page creators.

```
<META NAME="generator" CONTENT="Adobe GoLive">
```

CHAPTER 10

Formatting Text

Designers accustomed to desktop publishing programs are usually shocked to find how little control HTML offers over the display of the page. Before you get too frustrated, bear in mind that HTML was not developed as a method for designing how the page looks, but rather as a means of marking the structure of a document.

In fact, the tags that do provide specific display information (<center>, for example) are not true to the original HTML concept. In an ideal world, all style and presentation would go in style sheets, leaving HTML markup to work as originally designed. The W3C has made these intentions clear by deprecating in the HTML 4.01 specification nearly all tags that control presentation in favor of Cascading Style Sheet controls (see Chapter 17).

This chapter looks at the nature of text in web pages and reviews the HTML tags related to the structure and presentation of text elements.

Summary of Text Tags

This section is a listing of tags used for formatting text. It is divided into the following subgroups:

- Paragraphs and Headings (Block-Level Elements)
- Text Appearance (Inline Styles)
- Spacing and Positioning
- Lists

In this section, browser support for each tag is noted to the right of the tag name. Browsers that do not support the tag are grayed out. Tag usage is indicated below the tag name. Start and end tags are required unless otherwise noted. "Deprecated" means that the tag or attribute is currently supported but is due to be phased out of the HTML specification and is discouraged from use (usually in favor of similar style sheet controls). The attributes listed for each tag reflect those in common use. A more thorough listing of attributes for each tag, according to the HTML 4.01 specification, appears in Appendix A.

Paragraphs and Headings (Block-Level Elements)

Block-level elements are always formatted with a line break before and after, with most adding some amount of additional space above and below as well. The most commonly used block elements are paragraphs (`<p>`), headings (`<h1>` through `<h6>`), and blockquotes (`<blockquote>`).

Lists and list items are also block-level elements, but they have been grouped in their own section below.

`<address>`	NN 2, 3, 4, 6	MSIE 2, 3, 4, 5, 5.5, 6	HTML 4.01	WebTV	Opera5

`<address>...</address>`

Supplies the author's contact information, typically at the beginning or end of a document. Addresses are generally formatted in italic type with a line break (but no extra space) above and below.

`<blockquote>`	NN 2, 3, 4, 6	MSIE 2, 3, 4, 5, 5.5, 6	HTML 4.01	WebTV	Opera5

`<blockquote>...</blockquote>`

Enclosed text is a "blockquote" (lengthy quotation), which is generally displayed with an indent on the left and right margins and added space above and below the paragraph.

Note that:

- Some older browsers display blockquote material in italic, making it difficult to read.

- Browsers are inconsistent in the way they display images within blockquotes. Some align the graphic with the indented blockquote margin; others align the image with the normal margin of paragraph text. It is a good idea to test on a variety of browsers.

Attributes

`cite=URL`
> Provides information about the source from which the quotation was borrowed. Not often used in common practice.

`<div>`	NN 2, 3, 4, 6	MSIE 2, 3, 4, 5, 5.5, 6	HTML 4.01	WebTV	Opera5

`<div>...</div>`

Denotes a generic "division" within the document. This element can be used to add structure to an HTML document. When `<div>` was first introduced in HTML 3.2, only the alignment function (using the `align` attribute) was implemented by the major browsers. While it has no presentation properties of its own, it can be used in conjunction with the `class` and `id` attributes and then formatted with style

---

sheets (Chapter 17). Because divisions are block elements, they usually display with some added space above and below.

Attributes

`align=center |left |right`
> *Deprecated.* Aligns the text within the tags to the left, right, or center of the page.

`class=name`
> Assigns a name to an element or a number of elements. Elements that share a `class` identification can be treated as a group.

`id=name`
> Assigns a unique name to an element. There may not be two elements with the same `id` name in a document.

`style=style properties`
> Embeds formatting information to be applied to the division contents.

`<h1>` through `<h6>`   NN 2, 3, 4, 6   MSIE 2, 3, 4, 5, 5.5, 6   HTML 4.01   WebTV   Opera5

`<hn>...</hn>`

Specifies that the enclosed text is a heading (a brief description of the section it introduces). There are six different levels of headings, from `<h1>` to `<h6>`, with `<h1>` the largest and each subsequent level displaying at a smaller size. `<h5>` and `<h6>` usually display smaller than the surrounding body text.

Attributes

`align=center |left |right`
> *Deprecated.* Used to align the header left, right, or centered on the page. Microsoft Internet Explorer 3.0 and earlier do not support right alignment.

`<p>`   NN 2, 3, 4, 6   MSIE 2, 3, 4, 5, 5.5, 6   HTML 4.01   WebTV   Opera5

`<p>...</p>` *(end tag optional)*

Denotes the beginning and end of a paragraph. While many browsers will also allow the `<p>` tag to be used without a closing tag to start a new paragraph, the container method is preferred. When using Cascading Style Sheets with the document container, tags are required or the formatting will not work. Browsers ignore multiple empty `<p>` elements.

Attributes

`align=center |left |right`
> *Deprecated.* Aligns the text within the tags to the left, right, or center of the page.

Text Appearance (Inline Styles)

The following tags affect the appearance or meaning of text. With the exception of `<basefont>`, all of the tags listed in this section define inline styles, meaning they can be applied to a string of characters within a block element without introducing line breaks. (<basefont> is used to specify the appearance of type for a whole document or for a range of text.)

<abbr>

NN 2, 3, 4, 6   MSIE 2, 3, 4, 5, 5.5, 6   HTML 4.01   WebTV   Opera5

<abbr>...</abbr>

Identifies the enclosed text as an abbreviation. It has no inherent effect on text display but can be used as an element selector in a style sheet.

Attributes

title=*string*
> Provides the full expression for the abbreviation. This may be useful for non-visual browsers, speech synthesizers, translation systems, and search engines.

Example

```
<ABBR TITLE="Massachusetts">Mass.</ABBR>
```

<acronym>

NN 2, 3, 4, 6   MSIE 2, 3, 4, 5, 5.5, 6   HTML 4.01   WebTV   Opera5

<acronym>...</acronym>

Indicates an acronym. It has no inherent effect on text display but can be used as an element selector in a style sheet.

Attributes

title=*string*
> Provides the full expression for the acronym. This may be useful for non-visual browsers, speech synthesizers, translation systems, and search engines.

Example

```
<ACRONYM TITLE="World Wide Web">WWW</ACRONYM>
```

<b>

NN 2, 3, 4, 6   MSIE 2, 3, 4, 5, 5.5, 6   HTML 4.01   WebTV   Opera5

<b>...</b>

Enclosed text is rendered in bold.

<basefont>

NN 2, 3, 4, 6   MSIE 2, 3, 4, 5, 5.5, 6   HTML 4.01   WebTV   Opera5

<basefont> *(no end tag)*

Deprecated. Specifies certain font attributes for text following the tag. It can be used within the <head> tags to apply to the entire document, or within the body of the document to apply to the subsequent text.

Attributes

size=*value*
> *Deprecated.* Sets the basefont size using the HTML size values from 1 to 7 (or relative values based on the default value of 3). Subsequent relative size settings are based on this value.

Internet Explorer 3.0+ only

`color="#rrggbb"` *or name*

Sets the color of the following text using hexadecimal RGB values.

`face=font`

Sets the font for the following text.

\<big>   NN 2, 3, 4, 6   MSIE 2, 3, 4, 5, 5.5, 6   HTML 4.01   WebTV   Opera5

`<big>...</big>`

Sets the type one font size increment larger than the surrounding text.

\<blink>   NN 2, 3, 4, 6   MSIE 2, 3, 4, 5, 5.5, 6   HTML 4.01   WebTV   Opera5

`<blink>...</blink>`

Causes the contained text to flash on and off in Netscape browsers.

\<cite>   NN 2, 3, 4, 6   MSIE 2, 3, 4, 5, 5.5, 6   HTML 4.01   WebTV   Opera5

`<cite>...</cite>`

Denotes a citation—a reference to another document, especially books, magazines, articles, etc. Browsers generally display citations in italic.

\<code>   NN 2, 3, 4, 6   MSIE 2, 3, 4, 5, 5.5, 6   HTML 4.01   WebTV   Opera5

`<code>...</code>`

Denotes a code sample. Code is rendered in the browser's specified monospace font (usually Courier).

\<del>   NN 2, 3, 4, 6   MSIE 2, 3, 4, 5, 5.5, 6   HTML 4.01   WebTV   Opera5

`<del>...</del>`

Indicates deleted text. It has no inherent style qualities on its own but may be used to hide deleted text from view or display it as strike-through text via style sheet controls. It may be useful for legal documents and any instance where edits need to be tracked. Its counterpart is *inserted* text (`<ins>`). Both can be used to indicate either inline or block-level elements.

Attributes

`cite=URL`

Can be set to point to a source document that explains why the document was changed.

`datetime=YYYY-MM-DDThh:mm:ssTZD`

Specifies the date and time the change was made. Dates and times follow the format listed above where `YYYY` is the four-digit year, `MM` is the two-digit month, `DD` is the day, `hh` is the hour (00 through 23), `mm` is the minute (00 through 59), and `ss` is the seconds (00 through 59). The TZD stands for "Time Zone Designator" and its value can be `Z` (to indicate UTC, Coordinated

Universal Time), an indication of the number of hours and minutes ahead of UTC (such as +03:00), or an indication of the number of hours and minutes behind UTC (such as –02:20).

This is the standard format for date and time values in HTML. For more information, see *http://www.w3.org/TR/1998/NOTE-datetime-19980827.*

\<dfn\>

NN 2, 3, 4, 6   MSIE 2, 3, 4, 5, 5.5, 6   HTML 4.01   WebTV   Opera5

`<dfn>...</dfn>`

Indicates the defining instance of the enclosed term. Usually rendered in bold text, it calls attention to the introduction of special terms and phrases.

\<em\>

NN 2, 3, 4, 6   MSIE 2, 3, 4, 5, 5.5, 6   HTML 4.01   WebTV   Opera5

`<em>...</em>`

Indicates emphasized text. Nearly all browsers render emphasized text in italic.

\<font\>

NN 2, 3, 4, 6   MSIE 2, 3, 4, 5, 5.5, 6   HTML 4.01   WebTV   Opera5

`<font>...</font>`

Deprecated. Used to affect the style (color, typeface, and size) of the enclosed text.

Attributes

`color=color name` *or* `#RRGGBB`
> *Deprecated.* Specifies the color of the enclosed text. For information on how to specify color, see Chapter 16.

`face=typeface` *(or list of typefaces)*
> *Deprecated.* Specifies a typeface for the text. The specified typeface is used only if it is found on the user's machine. You may provide a list of fonts (separated by commas), and the browser uses the first available in the string.

`size=value`
> *Deprecated.* Sets the size of the type to an absolute value on a scale from 1 to 7 (3 is the default), or using a relative value *+n* or *–n* (based on the default or `<basefont>` setting).

\<i\>

NN 2, 3, 4, 6   MSIE 2, 3, 4, 5, 5.5, 6   HTML 4.01   WebTV   Opera5

`<i>...</i>`

Enclosed text is displayed in italic.

\<ins\>

NN 2, 3, 4, 6   MSIE 2, 3, 4, 5, 5.5, 6   HTML 4.01   WebTV   Opera5

`<ins>...</ins>`

Indicates text that has been inserted into the document. It has no inherent style qualities on its own but may be used to indicate inserted text in a different color via style sheet controls. It may be useful for legal documents and any instance in which edits need to be tracked. Its counterpart is deleted text (<del>). Both can be used to indicate either inline or block-level elements.

Attributes

cite=*URL*

> Can be set to point to a source document that explains why the document was changed.

datetime=*YYYY-MM-DDThh:mm:ssTZD*

> Specifies the date and time the change was made. See <del> for an explanation of the date/time format.

<kbd>   NN 2, 3, 4, 6   MSIE 2, 3, 4, 5, 5.5, 6   HTML 4.01   WebTV   Opera5

<kbd>...</kbd>

Stands for "keyboard" and indicates text entered by the user. It is usually displayed in the browser's monospace font (usually Courier). Some browsers also display it in bold.

<q>   NN 2, 3, 4, 6   MSIE 2, 3, 4, 5, 5.5, 6   HTML 4.01   WebTV   Opera5

<q>...</q>

Delimits a short quotation that can be included inline, such as "to be or not to be." It differs from <blockquote>, which is for longer quotations set off as a separate paragraph element. Some browsers automatically insert quotation marks. When used with the lang (language) attribute, the browser may insert language-specific quotation marks.

Attributes

cite=*url*

> Designates the source document from which the quotation was taken.

<s>   NN 2, 3, 4, 6   MSIE 2, 3, 4, 5, 5.5, 6   HTML 4.01   WebTV   Opera5

<s>...</s>

Deprecated. Enclosed text is displayed as strike-through text (same as <strike> but introduced by later browser versions).

<samp>   NN 2, 3, 4, 6   MSIE 2, 3, 4, 5, 5.5, 6   HTML 4.01   WebTV   Opera5

<samp>...</samp>

Delimits sample output from programs, scripts, etc. Sample text is generally displayed in a monospace font.

<small>   NN 2, 3, 4, 6   MSIE 2, 3, 4, 5, 5.5, 6   HTML 4.01   WebTV   Opera5

<small>...</small>

Renders the type smaller than the surrounding text.

`<span>`

NN 2, 3, 4, 6   MSIE 2, 3, 4, 5, 5.5, 6   HTML 4.01   WebTV   Opera5

`<span>...</span>`

Identifies a span of inline characters, but does not by default affect the formatting of those characters. It can be used in conjunction with the `class` and/or `id` attributes and formatted with Cascading Style Sheets (see Chapter 17).

Attributes

`class=name`

Assigns a name to an element or a number of elements. Elements that share a `class` identification can be treated as a group.

`id=name`

Assigns a unique name to an element. There may not be two elements with the same `id` name in a document.

`style=style properties`

Embeds style information to be applied to the division contents.

`<strike>`

NN 2, 3, 4, 6   MSIE 2, 3, 4, 5, 5.5, 6   HTML 4.01   WebTV   Opera5

`<strike>...</strike>`

Deprecated. Enclosed text is displayed as strike-through text (crossed through with a horizontal line). The HTML 4.01 specification prefers style sheet controls for this effect.

`<strong>`

NN 2, 3, 4, 6   MSIE 2, 3, 4, 5, 5.5, 6   HTML 4.01   WebTV   Opera5

`<strong>...</strong>`

Enclosed text is strongly emphasized. Nearly all browsers render `<strong>` text in bold.

`<sub>`

NN 2, 3, 4, 6   MSIE 2, 3, 4, 5, 5.5, 6   HTML 4.01   WebTV   Opera5

`<sub>...</sub>`

Formats enclosed text as subscript.

`<sup>`

NN 2, 3, 4, 6   MSIE 2, 3, 4, 5, 5.5, 6   HTML 4.01   WebTV   Opera5

`<sup>...</sup>`

Formats enclosed text as superscript.

`<tt>`

NN 2, 3, 4, 6   MSIE 2, 3, 4, 5, 5.5, 6   HTML 4.01   WebTV   Opera5

`<tt>...</tt>`

Formats enclosed text as teletype text. The text enclosed in the `<tt>` tag is generally displayed in a monospaced font such as Courier.

\<u> NN 2, 3, 4, 6   MSIE 2, 3, 4, 5, 5.5, 6   HTML 4.01   WebTV   Opera5

\<u>...\</u>

Deprecated. Enclosed text is underlined when displayed. The HTML 4.01 specification prefers style sheet controls for this effect.

\<var> NN 2, 3, 4, 6   MSIE 2, 3, 4, 5, 5.5, 6   HTML 4.01   WebTV   Opera5

\<var>...\</var>

Indicates an instance of a variable or program argument, usually displayed in italic.

Spacing and Positioning

The following tags give authors control over the line breaks, alignment, and spacing within an HTML document. Tables (discussed in Chapter 13) and style sheets (Chapter 17) offer better control over spacing and positioning than the minimal controls listed here.

**\
** NN 2, 3, 4, 6   MSIE 2, 3, 4, 5, 5.5, 6   HTML 4.01   WebTV   Opera5

\

Breaks the text and begins a new line but does not add extra space.

Attributes

clear=all|left|right|none
> Breaks the text flow and resumes the next line after the specified margin is clear. This is often used to start the text below an aligned image (preventing text wrap). none is the default, causing a simple line break.

\<center> NN 2, 3, 4, 6   MSIE 2, 3, 4, 5, 5.5, 6   HTML 4.01   WebTV   Opera5

\<center>...\</center>

Deprecated. Centers the enclosed elements horizontally on the page (a shortcut for \<DIV align=center>).

\<multicol> NN 2, 3, 4, 6   MSIE 2, 3, 4, 5, 5.5, 6   HTML 4.01   WebTV   Opera5

\<multicol>...\</multicol>

Netscape 4.x only. Displays enclosed text in multiple columns of approximately the same length. It is rarely used.

Attributes

cols=number
> *Required.* Specifies the number of columns.

gutter=number
> Specifies the amount of space (in pixels) to maintain between columns.

width=number
> Specifies the width of the columns in pixels. All columns within \<multicol> are the same width.

\<nobr\>   NN 2, 3, 4, 6   MSIE 2, 3, 4, 5, 5.5, 6   HTML 4.01   WebTV   Opera5

`<nobr>...</nobr>`

Nonstandard. Text (or graphics) within the "no break" tags always display on one line, without allowing any breaks. The line may run beyond the right edge of the browser window, requiring horizontal scrolling. The HTML 4.01 specification prefers style sheets for preventing line breaks.

\<pre\>   NN 2, 3, 4, 6   MSIE 2, 3, 4, 5, 5.5, 6   HTML 4.01   WebTV   Opera5

`<pre>...</pre>`

Delimits preformatted text, meaning that lines are displayed exactly as they are typed in, honoring multiple spaces and line breaks. Text within `<pre>` tags is displayed in a monospace font such as Courier.

Attributes

`width=value`
> *Deprecated.* This optional attribute determines how many characters to fit on a single line within the `<pre>` block.

\<wbr\>   NN 2, 3, 4, 6   MSIE 2, 3, 4, 5, 5.5, 6   HTML 4.01   WebTV   Opera5

`<wbr>`

Nonstandard. Indicates a potential word break point. The `<wbr>` tag works only when placed within `<nobr>`-tagged text and causes a line break only if the current line already extends beyond the browser's display window margins.

Lists

The following is a collection of tags used for formatting a number of different types of lists in HTML. Any list can be nested within another list.

\<dir\>   NN 2, 3, 4, 6   MSIE 2, 3, 4, 5, 5.5, 6   HTML 4.01   WebTV   Opera5

`<dir>...</dir>`

Deprecated. Creates a directory list consisting of list items `<li>`. Directory lists were originally designed to display lists of files with short names, but they have been deprecated with the recommendation that unordered lists (`<ul>`) be used instead. Most browsers render directory lists as they do unordered lists (with bullets), although some use a multicolumn format.

\<dl\>   NN 2, 3, 4, 6   MSIE 2, 3, 4, 5, 5.5, 6   HTML 4.01   WebTV   Opera5

`<dl>...</dl>`

Indicates a definition list, consisting of terms (`<dt>`) and definitions (`<dd>`).

Attributes

`compact`
> *Deprecated.* Makes the list as small as possible. Few browsers support the `compact` attribute.

\<dd>

NN 2, 3, 4, 6   MSIE 2, 3, 4, 5, 5.5, 6   HTML 4.01   WebTV   Opera5

`<dd>...</dd>` *(end tag optional)*

Denotes the definition portion of an item within a definition list. The definition is usually displayed with an indented left margin. The closing tag is commonly omitted but should be included when applying style sheets.

\<dt>

NN 2, 3, 4, 6   MSIE 2, 3, 4, 5, 5.5, 6   HTML 4.01   WebTV   Opera5

`<dt>...</dt>` *(end tag optional)*

Denotes the term portion of an item within a definition list. The closing tag is normally omitted but should be included when applying style sheets.

\<li>

NN 2, 3, 4, 6   MSIE 2, 3, 4, 5, 5.5, 6   HTML 4.01   WebTV   Opera5

`<li>...</li>` *(end tag optional)*

Defines an item in a list. It is used within the `<dir>`, `<ol>`, and `<ul>` list tags.

Attributes

The following attributes have been deprecated by the HTML 4.0 specification in favor of style sheet controls for list item display.

`type=`*format*
> *Deprecated.* Changes the format of the automatically generated numbers or bullets for list items.
>
> Within unordered lists (`<ul>`), the type attribute can be used to specify the bullet style (`disc`, `circle`, or `square`) for a particular list item.
>
> Within ordered lists (`<ol>`), the type attribute specifies the numbering style (see options under the `<ol>` listing) for a particular list item.

`value=`*number*
> *Deprecated.* Within ordered lists, you can specify the number of an item. Following list items increase from the specified number.

\<menu>

NN 2, 3, 4, 6   MSIE 2, 3, 4, 5, 5.5, 6   HTML 4.01   WebTV   Opera5

`<menu>...</menu>`

Deprecated. This indicates the beginning and end of a menu list, which consists of list items `<li>`. Menus are intended to be used for a list of short choices, such as a menu of links to other documents. It is little used and has been deprecated in favor of `<ul>`.

Attributes

`compact`
> Displays the list as small as possible (not many browsers do anything with this attribute).

`<ol>...</ol>`

Defines the beginning and end of an ordered (numbered) list, which consists of list items `<li>`. Item numbers are inserted automatically by the browser.

Attributes

`compact`

> *Deprecated.* Displays the list as small as possible (not many browsers do anything with this attribute).

`start=number`

> Starts the numbering of the list at *number* instead of at 1.

`type=1|A|a|I|i`

> *Deprecated.* Defines the numbering system for the list as follows:

Type value	Generated style	Sample sequence
1	Arabic numerals (default)	1, 2, 3, 4
A	Uppercase letters	A, B, C, D
a	Lowercase letters	a, b, c, d
I	Uppercase Roman numerals	I, II, III, IV
i	Lowercase Roman numerals	i, ii, iii, iv

`<ul>...</ul>`

Defines the beginning and end of an unordered (bulleted) list, which consists of list items `<li>`. Bullets for each list item are inserted automatically by the browser.

Attributes

`compact`

> *Deprecated.* Displays the list block as small as possible. Not many browsers support this attribute.

`type=disc|circle|square`

> *Deprecated.* Defines the shape of the bullets used for each list item.

Working with HTML Text

Formatting web page text is not like formatting text for print. In print, you have the luxury of knowing that text will stay where you put it. Web text, on the other hand, is more fluid. Many aspects of presentation are determined when the document flows into each user's browser window.

After establishing the skeleton of the document (see Chapter 9), a good place to begin formatting a web document is to establish the general structure of the contents by adding HTML tags that create paragraphs and heading levels in the raw text.

Paragraphs and Line Breaks

A browser starts a new paragraph or adds a line break only if it encounters a tag in the HTML source file that explicitly tells it to do so. Otherwise, it ignores the carriage returns and extra spaces in the HTML document. Without tags, all content in the HTML document wraps automatically to fill the width of the browser window. So even if you have written out your content with line spaces between the paragraphs, it will display as one block of text if it is not formatted with the appropriate HTML tags.

Paragraphs are the most rudimentary elements of a text document. In HTML they are indicated by enclosing a span of text in paragraph tags (`<p>...</p>`). A paragraph is an example of a *block-level element.* When browsers see block element tags, they start a new line and add an amount of extra space above and below the element. Other examples of block elements include headings (`<h1>`), blockquotes (`<blockquote>`), divisions (`<div>`), and various lists.

Technically, the end `</p>` tag is optional. Because browsers are clever enough to infer that a new opening tag indicates the end of the previous paragraph, many web authors leave off the closing `</p>` tag and insert `<p>`s as though they were line spaces. This is fine for most current web purposes, but it should be noted that lax coding may not be tolerated as well in future web page description languages (see Chapter 31). It is already important to tag paragraphs properly for use with Cascading Style Sheets. It's probably not a bad idea to get into the habit of closing all the tags you once left hanging.

If you want to break a line but not add any extra space, insert a line break with the `<br>` tag. The line break element does not have a closing tag; it can be placed in the flow of text where you want the line break to occur.

The following two figures show the difference between lines broken with a `<p>` tag and a `<br>`. In Figure 10-1, the line is broken by defining a paragraph block element, so extra space is introduced. In Figure 10-2, the `<br>` tag breaks the line but does not add space.

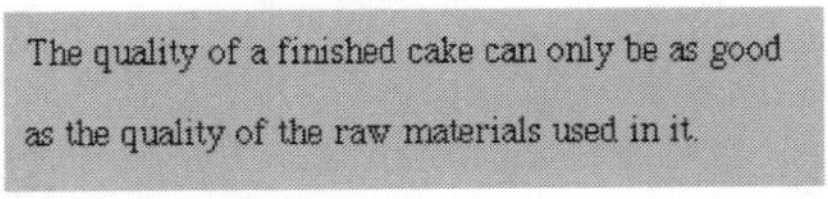


```
<P>The quality of a finished cake can only be as good</P>
<P>as the quality of the raw materials used in it.</P>
```

Figure 10-1: Vertical spacing is added above paragraphs

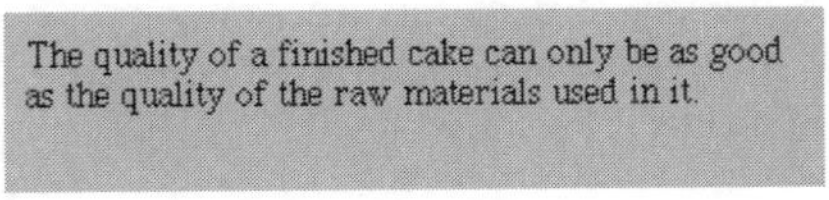


```
<P>The quality of a finished cake can only be as good
<BR>as the quality of the raw materials used in it.</P>
```

Figure 10-2: Breaking text with the <br> tag doesn't add vertical spacing

Headings

Headings are displayed in bold text with automatic line breaks and extra space above and below. There are six levels of HTML headings, ranging from <h1> (the top-level heading) to <h6> (the lowest level). Browsers display headings with a diminishing font size so that <h1>s are displayed in the largest possible font and <h6> are displayed in the smallest.

In fact, <h5> and <h6> are generally sized the same as or smaller than the default body text, making them not very commanding as headings. Figure 10-3 shows the relationship of the six heading levels as displayed in a browser.

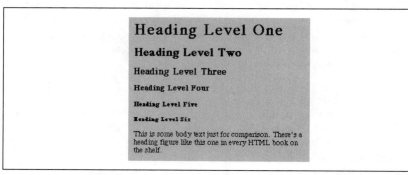

Figure 10-3: Results of the six heading tags, with regular body text for comparison

Legal HTML syntax requires that headings appear in order (i.e., an <h2> cannot precede an <h1>) for proper document structure. In practice, however, designers often pick and choose from heading levels to create desired presentation effects (most find the default <h1> display to be too large). Because browsers do not enforce correct structural hierarchies, web page authors have gotten away with these techniques. It is recommended that style sheets be used to control the display of properly structured heading tags, rather than choosing arbitrary heading levels based on presentation (see Chapter 17).

Inline Type Styles

Most HTML text tags indicate style or structural information for *inline* elements (strings of characters within the flow of text). Inline style tags affect the appearance of the enclosed text without adding line breaks or extra space. Closing tags are required for inline style tags in order to "turn off" the style attribute.

HTML inline styles fall into two conceptual categories: *logical* (or "content-based") styles and *physical* styles. This distinction does not affect the way you use the tags in an HTML document. However, in the movement toward removing style information from content, revived by the introduction of style sheets, logical tags are more in keeping with the ideal HTML model.

Logical Styles

Logical or content-based styles describe the enclosed text's meaning, context, or usage and leave the specific rendering of the tag to the discretion of the browser.

Using logical tags, you may indicate that a selection of text should be emphasized or displayed as code. Fortunately, browsers adhere to conventions for the display of logical styles; for instance, you can be pretty certain that emphasized text will be rendered in italics and code will appear in a monospaced font.

Table 10-1 gives a list of logical inline style tags. Refer to the "Summary of Text Tags" at the beginning of this chapter for complete browser support information.

Table 10-1: Logical inline style tags

Tag	Description	Usually displayed as
`<abbr>`	Abbreviation	Body text (requires style sheets for style information)
`<acronym>`	Acronym	Body text (requires style sheets for style information)
`<cite>`	Citation	Italic
`<code>`	Code	Monospace font
`<del>`	Deleted text	Body text (requires style sheets for style information); may be rendered as strike-through text.
`<dfn>`	Defining instance	Body text (requires style sheets for style information)
`<div>`	Division	Body text (requires style sheets for style information)
`<em>`	Emphasized	Italic
`<ins>`	Inserted text	Body text (requires style sheets for style information)
`<kbd>`	Keyboard text	Monospace font
`<q>`	Inline quotation	Italic (newer browsers only)
`<samp>`	Sample text	Monospace font
`<span>`	Span	Body text (requires style sheets for style information)
`<strong>`	Strong	Bold
`<var>`	Variable	Monospace or oblique (slanted) monospace font

Physical Styles

Physical styles provide specific display instructions, such as "italic" or "strike-through." Some physical styles affect the size of the text, such as "big" or "small." Several of these display-specific elements have been deprecated in favor of similar style sheet controls.

Table 10-2 lists the available physical inline style tags with their uses. Refer to the "Summary of Text Tags" at the beginning of this chapter for complete browser-support information.

Table 10-2: Physical inline style tags

Tag	Description	Function
`<b>`	Bold	Displays text in bold type
`<big>`	Big	Displays type slightly larger than the surrounding text
`<blink>`	Blink	Makes the text flash on and off (*Netscape Navigator only*)
`<font>`	Font	Specifies the font face, size, and color (discussed in "The <font> Tag" section later in this chapter) (*deprecated*)
`<i>`	Italic	Displays text in italic type

Table 10-2: Physical inline style tags (continued)

Tag	Description	Function
`<s>`	Strike-through	An alternative tag for `<strike>` (*deprecated*)
`<small>`	Small	Displays type slightly smaller than the surrounding text
`<strike>`	Strike-through	Displays strike-through text (crossed through with a horizontal line) (*deprecated*)
`<sub>`	Subscript	Displays the text at a smaller size, slightly below the baseline of the surrounding text
`<sup>`	Superscript	Displays the text at a smaller size, slightly above the baseline of the surrounding text
`<tt>`	Teletype	Displays the text in the user's default monospaced font
`<u>`	Underline	Underlines the text (*deprecated*)

<div> and <span>

The HTML specification provides two generic tags, `<div>` and `<span>`, that can be used to structure and label the contents of a web document.

The `<div>` tag divides a document into distinct sections (or divisions). It is a block-level element, which means that when you introduce a `<div>` tag, the enclosed content begins on a new line and space may be added above and below. The `<span>` tag is an inline element that can be applied to a string of text within a paragraph or other content flow. It does not introduce a line break.

The tags are used in much the same way. On their own, `<div>` and `<span>` have no inherent qualities and have no effect on the display of their contents. You can assign a `<div>` or `<span>` meaning (in effect, give it a name) by using the identifier attributes `class` and `id`. In a sense, it enables you to create your own tags so they can be called on later from a style sheet, hyperlink, script, applet, or other process.

The `class` attribute is used to identify various elements as belonging to a group. For example, if you want the glossary words in a document to display in green type, identify each word as a "glossary" word as shown here:

```
<SPAN class="glossary">resolution</SPAN> and
  <SPAN class="glossary">color depth</SPAN>
```

Then use a style sheet to affect the display of all "glossary" terms:

```
span.glossary {color: green}
```

The `id` attribute is used for unique instances in a document (in other words, the value of an id attribute cannot be repeated in the same document). The `id` attribute can be used in the same tag as the `class` attribute to call out one particular instance within a group.

 The `class` and `id` attributes can be used in nearly all HTML element tags. They are not limited to `<div>` and `<span>`.

The <font> Tag

The <font> tag is an inline style tag used to specify the size, color, and font face for the enclosed text using the `size`, `color`, and `face` attributes, respectively. It was created as an extension to HTML to give designers more control over the display of text. The dark side of the <font> tag is that it introduces very specific display information into the HTML markup. As noted several times in this book, in an ideal world, style would be kept separate from content. In HTML 4.01, the <font> tag and all its attributes have been deprecated in favor of the superior formatting capabilities of style sheets. Despite this, it continues to be quite popular (even the best authoring tools rely on it heavily), so it isn't likely to go away any time soon. That said, let's look at how the font tag is used.

A single <font> tag may contain all of these attributes as shown:

```
<FONT FACE="sans-serif" COLOR="white" SIZE="+1">
```

For an explanation of acceptable values for the `color` attribute, refer to Chapter 16.

Specifying Size with <font>

You can use the `size` attribute within the <font> tag to adjust type size. This attribute is supported by Versions 1.1 and higher of both Navigator and Internet Explorer.

Browsers measure HTML type on a relative scale from 1 to 7, where 3 is the default and will be displayed at the size specified by the user's preferences. These "virtual" sizes are relative, meaning they do not signify actual pixel or point adjustments. Each size is successively about 20 percent smaller or larger than the default size, 3.

The size value can be specified as an absolute value from 1 to 7 or as a relative value by means of a plus or minus sign. When relative values are given, the default value (which is 3, unless otherwise specified with a <basefont> tag) is increased or decreased by that relative amount. Type is never displayed larger than 7 or smaller than 1, even if the relative size results in such a value.

Absolute value	1	2	3	4	5	6	7
Relative value	−2	−1	−	+1	+2	+3	+4

Therefore, `<font size="4">block of text</font>` is the same as `<font size="+1">block of text</font>`, and both will result in a block of text that is 20 percent larger than the default text size.

It is interesting to note that when <font> tags are nested, the effects of their relative sizes are not cumulative, but rather are always based on the default or basefont size of the text. Therefore, if the default text size for a document is 3, any text in that document that is enclosed in `<font size="+1">` will result in text with a size of 4, even if that text is nested within a paragraph with `<font size="5">`.

Advantage of <font size="n">

- **Gives designers some control over type size** without resorting to inappropriate tags (such as heading tags) to adjust size.

Disadvantages of <font size="n">

- **Overrides viewers' preference for comfortable on-screen reading.** By changing sizes, you risk some viewers seeing type that is illegibly small or ridiculously big.

- **Introduces style information into the HTML document.** In addition to not abiding by the HTML standards, it makes it more difficult to make style changes because every single <font> tag needs to be edited individually.

Recommendations

- Limit the use of <font size="n"> to small blocks of text, such as copyright information, rather than applying a size adjustment to an entire page.

- If your content needs to be found by search engines that look for heading information, do not use the <font size="n"> tag as a substitute for HTML heading tags, which are weighted more heavily.

Specifying Fonts with <font>

Internet Explorer 1.0 introduced the proprietary `face` attribute to the <font> tag, which allows you to specify specific fonts for selected text. This attribute was adopted by Navigator in Versions 3.0 and higher (it does not work in Navigator 2.0 or earlier). If you are certain your audience is comprised of newer browser users, strive to use style sheets for all your page formatting.

The `face` attribute does not guarantee that the user will see your text in your specified font. Consider it merely a recommendation. Read "Why Specifying Type is Problematic" in Chapter 3 before gleefully sprinkling the <font> tag throughout your documents.

The quote-enclosed value of `face` is one or more display font names separated by commas as follows:

```
<FONT FACE="Verdana, Arial, sans-serif">block of text</FONT>
```

The browser looks at the string of font names until it finds one that is installed on the user's system and can be used for display. If none of the suggested fonts are installed, the default font is used instead.

You can include a generic font family (`serif`, `sans-serif`, `monospace`, `cursive`, or `fantasy`) as the last choice in your list, which allows the browser to choose any available font within that class should your named fonts not be found. It's sort of a last-ditch effort to get something like the font you want, without leaving it entirely to chance.

Advantages of <font face="fontlist">

- **Gives designers some influence over font selection.**

- **Degrades acceptably.** If the suggested fonts are not found (or if the tag is not supported), the text is simply displayed in the browser's default font specified by the user.

Disadvantages of <font face="fontlist">

- **Font specification (and other stylistic control) is better handled by style sheets.**

- **Not viable for specifying non-western fonts.** `<font face="fontlist">` uses simple mapping to match identifying character set numbers to character shapes ("glyphs") that may not translate correctly for the font you select.

Lists

The original HTML specification included tags for five different types of lists: numbered lists (called ordered lists), bulleted lists (called unordered lists), definition lists, menus, and directory lists. Since then, directory lists and menus have been deprecated with the recommendation that unordered lists be used for the same effect. In this section, we'll look at the structure of each type of list in current use.

Lists and the items within them are block-level elements, meaning that line spaces will automatically be added before and after them. Extra space may be added above and below the entire list element, but in general, if you want to add space between individual list items, you need to insert two `<br>` tags between them. It is also possible to use style sheets to control spacing around list items.

Unordered (Bulleted) Lists

An unordered list is used for a collection of related items that appear in no particular order. List items are displayed on an indent with a bullet preceding each list item. The bullet shape is automatically inserted by the browser when it encounters the list item, so you do not need to type a bullet character into your HTML source code.

An unordered list is delimited by the `<ul>...</ul>` tags, with each item indicated by an `<li>` tag. The closing `</li>` tag is usually omitted, but it should be included if you are using style sheets to control list item display.

Figure 10-4 shows the structure and display of a simple unordered list.

Figure 10-4: A simple unordered list

Changing the bullet shape

HTML provides only a minimal amount of control over the appearance of bullets. You can change the shape of the bullets for the whole list by using the `type` attribute within the `<ul>` tag. The `type` attribute allows you to specify one of three shapes: `disc` (the default), `circle`, or `square`. Figure 10-5 shows discs (left), circles (center), and squares (right). Like so many attributes that control how elements look, `type` has been deprecated in the HTML 4.01 specification.

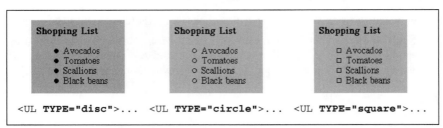

Figure 10-5: Specifying the bullet type with the TYPE attribute

The `type` attribute can be applied within a list-item tag (`<li>`) to change the shape of the bullet for that particular item. Figure 10-6 shows this effect.

<table>
<tr>
<td>
Shopping List
• Avocados
○ Tomatoes
□ Scallions
</td>
<td>
<pre><P><B>Shopping List</B></P>
<UL>
<LI TYPE="disc">Avocados
<LI TYPE="circle">Tomatoes
<LI TYPE="square">Scallions
</UL></pre>
</td>
</tr>
</table>

Figure 10-6: Changing the bullet type within list items

There is no method using HTML for specifying a graphic image for a bullet. If you want to use your own graphic as the bullet for a list, you need to simulate a list using a table for alignment. The table should have a narrow column of cells for the bullet graphic and a second column for the list item content. Omit all list tags to avoid redundant formatting. A better method is to take advantage of style sheet properties that allow you to specify a graphic to be used as a bullet while maintaining the integrity of the list markup.

Ordered (Numbered) Lists

Ordered lists are used when the sequence of the items is important. They are displayed on an indent, with a number (automatically inserted by the browser) preceding each list item. You do not need to type the numbers into your HTML source code.

Ordered lists follow the same basic structure as unordered lists: the entire list is contained within the `<ol>` and `</ol>` tags, and each individual list item is indicated with an `<li>` tag. Extra space will be added above and below the list.

Figure 10-7 shows the structure and display of a simple ordered list.

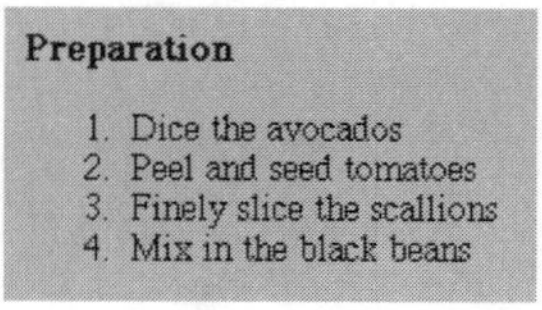

```
Preparation                     <P><B>Preparation</B></P>
                                <OL>
1. Dice the avocados            <LI>Dice the avocados
2. Peel and seed tomatoes       <LI>Peel and seed tomatoes
3. Finely slice the scallions   <LI>Finely slice the scallions
4. Mix in the black beans       <LI>Mix in the black beans
                                </OL>
```

Figure 10-7: A simple ordered list

Changing the numbering scheme

The type attribute can be used within ordered lists to specify the style of numbering. There are five possible values: 1 (numbers), A (uppercase letters), a (lowercase letters), I (uppercase roman), and i (lowercase roman). The value "1" is the default and is shown in Figure 10-7. Figure 10-8 shows the code and displays of the other four settings.

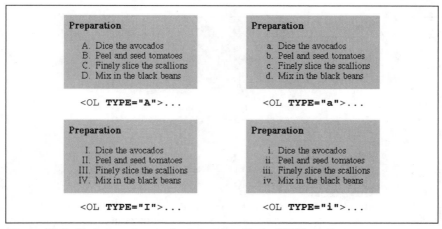

Figure 10-8: Changing the numbering style with the TYPE attribute

As with unordered lists, you can use the type attribute within individual <li> tags to mix-and-match styles within a list.

Setting the first number

If you want the list to start with some number (or letter value) other than 1, use the start attribute to specify the first number, as shown in Figure 10-9.

Definition Lists

The third type of list supported by HTML is the definition list, which follows a different structure than the other two. Definition lists consist of terms and definitions (any amount of descriptive text to be associated with the term) as in a glossary. In general, terms are positioned against the left edge of the page and definitions are positioned on an indent.

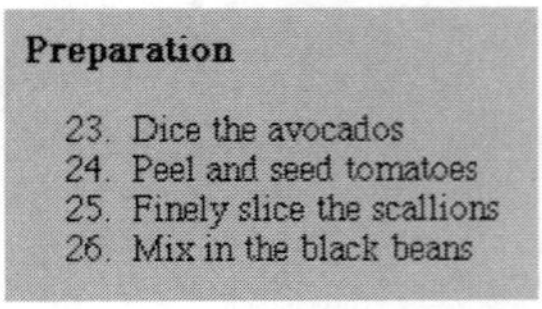

```
                             <P><B>Preparation</B></P>
Preparation                  <OL START="23">
  23.  Dice the avocados     <LI>Dice the avocados
  24.  Peel and seed tomatoes <LI>Peel and seed tomatoes
  25.  Finely slice the scallions <LI>Finely slice the scallions
  26.  Mix in the black beans <LI>Mix in the black beans
                             </OL>
```

Figure 10-9: Setting the first number in the list with the START attribute

Terms and definitions are block-level items, so line breaks are added around them, but if you want extra space between terms and definitions, you must insert two <br> tags between them.

A definition list is designated by the <dl>...</dl> tags. Within the list, each term is indicated with a <dt> and its definition is marked with a <dd>. Closing </dt> and </dd> tags may be safely omitted if style sheets are not in use. Figure 10-10 shows the display of a basic definition list and the code that created it.

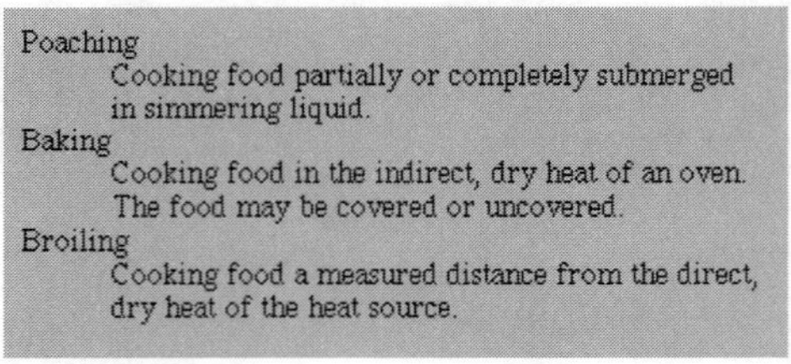

```
<DL>
    <DT>Poaching
    <DD>Cooking food partially or completely submerged
    in simmering liquid.
    <DT>Baking
    <DD>Cooking food in the indirect, dry heat of an
    oven. The food may be covered or uncovered.
    <DT>Broiling
    <DD>Cooking food a measured distance from the direct,
    dry heat of the heat source.
</DL>
```

Figure 10-10: Simple definition list

Nesting Lists

Any list can be nested within another list. For instance, you can add a bulleted list item under an item within a numbered list; numbered lists can be added within a definition; and so on. Lists can be nested several layers deep; however, since the left indent is cumulative, it doesn't take long for the text to end up pressed against the right margin.

It is helpful to use indents in your HTML source document to keep nesting levels clear. Be careful to close all the lists you start!

Nesting unordered lists

When unordered lists are nested within each other, the browser automatically displays a different bullet for each consecutive level, as shown in Figure 10-11.

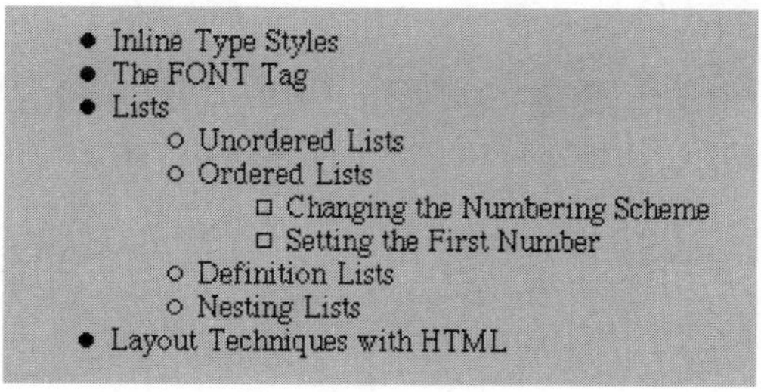

```
  • Inline Type Styles
  • The FONT Tag
  • Lists
      ○ Unordered Lists
      ○ Ordered Lists
          □ Changing the Numbering Scheme
          □ Setting the First Number
      ○ Definition Lists
      ○ Nesting Lists
  • Layout Techniques with HTML


<UL>
<LI>Inline Type Styles
<LI>The FONT Tag
<LI>Lists
    <UL>
    <LI>Unordered Lists
    <LI>Ordered Lists
        <UL>
        <LI>Changing the Numbering Scheme
        <LI>Setting the First Number
        </UL>
    <LI>Definition Lists
    <LI>Nesting Lists
    </UL>
<LI>Layout Techniques with HTML
</UL>
```

Figure 10-11: Nested unordered lists (bullet styles change automatically)

Nesting ordered lists

It would be nice if nested ordered lists automatically displayed in standard outline format, but unfortunately, browsers do not have the capacity to automatically change numbering schemes. By default, every level within a nested numbered list will display with numbers (arabic numerals). If you want standard outline format, you need to label each list manually with the type attribute, as shown in Figure 10-12.

Text Layout Techniques with HTML

First, let it be stated that "layout techniques with HTML" is an oxymoron. HTML was specifically designed to pass off all layout functions to the end user's browsing tool. The controls over presentation listed here are the result of either extensions to the original HTML standard or a "creative use" (or misuse, depending who you ask) of an existing tag.

```
        A.  Inline Type Styles
        B.  The FONT Tag
        C.  Lists
                1.  Unordered Lists
                2.  Ordered Lists
                        a.  Changing the Numbering Scheme
                        b.  Setting the First Number
                3.  Definition Lists
                4.  Nesting Lists
        D.  Layout Techniques with HTML
```

```
<OL TYPE="A">
<LI>Inline Type Styles
<LI>The FONT Tag
<LI>Lists
    <OL TYPE="1">
    <LI>Unordered Lists
    <LI>Ordered Lists
        <OL TYPE="a">
            <LI>Changing the Numbering Scheme
            <LI>Setting the First Number
        </OL>
    <LI>Definition Lists
    <LI>Nesting Lists
    </OL>
<LI>Layout Techniques with HTML
</OL>
```

Figure 10-12: Nested ordered list (numbered styles must be changed manually)

Several tags, such as <blockquote> or certain list tags, let you add text indents, while the <pre> tag gives you limited formatting control using "preformatted" text, and we'll look at these simple mechanisms here. HTML tables offer more precise control over positioning, which is covered in Chapter 13.

Ideally, of course, presentation should be controlled using style sheets.

Preformatted Text

Preformatted (<pre>) text is unique in that it is displayed exactly as it is typed in the HTML source code—including all line returns and multiple character spaces (in all other HTML text, returns and consecutive spaces are just ignored). Preformatted text is always displayed in a monospace font, which allows columns of characters to line up correctly.

The same block of source text was coded as <pre> text and as teletype (<tt>), another method for specifying a monospace font. The difference is obvious, as shown in Figures 10-13 and 10-14.

The <pre> tag is the only HTML tag that lets you know *exactly* how your text will line up when displayed in a browser. For this reason, it was adopted early on as a favorite cheat for controlling alignment in web pages. The downside is that all the text will be displayed in Courier.

```
                    Calories    Carb(g)     Fat(g)
French Fries          285         38          14
Fried Onion Rings     550         26          47
Fried Chicken         402         17          24
```

<PRE>

```
                    Calories    Carb(g)     Fat(g)

French Fries          285         38          14

Fried Onion Rings     550         26          47

Fried Chicken         402         17          24
```
</PRE>

Figure 10-13: Preformatted text

```
Calories Carb(g) Fat(g) French Fries 285 38 14 Fried
Onion Rings 550 26 47 Fried Chicken 402 17 24
```

<TT>

```
                    Calories    Carb(g)     Fat(g)
French Fries          285         38          14
Fried Onion Rings     550         26          47
Fried Chicken         402         17          24
```
</TT>

Figure 10-14: Teletype text

Note that <pre> is a block element, meaning that it is always preceded and followed by a line break (some browsers also add extra space above and below the block). For this reason, it is not possible to set text within a paragraph as preformatted. If you need a number of blank spaces within a sentence, use nonbreaking space characters ( ) instead.

Preventing Line Breaks

Text and graphics that appear within "no-break" (<nobr>) tags always display on one line, and are not wrapped in the browser window. If the string of characters or elements within <nobr> tags is very long, it continues off the browser window, and users must scroll horizontally to the right to see it, as shown in Figure 10-15.

The <nobr> tag can be used to hold together a row of graphics, such as the buttons of a toolbar, so they always display as one piece.

Adding a <br> within <nobr> tagged text causes the line to break.

The word-break tag (<wbr>) is an esoteric little tag that can be used in conjunction with the no-break tag. <wbr> is used to indicate a potential word break point within <nobr> tagged content. When the "no-break" segment extends beyond the browser window, the <wbr> tag tells it exactly where it is permitted to break the line, as shown in Figure 10-16. It keeps line lengths from getting totally out of hand.

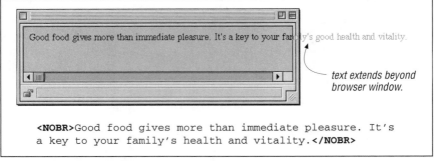

```
<NOBR>Good food gives more than immediate pleasure. It's
a key to your family's health and vitality.</NOBR>
```

Figure 10-15: Nonbreaking text

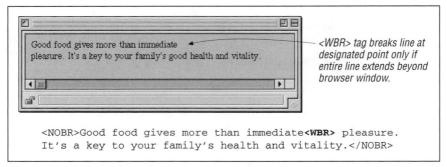

```
<NOBR>Good food gives more than immediate<WBR> pleasure.
It's a key to your family's health and vitality.</NOBR>
```

Figure 10-16: Use of the <wbr> tag within <nobr> text

It should be noted that both <nobr> and <wbr> are not part of the HTML 4.01 specification but are widely supported by popular browsers.

Centering Text Elements

There are two methods for centering text elements horizontally on a page: the align attribute and the <center> tag. Bear in mind that the <center> tag and align attribute have been deprecated by the HTML 4.01 specification in favor of style sheet controls (although browsers will continue to support the following tags for a while).

The align attribute

One way to center elements is to use the block-level tags' align attribute with its value set to center. The align attribute can be added to the paragraph tag (<p>), any heading tag (<h1> through <h6>), or a page division (<div>). Be sure to close the tags at the end of the element.

In Figure 10-17, each element is centered individually using align=center.

As an alternative, you could enclose all three elements in a <div> tag with align=center. Unfortunately, the align attribute in a <div> tag is only recognized by Internet Explorer Version 3.0 and higher and by Navigator Versions 4.0

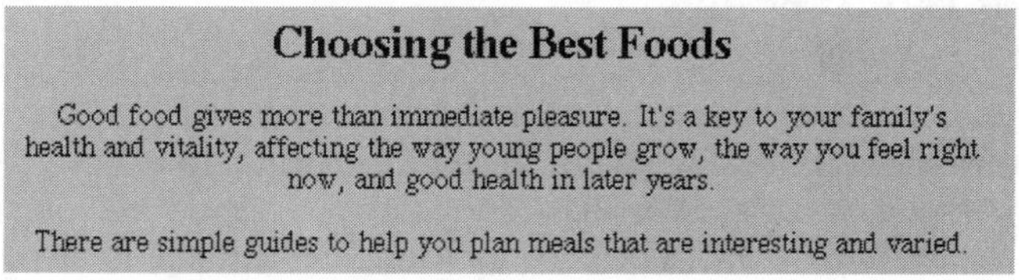

> ### Choosing the Best Foods
>
> Good food gives more than immediate pleasure. It's a key to your family's health and vitality, affecting the way young people grow, the way you feel right now, and good health in later years.
>
> There are simple guides to help you plan meals that are interesting and varied.

```
<H2 ALIGN="center">Choosing the Best Foods</H2>
<P ALIGN="center">Good food gives more than immediate pleasure.
It's a key to your family's health and vitality, affecting the
way young people grow, the way you feel right now, and good
health in later years.</P>
<P ALIGN="center">There are simple guides to help you plan meals
that are interesting and varied.</P>
```

Figure 10-17: Centering text

and up, so it is not a universal solution. The following code creates the same effect shown in Figure 10-17:

```
<DIV ALIGN="center">
<H2>Choosing the Best Foods</H2>
<P>Good food gives more than immediate pleasure. It's a key to your
family's health and vitality, affecting the way young people grow, the
way you feel right now, and good health in later years.</P>
<P>There are simple guides to help you plan meals that are interesting
and varied.</P>
</DIV>
```

The <center> tag

An extension to HTML, the <center> tag is extremely straightforward to use (and for that reason, it is used commonly)—just place the <center> and </center> tags around sections of the page you would like to be centered, as shown in the following code. This works the same as <div align=center>, but it is better supported. The <center> tag has been deprecated in the HTML 4.01 specification.

You can place your whole page within <center> tags or apply it just to certain paragraphs. The <center> tag can only be applied to block-level elements since it is illogical to center text within the flow of left-aligned text.

```
<CENTER>
<H2>Choosing the Best Foods</H2>
<P>Good food gives more than immediate pleasure. It's a key to your
family's health and vitality, affecting the way young people grow, the
way you feel right now, and good health in later years.</P>
<P>There are simple guides to help you plan meals that are interesting
and varied.</P>
</CENTER>
```

Right and Left Alignment

The `align` attribute is also used to specify left alignment and right alignment by setting its value to `left` or `right`, respectively. The alignment remains in effect until the browser encounters another alignment instruction in the source. You can break lines with the `<br>` tag within an aligned paragraph without losing the alignment. Figure 10-18 shows the effects of setting the attribute to `left` or `right`. Page elements are left-justified by default in left-to-right languages.

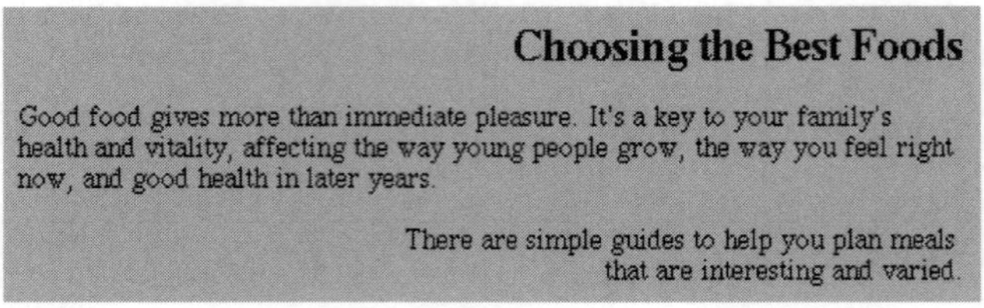

Choosing the Best Foods

Good food gives more than immediate pleasure. It's a key to your family's health and vitality, affecting the way young people grow, the way you feel right now, and good health in later years.

There are simple guides to help you plan meals that are interesting and varied.

```
<H2 ALIGN="right">Choosing the Best Foods</H2>
<P ALIGN="left">Good food gives more than immediate pleasure. It's
a key to your family's health and vitality, affecting the way
young people grow, the way you feel right now, and good health
in later years.</P>
<P ALIGN="right">There are simple guides to help you plan meals
<BR>that are interesting and varied.</P>
```

Figure 10-18: Left and right alignment

 Text aligned with the `align` attribute overrides any centering set with the `<center>` tag.

Creating Indents with HTML

Unfortunately, there is no specific function for creating indented text in HTML, so it has become common for web designers to make do with existing tags that have the side effect of producing an indent. This section looks at the more popular "cheats" for indenting text using only text-formatting tags.

Be aware, however, that it is poor HTML form to arbitrarily label elements just for their display features (like indenting). The recommended method is to use style sheets to specify margin indents (it's a much more precise method as well). You can also achieve indents using tables (see Chapter 13). Some designers place transparent graphics in the text to create white space, but this is strongly discouraged.

The following techniques are presented in the spirit of providing a thorough overview of current HTML solutions, and because you may also see them generated by WYSIWYG authoring tools. Their inclusion by no means represents an endorsement of the "old ways."

\<blockquote>

The blockquote element is intended to be used for lengthy quotations, but it has long been a favorite for adding white space along the left and right margins of a block of text. Browsers generally add approximately 40 pixels of space between the browser margin (*not* the window border) and the left and right edges of a blockquote element, as shown in Figure 10-19.

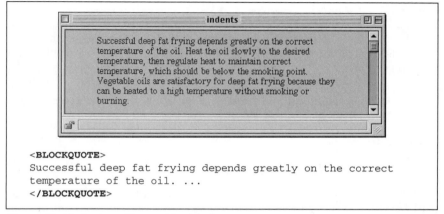

```
<BLOCKQUOTE>
Successful deep fat frying depends greatly on the correct
temperature of the oil. ...
</BLOCKQUOTE>
```

Figure 10-19: Setting off text with \<blockquote>

There are a few things you should know when using blockquotes. Some early browsers display blockquote material in italic, making it difficult to read on the screen. Also, if you plan to place aligned images in a blockquote, keep in mind that browsers are inconsistent in the way they display images within blockquotes. Some align the graphic with the indented blockquote margin; others align the image with the normal margin of paragraph text. It's a good idea to test on a variety of browsers.

Creating indents with list elements

Some web authors (and WYSIWYG authoring tools) take advantage of the automatic indentation that takes place when you specify text as a list. The two following methods are both syntactically incorrect and ought to be avoided, but they can be used in a pinch to create an indent from the left margin of the browser window. Either approach produces the result shown in Figure 10-20.

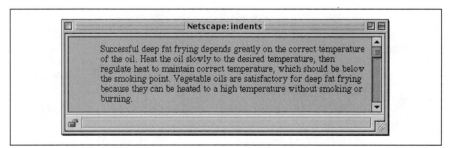

Figure 10-20: Indented text

A <ul> *with no items*

Marking a text element as an unordered list sets the text on a left-indent. As long as you don't add any list items (<li>) within the list, no bullets appear.

```
<UL>
Successful deep fat frying depends greatly on the correct temperature
of the oil. ...
</UL>
```

A <dd> *without its term*

A definition (<dd>) within a definition list (<dl>) is also set with the standard left indent. It's fine to omit the term from the list. I've seen definition lists set within definition lists to create deeper levels of indent (it's not pretty, but it works).

```
<DL>
<DD>Successful deep fat frying depends greatly on the correct
temperature of the oil. ...
</DD>
</DL>
```

Character Entity References

Characters not found in the normal alphanumeric character set, such as < and &, must be specified in HTML using character entities. Using the standard desktop publishing keyboard commands (such as Option-g for the © symbol) within an HTML document will not produce the desired character when the document is rendered in a browser. In fact, the browser generally displays the numeric entity for the character.

Character entities can be referenced by name (*&name;*) or by numeric value (*&#nnn;*). The browser interprets the string to display the proper character. Named entities are preferable because numeric values may be interpreted differently on different platforms.

Table 10-3 presents the character entities for commonly used special characters. The complete list appears in Appendix F.

Table 10-3: Common special characters and their character entities

Character	Description	Name	Number
	Character space (nonbreaking space)		
&	Ampersand	&	&
<	Less-than sign (useful for displaying tags on a web page)	<	<
>	Greater-than sign (useful for displaying tags on a web page)	>	>
"	Left curly quotes *(nonstandard entity)*	*(none)*	“
"	Right curly quotes *(nonstandard entity)*	*(none)*	”
™	Trademark *(nonstandard entity)*	*(none)*	™
£	Pound symbol	£	£
¥	Yen symbol	¥	¥
©	Copyright symbol	©	©
®	Registered trademark	®	®

CHAPTER 11

Creating Links

The HTML 4.01 specification puts it simply and clearly: "A link is a connection from one web resource to another." This ability to link one document to another is what makes HTML unique among document markup languages and is the key to its widespread popularity.

This chapter focuses on the HTML tags related to linking and building relationships between documents. It includes uses for the anchor tag, linking with imagemaps (both client- and server-side), affecting the appearance of hyperlinks, creating links with non-web protocols, and associating documents with the link tag.

Summary of Tags Related to Linking

In this section, browser support for each tag is noted to the right of the tag name. Browsers that do not support the tag are grayed out. Tag usage is indicated below the tag name. Start and end tags are required unless otherwise noted. "Deprecated" means that the tag or attribute is currently supported but is due to be phased out of the HTML specification and is discouraged from use (usually in favor of similar style sheet controls). The attributes listed for each tag reflect those in common use. A more thorough listing of attributes for each tag, according to the HTML 4.01 specification, appears in Appendix A.

\<a\>   NN 2, 3, 4, 6   MSIE 2, 3, 4, 5, 5.5, 6   HTML 4.01   WebTV   Opera5

\<a\>...\</a\>

Defines an *anchor* within the document. An anchor is used to link to another document or web resource. It can also serve to label a fragment within a document (also called a *named anchor*), which serves as a destination anchor for linking to a specific point in an HTML document.

Attributes

The attributes labeled "HTML 4.01" are new to the HTML 4.01 specification and are generally supported only by Internet Explorer 5.5 and higher and Netscape 6.

accesskey=*character*
> *HTML 4.01.* Assigns an access key (shortcut key command) to the link. Access keys are also used for form fields. The value is a single character. Users may access the element by hitting Alt-*key* (PC) or Ctrl-*key* (Mac).

charset=*charset*
> *HTML 4.01.* Specifies the character encoding of the target document. See Chapter 7 for information on character sets.

coords=*x,y coordinates*
> *HTML 4.01.* Specifies the x,y coordinates for a clickable area in an imagemap. HTML 4.0 proposes that client-side imagemaps be replaced by an <object> tag containing the image and a set of anchor tags defining the "hot" areas (with shapes and coordinate attributes). This system has not yet been implemented by browsers.

href=*url*
> Specifies the URL of the destination HTML document or web resource (such as an image, audio, PDF, or other media file).

id=*text*
> Gives the link a unique name (similar to the **name** attribute) so it can be referenced from a link, script, or style sheet. It is more versatile than **name**, but it is not as universally supported.

hreflang=*language code*
> *HTML 4.01.* Specifies the base language of the target document. See Chapter 7 for a list of two-letter language codes.

name=*text*
> Places a fragment identifier within an HTML document. Fragments are discussed further in the "Linking within a Document" section of this chapter.

rel=*relationship*
> Establishes a relationship between the current document and the target document. Common relationships include **stylesheet**, **next**, **prev**, **copyright**, **index**, and **glossary**.

rev=*relationship*
> Specifies the relationship from the target back to the source (the opposite of the **rev** attribute).

shape=rect|circle|poly|default
> *HTML 4.01.* Defines the shape of a clickable area in an imagemap. This is only used in the <a> tag as part of HTML 4.01's proposal to replace client-side imagemaps with a combination of <object> and <a> tags. This system has not yet been implemented by browsers.

tabindex=*number*
> *HTML 4.01.* Specifies the position of the current element in the tabbing order for the current document. The value must be between 0 and 32767. It is used for tabbing through the links on a page (or fields in a form).

`target=text`

> *Not supported by WebTV or Internet Explorer 2.0 and earlier.* Specifies the name of the window or frame in which the target document should be displayed. For more information, see "Targeting Windows" in this chapter and "Targeting Frames" in Chapter 14.

`title=text`

> Specifies a title for the target document. May be displayed as a "tool tip."

`type=MIME type`

> Specifies the content type (MIME type) of the defined content.

Link Examples

To a local file:

```
<A HREF="filename.html">...</A>
```

To an external file:

```
<A HREF="http://server/path/file.html">...</A>
```

To a named anchor:

```
<A HREF="http://server/path/file.html#fragment">...</A>
```

To a named anchor in the current file:

```
<A HREF="#fragment">...</A>
```

To send an email message:

```
<A HREF="mailto:username@domain">...</A>
```

To a file on an FTP server:

```
<A HREF="ftp://server/path/filename">...</A>
```

\<area\>

NN 2, 3, 4, 6   MSIE 2, 3, 4, 5, 5.5, 6   HTML 4.01   WebTV   Opera5

`<area>` *(no end tag)*

The **area** tag is used within the \<map\> tag of a *client-side imagemap* to define a specific "hot" (clickable) area. Client-side imagemaps are discussed later in this chapter.

Attributes

`alt=text`

> *Required.* Specifies a short description of the image that is displayed when the image file is not available.

`coords=values`

> Specifies a list of comma-separated pixel coordinates that define a "hot" area of an imagemap. The specific syntax for the coordinates varies by shape (see the "Imagemaps" section later in this chapter).

`href=url`

> Specifies the URL of the document or file that is accessed by clicking on the defined area.

`nohref`

Defines a "mouse-sensitive" area in an imagemap for which there is no action when the user clicks in the area.

`shape=rect|circle|poly|default`

Defines the shape of the clickable area.

`<base>`
NN 2, 3, 4, 6   MSIE 2, 3, 4, 5, 5.5, 6   HTML 4.01   WebTV   Opera5

`<base>` *(no end tag)*

Specifies the base pathname for all relative URLs in the document. Place this element within the `<head>` of the document.

Attributes

`href=url`

Required. Specifies the URL to be used.

`target=name`

Defines the default target window for all links in the document. Often used to target frames. (*This attribute is not supported in MSIE 2.0.*)

`<link>`
NN 2, 3, 4, 6   MSIE 2, 3, 4, 5, 5.5, 6   HTML 4.01   WebTV   Opera5

`<link>` *(no end tag)*

Defines a relationship between the current document and another document. This tag goes within the `<head>` portion of the document. It is often used to refer to an external style sheet.

Attributes

`href=url`

Identifies the target document.

`media=screen|tty|tv|projection|handheld|print|braille|aural|all`

Identifies the target medium for the linked document so an alternate style sheet can be accessed. The media attribute is explained in more detail in Chapter 5.

`rel=relation`

Describes the relationship from the current source document to the target. Common relationship types include `stylesheet`, `next`, `prev`, `copyright`, `index`, and `glossary`.

`rev=relation`

Specifies the relationship of the target document back to the source (the opposite of the `rel` attribute).

`title=text`

Provides a title for the target document.

`type=resource`

Shows the type of an outside link. The value `text/css` indicates that the linked document is an external cascading style sheet.

```
<map>...</map>
```

Encloses client-side imagemap specifications. Client-side imagemaps are discussed later in this chapter.

Attributes

`name=text`
> Gives the imagemap a name that is then referenced within the `<img>` tag. This attribute is required.

Simple Hypertext Links

The anchor (`<a>`) tag is used to identify a string of text or an image that serves as a hypertext link to another document. Linking to a string of text looks like this:

```
I am <A HREF="link.html">linking</A> to you!
```

To make an image a link, enclose the image tag within the anchor tags as follows:

```
<A HREF="link.html"><IMG SRC="pixie.gif"></A>
```

Most graphical browsers display linked text underlined and in blue by default, but this behavior can be altered. Linked graphics appear with a blue outline (unless you turn the outline off in the `<img>` tag by setting the border attribute to zero).

The URL is the pathname of the document you want to link to. URLs can be absolute or relative.

Absolute URLs

An *absolute URL* is made up of the following components: a protocol identifier, a host name (the name of the server machine), and the path to the specific file-name. When you are linking to documents on other servers, you need to use an absolute URL. The following is an example of a link with an absolute URL:

```
<A HREF="http://www.littlechair.com/web/index.html">...</A>
```

Here the protocol is identified as *http* (HyperText Transfer Protocol, the standard protocol of the Web), the host is *www.littlechair.com*, and the pathname is *web/index.html*.

Relative URLs

A *relative URL* provides a pointer to another document relative to the location of the current document. The syntax is based on pathname structures in the Unix operating system, which are discussed in Chapter 4. When you are pointing to another document within your own site (on the same server), it is common to use relative URLs.

For example, if I am currently in *resume.html* (identified here by its full pathname):

```
www.littlechair.com/web/work/resume.html
```

and I want to put a link on that page to *bio.html*, which is in the same directory:

```
www.littlechair.com/web/work/bio.html
```

I could use a relative URL within the link as follows:

```
<A HREF="bio.html">...</A>
```

Using the same example, to link to the file *index.html* in a higher level directory (*web*), I could use the relative pathname to that file as shown:

```
<A HREF="../index.html">
```

This relative URL is the equivalent to the absolute URL *http://www.littlechair.com/ web/index.html*.

By default, a relative URL is based on the current document. You can change that by placing the `<base>` element in the document header (`<head>`) to state explicitly the base URL for all relative pathnames in the document. The `<base>` tag can only appear in the `<head>` of the document, and it should appear before any other element with an external reference. The browser uses the specified base URL (not the current document's URL) to resolve relative URLs.

Linking Within a Document

By default, when you link to a page, the browser displays the top of that page. To aid in navigation, you can use the anchor tag to link to a specific point or section within a document. This navigation technique is only effective on long documents. Linking to specific destinations in a document is a two-step process in which you place a marker in the document and give it a name, and then you make a link to that marker.

Naming a fragment

First, identify and name the portion of the document (called a fragment) that you want to link to. The fragment is marked using the anchor (`<a>`) tag with its **name** attribute, giving the document fragment a name that can be referenced from a link. Named anchors receive no special style treatment by default (as `<a href>` links do).

To illustrate, let's set up a named fragment within a sample document called *dailynews.html* so users can link directly to the Stock Quotes section of the page. The following anchor tag marks the Stock Quotes title as a fragment named "stocks".

```
<H1><A NAME="stocks">Daily Stock Quotes</A></H1>
```

Fragments can also be named using the **id** attribute in any element tag. Keep in mind that the **id** attribute is a newer addition to the HTML specification, so it is not supported in older browsers. In this example, the heading itself serves as a marker:

```
<H1 ID="stocks">Daily Stock Quotes<H1>
```

The value of the **name** and **id** attributes must be unique within the document (in other words, two elements can't be given the same name).

Linking to a fragment

The second step is to create a link to the fragment using a standard anchor tag with its `href` attribute. Fragment identifiers are placed at the end of the pathname, preceded by the hash (#) symbol.

To link to the "stocks" fragment from within *dailynews.html*, the tag would look like this:

```
<A HREF="#stocks">Check out the Stock Quotes</A>
```

Linking to a fragment in another document

You can create a link to a named fragment of any document on the Web by using the complete pathname. (Of course, the named anchors would have to be in place already.) To link to the stocks section from another document in the same directory, use a relative pathname as follows:

```
<A HREF="dailynews.html#stocks">Go to today's Stock Quotes</A>
```

Use an absolute URL to link to a fragment on another site, as in the following example:

```
<A HREF="http://www.website.com/document.html#fragment">
```

Using named anchors

Named anchors are most often used as a navigational aid by creating a hyperlinked table of contents at the top of a very long scrolling web page. Users can see the major topics at a glance and quickly get to the portions that interest them. When linking down into a long page, it is generally a good idea to add links back to the top of the page or to the table of contents.

Affecting the Appearance of Links

As we all know by now, linked text is blue and underlined by default and graphics are identified by blue borders (unless you turn them off). But it doesn't have to be that way. Changing the color of links is easy with HTML, so you can make your links more coordinated with your chosen site palette. Style sheets offer even more control over the appearance of links.

You should exercise some caution in changing link appearance. The blue text and underlines have become a strong visual clue for "click here," so altering this formula may confuse your users. Use your knowledge of the savvy of your target audience to guide your design decisions. In general, as long as the link colors are consistent throughout a site and noticeably different from the default text style, changing the color is not a problem for the usability of the site.

Setting Colors in <body>

Link color specifications in the <body> tag are applied to the whole document. See Chapter 16 for instructions on providing color values for the following attributes.

Links	`<BODY LINK="color">`	Sets the color for hyperlinks. The default color for links is blue.
Visited Links	`<BODY VLINK="color">`	Sets the colors for links that have already been clicked. The default color for visited links is purple.
Active links	`<BODY ALINK="color">`	Sets the color for a link while it is in the process of being clicked. The default color for an active link is red.

Specifying Color for a Specific Link

You can override the color of a specific link by placing `<font>` tags *within* the anchor tags as shown in this example:

```
<A HREF="doc.html"><FONT COLOR="aqua">Specially colored link</FONT></A>
```

There is no way to set the visited link and active link colors for specific links. This feature is supported by Versions 3.0 and higher of Internet Explorer, and Netscape Navigator Versions 4.0 and higher. This technique is discouraged in the HTML 4.01 specification in favor of style sheet controls (see the next section).

Setting Global Link Colors with Style Sheets

You can apply almost any style sheet property to a link by using the anchor tag (`<a>`) as a selector. This example specifies a color for all the links in a document:

```
A {color: #rrggbb or colorname}
```

Note that the color will also be applied to text contained within `<a>` tags with the name attribute (named anchors). If that's not the effect you're after, try the `a:link` pseudo-class technique introduced next.

To change the color just for specific links, label them with a `class` attribute:

```
<A CLASS="internal" HREF="linkypoo.html">Go to another page</A>
```

and include the class in the selector of the style sheet rule as follows:

```
A.internal {color: #rrggbb or colorname}
```

CSS1 introduced a group of pseudo-classes (link, visited, and active) that replace the function of the `<body>` tag attributes listed in the section "Setting Colors in `<body>`" earlier in this chapter. The syntax for specifying colors with anchor pseudo-classes is as follows:

- To specify a color for unvisited links:

```
A:link {color: #rrggbb or colorname}
```

- To specify a color for visited links:

```
A:visited {color: #rrggbb or colorname}
```

- To specify a color for active links:

```
A:active {color: #rrggbb or colorname}
```

The advantage to setting colors with style sheets is that you separate style information from content. The major disadvantage is that style sheets (and particularly pseudo-classes) are not supported by all browsers, so you risk a portion of your audience not seeing your page as you intend.

See Chapter 17 for a better understanding of style sheet syntax and usage.

Turning Off Underlines

The `text-decoration` style sheet property can be used to turn off the under-lines for all the links in a document (it is supported by all browsers that support style sheets). Use this with caution, however, since most users rely on the under-line to indicate what is "clickable," particularly now that brightly colored HTML text is more prevalent. Be sure that your interface and system of visual cues is clear enough that links are still evident.

The style sheet rule for turning off underlines on hyperlinks and named anchors is as follows:

```
A { text-decoration: none }
```

To turn off underlines for specific links, label them with a `class` attribute:

```
<A CLASS="internal" HREF="linkypoo.html">Go to another page</A>
```

and include the class in the selector of the style sheet rule as follows:

```
A.internal { text-decoration: none }
```

Changing Status Bar Text with JavaScript

By default, when you position the mouse over a link, the browser displays the target URL in the status bar at the bottom of the browser. Use the following Java-Script command in an anchor tag to change the status bar message to whatever text you specify. In this example, the phrase "Samples of my web design work" will display in the browser's status bar.

```
<A HREF="web.html" onMouseOver="window.status='Samples of my web design
work'; return true;">The Web Lounge</A>
```

Be aware that many users value the ability to see the URL for a link, so if you are going to change the message, make sure that you substitute worthwhile and descriptive messages. Otherwise, you risk making your site less pleasant to use. Status bar messages are also easily overlooked, so don't rely on them to clarify navigation.

Targeting Windows

The problem with the hypertext medium is that when a users click on an inter-esting link on your page, they might never come back. One currently popular solution to this problem is to make the target document display in a second browser window. In that way, your page is still readily available in the background.

This technique is not without controversy, however. Many users find the loss of control over their browsing experience annoying. Windows users might not even realize a new window has opened in front of their current window if they have their browsers maximized to full screen. So keep both the good and the bad in mind when deciding whether to use pop-up windows.

Use the **target** attribute of the anchor tag to launch a new browser window for the linked document. Setting the **target** attribute to **"_blank"** causes the browser to open a fresh browser window. For example:

```
<A HREF="http://www.oreilly.com/" TARGET="_blank">...</A>
```

If you set every link on your page to target a **_blank** window, every link will launch a new window, potentially leaving your user with a mess of open windows.

A better method, especially if you have more than one link, is to give the targeted window a specific name, which can then be reused by subsequent links. The following link will open a new window called "display":

```
<A HREF="http://www.oreilly.com/" TARGET="display">...</A>
```

If you target every link on that page to the "display" window, each targeted document will open in the same second window.

The **target** attribute is most often used in conjunction with framed documents. The syntax and strategy for using the **target** attribute with framed documents is discussed in Chapter 14.

 Some browsers do not support the **target** attribute (including WebTV and Internet Explorer 2.0 and earlier). Furthermore, Netscape Navigator 4.0 has a bug that prevents an existing named window from coming to the front. To the user, this looks as though the link did not work since the target document loads into a browser window that is stuck behind the current window.

Imagemaps

Ordinarily, placing an image within anchor tags makes the entire image a link to a single document when the user clicks anywhere on the image. As an alternative, you can create multiple links, or "hot spots," within a single graphic. These graphics are called *imagemaps*. The effect is created with HTML tags and/or text files and scripts on the server; the image itself is an ordinary graphic file that just serves as a backdrop for the pixel coordinates.

There are two types of imagemaps: *client-side* and *server-side*. For client-side imagemaps, the coordinate and URL information necessary to create each link is contained right in the HTML document. The process of putting the pieces together happens in the browser on the user's machine (thus, client-side). For server-side imagemaps, as the name suggests, the map information resides on the server and is processed by the server or a separate CGI script.

Client-side imagemaps are a slightly newer technology and are not supported by first-version browsers (although nearly all current browsers know what to do). For

---

this reason, some web developers create redundant imagemaps (both client- and server-side) so that if the browser doesn't recognize the client-side map, the server's imagemap processor can take over.

Creating Imagemaps

The key to making imagemaps work is a map, based on the image, that associates pixel coordinates with URLs. This map is handled differently for client-side and server-side (as outlined in the following sections), but the outcome is the same. When the user clicks somewhere within the image, the browser passes the coordinates of the mouse pointer to the map, which, in turn, generates the appropriate link.

Available tools

Although it is possible to put together imagemap information manually, it is much easier to use a tool to do it. There are many imagemap creation tools available as shareware for both Windows and the Mac. Be sure to look for one that is capable of outputting both client- and server-side map information, such as the following:

Macintosh
> MapMaker 1.1.2 by Frederic Eriksson, available at *http://www.kickinit.com/mapmaker/*.

Windows
> MapEdit, by Tom Boutell, available at *http://www.boutell.com/mapedit/*. MapEdit is now also available for the Macintosh.

The full-featured WYSIWYG web authoring tools (such as Macromedia Dreamweaver and Adobe GoLive) have imagemap creation tools built in. This is particularly handy for creating client-side imagemaps right in the current document.

Creating the map

Regardless of the tool you're using, and regardless of the type of imagemap you're creating, the process for creating the map information is basically the same. Read the documentation for your imagemap tool to learn about features not listed here.

1. Open the image in an imagemap program.

2. Define areas within the image that will be clickable by using the appropriate shape tools: rectangle, circle, or polygon (for tracing irregular shapes).

3. While the outline of the area is still highlighted, enter a URL for that area in the text entry field provided, as shown in Figure 11-1.

4. Continue adding shapes and their respective URLs for each clickable area in the image.

5. For server-side imagemaps, you also need to define a default URL, which is the page that displays if users click outside a defined area. Many tools have a prominent field for entering the default URL, but on others you may need to look for it under a pull-down menu.

6. Select the type of imagemap (client- or server-side) you want to create.

7. Save or export the map information. Server-side imagemaps are saved in a map definition file (*.map*) that resides on the server. Client-side imagemaps are embedded directly in the HTML file.

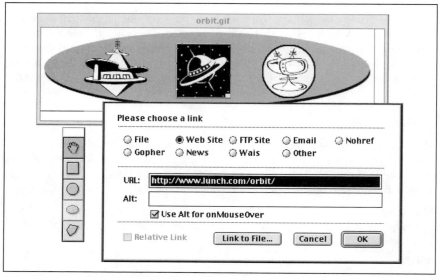

Figure 11-1: Creating map information (shown in MapMaker 1.1.2)

If you do not have an imagemap tool, it is possible to write out the map information by hand following the examples in this chapter. Simply note the pixel coordinates of the shapes as indicated in an image editing program (in Photoshop, they are provided in the Info palette) and type them into the appropriate place in the map file.

Client-Side Imagemaps

Client-side imagemaps have three components:

- An ordinary graphic file (*.gif, .jpeg,* or *.png*)

- A map delimited by <map> tags containing the coordinate and URL information for each area

- The usemap attribute within the image tag (<img>) that indicates which map to reference

There are many advantages to using client-side imagemaps. They are self-contained within the HTML document and do not rely on a server to function. This means you can test the imagemap on your local machine or make working site demos for distribution on disk. It also cuts down on the load on your server and improves response times. In addition, complete URL information displays in the status bar when the user mouses over the hot spot (server-side imagemaps display only coordinates).

The only disadvantage to client-side imagemaps is that because it is slightly newer technology, they are not universally supported. Netscape Navigator 1.0 and Internet Explorer 2.0 do not support client-side imagemaps. Experimental or obscure browser programs may not either. Fortunately, these browsers make up a miniscule portion of the current browser population.

Sample client-side imagemap

Figure 11-2 shows a sample imagemapped graphic. Example 11-1 provides the HTML document that contains the client-side imagemap.

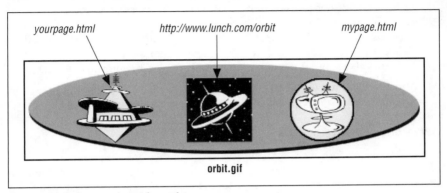

Figure 11-2: Imagemapped graphic

Example 11-1: HTML for client-side imagemap

```
<HTML>
<HEAD><TITLE>Client-side Imagemap Sample</TITLE></HEAD>
<BODY>
<MAP NAME="spacey">  A
<AREA SHAPE="RECT" COORDS="203,23,285,106"  B
HREF="http://www.lunch.com/orbit/">
<AREA SHAPE="CIRCLE" COORDS="372,64,40" HREF="mypage.html">  C
<AREA SHAPE="POLY"  D
COORDS="99,47,105,41,94,39,98,34,110,35,115,28,120,35,133,38,133,
42,124,42,134,58,146,56,157,58,162,63,158,67,141,68,145,72,155,
73,158,75,159,80,148,83,141,83,113,103,87,83,72,83,64,80,64,76,
68,73,77,72,79,63,70,59,67,53,68,47,78,45,89,45,99,47"
HREF="yourpage.html">
</MAP>
<IMG SRC="orbit.gif" WIDTH=500 HEIGHT=125 BORDER=0 USEMAP="#spacey">  E
</BODY>
</HTML>
```

A This marks the beginning of the map. You must give the map a name. Within the <map>, there are <area> tags for each hotspot within the image.

B Each area tag contains the shape identifier (shape), pixel coordinates (coords), and the URL for the link (href). In this case, the shape is the rectangle (rect) that corresponds to the black square in the center of the image. The value of the coords attribute identifies the top-left and bottom-right pixel positions of the rectangle (ooords="x1,y1,x2,y2"). Some browsers also support the nonstandard rectangle as an equivalent to rect, but this is not widely supported.

● This area corresponds to the circular area on the right of the image in Figure 11-2. Its shape is circle. For circles, the first two coordinates identify the position of the center of the circle and the third value is its radius in pixels (coords="x,y,r"). Some browsers also support the nonstandard circ as an equivalent to circle.

● This is the area tag for the irregular (polygon) shape on the left of the image in Figure 11-2. For polygons, the coordinates are pairs of x,y coordinates for each point or vertex along the path that surrounds the area (coords="x1,y1,x2,y2,x3,y3..."). At least three pairs are required to define a triangle; complex polygons generate a long list of coordinates. Some browsers also support the nonstandard polygon as an equivalent to poly.

● The USEMAP attribute is required within the image tag to indicate that this graphic is an imagemap that uses the <map> named "spacey".

Server-Side Imagemaps

Server-side imagemaps work with all browsers, but they are a bit more involved to create. In addition, they rely on the server, which makes them less portable than their client-side counterparts and increases the load on the server. For a number of reasons, server-side imagemaps are going out of style and aren't used nearly as often as their client-side counterparts.

Server-side imagemaps have four elements:

- An ordinary graphic file (.gif, .jpeg, or .png)

- HTML tags in the document: the ismap attribute within the graphic's <img> tag and an anchor tag that links the graphic to the .map file on the server

- A map definition file (.map) containing the pixel coordinate and URL information for each clickable area; the .map file resides on the server and the format is server-dependent

- A CGI script that runs on the server (or a built-in function of the server software) that interprets the .map file and sends the correct URL to the HTTP server

Because server-side imagemaps are so dependent on the configuration of the server, you need to coordinate with your server administrator if you plan to use them. You'll need to find out what type of .map file to create ("NCSA" and "CERN" are two possibilities, based on the type of server) as well as the pathname to which the imagemapped graphic should be linked (this usually includes a cgi-bin directory).

Sample map definition file (.map) file

Example 11-2 shows a server-side image map (called *spacey.map*) for the imagemapped graphic shown in Figure 11-2.

Example 11-2: Server-side imagemap

```
default index.html  Ⓐ
rect http://www.lunch.com/orbit/ 203,23 285,106  Ⓑ
circle mypage.html 372,64 412,104
poly yourpage.html 99,47 105,41 94,39 98,34 110,35 115,28 120,35 133,38
133,42 124,42 134,58 146,56 157,58 162,63 158,67 141,68 145,72 155,73
158,75 159,80 148,83 141,83 113,103 87,83 72,83 64,80 64,76 68,73 77,72
79,63 70,59 67,53 68,47 78,45 89,45 99,47
```

Ⓐ This establishes the default URL, which is what the browser displays if the user clicks outside one of the clickable areas. Set this to the current document if you want to give the impression that the click has no effect.

Ⓑ Each hot area in the image is defined by a shape name (rect, circle, poly), a URL, and a set of pixel coordinates. The syntax for the coordinates varies by shape and is generally the same as explained for client-side imagemaps above. The syntax for some shapes may vary from server to server. In this *.map* file, the coordinates are defined for use by an Apache server. Note that the coordinates defining the circle are different than in the client-side example. Apache's syntax for defining a circle is "x1,y1 x2,y2," which corresponds to the x,y coordinates of the circle's center point followed by the x,y coordinates for a point on the circle. Server-side imagemaps do not recognize the nonstandard shape values rectangle, circ, and polygon.

The HTML document

Within the HTML file, the image is treated as shown here:

```
<HTML>
<HEAD><TITLE>Server-side Sample</TITLE></HEAD>
<BODY>
<A HREF="/cgi-bin/imagemap/spacey.map">
<IMG SRC="orbit.gif" BORDER=0 ISMAP></A>
</BODY>
</HTML>
```

The anchor tag links the whole graphic to the map definition file (*spacey.map*), which is located within the *cgi-bin* directory on the server. This is a typical configuration; however, you should follow your server administrator's instructions.

The ismap attribute within the image tag tells the browser that the graphic is an imagemap.

When Not to Use Imagemaps

Imagemaps are not always the best solution and are actually waning somewhat in popularity as web design evolves. Slicing up a large image, each slice of which can be linked to a different document, and holding the pieces together with a table often offers functionality that an imagemap can't match. This technique is so popular that it is built into web graphics tools such as Macromedia Fireworks and Adobe Photoshop 6 and ImageReady. There is also a demonstration in Chapter 13.

Providing complete alternative text

When a user cannot view images (or has chosen to turn them off), the browser displays the text specified by the `alt` attribute within the `<img>` tag. Unfortunately, for each imagemap graphic you get only one alternative text message, which may not be useful for users with non-graphical browsers (although Lynx can construct a list of links based on the `href` values from each `area`).

One common solution to this problem is to provide a redundant set of links in HTML text somewhere else on the page so that users who cannot view graphics can still navigate the site.

If the image is divided into pieces rather than using an imagemap, you can provide alternative text for each linked piece, which alleviates the need to add the extra line of linked text to your HTML page.

Rollover buttons

Rollover buttons (graphics that change when the user rolls the mouse over them) are popular effects that use the power of JavaScript. Although it is possible to have an entire imagemap graphic change based on mouse-over cues, it is more efficient to break the image into pieces and swap out only the small portion that needs to change with the mouseover. You decrease the download time by preloading only the necessary small graphics. See Chapter 28 for sample JavaScript code for creating rollover effects.

Non-Web Links and Protocols

Linking to other web pages using the HTTP protocol is by far the most common type of link, but there are several other types of transactions that can be made using other standard Internet protocols.

Mail Link (mailto:)

The `mailto` protocol can be used in an anchor tag to automatically send an email message to the recipient, using the browser's email application or an external email application. Note that the browser must be configured to support this tag, so it will not work for all users. The `mailto` protocol has the following components:

```
mailto:username@domain
```

A typical mail link might look like this:

```
<A HREF="mailto:jen@oreilly.com">Send Jennifer email</A>
```

You can also experiment with adding information within the `mailto` URL that automatically fills in standard email fields such as Subject or cc:. As of this writing, these additional functions are supported only by Navigator 4.0 and higher, Internet Explorer 5 (Mac), and Internet Explorer 5.5 (Windows), so use them with caution and do lots of testing:

```
mailto:username@domain?subject=subject
mailto:username@domain?cc=person1
mailto:username@domain?bcc=person2
mailto:username@domain?body=body
```

Additional variables are appended to the string with an ampersand (&) symbol as follows:

```
mailto:username@domain?subject=subject&cc=person1&body=body
```

Spaces within subject lines need to be written as %20 (the space character in hexadecimal notation). The following is a sample mail link employing these additions:

```
<A HREF="mailto:jen@oreilly.com?subject=Like%20your%20book">Email for
Jen</A>
```

 A word of warning: when you put a link to an email address on a web page, the address is prone to getting "spidered" (automatically indexed) and added to spam mailing lists. If you don't want to risk getting junk email, keep the email address off the site.

FTP Link (ftp://)

You can link directly to a file on an FTP server. When the user clicks on the link, the file downloads automatically using the browser's built-in FTP functions and is saved on the user's machine. If the document is on an anonymous FTP server (i.e., no account name and password are required), the FTP link is simple:

```
<A HREF="ftp://server/pathname">...</A>
```

To link to an FTP server that requires the user to log in, the format is:

```
<A HREF="ftp://user:password@server/pathname">...</A>
```

For security purposes, it is highly recommended that you never include both the username and password to a server within an HTML document. If you use the syntax user@server/path, the user will be prompted to enter his or her password in a dialog box.

By default, the requested file is transferred in binary format. To specify that the document should be transferred as an ASCII file, add ;type=a to the end of the URL:

```
<A HREF="ftp://user:password@server/pathname;type=a">...</A>
```

The variable type=d identifies the pathname as a directory and simply displays its contents in the browser window. type=i specifies image or binary mode, which is the default but may also be given explicitly.

Following are some examples of FTP links:

```
<A HREF="ftp://pete@ftp.someserver.com/program.exe">...</A>
<A HREF="ftp://ftp.superwarehouse.com/games;type=d">...</A>
```

Other Links

The following URL types are not as well known or useful as mailto or ftp://, but they are available. As with other links, place these URLs after the HREF attribute within the anchor tag.

Type	Syntax	Use
File	`file://server/` `path`	Specifies a file without indicating the protocol. This is useful for accessing files on a contained site such as a CD-ROM or kiosk application, but it is less appropriate over networks (such as the Internet).
News	`news:newsgroup` `news:message_id`	Accesses either a single message or an entire news-group within the Usenet news system. Some browsers do not support news URLs, so you should avoid using them.

NTTP	`nntp://`
	`server:port/`
	`newsgroup/article`
		Provides a complete mechanism for accessing Usenet news articles. The article is served only to machines that are allowed to retrieve articles from this server, so this URL has limited practical use.

Telnet	`telnet://`
	`user:password@`
	`server:port/`
		Opens a telnet session with a desired server. The `user` and `password@` elements are optional and follow the same rules as described for `ftp://`.

Gopher	`gopher://` `server:port/path`	Accesses a document on a gopher server. The gopher document retrieval system was eclipsed by the World Wide Web, but some gopher servers are still operating.

Linking Documents with <link>

The `<link>` tag is used to define a relationship between the current document and another external document. It is always placed in the header (`<head>`) of the document. There can be multiple `<link>` tags in a document. The most important attributes are `href`, which points to the linked file, and `rel`, which describes the relationship from the source document to the target document. The `rev` attribute describes the reverse relationship (from the target back to the source).

A variety of attributes make the `<link>` tag very versatile, but it is not currently used to its full potential. The most popular application of the `<link>` tag is for referring to an external style sheet. In this example, the `type` attribute identifies the MIME content type of the linked document as a cascading style sheet:

```
<HEAD>
<LINK HREF="wholesite.css" REL="stylesheet" TYPE="text/css">
</HEAD>
```

Another use as recommended in the HTML 4.01 specification is to refer to an alternate version of the document in another language. The following example creates a link to a French version of the document:

```
<HEAD>
<LINK REL="alternate" HREF="translations/french.html"
      TYPE="text/html" HREFLANG="fr">
</HEAD>
```

By using the `next` and `prev` values for the `rel` attribute, you can establish the document's position in a sequence of documents, as shown in the following example. This information could be used by browsers and other tools to build navigation menus, tables of contents, or other link collections.

```
<HEAD>
<TITLE>Chapter 11: Creating Links</TITLE>
<LINK REL="prev" HREF="chapter10.html">
<LINK REL="next" HREF="chapter12.html">
</HEAD>
```

Table 11-1 lists the accepted values for the `rel` and `rev` attributes and their uses. These attributes and values can be used in the `<a>` tag as well as the `<link>` tag to define relationships for a specific link. Again, these features are not widely used, nor are they well supported by browsers, but they may grow in popularity.

Table 11-1: Link types using the REL attribute

Value	Relationship
alternate	Substitute version of the current document, perhaps in another language or optimized for another display medium
stylesheet	External cascading style sheet; used with `type="text/css"`
start	The first document in a collection or series
next	The next document in a series
prev	The previous document in a series
contents (or toc)	A document providing a table of contents
index	A document providing an index for the current document
glossary	A document containing a glossary of terms
copyright	A document containing copyright information for the current document
chapter	A document serving as a chapter in a collection of documents
section	A document serving as a section in a collection of documents
subsection	A document serving as a subsection in a collection of documents
appendix	A document serving as an appendix
help	A help document
bookmark	A document that serves as a bookmark; the `title` attribute can be used to name the bookmark

CHAPTER 12

Adding Images and Other Page Elements

This chapter focuses on the HTML tags available for placing elements such as rules, images, or multimedia objects on a web page.

Summary of Object Placement Tags

In this section, browser support for each tag is noted to the right of the tag name. Browsers that do not support the tag are grayed out. Tag usage is indicated below the tag name. Start and end tags are required unless otherwise noted. "Deprecated" means that the tag or attribute is currently supported but is due to be phased out of the HTML specification and is discouraged from use (usually in favor of similar style sheet controls). The attributes listed for each tag reflect those in common use. A more thorough listing of attributes for each tag, according to the HTML 4.01 specification, appears in Appendix A.

\<applet\>   NN 2, 3, 4, 6   MSIE 2, 3, 4, 5, 5.5, 6   HTML 4.01   WebTV   Opera5

`<applet>...</applet>`

Deprecated. This tag (first introduced in Netscape Navigator 2.0) is used to place a Java applet on the web page. `<applet>` and all its attributes have been deprecated in favor of the `<object>` element, but it is still widely used. Some applets require the use of the `<applet>` tag. Furthermore, Navigator 4 and earlier and Internet Explorer 4 do not support Java applets via object tags.

Attributes

`align=left|right|top|middle|bottom`
    Aligns the applet and allows text to wrap around it (same as image alignment).

`alt=text`
    Provides alternate text if the applet cannot be displayed.

`archive=urls`

Provides a space-separated list of URLs with classes to be preloaded.

`code=class`

Required. Specifies the class name of the code to be executed.

`codebase=url`

URL from which the applet code is retrieved.

`height=number`

Height of the initial applet display area in pixels.

`hspace=number`

Holds *number* pixels space clear to the left and right of the applet window.

`name=text`

Names the applet for reference from elsewhere on the page.

`vspace=number`

Holds *number* pixels space clear above and below the applet window.

`width=number`

Width of the initial applet display area in pixels.

`<embed>` 　　　　　 NN 2, 3, 4, 6　　MSIE 2, 3, 4, 5, 5.5, 6　　HTML 4.01　　WebTV　　Opera5

`<embed>...</embed>`

Embeds an object into the web page. Embedded objects are most often multimedia files that require special plug-ins to display (for example, Flash movies, Quicktime Movies, etc.). In addition to the standard attributes listed below, certain media types and their respective plug-ins may have additional proprietary attributes for controlling the playback of the file. The closing tag is not always required, but is recommended.

Attributes

`align=left|right|top|bottom`

NN 4.0+ and MSIE 4.0+ only. Controls the alignment of the media object relative to the surrounding text. The default is `bottom`. `top` and `bottom` are vertical alignments. `left` and `right` position the object on the left or right margin and allow text to wrap around it.

`height=number`

Specifies the height of the object in number of pixels. Some media types require this attribute.

`hidden=yes|no`

Hides the media file or player from view when set to `yes`. The default is `no`.

`name=name`

Specifies a name for the embedded object. This is particularly useful for referencing the object from a script.

`palette=foreground|background`

NN 4.0+ and MSIE 4.0+ only. This attribute applies to the Windows platform only. A value of `foreground` makes the plug-in's palette the foreground palette. Conversely, a value of background makes the plug-in use the background palette; this is the default.

pluginspage=*url*
> *NN 4.0+ and MSIE 4.0+ only.* Specifies the URL for information on installing the appropriate plug-in.

src=*url*
> *Required.* Provides the URL to the file or object to be placed on the page.

width=*number*
> Specifies the width of the object in number of pixels. Some media types require this attribute.

Internet Explorer only

alt=*text*
> Provides alternative text when the media object cannot be displayed (same as for the <img> tag).

code=*filename*
> Specifies the class name of the Java code to be executed.

codebase=*url*
> Specifies the base URL for the application.

units=pixels|en
> Defines the measurement units used by height and width. The default is pixels. En units are half the point size of the body text.

Netscape Navigator only

border=*number*
> Specifies the width of the border (in pixels) around the media object.

frameborder=yes|no
> Turns the border on or off.

hspace=*number*
> Used in conjunction with the align attribute, the horizontal space attribute specifies (in pixels) the amount of space to leave clear to the left and right of the media object.

pluginurl=*url*
> Specifies a source for installing the appropriate plug-in for the media file. Netscape recommends that you use pluginurl instead of pluginspage.

type=*MIME type*
> Specifies the MIME type of the plug-in needed to run the file. Navigator uses either the value of the type attribute or the suffix of the filename given as the source to determine which plug-in to use.

vspace=*number*
> Used in conjunction with the align attribute, the vertical space attribute specifies (in pixels) the amount of space to leave clear above and below the media object.

\<hr\>

`<hr>` *(no end tag)*

Adds a horizontal rule to the page.

Attributes

`align=center|left|right`
> *Deprecated.* If the rule is shorter than the width of the window, this tag controls horizontal alignment of the rule. The default is `center`.

`noshade`
> *Deprecated.* This displays the rule as a solid (non-shaded) bar.

`size=number`
> *Deprecated.* Specifies the thickness of the rule in pixels.

`width=number or %`
> *Deprecated.* Specifies the length of the rule in pixels or as a percentage of the page width. By default, rules are the full width of the browser window.

\<img\>

`<img>` *(no end tag)*

Places a graphic on the page.

Attributes

`align=type`
> *Deprecated.* Specifies the alignment of an image using one of the following attributes:

Type	Resulting alignment
absbottom	*Navigator 3.0 + and Internet Explorer 4.0 + only.* Aligns the bottom of the image with the bottom of the current line.
absmiddle	*Navigator 3.0 + and Internet Explorer 4.0 + only.* Aligns the middle of the image with the middle of the current line.
baseline	*Navigator 3.0 + and Internet Explorer 4.0 + only.* Aligns the bottom of the image with the baseline of the current line.
bottom	Aligns the bottom of the image with the text baseline. This is the default vertical alignment.
center	According to the W3C specification, this centers the image horizontally on the page; however, in practice, browsers treat it the same as `align=middle`.
left	Aligns the image on the left margin and allows subsequent text to wrap around it.
middle	Aligns the text baseline with the middle of the image.
right	Aligns the image on the right margin and allows subsequent text to wrap around it.
texttop	*Navigator only.* Aligns the top of the image with the ascenders of the text line. An ascender is the part of a lowercase letter (like "d") that rises above the main body of the letter.
top	Aligns the top of the image with the top of the tallest object on that line.

`alt=text`

> *Required.* Provides a string of alternative text that appears when the image is not displayed. Internet Explorer 4.0+ and Netscape 6 on Windows display this text as a "tool tip" when the mouse rests on the image.

`border=number`

> Specifies the width (in pixels) of the border that surrounds a linked image. It is standard practice to set `border=0` to turn the border off.

`height=number`

> Specifies the height of the image in pixels. It is not required, but is recommended to speed up the rendering of the web page.

`hspace=number`

> Specifies (in number of pixels) the amount of space to leave clear to the left and right of the image.

`ismap`

> Indicates that the graphic is used as the basis for a server-side imagemap (an image containing multiple hypertext links). See Chapter 11 for more information on server-side imagemaps.

`longdesc=url`

> Specifies a link to a long description of the image or an imagemap's contents. This may one day be used to make information about the image accessible to nonvisual browsers, but it is not currently supported.

`lowsrc=url`

> *Netscape Navigator (all versions) and Internet Explorer 4.0+ only.* Specifies an image (usually of a smaller file size) that will download first, followed by the final image specified by the `src` attribute.

`name=text`

> Assigns the image element a name so it can be referred to by a script or style sheet.

`src=url`

> *Required.* Provides the location of the graphic file to be displayed.

`usemap=url`

> Specifies the map containing coordinates and links for a client-side imagemap (an image containing multiple hypertext links). See Chapter 11 for more information on client-side imagemaps.

`vspace=number`

> Specifies (in number of pixels) the amount of space to leave clear above and below the image.

`width=number`

> Specifies the width of the image in pixels. It is not required, but is recommended to speed up the rendering of the web page.

Internet Explorer's dynsrc attribute

Using a `dynsrc` attribute, Internet Explorer Versions 2.0 and later also use the `<img>` tag to place a video on the page. The following attributes are related to the `dynsrc` function and work only with Internet Explorer:

controls
> Displays playback controls for the video.

dynsrc=*url*
> Provides the location of the video file to be displayed on the page.

loop=*number*|infinite
> Sets the number of times to play the video. It can be a number value or set to infinite.

start=fileopen|mouseover|fileopen, mouseover
> Specifies when to play the video. By default, it begins playing as soon as it's downloaded (fileopen). You can set it to start when the mouse pointer is over the movie area (mouseover). If you combine them (separated by a comma), the movie plays once when it's downloaded, then again every time the user mouses over it.

\<marquee\>

NN 2, 3, 4, 6   MSIE **2, 3, 4, 5, 5.5, 6**   HTML 4.01   **WebTV**   Opera5

<marquee>...</marquee>

Creates a scrolling-text marquee area.

Attributes

align=top|middle|bottom
> Aligns the marquee with the top, middle, or bottom of the neighboring text line.

behavior=scroll|slide|alternate
> Specifies how the text should behave. Scroll is the default setting and means the text should start completely off one side, scroll all the way across and completely off, then start over again. Slide stops the scroll when the text touches the other margin. Alternate means bounce back and forth within the marquee.

bgcolor=*#rrggbb* or *color name*
> Sets the background color of the marquee.

direction=left|right
> Defines the direction in which the text scrolls. IE 4.0+ also support the values up and down.

height=*number*
> Defines the height in pixels of the marquee area.

hspace=*number*
> Holds a number of pixels space clear to the left and right of the marquee.

loop=*number*|infinite
> Specifies the number of times the text loops as a number value or infinite.

scrollamount=*number*
> Sets the number of pixels to move the text for each scroll movement.

scrolldelay=*number*
> Specifies the delay, in milliseconds, between successive movements of the marquee text.

`vspace=number`

Holds a number of pixels space clear above and below the marquee.

`width=number`

Specifies the width in pixels of the marquee.

<noembed>

NN 2, 3, 4, 6   MSIE 2, 3, 4, 5, 5.5, 6   HTML 4.01   WebTV   Opera5

`<noembed>...</noembed>`

The text or object specified by **<noembed>** appears when an embedded object cannot be displayed (e.g., when the appropriate plug-in is not available). This tag is placed within the **<embed>** container tags.

<object>

NN 2, 3, 4, 6   MSIE 2, 3, 4, 5, 5.5, 6   HTML 4.01   WebTV   Opera5

`<object>...</object>`

A generic element used for placing an object (such as an image, applet, media file, etc.) on a web page. It is similar to the **<embed>** tag but is the W3C's approved method for adding elements to a page. Browser support for the **<object>** tag is not up to standards. Support in Navigator 4 is buggy, and in IE 4 (and even 5), the tag is generally useful only for ActiveX controls.

Attributes

`align=baseline|center|left|middle|right|textbottom|`
`  textmiddle|texttop`
Deprecated. Aligns object with respect to surrounding text. See the **<img>** tag for explanations of the **align** values.

`archive=urls`
Specifies a space-separated list of URLs for resources that are related to the object.

`border=number`
Nonstandard. Sets the width of the border in pixels if the object is a link.

`classid=url`
Identifies the location of an object's implementation. It is used with or in place of the **data** attribute. The syntax depends on the object type.

`codebase=url`
Identifies the base URL used to resolve relative URLs in the object (similar to **<base>**). By default, the codebase is the base URL of the current document.

`codetype=codetype`
Specifies the media type of the code. It is required only if the browser cannot determine an applet's MIME type from the **classid** attribute or if the server does not deliver the correct MIME type when downloading the object.

`data=url`
Specifies the URL of the data used for the object. The syntax depends on the object.

declare
> *HTML 4.01.* Declares an object but restrains the browser from downloading and processing it. Used in conjunction with the **name** attribute, this facility is similar to a forward declaration in a more conventional programming language, letting you defer the download until the object actually gets used.

height=*number*
> Specifies the height of the object in pixels.

hspace=*number*
> *Deprecated.* Holds *number* pixels space clear to the left and right of the object.

name=*text*
> Specifies the name of the object to be referenced by scripts on the page.

standby=*message*
> *HTML 4.01.* Specifies the message to display during object loading.

type=*type*
> Specifies the media type for the data.

usemap=*url*
> Specifies the imagemap to use with the object.

vspace=*number*
> *Deprecated.* Holds *number* pixels space clear above and below the object.

width=*number*
> Specifies the object width in pixels.

<param>

NN 2, 3, 4, 6   MSIE 2, 3, 4, 5, 5.5, 6   HTML 4.01   WebTV   Opera5

<param> *(no end tag)*

Supplies a parameter within the <applet> or <object> tag.

Attributes

name=*text*
> *Required.* Defines the name of the parameter.

value=*text*
> Defines the value of the parameter.

valuetype=data|ref|object
> Indicates the type of value: **data** indicates that the parameter's value is data (default); **ref** indicates that the parameter's value is a URL; **object** indicates that the value is the URL of another object in the document.

type=*content type*
> *HTML 4.01.* Specifies the media type of the resource only when the **valuetype** attribute is set to **ref**. It describes the types of values found at the referred location.

<spacer> *(no end tag)*

Holds a specified amount of blank space within the flow of a page. This is a proprietary tag introduced by Netscape; it met with controversy and is now rarely used in common practice. It can be used to maintain space within table cells for correct display in Navigator.

Attributes

type=vertical|horizontal|block
> Specifies the type of spacer: vertical inserts space between two lines of text, horizontal inserts space between characters, and block inserts a rectangular space.

size=*number*
> Specifies a number of pixels to be used with a vertical or horizontal spacer.

height=*number*
> Specifies height in number of pixels for a block spacer.

width=*number*
> Specifies width in number of pixels for a block spacer.

align=*value*
> Aligns block spacer with surrounding text. Values are the same as for the <img> tag.

Image Basics

Before jumping into the finer points of the <img> tag, let's back up and consider general graphics usage issues.

Inline Graphic Uses

Graphic files can be used in a number of ways on the Web. Images may be used as background tiles (added with the background attribute in the <body> tag as noted in Chapter 9). You can also create a link to a graphic file that displays either in the browser window or in a helper application if it is in a format that cannot be displayed by the browser.

This chapter focuses on inline images, graphics that are displayed in the browser window as part of the flow of the contents of the document. Inline images are placed on the page with the <img> tag. The overwhelming majority of graphics on the Web are used as inline images, including banners, buttons, logos, and so on. Graphics can serve a variety of functions:

As a simple graphic
> A graphic can be used on a web page much as it is used in print—as a static image that adds decoration or information, such as a company logo or an illustration.

As a link

A graphic can also be used to link to another document as an alternative to text links. Linked graphics are discussed later in this chapter.

As an imagemap

An imagemap is a single graphic with multiple "hotspots" that link to other documents. There is nothing special about the graphic itself; it is an ordinary inline image. Special coding and map files link pointer coordinates with their respective URLs. The usemap or ismap attribute within the <img> tag indicates to the browser that the graphic is used as a client-side or server-side imagemap, respectively. (A full explanation of how imagemaps work and how to create them appears in Chapter 11.)

As spacing devices

Because web pages are difficult for designers to control with HTML alone, some designers resort to using transparent graphics to invisibly control the alignment of text or the behavior of tables. Although it is one solution for arranging elements on the page, it is considered poor HTML form.

Netscape's solution for holding extra space on a web page is its proprietary <spacer> tag. Spacers can be used to hold a specified amount of horizontal or vertical space or a "block" of space with width and height measurements. The <spacer> tag and its attributes are listed earlier in this chapter. Because this is a proprietary tag that is useful to only a minority of web users, the use of the <spacer> tag is generally avoided.

Acceptable Graphics Formats

A graphic needs to be in either GIF or JPEG format to be displayed as an inline image by the vast majority of browsers. Furthermore, the files need to be named with the proper suffixes—*.gif* for GIF files, *.jpeg* or *.jpg* for JPEG—in order to be recognized by the browser.

There is a third format, PNG (pronounced "ping"), which was designed specifically with web distribution in mind; however, only Version 4 and higher browsers support PNG files (suffix *.png*) as inline graphics, and they don't support all of PNG's most attractive features. Until PNG gains better support, stick with either GIF or JPEG.

These graphics file formats, as well as other requirements for putting graphics online, are discussed in detail in the chapters of Part III.

The <img> Tag and Its Attributes

The <img> tag inserts a graphic image into the document's text flow. Placing graphics inline with the text does not introduce any line breaks or extra space. By default, the bottom of an image aligns with the baseline of surrounding text (ways to alter this are discussed later).

There are over a dozen attributes that can be added within the `<img>` tag to affect its display, but the only required attribute is `src`, which provides the URL of the graphic. The HTML 4.01 specification has declared the `alt` attribute (for alternative text, see explanation below) to be required as well, but the graphic will display just fine without it. The minimal HTML tag for placing an image on the page looks like this:

```
<IMG SRC="url of graphic">
```

Figure 12-1 shows an inline image and its HTML source.

```
<P>Star light <IMG SRC="star.gif"> Star bright.</P>
```

Figure 12-1: A graphic placed within a line of text

The URL of the graphic can be absolute (including the protocol and domain name) or relative to the current document (using a relative pathname). The conventions for relative pathnames are described in detail in Chapter 4.

Linked Graphics

To make a graphic a link, place anchor tags around the image tag just as you would around any string of text characters:

```
<A HREF="document.html"><IMG SRC="picture.gif"></A>
```

When a graphic is linked, the browser displays a two-pixel-wide border around the image in the same color as the text links on the page (bright blue by default). In most cases, this blue border is unacceptable, particularly around a graphic with transparent edges, but it is quite simple to turn it off using the `border` attribute.

The `border` attribute specifies the width of the border in number of pixels. Specifying a value of zero turns the borders off, as shown in the following example. Of course, if you are fond of the blue borders, you could just as easily make them really wide by setting a higher number value.

```
<A HREF="document.html"><IMG SRC="picture.gif" BORDER="0"></A>
```

Alternative Text

If a graphic cannot be displayed (either because the file is corrupted or cannot be found), the browser displays a generic broken graphic icon in its place. The browser will also display a generic graphic icon when the user has chosen to turn graphics off for faster browsing (and a lot of users do). The `alt` attribute allows you to specify a string of alternative text to be displayed in place of the graphic when the graphic is unavailable, as shown in Figure 12-2. It is also what non-graphical browsers display in place of images.

```
<P>First star <IMG SRC="star2.gif" ALT="[another star]"> I see tonight.</P>
```

Figure 12-2: Alternative text is displayed when graphics are unavailable

When alternative text is provided in the image tag, users at least know what they're missing. This is particularly important when graphics are links that make up the main navigation of the site. Readers can follow a link if they know where it goes, even if the graphic isn't visible. Without the alternative text, the page would be a big dead end.

Internet Explorer 4.0+ and Netscape 6 display alternative text as a pop-up "tool tip" when the mouse rests on the image area.

Taking the extra time to provide alternative text for your images is the simplest way to make your page accessible to the greatest number of readers. In fact, the HTML 4.01 specification has declared `alt` to be a required attribute within the `<img>` tag (although browsers are not currently enforcing this).

Specifying Width and Height

Although `src` is the only truly necessary attribute in the `<img>` tag, a few others come strongly recommended. The first is `alt`, discussed in the previous section. `width` and `height` are the others. The `width` and `height` attributes simply indicate the dimension of the graphic in pixels, such as:

```
<IMG SRC="star.gif" WIDTH="50" HEIGHT="50">
```

With this information, the browser can lay out the page before the graphics download. Without width and height values, the page may be redrawn several times (first without graphics in place, and again each time new graphics arrive). It is worthwhile to take the time to include accurate width and height information in the image tag.

Resizing images

If the values specified in the `width` and `height` attributes are different than the actual dimensions of the graphic, the browser resizes the graphic to match the specified dimensions. If you specify a percentage value for width and height, some later browsers resize the image to the desired proportions.

Although this effect can certainly be used strategically, as for resizing a single pixel graphic to hold a certain amount of space, it usually just results in a pixelated, poor image quality, as shown in Figure 12-3. It is better to resize images in a graphics program than to leave it up to the browser.

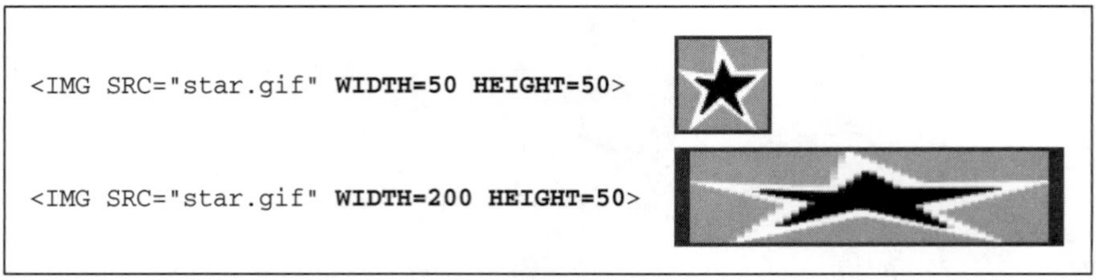

```
<IMG SRC="star.gif" WIDTH=50 HEIGHT=50>


<IMG SRC="star.gif" WIDTH=200 HEIGHT=50>
```

Figure 12-3: Scaling an image with width and height attributes

Using width and height to preload images

Preloading images refers to methods used for downloading images and storing them in cache before they actually need to be displayed on the page. One trick for preloading is to place the graphic on a page that will be accessed first (such as a home page), but with the width and height attributes set to one pixel. This causes the image to download with the rest of the page, but the only thing that will be visible is a one-pixel dot (which can be tucked away in a inconspicuous place).

```
<IMG SRC="bigpicture.gif" WIDTH="1" HEIGHT="1">
```

Ideally, the image finishes downloading quietly and is stored in the browser's cache while the user is still reading the first page. The graphic should then pop into view instantly when the user links to the page where the image is displayed at its full size.

Vertical Alignment

The `align` attribute is used to control how the graphic is positioned in relation to the flow of the text.

Vertical alignment controls the placement of the graphic in relation to points in the surrounding text (usually the baseline). The default alignment is `bottom`, which aligns the bottom of the image with the baseline of the surrounding text. Figure 12-4 shows the result for the following code with no vertical alignment settings:

```
<P>Star light <IMG SRC="star.gif"> Star bright.</P>
```

Figure 12-4: Default (bottom) alignment of image with text

The universally supported values for vertical alignment are `top`, `middle`, and `bottom`. Netscape Navigator introduced another (somewhat more subtle) set, which was then picked up for support in Internet Explorer 4.0. These are `absbottom`, `absmiddle`, `texttop`, and `baseline` (the same as `bottom`).

Figure 12-5 demonstrates the intended effects of each of these alignment values. The reality is slightly different. The `absbottom` value, for instance, seems to render the same as `bottom`, even in Navigator.

Figure 12-5: Vertical alignment values

Horizontal Alignment

The align attribute can be used to align a graphic on the left or right margin of the page by using the values left or right, respectively. What makes the left and right alignment special is that in addition to placing the graphic on a margin, it allows the text to flow around it.

Figure 12-6 shows how images are displayed when set to align to the left or right.

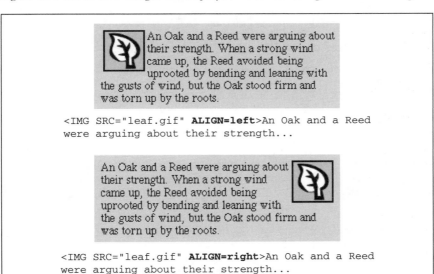

Figure 12-6: Text wraps around images when they are aligned to the left or right

Adding space around aligned images

When text flows around a graphic, it tends to bump up against the graphic's edge. Usually, it is preferable to have a little space between the graphic and the surrounding text. In HTML, this space is provided by using the **vspace** and hspace attributes within the <img> tag.

The **vspace** (vertical space) attribute holds a specified number of pixels space above and below an aligned graphic. Space to the left and the right is added with hspace (horizontal space). Note that space is always added symmetrically (both top and bottom, or on both sides), and it is not possible with these attributes to specify an amount of space along a particular side of the graphic (you can, however, do this with style sheets). Figure 12-7 shows an image aligned with the `hspace` attribute set to 12.

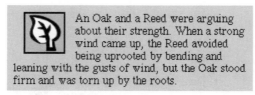

```
<IMG SRC="leaf.gif" ALIGN="left" HSPACE=12><P>An Oak and a Reed...
```

Figure 12-7: Image alignment with horizontal spacing

Stopping text wrap

Text automatically wraps to fill the space along the side of an aligned graphic (or other inline object). To stop the text from wrapping and start the next line against the margin (instead of against the image), insert a line break tag (`<br>`) with the `clear` attribute.

The `clear` attribute gives the browser directions on where to place the new line. It has three possible values: `left`, `right`, and `all`. If your graphic is aligned right, insert `<br clear=right>` to begin the text below the graphic against the right margin. For left-aligned graphics, use `<br clear=left>`. The `<br clear=all>` tag starts the text below the graphics on both margins (see Figure 12-8), so it may be the only value you'll ever need.

Tips for Placing Graphics

These are a few tips for graphics use that may not be obvious from simply looking at HTML code.

Link to large images

Remember that when designing for the Web, you must always consider the time it takes to download files. Images are particularly bandwidth-hungry, so you should

---

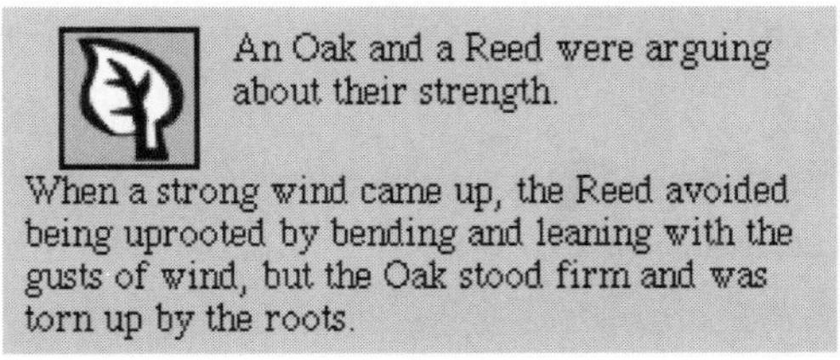

> An Oak and a Reed were arguing about their strength.
>
> When a strong wind came up, the Reed avoided being uprooted by bending and leaning with the gusts of wind, but the Oak stood firm and was torn up by the roots.

```
<IMG SRC="leaf.gif" ALIGN="left" HSPACE=12><P>An Oak and a Reed
were arguing about their strength.<BR CLEAR=all>When a strong...
```

Figure 12-8: The CLEAR attribute starts the next line below an aligned graphic

use them with care. One successful strategy for providing access to very large images (with correspondingly large file sizes) is to provide a postage-stamp-sized preview graphic that links to the full-size graphic.

The preview could be a reduction of the whole image or just an alluring fragment. Be sure to provide information necessary to help users decide whether they want to spend the time clicking the link, such as a description of what they're going to get and the file size of the image (so they can make an estimate of how long they'll need to wait).

Reuse images whenever possible

When a browser downloads a graphic, it stores it in the disk cache (a space for temporarily storing files on the hard disk). That way, if it needs to redisplay the page, it can just pull up a local copy of the HTML and graphics files without making a new trip out to the remote server.

When you use the same graphic repetitively in a page or a site, the browser only needs to download the graphic once. Every subsequent instance of the graphic is grabbed from the local cache, which means less traffic for the server and faster display for the end user.

The browser recognizes a graphic by its entire pathname, not just the file name, so if you want to take advantage of file caching, be sure that each instance of your graphic is pointing to the same graphic on the server (not multiple copies of the same graphic in different directories).

The lowsrc trick

Large graphics may take a long time to download via slow connection speeds, which means your viewers may spend moments staring at an empty space on the screen. The lowsrc attribute for the <img> tag (introduced by Netscape) provides one way to quickly give users some indication of the image to come while the "real" graphic is still downloading.

The lowsrc attribute provides the URL for an image file that the browser loads and displays when it first encounters the <img> tag. Then, once the document has completely loaded, the browser goes back and retrieves the image specified by the src attribute, as shown in Figure 12-9.

```
<IMG LOWSRC="lowres.gif" SRC="skyline.gif">
```

Figure 12-9: Code and images for using the lowsrc trick

To use this the way it was intended, the `lowsrc` image should contain the same image as the final graphic, but in a format that compresses to a much smaller file size. For instance, an image made up of only black and white pixels could stand in for a full-color JPEG.

With improving bandwidth speeds, this technique has grown a bit antiquated. When a page loads quickly, the initial image may appear as a brief flash or not be visible at all. The `lowsrc` attribute is not recognized in the HTML 4.01 specification and is supported only by Netscape Navigator.

Horizontal Rules

The simplest element you can add to a web page is a horizontal rule, plopped into place with the `<hr>` tag. In most browsers, horizontal rules display by default as an "embossed" shaded rule that extends across the full width of the browser window (or available text space). Horizontal rules are used as simple dividers, breaking an otherwise long scroll into manageable chunks.

Since it is a block-level element, a horizontal rule always creates a line break above and below. If you want additional space between the rule and the surrounding elements, insert `<p>` tags above and/or below the `<hr>`, as shown in Figure 12-10 (however, this is considered poor HTML form).

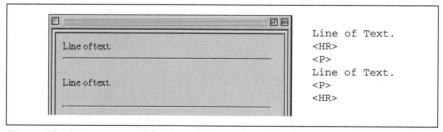

Figure 12-10: A <p> tag adds vertical space above or below a horizontal rule

There are a few attributes for the `<hr>` tag that allow authors to "design" rules more to their liking; however, all of them have been deprecated in HTML 4.01. They allow you to change the width, height, and alignment of the rule. You can also opt to turn off the 3-D shaded effect using the `noshade` attribute.

Specifying Thickness

The `size` attribute controls the thickness or weight of the rule. Size is specified in number of pixels. See Figure 12-11.

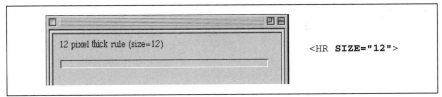

Figure 12-11: A 12-pixel rule

Specifying the Rule Length

Somewhat counterintuitively, the length of the rule is controlled by the `width` attribute (corresponding to the width of the parent element). The value for the rule width can be provided as a specific pixel length by entering a number, or as a percentage of the available page width. See Figure 12-12.

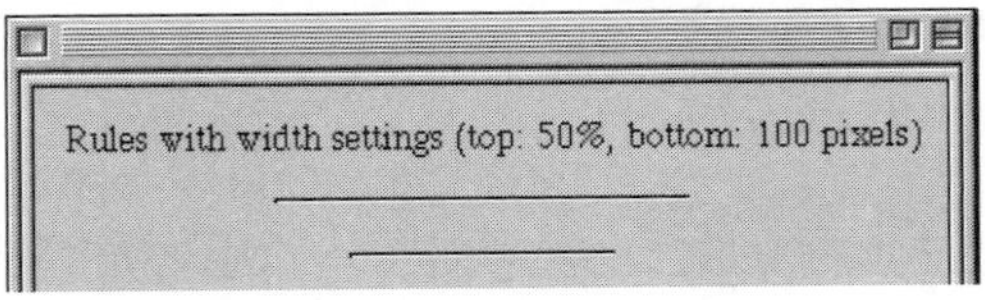

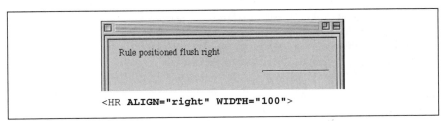

Figure 12-12: Rules set to 50% of page width (top) and 100 pixels (bottom)

Rule Alignment

If you've specified a rule length (using the `width` attribute) that is shorter than the width of the page, you can also decide how you would like the rule aligned: left, right, or centered. Like all other elements, horizontal placement is controlled using the `align` attribute and the values `left`, `right`, or `center`. See Figure 12-13.

Figure 12-13: Rule positioned flush right

Turning Off 3-D Shading

The `noshade` attribute allows you to turn off the 3-D shading for horizontal rules. This causes the rule to display as a solid black line. See Figure 12-14.

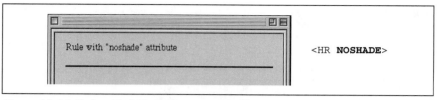

```
Rule with "noshade" attribute          <HR NOSHADE>
```

Figure 12-14: Rule with 3-D shading turned off

Creative Combinations

By using the available attributes in combination, you can get a little bit creative with horizontal rules. The most common trick is to set the width and size to the same value, creating a little embossed square that can be centered on the web page. Unfortunately, rules cannot be placed next to each other on a line (unless you put them in neighboring table cells). See Figure 12-15.

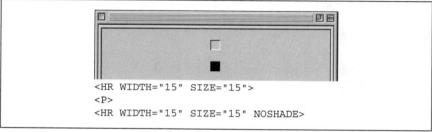

```
<HR WIDTH="15" SIZE="15">
<P>
<HR WIDTH="15" SIZE="15" NOSHADE>
```

Figure 12-15: Two 15-pixel-thick, 15-pixel-wide rules

Embedded Media Files

Images aren't the only things that can be displayed as part of a web page. You can also include content such as Quicktime movies, interactive Flash files, all manner of Java applets, and more. The browser renders embedded media files using the provided code (as in the case of an applet), using its built-in display devices (as for GIF or JPEG images), or by taking advantage of a plug-in or helper application.

The three tags that embed media in HTML are <object> (the HTML 4.01 preference for all media), <applet> (for Java applets; deprecated in HTML 4.01), and <embed> (for plug-in dependent media; not even recognized in HTML 4.01). Following are overviews of each of these tags and their uses.

The <object> Tag

The <object> tag is an all-purpose object-placer. It can be used to place a variety of object types on a web page, including applets (Java or ActiveX), multimedia objects, and even plain old images.

It began as a proprietary tag in Internet Explorer to support ActiveX and later Java applets. Netscape Navigator initially supported only <embed> and <applet> (discussed later in this chapter) for embedding media, but added limited <object> support in its Version 4 release, and full support in Version 6. Currently,

---

the `<object>` tag enjoys a hearty endorsement by the HTML 4.01 specification as the "right" way to add any media object to a web page.

The `<object>` tag has a large number of attributes that customize its use to the type of media being placed. It shares many attributes with the `<img>` tag for controlling placement on the page (such as align, width, height, vspace, and hspace). A complete list of attributes for the `<object>` tag is detailed in the "Summary of Object Placement Tags" section earlier in this chapter.

The syntax for the `<object>` tag varies with the type of content it is placing. The following examples should provide a general understanding of its use.

Adding an image

In this example, the `<object>` tag is used simply to place an image on the page.

```
<OBJECT DATA="daffodil.gif" TYPE="image/gif">
A color photograph of a daffodil.
</OBJECT>
```

Here, the data attribute specifies the source for the object (in this case a graphic file) and type tells the browser that the content type is a GIF image. The text enclosed within the `<object>` tags is used as alternative text if the object can't be rendered. While the syntax exists for adding images with the `<object>` tag, the `<img>` tag is still the most common way to go and isn't likely to be phased out of the HTML standard. This format is currently supported only by Internet Explorer 5+ and Netscape 6.

Adding plug-in media

The `<object>` tag can also be used to place media played by browser plug-ins and helper applications, such as Flash or Director movies. Note that some browsers support only the `<embed>` tag for embedding plug-in media, so in many cases you'll need to use a combination of the two tags. This is discussed in more detail in Part IV.

In this example, a Flash movie is added via the `<object>` tag (it has been abbreviated to emphasize the tag structure; see Chapter 26 for the full values).

```
<OBJECT CLASSID="clsid:D27..." CODEBASE="http://active.macromedia.com/"
    WIDTH="300" HEIGHT="150">
  <PARAM NAME="MOVIE" VALUE="moviename.swf">
  <PARAM NAME="LOOP" VALUE="false">
</OBJECT>
```

When used for a plug-in media type, classid functions like `<embed>`'s pluginurl attribute, which points to the place where the appropriate plug-in can be found and automatically installed. In this case, it points to an ActiveX control that will be used to play the movie for Internet Explorer users on Windows machines.

codebase provides a base URL based on which relative URLs for classid, data, and archive attributes should be evaluated.

Some plug-in media and applets require width and height values in order to play correctly, so be sure to read any documentation provided for your media type.

The <embed> Tag

The <embed> tag places a media object, such as a Flash movie or the controls for a RealAudio track, on a web page. It displays the media object in a rectangular area that behaves much like an inline image in terms of text flow positioning. The <embed> tag was originally created by Netscape for use with plug-in technologies. It is currently supported by both browsers; however, the HTML 4.01 specification prefers the use of the <object> tag with the data attribute for the placement of multimedia elements.

When the browser encounters the <embed> tag, it matches the suffix of the file name (Navigator also looks for the value of the type attribute) with the appropriate plug-in.

The following is a very simple example of the <embed> tag:

```
<EMBED SRC="url" HEIGHT="165" WIDTH="250" ALIGN="right" HSPACE="6">
</EMBED>
```

The src attribute is required to tell the browser the location of the media file to be played. Many media types require that the width and height values (the dimensions of the plug-in element in pixels) be specified in order for the plug-in to function.

If you are triggering plug-in functions from a script, you need to give the element a name using the name attribute.

Like images, media objects can be positioned using the align attribute and its related hspace and vspace settings. In Internet Explorer, you can also specify alternative text with the familiar alt attribute.

There are a few special attributes supported only by Version 4.0 and higher browsers that you might also want to include. To hide the media file or object from view, use the hidden attribute with a value of yes. The pluginspage attribute provides the URL of a page where the user can download information for the required plug-in should it not be found on the client machine. Netscape 4.0 introduced the pluginurl attribute, which specifies a link to a function that installs the plug-in automatically.

The complete list of attributes for the <embed> tag is detailed in the "Summary of Object Placement Tags" section earlier in this chapter.

Plug-in-specific attributes

In addition to these standard attributes, the <embed> tag may also contain plug-in–specific attributes for controlling the function of the player. The attributes loop, autostart, autoplay, and volume are examples of media-specific controls. Complete <embed> tags with their respective attributes are listed for several media types in Chapters 24, 25, and 26.

<noembed>

The <noembed> tag provides alternative content that displays if the browser cannot display the specified media file. In the following example, the browser would display the GIF file in place of the media object.

```
<EMBED SRC="cool.swf" HEIGHT="165" WIDTH="250" ALIGN="right" HSPACE="6">
<NOEMBED><IMG SRC="needplugin.gif"></NOEMBED>
</EMBED>fs
```

Java Applets

Java is an object-oriented programming language developed by Sun Microsystems (*http://www.sun.com*). It should be noted that it is not related to JavaScript, which is a scripting language developed by Netscape Navigator to run within an HTML document in a browser. Because Java is a full programming language (like C or C++), it can be used to create whole applications.

Java's primary contribution to the Web, however, has been in the form of Java *applets*, which are self-contained, mini-executable programs. These programs, named with the *.class* suffix, can be placed right on the web page, like a graphic.

Advantages and Disadvantages

Applets are ideal for web distribution for the following reasons:

*   They are platform-independent.
*   They download completely and run on the client, so there is no continued burden on the server.
*   Applet files are generally quite compact and download quickly.
*   They don't require a proprietary plug-in to be installed. All the major browsers are now Java-enabled, which means chances are good that users will be able to view the applet.

Of course, every utopian technology has its darker side, and unfortunately, in the real world, browsers can be temperamental in the way they handle Java applets. Browsers are notorious for crashing in the presence of a computation-hungry applet. In general, it also takes browsers a long time to initialize Java, which tends to chase users away. There was a great buzz among web developers when Java applets first hit the scene, but since then enthusiasm has waned in the face of performance issues and the development of other web multimedia solutions.

What Applets Can Do

What *can't* applets do?! Java applets are used for everything from simple animations to flight simulators. Because Java allows for computations on-the-fly, they are useful for programs that interact with user input. Not surprisingly, a large percentage of Java applets are games, but applets are also used for more practical purposes, such as calculators and spreadsheets. More interestingly, they can serve live data (news headlines, stock quotes, sports scores, etc.) and let users navigate through complex data relationships.

There are probably thousands of Java applets out there. The following is just a smattering of the types of things they can do:

- Utilities—calculators, calendars, clocks, spreadsheets
- Text effects—scrolling marquees, wiggling text, flashing colored text messages
- Audio effects—digital "guitars," radio buttons
- Games—Asteroids, crosswords, Hangman, Minesweeper
- Miscellaneous—biorhythm charts, flight simulators, daily quotes

Where to Get Applets

If you need a customized applet for your site, your best bet is to hire a programmer to create one to your specifications. However, there are a number of applets available for free or for a licensing fee that you can download from libraries on the Web.

A good place to start is the applets section of Sun's Java site at *http://java.sun.com/applets/*. This page provides a list of links to applet-related resources.

If you are looking for cool applets you can use right away, try the JavaBoutique at *http://javaboutique.internet.com*. Here you will find hundreds of applets available for download as well as clear instructions for their use. It's a great way to add interactivity to your site without learning any programming.

Downloading and Using Java Applets

In addition to these, there are a number of small businesses with Java applet packages for sale or available for a nominal licensing fee. Because the list is constantly changing, I recommend doing a search for "Java Applets" on Yahoo (*http://www.yahoo.com*) or your favorite search engine.

It is fairly easy to download an applet and add it to a web page. The steps below follow the instructions provided by the JavaBoutique for downloading applets from their site, but they can be used for applets from any resource.

1. Download the *.class* file along with any associated image or audio files. (Note that there is a bug in Navigator 4.0 that requires you to hold the Shift key before clicking the link for the *.class* file.) In some cases, you may be given the raw Java code, in which case you need to compile it using Sun's Java Developer Kit.

2. The *.class* file should be saved in the same directory as the HTML file, unless otherwise noted by the `codebase` attribute in the associated `<applet>` tag (this attribute gives the path for the applet). If the applet requires additional resources (such as image or audio files), be sure to save them in the same directory structure you found them (or follow the directions provided with the applet).

3. When getting an applet from a library such as JavaBoutique, the required HTML source is made available with the download, so you can just copy and paste it into your HTML document and adjust the parameters as necessary.

4. Test the applet in a browser or applet viewer. Because applets run client-side, you don't need a server to do your testing. Most problems with applets are due to elements not being in the right places. Make sure that your .*class* file is in the directory noted by the `codebase` attribute or in the same directory as the HTML file if no `codebase` is specified. Also be sure that your supporting resource files are in their correct directories and that everything is named correctly (remember that names in Java code are case-sensitive). Troubles may arise in setting all the parameters correctly, but these problems cannot be anticipated and need to be solved on a per-applet basis.

5. Last but not least, it is good form to credit the author of the applet as well as the online resource. The JavaBoutique provides a discreet logo you can place on the page with the applet.

Adding an Applet to a Page

There are currently two methods for adding an applet to a web page: the `<object>` tag, recommended by HTML 4.01, and the better-supported `<applet>` tag.

The W3C has deprecated the `<applet>` tag and all its attributes in favor of the `<object>` tag. Despite this, the `<applet>` tag may still be the better choice, because browser support for `<object>`-embedded applets is so inconsistent that it is difficult to find an approach that works in all browsers. In addition, some applets require that the `<applet>` tag be used, so read the documentation for the applet first. This section looks at both methods.

Adding applets with `<object>`

You can add a simple, self-contained applet to an HTML document using the `<object>` tag like this:

```
<OBJECT CLASSID="applet.class" CODEBASE="http://somedomain.com/classes/">
An applet with some useful function should display in this space.
</OBJECT>
```

The `classid` attribute points to the applet itself (its implementation). It has the same function as the `code` attribute in the `<applet>` tag when used for Java applets. `classid` may not contain any pathname information, so the location of the class file is provided by the `codebase` attribute.

When using `<object>` for Java applets, the object tag may contain a number of parameter (`<param>`) tags, as with the `<applet>` tag. (Note that Netscape 4.0 does not support `<param>` tags within the `<object>` tag, so it may not play applets correctly if placed this way.)

The following is an example of an applet with additional parameters:

```
<OBJECT CLASSID="applet.class" CODEBASE="http://somedomain.com/classes/">
  <PARAM NAME="param1" VALUE="value1">
  <PARAM NAME="param2" VALUE="value2">
  <PARAM NAME="param3" VALUE="value3">
An applet with some useful function should display in this space.
</OBJECT>
```

Adding applets with <applet>

The <applet> tag is a container for any number of parameter (<param>) tags. The following is an example of how an <applet> tag for a game might look:

```
<APPLET CODEBASE=class CODE="Wacky.class" WIDTH=300 HEIGHT=400>
<PARAM NAME="Delay" VALUE="250">
<PARAM NAME="Time" VALUE="120">
<PARAM NAME="PlaySounds" VALUE="YES">
</APPLET>
```

The opening applet tag contains a number of standard attributes:

code

> Tells the browser which applet will be used. Applets end with the suffix *.class* or *.jar*. This attribute is required.

codebase

> This tells the browser in which directory to find the applets. If the applets are in the same directory as the page, the codebase attribute is not necessary.

width, height

> These specify the pixel dimensions of the "window" the applet will occupy. These attributes are required for the Java applet to function properly.

The <applet> tag can also take many of the same attributes used for images, such as alt (for providing alternative text if the applet can not be displayed), align (for positioning the applet in the flow of text), and hspace/vspace (used in conjunction with align).

Special parameters for the applet are provided by any number of parameter tags (sometimes there are none). The <param> tag always contains the name of the parameter (name=) and its value (value=). Parameters provide special settings and controls that are specific to the particular applet, so you need to follow the parameter coding instructions provided by the programmer of the applet.

CHAPTER 13

Tables

HTML tags for creating tables were originally developed for presenting rows and columns of tabular data, but designers quickly co-opted them as a valuable tool for controlling the layout of web pages. Tables allow you to create columns of text, hold white space between elements, and restrict the dimensions of the page's content in ways other HTML formatting tags can't.

The HTML 4.01 specification on tables is a great deal more complex than the previous 3.2 standard. It makes an effort to bring context and structure to table data as well as to provide systems for incremental display during download and display on nonvisual display agents (such as speech- and Braille-based browsers). To read what the HTML 4.01 specification has to say about tables, see the W3C's site at *http://www.w3c.org/TR/html4/struct/tables.html*.

Summary of Table Tags

In this section, browser support for each tag is noted to the right of the tag name. Browsers that do not support the tag are grayed out. Tag usage is indicated below the tag name. Start and end tags are required unless otherwise noted. "Deprecated" means that the tag or attribute is currently supported but is due to be phased out of the HTML specification and is discouraged from use (usually in favor of similar style sheet controls). The attributes listed for each tag reflect those in common use. A more thorough listing of attributes for each tag, according to the HTML 4.01 specification, appears in Appendix A.

\<caption\>   NN 2, 3, 4, 6   MSIE 2, 3, 4, 5, 5.5, 6   HTML 4.01   WebTV   Opera5

`<caption>...</caption>`

Provides a brief summary of the table's contents or purpose. The caption must immediately follow the `<table>` tag and precede all other tags. The width of the caption is determined by the width of the table. The caption's position as displayed in the browser can be controlled with the `align` attribute (or `valign` in MSIE).

Attributes

`align=top|bottom|left|right`
> *Deprecated*. Positions the caption relative to the table. The default is `top`.

`valign=top|bottom`
> *Internet Explorer 3.0 and higher only*. Positions the caption above or below the table (`top` is the default).

\<col\>   NN 2, 3, 4, 6   MSIE 2, 3, 4, 5, 5.5, 6   HTML 4.01   WebTV   Opera5

`<col>` *(no end tag)*

Specifies properties for a column (or group of columns) within a *column group* (`<colgroup>`). Columns can share attributes (such as text alignment) without being part of a formal structural grouping.

Column groups and columns were introduced by Internet Explorer 3.0 and are now proposed by the HTML 4.01 specification as a standard way to label table structure. They may also be useful in speeding table display (i.e., the columns can be displayed incrementally without waiting for the entire contents of the table).

Attributes

`align=left|right|center|justify|char`
> *Deprecated*. Specifies alignment of text in the cells of a column. The default value is `left`.

`char=character`
> Specifies a character along which the cell contents will be aligned when `align` is set to `char`. The default character is a decimal point (language-appropriate). This attribute is generally not supported by current browsers.

`charoff=length`
> Specifies the offset distance to the first alignment character (`char`) on each line. If a line doesn't use an alignment character, it should be horizontally shifted to end at the alignment position. This attribute is generally not supported by current browsers.

`span=number`
> Specifies the number of columns "spanned" by the `<col>` element. The default value is 1. All columns indicated in the span are formatted according to the attribute settings in `<col>`.

`valign=top|middle|bottom|baseline`
> *Deprecated*. Specifies the vertical alignment of text in the cells of a column.

`width=pixels, percentage, n*`
> Specifies the width of each column spanned by the `<col>` element. Width can be measured in pixels or percentages, or defined as a relative size (`*`). For example, `2*` sets the column two times wider than the other columns; `0*` sets the column width at the minimum necessary to hold the column's contents. `width` in the `<col>` tag overrides the width settings of the containing `<colgroup>` element.

<colgroup>

<colgroup>...</colgroup> *(end tag optional)*

Creates a *column group*, a structural division within a table that can be appointed attributes with style sheets or HTML. A table may include more than one column group. The number of columns in a group is specified either by the value of the span attribute or by a tally of columns <col> within the group. Its end tag is optional.

Column groups and columns were introduced by Internet Explorer 3.0 and are now proposed by the HTML 4.0 specification as a standard way to label table structure. They may also be useful in speeding the table display (i.e., the columns can be displayed incrementally without waiting for the entire contents of the table).

Attributes

align=left|right|center|justify|char
> *Deprecated.* Specifies the alignment of text in the cells of a column group. The default value is left.

char=*character*
> Specifies a character along which the cell contents will be aligned when align is set to char. The default character is a decimal point (language-appropriate). This attribute is generally not supported by current browsers.

charoff=*length*
> Specifies the distance to the first alignment character (char) on each line. If a line doesn't use an alignment character, it should be horizontally shifted to end at the alignment position. This attribute is generally not supported by current browsers.

span=*number*
> Specifies the number of columns in a column group. If span is not specified, the default is 1.

valign=top|middle|bottom|baseline
> *Deprecated.* Specifies the vertical alignment of text in the cells of a column group. The default is middle.

width=*pixels, percentage, n**
> Specifies a default width for each column in the current column group. Width can be measured in pixels, percentages, or defined as a relative size (*). 0* sets the column width at the minimum necessary to hold the column's contents.

<table>

<table>...</table>

Defines the beginning and end of a table. The end tag is required, and its omission may cause the table not to render in some browsers.

Attributes

`align=left|right|center`

> *Deprecated.* Aligns the table within the text flow (same as `align` in the `<img>` tag). The default alignment is `left`. The `center` value is not universally supported, so it is more reliable to center a table on a page using tags outside the table (such as `<center>` or `<div>`).

`background=url`

> *Nonstandard.* Specifies a graphic image to be tiled in the background of the table. In Internet Explorer 3.0 and higher, the image tiles behind the entire table. In Netscape Navigator 4.0, the tile repeats in each individual cell (although its support is not officially documented).

`bgcolor="#rrggbb"` *or* `color name`

> Specifies a background color for the entire table. Value is specified in hexadecimal RGB values or by color name (see Chapter 16 for more information on specifying colors in HTML).

`border=number`

> Specifies the width (in pixels) of the border around the table and its cells. Set it to `border=0` to turn the borders off completely. The default value is 1. Adding the word `border` without a value results in a 1-pixel border.

`cellpadding=number`

> Sets the amount of space, in number of pixels, between the cell border and its contents. The default value is 1. For more information, see the "Space Between Cells" section in this chapter.

`cellspacing=number`

> Sets the amount of space (in number of pixels) between table cells. The default value is 2. For more information, see the "Space Between Cells" section in this chapter.

`frame=void|above|below|hsides|lhs|rhs|vsides|box|border`

> Tells the browser where to draw borders around the table. The values are as follows:

void	The frame does not appear (default)
above	Top side only
below	Bottom side only
hsides	Top and bottom sides only
vsides	Right and left sides only
lhs	Left-hand side only
rhs	Right-hand side only
box	All four sides
border	All four sides

> When the `border` attribute is set to a value greater than zero, the frame defaults to `border` unless otherwise specified. This attribute was introduced by Internet Explorer 3.0 and now appears in the HTML 4.01 specification. Netscape supports this attribute in Version 6 only.

height=*number, percentage*

    Nonstandard. Specifies the minimum height of the entire table. It can be specified in a specific number of pixels or by a percentage of the parent element.

hspace=*number*

    Holds a number of pixels space to the left and right of a table positioned with the `align` attribute (same as `hspace` in the `<img>` tag).

rules=all|cols|groups|none|rows

    Tells the browser where to draw rules within the table. Its values are as follows:

none	No rules (default)
groups	Rules appear between row groups (`thead`, `tfoot`, and `tbody`) and column groups
rows	Rules appear between rows only
cols	Rules appear between columns only
all	Rules appear between all rows and columns

    When the `border` attribute is set to a value greater than zero, rules default to `all` unless otherwise specified.

    This attribute was introduced by Internet Explorer 3.0 and now appears in the HTML 4.01 specification. Netscape supports it in Version 6 only.

summary=*text*

    Provides a summary of the table contents for use with nonvisual browsers.

vspace=*number*

    Holds a number of pixels space above and below table positioned with the `align` attribute (same as `vspace` in the `<img>` tag).

width=*number, percentage*

    Specifies the width of the entire table. It can be specified in a specific number of pixels or by percentage of the parent element.

Internet Explorer only

bordercolor="#*rrggbb*" *or color name*

    Specifies the color of the main center portion of a table border. (Table borders are rendered using three color values to create a 3-D effect.)

bordercolorlight="#*rrggbb*" *or color name*

    Specifies the color of the light shade used to render 3-D-looking table borders.

bordercolordark="#*rrggbb*" *or color name*

    Specifies the color of the dark shade used to render 3-D-looking table borders.

<tbody>...</tbody> *(start and end tags optional)*

Defines a row or group of rows as the "body" of the table. It must contain at least one row (<tr>).

"Row group" tags (tbody, thead, and tfoot) were introduced by Internet Explorer and are part of the HTML 4.01 specification. The attributes for <tbody> are currently not supported by any commercial browser. Row groups could speed table display and provide a mechanism for scrolling the body of a table independently of its head and foot. It could also be useful for printing long tables for which the head information could be printed on each page.

Attributes

align=left|center|right|justify|char
> *Deprecated.* Specifies horizontal alignment (or justification) of cell contents. The default value is left.

char=*character*
> Specifies a character along which the cell contents will be aligned. The default character is a decimal point (language-appropriate). This attribute is generally not supported by current browsers.

charoff=*length*
> Specifies the offset distance to the first alignment character (char) on each line. If a line doesn't use an alignment character, it should be horizontally shifted to end at the alignment position. This attribute is generally not supported by current browsers.

valign=top|middle|bottom|baseline
> *Deprecated.* Specifies vertical alignment of cell contents.

<td>...</td> *(end tag optional)*

Defines a table data cell. The end tag is not required but may prevent unpredictable table display, particularly if the cell contains images. A table cell can contain any content, including another table.

Attributes

align=left|center|right|justify|char
> *Deprecated.* Specifies horizontal alignment (or justification) of cell contents. The default value is left.

background=*url*
> Specifies a graphic image to be used as a tile within the cell. Netscape's documentation does not cover this tag, but it is supported by Version 4.0.

`bgcolor="#rrggbb"` *or* `color name`
> Specifies a color to be used in the table cell. A cell's background color overrides colors specified at the row or table levels.

`colspan=number`
> Specifies the number of columns the current cell should span. The default value is 1. According to the HTML 4.01 specification, the value zero (0) means the current cell spans all columns from the current column to the last column in the table; in reality, however, this feature is not supported in current browsers.

`height=number, percentage`
> *Deprecated.* Specifies the height of the cell in number of pixels or by a percentage value relative to the table height. The height specified in the first column will apply to the rest of the cells in the row. The height values need to be consistent for cells in a particular row. Pixel measurements are more reliable than percentages, which only work when the height of the table is specified in pixels.

`nowrap`
> *Deprecated.* Disables automatic text wrapping for the current cell. Line breaks must be added with a `<br>` or by starting a new paragraph. This attribute is only supported in Internet Explorer 5 and higher.

`rowspan=number`
> Specifies the number of rows spanned by the current cell. The default value is 1. According to the HTML 4.01 specification, the value zero (0) means the current cell spans all rows from the current row to the last row; in reality, however, this feature is not supported by any browsers.

`valign=top|middle|bottom|baseline`
> *Deprecated.* Specifies the vertical alignment of the text (or other elements) within the table cell. The default is `middle`.

`width=number`
> *Deprecated.* Specifies the width of the cell in number of pixels or by a percentage value relative to the table width. The width specified in the first row will apply to the rest of the cells in the column, and the values need to be consistent for cells in the column.

Internet Explorer only

`bordercolor="#rrggbb"` *or* `color name`
> Defines the border color for the cell.

`bordercolorlight="#rrggbb"` *or* `color name`
> Defines the dark shadow color for the cell border.

`bordercolordark="#rrggbb"` *or* `color name`
> Defines the light highlight color of the cell border.

New in HTML 4.01

These attributes are part of the HTML standard but are not supported by current browsers.

abbr=*text*
> Provides an abbreviated form of the cell's content.

axis=*text*
> Places a cell into a conceptual category, which could then be used to organize or search the table in different ways.

char=*character*
> Specifies a character along which the cell contents will be aligned. The default character is a decimal point (language-appropriate).

charoff=*length*
> Specifies the offset distance to the first alignment character (char) on each line. If a line doesn't use an alignment character, it should be horizontally shifted to end at the alignment position.

headers=*id reference*
> Lists header cells (by id) that provide header information for the current data cell. This is intended to make tables more accessible to nonvisual browsers.

scope=row|col|rowgroup|colgroup
> Specifies the table cells for which the current cell provides header information. A value of col indicates that the current cell is the header for all the cells that fall below. colgroup indicates the current cell is the header for the column group that contains it. A value of row means that the current cell is the header for the cells in the rest of the row. rowgroup means the current cell is the header for the containing rowgroup. This is intended to make tables more accessible to nonvisual browsers.

\<tfoot>

NN 2, 3, 4, 6   MSIE 2, 3, 4, 5, 5.5, 6   HTML 4.01   WebTV   Opera5

\<tfoot>...\</tfoot> *(end tag optional)*

Defines the foot of a table and should contain information about a table's columns. It is one of the "row group" tags introduced by Internet Explorer and proposed in the HTML 4.01 specification. A \<tfoot> must contain at least one row (\<tr>).

See \<tbody> for more information and a list of supported attributes.

\<th>

NN 2, 3, 4, 6   MSIE 2, 3, 4, 5, 5.5, 6   HTML 4.01   WebTV   Opera5

\<th>...\</th> *(end tag optional)*

Defines a table header cell. Table header cells function the same as table data cells (\<td>). Browsers generally display the content of table header cells in bold text centered horizontally and vertically in the cell (although some browsers vary). The end tag is optional.

Attributes

The \<th> tag uses the same attributes as the \<td> tag. See listing under \<td>.

<thead>

NN 2, 3, 4, 6   MSIE 2, 3, 4, 5, 5.5, 6   HTML 4.01   WebTV   Opera5

`<thead>...</thead>` *(end tag optional)*

Defines the head of the table and should contain information about a table. It must contain at least one row (`<tr>`). `<thead>` is one of the "row group" tags introduced by Internet Explorer and proposed in the HTML 4.01 specification.

See `<tbody>` for more information and a list of supported attributes.

<tr>

NN 2, 3, 4, 6   MSIE 2, 3, 4, 5, 5.5, 6   HTML 4.01   WebTV   Opera5

`<tr>...</tr>` *(end tag optional)*

Defines a row of cells within a table. A table row as delimited by `<tr>` tags contains no content other than a collection of table cells (`<td>`). Settings made in the `<tr>` tag apply to all the cells in that row, but individual cell settings override those made at the row level.

Attributes

`align=left|center|right|justify|char`
> *Deprecated.* Aligns the text (or other elements) within the cells of the current row. This attribute has been deprecated by the HTML 4.01 specification in favor of positioning with style sheets.

`bgcolor="#rrggbb" or color name`
> Specifies a color to be used in the row. A row's background color overrides the color specified at the table level.

`char=character`
> Specifies a character along which the cell contents will be aligned. The default character is a decimal point (language-appropriate). This attribute is generally not supported by current browsers.

`charoff=length`
> Specifies the offset distance to the first alignment character (`char`) on each line. If a line doesn't use an alignment character, it should be horizontally shifted to end at the alignment position. This attribute is generally not supported by current browsers.

`valign=top|middle|bottom|baseline`
> *Deprecated.* Specifies the vertical alignment of the text (or other elements) within cells of the current row.

Internet Explorer only

`background=url of image file`
> Specifies a graphic image to be used as a tile within the row.

`bordercolor="#rrggbb" or color name`
> Defines the border color for the row.

`bordercolorlight="#rrggbb" or color name`
> Defines the dark shadow color for the row border.

`bordercolordark="#rrggbb" or color name`
> Defines the light highlight color of the row border.

Introduction to Tables

Although there are no true classifications, tables can be used in the following general ways:

Table usage	Illustration
Data Table This is a table at its most basic (and as the creators of HTML intended)—rows and columns of textual data. Of course, data tables can be much larger and more complex than the one shown in this example.	
Text Alignment Tables are often used to clean up the display of text by creating effects common to print, such as columns, hanging indents, and extra white space. They are also useful for lining up text and input elements in forms.	
Page Template Many web designers use a large table as a container to give structure to a page. One common configuration is to create narrow columns for navigational items, as shown in this example. A template for a two-column table follows in the "Templates" section of this chapter.	
Multipart Image Container Tables can be used to hold together a large graphic that has been divided into separate sections to accommodate animations, rollovers, etc. In the example at right, the border was turned on to reveal the individual sections. Holding images together with tables is discussed at the end of this chapter.	

The HTML 4.01 specification proposal discourages the use of tables for page layout, favoring Cascading Style Sheets with absolute positioning instead. But until style sheets (particularly the positioning features) are more universally and consistently supported by the browsers in current use, tables remain a designer's most reliable tool for constructing complex page layouts.

Basic Table Structure

At their most basic, tables are made up cells, arranged into rows. You can control display characteristics for the whole table, for individual rows, and for individual cells.

Rows and Cells

The bare minimum tags for describing a table are `<table>`, `<tr>`, and `<td>`. The following HTML shows the basic structure for a four-cell table:

```
<TABLE>
<TR>
        <TD>cell 1</TD><TD>cell 2</TD>
</TR>
<TR>
        <TD>cell 3</TD><TD>cell 4</TD>
</TR>
</TABLE>
```

The `<table>` tag defines the beginning and end of the table. Its contents include a number of rows (two in our simple example). Each row is defined by `<tr>` tags and is made up of a number of data (or header) cells. Data cells are indicated by the `<td>` tag. A table cell may contain any data that can be displayed in an HTML document (formatted text, images, multimedia elements, and even other tables).

Figure 13-1 gives a visual representation of this concept. The image on the left shows that the table consists of two rows, each containing two cells. The image on the right shows how the HTML corresponds to the rows and cells.

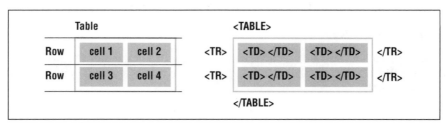

Figure 13-1: HTML table structure

Header cells use the `<th>` tag and function the same as data cells, but they are generally displayed in bold centered text (although some browsers vary). You may also add a caption to the table (using the `<caption>` tag), which provides a title or brief description of the table. The `<caption>` tag should be placed before the first row of the table; be sure that it is outside the row containers. Because tables are so often used as layout devices only, the caption feature is less often used than the other main table components.

The table system in HTML is very row-centric. Rows are labeled explicitly, but the number of columns is just implied by the number of cells in the longest row. In other words, if all the rows have three <td>s, then the table has three columns. If one row contains four <td>s and all the others contain two, the browser displays the table with four columns, adding blank cells to the shorter rows. HTML 4.01 includes an advanced system for describing table structure that includes explicit column tags. This system is discussed in the "Row and Column Groups" section of this chapter.

One of the tricks of designing tables is understanding what aspects of the table are controlled at the table, row, and cell levels.

Table-level controls

At the table level (using attributes within the <table> tag outlined previously), you can control:

- The width of the table and its position on the page
- The thickness of the border around the table and between cells
- The spacing within and between cells (using cellpadding and cellspacing, respectively)
- The background color of all its cells

Row-level controls

For each row (using attributes within the <tr> tag), you can control only:

- The vertical and horizontal alignment of the contents of all the cells in that row
- Background colors for all the cells contained in that row. Some browsers color the row background as well as the individual cell areas.

Row settings override table-level settings. Note that table row tags are merely containers for cell tags and contain no actual data themselves.

Cell-level controls

Much of a table's structure and appearance is controlled at the individual cell level using <td> or <th> attributes. Only the content within <td> or <th> tags is displayed in the browser. Within cells, you can control:

- The vertical and horizontal alignment of the cell's contents
- The color of the cell background
- The height and width of the cell (and the row and column that contain it)
- Whether the cell should span over more than one cell space in the table grid

Alignment and color specifications at the cell level override settings made at the row and table level.

Spanning Rows and Columns

Cells in a table can occupy the space of more than one cell in a row or column. This behavior is set within the <th> or <td> tags using the colspan and rowspan attributes.

Column span

In Figure 13-2, `<td colspan=2>` tells the browser to make "cell 1" occupy the same horizontal space as two cells ("span" over two columns). The resulting spanned cell is indicated in the figure on the left. Note that the row containing the spanned cell now only has one set of `<td>` tags instead of two.

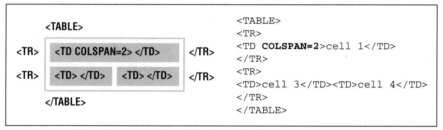

```
<TABLE>
<TR>
<TD COLSPAN=2>cell 1</TD>
</TR>
<TR>
<TD>cell 3</TD><TD>cell 4</TD>
</TR>
</TABLE>
```

Figure 13-2: The colspan attribute expands cells horizontally to the right

Setting the `colspan` to a number greater than the actual number of columns (such as `colspan=4` for our example) may cause some browsers to add empty columns to the table, possibly throwing your elements out of alignment. For example, in Netscape 4.5 and earlier, additional collapsed columns appear as an extra-wide border on the right of the table. The HTML 4.01 specification requests that empty cells not be added when the `colspan` exceeds the number of columns.

Row span

Similar to `colspan`, the `rowspan` attribute stretches a cell to occupy the space of cells in rows below. Include the `rowspan` attribute in the row where you want the cell to begin and set its value equal to the number of rows you want it to span.

In Figure 13-3, note that the bottom row now only contains one cell (the other has been incorporated into the vertical spanned cell). The resulting spanned cell is illustrated in the figure on the left. The browser ignores overextended `rowspan` values.

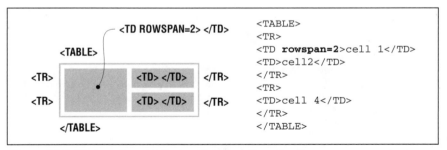

```
<TABLE>
<TR>
<TD rowspan=2>cell 1</TD>
<TD>cell2</TD>
</TR>
<TR>
<TD>cell 4</TD>
</TR>
</TABLE>
```

Figure 13-3: The rowspan attribute expands cells vertically

You may combine `colspan` and `rowspan` attributes to create a cell that spans both rows and columns.

Row and Column Groups

Internet Explorer 3.0 introduced a system for grouping rows and columns so they can be treated as units by style sheets or other HTML formatting tags. Row and column groups are mostly advantageous for long, complex tables containing actual data (as opposed to tables used strictly for page layout).

The system is reflected in the HTML 4.01 specification for tables, and it is now supported by Netscape 6 and other standards-compliant browsers. However, support for row and column groups is far from universal as of this writing, so keep them in mind but use them with caution. With careful coding, you can code tables with row and column groups in a way that will not disrupt display in older browsers.

The following is a brief introduction to row and column groups. For more information and examples, see the tables section of the HTML 4.01 specification (*http://www.w3c.org/TR/html4/struct/tables.html*). There is a useful article demonstrating the use of row and column groups at CNET's Builder.com at *http://www.builder.com/Authoring/Tagmania/020700/*.

Row groups

The rows in a table can be grouped into a table head (`<thead>`), a table foot (`<tfoot>`), and one or more table bodies (`<tbody>`). The head and foot should contain information about the document and may someday be used to display fixed elements while the body scrolls independently. For instance, the contents of the table head and foot would print on every page of a long table that has been divided over several pages. It is recommended by the W3C that the table foot (if there is one) appear before the body of the table so the table can render the foot before downloading all the (potentially numerous) rows of data.

You can use the `<tbody>` tag to define row groupings and then apply style sheet information to specific groups or add rules between sections of the table using the **rules** attribute, for example (see "Borders, Frames, and Rules" later in this chapter).

Column groups

Column groups create structural divisions within a table, explicitly identifying columns and enabling style information to be applied to all the cells within a specific column (traditionally, this would have had to be done within each individual cell). In addition, vertical rules can be added between column groups using the **rules** attribute (discussed later).

The `<colgroup>` tag delimits a conceptual group of columns. The number of columns included in the group is indicated with the **span** attribute or by the total of `<col>` elements (with their **span** values) within the column group. Attributes in the `<colgroup>` element apply to every column within that group.

The `<col>` element is used to apply attribute specifications to an individual column or across several columns without actually grouping them together structurally or conceptually. Like `<colgroup>`, you can specify the span (number of affected columns) and width (in pixels, percentages, or relative values) within the `<col>` tag.

Sample HTML

Example 13-1 is a bare-bones example of how row and column groups are integrated into the HTML table structure. Figure 13-4 shows the result.

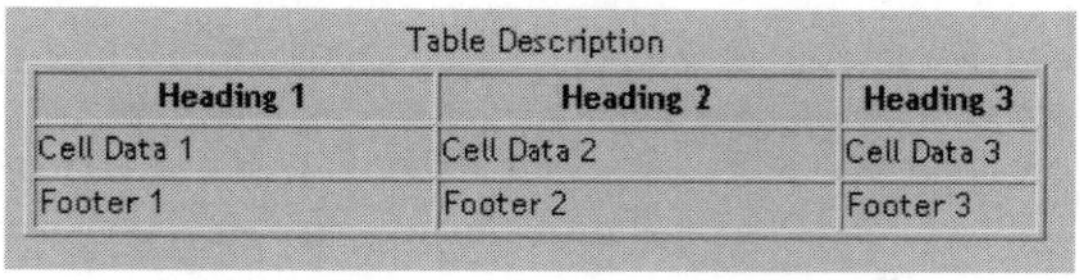

Heading 1	Heading 2	Heading 3
Cell Data 1	Cell Data 2	Cell Data 3
Footer 1	Footer 2	Footer 3

Figure 13-4: A table using the column and row groups to organize structure

Note again that row and column groups and their attributes are not universally supported at this time and can cause display problems. For instance, a browser that supports the <tfoot> element looks for it in the beginning of the document but knows to put its contents at the bottom of each page. In browsers that don't support this table structure, the footer information would be the second thing displayed on the page and would not be displayed again.

Example 13-1: Column and row groups

```
<TABLE BORDER=1>
<CAPTION>Table Description</CAPTION>

<COLGROUP>  Ⓐ
   <COL span=2 width=100>
   <COL span=1 width=50>
</COLGROUP>
<THEAD valign="top">  Ⓑ
<TR>
   <TH>Heading 1</TH><TH>Heading 2</TH><TH>Heading 3</TH>
</TR>
</THEAD>

<TFOOT>  Ⓒ
<TR>
   <TD>Footer 1</TD><TD>Footer 2</TD><TD>Footer 3</TD>
</TR>
</TFOOT>

<TBODY>  Ⓓ
<TR>
   <TD>Cell Data 1</TD><TD>Cell Data 2</TD><TD>Cell Data 3</TD>
</TR>
</TBODY>

</TABLE>
```

Ⓐ This table has a total of three columns. The <colgroup> element identifies the columns as part of the same structural group (there may be many column groups in a table, but for simplicity's sake, our example has just one). Within the colgroup, the first `<col>` element identifies two columns (span=2), each with a width of 100 pixels. The remaining `<col>` has a width of 50 pixels. If all the columns in the table were to be the same width, the width could have been specified in the `<colgroup>` element.

❸ The `<thead>` element defines a header for the table. The contents of the cells it contains may appear at the top of every page of the table.

❹ The `<tfoot>` defines a footer for the table. The cells in the footer row may appear at the bottom of every page. It should be defined before the actual contents of the table (`<tbody>`).

❺ The `<tbody>` element defines a number of rows that appear as the main content of the table.

Affecting Table Appearance

The HTML table standard provides many tags for controlling the display of tables. Bear in mind that, as with most formatting tags, browsers have their own way of interpreting your instructions, so results may vary among browser releases and platforms. This is particularly true of tables since the standard is still being nailed down. As always, it is best to test in a variety of viewing environments.

It is important to note that some of the attributes that affect appearance (`align`, `valign`, and `bgcolor`) have been deprecated by the HTML 4.01 specification in favor of achieving the same effects with style sheets. Expect the major browsers, however, to continue supporting the following methods until style sheets are universally supported.

Borders, Frames, and Rules

The traditional method for adding a border around a table is the **border** attribute, which affects the display of the borders around and within the table. For more finely tuned control, the HTML separates control over the outer edge of the table (its frame) from the lines between cells within the table (rules). Let's look at all three attributes.

The border attribute

By default, tables display with no borders. When the **border** attribute alone (with no value specified) is added to the `<table>` tag, a 1-pixel border is added around and between the cells, as shown in Figure 13-5.

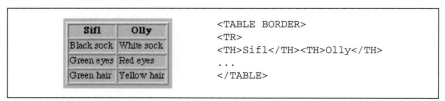

Figure 13-5: Table with a 1-pixel border

Baltimore County Public Library

10/16/2007

Thank you for using express checkout!

***********5543

31830986331861 Web design in a nutshell :
a desktop quick refer
Date Due: 06 Nov 2007

31831168805792 Animals
Date Due: 06 Nov 2007

31831237505918 Colors
Date Due: 06 Nov 2007

31831255497937 My first things that go boa
rd book
Date Due: 06 Nov 2007

Monday - Thursday 9:00 am - 9:00 pm
Friday - Saturday 9:00 am - 5:30 pm
Telephone: 410-887-7750
http://www.bcpl.info
Shelf Help 410-494-9063
No. Checked Out / No. Not Checked Out
4 / 0

You can also use the `border` attribute to specify a number value. Specifying a higher number for the border adds a thicker beveled border around the outside edges of the table (shown in Figure 13-6). The thickness of the borders between cells (default 2 pixels) is determined by the amount of cellspacing, described later.

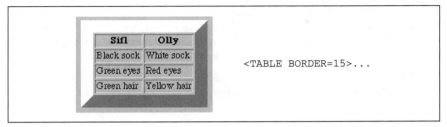

Sifl	Olly
Black sock	White sock
Green eyes	Red eyes
Green hair	Yellow hair

`<TABLE BORDER=15>...`

Figure 13-6: Table with a 15-pixel border

Even if you don't want a table to display with a border in your final design, turning the border on during the design process can help in visualizing the table structure; it is particularly useful for debugging problematic tables. Just remember to turn it off again before uploading.

The frame attribute

The `frame` attribute gives authors control over the display of a border around each of the outside edges of the table. By default, tables display with no frame (`void`). This attribute is supported by only the most recent browsers (Internet Explorer 5.5 and Netscape 6). The following is a list of all acceptable values for `frame`:

void	The frame does not appear (default)
above	Top side only
below	Bottom side only
hsides	Top and bottom sides only
vsides	Right and left sides only
lhs	Left-hand side only
rhs	Right-hand side only
box	All four sides
border	all four sides

The rules attribute

The `rules` attribute determines which rules appear between cells within a table. One use for this attribute might be to display rules only between certain sets of columns or rows, as defined by `<colgroup>` or the row group tags (`<thead>`, `<tbody>`, and `<tfoot>`). This attribute is supported by only the most recent browsers (5.5 and 6). The following is a list of all the accepted values for the rules attribute (the default is `none`):

none	No rules (default)
groups	Rules appear between row groups (`thead`, `tfoot`, and `tbody`) and column groups
rows	Rules appear between rows only
cols	Rules appear between columns only
all	Rules appear between all rows and columns

Positioning a Table on the Page

On current browsers (Navigator and Internet Explorer Versions 3.0 and higher), tables by default behave like paragraphs or other blocks, but they behave like images if floated to the left or right with the `align` attribute. Use the `align` attribute in the `<table>` tag to position the table against the left or right margin and allow text to flow around it. As with images, you can specify a number of pixels to hold clear to the left and right of the table using the `hspace` attribute. `vspace` holds space above and below the table.

The 4.0 browsers and later allow you to center a table on the page by setting the `align` attribute to `center`. Unlike left or right margin alignments, this setting does not allow text to flow around the table.

Because this attribute is not universally supported, it is best to center a table using HTML tags such as `<center>` or `<div>` outside the table.

Aligning Text in Cells

By default, the text (or any element) in a data cell (`<td>`) is positioned flush left and centered vertically within the available height of the cell, as shown in Figure 13-7.

Figure 13-7: Default placement of data within a cell

Table header text (`<th>`) is generally displayed in bold text centered horizontally and vertically in the cell. You can override these defaults using the `align` and `valign` attributes at either the row or cell level.

Row Settings

    Alignment settings specified within the `<tr>` tag affect all the table cells (`<td>` or `<th>`) within that row. This makes it easy to apply alignment changes across multiple cells.

Cell Settings

    Alignment attributes within a cell (`<td>` or `<th>`) apply to the current cell. Cell settings override row settings. Furthermore, alignment settings within the contents of the cell (e.g., `<p align=right>`) take precedence over both cell and row settings.

Horizontal alignment is specified with the `align` attribute, which takes the standard `left`, `right`, or `center` values. These values work the same as regular paragraph alignment. (The `align` attribute has been deprecated in favor of style sheet controls.)

Vertical alignment is controlled using the `valign` attribute, which can be set to `top`, `middle` (the default), `bottom`, or `baseline` ("first text line appears on a baseline common to all the cells in the row," but this setting is not as well supported).

By default, the text in a cell automatically wraps to fill the allotted space. There is a `nowrap` attribute which can be added within the table cell (`<td>` or `<th>`) to keep text on one line (unless broken by a `<br>` or `<p>`). Unfortunately, most browsers (except IE 5 and higher) ignore the attribute and wrap the text anyway. When `nowrap` is supported, the table cell resizes wider if it needs to accommodate the line of text.

Sizing Tables

You can control the size of the entire table as well as the size of rows and columns. By default, a table (and its rows and columns) are sized automatically to the minimum dimensions required to fit their contents. In many cases, it is desirable to assign a table or column a specific size (especially when using the table to build a page structure).

If the contents require a width greater than the specified size, the table generally resizes to accommodate the contents. Size specifications are treated as suggestions that will be followed as long as they don't conflict with other display directions. In effect, by specifying the size of a table you are merely specifying the minimum size. It is best to specify ample room to accommodate the contents of the cells.

Table dimensions

The `width` attribute is used within the `<table>` tag to specify the width of the table. You can specify an absolute value (measured in pixels) or a relative value (a percentage of the available width of the screen) as shown in the following table:

Style	Sample HTML	Result
Absolute value	`<TABLE WIDTH=600>`	Makes the table 600 pixels wide
Relative value	`<TABLE WIDTH=80%>`	Makes the table 80% of the screen width

To make a table fill the browser width, set the width to 100%.

Table height can be specified using the `height` attribute, which can also be defined by absolute or relative values. The `height` attribute is not part of the HTML standard, but it is well supported by browsers. If the contents of the table are longer than your specified height, the table expands to fit the contents. Therefore, the `height` attribute merely specifies a minimum, not an exact height for the table.

Cell dimensions

Use the **width** and **height** attributes within a cell tag (`<td>` or `<th>`) to specify the dimensions of that cell. A cell's width setting affects the width of the entire column it occupies, so column widths can be specified by setting the width of just one cell in the column (generally those in the top row); the remaining cells will follow.

Likewise, the cell's height may determine the height of all the cells in that row, so row height can be set using just one cell in each row.

Height and width values can be absolute measurements in pixels, or percentages relative to the dimensions of the table. Percentage heights don't work in table cells unless the height of the entire table is specified in pixels. Percentage measurements are problematic for Navigator 3.

Table Cell Spacing

There are two types of space that can be added in and around table cells: cell padding and cell spacing. The **cellpadding** and **cellspacing** attributes are used within the `<table>` tag and apply to the whole table (you can't specify padding or spacing for individual cells).

cellspacing

The amount of space between table cells is controlled by the **cellspacing** attribute within the `<table>` tag. Values are specified in number of pixels. Increasing the cell spacing results in wider shaded borders between cells. In the left image in Figure 13-8, the gray areas indicate the 10 pixels of cell spacing added between cells. The default value for **cellspacing** is 2; therefore, if no **cellspacing** is specified, browsers will automatically place 2 pixels of space between cells.

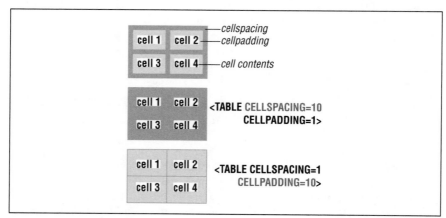

Figure 13-8: Cell spacing versus cell padding

cellpadding

Cell padding refers to the amount of space between the cell's border and the contents of the cell (as indicated in Figure 13-8). It is specified using the `cellpadding` attribute within the `<table>` tag. Values are specified in number of pixels; the default value is 1. Relative values (percentages of available space) may also be used.

Different effects can be created using different combinations of spacing and padding. If you want your table to be seamless, as when it is holding together an image, be sure to set the border, cellspacing, and cellpadding to 0, as follows:

```
<TABLE BORDER=0 CELLPADDING=0 CELLSPACING=0>
```

Coloring Tables

You can specify a background color for the entire table (`<table>`), for selected rows (`<tr>`), or for individual cells (`<td>` or `<th>`) by placing the `bgcolor` attribute in the appropriate tag. The `bgcolor` attribute is recognized by Internet Explorer Versions 2.0 and higher and Navigator Versions 3.0 and higher.

Color values can be specified by either their hexadecimal RGB values or a standard color name. For more information on specifying color in HTML, see Chapter 16.

Color settings in a cell override settings made at the row level, which override settings made at the table level. To illustrate, in the following example, the whole table is set to light gray, the second row is set to medium gray, and the furthest right cell in that row is set to dark gray. Figure 13-9 shows the results.

```
<TABLE BORDER=1 BGCOLOR="#CCCCCC">
<TR>
<TD></TD><TD></TD><TD></TD>
</TR>
<TR BGCOLOR="#999999">
<TD></TD><TD></TD><TD BGCOLOR="#333333"></TD>
</TR>
<TR>
<TD></TD><TD></TD><TD></TD>
</TR>
<TR>
<TD></TD><TD></TD><TD></TD>
</TR>
</TABLE>
```

Figure 13-9: Effects of setting background colors at cell, row, and table levels

Navigator and Internet Explorer treat background colors at the table level differently. Navigator fills every cell in the table with the specified color, but the border picks up the color of the document background. IE fills the entire table area, including the borders, with the specified color for a more unified effect. When you set background colors for individual cells or rows, it will be displayed the same way on both browsers (although Navigator uses the document background color for empty cells).

Table Troubleshooting

Despite the control they offer over page layout, tables are also notorious for causing major headaches and frustrations. This is partly due to the potential complexity of the code—it's easy to miss one little character that will topple a table like a house of cards. Another source of chaos is that browsers are inconsistent and sometimes quirky in the way they interpret table code. It is not uncommon to spend several careful hours crafting a table that looks perfect in browsers X and Y but crumbles into a little heap in browser Z.

Although not every problem can be anticipated, there are a number of standard places tables tend to go wrong. HTML tables have some inherent peculiarities that can make them frustrating to work with, but knowing about the potential pitfalls up front can make the design process go more smoothly. As always, it is necessary to test your designs on as many browser and platform configurations as possible.

Calculating Table Size

In some instances, your design may require that the dimensions of a table stay fixed at a certain pixel size. Unfortunately, setting the `width` and `height` attributes in the `<table>` tag is not a guarantee that your table will appear at that size when finally rendered. These attributes merely specify a minimum size, but the table will expand as necessary to accommodate its contents.

Tables also expand according to the border, cellpadding, and cellspacing settings, as shown in Figure 13-10. In order to keep a table at its specified size, all of these attributes must be set to zero, and the contents of the cell must fit comfortably within the allotted space (or just set the table dimensions to a size that takes into account your padding and spacing values). Bear in mind, also, that contents such as text or form elements can be unpredictable and may change the size of your table as well, as discussed in the next two sections.

Text in Tables

When designing tables that contain text, remember that text size can vary greatly from user to user. This adds an inherent level of unpredictability to the way your tables display.

Not only does text display larger on PCs than on Macs, each browser user can set the font size for text display. So although you've put a nice, tidy column of options in a table cell, for the user whose font is set to 16 points, the text may get some extra line breaks and change your table's dimensions.

In general, variable text sizes affect the height of cells and tables as the cells stretch longer to accommodate their larger contents (particularly if the width has been specified with an absolute pixel value). If you have HTML text in a cell, particularly if the cell needs to be displayed at specific pixel dimensions within the

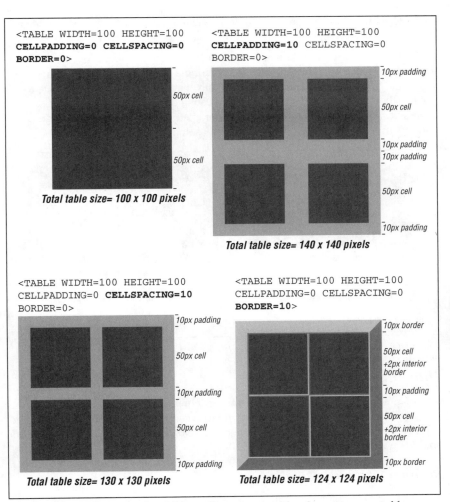

Figure 13-10: Effects of cellpadding, cellspacing, and border settings on table dimensions

table, be sure to give it lots of extra room and test your page with different browser font settings.

If you are using style sheets, you can control the size of the text by setting it to a specific pixel height; bear in mind, however, that many users still use browsers that do not support style sheets. For browsers that do, your pixel settings will override the browser's font size settings, which means that you risk annoying users by forcing text to be smaller than their preferences.

Form Elements in Tables

Like text, the way form elements display in a browser is dependent on the size of the default monospace (or constant width) font that is specified in the user's browser preferences. If the user has his monospace font set to 24 points (or to "largest" in Internet Explorer), your form elements (particularly text fields) will resize larger accordingly.

In the real-world example in Figure 13-11, I used a table to hold together a badge illustration, which contained a form for entering a name and password. In testing, we found that the target audience generally had their browser fonts set to 18 points (they were working on very high-resolution monitors), which caused the form text fields to resize and break the table apart. Making the badge image larger and incorporating lots of extra space was the solution in this case.

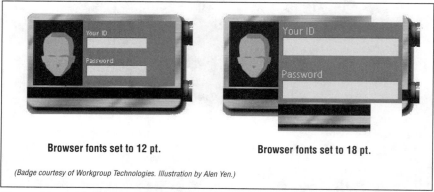

Browser fonts set to 12 pt.   Browser fonts set to 18 pt.

(Badge courtesy of Workgroup Technologies. Illustration by Alen Yen.)

Figure 13-11: The badge with browser fonts set to 12 points and 18 points

Unwanted White Space

It is common for extra white space to creep between table cells (or between the cells and the border). When you are trying to create a seamless effect with colored cells or hold together pieces of a larger image (such as Figure 13-12), this extra space is unacceptable.

Returns and spaces within <td> tags

The problem most often lies within the cell (<td>) tag. Some browsers render any extra space within a <td> tag, such as a character space or a line return, as white space in the table. This can occur when the cell contains text; however, the effect is most noticeable when the contents are images.

 Because <table> and <tr> tags are regarded only as containers for other tags, not as containers for actual content or data, spaces and returns within these tags are ignored.

If you want a seamless table, begin by setting the border, cellpadding, and cellspacing in the <table> tag to zero (0). In the code in Figure 13-12, a graphic is divided into four parts and held together with a table. The goal is to hold the graphic together seamlessly. As shown in the figure, the returns and extra spaces within the <td> tags add white space in each cell.

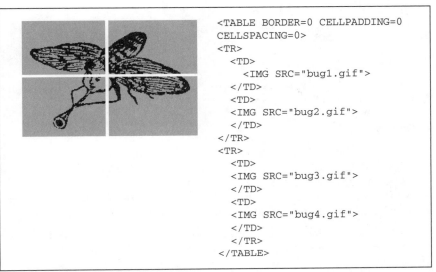

```
<TABLE BORDER=0 CELLPADDING=0
CELLSPACING=0>
<TR>
  <TD>
    <IMG SRC="bug1.gif">
  </TD>
  <TD>
  <IMG SRC="bug2.gif">
  </TD>
</TR>
<TR>
  <TD>
  <IMG SRC="bug3.gif">
  </TD>
  <TD>
  <IMG SRC="bug4.gif">
  </TD>
  </TR>
</TABLE>
```

Figure 13-12: Line breaks within <td> tags add white space to table cells

To keep out unwanted white space, be sure that the enclosing <td> and </td> tags are flush against the content of the cell, with no extra spaces or returns. In Figure 13-13, I've kept the <td> tags and their contents on one line, and the problem goes away.

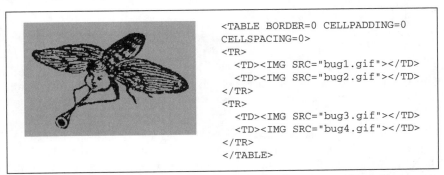

```
<TABLE BORDER=0 CELLPADDING=0
CELLSPACING=0>
<TR>
  <TD><IMG SRC="bug1.gif"></TD>
  <TD><IMG SRC="bug2.gif"></TD>
</TR>
<TR>
  <TD><IMG SRC="bug3.gif"></TD>
  <TD><IMG SRC="bug4.gif"></TD>
</TR>
</TABLE>
```

Figure 13-13: Removing line breaks from table cells creates a seamless table

Missing end tags

In most cases, cell end tags (</td>) are optional, but omitting them may add extra white space to the cell, because the line break to the next starting <td> tag is rendered as extra space.

The following code, in which the </td> tags have been left out, produces extra space (as in Figure 13-12):

```
<TABLE BORDER=0 CELLPADDING=0 CELLSPACING=0>
<TR>
  <TD><IMG SRC="bug1.gif">
```

```
    <TD><IMG SRC="bug2.gif">
<TR>
    <TD><IMG SRC="bug3.gif">
    <TD><IMG SRC="bug4.gif">
</TABLE>
```

For seamless tables, it is necessary to use end tags and keep them flush to the content, as shown in Figure 13-13.

Cellspacing in Navigator

According to the HTML specification, if you set `cellspacing=0` within the `<table>` tag, there should be no extra space between cells. There is a bug in Netscape's table implementation, however, that causes extra space to be added even when the cellspacing is set to 0. To eliminate all extra space for Netscape, you must explicitly include the `border=0` attribute in the `<table>` tag as well.*

The default value of the `border` attribute should be 0, but in Netscape it takes up space (even though it doesn't draw a shaded line) unless you explicitly set it to 0. These problems have been fixed in Netscape 6.

Collapsing Cells in Navigator

As of this writing, all versions of Netscape (even 6) collapse empty cells and do not render a background color in a collapsed cell. For that reason, all cells in a table need to contain *something* in order for it to render properly and with its background color. There are a number of options for filling cells for display in Netscape.

Nonrendering text

Sometimes, adding a simple nonbreaking space (` `) or a single line break (`<br>`) within a cell is enough for the cell to be displayed properly in Navigator. Neither of these text strings renders visibly when the table is displayed in the browser.

Be aware that a nonbreaking space occupies the height and width of a normal text character, even though nothing displays on the page. If you need to fill a very short cell with a specific pixel height, using a nonbreaking space may force the cell to be taller and throw off the dimensions of your table. Try a `<br>` or a single-pixel graphic instead if your table cell dimensions are misbehaving.

The single-pixel trick

Another popular work-around is to place a transparent one-pixel GIF file in the cell and set its width and height dimensions to fill the cell. If you choose this method, be sure to set both the `height` and the `width` attributes. If you set only one, many browsers will resize the image proportionally (into a big square), which may not be appropriate for the table.

---

* This tip taken with permission from *Creative HTML Design*, by Lynda Weinman and William Weinman, published by New Riders Publishing, 1998.

One drawback to this method is that a missing graphic icon will appear in the cell if the graphic doesn't load properly or if the viewer has the graphics turned off in the browser.

Using <spacer>

Table cells can also be held open with a **<spacer>** tag, which is Netscape's proprietary method for adding blank space on a web page. Set the spacer type to "block" and specify the width and height measurements as follows:

```
<TD><SPACER TYPE=block WIDTH=n HEIGHT=n></TD>
```

Although the **<spacer>** tag is Netscape-specific, the whole cell-collapsing problem is Netscape-specific as well, making spacers a good solution in this situation (although they're best avoided for general use). Browsers that don't understand the **<spacer>** element just ignore it, but chances are they won't need it to render the table properly anyway.

Restraining Row Heights

You might guess that the following code would create the table shown in Figure 13-14:

```
<TABLE CELLSPACING=0 CELLPADDING=0 BORDER=1>
<TR>
  <TD ROWSPAN=2><IMG SRC="red.gif"
  WIDTH=50 HEIGHT=150></TD>
  <TD HEIGHT=50><IMG SRC="blue.gif"
  WIDTH=100 HEIGHT=50></TD>
</TR>
<TR>
  <TD ALIGN=center>extra space</TD>
</TR>
</TABLE>
```

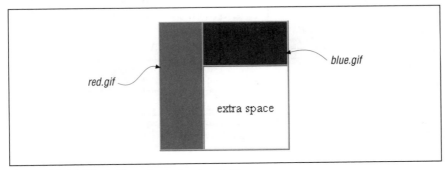

Figure 13-14: The table we're trying to create

However, what actually happens is that the bottom cell shrinks to fit the text it contains, and the cell containing the darker graphic on the right—despite being set to height=50—is stretched vertically, as shown in Figure 13-15.

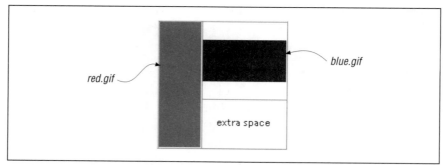

Figure 13-15: The actual result of the code

The problem is that the `height` attribute specifies a minimum, not a maximum, and a row defaults to the height of its tallest cell (determined by either the cell's contents or its height value). That's why the table doesn't work as intended—the text in the last cell isn't tall enough to force the desired effect. Since we can determine the exact height that we want in that last cell (by subtracting the height of *blue.gif* from the column height), giving it a `height=100` attribute will make it the proper height.

If you don't know the exact height—say, because other columns contain text—you may be better off removing the `rowspan` attributes and using a nested table instead (a table within a table). The nested table will size its rows based on their content only.*

Column Span Problems

If you want to create a table with multiple column spans, yet accurately control the width of each column, it is necessary to specify a width for at least one cell in each column. When column spans overlap, it is easy to get unpredictable results.

In order to create the table shown in Figure 13-16, it seems clear that we need a table that is 600 pixels wide with three columns of 200 pixels each. In each row, there is a 400-pixel-wide graphic that should straddle neatly over two columns.

Figure 13-16: The target layout: getting two graphics to span two columns

---

* This tip courtesy of Builder.com. It first appeared in the Builder.com article "Advanced HTML Tips," by Paul Anderson. It is reprinted here with permission of Builder.com and CNET. See *http://builder.com/Authoring/AdvHtml/index.html* for the complete article.

The first (failed) attempt at coding set the table to a specific width and provided column spans for the graphics, as shown in the following code:

```
<TABLE BORDER=1 CELLPADDING=0 CELLSPACING=0 WIDTH=600 BGCOLOR="#FFFFFF">
<TR>
    <TD COLSPAN=2><IMG SRC="2col.gif" ALIGN=top WIDTH="400"
        HEIGHT="50" BORDER="0"></TD>
    <TD ALIGN=center>width<BR>(should be 200 pixels)</TD>
</TR>
<TR>
    <TD ALIGN=center>width<br>(should be 200 pixels)
    </TD>
    <TD COLSPAN=2><IMG SRC="2col.gif" ALIGN=TOP WIDTH="400"
        HEIGHT="50" BORDER="0"></TD>
</TR>
</TABLE>
```

This code, however, doesn't give the browser enough information, particularly about the width of the center column, to accurately render the table. The unsuccessful result of this first code attempt is shown in Figure 13-17. The problem is that the center column is not defined anywhere.

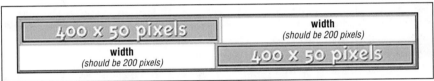

Figure 13-17: The result: middle column was not defined

The solution

The solution in this case, because the middle cell is eaten up by column spans in both rows, is to create a dummy row (shown in bold) that specifies an absolute width for all three columns as intended (200-pixels each). This row will not render in the browser because its height is set to 0, but it is enough to tell the browser what to do. Use this dummy row method when you have a table without any rows with all its cells intact.*

The following code produces the desired effect on all browsers that support tables—and on all platforms.

```
<TABLE BORDER=1 CELLPADDING=0 CELLSPACING=0 WIDTH=600 BGCOLOR="#FFFFFF">
<TR>
    <TD WIDTH="200" HEIGHT="0"></TD>
    <TD WIDTH="200" HEIGHT="0"></TD>
    <TD WIDTH="200" HEIGHT="0"></TD>
</TR>
```

---

* This tip is courtesy of Builder.com and appeared in the Builder.com article "Advanced HTML Tips," by Paul Anderson. It is reprinted here with permission of Builder.com and CNET. See *http://builder.com/Authoring/AdvHtml/index.html* for the complete article. The solution shown here was submitted by Steven Masters.

```
<TR>
    <TD colspan=2 WIDTH="400"><IMG SRC="2col.gif" WIDTH="400"
    HEIGHT="50" BORDER="0"></TD>
    <TD WIDTH="200" ALIGN=CENTER>width<BR>(should be 200
    pixels)</TD>
</TR>
<TR>
    <TD WIDTH="200" ALIGN=center>width<br>(should be 200
    pixels)</TD>
    <TD colspan=2 WIDTH="400"><IMG SRC="2col.gif" WIDTH="400"
    HEIGHT="50" BORDER="0"></TD>
</TR>
</TABLE>
```

Tips and Tricks

This section provides a few tricks of the trade for working with tables.

<font> and Tables

Unfortunately, placing <font> tags around a table will not affect the font of all the text contained within the table. You need to repeat the <font> tag and its attributes around the content in every cell of the table. For complex tables with lots of cells, the repetitive <font> tags can actually add significantly to the size of the HTML file (not to mention the visual clutter).

Cascading style sheets are the proper and much more efficient way to apply style information to the contents of a table. They result in smaller files and make life much easier when you need to make changes to the design.

Waiting for Tables to Display

Using the basic table tags, the browser must wait until the entire contents of a table have downloaded before it can begin rendering the page. Any text and graphics *outside* the table display quickly while the browser works on the table.

You can use this phenomenon to your advantage by placing elements you want your viewers to see first outside the table (can anybody say "banner ads"?).

Note that careful use of row and column groups can give the browser enough information to display the contents of the table incrementally, before all the data has downloaded.

Baseline Alignment Trick

If you want to align the first lines of text by their baselines across a row, you should be able to use valign=baseline; in reality, this setting is too unpredictable across browsers to be used reliably. A trick for achieving the same result is to add to each first line a nonbreaking space ( ) that is set the same size as the largest character. That way, you can set valign=top, and the baselines will all line up.

First look at simple top alignment. As shown in Figure 13-18, the top of the text is aligned, but the baselines are off. By adding a nonbreaking space at the larger text size (in bold), the baselines align neatly, as shown in Figure 13-19.*

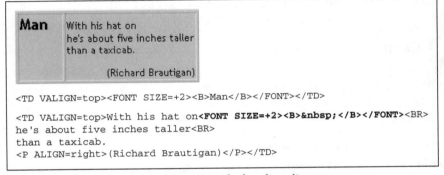

```
<TD VALIGN=top><FONT SIZE=+2><B>Man</B></FONT></TD>

<TD VALIGN=top>With his hat on<BR>
he's about five inches taller<BR>
than a taxicab.
<P ALIGN=right>(Richard Brautigan)</P></TD>
```

Figure 13-18: With top alignment, the baselines of the text don't line up

```
<TD VALIGN=top><FONT SIZE=+2><B>Man</B></FONT></TD>

<TD VALIGN=top>With his hat on<FONT SIZE=+2><B> </B></FONT><BR>
he's about five inches taller<BR>
than a taxicab.
<P ALIGN=right>(Richard Brautigan)</P></TD>
```

Figure 13-19: With a nonbreaking space, the baselines line up

Rowspans Made Easy

HTML 3.2 specifies that if a cell's `colspan` implies more columns than have been created up to that point in the table, the browser should create the additional columns. With `rowspan`, however, the specification states that browsers shouldn't create any extra rows. The existing browsers follow both these rules.

So if you have a cell that spans vertically to the bottom of the table, past rows that might vary in number or are too numerous to easily count, just give it a `rowspan` that you know is excessively high.

In Figure 13-20, we've set `rowspan` to 99. Even though there are only seven rows in the actual table, browsers won't generate any extra rows.

---

* This and the following tip are courtesy of Builder.com and first appeared in the Builder.com article "Advanced HTML Tips," by Paul Anderson. It is reprinted here with permission of Builder.com and CNET. See *http://builder.com/Authoring/AdvHtml/index.html* for the complete article.

```
<TABLE BGCOLOR="#ffff99" BORDER=1>
 <TR>
  <TD WIDTH=10 ROWSPAN=99
   BGCOLOR="#cc3333"> </TD>
  <TD>It</TD></TR>
 <TR><TD>doesn t</TD></TR>
 <TR><TD>matter</TD></TR>
 <TR><TD>how</TD></TR>
 <TR><TD>many</TD></TR>
 <TR><TD>rows</TD></TR>
 <TR><TD>are</TD></TR>
 <TR><TD>here</TD></TR>
</TABLE>
```

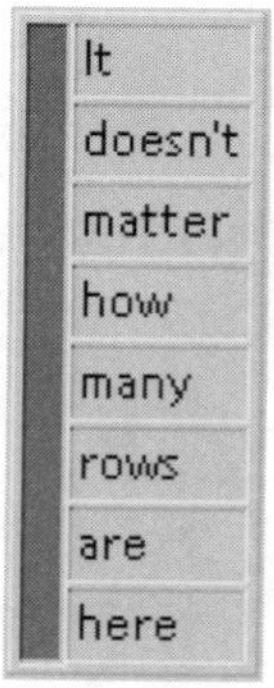

| It |
| doesn't |
| matter |
| how |
| many |
| rows |
| are |
| here |

Figure 13-20: The table contains only the actual number of rows needed

Standard Table Templates

Ever look at a table and wonder, "How'd they do that?" This section provides templates that give you shortcuts for creating standard table effects.

A Simple Announcement Box

Figure 13-21 depicts a simple one-cell table containing text. By setting the background to a bright color, it can be used as an effective attention-getting device for a special announcement. It could also be used as an alternative to a graphical headline for a page. By using the align attribute in the <table> tag, you can position the table along the left or right margin and allow text to wrap around it, making a nice space for a sidebar or callout.

You can use width and height attributes to make the bar any size. Try playing with the border and cell padding for different effects. Remember, placing the bgcolor within the cell will render differently than placing it in the <table> tag in Internet Explorer, so experiment and test to see what you like the best. Note that because height is a nonstandard attribute, it may not work in all browsers (including Version 6 browsers operating in "strict" rendering mode). 

headline or announcement!!

```
<TABLE BGCOLOR="#CCFF99" BORDER=2 CELLPADDING=12 CELLSPACING=0>
<TR>
   <TD ALIGN=center VALIGN=middle>headline or announcement!!</TD>
</TR>
</TABLE>
```

Figure 13-21: Announcement box

Centering an Object in the Browser Window

The table in the following code can be used to center an object in a browser window regardless of how the window is resized (as shown in Figure 13-22). It uses a single cell table with its size set to 100%, then centers the object horizontally and vertically in the cell.

```
<HTML>
<BODY>
<TABLE WIDTH=100% HEIGHT=100% BORDER=0 CELLSPACING=0 CELLPADDING=0>
<TR>
    <TD align=center valign=middle>your object here</TD>
</TR>
</TABLE>
</BODY>
</HTML>
```

Figure 13-22: Centering an object

Creating a Vertical Rule

This sample table creates a vertical rule between columns that resizes with the height of the table. The trick is to create an extra column only one pixel wide (or the desired thickness of the vertical rule) and fill it with a background color. This cell is indicated in bold. The result is shown in Figure 13-23.

The cell cannot be totally empty or it will collapse in Navigator and its background color won't display, so I've added a `<br>`. For this to display correctly, the cell padding must remain at zero, or the 1-pixel wide column will plump up with extra space. Add space between columns with the `cellspacing` attribute instead.

Creating a Box Rule

Although Microsoft Internet Explorer recognizes the proprietary `bordercolor`, `bordercolorlight`, and `bordercolordark` attributes, there is no method for specifying border colors using standard HTML for all browsers.

```
                          this

                          is

                          some

                          content

        <TABLE BORDER="0" CELLPADDING="0"  CELLSPACING="10">
        <TR ALIGN="LEFT" VALIGN="TOP">
           <TD WIDTH="50"><BR></TD>
           <TD WIDTH="1" BGCOLOR="darkred"><BR></TD>
           <TD>
              <P>this
              <P>is
              <P>some
              <P>content
           </TD>
        </TR>
        </TABLE>
```

Figure 13-23: A vertical rule that resizes with the depth of the table

To create a colored rule around a box of text using standard HTML, place one table within another as shown in Figure 13-24. To nest tables, place the entire contents of one table within a `<td>` of the other.

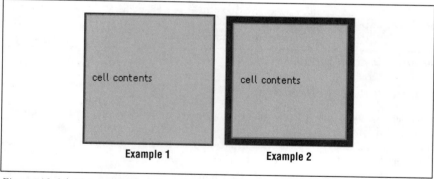

Figure 13-24: Two examples of creating box rules with nested tables

In Example 1 in Figure 13-24, cell width and height are set in the interior table. In the exterior table, a cell padding of 0 results in a one-pixel rule around the table. You can increase the thickness of the rule by increasing the `cellpadding` value. Note, however, that this will also increase the overall dimensions of the table. The color of the rule is specified by the `bgcolor` attribute in the `<table>` tag for the exterior table:

```
        <TABLE CELLPADDING=0 BORDER=0>
        <TR>
           <TD BGCOLOR="#333333" ALIGN=center VALIGN=center>
              <TABLE BORDER=0 WIDTH=200 HEIGHT=200 CELLPADDING=10>
```

```
        <TR><TD BGCOLOR="#999999">cell contents</TD></TR>
        </TABLE>
    </TD>
  </TR>
  </TABLE>
```

In Example 2 in Figure 13-24, to restrict the dimensions of the table, set specific dimensions for the exterior table and set the dimensions of the interior table slightly smaller (to a difference twice the desired rule thickness). In this example, the desired rule thickness is 10, so the interior table's dimensions are 20 pixels less than the exterior table's dimensions.

```
<TABLE WIDTH=200 HEIGHT=200 cellpadding=0 border=0>
<TR>
    <TD BGCOLOR="#333333" ALIGN=center VALIGN=center>
        <TABLE BORDER=0 WIDTH=180 HEIGHT=180 CELLPADDING=10>
        <TR><TD BGCOLOR="#999999">cell contents</TD></TR>
        </TABLE>
    </TD>
  </TR>
  </TABLE>
```

Two-Column Page Layouts

Many sites use a two-column table to lay out the structure of their pages. This grid creates a narrow column on the left for navigational options and a wider column on the right for the page's contents, as shown in Figure 13-25. These sample tables can be used to provide a basic structure to the page; you can place any elements (including other tables) within either table cell to create more complex layouts.

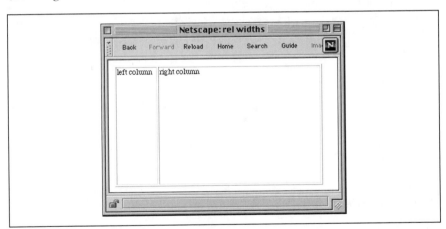

Figure 13-25: Typical two-column layout

First, a word about browser margins

When using a table to lay out the structure of a page, bear in mind that it will be placed in the page against the normal browser margins, not flush against the top and left edge of the browser window. The width of the margin varies from browser to browser (and platform to platform), but it generally ranges from 8 to 12 pixels. You should take this blank space into account when choosing measurements for your table and its column widths.

Getting rid of the browser margins for both Netscape Navigator and Microsoft Internet Explorer requires using redundant margin attributes in the <body> tag as shown here:

```
<BODY MARGINWIDTH=0 MARGINHEIGHT=0 LEFTMARGIN=0 TOPMARGIN=0>
```

If you are using style sheets, add the following rule:

```
BODY { margin:0; padding:0;}
```

Fixed-width columns

If it's predictability and control you're after, fixing the width of your table and its columns is the way to go. As long as the contents fit in the cells entirely, the table will hold its dimensions regardless of browser window size. If contents (such as graphics) are wider than the cell, the cell will usually expand to accommodate them.

Of course, you can change the specific width values to any pixel value you choose, but it is important that the total of the cell widths equals the width set for the entire table. If the values are different, browsers maintain the width setting for the table and resize all the columns proportionately within the allotted space. As a result, none of the column widths will display at the number of pixels you specified.

Note that the border in each of the following examples has been set to 1, but you can change it to any other value. Starting with the border set to 1 (as shown in Figure 13-25) makes it easier to see how the table is behaving. Once you get the table working properly, get rid of the border by setting the value to 0.

```
<HTML>
<BODY>
<TABLE BORDER=1 WIDTH=600>
<TR>
    <TD VALIGN=top WIDTH=150>left column</TD>
    <TD VALIGN=top WIDTH=450>right column</TD>
</TR>
</TABLE>
</BODY>
</HTML>
```

Relative column widths

Using relative values for the width of your table allows your page to resize itself to fill the width of the browser window. Many designers prefer this method because it is more flexible and suits any monitor configuration. Although the actual column widths will change when the browser window resizes (and their contents will rewrap), they will remain in proportion to one another.

Again, you can turn the border off by setting the value to zero. You may change the width values for the cell in each column, but be sure that they total 100%.

```
<HTML>
<BODY>
<TABLE BORDER=1 WIDTH=100%>
<TR>
    <TD VALIGN=top WIDTH=20%>left column</TD>
    <TD VALIGN=top WIDTH=80%>right column</TD>
</TR>
</TABLE>
</BODY>
</HTML>
```

Combination

At times, you may want to restrict the width of the left column but allow the right column to resize with the page—if you want the contents of the left column to stay aligned over a colored background image, for instance. Set the width of the left column to any pixel value you choose and do not specify a width for the right column.

This technique is not guaranteed to keep the width of the "fixed" column at its specified width. If the browser window is resized to be very narrow, the fixed column will be resized smaller and its contents will wrap.

```
<HTML>
<BODY>
<TABLE BORDER=1 WIDTH=100%>
<TR>
    <TD VALIGN=top WIDTH=150>left column</TD>
    <TD VALIGN=top>right column</TD>
</TR>
</TABLE>
</BODY>
</HTML>
```

The trick for maintaining a minimum width for a column is to place a graphic element in a cell that is sized to the desired column width. Some developers use a 1-pixel square graphic that is stretched using the width attribute.

Multipart Images in Tables

There are a number of reasons why you may want to slice a large image into pieces and use a table to reconstruct it seamlessly on a web page:

Rollovers
> If you want portions of the image—but not the whole image—to respond to the mouse passing over them (mouseover events or rollovers), it is more efficient to swap out just the bits that change instead of replacing the whole image. Rollover effects are created with JavaScript. See Chapter 28 for sample code.

Animations
> Similarly, if you want to add animation to small areas within an image, it is better to break up the image and animate just the portions that move. This will result in smaller files to download.

Better Optimization

At times, you may find that an image contains distinct areas of flat color and distinct areas of soft or photographic images. Breaking the image into sections allows you to save some sections as GIF (the flat color areas) and others as JPEG (for graduated tones), to achieve better optimization and image quality overall. For more information on optimizing images, see Chapters 19 and 20.

Imagemaps

Break the image into separated linked images instead of using an imagemap. This allows alternative text (using the `alt` attribute) to be added for each linked section of the image (instead of a single `alt` message for the whole imagemap). This makes the page more accessible for people using non-graphical or speech-based browsers.

In Figure 13-26, I've divided an image into sections so I can save the television image as a JPEG and the rest as GIFs (since they are flat, graphical images). It also allows me to swap out the television image based on rollovers elsewhere on the page. The table on the right has its border set to 1 to reveal the individual graphics that make up the image. When the border is set to zero, the effect is seamless, as shown on the left.

Figure 13-26: A multipart image held together by a table

Slicing and Dicing Tools

Multipart images in tables have been growing in popularity in recent years. Not surprisingly, software companies have responded with tools that make the production process much easier than the previously discussed method of splitting the graphic manually and writing the table code in an HTML editor. (This manual method is outlined a little later.)

Macromedia Fireworks, Adobe Photoshop 6.0, and Adobe ImageReady (all available for both Windows and Mac) include functions that slice up an image, export the individually numbered graphics (based on the position of guidelines), and automatically write the table code that holds them all together.

You can then just copy and paste the table code into your HTML file. One caution: you will need to adjust the pathnames if your graphics are to reside in a different directory from your HTML files. The automatically generated code writes relative pathnames assuming everything will be in the same directory. A simple find-and-replace in your HTML file should take care of this quickly.

Macromedia Fireworks

Fireworks makes its slicing tool available in the Toolbox. These are the basic steps for creating a sliced image and its accompanying HTML file:

1. Create or open your image. Using the Slice tool from the Toolbox palette, define rectangular segments of the image. Note that if you place a rectangular slice in the middle of a graphic, Fireworks automatically slices the remainder of the image into the fewest number of segments to contain the specified slice.

2. To set the default export settings (file format, bit depth, color palette, dithering, etc.) for the entire image, you must be sure that no slicing objects are selected, then adjust the settings in the Optimize palette. These settings will be applied to all slices after exporting.

3. You can override the default export settings for an individual slice—for instance, to reduce its palette, or to make it a different file format. Select the slice object, then adjust its properties in the Optimize palette (the word "slice" appears in the top bar when a slice is selected).

4. Once you have your slices chosen and configured, export the file by selecting File → Export. In the Export dialog box, select "Use Slice Objects" from the Slicing pop-up menu and set a base name for the graphics (Fireworks names them automatically based on the name you provide). You can also set a target directory for the files.

5. When you click Export, Fireworks creates all the graphic files and the HTML file for the sliced image. You can now copy the table code from the generated HTML file and paste it into your final document (be sure that the pathnames are correct).

For more information about Fireworks, see *http://www.macromedia.com/software/fireworks*.

Adobe ImageReady

ImageReady is a tool for advanced web graphics production that comes bundled with Photoshop Versions 5.5 and higher. The process for creating a sliced image in ImageReady is nearly the same as the one described for Fireworks.

1. Open the source image. Select Slices → Show Slices to make the Slices layer visible. You may also want to use guidelines to help control your selections. Use the Slice tool (it looks like a little knife) to outline the important elements in your design. When a slice is selected, its image appears in the Slice palette.

2. With the Slices layer turned off, you can use the Optimize palette to make export settings (file format, number of colors, etc.) for the entire image. You can override these settings for a particular slice by selecting it with the Slice Selection tool, then making adjustments in the Optimize palette.

3. When you are ready, save the file using File → Save Optimized. This gives you a dialog box where you can choose to have ImageReady save the images and the HTML file. Click the Options buttons next to each selection to access other relative options. For an explanation of these options, see the ImageReady manual. When you are ready, click Save.

Adobe Photoshop 6

Photoshop 6 is the first Photoshop release to feature slicing functions (slicing was delegated to ImageReady in previous versions). As with ImageReady, you can create slices using a special slicing tool from the toolbar. Adobe calls slices created with the slicing tool "user-slices." Photoshop will also generate slices based on pixel information in a layer (called "layer-slices").

This is particularly useful for making rollover buttons. Place the rollover element on a separate layer and create a slice from that layer (select "New Layer Based Slice" from the Layer menu). If you apply an effect to the layer that changes the pixel dimensions (such as a glow or a drop shadow), the layer-slice automatically resizes to encompass the new pixels.

Producing Images in Tables Manually

If you don't have Fireworks or the latest version of Photoshop, it's certainly possible to create the effect by hand. First, divide the image into separate graphic files using an image processor such as Paint Shop Pro or Photoshop 4 (used in the following example). Photoshop 5.5 and higher comes with a copy of ImageReady that does the work for you. Then write the HTML for the table using whichever HTML editor you like. These methods are demonstrated in the following sections.

Dividing the image (in Photoshop 4.0)

When dividing an image with Photoshop, it is important to set the guide preferences in a way that enables easy and accurate selections without redundant or overlapping pixels between image sections. This is described in steps 2 and 3.

1. Open the image in Photoshop. Make sure the rulers are visible by selecting View → Show Rulers.

2. Set your preferences to use pixels as the unit of measurement by selecting File → Preferences → Units & Rulers. Select "pixels" from the pop-up menu and hit OK.

3. Select View → Snap to Guides. This will snap your selection to the precise location of the guide.

4. Use the rectangle marquee (make sure feathering and anti-aliasing options are turned off) to select each area of the image (Figure 13-27). You can use the Info palette (Window → Show Info) to get accurate pixel measurements for each section as you select it. You'll need this information when you create the HTML file.

5. Copy and paste each section into a new file (Figure 13-27). Flatten the image and save it as a GIF or JPEG. You may want to develop a numbered naming scheme to keep the pieces organized.

Figure 13-27: Splitting up an image with Photoshop

Creating the table in HTML

Following is the HTML code that is used to hold together the image from Figures 13-26 and 13-27:

```
<TABLE BORDER="0" CELLPADDING="0" CELLSPACING="0" WIDTH="333">
  <TR>
  <TD><IMG SRC="part_1.gif" WIDTH="56" HEIGHT="92" BORDER="0"></TD>
  <TD><IMG SRC="part_2.gif" WIDTH="169" HEIGHT="92" BORDER="0"></TD>
  <TD><IMG SRC="part_3.gif" WIDTH="108" HEIGHT="92" BORDER="0"></TD>
  </TR>
  <TR>
  <TD><IMG SRC="part_4.gif" WIDTH="56" HEIGHT="133" BORDER="0"></TD>
  <TD><IMG SRC="part_5.gif" WIDTH="169" HEIGHT="133" BORDER="0"></TD>
  <TD><IMG SRC="part_6.gif" WIDTH="108" HEIGHT="133" BORDER="0"></TD>
  </TR>
  <TR>
  <TD><IMG SRC="part_7.gif" WIDTH="56" HEIGHT="82" BORDER="0"></TD>
  <TD><IMG SRC="part_8.gif" WIDTH="169" HEIGHT="82" BORDER="0"></TD>
  <TD><IMG SRC="part_9.gif" WIDTH="108" HEIGHT="82" BORDER="0"></TD>
  </TR>
</TABLE>
```

There is no difference between writing a table for piecing together graphics and writing any other kind of table; however, pay careful attention to the following settings if you want the image to piece back together seamlessly on all browsers:

- In the <table> tag, set the following attributes to zero: border=0, cellpadding=0, cellspacing=0.

- In the <table> tag, specify the width of the table with an absolute pixel value. Be sure that the value is exactly the total of the widths of the component images. You may also add the `height` attribute for thoroughness' sake, but it is not required.

- Don't put extra spaces or line returns between the `<td>` and the `<img>` tags (extra space within `<td>`s causes extra space to appear when the image is rendered). Keep them flush together on one line. If you must break the line, break it somewhere within the `<img>` tag.

- Set the `width` and `height` values in pixels for every image. Be sure that the measurements are accurate.

- Set `border=0` for every image.

- Specify the `width` and `height` pixel values for every cell in the table, particularly if it contains `colspans` and `rowspans`. Be sure that they match the pixel values set in the `<img>` tag and the actual pixel dimensions of the graphic. For simple grid-like tables (such as the one in Figure 13-26), you may not need to give individual cell dimensions because the enclosed images will force each cell to the proper dimensions.

- If your table has a lot of column spans, be sure there is at least one row with all its cells intact so you can declare the width of every column in the table. If there are no intact rows, add a dummy row (as described in "Column Span Problems" earlier in this chapter) to ensure the image segments line up correctly.

- Sometimes it is preferable to keep the table simple. For instance, the sample graphic could have been divided into just five portions (a top graphic, three middle graphics, and a bottom graphic) and held together with a table made up of three rows with a single cell each. These decisions are a matter of judgment and obviously depend on the individual project.

CHAPTER 14

Frames

Frames are a method for dividing the browser window into smaller subwindows, each displaying a different HTML document. This chapter covers the structure and creation of framed documents, controls for affecting their display and function, and some advanced tips and tricks.

Summary of Frame Tags

In this section, browser support for each tag is noted to the right of the tag name. Browsers that do not support the tag are grayed out. Tag usage is indicated below the tag name. Start and end tags are required unless otherwise noted. "Deprecated" means that the tag or attribute is currently supported but is due to be phased out of the HTML specification and is discouraged from use (usually in favor of similar style sheet controls). "Nonstandard" indicates that the attribute is not part of the HTML specification, but is supported by the major browsers. The attributes listed for each tag reflect those in common use. See "WebTV and Frames" at the end of this chapter for information on WebTV's special handling of framed documents.

A more thorough listing of attributes for each tag, according to the HTML 4.01 specification, appears in Appendix A.

\<frame>	NN 2, 3, 4, 6 MSIE 2, 3, 4, 5, 5.5, 6 HTML 4.01 WebTV Opera5

\<frame> *(no end tag)*

Defines a single frame within a \<frameset>.

Attributes

bordercolor="#*rrggbb*" *or color name*
    Nonstandard. Sets the color for frame's borders (if the border is turned on). Support for this attribute is limited to Netscape Navigator 3.0+ and Internet Explorer 4.0+.

frameborder=1|0 *(IE 3+ and W3C 4.0 Spec.)*; yes|no *(NN 3+ and IE 4.0+)*

Determines whether there is a 3-D separator drawn between the current frame and surrounding frames. A value of 1 (or **yes**) turns the border on. A value of 0 (or **no**) turns the border off. The default value is 1 (border on). You may also set the frameborder at the frameset level, which may be more reliable.

Because Netscape and Internet Explorer support different values, you need to specify the frameborder twice within <frame> to ensure full browser compatibility, as follows:

```
frameborder=yes frameborder=1 ...
```

longdesc=*url*

Specifies a link to a document containing a long description of the frame and its contents. This addition to the HTML 4.01 specification may be useful for nonvisual web browsers, but it is currently not well supported.

marginwidth=*number*

Specifies the amount of space (in pixels) between the left and right edges of the frame and its contents. The minimum value according to the HTML specification is 1 pixel. Setting the value to 0 in order to place objects flush against the edge of the frame works in Internet Explorer, but Netscape will still display a 1-pixel margin space.

marginheight=*number*

Specifies the amount of space (in pixels) between the top and bottom edges of the frame and its contents. The minimum value according to the HTML specification is 1 pixel. Setting the value to 0 in order to place objects flush against the edge of the frame works in Internet Explorer, but Netscape will still display a 1-pixel margin space.

name=*text*

Assigns a name to the frame. This name may be referenced by targets within links to make the target document load within the named frame.

noresize

Prevents users from resizing the frame. By default, despite specific frame size settings, users can resize a frame by clicking and dragging its borders.

scrolling=yes|no|auto

Specifies whether scrollbars appear in the frame. A value of **yes** means scrollbars always appear; a value of **no** means scrollbars never appear; a value of **auto** (the default) means scrollbars appear automatically when the contents do not fit within the frame.

src=*url*

Specifies the location of the initial HTML file to be displayed by the frame.

<frameset>

NN 2, 3, 4, 6   MSIE 2, 3, 4, 5, 5.5, 6   HTML 4.01   WebTV   Opera5

<frameset>...</frameset>

Defines a collection of frames or other framesets.

Attributes

`border=number`
    Nonstandard. Sets frame border thickness (in pixels) between all the frames in a frameset (when the frame border is turned on).

`bordercolor="#rrggbb"` *or* `color name`
    Nonstandard. Sets a border color for all the borders in a frameset. Support for this attribute is limited to Netscape Navigator 3.0 and higher and Internet Explorer 4.0.

`cols=list of lengths (number, percentage, or *)`
    Establishes the number and sizes of columns (vertical frames) in a frameset. The number of columns is determined by the number of values in the list. Size specifications can be in absolute pixel values, percentage values, or relative values (*) based on available space.

`frameborder=1|0` *(IE 3+);* `yes|no` *(NN 3+ and IE 4.0+)*
    Nonstandard. Determines whether 3-D separators are drawn between frames in the frameset. A value of 1 (or **yes**) turns the borders on; 0 (or **no**) turns the borders off.

    Because Netscape and Internet Explorer support different values, you may need to specify the frameborder twice within `<frameset>` to ensure cross-browser compatibility, as follows:

```
frameborder=yes frameborder=1 ...
```

`framespacing=number` *(IE only)*
    Internet 3.0 and higher only. Adds additional space (in pixels) between adjacent frames.

`rows=list of lengths (number, percentage, or *)`
    Establishes the number and size of rows (horizontal frames) in the frameset. The number of rows is determined by the number of values in the list. Size specifications can be in absolute pixel values, percentage values, or relative values (*) based on available space.

`<iframe>`
NN 2, 3, 4, 6   MSIE 2, 3, 4, 5, 5.5, 6   HTML 4.01   WebTV   Opera5

`<iframe> ... </iframe>`

Defines an inline (floating) frame within a document with similar placement tags to `<img>`. This element requires a closing tag. Any content contained within the `<iframe>` tags will display on browsers that do not support inline frames.

Attributes

`align=top|middle|bottom|left|right`
    Aligns the inline frame on the page within the flow of the text. Left and right alignment allows text to flow around the inline frame.

`frameborder=1|0`
    Turns on or off the displaying of a 3-D border for the inline frame. The default is 1, which displays the border.

height=*number*
> Specifies the height of the inline frame in pixels or as a percentage of the window size. Internet Explorer and Navigator use a default height of 150 pixels.

hspace=*number*
> *Nonstandard.* Used in conjunction with left and right alignment, this attribute specifies the amount of space (in pixels) to hold clear to the left and right of the inline frame.

longdesc=*url*
> Specifies a link to a document containing a long description of the inline frame and its contents. This addition to the HTML 4.01 specification may be useful for nonvisual web browsers.

marginheight=*number*
> Specifies the amount of space (in pixels) between the top and bottom edges of the inline frame and its contents.

marginwidth=*number*
> Specifies the amount of space (in pixels) between the left and right edges of the inline frame and its contents.

name=*text*
> Assigns a name to the inline frame to be referenced by targeted links.

scrolling=yes|no|auto
> Determines whether scrollbars appear in the inline frame (see the explanation of this attribute in **<frame>**, earlier in this chapter).

src=*url*
> Specifies the URL of the HTML document to display initially in the inline frame.

vspace=*number*
> *Nonstandard.* Used in conjunction with left and right alignment, this attribute specifies the amount of space (in pixels) to hold clear above and below the inline frame.

width=*number*
> Specifies the width of the inline frame in pixels or as a percentage of the window size. Internet Explorer and Navigator use a default width of 300 pixels.

<noframes> NN 2, 3, 4, 6   MSIE 2, 3, 4, 5, 5.5, 6   HTML 4.01   WebTV   Opera5

<noframes> ... </noframes>

Defines content to be displayed by browsers that cannot display frames. Browsers that do support frames ignore the content between <noframes> tags.

Introduction to Frames

Frames allow you to divide the browser window into smaller subwindows, each of which displays a different HTML document. Introduced by Netscape Navigator 2.0, frame support was soon added by other popular browsers. The basic frame specification works with Netscape Navigator 2.0 and higher as well as Microsoft Internet Explorer 3.0 and higher. As of this writing, frames have found their way into the World Wide Web Consortium's HTML 4.01 specification.

Despite the advanced navigational functionality that frames offer, they do present certain problems and peculiarities that have lead to their currently controversial status. In fact, they've become so notorious that it is not uncommon for web developers to encounter clients who, despite not knowing a lick of HTML themselves, strongly proclaim, "No frames!" at the beginning of a project.

Like most things, frames are neither all good nor all bad. It is your responsibility to be familiar with both sides of the coin so you can help present the best solution for your clients' needs.

Advantages

Consider these advantages to using frames:

- The main advantage to frames is that they enable parts of the page to remain stationary while other parts scroll. This is useful for elements you may not want to scroll out of view, such as navigational options or banner advertising.

- Frames unify resources that reside on separate servers. For instance, you may use frames to combine your own material (and navigation graphics) with threaded discussion material generated by software on a vendor's server.

- With the <noframes> tag, you can easily add alternative content for browsers that do not support frames. This degradability is built into the frames system.

Disadvantages

Also keep in mind these disadvantages:

- Frames are not supported by some browsers. (<noframes> may address this problem.)

- Frames may make site production more complicated because you need to produce and organize multiple files to fill one page.

- Navigating through a framed site may be prohibitively challenging for some users (especially users with disabilities who are using alternative browsing devices).

- Documents nested in a frameset may be more difficult to bookmark. Bookmarks identify only the top-level framed document in its initial state; there is currently no way to track the states of a frameset and therefore no way to bookmark individual states. There are workarounds in 4.0 browsers, however, such as opening the contents of the frame in a new window and bookmarking that page.

- A large number of frames on a page may significantly increase the load on the server because so much of the load on a server is initial document requests. Four requests for 1K files (the frameset and the contents of three frames) is more work for your server than a single request for a 4K document.

- Framed documents can be a nuisance for search engines. Content-level documents may be missed in searches. If a contained document is found by a search engine, it will probably be displayed out of context of its frameset, potentially losing important navigational options. For more information on searching framed documents, see "Helping Search Engines" later in this chapter.

- It is more difficult to track actual page (or ad) impressions when the pages are part of a framed document.

That said, let's look at how framed documents are constructed.

Basic Frameset Structure

A web page that is divided into frames is held together by a top-level *frameset* document.

Frameset documents are fundamentally different from other HTML documents in that they use the `<frameset>` element instead of a `<body>` element. The frameset element may not contain any content, but instead it defines and names some number of frames, arranged in rows and/or columns. Each frame is indicated with a `<frame>` tag within the `<frameset>`. A frameset document contains a standard header portion (as indicated with the `<head>` tag).

Figure 14-1 shows the structure of a basic frameset document that creates two frames, occupying two columns of equal width.

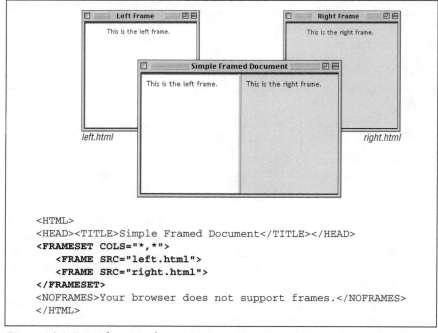

```
<HTML>
<HEAD><TITLE>Simple Framed Document</TITLE></HEAD>
<FRAMESET COLS="*,*">
   <FRAME SRC="left.html">
   <FRAME SRC="right.html">
</FRAMESET>
<NOFRAMES>Your browser does not support frames.</NOFRAMES>
</HTML>
```

Figure 14-1: Basic frameset document

The contents of framed documents come from separate HTML files that are displayed within each frame. For example, in Figure 14-1, the content that appears in the left frame is a standard HTML file called *left.html*. The samples throughout this chapter reference simple HTML documents similar to *left.html*, shown here:

```
<HTML>
<HEAD><TITLE>Left Frame Contents</TITLE></HEAD>
<BODY BGCOLOR="white">
This is the left frame.
</BODY>
</HTML>
```

At the *frameset* level (i.e., within the `<frameset>` opening tag), you establish the rows and columns and decide if you want borders to display between the frames (borders are discussed later in this chapter.)

At the *frame* level (within the `<frame>` tag), you identify the URL of the document to display in that frame and give the frame a name for future reference. You also have control over whether the frame has scrollbars, whether it can be resized by the user, and what its margins should be (if any). Each of these controls are discussed later in this chapter.

<noframes> content

Frameset documents should also have content contained within the optional `<noframes>` tag. Browsers that do not understand frames display the contents within `<noframes>` as though it were normal text. For instance, in nonframes browsers, the document in Figure 14-1 would simply display the text "Your browser does not support frames."

To treat the alternative content like a regular document, you may include the `<body>...</body>` tags within `<noframes>` (although, technically, it is not kosher HTML coding). This allows you to specify attributes such as document background color and text color for the page.

Establishing Rows and Columns

Rows (horizontal frames) and columns (vertical frames) are established within the `<frameset>` tag, using the `rows` and `cols` attributes, respectively. These attributes divide the frameset in a grid-like manner. Frames are filled from left to right for columns and from top to bottom for rows.

The size of each row (or column) is specified in a quote-enclosed, comma-separated list of values after the attribute. The number of values listed determines the number of rows (or columns). Figure 14-2 shows the most simple division of a framed document into two equal-sized rows (on the left) and columns (right).

Specifying sizes

Frame size can be listed in one of three ways:

Absolute pixel values
  The browser interprets an integer as an absolute pixel value. The frameset `<frameset cols="150,450">` creates two columns, one exactly 150 pixels

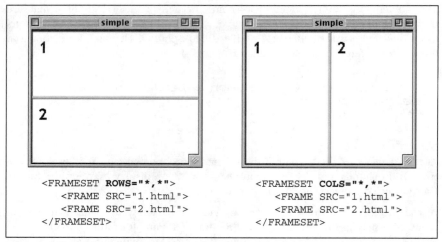

Figure 14-2: Simple horizontal and vertical frameset layouts

wide and the other exactly 450 pixels wide. If the browser window is larger than the total specified pixels, it enlarges each frame proportionally to fill the window. Unfortunately, Netscape Navigator 4.x and under converts pixel measurements to percentages, which can lead to unpredictable frame sizes. This bug is described under "Frame Sizes in Netscape Navigator" at the end of this chapter.

Percentages

Percentages are based on the total width of the frameset. The total should add up to 100%. The frameset `<frameset rows="25%,50%,25%">` creates three rows; the top and bottom frames each always occupy 25% of the height of the frameset, and the middle row makes up 50%, regardless of how the browser window is resized.

Relative values

Relative values, indicated by the asterisk (*) character, are used to divide up the remaining space in the frameset into equal portions (as shown in Figure 14-2). For instance, the frameset `<frameset cols="100,*">` creates two columns—the first is 100 pixels wide, and the second fills whatever portion is left of the window.

You can also specify relative values in multiples of equal portions and combine them with other measurement values. For example, the frameset defined by `<frameset cols="25%,2*,*">` divides the window into three columns. The first column always occupies 25% of the window width. The remaining two divide up the remaining space; however, in this case, the middle column will always be two times as big as the third. (You may notice that this results in the same division as the percentages example.)

Combining rows and columns

You can specify both rows and columns within a single frameset, creating a grid of frames, as shown in Figure 14-3. When both `cols` and `rows` are specified for a frameset, frames are created left to right in each row, in order. Rows are created top to bottom. The order of appearance of `<frame>` elements within the `<frameset>` determines where their contents display. The order in which documents are displayed is demonstrated in Figure 14-3.

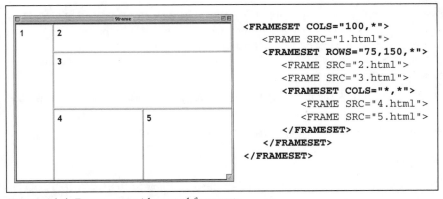

Figure 14-3: Frameset with rows and columns

Nesting Frames

It is possible to nest a frameset within another frameset, which means you can take one row and divide it into several columns (or, conversely, divide a column into several rows), as shown in Figure 14-4. Nesting gives you more page layout flexibility and complexity than simply dividing a frameset into a grid of rows and columns.

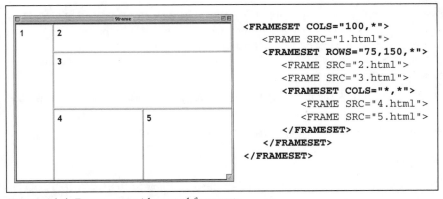

Figure 14-4: Document with nested framesets

In Figure 14-4, the top-level frameset contains one frame (100 pixels wide) and one frameset that occupies the remainder of the window. That frameset creates three rows; the last row is divided by another nested frameset into two columns. There is no limit on the number of levels that frames can be nested. If you nest frames, be careful to close each successive frameset or the document will not display correctly.

Frame Function and Appearance

By default, frames are separated by borders with 3-D beveled edges, and each frame has a scrollbar if its contents do not fit in their entirety. This section looks at the attributes that give you greater control over the display and function of frames.

Frame Borders and Spacing

By default, framed documents display with a 3-D border between each frame. These borders visually divide the sections and also serve as a handle for resizing. The HTML 4.01 specification allows for borders to be controlled only at the frame level (in the `<frame>` tag). However, browsers also support the nonstandard method of setting borders and border thicknesses for the whole page in the `<frameset>` tag.

Specifying borders can be unpredictable because Internet Explorer and Navigator developed their own methods for doing things early on. This has improved somewhat now that both are making an effort to be standards-compliant. It is still best to experiment to get the effect you want, and be sure to do plenty of testing (including in older browsers).

Frameset borders

Use the `frameborder` attribute in the `<frameset>` tag to turn the 3-D border on and off for all the frames on the page. Its values are 1 (on, the default) and 0 (off). For early versions of Navigator (pre-6), Netscape's documentation calls for the values **yes** (on) and **no** (off); however, in my experience, the traditional 1 and 0 values seem to work as far back as Navigator 3.0.

Turning the frameborder off removes only the 3-D border, but it leaves a gap between the frames. To remove this gap and give the page a smooth, seamless appearance, use the `border` attribute with a setting of 0 pixels. The border attribute can also be used to make the border as many pixels thick as you like. Internet Explorer uses the proprietary `framespacing` attribute for controlling the space between frames.

To turn all borders off in a way that is certain to work for all browsers, use the following redundant code in the `<frameset>` tag:

```
<FRAMESET FRAMEBORDER=0 FRAMESPACING=0 FRAMEBORDER=no BORDER=0>
```

Frame borders

The correct way to manipulate frame borders according to the HTML 4.01 specification is to use the `frameborder` attribute within each `<frame>` tag. With this method, you can turn borders on and off for individual frames and override settings at the frameset level. This gets tricky, however, when neighboring frames have conflicting border settings. In addition, there is no border attribute for the `<frame>` tag, which means that if you turn the 3-D frame off, you're still left with the offending gap. In addition, when `border` is set to 0 in the containing `<frameset>` tag, it cannot be overridden at the frame level. If you choose to grapple with individual frame settings, be sure to test thoroughly.

Border color

If you want to get extra fancy with your frame borders, you can assign them a color using the `bordercolor` attribute in the `<frame>` or `<frameset>` tags. This feature is supported by Navigator 3 and higher and Internet Explorer 4 and higher. It has not been adopted into the HTML standard.

Scrolling

The `scrolling` attribute within the `<frame>` tag controls whether scrollbars appear within the frame, regardless of the frame's contents.

The default setting is `auto`, which behaves like any browser window—no scrollbars display unless the contents are too big to fit entirely within the frame.

To make scrollbars always appear, even for mostly empty frames, set `scrolling=yes`. In Figure 14-5, the top frame has a scrollbar only because it was specified in the HTML source.

To make sure scrollbars never appear, such as when a frame is filled entirely by a graphic and it's OK if the edges are slightly obscured, set `scrolling=no`.

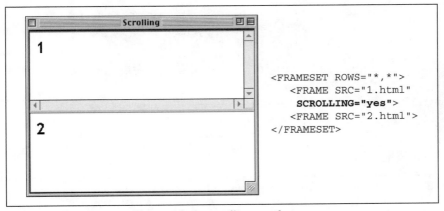

```
<FRAMESET ROWS="*,*">
    <FRAME SRC="1.html"
    SCROLLING="yes">
    <FRAME SRC="2.html">
</FRAMESET>
```

Figure 14-5: Setting scrollbars with the scrolling attribute

When scrollbars are visible, they take up some of the width of the current frame, so figure in the width of a scrollbar when calculating frame sizes in precise pixel measurements. On a Macintosh, both Navigator and Internet Explorer render scrollbars 15 pixels wide. On the PC, scrollbars are 12 pixels wide.

Disabling Resize

By default, any user can resize your frames—overriding your careful size settings—simply by clicking and dragging on the border between frames. You can prevent users from doing that (and messing up your cool design) by adding the `noresize` attribute within the `<frame>` tag.

Be careful that you're not disabling functionality the user needs, though; if the frame contains text, chances are good that some users may need to resize.

Frame Margins

As you probably already know, browsers hold a margin space on all borders of the browser window, preventing a document's contents from displaying flush against the edge of the browser. The width of the margin varies from browser to browser. In 4.0 browsers and higher, the margin can be adjusted using attributes in the <body> tag (see Chapter 9).

Frames have margin attributes that allow you to control (or remove) the margins on any frame-enabled browser. To adjust the top and bottom margins of a frame, specify a number of pixels for the `marginheight` attribute. Use the `marginwidth` attribute to specify the amount of space for the left and right margins. They can be combined as shown in the example in Figure 14-6.

Figure 14-6 shows the same HTML document (containing only a graphic) loaded into two frames within a frameset. The left frame has specific margins set. The right frame has its margins set to zero, allowing the contents of the frame to be positioned right up against the edges of the frame.

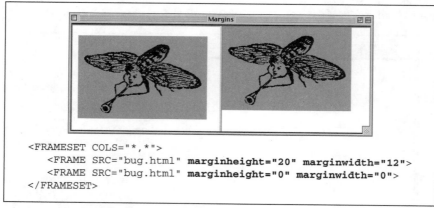

```
<FRAMESET COLS="*,*">
    <FRAME SRC="bug.html" marginheight="20" marginwidth="12">
    <FRAME SRC="bug.html" marginheight="0" marginwidth="0">
</FRAMESET>
```

Figure 14-6: Effects of setting frame margins

There is a slight bug in Netscape Navigator Versions 4.7 and earlier that causes it to display a 1-pixel margin even when the margins are set to 0 (zero). Fortunately, the Netscape 6 release works properly. The workaround for Navigator 4 is to set the `marginwidth` and `marginheight` in the <body> tag of the HTML source document for the frame in addition to the frame margin settings. Together, they will position the contents flush against the frame. For Navigator 2 and 3, there's not much you can do but camouflage the 1-pixel margin with a background color that matches the page contents. Fortunately, these browsers make up only a small percentage of browser usage today.

Targeting Frames

One of the challenges of managing a framed document is coordinating where linked documents display. By default, a linked document loads into the same window as the link; however, it is often desirable to have a link in one frame load a page into a different frame in the frameset. For instance, this is the desired effect for a list of navigation links in a narrow frame that loads content into a larger main frame on the page.

To load a new linked page into a particular frame, you first need to assign a name to the targeted frame using the name attribute in the <frame> tag, as follows:

```
<FRAME SRC="original.html" NAME="main">
```

Now you can specify that frame by name within any anchor (<a>) tag with the target attribute, as shown in this example:

```
<A HREF="new.html" TARGET="main">...</A>
```

The document *new.html* will load into the frame named "main".

If a link contains a target name that does not exist in the frameset, a new browser window is opened to display the document, and that window is given the target's name. Subsequent links targeted to the same name will load in that window.

The <base> tag

If you know that you want all the links in a given document to load in the same frame (such as from a table of contents into a main display frame), you can set the target once using the <base> tag instead of setting the target within every link in the document (saving a lot of typing and extra characters in the HTML document).

Placing the <base> tag in the <head> of the document, with the target frame specified by name, causes all the links in the document to load into that frame. The following is a sample targeted base tag:

```
<HEAD>
<BASE TARGET="main">
</HEAD>
```

Targets in individual links override the target set in the <base> tag at the document level.

Reserved target names

There are four standard target names for special redirection actions. Note that all of them begin with the underscore (_) character. You should avoid naming your frames with a name beginning with an underscore as it will be ignored by the browser. The four reserved target names are:

_blank
> A link with target="_blank" opens a new, unnamed browser window to display the linked document. Each time a link that targets _blank is opened, it launches a new window, potentially leaving the user with a mess of open windows. This can be used with any link, not just those in a frames context.

_self
> This is the default target for all <a> tags; it loads the linked document into the same frame or window as the source document. Because it is the default, it is not necessary to use it with individual <a> tags, but it may be useful within the <base> tag of the document.

_parent

A linked document with `target="_parent"` loads into the parent frame (one step up in the frame hierarchy). If the link is already at the top-level frame or window, it is equivalent to `_self`. Figure 14-7 demonstrates the effects of a link targeting the parent frame.

The `_parent` target name works only when the nested framesets are in separate documents. It does not work for multiple nested framesets within a single frameset document (such as the example shown under "Nesting Frames" earlier in this chapter).

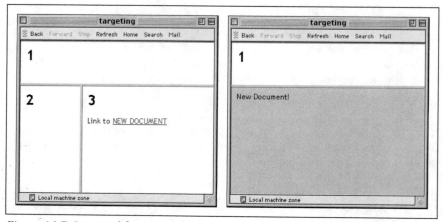

Figure 14-7: In nested framesets, the _parent target links to the parent frameset

_top

This causes the document to load at the top-level window containing the link, replacing any frames currently displayed. A linked document with `target="_top"` "busts out" of its frameset and is displayed directly in the browser window, as shown in Figure 14-8.

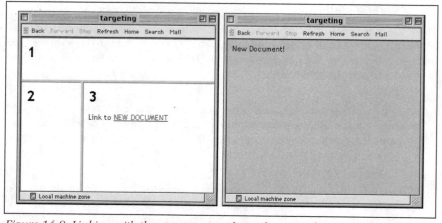

Figure 14-8: Linking with the _top target replaces the entire frameset

Inline (Floating) Frames

Microsoft Internet Explorer 3.0 introduced a feature called inline frames (also called floating frames), which are identified with the `<iframe>` tag. They enable a scrollable frame to be placed anywhere within the flow of an HTML document, much like an image.

As of this writing, inline frames are supported by Internet Explorer and Netscape 6. The `<iframe>` tag and its attributes are part of the HTML 4.01 specification. As older versions of Netscape fade away, we can begin to take advantage of this nifty feature with confidence that it will work for most users. (See "Faking an `<iframe>`" later in this chapter for an example of how to create a similar effect in a way that works in all frames-enabled browsers.)

Placing an inline frame is similar to placing an image on a page. As shown in the following code, within the `<iframe>` tag, specify the width and height of the frame and the HTML file you want it to display. As with images, you can align the frame on the page and specify hspace and vspace. As with frames, you can specify margins within the frame and border display. Figure 14-9 shows the results.

```
<HTML>
<HEAD><TITLE>IFRAME</TITLE></HEAD>
<BODY BGCOLOR="black" TEXT="white">

<H2>Inline (Floating) Frames</H2>

<IFRAME SRC="scrolly.html" WIDTH=200
HEIGHT=100 ALIGN=left HSPACE=12></IFRAME>

Microsoft Internet Explorer 3.0 introduced a feature called inline
frames...
</BODY>
</HTML>
```

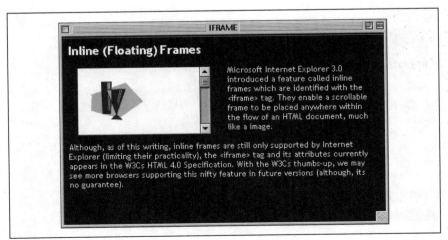

Figure 14-9: Inline frame with IE's `<iframe>` tag

Any content between the start and end `<iframe>` tags is rendered by browsers that do not support inline frames. You can use it to provide alternative text for the frame, as shown in this example:

```
<IFRAME SRC="scrolly.html">If your browser supported inline frames, you
would be seeing <A HREF="scrolly.html"> this page</A> in this space. To
view it correctly you need Internet Explorer or Netscape 6.</IFRAME>
```

Frame Design Tips and Tricks

Using frames effectively requires more than just knowing the HTML tags. This section provides a few pointers and tricks for framed documents.

All-Purpose Pages

Designing a web page to be part of a framed document doesn't guarantee that it will always be viewed that way. Keep in mind that some users might end up looking at one of your pages on its own, out of the context of its frameset (this is possible if a search engine returns the URL of the content, for example). Since frames are often used for navigation, this orphaned content page could be a big, fat dead-end for a user.

For that reason, you should try to design your content pages so that they stand up on their own. Adding a small amount of redundant information to the bottom of each page can make a big difference in usability. First, indicate the name of the site with a link to its home page on each content document. This helps to orient a newcomer who may have just dropped in from a search engine.

It is important to pay particular attention to the navigational options available on content pages viewed without their frameset. At the very least, provide a small link on every page to a more appropriate (and framed) starting point, such as the top level of your site. Be sure to set the `target="_top"` attribute so the link won't load the home page frameset within the current frameset.

As a backup measure, you could use JavaScript to ensure that a page is always viewed in its original frameset. This technique is discussed under "Keeping Pages in their Frames," later in this chapter.

External Links

In most cases, it is not appropriate to load whole external sites into the context of another framed document. By default, any link within a frame loads the new document into that same frame. To prevent external links from loading into the current frame, be sure to add `target="_top"` to all your external links; the new site will open in the full browser window. As an alternative, set the target to `"_blank"` to open the link in a new browser window.

Helping Search Engines

Search engines all work differently but pretty much uniformly do not understand frames or any content within a `<frameset>` or `<frame>` tag. This means search engines will not find any links that require burrowing through a site for indexing purposes, and all the content of your framed site will be missed.

There are a few measures you can take to make your site more friendly to search engines:

- **Include content in the frameset document.** Search engines read content within the <noframes> tag. It is a good idea to make it as descriptive as possible so search engines have something to index (instead of just "you need frames to see this site"). Adding a link within the noframes text to the HTML file containing all your navigational links helps search engines (and humans!) get to the content of your site without relying on the frameset.

- **Use descriptive titles.** Titles are the most important things that search engines index, so use descriptive titles on all content documents. Document titles do not display when the document is loaded into a frame, so it doesn't affect your frame design.

- **Use <meta> tags.** Although not all search engines use <meta> tag information, they can be a useful tool for those that do. If your top-level frameset document contains limited content within the <noframes> tag, you can add a site description and keywords to the page via <meta> tags for the search engine to index. The <meta> element is fully discussed in Chapter 9. The following is a sample of standard <meta> tags used to aid search engines:

```
<HEAD>
<TITLE>Littlechair Studios</TITLE>
<META name="description" content="Jennifer Niederst's resume and web
design samples.">
<META name="keywords" content="designer, web design, training,
interface design">
</HEAD>
```

For more information about search engines and how they work, see the Search Engine Watch site at *http://www.searchenginewatch.com* (from which the previous information was gathered).

Loading Two Frames from One Link

Ordinarily, a link can target only one frame, but there are a few options for creating links that change the contents of two frames at once. One involves simple HTML and the others use JavaScript controls.

Loading a framed document

In HTML, you can only load one document with a link, and that document can occupy just one window or frame. Loading two or more frames (essentially two documents) with a single click requires a bit of fakery. What you're actually doing is loading a single document that is divided into frames itself. What the user sees is a number of frames being replaced at once.

This effect cannot be achieved by nesting framesets as shown in Figure 14-4. Instead, the nesting happens as a product of a framed external document loading into a single frame.

For instance, the following code creates a frameset with two frames: a narrow "top" frame and a "main" bottom frame. This frameset is called *top.html*.

```
<FRAMESET ROWS=50,*>
<FRAME SRC="toolbar.html" NAME="top">
<FRAME SRC="two_frames.html" NAME="main">
</FRAMESET>
```

The bottom frame displays the contents of a document with two vertical frames called *two_frames.html*, shown here:

```
<FRAMESET COLS=250,*>
<FRAME SRC="left.html" NAME="leftframe">
<FRAME SRC="right.html" NAME="rightframe">
</FRAMESET>
```

It is assumed that there are a number of documents like *two_frames.html* that can be accessed by links in the top frame. Each link from the top frame loads one document in the "main" frame, but the contents of two frames change at once.

Of course, this method works only for neighboring frames.

Loading two frames with JavaScript

Adding an onClick JavaScript command within the link allows the browser to load documents into two frames based on one mouse click.* For this example, imagine a document that contains two frames, a list of options on the left and the contents in the main window on the right. We want a link in the left frame to change the contents on the right, but also to load a new list of options (perhaps with the current choice highlighted) into the left frame. The code is quite simple:

```
<A HREF="content.html" onClick="window.self.location='newlist.html'"
TARGET="display">Chocolate</a>
```

The text in bold is the JavaScript line that tells the browser to load *newlist.html* into the same window/frame as the link. The remaining code is the standard HTML link that will load *content.html* into the display frame on the right.

Another (and more robust) method for changing two frames with one click uses a function that changes the contents of two frames (named "toolbar" and "main"), as shown in this sample code:

```
<SCRIPT LANGUAGE="JavaScript">
<!--
function changePages (toolbarURL, mainURL) {
parent.toolbar.location.href=toolbarURL;
parent.main.location.href=mainURL;
}
-->
</SCRIPT>
```

---

* This tip was gathered from Webmonkey, an online magazine for web developers; see *http://www.webmonkey.com*.

Within the anchor tag, the additional code provides the URLs for the documents that will be used in the script (and loaded into the respective frames), as shown in the following example:

```
<A HREF="javascript:changePages('toolbar_document2.html',
'main_document 2.html');">
```

It is important to keep in mind that if JavaScript is turned off in the user's browser, this link will have no effect; therefore, you should use this method cautiously.

Faking an <iframe>

Inline (floating) frames are really cool, but unfortunately, they are not supported in all browsers (Navigator 4.7 and earlier lack support). The following code gives the effect of an inline frame using standard frames tags (but, of course, without all the text-wrap functionality). It creates a scrolling frame that is always centered in the browser window, regardless of how the window is resized, as shown in Figure 14-10.

```
<FRAMESET COLS="*,130,*" NORESIZE BORDER=0 FRAMEBORDER=0 FRAMEBORDER=no
FRAMESPACING=0>
    <FRAME SRC="black.html" SCROLLING=no>
    <FRAMESET ROWS="*,90,*"  NORESIZE BORDER=0 FRAMEBORDER=0
    FRAMEBORDER=no FRAMESPACING=0>
        <FRAME SRC="black.html" SCROLLING=no>
        <FRAME SRC="pix.html" SCROLLING=auto MARGINWIDTH=0
        MARGINHEIGHT=0>
        <FRAME SRC="black.html" SCROLLING=no>
    </FRAMESET>
    <FRAME SRC="black.html" SCROLLING=no>
</FRAMESET>
```

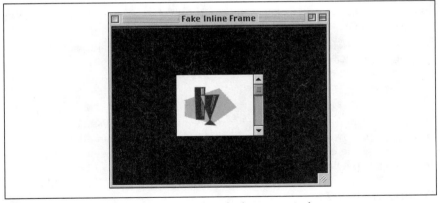

Figure 14-10: Scrolling frame centered in the browser window

The middle column setting in the first `<frameset>` is the width of the window in pixels. The middle row setting in the nested `<frameset>` gives the window's height. You can change the size of the window by adjusting these settings. You can also set the scrolling function of the frame in its `<frame>` tag.

In this example, all the remaining frames are filled with an HTML file with no contents and a black background. Of course, these frames could contain actual content as well.

Frame-Proof Your Site

Some sites may link to your site and load it into a single frame in their interface. If you really don't want to see your site squished into someone else's frame, you can add this tricky (yet simple) JavaScript to the `<head>` of your document, which makes your page always load into the top level of the browser window. (This script works for Netscape Navigator 3.0 and higher and Internet Explorer 3.0 and higher.[*])

```
<SCRIPT LANGUAGE="JAVASCRIPT">
<!-- Hide from old browsers
if (top != self)
top.location.href = location.href;
// Stop hiding from old browsers -->
</SCRIPT>
```

Preloading Images with Hidden Frames

"Preloading images" refers to methods used to download images and store them in the cache before they actually need to be displayed on the page. One method for doing this is to place all the images you'd like to download in a framed document that is hidden from view. The images download and are cached when the first frameset is loaded, but they won't be seen until the user links to a visible page that includes them.

The trick is to create a frameset with two rows (or columns). Set the size of the first row to 100%—this is the frame that will be used to display your first page. In the second row, the one that gets squeezed out of existence, specify the document that contains your images.

```
<FRAMESET ROWS="100%,0" NORESIZE BORDER=0 FRAMEBORDER=0 FRAMEBORDER=NO
FRAMESPACING=0>
    <FRAME SRC="firstpage.html">
    <FRAME SRC="thepictures.html">
</FRAMESET>
```

You can put a bunch of images there, but keep in mind that it's not a free download, just a predownload, so all the same rules about minimizing file sizes apply. There's always the chance that the user might request one of the images (via a link or by moving to a web page that contains it) before they've all arrived.

Frames in WebTV

While WebTV technically supports frames (i.e, it can display the information in a framed document), it does so by converting the framed document into a large

---

[*] Thank you to Vince Heilman for contributing this script.

table. Each "frame" (more like a table cell) displays the entire contents of the frame source. If a frame contains an HTML document that is quite long, the resulting "frame" in WebTV will be extended to display the entire file, regardless of the specified frame size. There is no scrolling function in WebTV.

In addition, WebTV "frames" do not remain in a fixed position like normal frames, but instead move off the screen when users page down through the content.

Frames done with JavaScript links (such as those discussed previously in this chapter) will break navigation in WebTV. If your site targets WebTV users, be sure to either keep frames simple or not use them at all.

For more information on WebTV's handling of frames, see *http://developer.webtv. net/authoring/frames/*.

Keeping Pages in Their Frames

In some cases, users might come across a content document independent of the frameset that is intended to contain it (such as from a link in search engine results). To prevent your content pages from appearing out of context, use this JavaScript code in the head of any document that needs to appear in a frameset:

```
<SCRIPT LANGUAGE="JavaScript">
<!--
if (top.location == self.location) {
    self.location.replace("frameset.html")
}
// -->
</SCRIPT>
```

The first line of the script checks to see if the topmost frame of the current window is the document. If it is, the second line of the script instructs the browser to replace the document with the frameset document (*frameset.html* in this example, but fill in your own file name in this location).

Frame Sizes in Netscape Navigator

Some framed page designs rely on precise pixel measurements to achieve a desired effect. While Internet Explorer (all versions) and Netscape 6 do not have a problem rendering frames with pixel accuracy, this is not the case for Netscape Navigator Versions 4.7 and earlier. They handle frames in a way that makes it nearly impossible to get the frame sizes you specify.

The reason is that Navigator's frame code (developed way back for Version 2.0) records all frame dimensions in percentages. Any pixel measurements provided in the rows or columns attributes are calculated as a percentage of the available screen space and then rounded off to the nearest percentage point. The rounding results in the rendered frame being up to 12 pixels different (usually smaller) than the specified size. If alignment is crucial for your design, 12 pixels of shift may be unacceptable.

Unfortunately, there is not much that you can do about this other than to use JavaScript to specify a new window with known `innerWidth` and `innerHeight` measurements, and then base your frame measurements on even percentages of those values. Otherwise, you may want to simply avoid pixel-dependent frame designs.

On the bright side, this problem was fixed in Netscape 6, and the older versions of Navigator make up an ever-diminishing percentage of overall browser use. Eventually this will be a non-issue, but in the meantime, just be aware that if your frames are misbehaving, it may be Navigator and not your code that's to blame.[*]

---

[*] This tip taken with permission from CNET's Builder.com. It appeared in an article by Paul Anderson entitled "Frame Quirks in Navigator" (12/6/99). You can read the original at *http:// www.builder.com/Authoring/Tagmania/120699/index.html*.

CHAPTER 15

Forms

Forms provide a method for true interaction between users and the publisher of a web site, with an immediacy that could never be achieved in print. With forms, you can solicit input from a user in order to provide a customized response on-the-fly or just collect the data for later use. Forms can be used for functions as simple as surveys and guestbooks or as complex as online commerce systems.

This chapter provides a detailed review of the available form elements and how to use them. It also provides a brief introduction to CGI, one of the available methods for processing form information.

Summary of Form Tags

In this section, browser support for each tag is noted to the right of the tag name. Browsers that do not support the tag are grayed out. Tag usage is indicated below the tag name. Start and end tags are required unless otherwise noted. "Deprecated" means that the tag or attribute is currently supported but is due to be phased out of the HTML specification and is discouraged from use (usually in favor of similar style sheet controls). The attributes listed for each tag reflect those in common use. A more thorough listing of attributes for each tag, according to the HTML 4.01 specification, appears in Appendix A.

\<button\> NN 2, 3, 4, 6 MSIE 2, 3, 4, 5.5, 6 HTML 4.01 WebTV Opera5

\<button\> ... \</button\>

Defines a "button" that functions similarly to buttons created with the input tag but allows for richer rendering possibilities. Buttons can contain content such as text and images (but not imagemaps).

Attributes

name=*text*
    Required. Assigns the control name for the element.

value=*text*
> Assigns the value to the button control. The behavior of the button is determined by the type attribute.

type=submit|reset|button
> Identifies the type of button: submit button (the default type), reset button, or custom button (used with JavaScript), respectively.

\<fieldset\>

NN 2, 3, 4, 6   MSIE 2, 3, 4, 5.5, 6   HTML 4.01   WebTV   Opera5

`<fieldset> ... </fieldset>`

Groups related controls and labels. The proper use of this tag should make documents more accessible to nonvisual browsers. It is similar to `<div>` but is specifically for grouping fields. It was introduced to improve form accessibility to users with alternative browsing devices.

\<form\>

NN 2, 3, 4, 6   MSIE 2, 3, 4, 5.5, 6   HTML 4.01   WebTV   Opera5

`<form> ... </form>`

Indicates the beginning and end of a form. There can be more than one form in an HTML document, but forms cannot be nested inside one another, and it is important that they do not overlap.

Attributes

accept=*content-type-list*
> Specifies a comma-separated list of file types (MIME types) that the server will accept and is able to process. Browsers may one day be able to filter out unacceptable files when prompting a user to upload files to the server, but this attribute is not yet widely supported.

accept-charset=*charset list*
> Specifies the list of character encodings for input data that must be accepted by the server in order to process the current form. The value is a space- and/or comma-delimited list of ISO character set names. The default value is unknown. This attribute is not widely supported.

action=*url*
> *Required.* Specifies the URL of the application that will process the form. The default is the current URL.

enctype=*encoding*
> Specifies how the values for the form controls are encoded when they are submitted to the server when the method is post. The default is the Internet Media Type (application/x-www-form-urlencoded). The value multipart/form-data should be used in combination with the file input element.

method=get|post
> Specifies which HTTP method will be used to submit the form data. With get (the default), the information is appended to and sent along with the URL itself.

target=*name*
>Specifies a target for the results of the form submission to be loaded so results of a form can be displayed in another window or frame. The special target values _bottom, _top, _parent, and _self may be used.

\<input type=button\>   NN 2, 3, 4, 6   MSIE 2, 3, 4, 5.5, 6   HTML 4.01   WebTV   Opera5

\<input type=button\> *(no end tag)*

Creates a customizable "push" button. Customizable buttons have no specific behavior but can be used to trigger functions created with JavaScript controls. Data from type=button controls is never sent with a form when a form is submitted to the server; these button controls are only for use with script programs on the browser.

Attributes

name=*string*
>*Required.* Assigns a name to the push button control. A script program uses this name to reference this control.

value=*string*
>*Required.* Specifies the value for this control.

\<input type=checkbox\>   NN 2, 3, 4, 6   MSIE 2, 3, 4, 5.5, 6   HTML4.0   WebTV   Opera5

\<input type=checkbox\> *(no end tag)*

Creates a checkbox input element within a \<form\>. Checkboxes are like on/off switches that can be toggled by the user. Several checkboxes in a group may be selected at one time. When a form is submitted, only the "on" checkboxes submit values to the server.

Attributes

checked
>When this attribute is added, the checkbox will be checked by default.

name=*text*
>*Required.* Assigns a name to the checkbox to be passed to the form-processing application if selected. Giving several checkboxes the same name creates a group of checkbox elements, allowing users to select several options with the same property.

value=*text*
>*Required.* Specifies the value of this control; this value is passed to the server only if the checkbox is selected. If no value is set, a default value of "on" is sent.

\<input type=file\>   NN 2, 3, 4, 6   MSIE 2, 3, 4, 5.5, 6   HTML 4.01   WebTV   Opera5

\<input type=file\> *(no end tag)*

Allows users to submit external files with their form submission. It is accompanied by a "browse" button when displayed in the browser.

Forms

Attributes

`accept=`*`MIME type`*
Specifies a comma-separated list of content types that a server processing the form will handle correctly. It can be used to filter out nonconforming files when prompting a user to select files to send to the server.

`name=`*`text`*
Required. Assigns a name to the control.

`<input type=hidden>`   NN 2, 3, 4, 6   MSIE 2, 3, 4, 5.5, 6   HTML 4.01   WebTV   Opera5

`<input type=hidden>` *(no end tag)*

Creates an element that does not display in the browser. Hidden controls can be used to pass special form-processing information to the server that the user cannot see or alter.

`name=`*`text`*
Required. Specifies the name of the control; this name (and the corresponding value) are passed to the form-processing application.

`value=`*`text`*
Required. Specifies the value of the element that is passed to the form-processing application.

`<input type=image>`   NN 2, 3, 4, 6   MSIE 2, 3, 4, 5.5, 6   HTML 4.01   WebTV   Opera5

`<input type=image>` *(no end tag)*

Allows an image to be used as a substitute for a `submit` button. If a `type=image` button is pressed, the form is submitted.

Attributes

`align=top|middle|bottom`
Aligns the image with respect to the surrounding text lines.

`alt=`*`text`*
Provides a text description if the image can not be seen.

`name=`*`text`*
Required. Specifies the name of the control; this name (and the corresponding value) are passed to the form-processing application, along with data giving the coordinates of the mouse on top of the control image.

`src=`*`url`*
Required. Provides the URL of the image.

`<input type=password>`   NN 2, 3, 4, 6   MSIE 2, 3, 4, 5.5, 6   HTML 4.01   WebTV   Opera5

`<input type=password>` *(no end tag)*

Creates a text-input element (like `<input type=text>`), but the input text is rendered in a way that hides the characters, such as by displaying a string of asterisks (*) or bullets (•). Note that this does *not* encrypt the information entered and should not be considered to be a real security measure.

Attributes

`maxlength=number`
> Specifies the maximum number of characters the user can input for this element. The default is an unlimited number of characters.

`name=text`
> *Required.* Specifies the name of this control to be passed to the form-processing application for this element.

`size=number`
> Specifies the size of the text-entry box (measured in number of characters) to be displayed for this element. Users can type entries that are longer than the space provided, causing the field to scroll to the right.

`value=text`
> *Required.* Specifies the value that will initially be displayed in the text box.

<input type=radio>   NN 2, 3, 4, 6   MSIE 2, 3, 4, 5.5, 6   HTML 4.01   WebTV   Opera5

`<input type=radio>` *(no end tag)*

Creates a radio button that can be turned on and off. When a group of radio buttons share the same control name, only one button within the group can be "on" at one time, and all the others are "off." This makes them different from checkboxes, which allow multiple choices to be selected within a group. Only data from the "on" radio button is sent when the form is submitted.

Attributes

`checked`
> Causes the radio button to be in the "on" state when the form is initially displayed.

`name=text`
> *Required.* Specifies the name of the control to be passed to the form-processing application if this element is selected.

`value=text`
> *Required.* Specifies the value of the parameter to be passed to the form-processing application.

<input type=reset>   NN 2, 3, 4, 6   MSIE 2, 3, 4, 5.5, 6   HTML 4.01   WebTV   Opera5

`<input type=reset>` *(no end tag)*

Creates a reset button that clears the contents of the elements in a form (or sets them to their default values).

Attributes

`value=text`
> Specifies a value for the reset button control. This appears as the button label (it will say "Reset" by default).

<input type=submit>
NN 2, 3, 4, 6 - MSIE 2, 3, 4, 5.5, 6   HTML 4.01 - WebTV - Opera5

<input type=submit> *(no end tag)*

Creates a submit button control; pressing the button immediately sends the information in the form to the server for processing.

Attributes

value=*text*
> Specifies a value for the submit button control. This appears as the button label (it will say "Submit" by default).

name=*text*
> *Required.* Specifies the name of this control to be passed to the form-processing application for this element.

<input type=text>
NN 2, 3, 4, 6   MSIE 2, 3, 4, 5.5, 6   HTML 4.01 - WebTV   Opera5

<input type=text> *(no end tag)*

Creates a text input element. This is the default input type, as well as the most useful and common.

Attributes

maxlength=*number*
> Specifies the maximum number of characters the user can input for this element. The default is an unlimited number of characters.

name=*text*
> *Required.* Specifies the name for the text input control. This name will be sent, along with the value, to the form-processing application.

size=*number*
> Specifies the size of the text-entry box (measured in number of characters) to be displayed for this element. Users can type entries that are longer than the space provided, causing the field to scroll to the right.

value=*text*
> Specifies the value that will initially be displayed in the text box.

<isindex>
NN 2, 3, 4, 6   MSIE 2, 3, 4, 5.5, 6   HTML 4.01   WebTV   Opera5

<isindex> *(no end tag)*

Deprecated. Marks the document as searchable. The server on which the document is located must have a search engine that supports this searching. The browser displays a text entry field and a generic line that says, "This is a searchable index. Enter search keywords." This method is outdated; more sophisticated searches can be handled with form elements and CGI scripting.

The <isindex> element is not part of the form system and does not need to be contained within a <form> element.

\<label\>

```
<label>...</label>
```

Used to attach information to controls. Each `label` element is associated with exactly one form control.

Attributes

`for=text`

> Explicitly associates the label with the control by matching the value of the `for` attribute with the value of the `id` attribute within the control element.

Example

```
<LABEL for="lastname">Last Name: </LABEL>
<INPUT type="text" id="lastname" size="32">
```

\<legend\>

```
<legend>...</legend>
```

Assigns a caption to a `<fieldset>` (it must be contained within a `<fieldset>` element). This improves accessibility when the `fieldset` is rendered nonvisually.

\<optgroup\>

```
<optgroup>...</optgroup>
```

Defines a logical group of `<options>`. This could be used by browsers to display hierarchical cascading menus. `<optgroups>` cannot be nested.

Attributes

`label=text`

> *Required.* Specifies the label for the option group.

\<option\>

```
<option> ... </option>
```
(end tag optional)

Defines an option within a select element (a multiple-choice menu or scrolling list). The end tag, although it exists, is usually omitted. The content of the `<option>` element is the value that is sent to the form processing application (unless an alternative value is specified using the `value` attribute).

Attributes

`label`

> Allows the author to provide a shorter label than the content of the option. This attribute is poorly supported.

`selected`

> Makes this item selected when the form is initially displayed.

`value=text`

> Defines a value to assign to the option item within the select control, to use in place of `<option>` contents.

Forms

`<select> ... </select>`

Defines a multiple-choice menu or a scrolling list. It is a container for one or more `<option>` tags. This element may also contain one or more `<optgroup>`s.

Attributes

`multiple`

This allows the user to select more than one `<option>` from the list. When this attribute is absent, only single selections are allowed.

`name=text`

Defines the name for select control; when the form is submitted to the form-processing application, this name is sent along with each selected option value.

`size=number`

Specifies the number of rows that display in the list of options. For values higher than 1, the options are displayed as a scrolling list with the specified number of options visible. When `size=1` is specified, the list is displayed as a pop-up menu.

The default value is 1 when `multiple` is *not* used. When `multiple` is specified, the value varies by browser (but a value of 4 is common).

<textarea>　　　　　　　NN 2, 3, 4, 6　　MSIE 2, 3, 4, 5.5, 6　　HTML 4.01　　WebTV　　Opera5

`<textarea>...</textarea>`

Defines a multiline text-entry control. The text that is enclosed within the `<textarea>` tags is displayed in the text-entry field when the form initially displays.

`cols=number`

Required. Specifies the visible width of the text-entry field, measured in number of characters. Users may enter text lines that are longer than the provided width, in which case the entry scrolls to the right (or wraps if the browser provides some mechanism for doing so).

`name=text`

Required. Specifies a name for the text input control. This name will be sent along with the control content to the form-processing application.

`rows=number`

Required. Specifies the height of the text-entry field in number of lines of text. If the user enters more lines than are visible, the text field scrolls down to accommodate the extra lines.

`wrap=off|virtual|physical`

Nonstandard. Sets word wrapping within the text area. `off` turns word wrapping off; users must enter their own line returns. `virtual` displays the wrap, but the line endings are not transmitted to the server. `physical` displays and transmits line endings to the server. Some browsers support the proprietary value `soft` as equivalent to `virtual`, and `hard` as equivalent to `physical`.

Introduction to Forms

HTML form tags alone don't make forms work; they merely provide an interface for gathering data. The real work is done by forms-processing applications on the server, such as CGI scripts, ASP, PHP, or Java servlets (see Chapter 4 for information on server-side scripting).

For simple forms processing, many web developers rely on CGI scripts. CGI (Common Gateway Interface) is the interface between HTTP/web server software (the program responsible for web transactions) and other programs on the server. There is an introduction to CGI scripts at the end of this chapter

If you are coming at web design from a designer's point of view (or even just as a novice to web design), chances are you will be handling the HTML form elements and leaving the programming to trained programmers. Often, ISPs provide a few canned CGI scripts, such as a guestbook or mailing function, that you can point to from within your form, but if you want something customized for your site, I recommend you hire a professional programmer to write it for you.

The Basic Form (<form>)

The <form> tag, which is used to designate a form, contains the information necessary for interacting with a program on the server. A form is made up of a number of controls (checkboxes, menus, text-entry fields, buttons, etc.) used for entering information. When the user has completed the form and presses the "submit" button, the browser takes the information, arranges it into name/value pairs, encodes the information for transfer, and then sends it off to the server.

You can have several forms within a single document, but they cannot be nested, and you must be careful they do not overlap. Figure 15-1 shows a very simple form and its <form> tag.

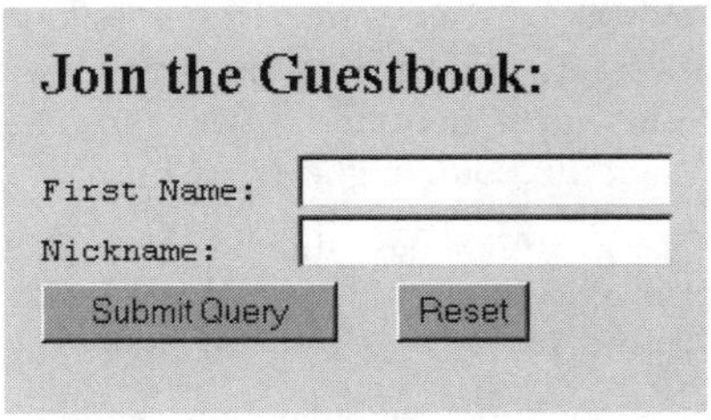

```
<H2>Join the Guestbook:</H2>

<FORM ACTION="/cgi-bin/guestbook.pl" METHOD="GET">
<PRE>
First Name: <INPUT TYPE="text" NAME="first">
Nickname:   <INPUT TYPE="text" NAME="nickname">
<INPUT TYPE="submit"> <INPUT TYPE="reset">
</PRE>
</FORM>
```

Figure 15-1: A simple form

The action Attribute

The `action` attribute in the `<form>` tag provides the URL of the program to be used for processing the form. In the example in Figure 15-1, the form information is going to a Perl script called *guestbook.pl*, which resides in the *cgi-bin* directory of the current server (by convention, CGI programs are usually kept in a directory called *cgi-bin*).

The method Attribute

The `method` attribute specifies one of two methods, either `get` or `post`, by which the information from the form can be transmitted to the server. Form information is typically transferred in a series of *name=value* pairs, separated by the ampersand (&) character.

Let's take into consideration a simple form with two fields: one for entering a name and the other for entering a nickname. If a user enters "Josephine" in the first field and "Josie" in the second, that information is transmitted to the server in the following format:

```
name=Josephine&nickname=Josie
```

With the `get` method, the browser transfers the data from the form as part of the URL itself (appended to the end and separated by a question mark) in a single transmission. The information gathered from the nickname example would be transferred via the `get` method as follows:

```
GET http://www.domainname.com/cgi-bin/guestbook.
pl?name=Josephine&nickname=Josie
```

The `post` method transmits the form input information separated from the URL, in essentially a two-part message. The first part of the message is simply the special header sent by the browser with each request. This header contains the URL from the form element, combined with a statement that this is a `post` request, plus some other headers we won't discuss here. This is followed by the actual form data. When the server sees the word `post` at the beginning of the message, it stays tuned for the data. The information gathered with the name and nickname form would read as follows using the `post` method:

```
POST http://www.domainname.com/cgi-bin/guestbook.pl HTTP1.0
... [more headers here]
name=Josephine&nickname=Josie
```

Whether you should use `post` or `get` may rely on the requirements of your server. In general, if you have a short form with a few short fields, use the `get` method. Conversely, long, complex forms are best sent via `post`. If security is an issue (such as when using the `<input type="password">` tag), use `post`, because it offers an opportunity for encryption rather than sending the form data straight away tacked onto the URL. One advantage of `get` is that the request can be bookmarked, since everything in the request is in the URL. This isn't true with `post`.

Encoding

Another behind-the-scenes step that happens in the transaction is that the data gets encoded using standard URL encoding. This is a method for translating spaces and other characters not permitted in URLs (such as slashes) into their hexadecimal equivalents. For example, the space character translates to %20, and the slash character is transferred as %2F.

The default encoding format, the Internet Media Type (application/x-www-form-urlencoded), will suffice for most forms. If your form includes a file input type (for uploading documents to the server), you should use the enctype attribute to set the encoding to its alternate setting, multipart/form-data.

In general, you will need to communicate with your server administrator to get all the necessary settings for the <form> tag to enable your form to function properly.

Form Elements

There are a variety of elements (also sometimes called "controls" or "widgets") that can be used for gathering information from a form. This section looks at each control and its specific attributes. Every form control (except submit and reset) requires that you give it a name (using the name attribute) so the form-processing application can sort the information. For easier processing of form data on the server, the value of the name should not have any character spaces (use underscores or periods instead).

Input Controls: <input>

The controls described in the following sections are entered as attribute options within the <input> tag.

Text entry (type=text)

The simplest type of form element is the text entry field (type=text), which is the default setting for the <input> element. This field allows the user to enter a single word or a line of text. By default, the browser displays a text-entry box that is 20 characters wide, but you can set it to be any length using the size attribute.

By default the user can type an unlimited number of characters into the field (the display scrolls to the right if the text exceeds the width of the supplied box), but you can set a maximum number of characters using the maxlength attribute.

Use the value attribute to specify text to appear when the form is loaded. This can be changed by the user. If you have a form that consists of only one text input element, hitting the Enter key submits the form without requiring a specific Submit button in the form. The following code creates a text field with a size of 15 characters, a maximum length of 50 characters, and the text "enter your name" displayed in the field (Figure 15-2).

```
<P>What is your name?</P>
<INPUT TYPE="text" NAME="name"  SIZE="18" MAXLENGTH="50" VALUE="enter
your name">
```

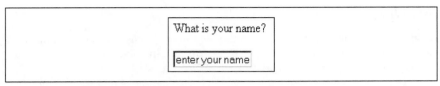

Figure 15-2: Text entry input

Password text entry (type=password)

A password field (`type=password`) works just like text entry, except the characters are obscured from view using asterisk (*) or bullet (•) characters (which one depends on the browser). Although the characters are not displayed in the browser (Figure 15-3), the actual characters are available in the form data, so this is not a secure system for transmitting passwords. For example, the following code text reveals the actual characters in the default value:

```
<P>What is your password?</P>
<INPUT TYPE="password" NAME="password"  SIZE="8" MAXLENGTH="8"
VALUE="abcdefg">
```

Figure 15-3: Password input

Hidden entry (type=hidden)

The hidden input (`type=hidden`) adds a control that isn't displayed in the browser. It is useful for sending information to be processed along with the user-entered data, such as labels used by the script to sort forms. Some scripts require specific hidden fields be added to the form in order to function properly. Here is a hidden element (Figure 15-4):

```
<P>This is a hidden element</P>
<INPUT TYPE="hidden" NAME="extra_info" value="important">
```

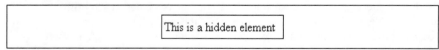

Figure 15-4: Hidden input

Checkbox (type=checkbox)

Checkboxes (`type=checkbox`) are typically used for multiple-choice questions. They work best when more than one answer is acceptable. When the box is checked, the corresponding value is transmitted with the form to the processing program on the server.

Checkboxes can be used individually to transmit specific name/value coordinates to the server when checked. By default a checkbox is not checked; to make it checked when the page loads, simply add the checked attribute to the corresponding <input> tag.

If you assign a group of checkboxes the same name, they behave like a multiple-choice list in which the user can select more than one option for a given property, as shown in the following code and in Figure 15-5.

```
<P>Which of the following operating systems have you used?</P>
<INPUT TYPE="checkbox" NAME="os" VALUE="Unix" CHECKED> Unix
<INPUT TYPE="checkbox" NAME="os" VALUE="Win98"> Windows 98
<INPUT TYPE="checkbox" NAME="os" VALUE="WinNT"> Windows NT
<INPUT TYPE="checkbox" NAME="os" VALUE="Mac" CHECKED> Macintosh 9.0
```

Which of the following operating systems have you used?

☑ UNIX ☐ Windows 98 ☐ Windows NT ☑ Macintosh 9.0

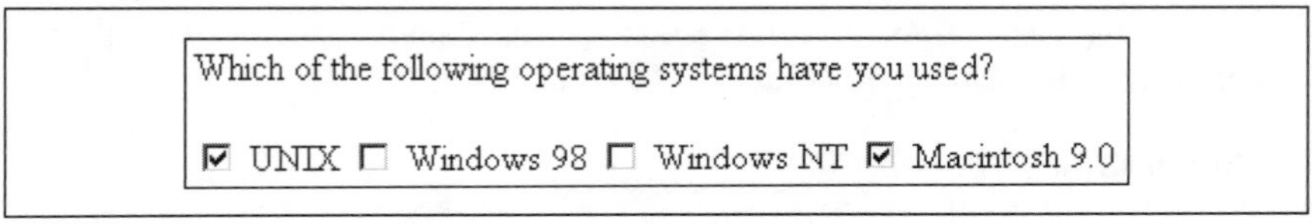

Figure 15-5: Multiple checkboxes in a group may be selected

Radio button (type=radio)

Radio buttons (type=radio) are used to select among choices. When a radio button is checked, its corresponding value is sent to the server for processing. Radio buttons are different from checkboxes in that when several radio buttons are grouped together by the same name, only one radio button can be selected at one time, as shown in the following code and in Figure 15-6.

```
<P>Which operating system do you like the best?</P>
<INPUT TYPE="radio" NAME="os" VALUE="Unix"> Unix
<INPUT TYPE="radio" NAME="os" VALUE="Win98"> Windows 98
<INPUT TYPE="radio" NAME="os" VALUE="WinNT"> Windows NT
<INPUT TYPE="radio" NAME="os" VALUE="Mac" CHECKED> Macintosh 9.0
```

Which operating system do you like the best?

○ UNIX ○ Windows 98 ○ Windows NT ⊙ Macintosh 9.0

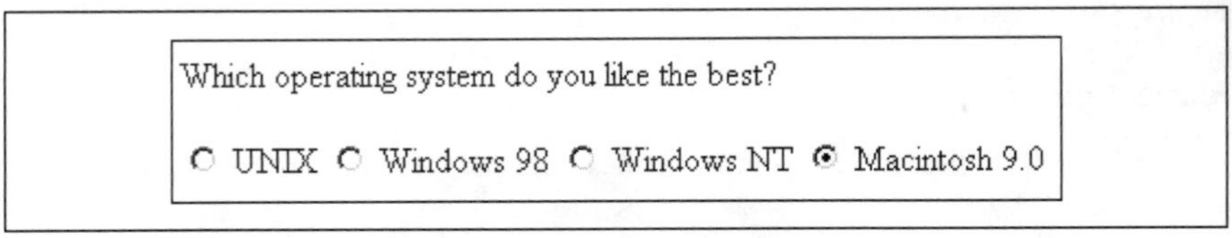

Figure 15-6: Only one radio button in a group may be selected

Submit and reset buttons (type=submit; type=reset)

Every form (unless it consists of exactly one text field) needs a submit button control to initiate the transmission of information to the server. By default, the submit button (type=submit) says "Submit" or "Submit Query," but you can change it by adding your own text after the value attribute.

The reset button (type=reset) reverts all form controls back to the state they were in when the form loaded (either blank or with default values). The default value (and hence the label for the button) is "Reset," but like the submit button, you can change its text by specifying its value, as shown in Figure 15-7.

```
<P>You have completed the form.</P>
<INPUT TYPE="submit"><INPUT TYPE="reset" VALUE="Start Over">
```

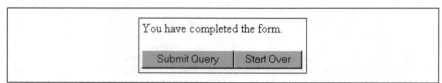

Figure 15-7: Submit and reset buttons

Some designers opt to leave the Reset button out entirely because there is no error-checking mechanism. If a user presses it accidentally, all the data already entered is lost. This isn't an uncommon occurrence.

Custom button (type=button)

This button (type=button) has no predefined function, but rather is a generic tool that can be customized with JavaScript. Use the value attribute to write your own text on the button, as shown in the following code and in Figure 15-8. It is supported only on Version 4.0 browsers and higher. The data from a type=button input element is never sent when a form is submitted; this type is only useful with JavaScript programs on the browser.

```
<P>This does something really exciting.</P>
<INPUT TYPE="button" VALUE="Push Me!">
```

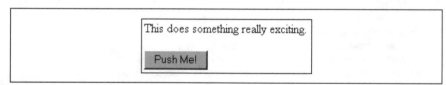

Figure 15-8: Custom button

Image button (type=image)

You can replace the submit button with a graphic of your choice by using the image input (type=image), as shown in the following code and in Figure 15-9. Clicking on the image submits the form to the server and includes the coordinates of the mouse click with the form data. You must provide the URL of the graphic with the src attribute. It is recommended that you use alternative text (with the alt attribute) for image buttons.

```
<INPUT TYPE="image" SRC="graphics/sendme.gif" ALT="Send me">
```

File selection (type=file)

The file-selection form field (type=file) lets users select a file stored on their computer and send it to the server when they submit the form. It is displayed as a

Figure 15-9: Using an image for a button

text entry field with an accompanying "Browse" button for selecting the file, as shown in the following code and in Figure 15-10. Like other text fields, you can set the `size` and `maxwidth` values as well as the field's default text. When using the `file` input type, you should specify `enctype="multipart/form-data"` in the `<form>` tag. Ask your server administrator to confirm this setting.

```
<FORM ENCTYPE="multipart/form-data">
<P>Send this file with my form information:</P>
<INPUT TYPE="file" SIZE="28">
</FORM>
```

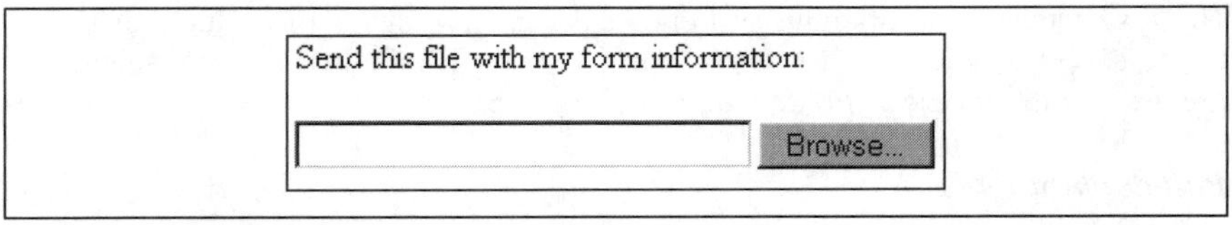

Send this file with my form information:

[   ] [Browse...]

Figure 15-10: The file-selection form field

Text Area: *<textarea>*

The `<textarea>` tag creates a multiline, scrollable text entry box that allows users to input extended text entries, as shown in the following code and in Figure 15-11. When the form is transmitted, the browser sends the text along with the name specified by the required `name` attribute.

Specify the number of lines of text the area should display using the `rows` attribute. The `cols` attribute specifies the width (measured in characters). These attributes are required according to the HTML 4.01 specification. Scrollbars are provided if the user types more text than fits in the allotted space.

Normally, the text is submitted just as it is typed in, with line returns only where the user presses the Enter key. However, you can use the `wrap` attribute to control text wrapping. When `wrap` is set to `virtual` or `soft`, the text wraps in the user's display. `Physical` or `hard` wrap settings transmit every new line with a hard-coded line return. When wrap is set to `off`, the default setting, the lines do not wrap. The wrap functions are browser-dependent.

The text that appears between `<textarea>` and its end tag `</textarea>` will be the initial contents of the text entry window when the form is displayed.

```
<P>What did you dream last night?</P>
<TEXTAREA NAME="dream" ROWS="4" COLS="45">Tell us your dream in 100 words
or less</TEXTAREA>
```

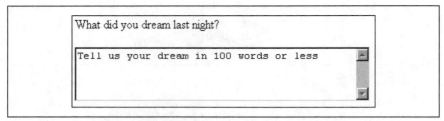

Figure 15-11: The textarea form field

Creating Menus with the <select> Tag

The <select> tag creates a menu of options that is more compact than group-ings of checkboxes or radio buttons. A menu displays as either a pull-down menu or as a scrolling list of choices, depending on how the size is specified. The <select> tag works as a container for any number of <option>s.

The text between the opening and ending <option> tags is the value that is sent to the server. If you want to send a value for that choice that is not displayed in the list, use the **value** attribute within the <option> tag.

Pull-down menus

The <select> element displays as a pull-down menu of options when no size specification is listed (the default) or when **size=1**. In a pull-down menu, only one item may be selected at a time. (Note that adding the **multiple** attribute turns the menu into a scrolling list, as described in the next section.) By default, the first <option> in the list displays when the form loads, but you can preselect another option by adding **selected** within its <option> tag.

```
<P>What is your favorite ice cream flavor?</P>
<SELECT NAME="ice_cream">
<OPTION>Rocky Road
<OPTION>Mint Chocolate Chip
<OPTION>Pistachio
<OPTION SELECTED>Vanilla
<OPTION>Chocolate
<OPTION VALUE="swirl">Fudge Ripple
<OPTION>Praline Pecan
<OPTION>Bubblegum
</SELECT>
```

Use the **selected** attribute in the <option> tag to indicate the default value for the menu (the option will be highlighted when the form loads). Clicking on the arrows or bar pops up the full menu, as shown in Figure 15-12.

Scrolling menus

To make the menu display as a scrolling list, simply specify the number of lines you'd like to be visible in the list using the **size** attribute, or add the **multiple** attribute to the <select> tag, as shown in the following code and in Figure 15-13.

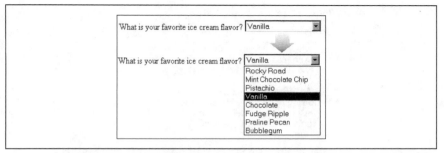

Figure 15-12: Items in a select menu can be set to display after menu is collapsed

The `multiple` attribute makes it possible for users to select more than one option from the list.

```
<P>What are your favorite ice cream flavors?<P>
<SELECT NAME="ice_cream" SIZE=6 MULTIPLE>
<OPTION>Rocky Road
<OPTION>Mint Chocolate Chip
<OPTION>Pistachio
<OPTION SELECTED>Vanilla
<OPTION SELECTED>Chocolate
<OPTION VALUE="swirl">Fudge Ripple
<OPTION>Praline Pecan
<OPTION>Bubblegum
</SELECT>
```

Figure 15-13: Use the size attribute to display a select menu as a scrolling list

New Form Attributes in HTML 4.01

The HTML 4.01 specification introduced a number of new attributes that make form elements more accessible and easier to use. As of this writing, they are still poorly supported by most browsers, but they do reveal the W3C's thinking regarding forms. Some attributes take into account efforts to improve accessibility and internationalization. Some can be used with Dynamic HTML to make form elements turn on and off, or become hidden or visible based on user input. Table 15-1 lists the new attributes along with the form elements to which they can be applied.

Table 15-1: New form attributes in HTML 4.0

Attribute	Description	Related tag(s)
accept-charset	Specifies the list of character encodings (character sets) that must be accepted by the server processing the form. This attribute is part of the W3C's internationalization efforts requiring alternative character sets to represent non-western writing systems. (This attribute is not widely supported.)	<FORM>
accesskey	Assigns an access key (keyboard shortcut) to an element for quicker access.	<BUTTON>, <INPUT>, <LABEL>, <LEGEND>, <TEXTAREA>
disabled	Disables the control for user input. It can only be altered via a script. Browsers may display disabled controls differently (grayed out, for example), which could be useful for dimming certain controls until required info is supplied.	<BUTTON>, <INPUT>, <OPTGROUP>, <OPTION>, <SELECT>, <TEXTAREA>
readonly	Prevents the user from changing the text in a field.	<INPUT type=text>, <INPUT type=password>, <TEXTAREA>
tabindex	Specifies position in the tabbing order. Tabbing navigation allows the user to cycle through the active fields using the Tab key.	<BUTTON>, <INPUT>, <SELECT>, <TEXTAREA>

Affecting the Appearance of Forms

A <form> element tends to be rendered by the browser, giving the designer little control over the appearance of the controls themselves. Not surprisingly, the same element may be rendered slightly differently on different browsers and platforms, as shown in Table 15-2.

If you really need to know the exact pixel dimensions of a form element on a specific browser or platform (perhaps for mock-up purposes), you can thank the fine folks at Webmonkey.com. They have taken the time to measure every last form element (among other browser display features) down to the pixel, and they posted their findings at *http://hotwired.lycos.com/webmonkey/99/41/index3a_ page5.html*. Knowing the largest possible dimensions for a form element may be useful in planning a page layout.

Navigator resizes form elements containing text (text fields, text areas, and scrolling lists) when the constant width font is resized in the browser preferences. So if a user's fonts are set to 18 points, a <textarea> could suddenly become huge and exceed the space you've allotted. Like many things on the Web, the way your forms will look is somewhat unpredictable.

Table 15-2. The appearance of form elements on major browsers

	Netscape 6.0 Macintosh	Netscape 6.0 Windows	Internet Explorer 5.0 Macintosh	Internet Explorer 5.5 Windows
Text Entry `<INPUT type="text">`	your name here	your name here	your name here	your name here
Password Entry `<INPUT type="file">`	••••••	*******	••••••	••••••
Checkbox (left) `<INPUT type="checkbox">`	☐ ☒	☐ ☑	☐ ☑	☐ ☑
Radio Button `<INPUT type="radio">`	◉ ○	○ ◉	◉ ○	○ ◉
Submit Button `<INPUT type="submit">`	Submit Query	Submit Query	Submit	Submit Query
Reset Button `<INPUT type="reset">`	Reset	Reset	Reset	Reset
File Selection Entry `<INPUT type="file">`	Browse...	Browse...	Browse...	Browse...
Text Area `<TEXT AREA COLS=20 ROWS=30>`	Default text here.	Default text here.	Default text here.	Default text here
Select Menu (pop-up) `<SELECT SIZE=1>`	Option 1 ▶	Option 1 ▶	Option 1 ◆	Option 1 ▶
Select Menu (scrolling list) `<SELECT SIZE=4>`	Option 1 / Option 2 / Option 3 / Option 4	Option 1 / Option 2 / Option 3 / Option 4	Option 1 / Option 2 / Option 3 / Option 4	Option 1 / Option 2 / Option 3 / Option 4

Styling Form Controls with CSS

As for any HTML element, you can use Cascading Style Sheets to alter the font, colors, and size of form controls. Unfortunately, CSS formatting will be lost on all but the most recent standards-compliant browsers (Internet Explorer 5.5 and Netscape 6). All other browsers ignore CSS styles for form controls and display the generic control (they'll still function just fine). For more information on how style sheet properties work, see Chapter 17.

One method for adding style information to a form element is to embed the style sheet right in the tag. The following example creates a black submit button with white text in the Impact font face (Figure 15-14):

```
<INPUT TYPE="submit" VALUE="SUBMIT" STYLE="font-family: Impact;
  color: white; font-size: 14px; background: black">.
```

Figure 15-14: A submit button altered with style sheets

You can also use the `class` and `id` attributes to apply styles to specific controls. Cascading Style Sheets rely on the `class` attribute to differentiate between input elements. In this example, a style sheet is used to highlight the required fields (last name and phone number) in a very simple form (Figure 15-15):

```
Style information in head of document
<STYLE TYPE="text/css">
<!--
input.required { background-color: darkred; color: white }
-->
</STYLE>

In the form...
<P>First Name: <BR>
<INPUT TYPE="text" NAME="first" SIZE="30"></P>
<P>Last Name: <BR>
<INPUT TYPE="text" NAME="last" SIZE="30" CLASS="required"></P>
<P>Phone Number: <BR>
<INPUT TYPE="text" NAME="number" SIZE="12" CLASS="required"></P>
```

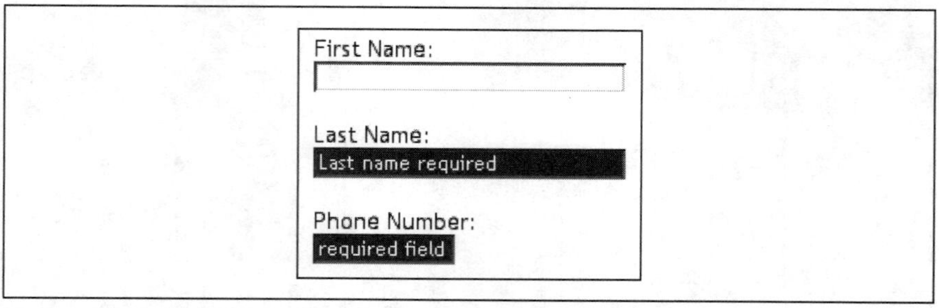

First Name:

Last Name:
Last name required

Phone Number:
required field

Figure 15-15: Style sheets alter the appearance of certain fields

Style sheets can be used to apply color to any form element, including check-boxes, radio buttons, specific options within menus, etc. You can even use them to specify the size of text entry fields in specific pixel dimensions (using the `width` and `height` properties), making it easier to predict page layouts. The only problem at this time is browser support. Because only the very latest browsers are on board, it will be a while before we can rely on these techniques for important interface cues.

Aligning Form Elements

A page with lots of form elements can get ugly in a hurry. The best favor you can do for a form is to align the elements in some orderly fashion. There are two methods for doing this: using the `<pre>` tag and using a table.

The `<pre>` tag

Unlike standard HTML body text, preformatted text (delimited by `<pre>` tags) is displayed exactly as it is typed in, honoring multiple character spaces and line breaks. Using characters wrapped in `<pre>` tags has long been a favorite cheat for aligning elements on a web page, going back to the Web's infancy.

If you put your entire form within `<pre>` tags, you can align the elements by columns of characters. The drawbacks to this method are that it does not offer much flexibility for page design and it may be tedious work. Another disadvantage is that any text displayed near the form elements will use a monospace font. The advantage to putting your whole form within `<pre>` tags is that it will be viewed the same way by all users, even those using browsers that don't support forms in tables (early browser versions, especially early versions of the AOL browser).

Using tables for form alignment

Tables are really the best tool available for tidying messy form elements. There is nothing special about tables used for forms; the same principles and guidelines outlined in Chapter 13 apply for this use. However, there are a few points to keep in mind for better results:

- Form elements tend to be rendered with extra space above and below. This can be problematic when trying to fit a form into a tight table cell. If you want to lay out a form with a table, it is better to put the `<table>` element within the `<form>` element instead of the other way around. Forms can contain all sorts of page elements, so it is not a problem for one to span over more of the page than just the form element. If you must put a form within a table, be sure to give it plenty of space.

- Remember that form elements that contain text (text entry fields, text areas, and scrolling lists) will resize in Navigator relative to the constant-width font size as set in the browser preferences. This is especially treacherous when form elements are placed in a meticulously sized table, as shown in Figure 15-16.

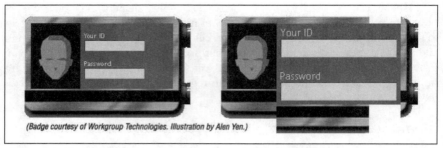

(Badge courtesy of Workgroup Technologies. Illustration by Alen Yen.)

Figure 15-16: Navigator expands forms to accommodate user-defined font sizes

Working with Menus

As mentioned earlier, browsers automatically generate form elements such as pull-down and scrolling menus; however, there are a few ways in which you can tweak their appearance.

First, your page may look neater overall if your menu elements are all the same width so they align nicely. The width of a menu element is automatically determined by the item with the most number of characters in the list. (The `size` attribute affects only the list's height.)

One way to give your lists the same width is to create a dummy option item (<option>) within each list and make it the desired width by filling it with a number of nonbreaking spaces ( ) or hyphens (-).

A dummy option item containing only a number of hyphens can also be used as a divider within the list. Select menus can not contain horizontal rules (<hr>), so adding a row of hyphens is the closest you can get to dividing the list items visually into groups, as shown in Figure 15-17.

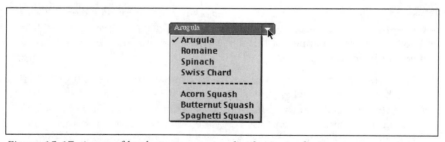

Figure 15-17: A row of hyphens serves as a divider in a select menu

The trick to doing this successfully is to make sure that if the user selects your dummy row (and there's nothing that can prevent users from doing so), the information will not be transferred to the server. The desired effect is to make it seem like nothing happens. This can be accomplished with JavaScript code such as the following, contributed to this book by Martin Burns of Edinburgh, Scotland:

```
<SCRIPT>
function checker(selector) {
```

```
   if(selector.options[selector.selectedIndex].text = '---------------') {
     selector.options.selectedIndex = selector.options.defaultIndex
   }
</SCRIPT>
<SELECT name="brand" size=1 onChange="checker(this)">
   <OPTION selected value="">Arugula
   <OPTION>Romaine
   <OPTION>Spinach
   <OPTION>Swiss Chard
   <OPTION>---------------
   <OPTION>Acorn Squash
   <OPTION>Butternut Squash
   <OPTION>Spaghetti Squash
</SELECT>
```

Demystifying CGI

Today, there are many options for processing forms on the server, such as ASP, PHP, and Java servlets. The traditional method is to use CGI scripts.

A CGI program (or script) can be written in a number of programming languages. It doesn't matter to the server which you use, as long as it can retrieve data and send data back. On Unix, the most popular language is Perl, but C, C++, Tcl, and Python are also used. On Windows, programmers write scripts in Visual Basic, Perl, and C/C++. On the Mac, AppleScript and C/C++ are common.

Often designers assume that the *cgi-bin* directory contains things beyond our comprehension. It's time to look behind the curtain! Although it is true that creating Perl and C scripts from scratch requires programming experience, you can still take advantage of the power of scripts by using one that is already made.

Many web-hosting services offer a library of standard CGI scripts that are already installed on their servers. In that case, all you may need to do is point to the script from your page. Some hosting providers also allow you to upload scripts of your own.

There are a number of great resources for CGI scripts on the Web, including scripts that process forms and send their contents in formatted email messages. Many of them are available for free and include exhaustive documentation that leads even a novice through the process of customizing and installing the script on the server. Some of the more popular CGI archives include:

Matt's Script Archive
> A collection of free and useful scripts written by Matt Wright (including Form-Mail discussed later in this chapter) with excellent documentation for configuring. See *http://www.worldwidemart.com/scripts/*.

The CGI Resource Index
> A complete index of over 1200 CGI-related resources. This site is compiled by Matt Wright of Matt's Script Archive. See *http://www.cgi-resources.com*.

Selena Sol's Public Domain CGI Script Archive

"A public service website developed out of the late-night scripting expeditions of Selena Sol and Gunther Birznieks." See *http://www.extropia.com/Scripts/*.

Freescripts.com

Like the name says, this is another site providing useful and free customizable CGI scripts. See *http://www.freescripts.com*.

Ask Your Server Administrator

Because adding scripts and programs to your web site relies heavily on your server and its configuration, you'll need to work with your server administrator to get things set up. Before you start, you should ask your administrator the following questions:

- **Does your web site-hosting package include access to CGI scripts?** Not all web site hosting services provide access to CGI scripts and functions.

- **Does the server have a script available that does what you're looking for?** Many web site-hosting services have standard scripts available for their customers' use. If there's one already installed, it may save you some time in development.

- **Can you upload your own scripts to the server?** Again, depending upon your arrangement for web site-hosting, you may not be permitted to upload your own scripts to the server, particularly if you are sharing a server with other sites.

- **Do you have upload privileges to the *cgi-bin* directory?** Assuming you can upload your own scripts to the server, you need to make sure that you have write privileges to the directory where the scripts are stored (usually called *cgi-bin*). Your administrator may need to set up an account for you that gives you access to the directory and allows you to make your scripts readable and executable by other users.

- **On what kind of server is your site hosted? What server software is it running?** Scripts are usually written to perform on a particular platform and web server software configuration. Before you spend time customizing a script, be sure that it can be run on your server.

- **What is the exact pathname to the script (once installed)?** You will need to include this in the `action` setting in a `<form>`, or wherever you need to reference the script.

In addition, there will usually be a few questions specific to your chosen script that will need to be answered by your administrator. For instance, in order to run a Perl script, the basic Perl interpreter needs to be installed on the server. Or if you want a script that automatically takes the contents of a form and sends it in an email message, you may need to know the exact pathname of the sendmail program on the server (as we'll see in the following example). You will need to find out what names to use for the form elements, since the CGI program will be expecting forms to use certain names for specific data. You should also ask whether to use the `post` or `get` method for transmitting form information.

Using Available Scripts

Let's take a look at the process for customizing a free script found on one of the CGI script archives. The purpose of this tutorial is to give you an idea of what to expect and to show that you don't need specific programming skills to do it.

In the following example, we use the FormMail script (written by Matt Wright), which takes the contents of a form and sends it to a specified user in a formatted email message. Although the script in its entirety (about nine book pages worth) is not shown here, you can easily download it from Matt's Script Archive (*http://www.worldwidemart.com/scripts/*).

1. First, make all the necessary arrangements with your server administrator as outlined in the previous section. You should have an understanding of how your particular server and account handle CGI scripts before proceeding.

2. Download the script. Upon downloading, you are given the script as well as a very complete ReadMe file that outlines, step by step, the process for using the script. Read the documentation carefully.

3. Configure the script. You may need to make changes within the script itself to customize it for your use. Following is a sample of the FormMail script. (Note that certain portions of this script have been omitted where indicated for purposes of fitting it in this chapter).

   The FormMail program requires only three variables to be changed (highlighted in bold type in this example):

   — The pathname of the Perl interpreter on your server (in the first line of the script)

   — The pathname of your server's sendmail program (after `$mailprog` in the sample below)

   — The list of domains on which you will allow forms to reside and use your FormMail script (following `@referers` in the sample below).

   These variables are clearly explained in the ReadMe file and are presented with labels in the beginning of the script for ease of customization. Furthermore, each section of the script is clearly labeled as to its function, if you are interested.

```
#!/usr/bin/perl
############################################################################
# FormMail                        Version 1.6                            #
# Copyright 1995-1997 Matt Wright mattw@worldwidemart.com                #
# Created 06/09/95                Last Modified 05/02/97                 #
# Matt's Script Archive, Inc.:    http://www.worldwidemart.com/scripts/#
############################################################################
# COPYRIGHT NOTICE                                                       #
# Copyright 1995-1997 Matthew M. Wright  All Rights Reserved.            #
```

[full copyright notice omitted]

```
##########################################################################
# Define Variables                                                       #
#         Detailed Information Found In README File.                      #

# $mailprog defines the location of your sendmail program on your unix   #
#           system.                                                       #

$mailprog = '/usr/lib/sendmail';

# @referers allows forms to be located only on servers which are         #
# defined in this field.  This security fix from the last version        #
# which allowed anyone on any server to use your FormMail script on      #
# their web site.                                                        #

@referers = ('worldwidemart.com','206.31.72.203');

# Done                                                                   #
##########################################################################
```

[section omitted]

```
sub check_url {

    # Localize the check_referer flag which determines if user is valid.#
    local($check_referer) = 0;

    # If a referring URL was specified, for each valid referer, make     #
    # sure that a valid referring URL was passed to FormMail.            #
if ($ENV{'HTTP_REFERER'}) {
        foreach $referer (@referers) {
            if ($ENV{'HTTP_REFERER'} =~ m|https?://([^/]*)$referer|i) {
                $check_referer = 1;
                last;
            }
        }
    }
    else {
        $check_referer = 1;
    }

    # If the HTTP_REFERER was invalid, send back an error.               #
    if ($check_referer != 1) { &error('bad_referer') }
}
```
[remaining script omitted]

4. Add mandatory controls to the form. The FormMail script relies on the following hidden input control, which must be included in the form. It tells the script who to mail the form results to.

```
<INPUT TYPE=hidden NAME="recipient" VALUE="email@your.host.com">
```

5. Add optional controls to the form. The FormMail documentation also provides a listing of other form controls you might include in your form and the exact HTML for creating them. The following is an example taken from the documentation that describes how to specify the "subject" field of an email message generated by the script:

Field

subject

Description

The subject field allows you to specify the subject you wish to appear in the email sent to you after this form has been filled out. If you do not have this option turned on, the script will default to a message subject: WWW Form Submission.

Syntax

If you wish to choose what the subject is:

```
<INPUT TYPE=hidden NAME="subject" VALUE="Your Subject">
```

To allow the user to choose a subject:

```
<INPUT TYPE=text NAME="subject">
```

6. Upload the script to the correct directory, following the instructions of your server administrator. Be sure that you have included the proper pathname to the script with the action attribute in the <form> tag.

Forms

CHAPTER 16

Specifying Color in HTML

You can specify the color of certain page elements using HTML tags. There are two methods for specifying colors in web documents: RGB values and color name.

Specifying Color by RGB Values

The most common and precise way to specify a color in HTML is by its numerical RGB (red, green, blue) values. For an explanation of RGB color, see "Color on the Web" in Chapter 3.

Once you've identified the red, green, and blue values of your chosen color (an image-editing tool helps with this task), you need to translate them to their hexadecimal equivalents in order to enter them into the HTML color tag. These values are written in HTML with the following syntax:

```
"#RRGGBB"
```

RR stands for the hexadecimal red value, GG stands for the hexadecimal green value, and BB stands for the hexadecimal blue value. Using these values, you can specify any color from the "true color" space (millions of colors).

Let's look at an example to put this in context. To set the background color of a document to dark olive green, first find the RGB values of the color (85, 107, 47) and convert them into their hexadecimal equivalents (55, 6B, 2F; explanation of conversion follows). Then the values can be placed in an HTML tag, in this case to change the background color of a page:

```
<BODY BGCOLOR="#556B2F">
```

The Hexadecimal System

The hexadecimal numbering system is base-16 (as compared to base-10 for decimal numbers). It uses the following 16 characters:

```
0, 1, 2, 3, 4, 5, 6, 7, 8, 9, A, B, C, D, E, F
```

A through F represent the decimal values 10 through 15.

Converting Decimal to Hexadecimal

You can calculate hex values in the 0 to 255 range by dividing a number by 16 to get the first digit, then using the remainder for the second digit. For example, dividing the decimal number 203 by 16 yields 12 with a remainder of 11. The hexadecimal value of 12 is C; the hex value of 11 is B. Therefore, the hexadecimal equivalent of 203 is CB.

Fortunately, there are simpler methods for converting numbers to hexadecimal:

- Use Table 16-1, which translates decimal values from 0 to 255.

- Use a hexadecimal calculator. On the Macintosh, you can download a copy of a utility called Calculator II (*ftp://ftp.amug.org/pub/mirrors/info-mac/sci/calc/ calculator-ii-15.hqx*). Windows users can find a hexadecimal calculator in the "Scientific" view of the Windows standard calculator.

- Use online resources. There are several resources online for calculating hexadecimal equivalents. Some allow you to enter all three values for red, green, and blue, and convert to hexadecimal while showing you a sample of your chosen color immediately. Examples of online calculations include:

Mediarama's Color Page Builder
> Plug in your decimal RGB values for page elements, and this page automatically generates a sample page with your color selections and the HTML code for the <body> tag. See *http://www.inquisitor.com/hex.html*.

URL Univox Internet: RGB 2 Hex
> This is a stripped-down, no-frills tool for converting decimal RGB values to their hex equivalents. See *http://www.univox.com/rgb2hex.html*.

Table 16-1: Decimal to hexadecimal equivalents

dec = hex	dec = hex	dec = hex	dec = hex	dec = hex	dec = hex
0 = 00	20 = 14	40 = 28	60 = 3C	80 = 50	100 = 64
1 = 01	21 = 15	41 = 29	61 = 3D	81 = 51	101 = 65
2 = 02	22 = 16	42 = 2A	62 = 3E	82 = 52	102 = 66
3 = 03	23 = 17	43 = 2B	63 = 3F	83 = 53	103 = 67
4 = 04	24 = 18	44 = 2C	64 = 40	84 = 54	104 = 68
5 = 05	25 = 19	45 = 2D	65 = 41	85 = 55	105 = 69
6 = 06	26 = 1A	46 = 2E	66 = 42	86 = 56	106 = 6A
7 = 07	27 = 1B	47 = 2F	67 = 43	87 = 57	107 = 6B
8 = 08	28 = 1C	48 = 30	68 = 44	88 = 58	108 = 6C
9 = 09	29 = 1D	49 = 31	69 = 45	89 = 59	109 = 6D
10 = 0A	30 = 1E	50 = 32	70 = 46	90 = 5A	110 = 6E
11 = 0B	31 = 1F	51 = 33	71 = 47	91 = 5B	111 = 6F
12 = 0C	32 = 20	52 = 34	72 = 48	92 = 5C	112 = 70
13 = 0D	33 = 21	53 = 35	73 = 49	93 = 5D	113 = 71
14 = 0E	34 = 22	54 = 36	74 = 4A	94 = 5E	114 = 72
15 = 0F	35 = 23	55 = 37	75 = 4B	95 = 5F	115 = 73
16 = 10	36 = 24	56 = 38	76 = 4C	96 = 60	116 = 74
17 = 11	37 = 25	57 = 39	77 = 4D	97 = 61	117 = 75
18 = 12	38 = 26	58 = 3A	78 = 4E	98 = 62	118 = 76
19 = 13	39 = 27	59 = 3B	79 = 4F	99 = 63	119 = 77

Table 16-1: Decimal to hexadecimal equivalents (continued)

dec = hex	dec = hex	dec = hex	dec = hex	dec = hex	dec = hex
120 = 78	143 = 8F	166 = A6	189 = BD	213 = D5	236 = EC
121 = 79	144 = 90	167 = A7	190 = BE	214 = D6	237 = ED
122 = 7A	145 = 91	168 = A8	191 = BF	215 = D7	238 = EE
123 = 7B	146 = 92	169 = A9	192 = C0	216 = D8	239 = EF
124 = 7C	147 = 93	170 = AA	193 = C1	217 = D9	240 = F0
125 = 7D	148 = 94	171 = AB	194 = C2	218 = DA	241 = F1
126 = 7E	149 = 95	172 = AC	195 = C3	219 = DB	242 = F2
127 = 7F	150 = 96	173 = AD	196 = C4	220 = DC	243 = F3
128 = 80	151 = 97	174 = AE	198 = C6	221 = DD	244 = F4
129 = 81	152 = 98	175 = AF	199 = C7	222 = DE	245 = F5
130 = 82	153 = 99	176 = B0	200 = C8	223 = DF	246 = F6
131 = 83	154 = 9A	177 = B1	201 = C9	224 = E0	247 = F7
132 = 84	155 = 9B	178 = B2	202 = CA	225 = E1	248 = F8
133 = 85	156 = 9C	179 = B3	203 = CB	226 = E2	249 = F9
134 = 86	157 = 9D	180 = B4	204 = CC	227 = E3	250 = FA
135 = 87	158 = 9E	181 = B5	205 = CD	228 = E4	251 = FB
136 = 88	159 = 9F	182 = B6	206 = CE	229 = E5	252 = FC
137 = 89	160 = A0	183 = B7	207 = CF	230 = E6	253 = FD
138 = 8A	161 = A1	184 = B8	208 = D0	231 = E7	254 = FE
139 = 8B	162 = A2	185 = B9	209 = D1	232 = E8	255 = FF
140 = 8C	163 = A3	186 = BA	210 = D2	233 = E9	
141 = 8D	164 = A4	187 = BB	211 = D3	234 = EA	
142 = 8E	165 = A5	188 = BC	212 = D4	235 = EB	

Hexadecimal Values for Web Palette Colors

The web palette is a set of 216 colors that will not shift or dither when rendered in browsers on 8-bit monitors (for a thorough explanation of the web palette, see Chapter 3). All colors in the web palette are made up of combinations of the following six hexadecimal values: 00, 33, 66, 99, CC, and FF.

Specifying Colors by Name

Colors can also be identified by one of 140 color names originally developed for the X Window System. The complete list appears in Table 16-2 (sorted alphabetically, with numerical values included) and Table 16-3 (grouped by hue). You can also view samples of each color at *http://www.learningwebdesign.com/colornames.html*.

To set the background color to a dark olive green using a color name, the complete HTML tag would look like this:

```
<BODY BGCOLOR="darkolivegreen">
```

Grays

There are also one hundred variants of gray numbered 1 through 100. "Gray1" is the darkest; "gray100" is the lightest. The color we generally think of as "gray" is roughly equivalent to "gray75." Both spellings "gray" and "grey" are acceptable.

Color Name Cautions

There are several pitfalls to using color names instead of numerical color values:

Browser support

Color names are supported only by Navigator Versions 2.0 and higher and Internet Explorer Versions 3.0 and higher. Internet Explorer 2.0 supports the following 16 color names:

```
aqua      gray      navy      silver
black     green     olive     teal
blue      lime      purple    white
fuchsia   maroon    red       yellow
```

These are also the only color names specified by the W3C in the HTML 4.01 Specification.

Color shifting

Of the 140 color names, only 10 represent nondithering colors from the web palette. They are aqua, black, blue, cyan, fuchsia, lime, magenta, red, white, and yellow.

When viewed on an 8-bit display, the remaining 130 colors shift to their nearest web palette equivalent (or system palette color). In many cases, the difference is drastic. Many of the pastels shift to solid white.

The "Nearest Web-safe Color" column in Table 16-2 lists the color that will actually be displayed for each color name on an 8-bit display.

Table 16-2: Color names with their numeric values

Color name	RGB values	Hexadecimal	Nearest web-safe color
aliceblue	240 - 248 - 255	F0F8FF	FFFFFF
antiquewhite	250 - 235 - 215	FAEBD7	FFFFCC
aqua	0 - 255 - 255	00FFFF	00FFFF
aquamarine	127 - 255 - 212	7FFFD4	66FFCC
azure	240 - 255 - 255	F0FFFF	FFFFFF
beige	245 - 245 - 220	F5F5DC	FFFFCC
bisque	255 - 228 - 196	FFE4C4	FFFFCC
black	0 - 0 - 0	000000	000000
blanchedalmond	255 - 255 - 205	FFFFCD	FFFFCC
blue	0 - 0 - 255	0000FF	0000FF
blueviolet	138 - 43 - 226	8A2BE2	9933FF
brown	165 - 42 - 42	A52A2A	993333
burlywood	222 - 184 - 135	DEB887	CCCC99
cadetblue	95 - 158 - 160	5F9EA0	669999
chartreuse	127 - 255 - 0	7FFF00	66FF00
chocolate	210 - 105 - 30	D2691E	996600
coral	255 - 127 - 80	FF7F50	FF6666
cornflowerblue	100 - 149 - 237	6495ED	6699FF

Table 16-2: Color names with their numeric values (continued)

Color name	RGB values	Hexadecimal	Nearest web-safe color
cornsilk	255 - 248 - 220	FFF8DC	FFFFCC
crimson	220 - 20 - 60	DC143C	CC0033
cyan	0 - 255 - 255	00FFFF	00FFFF
darkblue	0 - 0 - 139	00008B	000099*
darkcyan	0 - 139 - 139	008B8B	009999
darkgoldenrod	184 - 134 - 11	B8860B	CC9900
darkgray	169 - 169 - 169	A9A9A9	999999*
darkgreen	0 - 100 - 0	006400	006600
darkkhaki	189 - 183 - 107	BDB76B	CCCC66
darkmagenta	139 - 0 - 139	8B008B	990099
darkolivegreen	85 - 107 - 47	556B2F	666633
darkorange	255 - 140 - 0	FF8C00	FF9900
darkorchid	153 - 50 - 204	9932CC	9933CC
darkred	139 - 0 - 0	8B0000	990000*
darksalmon	233 - 150 - 122	E9967A	FF9966
darkseagreen	143 - 188 - 143	8FBC8F	99CC99
darkslateblue	72 - 61 - 139	483D8B	333399
darkslategray	47 - 79 - 79	2F4F4F	339999*
darkturquoise	0 - 206 - 209	00CED1	00CCCC
darkviolet	148 - 0 - 211	9400D3	9900CC
deeppink	255 - 20 - 147	FF1493	FF0099
deepskyblue	0 - 191 - 255	00BFFF	00CCFF
dimgray	105 - 105 - 105	696969	666666
dodgerblue	30 - 144 - 255	1E90FF	0099FF
firebrick	178 - 34 - 34	B22222	CC3333
floralwhite	255 - 250 - 240	FFFAF0	FFFFFF
forestgreen	34 - 139 - 34	228B22	339933
fuchsia	255 - 0 - 255	FF00FF	FF00FF
gainsboro	220 - 220 - 220	DCDCDC	CCCCCC*
ghostwhite	248 - 248 - 255	F8F8FF	FFFFFF
gold	255 - 215 - 0	FFD700	FFCC00
goldenrod	218 - 165 - 32	DAA520	CC9933
gray	128 - 128 - 128	808080	999999*
green	0 - 128 - 0	008000	009900
greenyellow	173 - 255 - 47	ADFF2F	99FF33
honeydew	240 - 255 - 240	F0FFF0	FFFFFF
hotpink	255 - 105 - 180	FF69B4	FF66CC
indianred	205 - 92 - 92	CD5C5C	CC6666
indigo	75 - 0 - 130	4B0082	330099
ivory	255 - 240 - 240	FFF0F0	FFFFFF
khaki	240 - 230 - 140	F0D58C	FFCC99
lavender	230 - 230 - 250	E6E6FA	FFFFFF*

Table 16-2: Color names with their numeric values (continued)

Color name	RGB values	Hexadecimal	Nearest web-safe color
lavenderblush	255 - 240 - 245	FFF0F5	FFFFFF
lawngreen	124 - 252 - 0	7CFC00	00FF00
lemonchiffon	255 - 250 - 205	FFFACD	FFFFCC
lightblue	173 - 216 - 230	ADD8E6	99CCFF
lightcoral	240 - 128 - 128	F08080	FF9999
lightcyan	224 - 255 - 255	E0FFFF	FFFFFF
lightgoldenrodyellow	250 - 250 - 210	FAFAD2	FFFFCC
lightgreen	144 - 238 - 144	90EE90	99FF99
lightgrey	211 - 211 - 211	D3D3D3	CCCCCC*
lightpink	255 - 182 - 193	FFB6C1	FFFFCC
lightsalmon	255 - 160 - 122	FFA07A	FF9966
lightseagreen	32 - 178 - 170	20B2AA	33CC99
lightskyblue	135 - 206 - 250	87CEFA	99CCFF
lightslategray	119 - 136 - 153	778899	669999
lightsteelblue	176 - 196 - 222	B0C4DE	CCCCCC
lightyellow	255 - 255 - 224	FFFFE0	FFFFFF
lime	0 - 255 - 0	00FF00	00FF00
limegreen	50 - 205 - 50	32CD32	33CC33
linen	250 - 240 - 230	FAF0E6	FFFFFF
magenta	255 - 0 - 255	FF00FF	FF00FF
maroon	128 - 0 - 0	800000	990000*
mediumaquamarine	102 - 205 - 170	66CDAA	66CC99
mediumblue	0 - 0 - 205	0000CD	0000CC
mediumorchid	186 - 85 - 211	BA55D3	CC66CC
mediumpurple	147 - 112 - 219	9370DB	9966CC
mediumseagreen	60 - 179 - 113	3CB371	33CC66
mediumslateblue	123 - 104 - 238	7B68EE	6666FF
mediumspringgreen	0 - 250 - 154	00FA9A	00FF99
mediumturquoise	72 - 209 - 204	48D1CC	33CCCC
mediumvioletred	199 - 21 - 133	C71585	CC0066
midnightblue	25 - 25 - 112	191970	000066*
mintcream	245 - 255 - 250	F5FFFA	FFFFFF
mistyrose	255 - 228 - 225	FFE4E1	FFFFFF*
moccasin	255 - 228 - 181	FFE4B5	FFFFCC
navajowhite	255 - 222 - 173	FFDEAD	FFCC99
navy	0 - 0 - 128	000080	000099*
oldlace	253 - 245 - 230	FDF5E6	FFFFFF
olive	128 - 128 - 0	808000	999900
olivedrab	107 - 142 - 35	6B8E23	669933
orange	255 - 165 - 0	FFA500	FF9900
orangered	255 - 69 - 0	FF4500	FF3300
orchid	218 - 112 - 214	DA70D6	CC66CC

Table 16-2: Color names with their numeric values (continued)

Color name	RGB values	Hexadecimal	Nearest web-safe color
palegoldenrod	238 - 232 - 170	EEE8AA	FFFF99
palegreen	152 - 251 - 152	98FB98	99FF99
paleturquoise	175 - 238 - 238	AFEEEE	99FFFF
palevioletred	219 - 112 - 147	DB7093	CC6699
papayawhip	255 - 239 - 213	FFEFD5	FFFFCC
peachpuff	255 - 218 - 185	FFDAB9	FFCCCC
peru	205 - 133 - 63	CD853F	CC9933
pink	255 - 192 - 203	FFC0CB	FFCCCC
plum	221 - 160 - 221	DDA0DD	CC99CC
powderblue	176 - 224 - 230	B0E0E6	CCFFFF
purple	128 - 0 - 128	800080	990099
red	255 - 0 - 0	FF0000	FF0000
rosybrown	188 - 143 - 143	BC8F8F	CC9999
royalblue	65 - 105 - 225	4169E1	3366FF
saddlebrown	139 - 69 - 19	8B4513	993300
salmon	250 - 128 - 114	FA8072	FF9966
sandybrown	244 - 164 - 96	F4A460	FF9966
seagreen	46 - 139 - 87	2E8B57	339966
seashell	255 - 245 - 238	FFF5EE	FFFFFF
sienna	160 - 82 - 45	A0522D	996633
silver	192 - 192 - 192	C0C0C0	CCCCCC
skyblue	135 - 206 - 235	87CEEB	99CCFF
slateblue	106 - 90 - 205	6A5ACD	6666CC
slategray	112 - 128 - 144	708090	669999
snow	255 - 250 - 250	FFFAFA	FFFFFF
springgreen	0 - 255 - 127	00FF7F	00FF66
steelblue	70 - 130 - 180	4682B4	3399CC
tan	210 - 180 - 140	D2B48C	CCCC99
teal	0 - 128 - 128	008080	009999
thistle	216 - 191 - 216	D8BFD8	CCCCCC*
tomato	253 - 99 - 71	FF6347	FF6633
turquoise	64 - 224 - 208	40E0D0	33FFCC
violet	238 - 130 - 238	EE82EE	FF99FF
wheat	245 - 222 - 179	F5DEB3	FFCCCC
white	255 - 255 - 255	FFFFFF	FFFFFF
whitesmoke	245 - 245 - 245	F5F5F5	FFFFFF
yellow	255 - 255 - 0	FFFF00	FFFF00
yellowgreen	154 - 205 - 50	9ACD32	66CC33

* These color names shift to the nearest Mac system palette color when viewed on a Macintosh using any browser except Netscape Navigator 4.0 (which shifts it to the nearest web palette color).

Table 16-3: Web color names by hue

black
white

Neutrals—cool

darkgray
darkslategray
dimgray
gainsboro
ghostwhite
gray
lightgray
lightslategray
silver
slategray
snow

Neutrals—warm

antiquewhite
cornsilk
floralwhite
ivory
linen
oldlace
papayawhip
seashell

Browns/Tans

bisque
beige
blanchedalmond
brown
burlywood
chocolate
khaki
moccasin
navajowhite
peru
rosybrown
sandybrown
sienna
tan
wheat

Oranges

darkorange
orange
orangered
peachpuff

Yellows

darkgoldenrod
gold
goldenrod

lemonchiffon
lightgoldenrodyellow
lightyellow
palegoldenrod
yellow

Greens

aquamarine
chartreuse
darkgreen
darkkhaki
darkolivegreen
darkseagreen
forestgreen
green
greenyellow
honeydew
lawngreen
lightgreen
lime
limegreen
mediumseagreen
mediumspringgreen
mintgreen
olive
olivedrab
palegreen
seagreen
springgreen
yellowgreen

Blue-greens

aqua
cyan
darkcyan
darkturquoise
lightcyan
lightseagreen
mediumaquamarine
mediumturquoise
paleturquoise
turquoise

Blues

aliceblue
azure
blue
cadetblue
cornflowerblue
darkblue
darkslateblue
deepskyblue

dodgerblue
indigo
lightblue
lightskyblue
lightsteelblue
mediumblue
mediumslateblue
midnightblue
navy
powderblue
skyblue
slateblue
steelblue

Purples

blueviolet
darkmagenta
darkorchid
darkviolet
lavender
lavenderblush
mediumorchid
mediumpurple
mediumvioletred
orchid
palevioletred
plum
purple
thistle
violet

Pinks

coral
darksalmon
deeppink
fuchsia
hotpink
lightcoral
lightpink
lightsalmon
magenta
mistyrose
pink
salmon

Reds

crimson
darkred
firebrick
indianred
maroon
red

Coloring Page Elements

Table 16-4 lists the HTML elements for which you can specify a color. Each tag's use is further explained in Chapters 9, 10, and 13 of this book.

Table 16-4: Summary of HTML tags with color attributes

Tag	Attribute	Description
<BODY>	BGCOLOR=*color*	Document background
<BODY>	TEXT=*color*	Regular text
<BODY>	LINK=*color*	Hypertext link
<BODY>	VLINK=*color*	Visited link
<BODY>	ALINK=*color*	Active link
<FONT>	COLOR=*color*	Colors a selection of text
<BASEFONT>	COLOR=*color*	Colors the following block of text (*IE only*)
<TABLE>	BGCOLOR=*color*	Applies color to all cells in a table
<TABLE>	BORDERCOLOR=*color*	Table border color (*IE only*)
<TABLE>	BORDERCOLORLIGHT=*color*	Table border highlight color (*IE only*)
<TABLE>	BORDERCOLORDARK=*color*	Table border shadow color (*IE only*)
<TR>	BGCOLOR=*color*	Table row background
<TD>	BGCOLOR=*color*	Table cell background
<TH>	BGCOLOR=*color*	Table header background
<FRAMESET>	BORDERCOLOR=*color*	Colors borders between all frames on a page
<FRAME>	BORDERCOLOR=*color*	Colors the border for one particular frame

Similarly, color can be applied to elements on a web page using Cascading Style Sheet properties. The CSS1 properties that take color values are listed in Table 16-5.

Table 16-5: CSS1 properties for specifying color

Property	Description
color	Sets the foreground color of a given element. When applied to a text element (such as H1 or P) it sets the text color.
background-color	Sets the background color of an element. The color fills the content area and padding and extends to the outer edge of the element's border.
border-color	Sets the color of the overall border of an element.

CHAPTER 17

Cascading Style Sheets

For those frustrated with the limited control over document presentation provided by straight HTML markup, Cascading Style Sheets (CSS) are a welcome advance in web design. They are also the official W3C standard for controlling all presentation, leaving HTML markup to indicate structure as it was designed to do.

Using Style Sheets

Like their counterparts in desktop publishing page-layout programs, style sheets in HTML allow authors to apply typographic styles and spacing instructions for elements on a page. The word *cascading* refers to what happens when several sources of style information vie for control of the elements on a page—style information is passed down from higher-level style sheets (and from parent to child element within a document) until it is overridden by a style command with more weight. (The cascading rules are discussed in detail later in this chapter.)

This comes as good news both for designers who want more control over presentation and for HTML purists who stand by the principle that style should be separate from content and structure. Style sheets make both these dreams possible, but it is important to be aware of their advantages and disadvantages.

Advantages

Style sheets offer the following advantages to web designers:

- **Greater typography and page layout controls**. With style sheets, you can specify traditional typography attributes such as font size, line spacing, and letter spacing. Style sheets also offer methods for specifying indents, margins, and element positioning, and they even use terminology from traditional and desktop publishing, such as points and em spaces.

- **Style is separate from structure**. HTML is designed for indicating the structure of a document, to which presentation is applied by the end user's browsing device. Over recent years, however, HTML has been extended to provide greater control over presentation (the <font> tag being the most infamous example). Style sheets, when done correctly, mark the return to the original intent of HTML by removing presentation instructions from HTML and placing them in a separate, optional area.

- **Potentially smaller documents**. Placing font specifications once at the beginning of the document instead of using a <font> description for every individual element can drastically cut down on the number of characters in the document, thus reducing its file size. As always with the Web, it is desirable to keep file sizes (and download times) as small as possible.

- **Easier site maintenance**. It is possible to link multiple HTML pages to a single style sheet, which means not only can you make one change that affects every instance of that element on a single HTML page, but you can also make style changes to hundreds or thousands of web pages by editing a single file.

- **It's easy to learn**. Creating basic style sheets is no more difficult than tagging documents, once you learn the syntax rules. To make the job even easier, style sheet functions are now built into web authoring tools like Macromedia Dreamweaver and Adobe GoLive.

Disadvantages

As of this writing, the sole drawback to implementing style sheets remains uneven browser support. First, style sheet information is not supported in browser versions earlier than Microsoft Internet Explorer 3.0 or Netscape Navigator 4.0. That is not as frustrating as the inconsistency of support among browsers and versions that claim they *do* support CSS.

The World Wide Web Consortium first published its recommendation for style sheets in 1996, and they were first implemented by Internet Explorer 3.0. Since then, as usual, Microsoft and Netscape have chosen diverging paths in the properties their browsers support and the way those properties are presented. The browser-support charts in Appendix E are evidence of the gap in style sheet implementations. A constantly updated browser support list is maintained online by Eric Meyer for WebReview at *http://www.webreview.com/style/css1/charts/mastergrid.shtml*.

The good news is that the outlook continues to improve with the release of standards-compliant browsers and as older versions fade away. Internet Explorer 5.5 and higher and Netscape 6 claim to support almost all of the CSS Level 1 specification and parts of CSS Level 2 (the latest version as of this writing). With an estimated 95% of web users surfing with 4.0 or higher version browsers, you can safely assume that basic styles (font, size, and color, for example) will reach the vast majority of your audience.

Strategies for Using Style Sheets Today

Although consistent browser support for style sheets remains a large issue, that does not mean that you should abandon them completely. In fact, many large commercial and consumer-oriented sites are taking advantage of the power of style sheets today. Here are a few strategies for adding styles to your site:

- **Include end tags.** While current browsers don't mind if you leave off the `</p>` or `</li>` tag, style sheets (and other web technologies such as XML) do mind. It is necessary to have clearly defined text elements, including both tags. If you think you may be adding style sheet functionality to your site in the future, get ready by closing all your tags today.

- **Use style sheets as "icing."** One way to create a site that degrades well to any browser is to first create a site free of style sheets that is acceptable on all browser and platform configurations. Once you are happy with it, add style sheet information that will not affect the display in older browsers (such as `<div>` and `<span>`, and the `class` attribute). Choosing properties that are fully supported by the major browsers (see Appendix E) will broaden the chances your design will be seen as you intend it.

- **Serve different styles to different browsers.** Another approach is to develop two versions of your site and deliver the proper version using a browser-detect JavaScript. You might have a fully-styled version that is aimed at the standards-compliant browsers (Internet Explorer 5.5+, Netscape 6, and Opera5) and another "vanilla" version that is stable without style sheets for everyone else. Since Navigator 4.x is particularly buggy, you can hold back certain style information from it using the `@import` method of style sheet application (which Navigator 4 does not support) along with or instead of `<link>`.

- **Use style sheets for intranets.** If you have the good fortune to be designing a site for which you know the exact browser/platform configuration for all your users (such as a corporate intranet or a self-contained kiosk display), feel free to use the supported style sheets to their limits.

The Future of Style Sheets

Despite a bumpy start, style sheets still hold great promise as the preferred method for specifying page presentation. The Web Standards Organization (*http://www. webstandards.org*), an industry watchdog group that educates the web community on the importance of standards, urges web authors and developers to begin using style sheets right away. Kiss your `<font>` tag goodbye!

In 1998, the W3C published its second style sheet proposal (CSS Level 2, or CSS2), which includes additional properties and advanced methods for absolute positioning that could make tables and frames as layout devices a thing of the past. Style sheets are also a key component to programming dynamic effects with DHTML. CSS Level 3 is already being considered. (Both CSS2 and CSS3 are discussed later in this chapter.)

For Further Reading

Not surprisingly, the place to go for information on Cascading Style Sheets is the W3C's site at *http://www.w3.org/style/CSS*. The full CSS1 recommendation is located at *http://www.w3.org/TR/REC-CSS1*; for CSS2, see *http://www.w3.org/TR/REC-CSS2*.

Another great resource (and one that's easier to digest than the specs themselves) is the book *Cascading Style Sheets: The Definitive Guide* by Eric Meyer (O'Reilly, 2000). Eric has also written many useful articles on style sheets for WebReview magazine (*http://www.webreview.com*). There you'll also find his CSS browser compatibility charts (*http://www.webreview.com/style/*).

How Style Sheets Work

The key to working with style sheets is understanding how to define rules and then attach those rules to one or more HTML documents.

Rule Syntax

Style sheets consist of one or more rules for describing how a page element should be displayed. The following sample contains two rules. The first makes all the H1s in a document red; the second specifies that paragraphs should be set in 12 pixel high Verdana or some sans-serif font:

```
H1 {color: red}
P {font-size: 12px;
   font-family: Verdana, sans-serif;
   }
```

Figure 17-1 shows the components of a style sheet rule.

Figure 17-1: Parts of a style sheet rule

The two main sections are the *selector* (which identifies the element to be affected) and the *declaration* (the style or display instructions to be applied to that element). In the sample code above, H1 and P are the selectors. The different types of selectors that may be used are discussed in the "Selectors" section of this chapter.

The declaration, enclosed in curly brackets, is made up of a *property* and its *value*. Properties are separated from their values by the colon (:) character followed by a space. A property is a stylistic parameter that can be defined, such as color, font-family, or line-height.

A declaration may contain several property/value pairs. Multiple properties must be separated by semicolons (;). Technically, the last property in a string does not require a semicolon, but developers usually include it anyway to make it easy to append the rule later. In addition, the inclusion of the trailing semicolon avoids a rare bug in older browsers.

Values are dependent on the property. Some properties take length measurements, some take color names, and others have a predefined list of accepted values. The syntax for length measurement and color values are discussed later in this chapter.

Adding Styles to an HTML Document

Rules (and sets of rules) can be applied to HTML documents in three ways: as inline style directions, as style elements embedded at the top of the HTML file, and as external files that can be either linked to or imported into the document.

Inline styles

Style information can be added to an individual element by adding the `style` attribute within the HTML tag for that element. The value of the style attribute is one or more standard style declarations, as shown here:

```
<H1 STYLE="color: red">This Heading will be Red</H1>

<P STYLE="font-size: 12pt; font-family: Verdana, sans-serif">
This is the content of the paragraph to be set with the
described styles.</P>
```

Although a perfectly valid use of style information, inline styles are equivalent to the `<font>` tag in that they "pollute" the document with presentation information. Style information is still tied to each individual content element, and any changes need to be made in every tag, in every file, rather than globally. Inline styles are best used only occasionally to override higher-level rules.

Embedded style sheets

A more compact method for adding style sheets is to embed a style block in the top of the HTML document using the `<style>` element, summarized here:

`<style>`   NN 2, 3, 4, 6   MSIE 2, 3, 4, 5, 5.5, 6   HTML 4.01   WebTV   Opera5

`<style>...</style>`

Allows authors to embed style sheet rules in the head of the document There may be any number of `<style>` elements in a document.

Attributes

`media=screen|tty|tv|projection|handheld|print|braille|aural|all`
    Specifies the target medium to which the style sheet applies.

`type=content-type`
    Required. Specifies the style sheet language of the element's contents. The only viable type at this time is `text/css`.

`title=text`
    Provides a title for the element.

The following example shows our sample rules embedded in a simple HTML document:

```
<HTML>
<HEAD>
<STYLE TYPE="text/css">
```

```
<!--
   H1 {color: red}
   P {font-size: 12pt;
       font-family: Verdana, sans-serif;
       }
-->
</STYLE>
<TITLE>Style Sheets</TITLE>
</HEAD>
...
</HTML>
```

The `<style>` element must be placed within the `<head>` tags in the document. In addition, it is usually necessary to place HTML comment tags (`<!--` and `-->`) around the `<style>` contents. This hides the style information from browsers that don't understand the `<style>` tag. (Otherwise, they might display the rules as text in the browser window.)

Currently, Cascading Style Sheets is the only widely supported style sheet language, but the W3C has prepared for the possibility of additional languages to be added in the future by providing the `type` attribute within the `<style>` element. The only viable style type as of this writing is `text/css`. If the `type` attribute is omitted, some browsers may ignore the entire style sheet.

External style sheets

The most powerful way to use styles is to collect them all in a separate text document and create links to that document from all the HTML pages in a site. In this way, you can make stylistic changes consistently across a whole site by editing the style information in a single document. This is a powerful tool for large-scale sites.

The style sheet document is a simple text document that contains a collection of style sheet rules. It may *not* contain HTML tags (after all, it isn't an HTML document). It also may not include HTML comments. In fact, the contents of a style sheet would look just like the sample code under "Rule Syntax" earlier in this chapter.

There are two ways to refer to external style sheets (which should be named with the *.css* suffix) from within an HTML document:

Linking

The most standard and best-supported method is to create a link to that document using the `<link>` tag in the `<head>` of the document, as shown here:

```
<HEAD>
<LINK REL="STYLESHEET" HREF="/pathname/stylesheet.css" TYPE="text/
css">
</HEAD>
```

The `rel` attribute defines the linked document's relation to the current document—a "style sheet." The `href` attribute provides the URL to the file containing the style sheet information. Authors can link to more than one style sheet in a document.

Importing

An alternative to linking is to import external style sheets into the `<style>` element using the `@import` function:

```
<!--
<STYLE TYPE="text/css">
    @import url(http://pathname/stylesheet.css);
</STYLE>
-->
```

`@import` commands must come *before* any style rules.

As in linking, importing allows multiple style sheets to be applied to the same document. When additional `@import` functions are added within the `<style>` element, the style information from the last file read (the one at the bottom of the list) takes precedence over the previous ones. The drawback to `@import` is limited browser support (it is currently supported only by Internet Explorer 4.0+ and Netscape 6).

Inheritance

An important feature of style sheets is the concept of inheritance, in which style properties are passed down from an element (the parent) to any element contained within it (the child). An element is said to *inherit* properties applied to elements higher in the HTML hierarchy. In CSS most properties can be inherited, but some (such as margins) cannot—the CSS specifications later in the chapter point out if the property inherits or not.

For example, if you set the text color for a `<ul>` list, then this color will be inherited by every list item (`<li>`) within that list. If you specify that the `<body>` of a document should be red, all text elements contained in the body of the document will be red (unless specified otherwise).

Styles applied to specific elements override settings higher in the hierarchy. With planning, inheritance can be used to make style specification more efficient. For example, if you'd like all the text on the page to be blue except for list items, you can set the color property at the `<body>` level to apply to the whole document and then use another rule to make `<li>`s a different color. The more specific rules override more general rules.

If two rules of equal weight are listed in a style sheet, whichever one is later in the style sheet will apply.

Conflicting Style Sheets: The Cascade

Style sheets are said to be cascading because many different style sheet rules, coming from many different possible style sheets (inline, embedded, or external) can simultaneously affect the presentation of a single document. For example, it is possible to add inline styles to a document that is already linked to an external style sheet: the final look will result from all these style components cascading together.

With several styles applied to a document, conflicts are certain to arise. For example, when an inline style says the paragraph should be maroon, but the external style sheet says all paragraphs are blue, which style gets used?

The W3C anticipated this situation and devised a hierarchical system that assigns different weights to each type of style information. This cascade order provides a set of rules for resolving conflicts between competing style sheets. Styles with more weight (those defined at the more specific level) take precedence over styles set in a higher-level style sheet.

As in inheritance, more specific rules override more general rules. This allows you to design a general style for a whole site, then modify it for particular pages or elements, alleviating redundancy.

The following list shows the hierarchy of style instructions from general to specific, such that elements lower in the list have more weight and override styles above them.

- Browser default settings.
- User style settings (set in browser as a "reader style sheet").
- Linked external style sheets. A document may have many linked style sheets. When multiple style sheets are linked to a document, the commands from the last file read take precedence over the first ones listed.
- Imported style sheets. When multiple styles are imported, the commands from the last file read take precedence over the first ones listed.
- Embedded style sheets (rules within the `<style>` element). Later rules have greater weight than earlier rules.
- Inline style information.

If you want a rule never to be overridden by a subsequent rule, include the `!important` indicator just after the property value and before the semicolon for that rule. For example, to always set all paragraph text to blue, use the following rule in a style sheet for the document:

```
p {color: blue !important;}
```

Even if the browser encounters an inline style later in the document (which should override a document-wide style sheet), such as the following, that paragraph will still be blue because the rule with the `!important` indicator can not be overridden.*

```
<p style="color: red">
```

Selectors

Selectors are the parts of the rule that identify the element (or elements) to which the style will be applied. There are several methods for identifying elements.

---

* In CSS1, `!important` rules in style sheets generated by the author take precedence over reader style sheets. However, in CSS2, `!important` rules in reader style sheets take precedence over all other style sheets.

Type Selector

The simplest type of selector calls an HTML element by its tag, as shown:

```
H1 {color: blue}
H2 {color: blue}
P {color: blue}
```

Type selectors can be grouped into comma-separated lists so a single property will apply to all of them. The following code has the same effect as the previous code:

```
H1, H2, P {color: blue}
```

<div> and <span>

Two HTML elements, div and span, are generic identifiers ideal for use with style sheets. These elements have no inherent formatting properties of their own, but they can be used to designate elements on a web page that should be affected by style sheet instructions. These instructions are ignored by browsers that do not understand them.

The <div> tag is used to delimit block-level tags and can contain other HTML elements within it:

```
<DIV STYLE="color: blue">
<H1>Headline!</H1>
<P>This is a whole paragraph of text.</P>
</DIV>
```

The <span> tag is used inline to change the style of a set of characters:

```
<P>This is a paragraph and <SPAN STYLE="color: blue">this area will be
treated differently</SPAN> from the rest of the paragraph</P>
```

When used with the class and id attribute selectors (discussed later in this chapter), these tags can be used to create custom-named elements, sort of like creating your own HTML tags.

Contextual Selectors

You can also specify style attributes for HTML elements based on the context in which they appear.

As we've seen already, a simple selector specifies that all emphasized text within a document should be red:

```
EM {color: red}
```

Using a contextual selector (written as a list of simple selectors separated by white space) you can specify that only the emphasized text that appears within a list item will be green:

```
LI EM {color: green}
```

In other words, this affects emphasized text when it appears *in the context of* a list item element. If both of these rules for emphasized text were to appear in the

CSS

same document, the contextual selector (because it is more specific) would take precedence over the simple selector.

Like simple type selectors, contextual selectors can also be grouped together in comma-separated lists. The following code makes bold (<B>) text red only when it appears in the context of a heading:

```
H1 B, H2 B, H3 B {color: red}
```

class and id Attribute Selectors

Attribute selectors allow web page authors to apply style rules based on special identifying attributes placed within HTML element tags. There are currently two available attribute selectors: `class` and `id`. They can be applied to all HTML elements except `<base>`, `<head>`, `<html>`, `<meta>`, `<script>`, `<style>`, and `<title>`. (In addition, class may not be used in `<basefont>` and `<param>`.)

class selector

Use the `class` attribute to identify a number of elements as being part of a conceptual group. Elements in a class can then be modified with a single style rule. For instance, you can identify all the items in the HTML document that you classify as "important":

```
<H1 CLASS="important">Attention!</H1>
<P CLASS="important">Your account is past due.</P>
```

To specify the styles for elements of a particular class, add the class name to the HTML selector, separated by a period (.). Note that `class` names cannot contain spaces; use hyphens or underscores instead if necessary (although underscores are discouraged due to lack of support in some browsers).

```
H1.important {color: red}
P.important {color: red}
```

To apply a property to all the elements of the same class, omit the tag name in the selector (be sure to leave the period—it is the character that indicates a class):

```
.important {color: red}
```

id selector

The `id` attribute is used similarly to `class`, but it is used for targeting a single element rather than a group. `id` must be used to name an element uniquely (in other words, two elements can't have the same `id` name in the same document). If you have several elements that need a similar treatment, use `class` instead.

In the following example, a paragraph is given a specific id (note that the value of an `id` attribute must always begin with a letter):

```
<P ID="j042801">New item added today</P>
```

`id` selectors are indicated by the hash (#) symbol within the style sheet as follows:

```
P#j061998 {color: red}
```

The HTML tag name may be omitted:

```
#j061998 {color: red}
```

Pseudo-Selectors

The CSS1 Specification provides several pseudo-elements and pseudo-classes that are not based on structural elements of a document. They can be used as selectors, but the code does not appear in the HTML source; rather, they are interpreted by the browser based on context and function. Pseudo-selectors are indicated by the colon (`:`) character. As of this writing, only Internet Explorer 5.5+ (Windows), Internet Explorer 5 (Mac), Netscape 6, and Opera support pseudo-selectors reliably.

Pseudo-elements

In CSS1, the pseudo-elements (subparts of existing elements) are `first-line` and `first-letter`. They can be used to apply styles to the first line or letter of an HTML element as it is displayed in the browser window. The following code adds extra letter spacing in the first line of text for every paragraph:

```
P:first-line {letter-spacing: 6pt}
```

Pseudo-elements can be combined with class information, so you can apply first-line or -letter effects to only a certain class of element. The following sample makes the first letter of any paragraph classified as "opener" big and red:

```
P.opener:first-letter {font-size: 300%; color: red}
```

Pseudo-classes

CSS1 provides three pseudo-classes that can be applied to the anchor (`<a>`) tag: `link`, `visited`, and `active` (referring to the various link states as interpreted by the browser). These do not apply to named anchors, only those containing the `HREF` attribute.

```
A:link {color: red}
A:visited {color: blue}
A:active {color: maroon}
```

This style information provides the same functionality as specifying link colors in the `<body>` of a document, but it has the advantages that style sheets provide. Netscape's support for pseudo-classes is pretty buggy prior to Version 6.

Specifying Values

It is important to use the proper syntax for specifying length and color values in style sheet rules.

Length Units

Table 17-1 lists units of measurements that can be specified in style sheet values.

Table 17-1: Units of measurements for style sheet values

Code	Unit	Description
px	Pixel	Pixel units are relative to the monitor resolution.
pt	Point	A traditional publishing unit of measurement for type. There are approximately 72 points in an inch.
pc	Pica	A traditional publishing unit of measurement equal to 12 points (or 1/6 of an inch).
em	Em	A relative unit of measurement that traditionally equals the width of the capital letter M in the current font. In practical terms, it is equal to the point size of the font (e.g., an em space in 24pt type is 24 points wide).
ex	Ex	A relative unit of measurement which is the height of the letter "x" for that font (approximately half the length of an em).
in	Inches	Standard unit of measurement in the U.S.
mm	Millimeters	Metric measurement.
cm	Centimeters	Metric measurement.

Some values can be specified as percentages that are relative to the font size or bounding box of the element. The following example makes the line height 120% of the element's font size:

```
P {line-height: 120%}
```

Designers should keep in mind that the specific unit measurements listed above (pt, pc, in, mm, and cm) are not good choices for screen design because of the variation in size from monitor to monitor. It is preferable to specify sizes using relative measurements such as em and ex. Pixels (px) are acceptable as measurements for elements, but not necessarily for text. See the section "Specifying Text in Pixels" later in this chapter for the pros and cons.

Specifying Color

As in HTML tags, there are two methods for specifying color in style sheets: by name and by numerical values.

By name

You can specify color values by name as follows:

```
H1 {color: olive}
```

The CSS1 Specification specifically lists only 16 color names that can be used in style sheets; they are:

```
aqua        gray        navy        silver
black       green       olive       teal
blue        lime        purple      white
fuchsia     maroon      red         yellow
```

Other names from the complete list of color names may be supported by some browsers. For the complete list, see Chapter 16.

By RGB values

Within style sheets, RGB colors can be specified by any of the following methods:

```
H1 {color: #0000FF}
H1 {color: #00F}
H1 {color: rgb(0,0,255)}
H1 {color: rgb(0%, 0%, 100%)}
```

The first method uses three two-digit hexadecimal RGB values (for a complete explanation, see Chapter 16). The second method uses a three-digit syntax, which is essentially converted to the six-digit form by replicating each digit (therefore, 00F is the same as 0000FF).

The last two methods use a functional notation specifying RGB values as a comma-separated list of regular values (from 0 to 255) or percentage values (from 0 to 100%). Note that percentage values can use decimals, e.g., `rgb(0%, 50.5%, 33.3%)`.

Properties

The real meat of style sheets lies in the collection of properties that can be applied to selected elements. The properties reviewed in this chapter reflect those provided in the CSS Level 1 specification (CSS1). The CSS Level 2 specification, released in May 1998, contains many additional properties and additional values for existing properties (see "What's New in CSS2" later in this chapter). However, because only the latest browser releases are up to speed with CSS1, these properties should be enough to give you a good start in working with style sheets.

First, a disclaimer—the explanations provided here describe how each property *ought* to work according to the specification. Many of these are either unsupported or buggy in Version 3 and 4 browsers. For a listing of which browsers support which properties, see the charts in Appendix E.

Type-Related Properties

Style sheets offer controls for type presentation similar to those found in desktop publishing. The following group of properties affects the way type is displayed, both in terms of font and text spacing.

font-family

You can specify any font (or list of fonts, separated by commas) in the `font-family` property. Bear in mind, however, that the font needs to be present on the user's machine in order to display, so it is safest to stick with common fonts.

You may (and it is advisable) include a generic font family as the last option in your list so that if the specific fonts are not found, a font that matches the general style of your choices will be substituted. The five possible generic font family values are:

- Serif (e.g., Times)

- Sans-serif (e.g., Helvetica or Arial)

CSS

- Monospaced (e.g., Courier or New Courier)
- Cursive (e.g., Zapf-Chancery)
- Fantasy (e.g., Western, Impact, or some display-oriented font)

Note that in the example, the first font is enclosed in quotes. Font names that contain character spaces must be enclosed in quotation marks (single or double). Generic family names must never be enclosed in quotation marks.

Values:	`family name, generic family name`
Example:	`P {font-family: "Trebuchet MS", Verdana, sans-serif}`
Applies to:	All elements
Inherited:	Yes

font-style

The `font-style` property selects between `normal` (the default) and `italic` or `oblique` faces within a font family. Oblique type is just a slanted version of the normal face. Italic is usually a separate face design with more curved characters. Note that `bold` is part of `font-weight`, not `font-style`, in style sheet syntax.

Values:	`normal|italic|oblique`
Example:	`H1 {font-style: italic}`
Applies to:	All elements
Inherited:	Yes

font-variant

Use the `font-variant` property to specify that an element display in small caps. If a true small caps font face is not available, the browser may simulate small caps by displaying all caps at a reduced size. More values may be supported for this property in future style sheet versions.

Values:	`normal|small-caps`
Example:	`P:first-line {font-variant: small-caps}`
Applies to:	All elements
Inherited:	Yes

font-weight

The `font-weight` property specifies the weight, or boldness, of the type. It can be specified either as a descriptive term (`normal, bold, bolder, lighter`) or as one of the nine numeric values listed above. The default font weight is `normal`, which corresponds to 400 on the numeric scale. Typical `bold` text corresponds to 700 on the numeric scale. There may not be a font face within a family that corresponds to each of the nine levels of boldness (some may come in only `normal` and `bold` weights).

Unfortunately, the current browsers are inconsistent in support of the `font-weight` property. Of the possible values, only `bold` will render reliably as bold text.

Values: `normal|bold|bolder|lighter|100|200|300|400|500|600|700|800|900`

Example: `STRONG {font-weight: 700}`

Applies to: All elements

Inherited: Yes

font-size

As the name suggests, the `font-size` property specifies the size of the text element. There are four methods for specifying font size:

`absolute size`

    Values: `xx-small|x-small|small|medium|large|x-large|xx-large`

    Example: `H1 {font-size: x-large}`

    Absolute sizes are descriptive terms that reference a table of sizes kept by the browser.

`relative size`

    Values: `larger|smaller`

    Example: `H1 { font-size: larger }`

    These values specify the size of the type relative to the parent object.

`length`

    Values: *number* + `em|ex|px|pt|pc|mm|cm|in`

    Example: `H1 {font-size: 24pt}`

    You can also specify font size using any of the length values described in the "Length Units" section earlier in this chapter.

`percentage`

    Values: *n*`%`

    Example: `H1 {font-size: 125%}`

    This specifies font size as a percentage of the inherited size. For instance, in this example the H1 will be 125% larger than the size of regular body text.

Values: *absolute size|relative size|length|percentage*

Applies to: All elements

Inherited: Yes

font

The `font` property is a shorthand property for specifying all the available font controls in a single rule. Values should be separated by character spaces. In this property, the order of the enclosed values is important (although not every value needs to be present) and must be listed as follows:

```
{ font: weight style variant size/line-height font-name(s) }
```

A valid font value must contain the size and the font name, in that order; otherwise, the value should be ignored (and is by most browsers).

Values:

> *font-style|font-variant|font-weight|font-size|line-height|font-family*

Example: `EM {font: 12pt Times, serif}`
                     `H1 {font: oblique bolder 18pt Helvetica, sans-serif}`

Applies to: All elements

Inherited: Yes

color

This property is used to describe the text (a.k.a. "foreground") color of an element. For an explanation of specifying color values, see the "Color Values" section earlier in this chapter.

Values: *color name|RGB color value*

Example: `BLOCKQUOTE {color: navy}`
                     `H1 {color: #666633}`

Applies to: Block-level elements

Inherited: Yes

line-height

In simplified terms, the `line-height` property sets the distance between the baselines of adjacent lines of text (the real calculation method is a great deal more complicated). In traditional publishing, this measurement is called "leading" and can be used to create different effects by adding white space to the block of text.

The default value is `normal`, which corresponds to 100–120%, depending on the browser's interpretation of the tag. When a number is specified alone, that number is multiplied by the current font size to calculate the `line-height` value. Line-heights can also be specified using any of the length units described earlier. Percentage values relative to the current (inherited) font size may also be used.

These examples demonstrate three alternative methods for the same amount of line spacing. For example, if the point size is 12 pt, the resulting line-height for each of the examples listed would be 14.4 pts.

Values: *normal|number|length|percentage*

Example:

```
P {line-height: 1.2}
P {line-height: 1.2em}
P {line-height: 120%}
```

Applies to: All elements

Inherited: Yes

word-spacing

This property specifies an additional amount of space to be placed between words of the text element. Note that when specifying relative lengths (such as em, which is based on font size), the *calculated* size will be passed down to child elements, even if they have a smaller font size than the parent.

Values: normal|*length*

Example: H3 {word-spacing: .5em}

Applies to: All elements

Inherited: Yes

letter-spacing

This property specifies an amount of space to be added between characters. Note that when specifying relative lengths (such as em, which is based on font size), the *calculated* size will be passed down to child elements, even if they have a smaller font size than the parent.

Values: normal|*length*

Example: P.opener:firstline {letter-spacing: 2pt}

Applies to: All elements

Inherited: Yes

text-decoration

This applies a "decoration" to text, such as underlines, overlines (a line over the text), strike-throughs, and the ever-beloved blinking effect.

Values: none|underline|overline|line-through|blink

Example: A: link, A:visited, A:active {text-decoration: underline}

Applies to: All elements

Inherited: No, but a text decoration is "drawn through" any child elements

vertical-align

The vertical-align property, as it sounds, affects the vertical alignment of an element. The possible values are as follows:

baseline
> Aligns the baseline of text (or bottom of an image) with the baseline of the parent element (this is the default)

bottom
> Aligns the bottom of the element with the bottom of the lowest element on the line

CSS

middle

Aligns the "vertical midpoint of the element (typically an image) with the baseline plus half the x-height of the parent" (in the words of the CSS1 Specification)

sub

Lowers the element relative to the baseline

super

Raises the element relative to the baseline

text-bottom

Aligns the bottom of the element with the bottom of the parent element's font (its descenders)

text-top

Aligns the top of the element with the top of the parent element's font (its ascenders)

top

Aligns the top of the element with the tallest element on the line

percentage values refer to the value of the `line-height` property of the element.

Values:

    `baseline|bottom|middle|sub|super|text-bottom|text-top|top|`*percentage*

Example: `IMG.capletter {vertical-align: text-top}`

Applies to: Inline elements

Inherited: No

text-transform

This property affects the capitalization of the element. The possible values are as follows:

none

Displays the element as it is typed in the HTML source and neutralizes any inherited value

capitalize

Displays the first letter of every word in uppercase characters

lowercase

Displays the whole element in lowercase characters

uppercase

Displays the whole element in uppercase characters

Values: `none|capitalize|lowercase|uppercase`

Example: `H1.title {text-transform: capitalize}`

Applies to: All elements

Inherited: Yes

text-align

This affects the horizontal alignment of the contained text within an element. The possible values are center, left, right, and justify (aligns both the left and right margins).

Values: center|justify|left|right

Example: DIV.center {text-align: center}

Applies to: Block-level elements

Inherited: Yes

text-indent

This property specifies an amount of indentation (from the left margin) to appear in the first line of text in an element. The value of text-indent may be negative to create hanging-indent effects, although this feature is poorly supported. Values can be specified in any available unit of length or as a percentage of the line length.

Values: length|percentage

Example: P.first {text-indent: 3em}

Applies to: Block-level elements

Inherited: Yes

Box Properties

Style sheets treat each element on a page as though it were contained within a box (imagine four lines drawn against the edges of this paragraph). More accurately, each element is in a series of containing boxes, beginning with the content itself, surrounded by padding, then the border, which is surrounded by the margin. The margin padding and border parts, as well as an element's width and height, are illustrated in Figure 17-2.

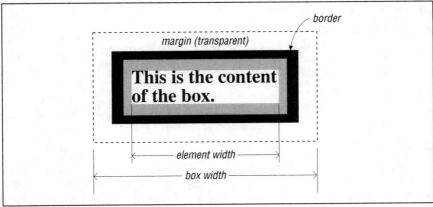

Figure 17-2: The box formatting model for page elements

The content itself is contained within the element's width. Any background applied to an element extends into the padding space and under the border, but not beyond the border's outer edge. The entire box's width extends to the outer edges of the margin. The boundary of the margin is not visible but is a calculated amount.

The CSS1 provides many properties for controlling the presentation of an element's box, including setting the amount of padding and margin, the appearance of the borders, and the background color (discussed in the next section). The box model is also the basis for absolute positioning (discussed later in this chapter), so it is important to get a feel for how they work. For more information on how box elements are formatted and interact with each other, see Section 4, "Formatting Model" in the CSS specification online at *http://www.w3.org/TR/REC-CSS1/*.

Box Measurements in Internet Explorer

Internet Explorer Version 6 is the first version of IE to comply perfectly with the CSS standard for box model measurements (as illustrated in Figure 17-2). Previous versions (which only partially supported box properties anyway) calculated the size of an element to include its padding, border, and margin. According to the standard, the width of the element is the same as content width.

---

margin-top, margin-right, margin-bottom, margin-left

These properties specify the amount of margin on specific sides of the element (as called by name). Values for `margin-right` and `margin-left` can be specified in length units, as a percentage based on the size of the element's overall box width, or as `auto`, which automatically fills in a margin amount based on other elements on the page. `margin-top` and `margin-bottom` may be specified in length units or `auto` (not in percentages).

Values: `length|percentage|auto`

Example: `IMG {margin-top: 0px}`
               `IMG {margin-right: 12px}`
               `IMG {margin-bottom: 0px}`
               `IMG {margin-left: 12px}`

Applies to: All elements

Inherited: No

margin

This is a shorthand property for specifying all the margins of an element. Values can be entered as length units, as a percentage based on the size of the element's overall box width, or as `auto`, which automatically fills in a margin amount based on other elements on the page.

If a single value is given, as in the first example, that value will apply to the margins on all four sides of the box.

You can combine values for each of the four sides in a list, as shown in the second example. It is important to note that the values always follow a clockwise order, as follows:

```
{ margin: top right bottom left }
```

(Note that the second example duplicates the four separate rules illustrated for the margin-top, etc., properties.)

When you specify three values, the second value will apply to both the right and left margins:

```
{ margin: top right/left bottom }
```

Two values, as shown in the third example, are interpreted as follows:

```
{ margin: top/bottom right/left }
```

(Note that in the examples at the beginning of this section, the third example has the same effect as the second example.)

If the browser doesn't find a value for the left margin, it just duplicates the value for the right; if the bottom margin value is missing, it duplicates the value for the top.

Values: length|percentage|auto

Example: IMG {margin: 20px}
            IMG {margin: 0px 12px 0px 12px}
            IMG {margin: 0px 12px}

Applies to: All elements

Inherited: No

padding-top, padding-right, padding-bottom, padding-left

These properties specify an amount of padding to be added around the respective sides of an element's contents (the side indicated by the property name). Values are the same as explained for the margin property.

Values: length|percentage

Example: P.sidebar {padding-top: 1em}

Applies to: All elements

Inherited: No

padding

This is a shorthand property for specifying the padding for all sides of an element. A single value will apply the same amount of padding on all sides of the content. More than one value will be interpreted as described for the margin property (top, right, bottom, left).

Values: length|percentage

Example: P.sidebar {padding: 1em}

CSS

Applies to: All elements

Inherited: No

border-top-width, border-right-width, border-bottom-width, border-left-width

These properties specify the border widths of the respective sides of an element's box. The keywords `thin`, `medium`, and `thick` will be interpreted by the browser and are consistent throughout the document (i.e., they are not affected by the font size of the element). You can also specify a length unit.

Values: thin|medium|thick|*length*

Example:

```
P.sidebar {border-right-width: medium; border-bottom-width: thick}
```

Applies to: All elements

Inherited: No

border-width

This is a shorthand property for specifying the width of the border for all four sides of the element box. A single value will set the same border width for all four sides of the box. More than one value will be interpreted as described for the `margin` property (top, right, bottom, left).

Values: thin|medium|thick|*length*

Example: P.warning {border-width: thin}

Applies to: All elements

Inherited: No

border-color

This property sets the border color for each of the four sides of an element box. A single value will apply to all four borders of the box. More than one value will be applied as described for the `margin` property (top, right, bottom, left).

Values: color name|*RGB value*

Example: BLOCKQUOTE {border-color: red blue lime yellow}

Applies to: All elements

Inherited: No

border-style

This property sets the style of border for an element box. The different styles are illustrated in Figure 17-3. A single value will result in a box with the same style border on all four sides. More than one value will be interpreted as described for the `margin` property (top, right, bottom, left). The example given would create a box with a solid line on the top and bottom and with dashed rules on the left and right sides.

Values: none|dotted|dashed|solid|double|groove|ridge|inset|outset

Example: P.example{border-style: solid dashed}

Applies to: All elements

Inherited: Yes

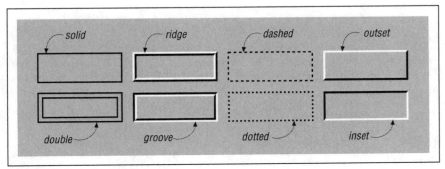

Figure 17-3: Potential border styles

border-top, border-right, border-bottom, border-left

Each of these properties is a shorthand property for setting the width, style, and color of a specific side of a box (as named). The example given would create a solid blue border .5 em thick on the left side of the H1 element only.

Values: border-top-width|border-style|border-color

Example: H1: {border-left: .5em solid blue}

Applies to: All elements

Inherited: No

border

This is a shorthand property for setting the border width, style, and color for all four sides of an element box. The values specified in **border** will always apply to all four sides of the box (unlike other shorthand border properties described earlier, **border** cannot accept values for separate sides).

Values: border-width|border-style|border-color

Example: P.example {border: 2px dotted #666633}

Applies to: All elements

Inherited: No

width

This property sets the width of the element and can apply to blocks (like paragraphs) in addition to things like images. If you use this on an image, be sure also to specify the height. Percentage values pertain to the width of the containing block.

Values: length|percentage|auto

Example:

```
    IMG.photo {width: 300px; height:300px;} P.narrow {width: 75%}
```

Applies to: Block-level elements and replaced elements (such as graphics)

Inherited: Yes

height

This property sets the height of the element and can apply to blocks (like paragraphs) in addition to things like images. If you use this on an image, be sure also to specify the width. CSS1 does not allow percentage values for height, although CSS2 does. The percentage is still taken as a percentage of the containing block's width, oddly enough.

Values: length|percentage|auto

Example: IMG.photo {height: 100px; width: 100px;}
            P.sidebar {height:20em}

Applies to: Block-level elements

Inherited: Yes

float

The float property works much like the HTML align attribute for images; it positions an element against the left or right border and allows text to flow around it. Support for the float property is poor as of this writing, but it should prove useful in the future for creating drop caps and similar effects.

Values: left|right|none

Example: P.sidebar {float: right}

Applies to: All elements

Inherited: No

clear

This property specifies whether to allow floating elements on an image's sides (more accurately, the sides along which floating items are *not* accepted). none means floated elements are allowed (but not required) on both sides.

Values: none|left|right|both

Example: H1, H2, H3 {clear: left}

Applies to: Block-level elements

Inherited: Yes

Background Properties

Background properties are applied to the "canvas" behind an element. Ideally, background color appears behind the content and its padding, stopping at the border. Background properties are not inherited, but since the default value is transparent, the parent's background color or pattern shows through for child elements.

background-color

Sets the background color of the element (creating a colored rectangle). The default is `transparent`. Navigator 4.x renders `transparent` as black.

Values: color name or RGB value|transparent

Example: P.warning {background-color: red}

Applies to: All elements

Inherited: No

background-image

Sets a background image for the element. If a background color is also specified, the image will be overlaid on top of the color.

Values: URL|none

Example: BODY {background-image: url(stripes.gif)}

Applies to: All elements

Inherited: No

background-repeat

When a background image is specified, this property specifies whether and how the image is repeated. The position from which the image does or doesn't repeat is set by the `background-position` property (discussed later).

repeat
> Allows the image to repeat both horizontally and vertically

repeat-x
> Allows the image to repeat only horizontally in both directions

repeat-y
> Allows the image to repeat only vertically in both directions

no-repeat
> Displays the image only once (does not repeat)

Values: repeat|repeat-x|repeat-y|no-repeat

Example:

> BODY { background-image: url(oldmap.gif); background-repeat: no-repeat}

Applies to: All elements

Inherited: No

background-attachment

This determines whether the background image scrolls along with the document (`scroll`, the default) or remains in a fixed position (`fixed`).

Values: scroll|fixed

Example:

```
BODY {background-image: url(oldmap.gif); background-attachment: scroll}
```

Applies to: All elements

Inherited: No

background-position

When a background image has been specified, this property specifies its initial position relative to the upper-left corner of the box that surrounds the content of the element (not including its padding, border, or margin).

The CSS methods for specifying position get a bit complicated. Values are given in horizontal/vertical pairs, with a default value of 0%/0%, which places the upper-left corner of the image in the upper-left corner of the element. A value of 100%/100% would place the image in the bottom-right corner of the element.

Length values from the left and top margin can also be specified. Or you can use the keywords, which correspond to the percentage values 0%, 50%, and 100%, respectively. The two examples given create the same result, with the bottom-left corner of the image placed in the bottom-left corner of the element.

Values: percentage|length|top/center/bottom|left/center/right

Example:
```
BODY {background-image: url (oldmap.gif);
  background-position: bottom left}
BODY {background-image: url (oldmap.gif);
  background-position: 100% 0%}
```

Applies to: Block-level elements and replaced elements

Inherited: No

background

This is a shorthand property for specifying all the individual background properties in a single declaration.

Values:

background-color|background-image|background-repeat|background-attachment|background-position

Example:

```
BODY {background: silver url(nightsky.gif) no-repeat fixed}
BODY {background: url(oldmap.gif) bottom left}
```

Applies to: Block-level elements

Inherited: Yes

Classification Properties

These properties classify elements into categories rather than setting specific visual parameters.

display

This property defines how and if an element is displayed. A value of none turns off the display and closes up the space the element would otherwise occupy. (The second example given turns off all images, for instance.) block opens a new box that is positioned relative to adjacent boxes. list-item is similar to block except that a list-item marker is added. inline results in a new inline box on the same line as the previous content.

Values: block|inline|list-item|none

Example: P {display: block}
                IMG {display: none}

Applies to: All elements

Inherited: No

white-space

This property defines how white space in the source for the element is handled. The normal value treats text normally, with consecutive spaces collapsing to one. The pre value displays multiple characters, like the <pre> tag in HTML, except that the element is not displayed in a monospace font, unless you use CSS to specify such a font face as well. nowrap prevents the text element from wrapping unless designated by a <br> tag.

Values: normal|pre|nowrap

Example: P.haiku {white-space: pre}

Applies to: Block-level elements

Inherited: Yes

list-style-type

This attribute specifies the appearance of the automatic numbering or bulleting of lists. Values are the same as for the type attribute within a list item (<li>). (In the example given, decimal corresponds to list items numbered 1, 2, 3, etc., and upper-roman results in A, B, C, etc.) These numbers/bullets will be displayed when no list-item image is specified or if the image cannot be found.

Values: disc|circle|square|decimal|lower-roman|upper-roman|
                lower-alpha|upper-alpha|none

Example: OL {list-style-type: decimal}
                OL {list-style-type: upper-roman}

Applies to: Elements with the display property set to list-item

Inherited: Yes

list-style-image

This property specifies a graphic to be used as a list-item marker (bullet).

Values: URL|none

Example: UL {list-style-image: url(3dball.gif)}

Applies to: Elements with the `display` property set to `list-item`

Inherited: Yes

list-style-position

This property specifies whether list items should be set with a hanging indent. The `inside` value makes subsequent lines of a list item wrap all the way to the left margin of the list item (under the list item marker). The `outside` value starts subsequent lines under the first word of the list item, creating a hanging indent.

Values: inside|outside

Example: OL {list-style-position: outside}

Applies to: Elements with `display` property set to `list-item`

Inherited: Yes

list-style

This is a shorthand property for setting the `list-style` type, image, and position (inside, outside) in one declaration.

Values: list-style-type|list-style-image|list-style-position

Example: UL {list-style: list-item url(3dball.gif) disc inside}
               UL UL {list-style: circle outside}

Applies to: Elements with `display` property set to `list-item`

Inherited: Yes

Positioning with Style Sheets

In August of 1997, the W3C published its working draft of specifications for style sheet properties for positioning HTML elements on the page and in three-dimensional space. This greater control over object placement can be used for more tightly designed static page layout as well as for creating and tracking motion effects with DHTML.

This effort was initiated by Netscape and Microsoft, who began supporting some positioning properties in their Version 4.0 browsers. The positioning concepts and properties were picked up and developed further in the CSS Level 2 specification, which was released in May of 1998.

Style sheet positioning is a rich and complex topic that is beyond the scope of this chapter, but this section aims to introduce some basic positioning concepts. For complete positioning information, see the W3C's CSS2 specification online at *http:// www.w3.org/TR/REC-CSS2/*.

While the positioning properties are reviewed here, they come with a word of warning. Positioning is one of the most inconsistently implemented and buggy aspects of style sheets. It will be a while before a single solution works across all platforms and browsers in a predictable fashion. This is particularly unfortunate because positioning is a tempting feature and essential to some DHTML effects. If you use positioning in your pages, be sure to test thoroughly.

The position Property

The `position` property has three possible values: `absolute`, `relative`, and `static`.

It works in conjunction with the `top` and `left` properties (used for specifying distances from the top and left starting point), the `bottom` and `right` properties, and the `width` and `height` properties (for specifying the width and height of the element, including its padding and border). Values for these properties can be specified as either length units or percentages.

Relative positioning

Relative positioning places the element relative to its initial position in the flow (i.e., where it would be if it weren't being positioned). Once the element is moved, the space it previously occupied is held blank. The resulting position may cause the element to overlap other elements on the page. Relative positioning is the most reliable of the CSS2 positioning values and is handled fairly well by the current browsers (Versions 4 and higher).

Measurements are taken as an offset from the appropriate sides of the element box, so using `right` and `top` defines offsets from the top and right sides of the containing block. Adding a positive top value moves the element down the specified amount from its initial top position. Adding a positive value for the left property moves the element that amount to the right. You can also specify negative values to move an element up and to the left. In Figure 17-4 and the following code, the emphasized text is moved 20 pixels down and 12 pixels to the right of its initial position.

```
<HEAD>
<STYLE TYPE="text/css">
<!--
EM {position: relative; top: 20px; left: 12px;}
-->
</STYLE>
</HEAD>

<BODY>
<P>This line contains some <EM>emphasized</EM> text that will be
repositioned.</P>
<P>This is some more text that follows the line with emphasized text.</P>
</BODY>
```

Figure 17-4: Word moved down and to right with relative positioning

Absolute positioning

Absolute positioning places the element in an arbitrary position, but technically it is still relative to the containing block of another element or to the document coordinates (it will scroll when the document scrolls). Measurements in absolute positioning are relative to the sides of the document itself (or the containing block of the "positioned" block the element is inside). Again, negative values can be specified.

When an element is positioned absolutely, the space it previously occupied is closed up, as shown in Figure 17-5 and the following code. In its new position, the element may overlap other elements on the page. An absolutely positioned element has a margin of zero by default—changing the width of the element's margin results in a corresponding shift in the element's position.

```
<HEAD>
<STYLE TYPE="text/css">
<!--
EM {position: absolute; top: 20px; left: 12px;}
-->
</STYLE>
</HEAD>

<BODY>
<P>This line contains some <EM>emphasized</EM> text that will be
repositioned.</P>
<P>This is some more text that follows the line with emphasized text.</P>
</BODY>
```

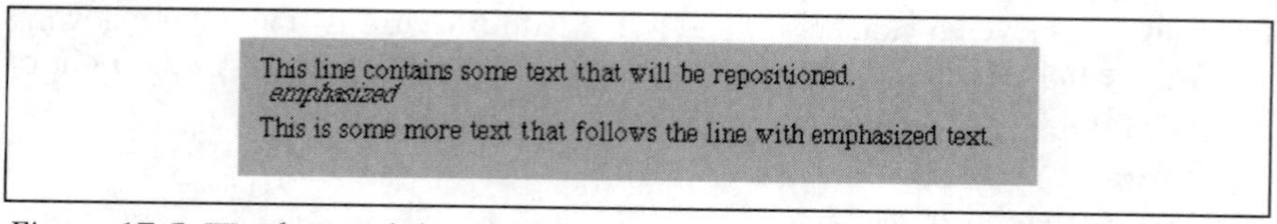

This line contains some text that will be repositioned.
emphasized
This is some more text that follows the line with emphasized text.

Figure 17-5: Word moved down and to the right with absolute positioning

If its parent element (or an element somewhere above the parent) is specified to have relative positioning (whether or not it is actually moved), the absolutely positioned child element will be placed relative to the position of the top-left corner of this "relatively positioned" parent. One possible application of this is keeping notations near their source paragraphs.

Static positioning

Static is the default value for the position property. Static elements can never serve as a context for child element placement (as discussed in the explanation of absolute positioning). Static elements cannot be positioned or repositioned.

Z-Order

Z-order refers to the overlapping of elements that can occur when elements are positioned outside of their normal flow. The CSS2 specification provides a special property, z-index, for handling the placement of objects in three-dimensional space. Unfortunately, it is not consistently supported by current browsers.

Elements with higher z-index values obscure those with lower values. When z-index is not specified, elements appear from back to front in the order in which they appear in the HTML source.

In Figure 17-6, two ordinary transparent GIFs, *A.gif* and *B.gif*, are "stacked" using z-index settings. In the top image, *B.gif* is given a higher z-index value and thus overlaps *A.gif*. In the bottom image, the positioning code is the same, but this time, *A.gif* is given the higher z-index value and comes out on top.

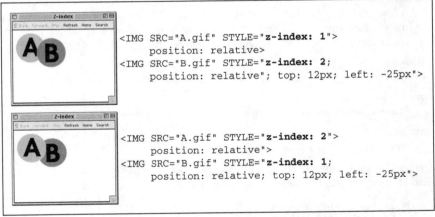

Figure 17-6: Graphic file with higher z-index value is positioned on top

Visibility

The CSS2 specification also includes a new property called visibility, which takes the values visible (the default) or hidden. When an element is hidden, it is not displayed on the page, and the space it occupies is held blank as shown in Figure 17-7 and the following code.

```
<STYLE TYPE="text/css">
<!--
EM {visibility: hidden;}
-->
</STYLE>
```

. . .

```
<P>This line contains some <EM>emphasized</EM> text, which will be
hidden.</P>
```

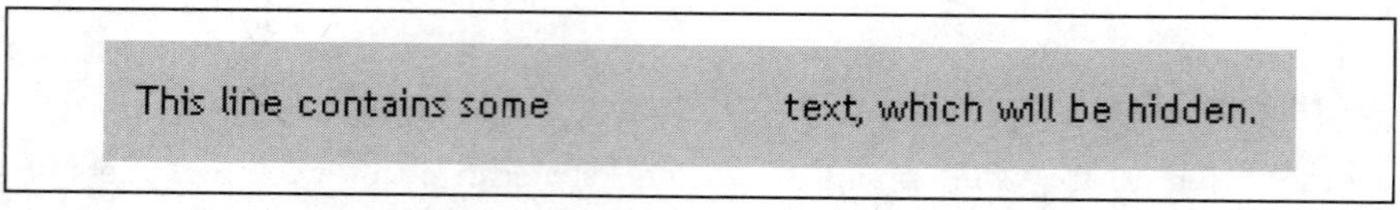

Figure 17-7: Word is hidden using visibility property

This is different from `display:none` (another method for hiding elements) in that `display:none` removes the element completely from the display and closes up the space that would have been taken up by the element.

Overflow

Another new property first proposed in the Positioning Specification is `overflow`, which provides alternative ways for handling text that does not fit in the box dimensions as specified. It has four possible attributes:

`visible`
> Allows the overflowed content to "flow out" of the fixed box dimensions for the element (Internet Explorer 5 for Windows and other older browsers incorrectly resize the box dimensions to contain the text)

`hidden`
> Hides from view the portion of the element that does not fit in the box

`scroll`
> Places a scroll bar in the box so the user can scroll down to read its contents

`auto`
> Places a scroll bar only when necessary

Figure 17-8 shows the effects of different overflow settings on a text element specified at 200×100 pixels (`visible`, `hidden`, and `scroll`, respectively).

What's New in CSS2

The CSS Level 2 (*http://www.w3.org/TR/REC-CSS2/*) specification expands significantly on the work done in CSS1. Not surprisingly, it includes dozens of new properties (and pseudo-elements) and a fair number of additional values for existing properties (see the following tables).

CSS2 incorporates and refines the set of properties used for positioning to give designers more control over page layout and DHTML authors the ability to create dynamic motion effects.

It provides more controls over traditional typesetting elements such as widows, orphans, and page breaks. This shows that style sheets are being developed with a mind to developing documents for both HTML display and print output.

CSS2 also introduces properties that give additional control over table element presentation.

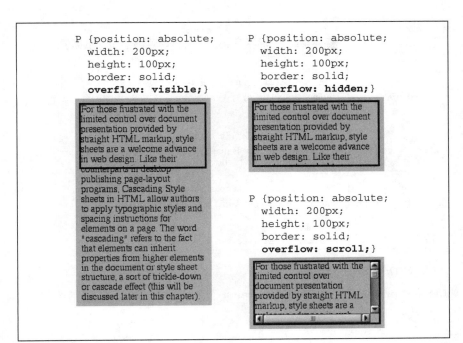

Figure 17-8: Overflow settings: visible, hidden, and scroll

As part of the W3C's efforts to make web pages accessible to all users, the latest style sheet specification includes a number of new properties that pertain to the nonvisual display of web pages. These new attributes provide controls for speech-delivery and sound controls.

The following list of new CSS2 elements was compiled and graciously contributed to this book by CSS guru Eric Meyer. It reflects the state of the final CSS2 specification, which was made a W3C Recommendation in May 1998. Unfortunately, as of this writing, no browsers are supporting CSS2 in its entirety, and no promises have been made on when that day will come.

New Selectors

The following table lists the new CSS2 selectors.

Selector	Description
*	Matches any element. Example: `*{font-family:serif;}`
A>B	Matches any element B that is a child of any element A. Example: `DIV.main>P{line-height:1.5;}`
A+B	Matches any element B that immediately follows any element A. Example: `P+UL{margin-top:0;}`

CSS

Selector	Description
A[att]	Matches any element A that has the given attribute defined, whatever its value. Example: `TABLE[border]{background-color:white;}`
A[att="val"]	Matches any element B that has the specified attribute set to the specified value. Example: `TABLE[border="3"]{background-color:yellow;}`
A[att~="val"]	Matches any element B that has the specified value as one of the values in a list given to the specified attribute. Example: `TABLE[class~="example"]{background-color:orange;}`
A[lang|="val"]	Matches any element A that has the given value as one of the values for the `lang` attribute. Example: `P[lang|="en"]{text-align:left;}`

New Properties

The following are the new CSS2 properties:

text-shadow
font-size-adjust
font-stretch
unicode-bidi

cursor
outline
outline-color
outline-style
outline-width

content
quotes
counter-reset
counter-increment
marker-offset

border-top-color
border-right-color
border-bottom-color
border-left-color
border-top-style
border-right-style
border-bottom-style
border-left-style

position
direction

top
right
bottom
left
z-index

min-width
max-width
min-height
max-height
overflow
clip
visibility

page
page-break-before
page-break-after
page-break-inside
orphans
widows
size
marks

row-span
column-span
border-collapse
border-spacing

table-layout
border-spacing
empty-cells
caption-side
speak-header-cell

volume
speak
pause-before
pause-after
pause
cue-before
cue-after
cue
play-during
azimuth
elevation
speech-rate
voice-family
pitch
pitch-range
stress
richness
speak-punctuation
speak-date
speak-numeral
speak-time

Font Descriptors

The following new CSS2 font descriptors (properties) are used to identify particular font properties for downloading, font matching, or alignment:

unicode-range	slope	bbox
units-per-em	cap-height	definition-src
src	x-height	baseline
panose-1	ascent	centerline
stemv	descent	mathline
stemh	widths	topline

(Note that these properties are used only for font matching and description; most authors will not need to use them.)

New Pseudo-Selectors

Pseudo-selectors allow the author to assign styles to structures that don't necessarily exist in the document, or to things that are inferred by the state of certain elements or the document itself. The following are the new CSS2 pseudo-selectors:

Pseudo-selector	Description
:after	Inserts generated content after an element's content
:before	Inserts generated content before an element's content
:first	Applies a style to the first page of a document
:first-child	Matches an element that is the first child of some other element
:focus	Applies a style while an element is "in focus"
:hover	Applies a style when the curser hovers over an element
:lang	Matches an element based on its language
:left	Applies a style to left-hand pages
:right	Applies a style to right-hand pages

New "at-rules"

The following are the new CSS2 functions:

Pseudo-selector	Description
@charset	Specifies the name of a character encoding (e.g., "ISO-8859-1")
@font-face	Specifies values for every font descriptor, either implicitly or explicitly
@media	Specifies the media for which the style applies
@page	Specifies the dimensions, orientation, margins, etc., of a page box when using paged-media style sheets

CSS

New Values for Existing Properties

The following are the new CSS2 values for existing properties:

all properties
  inherit

display
  run-in, compact, marker, table, inline-table, table-row, table-row-group, table-column, table-column-group, table-cell, table-caption, table-header-group, table-footer-group

font
  caption, icon, menu, message-box, small-caption, status-bar

list-style-type
  hebrew, armenian, georgian, cjk-ideographic, hiragana, hiragana-iroha, katakana, katakana-iroha

<color> *values*
  (These values are used to borrow colors from the user's system setup to be applied within the web document. They are case-insensitive, but use of the capitalization is encouraged for the sake of readability.)

  ActiveBorder, ActiveCaption, AppWorkspace, Background, ButtonFace, ButtonHighlight, ButtonText, CaptionText, GrayText, Highlight, HighlightText, InactiveBorder, InactiveCaption, InfoBackground, InfoText, Menu, MenuText, Scrollbar, ThreeDDarkShadow, ThreeDFace, ThreeDHighlight, ThreeDLightshadow, ThreeDShadow, Window, WindowFrame, WindowText

Style Sheet Tips and Tricks

The following Cascading Style Sheet tips and tricks are courtesy of Eric Meyer (author of O'Reilly's *Cascading Style Sheets: The Definitive Guide*).

Style Sheet MIME Types

Some authors have reported trouble with gettting their ISPs to correctly serve up CSS files. Apparently, with some Web servers, *.css* is mapped to the MIME-type x-application/css, or "Continuous Slide Show," instead of the MIME-type text/css. The style sheet gets mangled into something else. If you find you're having this problem, you'll need to contact your ISP and explain the problem. Because *.css* is now an IANA-registered MIME-type, service providers really have no excuse for not supporting it for style sheets. If they refuse to fix it, and style sheets are a necessary part of your site, you may have to consider switching ISPs.

Specifying Text Size in Pixels

One of the great frustrations in designing web pages is that fonts are rendered so differently from platform to platform, especially with regard to point size. The same point size will be rendered much larger on a PC than on a Mac, making it difficult to anticipate how much type will fit on the page. (See "Why Specifying Type is Problematic" in Chapter 3.)

Style sheets introduce the ability to specify type size in pixels. This translates better across platforms because the size of the type stays fixed in relation to the other elements (like graphics) on the page. The result is more predictable page layouts.

Most web developers discourage specifying text in pixels because it is not a flexible system. Pixel-sized text will be of different physical sizes on different monitors and under different resolutions. In very high-resolution environments, small pixel measurements (such as 10 pixels) might be unreadable. In general, relative measurements (`em`, `%`, `x-large`, `larger`, etc.) are a more Web-friendly way to go.

Creating a Drop Cap

As an alternative to the `:firstletter` pseudo-element (which is not universally supported), you can create a drop cap using a <span> to isolate the first letter of the paragraph.

The `float` property also has spotty support. The `width` property was added to the following example in order to get `float` to work with Internet Explorer (and it still doesn't function properly on a Mac). Without the `float` property, the capital letter will stand taller than the rest of the line, which may still be an acceptable effect. Figure 17-9 shows a drop cap created with the following style sheet code.

```
<STYLE TYPE="text/css">
<!--
    .dropcap {font: bold 200% sans-serif;
              color: teal;
              width: 24pt;
              float: left;}
-->
</STYLE>

<P><SPAN CLASS="dropcap">F</SPAN> or those frustrated...</P>
```

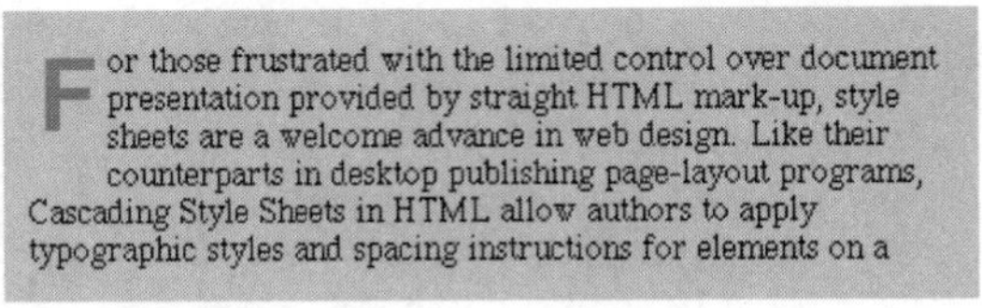

For those frustrated with the limited control over document presentation provided by straight HTML mark-up, style sheets are a welcome advance in web design. Like their counterparts in desktop publishing page-layout programs, Cascading Style Sheets in HTML allow authors to apply typographic styles and spacing instructions for elements on a

Figure 17-9: Drop cap created with float property

Table Troubles in Older Browsers

According to proper style sheet behavior, styles set for the <body> element should be inherited by all the elements on the page. Unfortunately, Navigator 4.x and Internet Explorer 4 and 5 have problems properly inheriting font and color styles (among others) into tables. To set global styles for a document that contains tables, explicitly list table elements in the selector for the page as follows:

```
BODY, TD, TH {font-family: georgia; color: blue;}
```

This problem has been fixed in standards-compliant versions of each browser (Netscape 6 and Internet Explorer 5.5+).

Making Backgrounds Behave in Navigator 4.x

Although a background should always fill an element's padding out to its border, Netscape Navigator 4.x needs a little extra help to get it right. Anywhere padding is used with a background color, add the following declaration:

```
{border: 1px solid none;}
```

This will have no visual effect, but in the course of telling Navigator to draw a one pixel, solid, transparent border, padding will suddenly start to inherit the background color. If you leave out this statement, many versions of Navigator will not extend the background color into the padding. (Again, this is just a workaround to compensate for bugs in Navigator 4.x—this is *not* how CSS1 is defined to behave. The problem has been corrected in Netscape 6.)

Beware Box Properties in Navigator 4.x

Some box properties are problematic for Navigator 4.x. For instance, applying borders, padding, or margins to inline elements can trip terrible bugs. Applying them in table cells can trigger browser crashes. It is best to avoid these features or put them in a separate style sheet that can be selectively not served to Navigator 4.x browsers (via browser-detect scripts or by adding it via @import, which is not supported by Netscape 4).

Browser Support Charts

Appendix E in this book contains charts with browser support for style sheet properties, current as of this writing. They were compiled and continue to be maintained by Eric Meyer for *WebReview* magazine. To get up-to-date statistics on browser support, WebReview's Style Sheets Reference Guide online at *http://style. webreview.com*.

CHAPTER 18

Server Side Includes

In layperson's terms, Server Side Includes (SSI) are special placeholders in an HTML document that the server replaces with actual data just before sending the final document to the browser. By the time the document gets to the browser, it looks just like any other HTML page (even if someone happens to "view source"), as though you typed the data into the HTML source by hand.

When the server looks through the file for placeholders (SSI commands), it is said to *parse* the file. The server then inserts the requested data, which could be anything from the current date and time to other HTML documents to the results of a CGI script. (The complete list of information available via Server Side Includes is listed later in this chapter.)

How SSI Is Used

SSI allows you to create the framework for pages that will be dynamically generated by the server. For the web author, this can be a powerful tool for managing site production and increasing efficiency. The following are just a few examples of the ways SSI can be used:

- Placing elements that you use over and over again. If you have an element that appears on every page of your site, such as a complex navigational header, you can use a single SSI command that just sources it in instead. If you make changes to the header, such as changing a URL or a graphic, you need to make the change only once, and it will be updated automatically on all pages of your site.

- Placing a constantly changing element on your page with a single line. For example, if you maintain a home page that has a message that changes every day, you can use a Server Side Include command (and a script on the server) to replace the message automatically. You never need to touch the source code for the home page—you just let the server do the work.

- Show the date and time the page was last updated, or show the current date and time in the user's time zone.

- Allow multiple users to submit content for inclusion on a web page without giving them access to the HTML source. For example, staff members could send in weekly updates via email. The server could run a script that turns the email into a text file, which is then inserted into the web page via an SSI command.

- Serve an appropriate web page based on the browser making the request. You can even serve documents based on the user's domain name. (Note that not all servers can perform conditional functions. This is discussed later in this chapter.)

Obviously, these are just a handful of possibilities, but they demonstrate the sort of tasks well suited for Server Side Includes.

Advantages

Server Side Includes offer the following advantages:

- It's easy to learn the basic SSI syntax and start implementing simple SSI.

- Most servers provide support for SSI or can add it quickly (check with your server administrator first).

- Pages can be dynamically generated, including up-to-the-second information and content served based on information about the users' viewing environment.

- It isn't browser-dependent like JavaScript, so it works for everyone (as long as it works on your server).

- The commands don't display in the browser, so your methods are invisible to the user.

- It's less work for the server than processing CGI programs for the same functions.

Disadvantages

There are few disadvantages:

- Parsing a file and adding information requires slightly more work for the server than serving a straight HTML document.

- Enabling Server Side Includes on the server may pose a security risk. Talk to your server administrator to find out the policy for SSI on your server.

- SSI is not as robust a solution for dynamic page generation as other scripting methods such as ASP or PHP.

Getting the Most Out of SSI

The examples in this chapter illustrate the basic form and function of SSI commands. On their own, Server Side Includes provide some useful, though limited, tools for dynamic page generation. The real power of Server Side Includes comes in the combination of SSI commands with CGI scripts running on the server. The CGI programs do the necessary processing before the information is ready to be placed in the HTML page.

If you focus on front-end web design, you can get started right away using the elements and variables listed in this chapter, but you may need to consult a CGI programmer to design the back-end for more advanced SSI solutions.

SSI and the Server

It should come as no surprise that the function of SSI depends heavily on the configuration of the server. This is another instance in which you need to communicate with your system administrator to find out whether your server supports SSI and, if so, which syntax to follow.

The instructions in this chapter use SSI commands that work for the Apache web server; the functionality is provided by Apache's `mod_include` module. Apache is a freely distributed and highly sophisticated server software package that makes up a large percentage of servers on the Web. If you aren't using the Apache web server, the instructions and examples shown in this chapter may not work with your server, so be sure to check with an administrator first.

Adding SSI Commands to a Document

Server Side Include commands have the following format:

```
<!--#element attribute="value" -->
```

The `element` is one of the predefined functions that Server Side Includes can perform, such as `include` or `echo` (we'll talk more about specific elements later).

The command also includes one or more `attribute/value` pairs that provide the specific parameters to the function.

There are a few important things to note about SSI command syntax:

- The whole command must be enclosed in comment indicators (`<!-- ... -->`).

- The comment terminator (`-->`) must be preceded by a space to make it clear it is not part of the SSI information.

- The whole command must be kept on one line (line breaks between the comment tags may cause the SSI not to function).

- The `#` symbol is an important part of the command and must not be omitted.

Example: Virtual Includes

The simplest type of Server Side Include is a "virtual include," which tells the server to add information to a file before sending it to the browser.

In this example, let's take a page from within a web site that uses a standard navigational toolbar held together with a table. Instead of placing the table in the

HTML source for every web page in the site, we can just insert it into each document as follows:

```
<HTML>
<HEAD><TITLE>News</TITLE></HEAD>
<BODY>
<!--#include virtual="navtable.html" -->
<H1>Today's Headlines</H1>
...page contents...
</BODY>
</HTML>
```

Documents that contain SSI commands should be saved with an identifying suffix, which indicates to the server that the file should be parsed before being sent to the browser. In most cases, the suffix is *.shtml* (the default), but this can be configured to be any suffix, so check with your server administrator first.

The command in the above example uses the `include` element, which inserts the text of another document into the parsed file. The `include` element uses the `virtual` parameter to specify the URL of the document to be inserted, in this case, *navtable.html*. The following shows the entire contents (simplified for sake of space) of *navtable.html*:

```
<TABLE>
<TR><TD><IMG SRC="toolbar.gif"></TD></TR>
...complicated toolbar stuff...
</TABLE>
```

Technically, this should be just a fragment of an HTML document in which the structural tags (<html>, <head>, and <body>) have been omitted. This is one way to ensure the final document doesn't end up with a double (and conflicting) set of structural tags. If you have a very good reason for leaving them in, be sure they match the parsed document exactly, and keep in mind that double <body> tags aren't received well by some browsers. Otherwise, play it safe and omit them.

Many web masters label these fragments with the *.htmlf* suffix to keep them distinct from normal HTML documents, although it's not necessary.

The server puts the fragment in the spot indicated by the virtual include command. When the document is sent to the browser, the source looks like this:

```
<HTML>
<HEAD><TITLE>News</TITLE></HEAD>
<BODY>
<TABLE>
<TR><TD><IMG SRC="toolbar.gif"></TD></TR>
...complicated toolbar stuff...
</TABLE>
<H1>Today's Headlines</H1>
... page contents...
</BODY>
</HTML>
```

The `include` element is just one of the elements available through SSI. The full list of Apache 1.3 elements appears in the "SSI Commands" section later in this chapter.

Using Environment Variables

In the example in the previous section, the information placed in the document was prepared ahead of time and saved in a file on the server for future use.

Another type of information that can be used by an SSI element is *environment variables*. These are bits of information that the operating system (or the HTTP server) always keeps track of and makes available for use by CGI programs and SSI. The current date and time, the modification times of local files, and the user's browser version are all examples of environment variables. To use one in an SSI, call it by its specific variable name (DATE_LOCAL, LAST_MODIFIED, and HTTP_ USER_AGENT, respectively, for the previous examples) in the command. Note that variable names can vary for different server software. The complete list is available under "Include Variables" later in this chapter.

Example: Printing the Date and Time

Let's look at a very simple example of how environment variables work. In the following example, we'll display the current date and time on the web page using the echo element (which prints a specified variable to the screen) and the DATE_ LOCAL variable. If I put the following SSI command in my HTML source:

```
<!--#echo var="DATE_LOCAL" -->
```

the server prints the following in its place:

```
Thursday, 28-Apr-01 16:39:24 EST
```

 If the date and time format looks a little dry to you, you can change it using the config element and SSI time formats as explained later in this chapter.

XSSI

Apache also supports XSSI (eXtended Server Side Includes), which provides more advanced command functions (and, consequently, uses code that is a bit more complicated for non-programmer types).

This section presents a brief overview of features unique to XSSI. For the nitty-gritty how-to information, see the Apache 1.3 mod_include documentation at *http://www.apache.org/docs/mod/mod_include.html*. There are several good articles on XSSI available on the Webmonkey site (*http://hotwired.lycos.com/ webmonkey/backend/apache_xssi/index.html*), which provide good explanations and examples of real-world implementations of XSSI. Despite being several years old, the information is still valid.

Flow Control Elements

Flow control elements are a set of if/else commands (similar to if statements used in a programming language) that allow authors to create conditional commands.

Using flow control elements, authors can make documents display differently based on specific variables (the "test conditions"). For instance, you could publish one version of your page for users accessing it with the Navigator browser and another for Internet Explorer users.

The basic flow elements are:

```
<!--#if expr="test_condition" -->
<!--#elif expr="test_condition" -->
<!--#else -->
<!--#endif -->
```

The first command contains the `if` statement that causes the server to test for a condition (e.g., if the browser is Navigator). If it is found to be true, the server prints the text or executes any SSI commands immediately following the `if` command. If the test condition posed by the `if` statement is false, the `elif` statement (which stands for "else if") is tried next. If the `elif` test condition is true, the server prints or executes whatever follows it.

Otherwise, the server prints or executes whatever comes after `else`, which acts as a catch-all for every other condition that might exist. An if/else statement like this can have as many `elifs` as you want to add, each of which is tested in turn, and it does not require that you have an `else` statement at the end—in which case, if none of the `if` or `elif` statements are found to be true, the server does not do anything.

The `endif` element ends the `if` element and is required.

In the following example, a greeting is customized based on the user's browser:

```
<!--#if expr="\"$HTTP_USER_AGENT\" = \"Mozilla\"" -->
Welcome Netscape User!
<!--#elif expr="\"$HTTP_USER_AGENT\" = \"Explorer\"" -->
Welcome Internet Explorer User!
<!--#else -->
Welcome!
<!--#endif -->
```

As you can see, this is where a little programming knowledge comes in handy for getting the most out of SSI.

Setting Variables

The standard available environment variables were introduced earlier in this chapter. XSSI adds the capability to create your own variables using the `set` element as follows:

```
<!--#set var="category" value="help" -->
```

Your customized variables can then be used as test conditions using the flow control elements listed earlier.

SSI Commands

The following section describes the primary Server Side Includes and their respective attributes.

config

```
config errmsg|sizefmt|timefmt="string"
```

Controls various aspects of SSI.

Attributes

errmsg

Defines the default message sent if an error occurs while parsing the document.

sizefmt

Sets the format to be used when displaying the size of the file. Valid values are **bytes** or **abbrev**, which rounds the size up to the nearest kilobyte.

timefmt

Sets the format for dates and times. The full range of formats and examples are provided in the section "Time Formats for SSI Output."

Example

```
<!-- #config errmsg="Error: File not found" -->
<!-- #config sizefmt="abbrev" -->
```

echo

```
echo var="environment or set variable"
```

Prints (displays in the document) the value of the variable. For an list of available variables, see "Include Variables" later in this chapter.

Attributes

var

The value is the name of the variable to print.

Example

```
<!--#echo var="DATE_GMT" -->
```

exec

```
exec cmd|cgi="string"
```

Executes an external program and inserts the output in the current document.

Attributes

cgi

Provides the relative URL path to the CGI script.

cmd

Specifies any shell program on the server. The SSI variables are available to the command.

Example

```
You are visitor number <!--#exec cgi="/cgi-bin/counter.pl" -->
<!--#exec cmd="/bin/finger $REMOTE_USER@$REMOTE_HOST" -->
```

fsize

```
fsize file|virtual="path"
```

Inserts the file size of a specified file. The size follows the `sizefmt` format configuration.

Attributes

`file`

> Specifies the location of the file as a pathname relative to the directory of the document being parsed. This attribute is not recommended for use (it is there for backwards compatibility with old NCSA scripts).

`virtual`

> Specifies the URL path relative to the current document being parsed. If it does not begin with a slash (/) it is taken to be relative to the current document.

Example

```
The size of this file is <!--#fsize file="thisfile.html" -->
```

flastmod

```
flastmod file|virtual ="path"
```

Inserts the last modification date of a specified file. The date follows the `timefmt` format configuration.

Attributes

`file`

> Specifies the location of the file as a pathname relative to the directory of the document being parsed. This attribute is not recommended for use (it is there for backwards compatibility with old NCSA scripts).

`virtual`

> Specifies the URL path relative to the current document being parsed. The URL cannot contain a scheme or hostname, only a path (and optional query string). If it does not begin with a slash (/), it is taken to be relative to the current document.

Example

```
That file was last modified on
  <!--#flastmod virtual="/mydocs/thatfile.html" -->
```

include

```
include file|virtual = "path"
```

Inserts the contents of another document or file into the parsed file.

Attributes

`file`

> Specifies a path relative to the directory of the parsed file (i.e., it cannot include ../ nor can it be an absolute path). The virtual attribute should always

be used in preference to this one. This attribute is not recommended for use (it is there for backwards compatibility with old NCSA scripts).

`virtual`

> Specifies a URL relative to the document being parsed. The URL cannot contain a scheme or hostname. If it does not begin with a slash (/), it is taken to be relative to the current document.

printenv

`printenv`

Prints out a listing of all existing variables and their values.

Example

```
<!--#printenv -->
```

set

`set`

Sets the value of a variable.

Attributes

`var`

> The name of the variable to be set.

`value`

> The value given to the variable.

Example

```
<!--#set var="password" value="mustard" -->
```

Include Variables

These variables are available to the echo command, if, elif, and any program on the server invoked with the exec command:

`DATE_GMT`

> The current date (at the server) in Greenwich Mean Time

`DATE_LOCAL`

> The current date (at the server) in the local time zone

`DOCUMENT_NAME`

> The name of the current file (excluding directories)

`DOCUMENT_URI`

> The (%-decoded) URL path of the current file

`LAST_MODIFIED`

> The last modification date and time for the current file

`QUERY_STRING_UNESCAPED`

> Contains the "unescaped" version of any search query (GET) sent by the browser. Any special characters are escaped using the backslash (\) character.

Other Available Variables

The following are just a few of the many standard environment variables available to both CGI programs and Server Side Includes:

HTTP_ACCEPT

> A list of the media types the client can accept

HTTP_REFERER

> The URL of the document the client was viewing before selecting the link (or form) that accessed the SSI page or CGI script

HTTP_USER_AGENT

> The browser the client is using to issue the request

REMOTE_ADDR

> The remote IP address from which the user is making the request

REMOTE_HOST

> The remote hostname from which the user is making the request (can be useful for detecting top level domain suffixes such as *.com*, *.edu*, etc.)

Time Formats for SSI Output

SSI provides a rich set of date and time formats that can be used with the `timefmt` attribute of the `config` command. To format the date, insert the code for the format, separated by commas as you intend it to display in the inserted text:

```
<!--#config timefmt="%A, %B %e, %Y" -->
Good morning! It is now <!--#echo var="DATE_LOCAL" -->
```

This would result in the date and time displayed in this manner:

```
Good morning! It is now Friday, June 22, 2001
```

As you can see, `%A` specifies the full day name, `%B` specifies the full month name, etc. Commas placed within the list will display in the inserted date and time.

Table 18-1 provides the standard SSI time format codes and their meanings.

Table 18-1: SSI time formats

Status code	Meaning	Example
%a	Day of the week abbreviation	Sun
%A	Day of the week	Sunday
%b	Month name abbreviation (also %h)	Jan
%B	Month name	January
%d	Day of the month	01
%D	Date as "%m/%d/%y"	07/19/65
%e	Day of the month	1 (*not* 01)
%H	24-hour clock hour	13
%I	12-hour clock hour	01
%j	Decimal day of the year	148
%m	Month number	11
%M	Minutes	08

Table 18-1: SSI time formats (continued)

Status code	Meaning	Example
%p	AM | PM	AM
%r	Time as "%I:%M:%S %p"	01:50:40 AM
%S	Seconds	09
%T	24-hour time as "$H:%M:%S"	20:15:30
%U	Week of the year (also %W)	37
%w	Day of the week number (starting with Sunday=0)	2
%y	Year of the century	01
%Y	Year	2001
%Z	Time zone	EST

Server Side
Includes

PART III

Graphics

CHAPTER 19

GIF Format

GIF (Graphic Interchange Format) was the first graphic file type to be displayed by early web browsers, and it remains the most popular and versatile format for distributing color images on the Web to this day. Any image can be saved as a GIF, but they excel at condensing graphical images with areas of flat color.

GIFs are completely platform-independent, meaning a GIF created on any platform can be viewed and edited on any other platform. They were originally developed by CompuServe to distribute images over their network to a variety of platforms (this is why you sometimes see GIFs referred to as "CompuServe GIF").

It is also the only graphic file format that is universally supported by all graphical browsers, regardless of version. If you want to be absolutely sure everyone will see your graphic, make it a GIF.

GIF87a Versus GIF89a

There are technically two types of GIF file: GIF87a and the newer, improved GIF89a. Both are fully supported on most browsers, and both use *.gif* as their file name suffix.

GIF87a is the original format for indexed color images. It uses LZW compression and has the option of being interlaced.

GIF89a is the same, but also includes transparency and animation capabilities (animation is discussed in Chapter 23). If you want to add these features to your graphic, you'll need to create the graphic with a tool that supports the GIF89a format. These features have become so popular with web developers that this format has become the de facto standard on the Web today. Detailed descriptions of each feature appear in the following sections of this chapter.

8-Bit Indexed Color

GIF files are indexed color images that can contain a maximum of 8-bit color information (they can also be saved at lower bit rates). This means they can contain up to 256 colors—the maximum number that 8 bits of information can define ($2^8 = 256$). Lower bit depths result in fewer colors and also reduce file size. This is discussed in "Minimizing GIF File Sizes" at the end of this chapter.

"Indexed color" means that the set of colors in the image, its *palette*, is stored in a color table. Each pixel in the image contains a reference (or "index") to a table cell containing the color for that pixel. In Photoshop, you can view the table for an indexed color image by selecting Image → Mode → Color Table.

When you convert a 24-bit (millions of colors) image to GIF, it is necessary to first convert the image to Indexed Color mode, and as part of that process, reduce the number of colors to a palette of 256 or fewer colors. The image-editing tool does its best to approximate the full color range by using the most appropriate colors to approximate the image (an "adaptive" palette). You can specify an alternate set of colors to use in this process, such as the web palette. See the sidebar "Common Palettes" in Chapter 22 for descriptions of other color palette options.

GIF Compression

There are two main things to know about GIF compression. First, it is a "lossless" compression, meaning no image information is lost in the compression process, and the decompressed image is identical to the original. (Note that some information may be lost in the conversion process from RGB to indexed color format, but once it is converted, the compression itself is lossless.)

Second, GIF uses LZW (Lempel-Zev-Welch) compression, which takes advantage of repetition in data streams. Translated into graphic terms, this means that LZW compression is extremely efficient at condensing rows of pixels of identical color. To use a simplified example, when the compression scheme hits a row of 15 identical blue pixels, it can store the information as "15 blue," but when it encounters a row that has a gentle gradation from blue to black, it needs to store a description for every pixel along the way, therefore requiring more data. This is why GIFs are efficient at storing simple graphical images; the areas of flat color take advantage of the LZW compression.

On a historical note, Unisys, the company that holds the patent on LZW compression, caused quite a stir on the Internet in 1994 when they announced that it would begin charging licensing fees to developers incorporating GIF compression into their products. In the face of fees and legal hassles, the Internet population rushed to find nonproprietary alternatives to the GIF format, leading to the development of PNG (see Chapter 21). Unisys does enforce its patent and charges software companies fees for including GIF support, but GIF shows no sign of disappearing any time soon.

When to Use GIFs

GIF is a versatile format for condensing color images for use on the Web. It is particularly well suited for any image with areas of flat color, such as logos, line art, icons, cartoon-like illustrations, etc. (Figure 19-1). It compresses them cleanly (since it is a lossless compression) and efficiently (LZW compression looks for repetition of pixel colors). Even if the image contains some photographic elements, if the majority is flat colors, GIF is your best bet.

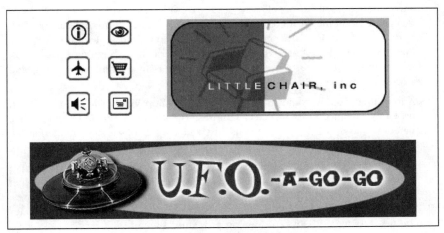

Figure 19-1: Examples of images well suited for GIF format

You will also need to use GIF format if you want a portion of the image to be transparent, because it is the only format that has this ability and is universally supported by browsers. PNG files can contain transparency information (actually, in a more sophisticated way than GIF), but as of this writing, browser support is too spotty to use them confidently.

GIF is also a good option for adding simple animation to your page without relying on plug-in technology, Java programming, or server-intensive methods. Most browsers display an animated GIF as easily as any other GIF. See Chapter 23 for more information on GIF animation.

GIFs are not particularly good for photographic images. With the 8-bit limit, true color information is lost and the subtle gradations of tone become pixelated when the image is reduced to 256 colors. The quality of the image may be greatly reduced. In addition, GIF is not able to condense photorealistic image content efficiently.

In many cases (especially for very small images), GIF works just fine for all image types, but you will get much better image quality and smaller file sizes if you save photographs and continuous-tone images as JPEGs (see Chapter 20 for more information).

Tools Overview

GIFs can be created with a wide variety of graphics programs and utilities.

Image-editing software

There are many tools available for creating GIF files. The professional industry standard remains Adobe Photoshop (Version 6 is available as of this writing), a full-featured image-editing application (see *http://www.adobe.com* for more information). However, if you work on a PC, you may want to try Paint Shop Pro, which has some of the same features at a lower cost. You can download a demo at *http://www.jasc.com*.

Web graphics tools

Two tools, Adobe ImageReady and Macromedia Fireworks, have been designed from the ground up to address the special requirements of Web graphics. In addition to providing superior optimization features for web delivery, they also offer web design shortcuts, such as building imagemaps, slicing images into sections (to be held together by a table), animation, and adding rollover effects.

Adobe ImageReady comes bundled with Photoshop Version 5.5 and higher. It provides advanced optimization features, optimization previews, interactive palettes, and all of the functions listed previously. It has a similar interface to Photoshop, and it is easy to bounce back and forth between the two.

Macromedia Fireworks combines a vector-drawing application with a bitmap editor. Among its many impressive features are editable text, "live" effects that can be edited at any time, side-by-side export previews, animation features, rollover buttons, advanced image-slicing tools, and much more. It alleviates the need to switch between drawing programs, bitmap programs, and special-ized web utilities. For more information, see Macromedia's site at *http://www. macromedia.com*.

Both Fireworks and ImageReady provide GIF creation capabilities along with many fine-tuning controls over bit depth, dithering, and palette selection, that many standard image editing programs lack. Both programs condense GIF files very efficiently.

Vector-drawing programs

With the growing demand for web graphics, many vector-based drawing applications now offer the ability to save bitmapped GIF files without exporting the files and opening them in a program such as Photoshop (a big time saver). In addition, simple graphics with solid fills, typical of images created in vector-based drawing tools, are ideal for GIF compression. Vector-drawing tools such as Macromedia Freehand (Version 7 and higher), Adobe Illustrator (Version 7 and higher), Corel Draw, and Corel Xara offer basic GIF creation capabilities. They are not as effective at optimizing file sizes as web graphics tools.

Plug-ins

There are also a host of third-party plug-ins that can enhance the function-ality of Photoshop and other software that supports Photoshop plug-ins. The most notable of these are PhotoGIF from BoxTop Software (*http://www. boxtopsoft.com*) and HVS ColorGIF from Digital Frontiers (*http://www. digfrontiers.com*). Each provides tools that exceed Photoshop's built-in features for fine-tuning GIFs.

Shareware utilities

In addition, there are dozens of utilities for both Mac and PC that perform simple and specialized tasks. These utilities can be downloaded for free and can be registered for a very modest fee. One example is GifConverter, which

---

will convert most existing graphic formats into GIF and also allows you to add interlacing. Another is Ulead GifSmartsaver, a very nice standalone GIF optimization utility. Shareware.com is a valuable resource for finding such utilities (search for "gif" at *http://www.shareware.com*).

Interlacing

Normal GIFs are either displayed one row of pixels at a time, from top to bottom, or all at once when the entire file has downloaded. On slow connections, this can mean potentially long waits with empty space and generic graphic icons on the screen.

As an alternative, you can save a GIF87a or 89a with interlacing. An interlaced GIF is displayed in a series of four passes, with the first hint of the upcoming image appearing after only 1/8th (12.5%) of the file has downloaded. The first pass has the appearance of a blurry mosaic; as more data flows in, the blurred areas are filled in with real image information and the image becomes more defined (Figure 19-2). The three subsequent passes fill in 25%, 50%, and 100% of the image information, respectively.

Graphics programs that support the GIF format provide an interlacing option (usually a checkbox) in the Save as or Export dialog box. Simply turn the interlacing on or off when you save the GIF.

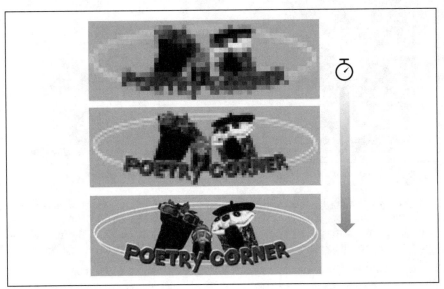

Figure 19-2: Interlaced GIFs display in a series of passes

Advantages

The advantage to using interlacing is that it quickly gives the viewer some idea of the graphic to come. This peek may be enough to make some important decisions. For instance, if the graphic is a familiar imagemap, the user can use the link to go to another page before the entire image has downloaded. In some cases, the partially downloaded image might be enough for the viewer to decide that she doesn't want to wait for the rest.

Disadvantages

The main trade-off in choosing to make a GIF interlaced is that it slightly increases the file size of the resulting graphic. There are also aesthetic considerations involved that come down to a matter of personal taste. Some viewers would rather see nothing at all than look at the temporary visual chaos an interlaced GIF creates. For these reasons, you may choose to limit interlacing to instances when it makes sense, such as for large imagemaps, instead of using it for every small graphic on a page.

Transparency

The GIF89a format introduced the ability to make portions of graphics transparent. Whatever is behind the transparent area (most likely the background color or pattern of the page) will show through. With transparency, graphics can be shapes other than rectangles (Figure 19-3)!

Figure 19-3: The same GIF image with transparency (left) and without (right)

In most graphics tools, the transparent area is specified by selecting a specific pixel color in the image with a special transparency pointer or eyedropper tool (in Paint Shop Pro, it needs to be specified numerically). All pixels in the image that match the selected color will be transparent when they are rendered in a browser.

To understand how transparency works, you need to start with the color table (the table that contains the palette) for the indexed color image. In transparent GIFs, one position in the color table is designated as "transparent," and whatever pixel color fills that position is known as the Transparency Index Color (usually gray by default). All pixels in the image that are painted with that color will be transparent when viewed in a browser.

Let's look at techniques for working with transparent GIFs. These techniques use Adobe Photoshop for its layering features. The first provides strategies for getting rid of "halos" (or fringe) around transparent graphics. The next gives pointers for preventing unwanted transparency within your image.

Preventing "Halos"

Far too often, you see transparent graphics on the Web with light-colored fringe around the edges (called a "halo") that doesn't blend into the background color (see Figure 19-4).

Figure 19-4: A "halo" effect created by anti-aliased edges in a transparent graphic

This effect is the result of *anti-aliasing*, the slight blur used on curved edges to make smoother transitions between colors (like the image on the right in Figure 19-5). Aliased edges, by contrast, are blocky and stair-stepped (like the image on the left). The images below have been enlarged to make pixel-level detail more prominent.

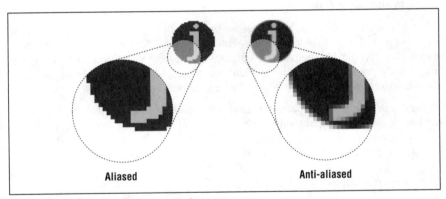

Figure 19-5: Aliasing versus anti-aliasing

When the color around an anti-aliased edge is made transparent, the blur along the edge remains intact, and you can see all those shades of gray between the graphic and the darker background. Halos make graphics look messy and unprofessional.

Unfortunately, once an image is saved as a GIF, the only way to fix a halo is to get in there and erase the anti-aliased edge, pixel by pixel. Even if you get rid of all the edges, you'll be left with blocky edges and the quality of the image will suffer.

However, halos are very easy to prevent. Following are a few techniques to avoid that unwanted fringe in transparent graphics.

Use aliased edges

One way to avoid halos is to keep your image and text edges aliased (as shown in Figure 19-6). That way there are no stray pixels between your image and the background color.

Figure 19-6: Transparent graphic with aliased edges (no halo effect)

In Photoshop, the marquee, lasso, and magic wand selection tools all have the option of turning off anti-aliasing in their respective Option palettes. You can also choose to turn off anti-aliasing when creating text.

The advantages to aliased edges are that they are halo-proof and require fewer pixel colors (which potentially means smaller file sizes). The disadvantage is that the blocky edges often just look bad.

Use a matte color tool

If you are using Fireworks, ImageReady, or Photoshop (5.5 and higher), the best way to prevent a halo is to use the Matte color tool. The tool requires that you start with a layered file that already contains transparent areas. In other words, the image must not have already been "flattened." The parts of the layered image that are transparent will remain transparent when exported to GIF format.

In the tool's optimization palette, simply set the Matte color to the same color as the background of the page on which the GIF will appear (Figure 19-7). When the GIF is exported with Transparency selected, the anti-aliased edges of the image blend with the selected Matte color. That blend ensures there will be no halo.

Use a colored background layer

If you are working with Paint Shop Pro or an earlier version of Photoshop, there is an easy technique for avoiding halos, but it also requires that you begin with a layered file. If you are starting with a flattened image, such as from a CD-ROM or scan, you first need to use a selection tool to cut the image from the background (using an anti-aliased selection tool) and paste it on a layer of a new file.

1. In your layered file, create a new layer at the bottom of the layer "stack."

2. Fill the whole layer with a color that is the same as, or as close as possible to, the background color of your web page (Figure 19-8). If you are using a tiled background pattern, choose a color that approximates its dominant color value. If you cannot select the exact color, it is better to guess a little darker.

3. When the layers are flattened as a result of converting to Indexed Color, the anti-aliased text and other soft edges will blend into the color of the bottom

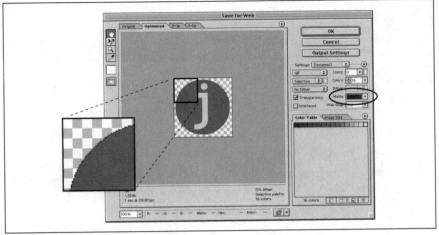

Figure 19-7: The matte color tool (shown in Photoshop 6)

layer. The transition pixels will be the appropriate color, and they won't stand out when placed against the background color on your web page.

4. Select the background color to be transparent (using the transparency tool or specifying its RGB values) upon export.

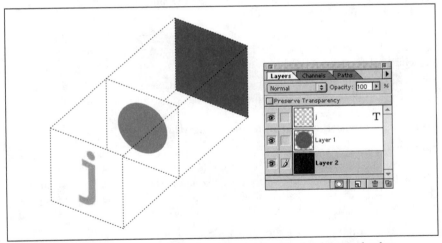

Figure 19-8: Filling a layer with a color that matches the background color

Preventing Unwanted Transparent Areas

In some instances, you'll find that the color around the edge of your image also appears within the image. This means that if you use an eyedropper tool to select the edge color for transparency, parts of your image will disappear as well.

The easiest way to prevent this is the handy Matte color feature of a web graphics application (discussed earlier), because it does not rely on an eyedropper tool for transparency. Rather, the transparent areas of the layered file are preserved upon export, and the solid pixels in the image area are unaffected.

However, if you are using a tool that does not have a Matte color feature, such as an early version of Photoshop or PaintShop Pro, there is a trick for preventing unwanted transparency. For this example, consider an image that has a white background, but also white text within the image area. The goal is to turn the white pixels around the image transparent, but to keep the white text white.

Creating a distinct color for transparency

Follow these steps to create a distinct color for transparency:

1. Flatten your image so any anti-aliased edges will merge with your chosen background color (see "Use a colored background layer," earlier in this chapter). If you are starting with an Indexed Color image, change it to RGB so you can add a color to its palette.

2. Using the Magic Wand tool with the tolerance set to 1 and anti-aliasing turned *off* (these settings are important!), select the areas in the image that you'd like to be transparent. Holding down the Shift key allows you to add to your selection. (Don't use "Select Similar" or you will select *all* the pixels in the image, which is what you're trying *not* to do!)

3. Using the Fill tool (or doing it by hand), fill your selection with a distinct color that does not appear anywhere in the image (one of the obnoxious bright colors usually works well).

4. Check the image to be sure that all areas you wish to be transparent are filled with the obnoxious color (and, of course, that no pixels in your image have changed).

5. Now you can convert the image to Indexed Color, save as GIF format, and select the distinct color to be transparent as you would normally.

Changing the distinct color without losing transparency

The following is an optional addition to the preceding technique. If for some reason you are unhappy with the new color in your file, or if you worry that it will be visible if transparency isn't supported (not likely these days), you can turn the new color back to its original color value (white in our example) while keeping it distinct from nontransparent pixels sharing that color (the white in the text areas).

1. Create a distinct color for the transparency (as described previously).

2. After the image has been converted to Indexed Color, open the Color Table (Image → Mode → Color Table).

3. Find the new, distinct color in the Color Table (if you made it obnoxious enough, it should be easy to find), and click on it.

4. Edit the RGB values in the dialog box to set the color back to the color it was before (white in our example). By doing this, you are assigning a color (white) to two positions in the Color Table; one will be made transparent, and the other will remain visible.

5. For some transparent-GIF creation tools, it is important to know the position of the new white in the Color Table, so you may want to pay attention to the neighboring colors in the table.

6. Once the color is changed, close the dialog boxes and Export to GIF89a, selecting the background area to be transparent. You'll know you've selected the correct white because the areas will be filled with the Transparency Index Color in the preview.

Minimizing GIF File Sizes

When you are designing and producing graphics for the Web, it is of utmost importance to keep your file sizes as small as possible. The standard guideline for estimating download time over a modem is 1 second per kilobyte. Of course, actual download times will vary widely, but this gives you a ballpark number to use for comparisons.

There are a few simple strategies you can follow to minimize the size of your GIF files, described in the following sections.

Tools for Optimizing GIFs

There are several software tools available specifically for creating and optimizing graphics for the Web. One of the greatest benefits is that they offer previews of your optimization settings (even providing side-by-side comparisons), so you can make adjustments to the settings while keeping an eye on the resulting file size and overall image quality.

The big two are Adobe Photoshop/ImageReady and Macromedia Fireworks. Both offer very similar controls for file format, color depth, palette dithering, loss, and color palette editing. If you want to make professional-level web graphics, it is highly recommended you use one of these tools. The one you choose is up to your personal preference. Photoshop has the advantages of being the industry standard program for digital imaging and an interface that many designers are already familiar with. Fireworks provides an all-in-one package, impressive compression rates, and good integration with Dreamweaver, the industry-standard web authoring program.

If you are really serious about making your GIFs as small as possible, consider using HVS ColorGIF (*http://www.digfrontiers.com*), a third-party plug-in designed specifically for GIF optimization. HVS ColorGIF is in a class by itself when it comes to GIF optimization. In all the tests I've run, HVS ColorGIF's compression algorithms produce the smallest GIFs while maintaining the highest image quality compared to other optimizing tools. It can be used with Photoshop, ImageReady, Fireworks, Paint Shop Pro, and any graphics application that supports plug-ins.

Design Strategies

You can help keep file size under control by the design decisions you make. After a while, designing graphics for the Web becomes second nature.

Limit dimensions

Though it may seem obvious, the easiest way to keep file size down is to limit the dimensions of your graphic. There aren't any numerical guidelines here; just don't make graphics larger than they need to be.

- Scale large images down (see "Resizing tips" in Chapter 3).

- Crop out any extra space around the important areas of your image.

- Avoid large graphics if they are not absolutely necessary.

Design with flat color

If you design your graphics with flat color from the beginning, you are basically giving the LZW compression the kind of file it likes—rows of repetitive pixel colors.

- Fill areas with solid colors rather than gradients (fades from one color to another).

- Limit the amount of photographic material in your GIFs (use JPEGs for photo images).

- Favor horizontal fields of color in your designs when applicable; for example, horizontal stripes condense better than vertical stripes.

- Turn off anti-aliasing when it isn't necessary. The blur that makes smooth (not stair-stepped) contours also adds to the number of colors in the image.

Reduce number of colors (bit depth)

Although GIF format can support 8-bit color information with a maximum of 256 colors, you don't necessarily have to use all of them. In fact, you can reduce the size of a file considerably by saving it at a lower bit depth, which corresponds to fewer number of colors. Adobe Photoshop Versions 5 and higher allow you to select the number of colors you'd like in the image. Other tools ask you to choose from a list of bit depths. The effect is the same; it's just useful to know how bit depth translates into numbers of colors for the latter (see Table 19-1 for translations).

Table 19-1: Color depth equivalents for bit depths

Bit depth	Number of colors
1-bit	2 (black and white)
2-bit	4
3-bit	8
4-bit	16
5-bit	32
6-bit	64
7-bit	128
8-bit	256

The goal is to find the minimum number of colors (smallest bit depth) that still maintains the integrity and overall character of the image. You may be surprised to find how many images survive a reduction to just 32 colors. Of course, the bit-depth at which the image quality becomes unacceptable depends on the specific image and your personal preferences.

Reducing the number of colors reduces file size in two ways. First, lower bit depths have less data in the file. In addition, clusters of similarly colored pixels suddenly become the same color, creating more pockets of repeating pixels for LZW compression to work on. For that reason, fewer image colors take better advantage of GIF's compression scheme, resulting in smaller files. The real file size savings kicks in when there are large areas of flat color. Even if an image has only eight pixel colors, if it has a lot of blends and gradients, you won't see the kind of file size savings you might expect with that kind of severe color reduction.

Limit dithering

When an RGB image (made up of colors from the true color space of millions of colors) is reduced to an Indexed Color palette of only 256 colors, dithering usually occurs. *Dithering* is the random dot pattern that results when colors are approximated by mixing similar and available colors from a limited palette. Dithering is relevant to GIF file size because it interrupts the clean areas of flat color that are conducive to efficient LZW compression, and can make the file size larger than it needs to be.

Nearly all image editing tools allow you to turn on and off dithering. Current web graphics tools (Fireworks and Photoshop/Imageready) go one step further by allowing the amount of dithering to be selected on a sliding scale from 0 to 100. You can preview the results of various settings, making it easy to select the best balance of file size and image quality.

Bear in mind, however, that dithering also enables you to maintain image quality and character at lower bit depths, and in this respect can be considered a friend of optimization. Lower bit depths generally result in smaller file sizes.

Lossy GIFs

As explained earlier in this chapter, GIF compression is "lossless," meaning every pixel in the image is preserved during compression. The current web graphics tools allow you to force some pixels out during the conversion process using the "Loss" or "Lossy" setting. Throwing out stray pixels is all in the name of maximizing the number of uninterrupted rows of pixel colors, thus allowing the LZW compression to work more efficiently. Depending on the image, a loss value of 5-30% will maintain the integrity of the image while reducing file sizes significantly. This technique works best on images with areas of continuous tone (blended colors) and photographic content.

Weighted Optimization (Photoshop 6/ImageReady 3)

Photoshop 6 and ImageReady 3 offer yet another advance in graphic optimization. Their weighted optimization feature allows you to apply varying amounts of optimization to different parts of the image. This preserves the integrity of the most important areas while maximizing file size savings for the remainder.

Weighted optimization uses an alpha channel (called a mask) to select areas of the image for various optimization levels. The white areas of the mask correspond to the highest level of image quality, while black areas describe the lowest (gray areas are on a linear scale in between). Channels can be used to control color reduction, dithering, and lossiness in a GIF image.

To access the Modify dialog box (Figure 19-9), click the Channel button next to each of these controls on the Optimization palette. In the dialog box, use the sliders to set the maximum (white tab on the left) and minimum (black tab on the right) levels of optimization.

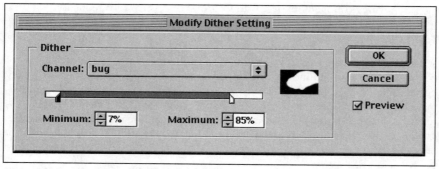

Figure 19-9: Weighted Optimization dialog box in ImageReady 3

In Photoshop, create the alpha channel by saving a selection and giving the channel a name (the channel can then be accessed from the Modify dialog boxes). In ImageReady, you can create a new channel based on a selected image area on the fly when you click the Channel button.

Weighted color reduction

When you use the alpha channel to reduce colors in parts of an image, the white areas of the mask determine what areas of the image are most important. Colors in those areas will be weighted more heavily when calculating the color table for the image.

Weighted dithering

When using the alpha channel with dithering, the white areas of the mask correspond to the areas that receive the most dithering. Black areas yield the least dithering. Set the percentage amounts for each using the black and white tabs on the slider.

Weighted lossiness

Similarly, when using the alpha channel with lossiness, the white areas of the mask correspond to the highest image quality. However, because more lossiness results in less quality, the settings are reversed. To set the highest level of quality (with the white tab) or enter a value in the Minimum text box. For lowest level of quality, drag the right (black) tab or enter a value in the Maximum text box.

Optimize to a File Size in Photoshop 5.5+

In some cases, you may know ahead of time what you'd like the file size of your GIF file to be, for example, when designing an ad banner with a specific file size limitation.

Photoshop 5.5 and higher offers an "Optimize to File Size" function that automatically optimizes an image to meet a target file size. This enables you to achieve your desired file size without having to test a variety of file size settings. The Optimize to File Size function is accessible from the "Save for Web" dialog box as shown in Figure 19-10.

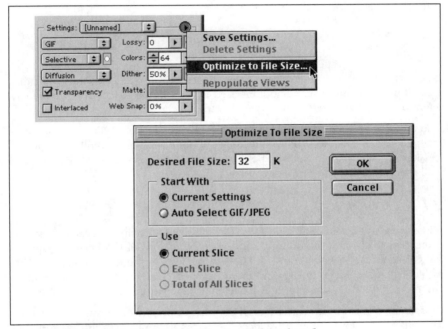

Figure 19-10: "Optimize to File Size" shown in Photoshop 6

This function works about the same in Versions 5.5 and 6.0, but 6.0 adds the ability to set a target size for a single slice (a portion created with the slicing tool) of an image.

CHAPTER 20

JPEG Format

JPEG (which stands for Joint Photographic Experts Group, the standards body that created it) is a compression algorithm used by files in the JFIF format, commonly referred to as "JPEG files." JPEGs use either the *.jpg* or *.jpeg* suffix.

Like any graphics file format in widespread use on the Web, JPEGs are platform-independent. In addition, JPEGs are fully supported for use as inline images in Versions 2.0 and higher of Netscape Navigator and Microsoft Internet Explorer, as well as in nearly all other current browsers.

24-Bit Color

JPEG images contain 24-bit RGB color information, which means they are comprised of colors from the true color space of millions of colors (see Chapter 3 for a description of 24-bit color). JPEG files can also carry grayscale images. This results in higher image quality and more rich and subtle color variations. Unlike GIF files, JPEGs do not use palettes for referencing color information.

Bear in mind, however, that when JPEGs are displayed on a system that only supports 8-bit color, a browser reduces the colors in the image to its built-in web palette, and some dithering occurs. In general, however, dithering is often acceptable in photographic image areas. For an explanation of the web palette, see Chapters 3 and 22.

JPEG Compression

JPEG uses what is known as a "lossy" compression scheme, meaning that some image information is actually thrown out in the compression process. Fortunately, for photographic images at most compression levels, this loss is not discernible to the human eye, particularly when the image is displayed on a monitor at screen resolution (and even less so for images saved at print resolutions).

Using "lossy" compression algorithms, JPEG is able to achieve 10:1 to 20:1 data-compression ratios without visible loss in quality. Of course, the savings in file size at any given compression is dependent on the content of the specific image, and results vary. If maintaining high image quality is not a priority, these ratios can go even higher.

The efficiency of JPEG compression is based on the *spatial frequency*, or concentration of detail, of the image. Image areas with low frequency (smooth gradients, like a blue sky) are compressed much further than areas with higher frequency (lots of detail, like blades of grass). Even a single sharp color boundary, although not giving "lots of detail," represents a surge in spatial frequency and therefore poses problems for JPEG compression.

The compression algorithm samples the image in 8×8-pixel squares and then translates the relative color and brightness information into mathematical formulas. These sampling squares may become visible when images are compressed with the highest compression ratios (lowest quality settings).

It is perhaps most meaningful to compare JPEG and GIF compression on photographic images. A detail-rich photographic image that takes up 85K of disk space as a GIF image would require only 35K as a JPEG. Again, the rate of compression depends on the specific image, but in general, a JPEG compresses a photographic image two to three times smaller than GIF. For flat-color graphics, however, GIF is far more efficient than JPEG.

Image Loss

Be aware that once image quality is lost in JPEG compression, you can never get it back again. Loss in image quality is also cumulative, meaning you lose a little bit more information each time you decompress and compress an image. Each time you open a JPEG and resave it, you degrade the image further. Not only that, you may introduce new artifacts to the image that prevent the second compression from working as efficiently as the first, resulting in higher file sizes.

It is a good idea to hang on to one copy of the original digital image if you anticipate having to make changes, so your final image only goes through the compression process once. You should also start from an original image each time to experiment with different compression levels. The new web graphics tools (Fireworks, Photoshop 5.5 and higher, and ImageReady) make this easy because they always retain the original and allow you to export graphics with your chosen settings.

Variable Compression Levels

One advantage to JPEGs is that you can control the degree to which the image is compressed. The higher the quality, the larger the file. The goal is to find the smallest file size that still maintains acceptable image quality.

The quality of a JPEG image is denoted by its "Q" setting, usually on a scale from 0 to 100. In nearly all programs, the lower numbers represent lower image quality but better compression rates (and smaller files). The higher numbers result in better image quality and larger files.

For the most part, the Q setting is an arbitrary value with no specific mathematical significance. It is just a way to specify the image quality level you'd like to maintain. When JPEG compression goes to work, it compresses as much as it can while maintaining the targeted Q setting. The actual compression ratio depends on the content of the individual image.

The scales for specifying Q-settings (or "Quality") vary among tools that create JPEGs. Most current web tools use a scale from 0 to 100; however, you will still find some that use a scale from 0 to 10 or 0 to 12. The numbers themselves are not significant (a 30 in one program may be radically different than 30 in another); what matters is the way the image looks and its resulting file size.

JPEG Decompression

JPEGs need to be decompressed before they can be displayed; therefore, it takes a browser longer to decode and assemble a JPEG than a GIF of the same file size. Bear in mind that a small portion of the download time-savings gained by using a JPEG instead of a GIF is lost to the added time it takes to display. (Not much though, so don't sweat it.)

When to Use JPEGs

As mentioned earlier, JPEGs, with their 24-bit color capacity and specialized compression scheme are ideal for photographic and other continuous-tone images, such as paintings, watercolor illustrations, and grayscale images with the 256 shades of gray (see Figure 20-1).

Figure 20-1: Examples of images appropriate for JPEG format

JPEGs are notably *not* good at compressing graphical images with areas of solid color, such as logos, line art, type, and cartoon-like illustrations. JPEG's lossy compression makes flat colors blotchy and pixelated, resulting in unacceptable loss of quality in some cases. Not only that, the files are generally quite a bit larger than a GIF file of the same image. JPEG compression is also not good at sharp edges or typography since it tends to leave artifacts that "ripple" the edges.

It is usually best to let JPEGs handle photographic material and leave the flat graphics (including graphics containing text) to GIF.

Progressive JPEGs

Progressive JPEGs are just like ordinary JPEGs except they display in a series of passes (like interlacing in the GIF format), each pass containing more detailed information, until the whole image is rendered clearly. Graphics programs allow you to specify the number of passes it takes to fill in the final image (3, 4, or 5 scans). Bear in mind that over a fast Internet connection, the image may load and render so quickly the user may not see any passes at all.

Advantages

One advantage to using Pro-JPEGs is that like interlaced GIFs, they provide some indication of the full image for the reader to look at without having to wait for the entire image to download. Progressive JPEGs are also generally slightly smaller than standard JPEG files.

Disadvantages

One disadvantage to Progressive JPEGs is that they require more processing power to display. The higher the specified number of passes, the more power it takes the user's machine to render them.

The other disadvantage is that they are not supported on older browser versions. Netscape Navigator 2.0 and Internet Explorer 2.0 display Pro-JPEGs inline but may not support the progressive display. Pro-JPEGs are fully supported by Versions 3.0 and higher of both Netscape and MSIE. If a browser cannot identify a Pro-JPEG, it displays a broken graphic image.

Creating JPEGs

Because JPEG is a standard file format, it is supported by all the popular graphics tools. Adobe Photoshop/ImageReady, JASC Paint Shop Pro, and Macromedia Fireworks all provide similar options for saving JPEGs.

All of these products allow you to set the quality/compression level and save images in Progressive JPEG format. In Paint Shop Pro and Photoshop 5.0 and earlier, select "Save As" from the File menu and select JPEG from the available file formats. Photoshop Versions 5.5 and higher (including ImageReady) and Fireworks provide more advanced optimization options, side-by-side previews of the image and resulting file sizes, and an export function that preserves the original image.

There are also plug-in utilities especially for JPEG creation, such as ProJPEG from Boxtop Software (*http://www.boxtopsoft.com*) and HVS JPEG 2.1 from Digital Frontiers (*http://www.digfrontiers.com*). These plug-ins work with all of the programs mentioned here.

Regardless of the tool you use, the following guidelines apply:

- Make sure your file is in RGB or grayscale format. You can apply JPEG compression to CMYK files in some applications, but these files are not compatible with web browsers.

- Layered images must be flattened before they can be saved as a JPEG. Photoshop 5.5+, ImageReady, and Fireworks allow you to export flattened JPEG images while preserving the layered original.

- Name your file with the suffix *.jpg* or *.jpeg*. This is necessary for the browser to recognize it as a readable JPEG file type.

Minimizing JPEG File Size

As for all files intended for Web delivery, it is important to optimize JPEGs to make them as small as possible. Because JPEGs are always 24-bit by nature, reducing bit-depth is not an option. For the most part, all you have to play with is the quality setting, but it is possible to prepare an image prior to compression. There are a number of specialized tools available for making JPEGs as small as they can be while letting you make decisions about image quality.

Aggressive Compression Ratios

The most direct way of optimizing a JPEG is to adjust its Quality setting. If your image has a lot of continuous tone or gradient colors, you can be pretty aggressive with the compression level and not worry too much about loss of quality in the resulting JPEG. Even at some of the lowest quality settings, the image quality is still suitable for viewing on web pages. Of course, this depends on the individual image. A low quality setting (below 40) usually results in a blocky or blotchy effect in areas of flat color, which may be unacceptable to you.

Each tool provides sliders for controlling quality/compression ratios, although they use different numbering systems. Fireworks uses a percentage value from 1 to 100%. Paint Shop Pro uses a scale from 1 to 100, but it works as the inverse of the standard scale: lower numbers correspond to higher image quality and less compression.

Photoshop uses a scale of 0 to 12 when you select JPEG from the "Save As" dialog box. When you "Save for Web" in Photoshop/ImageReady, the quality rating is on a scale from 0 to 100. It should be noted that Photoshop is much less aggressive with its numbering; 0 on the Photoshop scale corresponds to about 30 on the standard scale.

The easiest way to get the balance of compression and image quality just right is to use a tool that offers a preview of the image (and its file size) with your settings. Photoshop 5.5+/ImageReady, Fireworks, and the third party JPEG plug-ins offer previews. If your image editor does not have a preview function, you may need to do some testing to find the compression level that works best (save the file, then preview it in a browser). Be sure to save a copy of the original image so you can do a fresh JPEG compression with each test.

"Optimized" JPEGs

Standard JPEGs use a precalculated, general purpose compression table (called the Huffman table) for compressing an image. Some tools offer the ability to create an "optimized" compression table that is customized for the particular image. This results in better color fidelity and slightly smaller file sizes. This format is supported on current browsers, but some (mostly older) browsers may have trouble displaying optimized JPEGs.

The optimization option is presented differently in each tool:

Photoshop 5.5 and higher (and ImageReady)
Check the "Optimized" checkbox in the Optimize palette.

Photoshop (4.0 and 5.0)
Select the "Baseline (Optimized)" option in the JPEG dialog box.

Pro-JPEG (BoxTop Software)
Check the "Optimize Huffman Codes" checkbox in the Pro-JPEG dialog box.

HVS JPEG (Digital Frontiers)
In addition to optimizing Huffman Codes, HVS JPEG utilizes a different (and unique) method of optimization that, according to Digital Frontiers, uses a proprietary algorithm to base compression rates on a spatial frequency analysis of the image.

These optimization controls are grouped under the "Q-Table" options in the dialog box. "General" uses the standard compression table. "Generate Optimized Q-Table" creates a customized table for the image.

In addition to these, HVS JPEG provides two predefined tables for optimizing certain image types. "Portraits" is best used on images with smooth tones. "Textured" is for images where it is important to preserve detail and texture.

Softening the Image for Better Compression

JPEG compression does an admirable job of condensing photographic images without requiring much extra attention. However, if you are serious about making your JPEGs as compact as possible, you may want to maximize JPEG compression's strengths by feeding it the kind of image it likes—an image with subtle gradations, fewer details, and no hard edges. By applying a slight blur to all or part of the image, you allow the compression scheme to do its work more efficiently.

If you are using one of the newer web graphics tools, you will find a setting with the optimization options that softens the image. In Photoshop 5.5 and higher, the tool is called "Blur"; in Fireworks, it's "Smoothing." If you apply a soft blur, the JPEG compression works better, resulting in a smaller file. If you don't have these tools, you can soften the whole image by applying a slight blur to the image with the "Gaussian Blur" filter (or similar). Compare the file sizes of the original image (left) and the slightly blurred image (center) in Figure 20-2.

A more sophisticated approach is to apply aggressive blurs to areas of the image that are not important and leave areas of detail alone. For instance, if you are working with a portrait, you could apply a blur to the background while maintaining detail in the face, as shown in the example on the right in Figure 20-2.

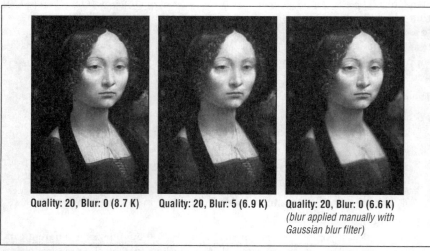

Quality: 20, Blur: 0 (8.7 K)   Quality: 20, Blur: 5 (6.9 K)   Quality: 20, Blur: 0 (6.6 K)
(blur applied manually with Gaussian blur filter)

Figure 20-2: Blurring all or part of an image results in smaller file sizes

Using the HVS JPEG Plug-in

HVS JPEG has some unique features for pushing JPEG compression while maintaining image quality. The Edge-Preserving Detail Filter (in the upper-left corner of the dialog box shown in Figure 20-3) smooths out texture detail while working to maintain the edges. This results in higher compression with better overall image quality and without edge artifacts.

If you have an image that has a lot of detail, position the Detail slider towards the left. If your image is soft, you can slide the Detail slider to the right for a more

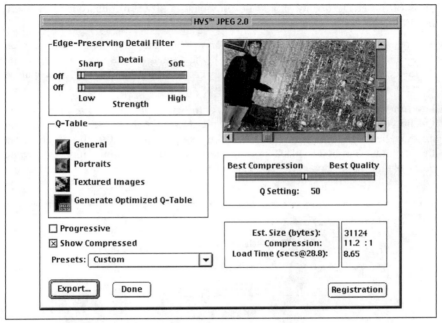

Figure 20-3: HVS JPEG dialog box

aggressive application of the prefilter. Note that if either of the edge-preserving sliders is positioned all the way to the left, no prefilter will be applied.

Once you've set the Detail slider to match the general quality of the image, you can experiment with various amounts of blur using the Strength slider. This is not a scientific process—it's a matter of finding the point at which you are comfortable with the image quality while minimizing the file size.

Always apply the prefilters first (that's why they're called "pre" filters), because the optimization tables and compression ratios will be based on these settings. After applying the filters and optimization, you may be able to reduce the compression Q-setting a bit without noticeable change in image quality.

Optimize to File Size in Photoshop 5.5+

If you know ahead of time the size you'd like your JPEG to be, try using the "Optimize to File Size" feature in Photoshop 5.5 and higher. Optimize to File Size (accessible via the "Save for Web" dialog box) allows you to achieve your target file size automatically without trying out lots of different optimization settings. Photoshop handles it all for you! The Optimize to File Size function is also discussed in Chapter 19 (see Figure 19-10).

Weighted Optimization (Photoshop 6/ImageReady 3)

Photoshop 6 and ImageReady 3 offer a "weighted optimization" function that lets you smoothly vary the optimization settings across an image using an alpha channel (also called a mask). This allows you to let Photoshop know for which areas of the image quality should be preserved, and where quality may be sacrificed in order to achieve a smaller file size.

To save a JPEG with weighted optimization in Photoshop 6, first select the portion of the image that you want to retain the highest quality. Save the selection (using the Select menu) and give it a name. This creates the alpha channel that will be referenced when optimizing the image.

From the "Save for Web" dialog box, select the channel button to the right of the Quality text box (see Figure 20-4). In the Modify Quality Setting dialog that appears, select your named channel from the pop-up menu. Use the sliders to set the minimum (applied to black areas of the mask) and maximum (applied to white areas of the mask) quality levels. The results of your settings can be seen in the Optimized Preview.

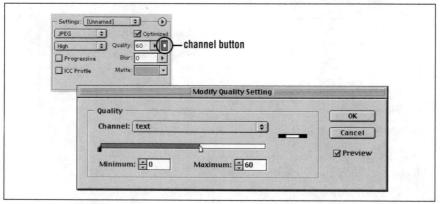

Figure 20-4: Weighted optimization for JPEGs using Photoshop 6

In ImageReady, you can create a new channel based on a selected image area on the fly when you click on the Channel button.

CHAPTER 21

PNG Format

The *Portable Network Graphic* format (PNG for short—pronounced "ping") is a versatile and full-featured graphics file format that has been lurking in the shadows for several years. Despite some attractive features and the fact that it was created with web use specifically in mind, the PNG has been largely avoided by the web design community. This is primarily due to abysmal browser support and a lack of tools that can compress PNGs well enough to make them compete with GIFs.

The good news is that both browser and tool support has been gradually improving over the last several years. It remains to be seen, however, whether PNG will ever be permitted to live up to its potential.

The PNG Story

PNG was developed in January and February 1995 as an effort to find a non-proprietary alternative to GIF when Unisys threatened to enforce its patent on LZW compression and collect licensing fees from developers of GIF-supporting programs. This caused a flurry of outrage and activity on the Internet.

Days after the announcement, Thomas Boutell posted the first draft of the PNG specification to the *comp.graphics* newsgroup. A community of programmers then quickly cooperated in specifying and implementing an impressive list of features:

- 8-bit palette support (like GIF), support of 16-bit grayscale, and up to 48-bit truecolor (RGB) support

- A lossless compression scheme and better compression than GIF for indexed color (palette) images

- Two-dimensional progressive display that is more sophisticated than GIF's one-dimensional interlacing

- An alpha channel that can contain 8-bit or 16-bit transparency information, which means pixels can have up to 65,000 shades of transparency (not just "on" or "off" like GIF); 8-bit (256 shades of transparency) is far more common

- Gamma correction information to make the PNG display with its intended brightness regardless of platform
- Several methods for checking file integrity and corruption
- Text storage capabilities for keyword information, such as copyright
- Nonpatented compression free from licensing restrictions

The PNG format became an official W3C Recommendation in October of 1996 (see *http://www.w3.org/Graphics/PNG/*). Since then, browser and software developers have given the format more attention, but there is still a long way to go.

MNG for Motion

Here's another acronym for your graphic format arsenal—the MNG (Multiple-image Network Graphic). As the name implies, MNG was designed based on the PNG format to handle animated (multi-image) graphics. It shares a number of PNG's best features. In addition, it offers a number of interesting animation features, including:

- Object- or sprite-based animation
- Nested loops for complex animations
- Much better compression than animated GIFs
- Support for frame differencing (for maximizing compression)

The MNG format is still in development, but it is already being supported by a number of programs, including Netscape 6. For complete information, see the official MNG home page at *http://www.libpng.org/pub/mng/*.

When to Use PNGs

Unfortunately, as of this writing, PNGs are still not universally supported, so you run the risk that some users will not be able to see inline PNGs. Even the browsers that do support it, don't fully support the more useful and interesting features.

But in a perfect world, where PNG is fully implemented on all browsers, PNG is capable of supporting both indexed and truecolor image types, so there's no bitmapped graphic it can't handle.

Not a JPEG Substitute

Although PNG does support 24-bit color and higher, its lossless compression scheme nearly always results in larger files than JPEG's lossy compression when applied to the same image. The high bit depth support was developed so PNGs could take the place of TIFF files for saving highly detailed images where loss of image information is unacceptable (such as medical images). For web purposes where every byte counts, photographic and continuous tone images are still best saved as JPEGs.

Potential GIF Substitute

PNGs are recommended for the type of image that would typically be saved as a GIF (graphics with areas of flat color or sharp edges). PNG's better compression engine can result in a file size that is smaller than a GIF compression of the same image. Bear in mind, however, that the efficiency of compression largely depends on how well the PNG format is implemented in the graphics program being used. PNG also has a more sophisticated interlacing technique than GIF and starts displaying the image in 1/8 the time.

Platform/Browser Support

PNG was designed to be network-friendly, so naturally it is recognized and supported on all platforms. While PNG graphics can be viewed on the majority of browsers in use today (Versions 4 and up of the "Big Two," except IE4 on the Mac), support for advanced features such as alpha-transparency and gamma correction remains inconsistent, buggy, and conspicuously broken.

Initially, in Navigator and Internet Explorer, PNGs could only be handled as embedded objects (placed with the `<embed>` tag) and viewed with plug-ins such as PNG Live. Eventually, PNGs became supported as inline images (placed with the `<img>` tag, like any other web graphic).

As of this writing, the leader in complete PNG implementation is Internet Explorer 5.0 for the Macintosh (unfortunately, the PC team has not followed suit, and PNG support on IE remains buggy for Windows). Netscape 6 also does a good job of supporting PNG's more interesting features.

Table 21-1 lists the more popular browsers capable of displaying PNGs and the features they support. Note that there are a myriad of lesser-known browsers out there that also support PNG in all its glory. For a complete list of PNG behavior on all browsers, see the browser support page on the official PNG web site at *http://www.libpng.org/pub/png/pngapbr.html.*

Table 21-1: Browser support for PNG

Browser	Progressive display	Binary transparency	Alpha-channel transparency	Gamma correction
Windows				
IE 6 (beta)	Yes	partial	—	Yes
IE 5.5	Yes	partial	—	Yes
IE 4.0	Yes	partial	—	—
NN 6	Yes	Yes	Yes	Yes
NN 4.x	Yes	—	—	—
Opera 5	Yes	broken	—	Yes
Macintosh				
IE 5	Yes	Yes	Yes	Yes
NN 6	Yes	Yes	Yes	Yes
NN 4.x	Yes	—	—	—
iCab	—	Yes	Yes	—

Table 21-1: Browser support for PNG (continued)

Browser	Progressive display	Binary transparency	Alpha-channel transparency	Gamma correction
Unix				
IE 6 beta	Yes	partial	—	Yes
IE 5.5	Yes	partial	—	Yes
IE 5.	Yes	partial	—	Yes
NN 6	Yes	Yes	Yes	Yes
WebTV	—	Yes	Yes	Yes

8-Bit Palette, Grayscale, and Truecolor

PNG was designed to replace GIF for online purposes and the inconsistently implemented TIFF format for image storage and printing. As a result, there are three types of PNG files: indexed color (palette images), grayscale, and truecolor.

8-Bit Palette Images

Like GIFs, PNGs can be saved as 8-bit indexed color. This means they can contain up to 256 colors, the maximum number that 8 bits of information can define. Indexed color means the set of colors in the image, its palette, are stored in a color table. Each pixel in the image contains a reference (or "index") to its corresponding color and position in the color table.

Although 8-bit is the maximum, PNGs may be saved at lower bit-depths (1-, 2-, and 4-bit, specifically) as well, thus reducing the maximum number of colors in the image (and the file size).

Indexed color PNGs are also capable of containing multiple transparency levels within the index color palette itself (performing a task usually assigned to an Alpha Channel).

Grayscale

PNGs can also support 16-bit grayscale images—that's as many as 65,536 shades of gray (2^{16}), enabling black and white photographs and illustrations to be stored with enormous subtlety of detail. This is useful for medical imaging and other types of imaging where detail must be maintained, but it is not much of an advantage for images intended for web delivery due to the inherent limitations of low-resolution images. Grayscale images are supported at 1-, 2-, 4-, and 8-bit depths as well.

Truecolor

PNG can support 24-bit and 48-bit truecolor images. "Truecolor" (or the "true color space" as it is referred to in this book) refers to the full color range (millions of colors) that can be defined by combinations of red, green, and blue (RGB) light on a computer monitor. Truecolor images do not use color tables and are limited only by the number of bits available to describe values for each color channel. In PNG format, each channel can be defined by 8-bit or 16-bit information. It should be noted that 48-bit images are useless for the Web. Even 24-bit should be used with care (other formats offer smaller file sizes with acceptable image quality).

PNG Compression

The most notable aspect of PNG compression is that it is "lossless," meaning no information is lost in the compression process. A decompressed PNG image is identical to the original.

PNGs use a "deflate" compression scheme (the same engine used to "zip" files with gzip, WinZip, etc.). Like GIFs, PNG's compression works on rows of pixels, taking advantage of repetition in bytes of information. By use of internal filters, it can take advantage of some vertical patterns as well. PNG's compression engine typically compresses images 5–25% better than GIF (and up to 39% better under optimal conditions). Unfortunately, with the currently available tools, it is difficult to achieve such file savings. See "Creating PNG Files" later in this chapter.

Filters

Before PNG compresses an image, it first runs the image data, row by row, through one of five filters (Sub, Up, Average, Paeth, Adaptive). The filters use different methods for finding patterns in the image information that can then be condensed more efficiently. The process is similar to how LZW compression takes advantage of horizontal repetition in GIFs, but PNG can look for vertical repetition as well.

In most applications, the filters are applied internally and are hidden from the end user (as they should be). If your tool provides filter options, there are only two you need to remember:

- Use "None" for all indexed color images (or grayscale images with fewer than 16 shades).

- Use "Adaptive" for all other image types.

Special Features

You may choose to use a PNG (in that perfect world) for some of its advanced features that no other graphic offers, such as variable transparency levels and full color management systems for automatic image correction, including gamma and color balance corrections.

Interlacing (Progressive Display)

Like GIFs, PNGs can be encoded for interlaced display. When this option is selected, the image displays in a series of passes, the first displaying after only a portion of the file has been downloaded, and each subsequent pass increasing in detail and clarity until the whole image is rendered.

Interlaced PNGs display over a series of seven passes (using a method known as "Adam7," named for its creator, Adam Costello). The first rendering of the image appears after only 1/64 of the file has downloaded (that's eight times faster than GIF). Unlike GIF, which fills in horizontal rows of information, PNGs fill in both horizontally and vertically (the effect looks more like the display of progressive JPEGs). Interlacing can add to the file size of PNGs, especially on small images (which don't really need to be interlaced anyway). To keep file sizes as small as possible, turn interlacing off.

Gamma Correction

Briefly stated, *gamma* refers to the brightness setting of a monitor (for more information on gamma, see Chapter 3). Because gamma settings vary by platform (and even by manufacturer), the graphics you create may not look the way you intend. In general, graphics created on Macs look dark on PCs and graphics created on PCs look washed out on Macs.

PNGs can be tagged with information regarding the gamma setting of the platform on which they were created. This information can then be interpreted by software on the user's end (the browser) to make appropriate gamma compensations. When this is implemented on both the creator and end-user's side, the PNG retains its intended brightness and color intensity.

Transparency

Both 24-bit and 8-bit indexed color PNGs can have variable levels of transparency. This sophisticated transparency function allows for smooth transitions between foreground and background elements. Grayscale images can also have variable transparency. PNGs can also use simple binary transparency (like transparent GIFs), in which a pixel is either totally transparent or totally opaque.

PNGs handle transparency in two ways: using an alpha channel (think of it as a separate layer that keeps track of the transparent areas of the image) or adding transparency information within the index color table for 8-bit palette images. The 8-bit palette transparency results in smaller file sizes for the same effect and is preferable for Web use. Both methods are discussed further below.

As of this writing, the only common tools that allow you to create transparency information in PNGs are Adobe Photoshop (4.0 and higher), Adobe ImageReady, Macromedia Fireworks, the GIMP (an image-editing tool for Unix, Linux, and OS/2), and PaintShop Pro (4.0 and higher). Photoshop currently supports only 24-bit transparency, which results in unacceptably large files. ImageReady and Fireworks both support the more complicated 8-bit, palette-based transparency.

Transparency techniques are discussed in the "Creating PNG Graphics" section of this chapter.

Bear in mind that even if you manage to make a PNG file with transparency, it may be a challenge finding a browser to display it correctly (particularly the preferable 8-bit indexed color transparency). Refer back to Table 21-1 for browser support information.

Alpha channel transparency

In addition to the standard channels for RGB color values for truecolor images, PNGs may contain an additional alpha channel used for transparency information. Each pixel is then defined by its RGBA values. For 24-bit images, the alpha channel can contain up to 8 bits of information for 256 levels of transparency for every pixel in the image. The alpha channel may also contain simple binary transparency information, like GIFs. Keep in mind, however, that an RGB PNG file with alpha channels will be about 20% larger than one without.

48-bit PNGs may contain an alpha channel with 16 bits of information—that's over 65,000 levels of transparency! 48-bit images, however, are inappropriate for the Web.

In practical terms, this means you can create glows and soft drop shadows that allow background patterns and underlying images to show through in a realistic manner. Figure 21-1 illustrates the effect of graphics showing through areas with variable levels of transparency.

Figure 21-1: Variable transparency allows PNGs to blend with background patterns

8-bit transparency

Indexed color PNGs can also contain variable levels of transparency (up to 256 levels); however, this information is not handled in a distinct alpha channel as for 24-bit images. Instead, transparency information for each color occupies positions in the color table. So, if you have a red area that fades out using eight levels of transparency, that red would be present in eight slots in the color table, each with its own transparency setting. In other words, each slot in the color table can store RGBA information. Other than adding to the number of pixel colors in the color table, adding transparency to an 8-bit PNG does not significantly increase its file size, making it the way to go for web graphics where file size is crucial.

Embedded Text

PNGs also have the ability to store strings of text. This is useful in permanently attaching text to an image, such as copyright information or a description of what is in the image. Unfortunately, the only browser that supports embedded text is

Internet Explorer 5 for the Mac, but someday it may be available via a right-button context menu or some other method on all browsers and platforms. The only tools that allow text annotations to PNG graphics are Paint Shop Pro and the GIMP (a free image editor for the X Windows system on Unix). Fireworks will preserve embedded text information in PNGs.

Creating PNG Files

The good news is that there are quite a few tools out there for both PCs and Macs that can save files in PNG format. The bad news is that not many support special features such as alpha channel transparency or gamma correction. Furthermore, some programs that create PNG files do not compress them as well as they could (including Adobe Photoshop 4.0 and PaintShop Pro).

Table 21-2 lists PNG feature support in a number of popular graphics tools. For a more comprehensive list of image editing tools and graphics file converters that support PNG compression (as well as their known bugs), see *http://www.libpng. org/pub/png/pngaped.html.*

Table 21-2: Graphics applications that support PNG format

Application	Alpha-channel Transparency	Binary 8-bit Transparency	Multilevel 8-bit Transparency	Gamma Correction
Adobe Photoshop 5.5/ ImageReady 2	Yes	Yes	—	—
Adobe Photoshop 4.0/5.0	Yes	—	—	—
JASC PaintShopPro 4 and higher[a]	partial	Yes	—	—
JASC PaintShopPro 3[a]	—	Yes	—	—
Macromedia Fireworks 4.0[b]	Yes	Yes	Yes	—
Macromedia Freehand 8 and higher	Yes	—	—	—
Macromedia Freehand 7	Yes[c]	—	—	—
Adobe Illustrator 7.0 and higher	—	—	—	—
CorelDRAW 7 and higher	read-only	—	—	—
The GIMP	Yes	Yes	Yes	Yes

[a] PaintShop Pro 3 reportedly creates unnecessarily large palette files. This is fixed in Versions 4.0 and later.
[b] PNG is the native file format for Macromedia Fireworks and is supported in all versions.
[c] Freehand 7 preserves alpha channel information when 32-bit depth and Save Alpha Channel options are selected during export. It does not provide a way to create an alpha channel.

Fireworks (2 and higher)

Macromedia Fireworks 4 is currently the best commercial software for creating PNG graphics. Not only does it have the most efficient PNG compression among its competitors, it also supports all varieties of PNG transparency, including the coveted multilevel 8-bit palette transparency. Fireworks also uses PNG as its native source file format because of its lossless compression.

When creating a PNG in Fireworks, it is important to use the Export function rather than just saving the file (resulting in a Fireworks native PNG file with loads of extra data). The Export Preview dialog box (shown in Figure 21-2) allows you to choose 8-bit, 24-bit, or 32-bit PNG format. The 8-bit PNG option gives you the same controls used for GIF compression: palette selection, color reduction, dither control, and transparency.

Figure 21-2: Fireworks' Export Preview dialog box showing PNG options

In "PNG 8" mode, the transparency pop-up menu allows you to select from alpha channel or index (palette) transparency. Index transparency generally results in smaller file sizes and therefore is more appropriate for the Web. Note that there must be transparent areas in the original layered image; Fireworks merely preserves the transparent areas on export (including soft fades and anti-aliased edges).

Fireworks keeps the file sizes small as well, delivering on the PNG promise to be smaller than their GIF counterparts. For the image in Figure 21-2, with exactly the same settings, the resulting GIF weighed in at 11,187 bytes, while the 8-bit PNG was 10,287 bytes (an 8% savings). Of course, file size savings varies depending on the image type.

Photoshop 5.5/ImageReady (and Higher)

Photoshop has offered read/write PNG capabilities since Version 4. For the best results, use the optimization features in the "Save for Web" option in Versions 5.5 and higher. The same export features are available in ImageReady (the web graphics tool that comes bundled with Photoshop 5.5 and higher).

From the Save For Web dialog box (Figure 21-3), PNG-8 format has the same settings as a GIF image. Only binary transparency is available for 8-bit PNGs (the same on/off style as transparent GIFs) with the Matte tool for blending into the page background. Multilevel transparency can be preserved for 24-bit PNGs.

Unfortunately, Photoshop does not squeeze PNGs down as small as it could. For the image in Figure 21-3, with exactly the same settings, the resulting PNG was 11,666 bytes, versus the GIF at 10,789 bytes. Photoshop's PNG was 8% *larger* than its GIF, and 4% larger than the Fireworks-generated PNG. A detailed list of other PNG bugs in Photoshop is available on the official PNG web site at *http://www. libpng.org/pub/png/pngaped.html.*

Figure 21-3: PNG-8 options in Photoshop 6's Save For Web dialog box

The GIMP

The GIMP (GNU Image Manipulation Program) is a free, Photoshop-like image-editing tool that runs on the X Window system under Unix. There is also a Microsoft Windows port available. The GIMP is virtually unknown by most professional graphic designers, but it bears mention here due to its superior implementation of the PNG format.

The GIMP offers excellent compression, full transparency support, gamma correction, and embedded text entry. You can apply compression incrementally using the deflate "compression level knob" (a sophisticated tool that no other image program offers). For more information about the GIMP, see *http://www.gimp.org*.

PNG Optimization Strategies

The following are a few strategies for keeping PNG file size small and for using PNGs wisely.

- **Use 8-bit (or smaller) PNGs.** Index color PNGs will always be smaller than their 24-bit RGB counterparts.

- **Use JPEGs instead of RGB (24-bit) PNGs.** Photographic images are best saved in JPEG format for use online. The resulting file sizes are smaller (with only minimal image quality loss) and more appropriate for web delivery.

- **Use GIF optimization techniques.** 8-bit PNGs benefit from all the same tactics used to minimize GIFs, including limiting dithering and reducing the number of colors and bit-depth. See Chapter 19 for more information on optimization methods.

- **Avoid interlacing.** Interlacing always adds to the size of a PNG. It is usually unnecessary anyway for small graphics or any graphic accessed via a high-bandwidth connection or locally (as from disk or CD-ROM).

- **Use maximum compression (if available) for final images.** If your image tool offers control over compression, use level 9 (or "max" or "slowest") for the final version of your image. Use lower compression (3 or 6) for intermediate saves. Many commercial programs (such as Fireworks) handle compression and filter application internally, so you may not have control over specific levels.)

- **Create PNGs from GIFs.** Depending on the tool you're using, you may be able to squeeze extra bytes out of a PNG by creating it from a GIF (which is already in indexed color format) instead of from an RGB source. If your tool offers only a "Save as" function, this ensures that you will end up with an 8-bit PNG. If you are starting with an RGB image, first save it as a GIF, then open it again and save it as a PNG. This method is unnecessary for more sophisticated web graphics tools such as Fireworks and Photoshop/ImageReady (but Fireworks did reduce the "sweetpea" sample image by 140 bytes when re-exported from a GIF).

- **Try the *pngcrush* utility.** If you are serious about optimizing PNGs, you should download Glenn Randers-Pehrson's *pngcrush* application (freeware, available at *http://pmt.sourceforge.net/pngcrush/*). It is a command-line DOS application, but it can run in batch mode. *pngcrush* takes existing PNGs and makes them smaller, losslessly.

- **Convert transparency with the *pngquant* utility.** The *pngquant* command-line utility (written by Greg Roelofs, one of the creators of the PNG format) converts RGB alpha-channel transparency (32-bit) into 8-bit palette transparency. The resulting PNG will be significantly smaller and more suitable for web use.

PNG

For Further Reading

If you are interested in learning more about the PNG format, definitely check out *PNG: The Definitive Guide* (O'Reilly, 1999) by Greg Roelofs. Many thanks to go Greg for his generous contributions to this chapter.

There are also a few good resources available online:

PNG Home Page
> *http://www.libpng.org/pub/png/*
>
> This site is written and maintained by Greg Roelofs. It contains a complete history of PNG's birth, descriptions of its features, and up-to-date lists of applications that support the new format. It also includes a copy of the PNG Specification and the official PNG extensions documents (as well as the draft MNG Spec). All of it is written with so much enthusiasm that you can't help but become a PNG fan! It is the source of much of the information in this chapter.

PNG Specification
> *http://www.w3.org/TR/png.html*
>
> This is the complete PNG specification (Version 1.0) as published by the W3C. For a technical document, it is very user-friendly to nonprogrammers and offers detailed information on how PNGs work, as well as some useful background information and tutorials. The updated Version 1.2 of the specification is available at the PNG web site at *http://www.libpng.org/pub/png/spec/*.

CHAPTER 22

Designing Graphics with the Web Palette

The web palette is a set of 216 colors that will not dither on Macs or PCs and is built into all the major browsers (it is discussed in more detail in Chapter 3). When a browser is running on a computer with an 8-bit monitor (capable of displaying only 256 colors at a time), the browser refers to its internal web palette to make up the colors on the page.

If the browser is running on a 24-bit display, the web palette does not come into effect and all colors are displayed accurately. See the sidebar "When Not to Worry about the Web Palette" for other instances when the web palette does not apply.

Most often, remapping images to the web palette in the browser results in undesirable dithering. Not only that, sometimes flat colors shift to the nearest web-safe colors without dithering. The algorithm for deciding which colors to shift and which to dither (as well as choosing *where* to shift) differs depending on the browser brand and version.

All of this shifting and dithering means unpredictable image quality on 8-bit monitors. But there is one thing that is predictable—the web palette. If you use colors from the web palette in the image in the first place, you have the advantage of controlling how the image appears on 8-bit monitors. It requires a little extra effort and an adjustment to a limited color choice, but the payoff is that you, not the browser, control whether and how the image dithers.

There are two opportunities to apply the web palette in the image creation process. The first is to choose web-safe colors when you design the image (particularly for areas of flat color). The web palette can also be applied to the image when reducing it to Indexed Color.

This chapter looks at both approaches to using the web palette in graphics. The techniques apply to graphics that use 8-bit palettes such as GIF or PNG. Because PNG is not widely supported at this time, GIF is featured in the following examples.

Designing with Web-Safe Colors

If you are creating graphics from scratch, especially graphics such as logos or simple illustrations that contain areas of flat color, you can use web palette colors right from the start. In this way, you can be certain that your graphics will look the same for all users. Figure 22-1 shows how dithering could have been avoided if the image had used colors from the web-safe palette. Remember, it's the flat color areas where using web-safe colors makes the most difference.

The major drawback is that with only 216 colors to choose from (a good 30 of which you'd never be caught dead using for anything), the selection is extremely limited. (See the "Color Blenders" section of this chapter for one approach to overcoming the limited choice of colors.)

The trick is to have the web palette colors available in a Swatches palette or in whatever device your graphics program uses for making colors handy. You should be aware, however, that even if you select web colors for fills, any shades of colors created by soft drop shadows or anti-aliased edges between areas of color will probably not be web-safe.

This GIF is designed with non-web-safe colors, resulting in dithering on 8-bit monitors.

On a 24-bit monitor, the solid colors are smooth and accurate.

On an 8-bit monitor, the colors are approximated by dithering colors from the web palette.

If the flat areas are filled with web-safe colors, the photograph still dithers, but the flat colors stay flat.

Figure 22-1: Designing with web-safe colors prevents dithering

Tools with Built-in Web Palettes

Not surprisingly, with the explosion of the Web's popularity, the web palette is finding its way into many commercial graphics tools. The web palette is known by many names, including Netscape Palette, Web 216, Browser-safe Palette, Non-Dithering Palette, the 6×6×6 Cube, and so on—but you should recognize it when you see it.

Adobe Photoshop 5+
Version 5 and up ships with the Web Safe Colors CLUT file (see the following section) in its Color Palettes directory. These can be easily loaded into the Swatches palette by selecting Replace Swatches or Load Swatches from the Swatches pop-up menu.

Adobe ImageReady (bundled with Photoshop 5.5 and higher)
ImageReady was created specifically for the optimization of web graphics, so the web palette comes preloaded in the Swatches palette.

Macromedia Fireworks
Fireworks also has the web palette available in its Swatches palette by default. In fact, it is difficult to use non-web-safe colors in Fireworks.

Adobe Illustrator 7.0 and higher
Version 7.0 of Adobe Illustrator introduced the ability to work within the RGB color space (instead of being limited to CMYK as in previous versions), so you can color your graphics and even export them directly to GIF format. To select colors from the 216 web-safe colors, select Windows → Swatch Libraries → Web.

Web Palette on 16-Bit Displays

Because 16-bit (also called "high color") displays must mathematically approximate colors from the true color space, slight color shifting and dithering occurs even if you choose colors from the "safe" web palette. Unfortunately, over half of web users today use 16-bit monitors, which means that your colors aren't looking the way you think over half the time.

This is most noticeable for pages with graphics that are intended to blend seamlessly with a tiled background graphic or specified background color. Although the foreground and background elements may have identical web-safe RGB values, on 16-bit displays, colors shift and dither in a way that causes the "seams" to be slightly visible.

Which elements shift and which get dithered seems to depend on the browser and operating system combination, so it's difficult to anticipate. If the mismatched colors concern you, making the edges of your graphics transparent instead of a matching color may help eliminate the dithered rectangles on 16-bit displays.

Webmonkey (an online developers' magazine) has an article called "Death of the Websafe Color Palette?" by David Lehn and Hadley Stern that does a great job of explaining how web-safe colors fail in the 16-bit environment. It includes a thorough technical explanation of how 16-bit color works as well as results of their web palette testing. It is available at *http://hotwired.lycos.com/webmonkey/00/37/index2a.html.*

Macromedia Freehand 7.0 and higher

You can select colors from the Websafe Color Library, under Options on the Color Palette. Colors appear with their decimal and hexadecimal RGB values.

Macromedia Director 5.0 and higher

You can find the web palette under the Xtras pull-down menu. Look for the palette called "Netscape."

Macintosh System OS8

MacOS8 comes with an HTML Color Picker in addition to the standard Color Picker. This tool makes selecting web-safe colors extremely easy via slider bars that snap into place at the safe color values. It also translates the colors into the hexadecimal values that HTML and browsers understand. (See Chapter 16 for more information on hexadecimal numbering.)

Pantone ColorWeb Pro

ColorWeb Pro is a Mac-only product that enables designers to select web-safe colors via an addition to the Macintosh Color Picker. It also has printed swatch books that provide Pantone color equivalents for the web palette when you need to coordinate your web page with a printed piece. Another swatch book lists traditional Pantone ink colors, but lists their digital equivalents in decimal and hexadecimal RGB values.

Color Look-Up Tables (CLUT Files)

Photoshop and some other graphics tools save palettes in files called CLUTs (Color Look-Up Table). To make the web palette available in the Swatches palette, you need to load the appropriate web CLUT file using Load Swatches, Replace Swatches, or some equivalent command.

Creating a CLUT file in Photoshop 4.0

Photoshop 5.0 ships with the Web Safe Colors CLUT file in its Color Palettes folder, but Photoshop 4.0 does not. If you are using Version 4.0, it's easy enough to create one as follows:

1. Convert any RGB image to Indexed Color.
2. In the Indexed Color dialog, select Web from the Palette pop-up menu. Click OK.
3. Select Image → Mode → Color Table. Although the Table pop-up lists Custom as the current option, the table itself contains the 216 browser-safe RGB values.
4. Click the Save button, and save the color palette. Name it descriptively and save it into Photoshop's Color Palettes folder.
5. Load these colors into the Swatches Palette by choosing Replace Swatches from the Swatches Palette submenu.

Now you can select from swatches of web-safe colors to fill areas of your graphic. If you don't want to create the CLUT file yourself, you can download it from Lynda Weinman's FTP site, as explained in the following section.

CLUT files for other graphics programs

Many commercial tools that don't ship the web palette in their color selector tools (including Photoshop) allow you to load in palette files. Lynda Weinman, author of a well-known series of books on web design, has created a collection of browser-safe palette files that can be loaded into the following software packages:

Software Package	CLUT filename
Adobe Photoshop	bclut2.aco
Paint Shop Pro	netscape.pal
Photo-Paint	216clut.cpl
MetaCreations Painter	clut (in Painter folder)
Macromedia Freehand	clut.BCF

All of these files can be downloaded from Lynda's site: *http://www.lynda.com/downloads/CLUTS/*.

Converting to the Web Palette

Designing with web colors is one method to prevent dithering. The other opportunity is to add (or preserve) web-safe colors in the conversion process from RGB to

Indexed Color. As part of this process, you will be asked to select a palette for the image. The colors from the palette will be used to approximate the full color range from the original RGB graphic. See the sidebar "Common Palettes" for descriptions of palette options in popular graphics programs.

Applying the Strict Web Palette

In current graphics tools, one of the palette options is likely to be "Web" or "Web216," which means that the resulting 8-bit image will be made up exclusively of colors from the 216 color web-safe palette. Many beginners make the mistake of applying the web palette to every graphic that is going on a web page. While "Web" may seem like the logical palette choice, it isn't appropriate for most images and can reduce potential quality.

The problem with applying the strict web palette is that it doesn't take into account the colors or content of your original image—everything will be forced into web colors. Extra dithering may be introduced in the conversion which may increase file size. The web palette is also made up of some fairly strange and extreme colors that won't do your image any favors.

"Snapping" to Web Colors

The newer graphics tools (Fireworks and Photoshop 5.5+/ImageReady) offer more sophisticated methods for applying and preserving web-safe colors in the conversion process. Instead of changing all the pixel colors in the image, these tools find the colors that are close in value to web-safe, and then shift (or "snap") them to their nearest web-safe neighbor. The snap feature is especially effective for images that contain a combination of full-color photographic images and flat, web-safe colors.

Macromedia Fireworks

Fireworks gives the option of saving with the "Web Adaptive" palette. It is an adaptive palette, so the set of colors will be customized for the image, but any colors that are near in value to web palette colors will shift to the closest web safe equivalent. A color shifts if it is within 7 bits of a web safe value (e.g., 57-57-57 shifts to 51-51-51, but 60-57-57 does not). There is no way to adjust this tolerance. Palettes are chosen from the Optimize palette (Figure 22-2) or the Export Preview dialog box.

Adobe ImageReady (Photoshop 5.5 and higher)

In ImageReady (and within Photoshop 5.5+ using the "Save For Web" feature), you can control how many colors shift to their nearest web-safe neighbor using the "Web Snap" slider tool (Figure 22-3, left). The higher you set the slider, the more colors shift. This allows the tool to construct a custom color table for the image while keeping areas web-safe. (You may need to select "Show Options" using the small arrow button in the top-right corner to expose the Web Snap slider in the Optimize palette.)

Common Palettes

All 8-bit Indexed Color images (such as GIF or PNG-8) use a palette of colors to define the colors in the image. The web palette is just one of infinite palette possibilities. There are several standard palettes you can choose from within popular graphics programs.

Exact

> If the image contains fewer than 256 colors, choosing the Exact palette option makes a palette out of the actual colors that are found in the image.

Adaptive

> This is a custom palette generated with the most commonly used pixel colors in the image. It allows for color-depth reduction while preserving the original character of the image. Because the number of colors is being reduced, some dithering and color-shifting will occur.

Perceptual (Adobe Photoshop/ImageReady only)

> This creates a custom palette by giving priority to colors for which the human eye has greater sensitivity. Unlike Adaptive, it is based on algorithms, not just a pixel count. It generally results in images with better color integrity than adaptive palette images.

Selective (Adobe Photoshop/ImageReady only)

> This is similar to Perceptual, but it gives preference to areas of broad color and the preservation of web-safe colors. It is the preferred palette for web graphics created with Photoshop/ImageReady.

WebSnap Adaptive (Macromedia Fireworks only)

> An adaptive palette in which colors that are near in value to web palette colors are converted to the closest web palette color.

System (Mac/Windows)

> Choosing either system palette converts the image to the palette of 256 colors as defined by each operating system.

Uniform

> This palette contains an evenly stepped sampling of colors from the RGB spectrum.

Custom

> This allows you to load a palette that was previously saved and apply it to the current image.

Optimized Median Cut (Paint Shop Pro only)

> This reduces the image to a few colors using something similar to an adaptive palette.

Optimized Octree (Paint Shop Pro only)

> Use this palette if the original image has just a few colors and you want to keep those exact colors.

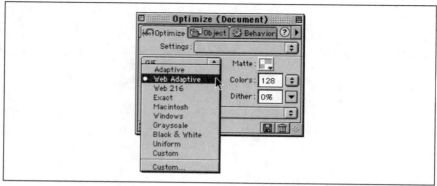

Figure 22-2: Palette options in Fireworks' Optimize palette

The slider works in coordination with one of the adaptive palette choices ("Adaptive," "Perceptual," or "Selective"). If your image contains broad areas of flat color, particularly web-safe color, "Selective" is the best choice. If the image is mostly photographic, use "Perceptual."

ImageReady also allows you to shift colors to their nearest web equivalents manually using the Color Table palette (Figure 22-3, right). Clicking on a color in the table and then the cube icon below shifts it to web-safe (indicated by a diamond in the center of the swatch). This shifts all the corresponding pixels within the image. The color can then be locked down with the lock icon.

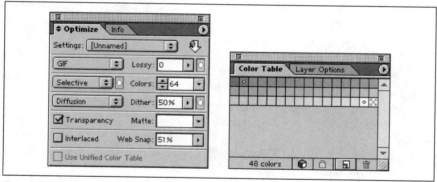

Figure 22-3: ImageReady's Optimize options (left) and Color Table palette (right)

Web Scrubber plug-in filter (Furbo Filters)

If you work on a Mac and haven't yet invested in a web graphics tool such as ImageReady or Fireworks, you can lay out a smaller chunk of change for special web utilities that work as plug-ins for PaintShop Pro, Photoshop 3+, or any program that accepts Photoshop-compatible plug-ins.

Web Scrubber from Furbo Filters provides "web-snap" abilities similar to Image-Ready and allows you to reduce the number of colors in a paletted image. It is particularly good at optimizing images that contain a combination of photographic imagery and areas of flat, web-safe color.

As of this writing, Web Scrubber is available only for the Mac as part of Furbo Filters' Webmaster series of plug-ins. These plug-ins are available at *http://www. furbo-filters.com.*

Web Palette Strategies

There are no hard and fast rules, since every image has its own requirements. The following are some basic guidelines for using—and resisting—the web palette.

Flat Graphical Images

Goal: Keep flat color areas from dithering while maintaining smoothness in the anti-aliased edges.

Strategy: Use colors from the web palette to fill flat color areas when you are designing the image. Do not apply the strict web palette option when saving or exporting because you'll lose the gradations of color in the anti-aliasing. It is better to choose an adaptive palette with a "web snap" option, if it is available. In Photoshop, set the amount of web snap with the slider scale. In Fireworks, apply the Web Adaptive palette. This will maintain the web colors in your flat areas but allow some non-web-safe colors in the anti-aliasing and other blends to remain.

Photographic Images

Goal: To maintain clarity and color fidelity for the maximum number of users.

Strategy: First, if it is an entirely photographic image, consider saving it in JPEG format. Otherwise, choose an Adaptive palette (or Perceptual in Photoshop 5.5 and up) to preserve the original color range in the image. That way, the image will look the best it possibly can for users with 16- and 24-bit monitors (the vast majority). For users with 8-bit monitors, the image will map again to the web palette, but dithering is usually not detrimental in photographic images. The only advantage to applying the web palette to a continuous-tone image in the saving process is that you know it will look equally bad to everyone.

Combination Images (Flat and Photographic Areas)

Goal: To keep the flat areas from dithering while allowing the continuous tone areas to dither with an adaptive palette.

Strategy: Use web-safe colors in the flat areas when you are designing the image. When it's time to save or export to GIF format, choose an adaptive palette with a "web snap" option if it is available. The adaptive palette preserves the color fidelity in the photographic areas while the web snap option preserves the web-safe colors in the flat areas.

Color Blenders

The problem with the web palette is that it has only 216 colors to choose from (and they probably wouldn't be your first choices). If you are bored with your color options, you may want to try a *color blender.* Color blenders approximate any RGB color by mixing two colors from the web palette in a tiny checkerboard pattern. You can use these "hybrid colors" to fill areas of graphics or to create a background tile.

Color blenders all work about the same way. Simply select an RGB color (such as from an image using an eyedropper tool) and the blender converts it to a 2×2-pixel tile made up of two web-safe colors. The hybrid color is then available as a fill color to be applied to a selected object or marquee selection.

The Pros and Cons of Color Blenders

No technology is either all good or all bad, so let's look at the ups and downs of color blenders:

Advantages

- Color blenders allow you to choose colors off the beaten path of the 216-color web-safe palette, yet still be certain they will look the same on 24- and 8-bit monitors.

Disadvantages

- The controlled dither adds to the file size if used as a fill for large areas of the graphic, because it interferes with the GIF's LZW compression.
- It is more difficult to get inline images to blend seamlessly over a background tiled with a hybrid color. For instance, an image with a hybrid blue background may not line up correctly with the same hybrid blue in the browser background. For best results, create the original image with a background that is similar to the hybrid blue, and use transparency.

Creating Hybrid Colors

Color blenders are built into Fireworks, Photoshop 5.5+, and ImageReady. If you don't have these tools yet, try the less expensive ColorSafe from BoxTop Software (*http://www.boxtopsoft.com*), which has nearly identical features to DitherBox in ImageReady (shown later).

Photoshop/ImageReady

Photoshop and ImageReady use the DitherBox plug-in filter for creating "custom dither patterns" from web-safe colors (Figure 22-4). To use it, select an RGB color that you want to simulate. Then select the part of your image that you want to fill and choose Filter → Other → DitherBox. The DitherBox window shows you a close-up the tile used to make up your target color as well as a preview at actual size. When you are ready, click "Fill" to fill your selection with the dither pattern.

Fireworks

In Fireworks, the color blender (called Web Dither) is located on the Fill palette (Figure 22-5). Select an object containing a non-web-safe color. When you select

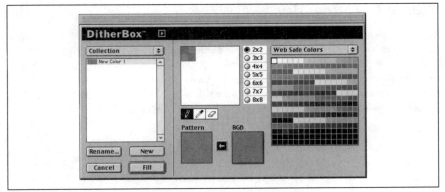

Figure 22-4: DitherBox filter in Photoshop and ImageReady

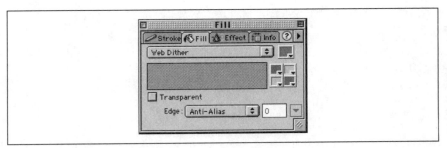

Figure 22-5: Web Dither tool in Fireworks

Web Dither, the tiled pattern is applied to the selected object and becomes the active fill color. Be sure also to select the Hard Edge option to maintain web-safe colors. You can also use the Web Dither tool to simulate a transparent effect when you click the Transparency box.

Creating Hybrid Background Tiles in Photoshop

When creating a background tile filled with hybrid colors, the key is to set the width and height to an even number of pixels so the pattern repeats correctly. You can make the tile quite small (10 or 12 pixels square) to limit file size.

1. Create a new graphic and fill the whole area with the color you'd like your background to be.

2. Select the DitherBox filter from the Filters menu. You can adjust the color using the RGB controls.

3. Fill your image with the new hybrid color.

4. Convert the image to Indexed Color using the Exact Palette and either Save as or Export to GIF format.

5. Insert your graphic into the HTML document by adding the `background` attribute identifying your tile to the `<body>` tag as follows:

```
<BODY BACKGROUND="tilegraphic.gif">
```

Where to Learn More

The champion of the web palette is undeniably Lynda Weinman, author of many fine books on web design. Her book *Designing Web Graphics, Third Edition,* (New Riders Publishing) includes samples and instructions for working with the browser-safe palette. For a more in-depth look at the palette as well as suggestions on hundreds of pleasing combinations that can be created with it, check out Lynda's book *Coloring Web Graphics* (New Riders Publishing).

CHAPTER 23

Animated GIFs

These days, it's just about impossible to browse the Web without seeing the flashing, bouncing, and wiggling of GIF animation. The animated GIF is ubiquitous, and there are many good reasons for its popularity.

- **Users need no special software or plug-in.** All they need is a browser that supports animation—which is fortunately the overwhelming majority of browsers in use as of this writing.

- **GIF is the standard file format for the Web.** Animated GIFs are not a unique file format in themselves, but merely take advantage of the full capabilities of the original GIF89a specification. Even if a browser cannot display all of its frames, the GIF will still be visible as a static image.

- **They're easy to create.** There are scores of GIF animation tools available (some are built into larger web graphics applications), and they're simple to learn and use.

- **They require no server configuration.** Because they are standard GIF files, you do not need to define a new file type on the server.

- **They use streaming technology.** Users don't need to wait for the entire file to download to see something. Each frame displays as soon as it downloads.

The only drawbacks to animated GIFs are that they can contain no sound or interactivity (you can't make different parts respond to mouse actions), and they may cause some extra work for the user's hard disk to keep refreshing the images.

How They Work

Animated GIFs work a lot like traditional cell animation. The file contains a number of frames layered on top of each other. In simple animations, each frame is a complete scene. In more sophisticated animations, the first frame provides the background and subsequent frames just provide the changing portion of the image.

The GIF animation consists of a number of images and a set of instructions that specify the length of delay between frames, as well as other attributes like transparency and palettes.

Using Animated GIFs

Nowhere has GIF animation made a larger impact than in banner advertising. Ad agencies aren't stupid; they know that adding motion and flashing lights to a web page is a sure-fire way to attract attention. And it's true—adding animation is a powerful way to catch a reader's eye.

But beware that this can also work against you. Many users complain that animation is *too* distracting, making it difficult to concentrate on the content of the page. Although it adds a little "pizzazz" to the page, overall, too much animation can quickly spoil the user's enjoyment of your page.

Use animated GIFs wisely. A few recommendations:

*   Avoid more than one animation on a page.
*   Use the animation to communicate something in a clever way (not just as gratuitous flashing lights).
*   Avoid animation on text-heavy pages that might require concentration to read.
*   Consider whether the extra bandwidth to make a graphic "spin" is actually adding value to your page.
*   Decide whether your animation needs to loop continuously.
*   Experiment with timing. Sometimes a long pause between loops can make an animation less distracting.

Browser Support

Versions 2.0 and higher of both Netscape Navigator and Microsoft Internet Explorer have some degree of support for GIF animation, with the implementation improving with each subsequent release. Still, there are a few specific aspects of animation that prove to be particularly problematic for some early-version and lesser-known browsers.

If your animation uses one of the following, you may want to do some cross-browser, cross-platform testing:

Looping
>   Very early browsers do not support looping at all. More commonly, looping is supported, but settings for a specific number of loops may be ignored. If you specify the number of repetitions, be aware that some users will experience nonstop looping instead. Internet Explorer Versions 2 and 3 support only one-loop animation.

Revert to previous
>   This disposal method does not work on Navigator 2.0, 3.0, and the Mac version of 4.0 (it treats it as "do not dispose.") (See the "Disposal Methods" section later in this chapter.) Revert to Previous is supported only by Internet

Explorer Versions 3.0 and higher. Although it can result in slightly smaller file sizes, it is recommended to avoid this setting. This and other disposal methods are more thoroughly discussed later in this chapter.

Browsers that do not support GIF animation display a static image. The problem is that some browsers display the first frame and others display the last frame. If possible, it is advisable to make both your first and last frames meaningful (particularly if it contains important information, like the name of your company).

Tools

You don't need to search very far to find a GIF animation tool—there seem to be scores of them available. Regardless of the tool you choose, the interface is basically the same. Tools tend to differ somewhat in the degree to which they are able to optimize (shrink the file size of) of the resulting graphic. The following sections provide an overview of the most popular and/or recommended tools.

Applications That Include GIF Animation Tools

GIF animation tools are built in or bundled with many popular graphics applications, eliminating the need to jump between different software packages.

Macromedia Fireworks (Mac and Windows)
Macromedia Fireworks was designed specifically for the creation of web graphics. It supports multiple layers that can be converted to multiple animation frames. Among other features are automatic super-palette optimization and the ability to perform LZW optimization. For more information, see Macromedia's site at *http://www.macromedia.com/software/fireworks/*.

Adobe ImageReady (Mac and Windows)
Adobe ImageReady is a tool (bundled with Photoshop 5.5 and higher) especially for preparing and optimizing web graphics. It includes a GIF animation tool that converts layers into frames and allows easy layer editing. Image-Ready 3 offers advanced optimization methods for making the smallest possible animations. For more information, see Adobe's site at *http://www.adobe.com*.

Animation Shop & Paint Shop Pro (Windows only)
Animation Shop is a tool that comes bundled with the latest version of Paint Shop Pro, an inexpensive and powerful graphics creation application from JASC Software, Inc. For more information, see JASC's web site at *http://www.jasc.com*.

GIF Animation Utilities

The following are just a few dedicated tools for creating animated GIF files. For an extended list and a description of their features, see the article on GIF animation in WebReference.com (*http://www.webreference.com/dev/gifanim/*).

GIFmation 2.3 (Mac and Windows)
This is commercial software from BoxTop Software that comes highly recommended by web developers. It features sophisticated palette-handling options

and a bandwidth simulator. It also uses the efficient "frame differencing" method (discussed later in this chapter) for optimizing animations significantly better than its competition. GIFmation costs $49.95 and is available at *http://www.boxtopsoft.com.*

GifBuilder 0.5 (Mac only)

GifBuilder, developed by Yves Piguet, is the old standby for creating animated GIFs on the Macintosh. It's freeware that's easy and intuitive to use. Its method of optimization, although adequate, is not as efficient as some other programs. It is available for download at *http://www.mac.org/graphics/gifbuilder/.*

Ulead GIF Animator 5.0 (Windows only)

Ulead's GIF Animator features wizards for quickly and easily constructing animations, 200 levels of undo, pixel-level optimization, built-in transition and animation effects, a plug-in architecture for adding new animation modules, and support for AVI and QuickTime videos and layered Photoshop files. Download a preview copy from *http://www.ulead.com.* Registration is $44.95.

Creating Animated GIFs

Regardless of the tool you choose, the process of creating an animated GIF is about the same and involves making decisions about a standard set of features and options. Some of the following descriptions use GIFBuilder's terminology, but the concepts and settings are consistent across tools.

Frame Delay

Also called "interframe delay," this setting specifies the amount of time between frames. Frame delays are measured in 1/100ths of a second. You can apply a different delay time to each frame in the animation to create pauses and other timing effects. This differs from digital video formats, in which the delay between all frames is consistent.

Transparency

You can set transparency for each frame within an animation. Previous frames will show through the transparent area of a later frame if disposal methods are set correctly.

If the background frame is made transparent, the browser background color or pattern will show through.

 There is a bug in early versions of Navigator in which transparency works only with background patterns, not colors specified in HTML.

Don't be surprised if the transparent areas you specified in your original graphics are ignored when you import them into a GIF animation utility. You may need to set transparency in the animation package. Some standard transparency options include:

None
> No transparency.

White
> All the white pixels in the image will become transparent.

Based on first pixel
> The color of the "first pixel"—that is, the top left pixel, the one at coordinates 0,0—is transparent. This is a handy option since you'll often have an image in the center, and the four corners will be transparent.

Other
> This option lets you select one of the palette colors as transparent.

Disposal Methods

Disposal method gives instructions on what to do with the previous frame once a new frame is displayed.

Most GIF animation utilities offer "optimization," a file-size reducing process that takes advantage of the fact that previous frames will "show through" transparent areas of a later frame. In order for this process to work, the disposal method must be set to Do Not Dispose (or Leave Alone, Leave As Is, etc.). With this method, areas of previous frames continue to display unless covered up by an area in a succeeding frame. The four choices are:

Unspecified (Nothing)
> Use this option to replace one full-size, nontransparent frame with another.

Do Not Dispose (Leave As Is)
> In this option, any pixels not covered by the next frame continue to display. Use this when you want a frame to continue to show throughout the animation.

Restore to Background
> The background color or background tile shows through the transparent pixels of the new frame (replacing the image areas of the previous frame).

Restore to Previous
> This option restores to the state of the previous, undisposed frame. For example, if you have a static background that is set to Do Not Dispose, that image will reappear in the areas left by a replaced frame.
>
> This disposal method is not correctly supported in Netscape Navigator (it is treated like Do Not Dispose), leading to all the frames being visible and stacking up. Although it can produce better optimized animation files, it is safest not to use it.

The effects of each of these disposal methods are compared in Figure 23-1.

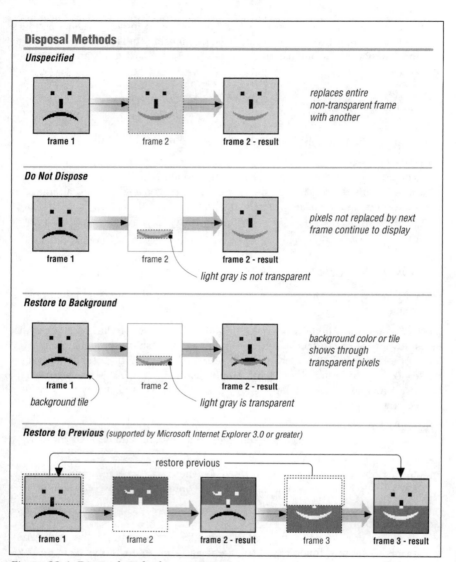

Disposal Methods

Unspecified

frame 1 → frame 2 → frame 2 - result

replaces entire non-transparent frame with another

Do Not Dispose

frame 1 → frame 2 → frame 2 - result

pixels not replaced by next frame continue to display

light gray is not transparent

Restore to Background

frame 1 → frame 2 → frame 2 - result

background color or tile shows through transparent pixels

background tile *light gray is transparent*

Restore to Previous (supported by Microsoft Internet Explorer 3.0 or greater)

restore previous

frame 1 → frame 2 → frame 2 - result → frame 3 → frame 3 - result

Figure 23-1: Disposal method comparison

Color Palette

Animated GIFs, like static GIF files, use a list of up to 256 colors that can be used in the image. They can have multiple palettes (one for each frame) or one global palette. The palette choice affects how well the images appear on the inevitable variety of systems and monitor setups.

One problem with using multiple, frame-specific palettes is that they can cause a flashing effect on some early versions of Navigator (it cannot load the frames and their respective palettes in sync). In any case, multiple palettes dramatically increase file size. It is recommended you use one global palette for the whole animation. GifMation and Ulead GIF Animator allow you to create a customized global palette. In fact, any image editor can be used to create a global palette. Just place all images to be used in one document, then index the document. The resulting palette will be a global palette for the entire animation.

Other palette options include:

System palette
> You can apply the Mac or Windows system palettes to your animation if you know it will be viewed exclusively on one platform.

Grayscale
> This converts your image to 256 shades of gray. Keep in mind, however, that browsers running on 8-bit monitors will try to convert the various shades of gray to the web palette. Since there are only a few true grays in the web palette, a grayscale image may not look very good on those monitors.

Adaptive palette
> Either ask your utility to create a global palette from the colors in the animation, or import one you created in another program. For most animations, this is your best bet.

Web palette (6× 6× 6 palette)
> Use the web palette if your animation is composed largely of flat colors and you want to be sure they don't dither on 8-bit displays. The web palette is explained in Chapters 3 and 22.

Other Options

The following are descriptions of other aspects of animated GIF files that can be set within most animation programs.

Loop
> You can specify the number of times an animation repeats—none, forever, or a specific number. As noted earlier, not all browsers support a specific number of loops (the animation either loops or does not). One workaround to this problem is to build looping right into a file by repeating the frame sequence a number of times; of course, this increases the file size and download time.

Interlaced
> Like ordinary GIF89a graphics, animated GIFs can be set to be interlaced, which causes them to display in a series of passes (starting blocky, finishing clear). It is recommended that you leave the interlacing option set to "no" or "off" because each frame is on the screen for only a short amount of time.

Depth
> This option allows you to limit the bit depth of the image to some number less than 8 (the default for GIF). Bit depth and its effect on file size is discussed in detail in Chapter 19. Note that if you select the web (6×6×6) palette, you will need to keep the bit depth set to 8.

Dithering

Dithering is a way to simulate intermediate color shades. It should be used with continuous-tone images.

Background Color

Regardless of what color you select in the background color option, Navigator and Internet Explorer display the background color or image you specify in your HTML page. So, this option doesn't affect the display of the GIF in a browser, only within the tool itself.

Starting Points

These settings are a good starting point for creating full-frame animations:

Color Palette: Global, adaptive palette
Interlacing: Off
Dithering: On for photographic images; Off for drawings with few colors
Image Size: Minimum Size
Background Color: Black
Looping: None or Forever
Transparency: Off
Disposal Method: Do Not Dispose

Optimizing Animated GIFs

As with any file served over the Web, it is important to keep animated GIFs as small as possible. I highly recommend reading "Optimizing Animated GIFs," an article and tutorial by Andrew King in WebReference.com, from which many of the following tips were summarized (with permission). You can find it at *http://www.webreference.com/dev/gifanim/index.html.*

Image Compression

Start by applying the same file-size reduction tactics used on regular, static GIF files to the images in your animation frames. For more information, see "Minimizing GIF File Sizes" in Chapter 19. These measures include:

• Reducing the number of colors.

• Reducing the bit depth.

• Eliminating unnecessary dithering.

• Applying the "loss" feature available in Adobe ImageReady and Macromedia Fireworks. ImageReady 3 allows you to do weighted optimization where loss can be applied more agressively to selected areas of the image. If your tool does not include a loss function, you can manually remove stray pixels from otherwise solid areas.

Optimizing Methods

In addition to the standard image-compressing methods, GIF animation tools optimize animations by eliminating the repetition of pixels in unchanging image areas.

Only the pixels that change are recorded for each frame. Different tools use different optimizing methods, which are not equally efficient. These methods, in order from least to most compression, include:

Minimum bounding rectangle
In this method, the changed portion of the image is saved, but it is always saved in the smallest rectangular area necessary to contain the changed pixels.

Frame differencing
In frame differencing, *only* the individual pixels that change are stored for each frame. This is a more efficient method than Minimum Bounding Rectangle, which includes a lot of unnecessary pixel information to make up the rectangle. Of the tools listed above, only GIFmation and ImageReady 3 use the frame differencing method for optimization. In ImageReady, be sure to select the "Transparency" option in the optimization dialog box to turn on frame differencing.

LZW interframe optimization
This optimization method uses the LZW compression scheme to minimize the frequency of changes in pixel patterns between frames. This compression method, when used in conjunction with frame difference, is capable of producing the smallest possible file sizes. Macromedia Fireworks 3, SuperGIF 1.0, and WebPainter 3 all take advantage of LZW compression for animations.

PART IV

Multimedia and Interactivity

CHAPTER 24

Audio on the Web

Simple audio files found their way onto the Web in its earliest days when they could be linked to and downloaded like any other file. The drawback to this technique is that traditional audio files are generally quite large and may take a prohibitively long time to download. As the Web evolved, we've seen some major breakthroughs in web audio. First, streaming audio (files that play as they download) made long-playing audio and even live broadcasts possible. Then the MP3 format exploded into popularity around 1999. MP3's ability to crunch audio files to one-tenth their original size while maintaining very good quality made it a perfect solution for sharing music over the Internet.

Obviously, audio, even specialized for the Web, is a rich and complex topic that cannot be thoroughly treated in a single chapter of a Nutshell reference book. If you are interested in learning about all the ins and outs of creating professional-quality audio for a web site, I recommend starting with *Designing Web Audio* by Josh Beggs and Dylan Thede (O'Reilly, 2001). It contains information on recording, editing, and optimizing audio content, as well as in-depth discussions of popular web audio formats.

This chapter introduces general audio concepts and a number of popular web audio file formats, including WAV, AIFF, MP3, QuickTime, MIDI, RealAudio, Windows Media, Liquid Audio, Flash audio, and Beatnik's Rich Media Format. It also discusses the many options for adding audio to a web site. It begins with an introduction to basic audio terminology that will be useful to know when it comes time to create and optimize sound files.

Basic Digital Audio Concepts

In order to distribute recorded speech or music over the Internet, an analog signal must be converted to digital information (described by bits and bytes). This process is called *encoding*. It is analogous to scanning a photograph to a digital bitmap format, and many of the same concepts regarding quality and file size apply. Some audio file formats (such as MPEG) are compressed in size during encoding using a specialized audio compression algorithm to save disk space. In the encoding process, you may be asked to provide settings for the following aspects of the audio file.

Sampling rate

To convert an analog sound wave into a digital description of that wave, samples of the wave are taken at timed intervals (see Figure 24-1). The number of samples taken per second is called the *sampling rate*. The more samples taken per second, the more accurately the digital description can recreate the original shape of the sound wave, and therefore the better the quality of the digital audio. In this respect, sampling rate is similar to image resolution for digital images.

Sample rates are typically measured in kilohertz (KHz). On the high end, CD-quality audio has a sampling rate of 44.1 KHz (or 44,100 samples per second). On the low end, 8 KHz produces a thin sound quality that is equivalent to a transistor radio. Standard sampling rates include 8 KHz, 11.025 KHz, 11.127 KHz, 22.05 KHz, 44.1 KHz, and 48 KHz. The new emerging high-end standard is 96K, which may be seen in DVD audio but is not applicable to the Web. The higher the sampling rate, the more information is contained in the file, and therefore the larger the file size.

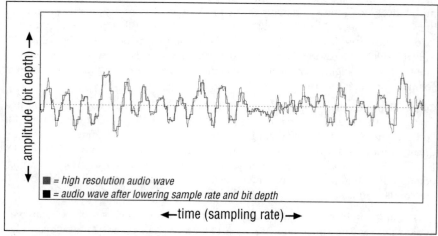

Figure 24-1: Audio wave after lowering sample rate and bit depth

Bit depth

Like images, audio files are also measured in terms of their bit depth (also called sampling resolution or word length). The bit depth corresponds to the resolution of the amplitude (or volume) of the sound file. The more bits, the better the quality of the audio, and of course, the larger the resulting audio file. This is similar to bit depth in images—the more bits, the more colors the image can contain.

Some common bit depths are 8-bit (which sounds thin or tinny, like a telephone signal) and 16-bit, which is required to describe music of CD quality. High end digital audio is now capable of 20-, 24-, 32-, and 48-bit depths.

Channels

Audio files can support from one to six separate channels of audio information. The most familiar of these are mono (one channel) and stereo (two channels), but some formats can support three-, four-, or six-channel (also referred to as 5.1-channel) surround sound. Most file formats support only mono and stereo, but we will be seeing a lot more support for multichannel surround formats in the coming years.

Bit rate

Audio files are also measured in terms of bit rate, the number of bits per second devoted to storing audio data. Bit rate is a function of the file's bit depth and sampling rate, so you reduce the bit rate by reducing a combination of those settings. Bit rate is measured in kilobits per second (Kbps) and can be calculated by dividing the file size by the length of the audio clip in seconds. In general, it is advisable for the bit rate of streaming audio files to be lower than the bit rate of the user's connection to the Internet to ensure smooth playback.

It stands to reason that before you can put your own audio files on the Web, you first need to create them. Your options are to find existing audio resources (such as from a royalty-free CD) or to record them yourself.

Using Existing Audio

The simplest way to add audio to a site is to use found music, sound effects, or other resources. But before you start featuring music and sound effects from your personal CD collection, it is important to be aware of copyright issues.

Copyright Restrictions

With few exceptions, it is illegal to reproduce, distribute, or broadcast a sound recording without the permission of the copyright owner. Copyright issues have been brought to the forefront with the growing popularity of MP3 distribution through Napster and other peer-to-peer networks, but they apply to all audio published on the Internet. To get permission, you usually need to pay licensing fees.

Be aware that simply posting somebody else's music or recordings from a CD without their expressed written permission is a copyright violation. Record companies, entertainment corporations, and the RIAA (Recording Industry Association of America) are taking measures to crack down on the illegal use of copyrighted material. So be smart and be sure that you have the rights to the sound you use on your site.

Royalty-Free Audio Resources

Fortunately, collections of prerecorded sound effects and music are available for multimedia and Internet use. Many are royalty-free, meaning once you've purchased the package of sounds, you can use them however you wish and pay no licensing fees. Some collections include:

- Digital Kitchen: *http://www.dkitchen.com*
- DXM Production's Earshot SFX Library: *http://www.earshotsfx.com*
- Creative Support Services: *http://www.cssmusic.com*
- SampleNet: *http://samplenet.co.uk*

Preparing Your Own Audio

Recording and producing your own audio requires a significant investment in hardware, software, and time spent learning. If you need to put professional-quality audio on your site but aren't likely to make the investment in time and equipment yourself, consider outsourcing the work to professionals.

The final product may be anything from a simple personal greeting to a live concert broadcast. The preparation of original audio requires a number of standard steps: recording, basic sound editing, then optimization for web delivery.

Recording

The first step is to make a recording of the music, spoken word, or sound effects for your site. As for most things, when it comes to sound quality, you get what you pay for. It is possible to capture sound using available resources (like the microphone that came with your computer), but the quality will not be appropriate for a professional site. The cost of recording equipment escalates quickly for each level of sound quality. An investment of $800 to $4000 in equipment (not counting the computer) is enough to get started on creating a home (or small business) studio. Getting a studio up and running also requires investments of time, effort, and education.

Although this may be a good choice for a business, it may be too expensive for many hobbyists and garage bands. It may be more cost-effective for an individual or organization on a strict budget or tight deadline to hire the services of a professional studio. Depending on how well the studio is equipped, it can cost from $30 to $250 per hour, and up.

Basic Sound Editing and Effects

Once you've recorded raw audio, the next step is to clean up the recording. This can involve removing unwanted sounds, setting the beginning and end of the file, and/or making a loop. You may want to apply digital effects to the sound, such as reverb or a delay.

Consider also using mastering processing techniques such as normalization or compression that can balance out the level of your audio such that no part is too loud or too quiet.

There is a huge selection of software for audio editing and format conversion. The software ranges from single-purpose utilities available via free download to professional digital-audio editing suites costing thousands of dollars. Some popular professional-level tools are listed in the following sections.

Windows audio tools

The following tools are available for use on Windows:

Sound Forge by Sonic Foundry
  http://www.sonicfoundry.com
  Sound Forge is limited to editing stereo files, but it includes many plug-ins for effects such as chorus, delay, distortion, reverb, and compression. Street price is about $400.

Cool Edit by Syntrillium
  http://www.syntrillium.com
  For only $69, Cool Edit offers up to four tracks of audio editing and includes plug-ins for audio restoration as well as the usual reverbs, delays and so on. At $400, Syntrillium's flagship product is Cool Edit Pro, which offers up to 64 channels in a full multitrack recording environment.

Mac audio tools

These tools can be used on Mac systems:

Peak by Bias
  http://www.bias-inc.com
  With built-in batch processing and a street price of less than $400, this application has been the Mac standard when it comes to stereo editing. Bias also offers the more streamlined Peak LE for $99. This "Light Edition" may be sufficient for most entry-level users.

Spark by TCWorks
  http://www.tcworks.de
  A more recent entry into the Mac stereo editing game, Spark is quickly making an impact. This program focuses on effects and offers support for VST plug-ins, but it also offers all of the editing features standard for professional work. Street price is around $400.

Digital Performer by MOTU
  http://www.motu.com
  Performer software has evolved from a MIDI sequencing application into a full fledged digital recording studio environment offering top quality effects plug-ins and audio editing. Musicians can make entire recordings with this software, but it is also just as capable at adding audio to video or mixing radio programs. Street price is around $550.

Tools for both Mac and Windows systems

These tools are available for both Windows and Mac systems:

Cubase by Steinberg
  http://www.steinberg.net
  Similar to Digital Performer, this cross-platform multitrack recording environment offers both MIDI and audio editing with lots of effects plug-ins, virtual instruments, and recording tools for creating an entire virtual studio inside your computer. Street price is around $600.

ProTools by Digidesign
   http://www.digidesign.com
   Long the industry standard for multitrack computer recording, ProTools offers everything you'd ever need for a professional quality recording studio in your computer. Their high end "Mix" systems, including both software and custom hardware, start at $7000 and go up from there, but they have recently started making consumer-level solutions such as the Digi001, which offers ProTools software and a hardware input/output box for around $900. Digidesign also offers "ProTools Free," a free version of ProTools (limited to eight tracks), at *http://www.digidesign.com/ptfree/*.

Optimizing for the Web

After the sound files have been recorded and edited, it is time to convert them to their target web audio format and make them as small as possible for web delivery. The tool you use may depend on the file format. For instance, RealAudio and LiquidAudio have their own creation tools. There are also several tools specialized for the creation of MP3s. Tools are discussed with their respective file formats later in this chapter.

One great all-purpose tool is Cleaner 5, from Terran Interactive available for the Mac and Windows systems. This program is designed to get the best quality files at the smallest size in whatever format you choose. Cleaner can compress a number of file formats, including Quicktime and RealMedia. It can also do batch processing. The program sells for $599 as of this writing. (Cleaner is the newer and renamed version of MediaCleanerPro.)

Regardless of the tool you use, there are standard ways to reduce the size of an audio file so it is appropriate for downloading via a web page. Not surprisingly, this usually requires sacrificing quality. The aspects of the audio file you can control are:

Length of the audio clip
   It might seem obvious, but you should keep the audio sample as short as possible. For example, consider providing just part of a song rather than the whole thing. If you are recording a greeting, make it short and sweet.

Number of channels
   A mono audio file requires half the disk space of a stereo file and and may be adequate for some audio uses.

Bit depth
   Audio files for the Web are often saved at 8 bits, which will result in a file that is half the size of a 16-bit file. MP3s can handle 16-bit due to their efficient compression.

Sampling rate
   Cutting the sampling rate in half will cut the file size in half (e.g., a sampling rate of 22.05 KHz requires half the data than one of 44.1 KHz). As a general guideline, audio files that are voice-only can be reduced down to 8 KHz. Sound effects work at 8 Khz or 11.025 KHz. Music sounds acceptable at 22 Khz.

Using these guidelines, if we start with a one-minute music sample at CD quality (10 MB) and change it to a mono, 8-bit, 22 Khz WAV file, its size is reduced to 1.25 MB, which is much more reasonable for downloading. Using MP3 compression, we can keep the quality of that one-minute sample at 16-bit, 44.1 kHz stereo (similar to CD quality) with a resulting file size of under 1MB. Combining these methods (a mono, 8-bit, 22Khz MP3), you can offer one minute clips at acceptable audio quality at only a few hundred K.

Obviously, just how stingy you can be with your settings while retaining acceptable quality depends on the individual audio file. You should certainly do some testing to see how small you can make the file without sacrificing essential audio detail.

Streaming Audio

Once upon a time, the only way to play audio from a web page was to link to it and wait for it to download to the hard drive so it could be played. With this method, once the file finishes downloading, the browser either launches an external player or uses a plug-in to play the audio.*

Downloaded audio has a few distinct disadvantages. First, because the file needs to download to the hard disk in its entirety before it can begin playing, users may be faced with a very long wait before they hear any sound. In addition, because the audio file is copied to the hard drive, it is more difficult for artists and publishers to limit distribution and protect copyrights.

Although it is still possible and common to deliver static audio files in this manner, it is far more effective to use one of several streaming media technologies. Streaming media (be it audio or video) begins playing almost immediately after the request is made, and continues playing as the audio data is being transferred. Streaming audio technology was developed to address the problem of unacceptable download times. It can even be used to broadcast live programs, such as concerts or baseball games.

The following are some advantages to streaming audio:

- Audio begins playing soon after the stream begins.

- Using new technologies and formats, sound quality doesn't need to be as severely sacrificed.

- Artists and publishers can better control distribution and protect copyright because the user never gets a copy of the audio file.

---

* Some common Macintosh external players include QuickTime and iTunes. MediaPlayer is a common player on the Windows operating system. Internet Explorer Versions 3 and higher can play many audio file formats natively. Netscape Navigator 3.0 and 4.0 uses the LiveAudio plug-in to play most audio files. The QuickTime player is available for both platforms and as a plug-in to both browsers.

Consider also these disadvantages:

- The potentially high cost of server software may be prohibitive.

- Some formats require a dedicated or preconfigured server, which may be problematic with some hosting services.

- Sound quality and stream may be adversely affected by low speed or inconsistent Internet connections.

Streaming File Formats

It used to be that if you wanted audio to stream, you had to use RealAudio technology. Not so anymore. As it became obvious that streaming was the best way to deliver sound to the Web, we've seen the development of a number of compteting proprietary technologies, as well as solutions for streaming standard file formats such as MP3 and QuickTime. The following formats have streaming functionality:

RealNetwork's RealMedia (and RealAudio)
Apple's QuickTime
Microsoft's Windows Media (Netshow)
Streaming MP3s (using a streaming MP3 server like SHOUTcast)
Macromedia Flash and Shockwave
Liquid Audio
Beatnik's Rich Music Format (RMF)

These file formats are discussed in more detail later in this chapter.

Server Software and Protocols

True streaming relies on special server software that permits the uninterrupted flow of data. The information in the song is broken up into little "packets" and sent out in order over the lines. These packets are then reassembled on the user's end. The audio player collects a number of packets before playback begins (a process called *buffering*) to increase the likelihood of smooth playback.

Streaming media takes advantage of either UDP (User Datagram Protocol), RTSP (RealTime Streaming Protocol), or RTP (RealTime Transfer Protocol) for the transmission of data. What makes these protocols effective at streaming is that if a packet of information is dropped or missing, the data transmission continues on without it. This is in contrast to traditional HTTP, the traditional protocol of the Web, which stops and tries to resend lost packets, potentially halting the stream.

UDP was the first protocol used for streaming media because of its improvements over HTTP. The newer RTSP is more efficent than UDP. RTSP is a two-way streaming protocol, allowing the user to send messages back to the server (such as rewinding the tape). By contrast, RTP (used by Apple QuickTime) is a one-way stream (similar to HTTP in this regard), only the file never downloads completely to the user's hard drive as it does in HTTP or FTP transfers.

Commercial streaming server software, such as RealServer, can handle thousands of simultaneous streams. It provides robust administrative tools and offers advanced functions such as bandwidth negotiation (where the proper bit rate version is delivered based on the connection speed). The software and hardware to set up a dedicated streaming server can be quite costly. On top of that, RealNetworks charges licensing fees based on number of streams.

Pseudo-Streaming

Some media formats are designed to begin playing before they've completely downloaded, producing a streaming effect even when the files are served from an HTTP server. This is known as pseudo-streaming or HTTP-streaming.

The advantage to pseudo-streaming is that it requires no special (and costly!) server software. You just put the files on your server as you would a GIF or JPEG. This is a good solution for broadcasting relatively short audio tracks to just a few simultaneous listeners.

There are a number of key limitations to serving streaming media from a web server. It can not handle heavy server loads and multiple simultaneous connections. You also sacrifice the advanced administration tools and bandwidth negotiation (users have to choose the appropriate file for themselves). This method also makes it impossible to do live broadcasts since the whole file needs to be available for download.

With the proper player on the user's end, RealMedia, QuickTime, MP3, Flash, and Shockwave files will pseudo-stream from an HTTP server.

Web Audio Formats

At last, we get to the heart of web audio—the various file formats. This section provides an introduction to some of the most common formats for web audio.

WAV/AIFF (.wav, .aif, .aiff)

The WAV and AIFF audio formats are very similar in peformance. The Waveform Audio File Format (.wav) was originally developed as the standard audio format for the Microsoft Windows operating system, but it is now supported on the Macintosh as well. WAV files can support arbitrary sampling rates and bit depths, although 8 KHz and 11.025 KHz at 8- or 16-bit are most common for Web use.

The Audio Interchange File Format (.aif or .aiff) was developed as the standard audio format for the Macintosh platform, but it is now supported by Windows and other platforms. It can support up to six channels and arbitrary sampling rates and bit depths, with 8 KHz and 11.127 KHz at 8- and 16-bits being the most common online.

WAV and AIFF files are less commonly used on the Web than they once were, now that we have audio formats that are better suited for web delivery (MP3) or designed specifically for the Web (streaming formats). WAV and AIFF files are typically used as the source format for audio that then gets compressed into more web-friendly formats, like RealAudio. They sound good when uncompressed, but they suffer drastic loss of quality when compressed to small file sizes. For this reason they are useful for very short, downloadable audio clips, such as short greetings. They are usually added to web pages via a link for download.

The following summarizes the WAV and AIFF formats:

Good for	Storing high-quality source audio before converting to web formats, delivering short clips where pristine sound quality is not important, reaching the lowest common denominator (since everyone can play them).
Delivery	Download.
Creation tools	The majority of sound editing tools can save files in WAV and AIFF format.
Player	WAVs and AIFFs generally play using the browser's default function for sound handling (such as Windows MediaPlayer or the QuickTime plug-in).

MP3 (.mp3)

MP3's explosion in popularity is nothing short of a phenomenon and has changed the way we use and view the Internet. The key to its success is MP3's ability to maintain excellent sound fidelity at very small file sizes. In fact, its compression scheme can reduce an audio source to just one-tenth of its original size. For instance, four minutes of high-quality music in WAV format requires 40 MB of disk space; as an MP3, the same file weighs in at just 3.5 MB! With the discovery of MP3, it was suddenly feasible to transfer songs over the Internet without prohibitive download times. The rest is history.

MPEG compression

The MP3s that we've grown to love are technically MPEG-1, Layer-III files. MPEG is actually a family of multimedia standards created by the Moving Picture Experts Group. It supports three types of information: video, audio, and streaming (which, in the context of MPEG compression, is synchronized video and audio).

MPEG uses a lossy compression scheme that is based on human auditory perception. Sounds that are not discernible to the human ear are thrown out in the compression process. The resulting file sounds nearly the same, but contains much less data than the original.

There are a number of MPEG standards: MPEG-1 was originally developed for video transfer at VHS quality and is the format used for MP3s; MPEG-2 is a higher-quality standard that was developed for television broadcast; other MPEG specs that address other needs (such as MPEG-4 and -7) are currently in development. MPEGs can be compressed using one of three schemes: Layer-I, -II, or -III (the "3" in MP3 refers to its compression scheme layer). To learn more about MPEG, visit the MPEG web site (*http://www.mpeg.org*).

Creating MP3s

Any audio source file (usually a WAV or AIFF file) can be turned into an MP3 using an MP3 encoder such as Xing AudioCatalyst, iTunes (Mac), or MusicMatch Jukebox. For a complete list of MP3 creation tools, see MP3-Converter.com (*http://www.mp3-converter.com*).

To make an MP3, begin with raw audio saved in WAV or AIFF format. If the audio is coming from a CD, it will need to be "ripped" first (extracted from the CD format and saved in a format a computer can understand). The next step is to encode the raw audio into the MP3 format. Many MP3 tools rip and encode audio tracks in one step.

When encoding, you'll be asked to set the quality level, or bit rate. The standard quality setting for putting music on the Internet is 128 Kbps (which is near-CD quality sound) at 44.1 kHz. For personal use (to play from your computer or portable MP3 player), you can use the next higher levels (160 or 192 Kbps). To keep file sizes extra small, choose 112 Kbps or lower, but expect a loss in audio quality. In order to stream MP3s at rates acceptable for 28.8 modem users, many MP3 online "radio" stations use 22.05K mono files compessed at a mere 24 Kbps.

You'll also need decide whether you want to make CBR (contant bit rate) or VBR (variable bit rate) files. Variable bit rate MP3s adjust their bit rate based on the complexity of the current audio passage. Variable bit rate MP3s can provide an enormous increase in quality at similar bit rates, but because VBR is inconsistently supported, the most reliable choice is CBR. Most of the new MP3 players support VBR, so keep an eye out for VBR to gain more support in the coming years.

Serving MP3s

MP3s can be served from a traditional FTP or HTTP server. MP3s can also be streamed using server solutions such as SHOUTcast (discussed later in this section) or RealServer 8. Along with the main advantages of streaming, this means that the MP3 file is not actually downloaded to the user's computer, providing better copyright protection.

And speaking of copyright, remember that while there is no problem creating MP3s for your own personal use, it is illegal to upload and distribute audio if you do not hold the copyright for it.

One of the most popular software packages used for streaming MP3s is SHOUTcast from Nullsoft. It makes it possible for people to broadcast audio from their PCs with a minimum amount of hardware and knowledge, over any speed Internet connection (although more bandwidth certainly helps). You can broadcast MP3s to individual users or to many users at once by redirecting your stream to a high-bandwidth server. To listen to a SHOUTcast server stream, open Winamp (or any other stream-capable MP3 player) and bring up the Open Location dialog box. Enter the URL of the server you want to listen to and hit Enter. For a list of SHOUTcast servers (and for more information), visit *http://www.shoutcast.com*. SHOUTcast is free for download for general non-profit use. For commercial use, there is a one-time licensing fee of $299 (as of this writing).

The following summarizes the MP3 format:

Good for	Distribution and sale of high-quality audio (like music tracks), radio broadcast-style transmissions at lower bit rates.
Delivery	Streaming, download.
Creation tools	One of dozens of MP3 encoding programs. See *http://www.mp3-converter.com* for a complete list.
Player	One of dozens of free MP3 players, such as WinAmp (Windows), MPEG Audio Player (Mac), or iTunes (Mac); browsers may support MPEG audio via the QuickTime Plug-in. You can select a program for MP3 playback in the browser's application preferences.

Apple QuickTime Audio (.mov)

Although QuickTime is best known as a video technology, it is also possible to create audio-only QuickTime Movies (.mov). QuickTime is a container format, meaning it can contain a wide variety of media. In fact, the QuickTime 5 format can store still images (JPEG, BMP, PICT, PNG, and GIF), a number of movie formats including MPEG-1, 360-degree panoramic images, Flash movies, MP3 audio, and other audio formats. Once you package up media in a QuickTime .mov file, you can take advantage of QuickTime features such as dependable cross-platform performance, excellent compression, and true streaming.

Although the QuickTime system extension is needed to play a .mov file, it is widely distributed and available for both Windows and Macintosh systems. In addition, recent versions of both Netscape Navigator and Internet Explorer come with the QuickTime plug-in, so a QuickTime audio player can be embedded right on the page. It is a reliable format since you can assume most users have the appropriate plug-in or player.

QuickTime is discussed further in Chapter 25. For more information on Quick-Time, see *http://www.apple.com/quicktime/*.

The following summarizes the QuickTime format:

Good for	Continuous-play audio (music, narration).
Delivery	True streaming via RTP or RTSP (using QuickTime Server on Mac OS X Server or the open source Darwin Streaming Server on Unix and NT), pseudo-streaming on HTTP servers, download.
Creation tools	Most audio and multimedia editors support QuickTime, or use Apple's basic editing tool QuickTime Pro for $29.95.
Player	QuickTime plug-in (part of Netscape Navigator and Internet Explorer) for viewing within a web browser or QuickTime Player (standalone utility).

MIDI (.mid)

MIDI (which stands for Musical Instrument Digital Interface) is a different breed of audio file format. It was originally developed as a standard way for electronic musical instruments to communicate with each other.

A MIDI file contains no actual audio information (the digital representation of analog sound), but rather numeric commands that trigger a series of notes (with instructions on each note's length and volume). These notes are played by a MIDI player using the available "instrument" sounds on a computer's sound card. The function is similar to the way a player piano roll creates a song when run through on the player piano.

As a result, MIDI files are incredibly compact and ideal for low-bandwidth delivery. They are capable of packing a minute of music into just 10K, which is 1,000 times smaller than a one-minute WAV file (approximately 10 MB).

QuickTime and most other MIDI file handlers install a General MIDI (GM) soundset with instruments like piano, drums, bass, orchestral strings, and even vocal "oohs" and "aahs" in standardized MIDI locations. While these sounds may vary in quality and timbre from player to player, General MIDI files can depend on getting a piano sound when they send to Program 1, Channel 1 of the GM Player (built into QuickTime, etc.). These sound sets can be surprisingly good, but they still can't compete with recordings created in a studio. In general, MIDI files will always sound "computery."

Despite this limitation, MIDIs are an extremely attractive alternative for adding instrumental music to your web site with very little download time.

The following summarizes the MIDI format:

Good for	Background music and loops.
Delivery	Download.
Creation tools	Requires special MIDI sequencer software, such as Vision, Cakewalk, and Digital Performer. Creating and editing MIDI files can be complicated. Consider using an existing MIDI file if you are inexperienced with music composition and digital audio.
Player	QuickTime plug-in or Windows Media Player. MIDI sound engines are built into Internet Explorer and Navigator 4.0 and higher.

RealMedia/RealAudio (.rm, .ra)

RealNetworks (once Progressive Networks) was a pioneer in producing a viable technology for bringing streaming audio to the Web. Despite heavy competition, it continues to lead the pack in terms of widespread use and popularity, and it has grown to be the standard for streaming audio, including live broadcasts.

RealAudio is a server-based streaming audio solution. The RealServer offers advanced features for streaming audio delivery, including bandwidth negotiation (the proper bit rate version is delivered based on the speed of the connection), RTSP transmission for smooth playback, and administrative tools for tracking usage and minimizing server load. Using the SureStream feature, the bandwidth can be adjusted on the fly (while the file is streaming) to accommodate bit rate fluctuations.

A robust RealServer system can allow thousands of simultaneous listeners. The server software requires a large investment (starting at around $2000 for the basic package), and RealNetworks charges licensing fees for the number of streams. There is, however, a free version that allows 25 simultaneous listeners. For more information, see the RealNetworks site at *http://www.realnetworks.com*.

If you aren't ready to commit to a RealServer, RealMedia and RealAudio files can be pseudo-streamed from an ordinary HTTP server for sites with a limited amount of traffic.

To listen to RealAudio files, users must have RealPlayer, which is available for Windows, Mac, and Unix systems. The RealPlayer plug-in comes installed with Netscape Navigator and Internet Explorer and makes it possible to embed a RealMedia player right in the web page.

RealNetworks also offers tools for creating RealAudio and RealMedia files. The latest version (as of this writing) is RealSystem Producer Plus, which provides complete tools for converting audio and video to streaming format. Earlier creation

Audio

tools include RealEncoder, for simple conversions, and RealPublisher, with advanced features such as wizards for creating HTML and FTP support. Audio can be saved in either the current and preferred RealMedia format (*.rm*) or the RealAudio format (*.ra*) for support in older versions of RealPlayer (5 and earlier).

The process for adding RealAudio to a web page is covered in detail later in this chapter. For more information, visit the RealNetworks site at *http://www. realnetworks.com*. For consumer-oriented information and downloads, see *http:// www.real.com*.

The following summarizes the RealAudio format:

Good for	Continuous-play audio and live broadcasts to large numbers of people.
Delivery	Streaming (via RTSP), pseudo-streaming (via HTTP).
Creation tools	One of the RealNetworks encoders (such as RealSystem Producer Plus) or a third-party tool such as Cleaner 5 from Terran Interactive.
Player	Freely available RealPlayer, Commercial RealPlayer Plus (with added features), RealPlayer plug-in in Netscape Navigator and Internet Explorer.

Windows Media (.wma, .asf)

Microsoft's Windows Media is a streaming media system similar to RealMedia. Like RealMedia, it comes with the standard components for creating, playing, and serving Windows Media files. Windows Media wraps all media elements into one Active Streaming File (*.asf*), Microsoft's proprietary streaming media format. Audio may also be saved as nonstreaming Windows Media Audio format (*.wma*). Because Media Player is part of the Windows operating system, it is widely distributed and stable on the Windows platform. A considerably less supported version of Media Player is available for the Mac as well.

Windows Media Audio files are encoded using the special Windows Media Audio codec (currently in Version 8) which is ideal for all types of audio at bit rates from 16 Kbps to 192 Kbps. Users must have the Version 8 player to hear audio encoded with the Version 8 codec, so use Version 7 if you don't wish to force your users to upgrade. For voice-only audio at low bit rates (8 Kbps), use the alternative ACELP codec.

The Windows Media system has its advantages and disadvantages. On the good side, the server software comes free with Windows NT Server 4.0 and later, and there are no charges for streams as there is with RealMedia. Administration tools make it easy to track performance and bill per view or per minute. The disadvantages to Windows Media are that the server only runs on Windows NT and it doesn't support Flash or SMIL (Synchronized Multimedia Integration Language) like RealMedia. Also, although there is a Windows Media Player for the Mac, it lags behind the Windows version in terms of features and performance, so Mac users may miss your content.

For more information on Windows Media, see *http://www.microsoft.com/windows/ windowsmedia/en/default.asp*. The FAQ is a good starting point.

The following summarizes the Windows Media format:

Good for   Continuous-play audio and live broadcasts.
Delivery   Streaming, download.
Creation tools Windows Media Encoder for converting to Windows Media format, Windows Media Author for creating synchronized multimedia presentations. See the Windows Media site for a complete list of creation tools at *http://www.microsoft.com/Windows/windowsmedia/en/overview/components.asp.*
Player   Media Player (shipped with Windows OS), available as download for the Mac as well as a variety of handheld devices that support Windows CE.

Liquid Audio

Liquid Audio specifically targets the needs of the music industry by "providing labels and artists with software tools and technologies to enable secure online preview and purchase of CD-quality music." LiquidAudio is not just a file format; it's a professional utility for controlling music sales and distribution. It is very effective in what it sets out to do, but it is not an all-purpose web audio solution.

Liquid Audio delivers CD-quality audio (including streaming MP3s) and is the only streaming format that offers Dolby encoding. Audio files can be watermarked with copyright, owner, and purchaser information, discouraging piracy and copyright violation. The Liquid MusicServer offers a suite of integrated proprietary tools for encoding, serving, and playing Liquid Audio files.

Liquid Player can offer views of album graphics, lyrics, credits, and up-to-date promotions or announcements (such as tour dates). The player works with the Liquid MusicServer (which is easily tied into SQL databases) to enable individual tracks or entire CDs to be purchased online.

For more information, see the Liquid Audio web site at *http://www.liquidaudio.com.*

The following summarizes the Liquid Audio format:

Good for   Distribution and sales of music.
Delivery   Streaming via Liquid Server.
Creation tools Liquifier Pro.
Player   Liquid Player.

Flash (.swf) and Shockwave (.dcr)

If you want to add short interactive sound effects to a page, such as button rollover noises, consider using a Flash movie (*.swf*). Flash, developed by Macromedia, is an ideal format for adding high-impact interactivity and animation to web sites. Audio (from short clips to long-playing audio) can be embedded in a Flash movie and triggered instantly by user actions. With other file formats (particularly streaming audio), there is an inevitable delay between the request and playback, making it inappropriate for interactive presentations.

Macromedia also offers Shockwave for putting CD-ROM-like interactive media files on web pages. Shockwave takes Director files (which can take advantage of the robust Lingo scripting language for advanced functionality) and compresses them down for web delivery as .dcr files. Shockwave files may contain internal sound effects and streaming audio in the Shockwave Audio (SWA) format. Despite compression, Shockwave files are not well suited for low-bandwidth connections.

Flash and Shockwave are covered in more detail in Chapter 26. For more information, see Macromedia's site, *http://www.macromedia.com*.

The following summarizes the Flash and Shockwave formats:

Good for	Interactive sound effects, specialized web applications with embedded long-playing sound.
Delivery	Streaming (via QuickTime 8 or RealServer), pseudo-streaming (via HTTP), download.
Creation tools	Macromedia Flash, Adobe LiveMotion.
Player	Flash Player or Shockwave browser plug-in (two of the most widely distributed plug-ins).

Beatnik's Rich Music Format (.rmf)

Beatnik's Rich Music Format (RMF) is an HTML-based format that uses scripting languages (like JavaScript) to synchronize interactive soundtracks. RMF uses an advanced collection of MIDI sounds (some proprietary) combined with user-configured samples. The result is excellent sound quality in extremely small files that download fast. Beatnik is another option for adding interactive (user-triggered) sound effects to a web page.

One of Beatnik's claims to fame (besides being co-founded by pop legend Thomas Dolby Robertson) is its Mixman eMix remixers. By clicking on different buttons, users can remix popular songs and send their creations to their friends. For more information, go to *http://www.mixman.com*.

The Beatnik system is comprised of Beatnik Player (the browser plug-in required for playing .rmf files), Beatnik Audio Engine (a software audio mixer), Beatnik Methodizer (an automated JavaScript generator for adding Beatnik to web pages), and Beatnik Editor (for creating customized digital audio samples). The learning curve is fairly steep, and you must know some JavaScript to get the most out of the system.

Beatnik's disadvantages are its reliance on the Beatnik Player plug-in, which users must download, and the complexity of its authoring environment. It is also not well suited for long-format audio files. But for short, interactive sound effects, Beatnik offers a big bang for a few bytes. For more information, see the Beatnik web site at *http://www.beatnik.com*.

The following summarizes the Rich Music Format:

Good for	Interactive sound effects, background sound loops, specialized online apps like remix machines.
Delivery	Download.
Creation tools	Beatnik Audio Engine, Beatnik Methodizer, and Beatnik Editor.
Player	Beatnik Player (currently not part of standard browser download, but Beatnik is still lobbying for greater distribution).

Choosing an Audio Format

Which audio format or system you choose depends on your communication goals, the scale of your site, and your budget. Table 24-1 provides suggestions for some common scenarios. Consider them only as starting points for researching the solution that best meets your needs.

Table 24-1: Suggested audio formats

Audio needs	Suggested formats
Short voice greetings	WAV, AIFF, QuickTime (via regular HTTP server), MP3
Narration (news broadcasts, interviews, and other voice-only content)	Streaming solutions such as RealAudio, Windows Media, or QuickTime for large audiences; RealAudio or QuickTime via HTTP server for limited traffic and few simultaneous listeners
Background music (ambient sound loops)	MIDI, Beatnik, WAV
Short interactive sound effects (such as button rollover and transition sounds)	Flash, Shockwave, Beatnik
Music samples for a limited audience	MP3, RealMedia, or QuickTime via HTTP server
Music samples for a large-scale site with heavy traffic	Complete streaming solution, such as RealSystem or Windows Streaming Media
Radio-style music broadcasting	RealMedia System, streaming MP3s (via a streaming server such as SHOUTcast), Windows Media System
Distribution and sale of CD-quality audio	MP3, Liquid Audio
Live broadcasting	RealMedia System, QuickTime, Windows Media System
Musical e-greeting card	Flash, Beatnik, MIDI or WAV background sound
Specialized audio applications (such as virtual CD players, mixers, etc.)	Flash, Shockwave, Beatnik, QuickTime

Adding Audio to a Web Page

There are a number of ways to add audio to a web page. This section covers the most common techniques.

A Simple Link

You can use a simple anchor tag (<a>) to link to an audio file from a web page, as follows:

```
<A HREF="audio/song.wav">Play the song (3.5 MB)</A>
<A HREF="groovy.mp3"><IMG SRC="buttons/playme.gif"></A>
```

When the reader clicks on the linked text or graphic, the browser retrieves the audio file from the server and launches a helper application (or plug-in, if the browser is so configured) to play the file. Files accessed in this manner are typically downloaded to the user's hard drive (stored in cache).

If the browser uses an external player, a new small window from the helper application opens with the controls for playing the audio. If the browser is configured to use a plug-in player (such as the popular QuickTime plug-in), a control panel may load right in the browser window, replacing the original web page. You may want to advise readers to use the Back button to return to the original page should this happen.

It is also good web etiquette to warn readers of the size of an audio file so they can make an informed decision as to whether they want to spend the time downloading the file.

Background Sound

There are several ways (mostly browser-specific) to make an audio file start playing automatically when a web page loads. Note that the disadvantage of using background sounds is that the user has no way of turning the sound off if she does not like it. Also, if the audio file is large, you are forcing a potentially lengthy download on the user. This is particularly bad web etiquette.

To add a background sound to a web page, try these methods:

- For Internet Explorer 2.0+ (no other browsers support this tag), use the <bgsound> tag, as follows:

    ```
    <BGSOUND SRC="audio/song.mid" LOOP=3>
    ```

    where src gives the URL for the audio file and loop is the number of times you want the audio to play (this attribute can be set to "infinite"). WAV, AIFF, and MIDI sound files can be played as background sounds using this method.

- To set a background sound that works with both Netscape Navigator and Internet Explorer, use a combination of the background sound tag (for IE) and an <embed> tag (for Navigator) with the control panel hidden, as follows:

    ```
    <EMBED SRC="audio/song.mid" autostart=true hidden=true>
    <NOEMBED><BGSOUND="audio/song.mid"></NOEMBED>
    ```

- For Netscape Navigator and Internet Explorer (5 and higher), you can make audio play automatically with client-pull by using the <meta> tag as follows:

    ```
    <META http-equiv="refresh" content="1;url=audio/song.mid">
    ```

    which causes the page to refresh (and the audio to play) after one second. This use of the <meta> tag is discouraged by the W3C in HTML 4.01.

Adding RealMedia

RealMedia (including RealAudio) files can be added to a web page via two methods. The first triggers the browser to launch RealPlayer as an external application. The second plays the media file in a player embedded directly in the browser window using the RealPlayer plug-in.

In either case, you do not create a link directly to the RealMedia file itself, but rather to a special reference file, called a *metafile*. The metafile is a simple text document that contains the URL of the RealMedia file. These reference files are generally kept in the same directories as the HTML documents, although that is not a requirement.

There is a three-step process from click to playback. First, clicking the HTML link downloads the metafile from the server to the browser. Once it arrives at the browser, the metafile tells the browser to launch the RealPlayer and provides the player with URL information. Finally, the player uses the URL to request the actual media file from the server and begins playing the stream.

Metafiles are useful for maintenance and control purposes. To change the audio, all you have to do is change the tiny metafile, rather than having to dig through HTML source code. You can also do things like calling multiple streaming media files from one metafile. One link to the metafile plays all the files.

This indirect linking process is demonstrated in the following two examples.

Linking to RealMedia (external player)

When the user accesses RealMedia via a link (using the `<a>` tag), the browser launches the external RealPlayer application.

In the HTML document, make a link to the metafile that points to the RealMedia file as follows:

```
<A HREF="song.ram">Link to the song</A>
```

When linking to RealMedia, the metafile uses the *.ram* suffix. The metafile is a small text-only file that contains only the URL that points to the RealAudio file (suffix *.rm* or *.ra*):

```
pnm://domainname.com/song.rm
```

Embedding RealPlayer on the page

To place the RealPlayer controls in the web page itself, use the `<embed>` tag for Netscape Navigator (Version 4 and earlier) and the standards-compliant `<object>` tag for Internet Explorer (all versions) and Netscape 6. To reach both browsers, you may use a combination of the two as shown in the following examples. This method uses the RealPlayer plug-in for playback.

It should be noted that the audio stops playing when the user leaves the page. Also, it is more difficult to get consistent cross-browser performance when the player is embedded. For these reasons, it is generally preferable to link to the audio and use the external player.

The following sample code uses both the `<object>` (with parameters) and `<embed>` tags to embed the player on the page. When RealMedia is embedded, the suffix of the metafile should be *.rpm*. This tells the browser to start playing the media in the browser window.

```
<OBJECT ID="oakshoessong"
    CLASSID="clsid:CFCDAA03-8BE4-11cf-B84B-0020AFBBCCFA"
    HEIGHT="150" WIDTH="250" BORDER="0">
<PARAM NAME="SRC" VALUE="realmedia/oakshoes.rpm">
<PARAM NAME="CONTROLS" VALUE="all">
```

Audio

```
<EMBED SRC="realmedia/oakshoes.rpm" HEIGHT="150" WIDTH="250"
    AUTOSTART="false" CONTROLS="all" BORDER="0">
```

```
</OBJECT>
```

Let's start by looking at the <embed> tag, which is used by older versions of Netscape. It contains attributes for pointing to the metafile (src), specifying the size of the embedded player (width, height), whether the file starts playing automatically (autostart), whether it displays control buttons (control), and a border (border).

These same settings are made in the <object> tag using attributes and additional parameters (indicated by the <param> tag). It important that the classid attribute be specified *exactly* as it is shown in the example, as it is the unique identifier of the RealAudio plug-in. This may not be changed.

The easiest way to create the HTML code for handling RealAudio is to use the RealProducer or RealPublisher tool and allow it to do the work for you. RealNetworks also provides developer information at *http://www.realnetworks.com/devzone/*. The process for naming and accessing RealAudio has changed several times over the last few years, so be sure to refer to current documentation for up-to-date instructions.

Adding Windows Media

Before linking to Windows Media files (*.asf* or *.wma*), be sure they are saved in the *ASFROOT* directory on the NT Server running the Windows Media Administrator.

To link to a downloadable (nonstreaming) Windows Media Audio file (*.wma*), use a simple link directly to the audio file:

```
<A HREF="song.wma">Link to the song</A>
```

Linking to streaming Windows Media works much like the process described for RealAudio above. Streaming Windows Media use a go-between reference file called an "active stream redirector" file (*.asx*), similar to RealAudio's metafile. The ASX file contains the URL information that points the player to the actual media file. This method of providing a single stream to a single user on demand is called *unicasting*. In the HTML document, create a link to the redirector file as shown in this example:

```
<A HREF="streamingsong.asx">Stream the song</A>
```

The content of the *.asx* file looks like this:

```
<ASX version="3">
    <Entry>
        <ref href="path/streamingsong.asf" />
    </Entry>
</ASX>
```

Change the path in the <ref> tag so that it points to your Windows Media file. The *.asx* file should be saved in the same directory as the Windows Media file.

Another method for delivering Windows Media is *multicasting*, in which a single media stream is delivered (at a time determined by the publisher) and multiple

---

users share the stream. You can multicast prerecorded or live content. To add a multicast to your site, it is recommended that you use the tools and wizards provided by the Windows Media Administrator program. For more information, see the Windows Media Technologies pageSG located at *http://www.microsoft. com/Windows/windowsmedia/en/serve/basics_WM4.asp.*

For Further Reading

There are a number of books available that deal specifically with putting audio on the Web:

Designing Web Audio, Josh Beggs and Dylan Thede (O'Reilly & Associates, 2000).

Cutting Edge Web Audio, Ron Simpson, Jr. (Prentice Hall, 1998).

Audio on the Web: The Official IUMA Guide, Jeff Patterson, Ryan Melcher (Peachpit Press, 1998).

Web Developer.com® Guide to Streaming Multimedia, Jose Alvear (John Wiley & Sons, 1998).

CHAPTER 25

Video on the Web

Like audio, video clips were linked to web pages in the Web's earliest days. Delivering video via the Web is especially problematic because video files require huge amounts of data to describe the video and audio components, making for extremely large files. Few people will sit and wait an hour for a couple of minutes of video fun.

Many of the same technologies that have improved the experience of receiving audio over the Web have been applied to video as well. As with audio, you have the option of simply linking a video to your web page for download and playback, or you can choose from a number of streaming solutions. "Streaming" means the file begins playing almost immediately after the request is made and continues playing as the data is transferred; however, the file is never downloaded to the user's machine. For a more complete description of streaming versus nonstreaming media, see Chapter 24.

Many of the principles for developing and delivering video content for the Web are the same as those for audio (in fact, some of the file formats are the same as well). This chapter introduces you to basic video technology and concepts, including introductions to the video file formats QuickTime, RealMedia, Windows Media, AVI, and MPEG. If you are interested in learning how to produce video files for the Web, the books listed at the end of this chapter are a good start.

Basic Digital Video Concepts

The following is a list of aspects of digital video that can be manipulated with standard video-editing software. It is important to be familiar with these terms so you can create video optimized for web delivery.

Movie length

It's a simple principle—limiting the length of your video clip limits its file size. Videos longer than a minute or two may cause prohibitively long download times. If you must serve longer videos, consider one of the streaming video solutions.

Frame size

Obviously, the size of the frame has an impact on the size of the file. "Full-screen" video is 640×480 pixels. The amount of data required to deliver an image of that size would be prohibitive for most web applications. The most common frame size for web video is 160×120 pixels. Some producers go as small as 120×90 pixels. It is not recommended that you use a frame size larger than 320×240 with current technology. Actual size limits depend mostly on CPU power and bandwidth of the user's Internet link.

Frame rate

The frame rate is measured in number of frames per second (fps). Standard TV-quality video uses a frame rate of 30 frames per second to create the effect of smooth movement. For the Web, a frame rate of 15 or even 10 fps is more appropriate and still capable of producing fairly smooth video playback. For "talking head" and other low-motion subjects, even lower frame rates may be satisfactory. Commercial Internet broadcasts are routinely done as low as 0.5, 0.25, or even 0.05 frames per second (resulting in a slideshow effect rather than moving video).

Quality

Many video-editing applications allow you to set the overall quality of the video image. The degree to which the compression algorithms crunch and discard data is determined by the target quality setting. A setting of Low or Medium results in fairly high compression and is appropriate for web delivery. Frame rate and quality are often traded off in different degrees in relation to each other, depending on the application, to reduce bandwidth requirements.

Color bit depth

The size of the video is affected by the number of pixel colors in each frame. Reducing the number of colors from 24- to 8-bit color will drastically reduce the file size of your video, just as it does for still images. Of course, you also sacrifice image quality.

Data rate (bit rate)

This is the rate at which data must be transferred in order for the video to play smoothly without interruption. The data rate (also called "bit rate") for a movie is measured in kilobytes per second (K/sec or Kbps). It can be calculated by dividing the size of the file (in K) by the length of the movie (in seconds). So, for example, a highly compressed movie that is 1900K (1.9 MB) and 40 seconds long has a data rate of 47.5K/sec.

For streaming media in particular, a file's data rate is more important than its total size. This is due to the fact that the total bandwidth available for delivery may be severely limited, particularly over a dial-up connection. For example, even an ISDN line at 128 Kbps offers a capacity to deliver only 16K of data per second.

Compression

Digital video wouldn't be possible without methods for compressing the vast amounts of data necessary to describe sound and frame images. Video files can be compressed in a number of ways. This section looks at a variety of compression schemes and introduces the methods they use for achieving compression rates. Understanding your options can help you make better decisions for optimizing your video files.

Lossless Versus Lossy Compression

Compression can be "lossless," which means no information is lost and the final file is identical to the original.

Most compression schemes use forms of *lossy compression*. Lossy compression sacrifices some data from the file to achieve much higher compression rates. Lossy compression schemes, such as MPEG, use complicated algorithms that toss out data for sound and image detail that is not discernible to the human ear or eye. The decompressed file is extremely similar in character to the original, yet is not identical. This is similar to the way JPEG handles still images.

Spatial Versus Temporal Compression

Spatial (or *intraframe*) compression takes place on each individual frame of the video, compressing the pixel information as though it were a still image.

Temporal (or *interframe*) compression happens over a series of frames and takes advantage of areas of the image that remain unchanged from frame to frame, throwing out data for repeated pixels.

Temporal compression relies on the placement of *key frames* interspersed throughout the frames sequence. The key frames are used as masters against which the following frames (called delta frames) are compared. It is recommended that a key frame be placed once every second; therefore, if you have a frame rate of 15 fps, set your key frame rate once every 15 frames.

Videos without a lot of motion, such as talking head clips, take the best advantage of temporal compression. Videos with pans and other motion are compressed less efficiently.

Video Codecs

There are a number of *codecs* (compression/decompression algorithms) that can be used to compress video files for the Web. Many of these codecs can be applied to several different file formats (discussed in the next section of this chapter).

Video-editing software packages often offer a long list of codecs in their compressor list options. Here we focus on just those that are relevant to video intended for web delivery.

Radius Cinepak

Cinepak provides decent compression/decompression rates and is compatible with both QuickTime or AVI formats. It employs both spatial and temporal compression and a lossy compression scheme at lower quality levels. Low to medium quality settings will produce acceptable quality video. It is also well supported, so if you want your video to be viewable by the widest possible audience, choose Cinepak.

Sorenson

The Sorenson Video codec was designed for low-bandwidth applications and is capable of producing files with lower data rates (if you select the Limit Data Rate option) than Cinepak while maintaining excellent quality. It is the ideal codec for web delivery, with some concessions. First, because it uses complicated compression algorithms, it requires a lot of processing power and may not run smoothly on older machines. It also requires that users install Quick-Time Version 3 or higher. While growing in popularity, it will be a while before it is completely risk-free.

Intel Indeo

The Indeo codec provides compression rates similar to Cinepak by the use of spatial and temporal compression, with lossy compression at low quality levels. Its drawbacks are that it does not maintain quality at data rates as low as Cinepak, and it requires high-end machines to perform at its best.

Animation

If your video clip is all computer-generated graphical imagery (i.e., not sourced from videotape), you may want to try the Animation compressor. Depending on the type of image, the Cinepak codec may work just as well (or better) for these types of files.

MPEG

The MPEG codec can only be used when the final video file will be in MPEG format (it is not compatible with other file types). It uses a lossy compression scheme (although it may be lossless at high-quality settings) and spatial and temporal compression. MPEG offers the best compression possible, but MPEGs are not yet as widely supported on the Web as other video formats.

Video File Formats

As with audio, in the early days of the Web, adding video to a web page meant using one of the currently available video formats (such as QuickTime or AVI) and linking it to a page for download. The evolution of streaming media has changed that, and now adding video content like movie trailers, news broadcasts, even live programming to a web site is much more practical and widespread.

This section looks at the video formats that are most common for web delivery.

QuickTime Movie (.mov)

QuickTime is a highly versatile and well-supported media format. While originally developed as a video format, it has evolved into a container format capable of storing all sorts of media (still images, audio, video, Flash, and SMIL presentations). For the complete list of file formats supported by QuickTime, see *http://www.apple.com/quicktime/specifications.html*.

QuickTime, a system extension that makes it possible to view audio/video information on a computer, was introduced by Apple Computer in 1991. Although developed for the Macintosh, it is also supported on PCs via QuickTime for Windows. QuickTime has grown to be the industry standard for multimedia development, and most hardware and software offer QuickTime support. Both Netscape

Navigator 3.0+ and Internet Explorer 3.0+ come with QuickTime plug-in players, so the majority of web readers are able to view QuickTime movies right in the browser.

Streaming

QuickTime movies can be streamed using a number of streaming server packages, including Apple's QuickTime Server for Mac OS X or its open source Darwin Streaming Server for Unix. To give the illusion of streaming from an HTTP server (pseudo-streaming), create FastStart Quicktime movies, which begin playing right away and continue playing as the file downloads.

Creating QuickTime movies

You can take care of rudimentary video editing, such as deleting and rearranging, right in Apple's free QuickTime Player. The QuickTime Pro version ($29.95) offers more features and is sufficient for most basic tasks. For advanced video editing, use a professional video editing tool such as Adobe Premier or AfterEffects (most video editors support QuickTime). You may also use a file converter, such as Cleaner from Terran Interactive (*http://www.terran.com*) to convert existing files to QuickTime format.

Other video editing applications for the Mac include iMovie (which ships free on newer Macintoshes) and Final Cut Pro, a more professional video editing program.

An important step to remember when saving a movie is to make it *self-contained*. This process resolves all data references and prepares the file to go out on the Internet on its own. You will also be asked to pick a codec (QuickTime supports several). Cinepak is a good general purpose codec; Sorenson is more efficient but not as well supported.

Reference movies

Another interesting feature of Version 2.0 and higher of the QuickTime plug-in is its support for reference movies. Reference movies are used as pointers to alternate versions (or "tracks") of a movie, each optimized for a different connection speed. When a user downloads the reference movie, the plug-in ensures that the best track for the current connection speed is played.

You could also save a version of your movie that doesn't use the Sorenson codec in the reference file. This movie will play for users who don't have the latest plug-in version, ensuring backwards compatibility.

For more information

The process for adding QuickTime to a web page is discussed later in this chapter. For general information on QuickTime, see Apple's site at *http://www.apple.com/ quicktime/*. For complete information on all aspects of QuickTime creation and delivery, I recommend the book *QuickTime for the Web: A Hands-On Guide for Webmasters, Site Designers, and HTML Authors* by the folks at Apple Computer, Inc. (Morgan Kaufmann, 2000). It is an excellent reference if you are serious about QuickTime for adding multimedia elements to your site.

The following summarizes the QuickTime format:

Good for	Delivering video to a wide audience (very good support).
Delivery	True streaming via RTP or RTSP (using QuickTime Server on Mac OS X Server or the open source Darwin Streaming Server on Unix and NT), pseudo-streaming on HTTP servers, download.
Creation tools	Most video editing and conversion tools support QuickTime, or use Apple's basic editing tool QuickTime Pro for $29.95.
Player	QuickTime plug-in (part of Netscape Navigator and Internet Explorer) for viewing within a web browser or QuickTime Player (standalone utility).

RealMedia (.rm)

RealMedia is the industry standard streaming media format. RealNetworks (which used to be Progressive Networks) first launched its streaming video capabilities in Version 3.0 of its RealMedia line of products (of which RealAudio is the star component). RealMedia files (*.rm*) are viewed using RealPlayer 3 and higher. The wide distribution of RealPlayer and a proven track record of effective playback have made RealNetworks' products the de facto standard for adding streaming media to a web site.

The components of the RealMedia system (RealPlayer for playback, RealServer for serving simultaneous streams, and RealProducer for creating *.rm* files) are the same as for RealAudio. The descriptions of each component as discussed in Chapter 24 apply to video as well. RealMedia movies are encoded using a proprietary codec built into RealProducer and RealPlayer.

For more information, visit the RealNetworks site at *http://www.realnetworks.com*. For consumer-oriented information and downloads, see *http://www.real.com*.

The following summarizes the RealAudio format:

Good for	Long-playing video clips and live broadcasts to large numbers of people.
Delivery	Streaming (via RTSP), pseudo-streaming (via HTTP).
Creation tools	One of the RealNetworks encoders (such as RealSystem Producer Plus) or a third-party tool such as Cleaner 5 from Terran Interactive.
Player	Freely available RealPlayer, Commercial RealPlayer Plus (with added features), RealPlayer plug-in in Netscape Navigator and Internet Explorer.

Windows Media (.wmv or .asf)

Windows Media is the new standard for audio and video, created by Microsoft and therefore very closely integrated with the Windows OS. The Windows Media Player is capable of playing Microsoft's proprietary Windows Media Video (*.wmv*) and Advanced Streaming Format (*.asf*), as well as a number of other formats such as AVI, MPEG, MP3, and QuickTime.

The Windows Media system is also comprised of Windows Media Server (which runs only on Windows NT/2000) and tools for creating *.wmv* and *.asf* files (Windows Media Author and Windows Media Encoder, which are both Windows only). These components, as well as the methods for adding Windows Media to a web page, are discussed in Chapter 24.

Windows Media movies are encoded using the proprietary Windows Media Video codec (currently in Version 8) designed especially for the Windows Media system. Users must have the Windows Media Player 8 in order to play movies encoded with the Version 8 codec. Use Version 7 if you don't want to force your users to upgrade (or if the processing power of your PC cannot handle the demands of the Version 8 encoder).

For more information about Window Media, visit Microsoft's site at *http://www. microsoft.com/windows/windowsmedia/*.

The following summarizes the Windows Media format:

Good for	Long-playing video and live broadcasts.
Delivery	Streaming, download.
Creation tools	Windows Media Encoder for converting to Windows Media format, Windows Media Author for creating synchronized multimedia presentations. See the Windows Media site for a complete list of creation tools at *http://www.microsoft.com/Windows/windowsmedia/en/ overview/components.asp.*
Player	Media Player (shipped with Windows OS), available as download for the Mac as well as a variety of handheld devices that support Windows CE.

AVI (.avi)

AVI (which stands for Audio/Video Interleaved) was introduced by Microsoft in 1992 as the standard movie format to work with its Video for Windows (VFW) multimedia architecture for Windows 95. The AVI format has been replaced by the more robust Windows Media as the standard media format for Windows. Macintosh users can view AVI files using the QuickTime player. In AVI files, the audio and video information is interleaved every frame, which in theory produces smoother playback.

With the growing (and well-deserved) popularity of streaming media systems, AVI movies are not as common as they once were for web distribution. More often, they serve as the high-quality source file for the video which is then converted into a more web-friendly format.

The following summarizes the AVI format:

Good for	Short web video clips, high quality video source files.
Delivery	Download.
Creation tools	Most video editing tools support AVI.
Player	Windows Media, QuickTime, (or Video for Windows on older machines).

MPEG (.mpg or .mpeg)

MPEG is a set of multimedia standards created by the Moving Picture Experts Group. It supports three types of information: video, audio, and streaming (which, in the context of MPEG compression, is synchronized video and audio). MPEG was initially popular as a web format because it was the only format that could be produced on the Unix system.

MPEG files offer extremely high compression rates with little loss of quality. They accomplish this using a lossy compression technique that strips out data that is not discernible to the human ear or eye.

There are a number of MPEG standards: MPEG-1 was originally developed for video transfer at VHS quality; MPEG-2 is a higher-quality standard that was developed for television broadcast; other MPEG specs that address other needs (such as MPEG-4 and -7) are currently in development. MPEGs can be compressed using one of three schemes, Layer-I, -II, or -III. The complexity of the coding (and therefore the processor power needed to encode and decode) increases at each level. Due to this complexity, you need special encoding tools to produce MPEG videos.

MPEG-1 (which uses the *.mpg* or *.mpeg* suffix) is the most appropriate format for web purposes. MPEG-2 files are rare except in broadcast studios and on DVDs and are not well suited for web delivery.

To learn more about MPEG, visit the MPEG web site (*http://www.mpeg.org*).

The following summarizes the MPEG movie format:

Good for	High-quality video.
Delivery	Streaming, download.
Creation tools	Cleaner 5 by Terran Interactive (*http://www.terran.com/cleaner/*).
Player	Windows Media Player, QuickTime Player.

Which Format to Choose

To deliver long-playing video (like a full movie trailer) or live video broadcasts, you should definitely use one of the streaming media solutions (RealMedia, Windows Media, or streaming QuickTime). Which you choose will come down to the individual requirements of your site. If you expect heavy traffic and many simultaneous streams, definitely invest in a dedicated true streaming system.

If you have just a few short clips to share with a limited number of visitors, you may be able to get away with pseudo-streaming RealMedia or FastStart QuickTime movies on your regular web server.

Since all streaming video formats are capable of supporting multiple file formats, are fairly stable, and feature well but not universally distributed players and plugins, the decision will likely come down to which server matches your budget or expertise.

Adding Video to an HTML Document

This section looks at the ways video files can be linked to or embedded within an HTML document.

A Simple Link

Like audio, downloadable video files (AVI, MPEG, and QuickTime) can be linked to HTML documents using the standard `<a>` tag:

```
<A HREF="video.mov">Check out the video (1.3MB)</A>
```

Video

When the user clicks on the link, the browser looks at the file type (as defined in the filename suffix) and launches an external player application or uses a plug-in to play the movie right in the browser window. Which player it uses depends on how that user has the browser configured, so it is out of the control of the web page designer.

Streaming Video

As in audio, streaming media in the RealMedia (*.rm*) and streaming Windows Media (*.asf*) formats are added to web pages via linked or embedded reference files (also called metafiles). The process, covered in detail at the end of Chapter 24, is exactly the same for video as for audio. See the audio chapter for more thorough coverage.

RealMedia

In brief, to link to a RealMedia movie, create a link to a RealMedia metafile (*.ram*) as shown in this example:

```
<A HREF="movie.ram">Link to the streaming movie</A>
```

The metafile is a small text-only file that contains only the URL for the RealMedia file (suffix *.rm*). When the user clicks the link, the browser accesses the metafile, which launches the player and passes it the URL of the actual media file:

```
pnm://domainname.com/song.rm
```

To embed a RealMedia movie on a web page, use the following code:

```
<OBJECT ID="spacestress"
   CLASSID="clsid:CFCDAA03-8BE4-11cf-B84B-0020AFBBCCFA"
   HEIGHT="160" WIDTH="320" BORDER="0">
<PARAM NAME="SRC" VALUE="realmedia/spacestress.rpm">
<PARAM NAME="CONTROLS" VALUE="all">

   <EMBED SRC="realmedia/oakshoes.rpm" HEIGHT="150" WIDTH="250"
   AUTOSTART="false" CONTROLS="all" BORDER="0">

</OBJECT>
```

The value of the classid should be copied exactly as it is shown here as this points to the RealMedia player. Note that when embedding, the metafile suffix is *.rpm* (rather than *.ram*).

Windows Media

To link to a Windows Media Video file for download and playback, create a link directly to the video file:

```
<A HREF="movie.wmv">See the movie</A>
```

To link to a streaming Windows Media file for unicasting (a single stream triggered by a user request), make a link to an active stream redirector file (*.asx*), that works like a RealMedia metafile:

```
<A HREF="streamingmovie.asx">See a streaming movie</A>
```

The content of the *.asx* file looks like this:

```
<ASX version="3">
   <Entry>
       <ref href="path/streamingmovie.asf" />
   </Entry>
</ASX>
```

For multicasting (a publisher-controlled broadcast of a single stream that is viewed by many users simultaneously), it is recommended that you generate code using the tools and wizards provided by the Windows Media Administrator program. For more information, see the Windows Media Technologies page located at *http:// www.microsoft.com/Windows/windowsmedia/serve/basics_WM4.asp.*

Embedded QuickTime Movies

In addition to simply linking to a QuickTime movie, you can also place the player right in the web page like an image using the <embed> tag. The QuickTime plug-in is required to play *.mov* files inline, but it is bundled with the two major browsers, making it a relatively safe way to put a video right on a page. The method listed here is supported by Internet Explorer 3+ and Navigator 3+.

A simple <embed> tag looks like this:

```
<EMBED SRC="cool.mov" AUTOPLAY=false WIDTH=160 HEIGHT=136
       CONTROLLER="true">
```

In this example, the actual height of the movie is 120 pixels, but I've added 16 pixels (for a total of 136) so the QuickTime control strip can display below the movie.

Browser <embed> attributes

The <embed> tag has a number of standard attributes that control various aspects of playback and display. These attributes are recognized by every browser that supports the <embed> tag and are supported by the QuickTime plug-in as well.

src=*url*
> *Required.* This attribute points to the video file you want to play.

width=*number*
height=*number*
> *Required.* These attributes set the width and height in number of pixels for the video frame. It is important that the values of width and height be at least 2, even when the player is set to be hidden. A value of less than 2 results in crashes in some browsers. Add 16 pixels to the height of your movie if you have also set the controller tag to true, so that the Quick-Time controller strip has room to display.

hidden=true|false
> When set to true, the plug-in player is not displayed. Be sure that the height and width are set to at least 2 even if the player is hidden to prevent crashes. This attribute is listed here for thoroughness' sake, but it is more appropriate for QuickTime audio (used as a background sound) than for video.

Video

`pluginspage="http://www.apple.com/quicktime/download/"`

> This provides a link to a source to acquire the QuickTime plug-in if the browser can't find it on the system.

`loop=true|false|palindrome`

> `true` causes the video to loop continuously. `false` (the default) causes the video to play through once. `palindrome` makes the video play through, then play in reverse, then play through, continuously.

`href=url`

> This attribute makes your movie a link to another page.

`align=left|right|top|bottom`

> Sets the alignment of the movie on the page (similar to an image).

`border=number`

> Sets the width of the border around the plug-in.

`hspace=number`
`vspace=number`

> Holds space to the left and right (`hspace`) and above and below (`vspace`) the plug-in when positioned with the `align` attribute.

`name=text`

> Assigns a name to the embedded object for use with a scripting language.

`type=MIME type`

> Specifies the MIME type of the file (such as `video/quicktime` or `image/x-quicktime`) if you aren't sure the web server will provide it (it usually does).

Special QuickTime <embed> attributes

There are dozens of specialized attributes that are recognized by the QuickTime plug-in. The list below includes only a few of the most common. A complete list is available online at *http://www.apple.com/quicktime/authoring/embed.html*.

`autoplay=true|false`

> The video will start playing automatically if this attribute is set to `true`. The default depends on the user's settings, but it is generally `false` (meaning the user will have to start the video with the Play button).

`controller=true|false`

> A control bar for the video will be visible when this is set to `true` (or by default). Although it is possible to turn off the controls, it is usually advisable to leave them visible and available for use.

`volume=percent (0-300)`

> By default, audio is played at full volume (100%). You can set it lower to compensate for an especially loud audio track. Setting it higher than 100% is discouraged because it causes distortion and lessens audio quality.

`playeveryframe=true|false`

> When set to `false` (the default), you allow the video to skip frames in order to ensure smooth playback. Do not set this attribute to `true` if you have audio with your movie as it will be muted during playback.

The dynsrc Attribute

Internet Explorer allows you to embed a video on a page using the nonstandard dynsrc attribute in the <img> tag. Note: This tag does not work with any version of Netscape Navigator, so using it may alienate a portion of your audience.

An <img> tag with a dynsrc attribute is placed in the document like an ordinary <img> tag. The dynsrc attribute replaces the traditional src attribute, but otherwise you can use all the same <img> attributes such as alignment, horizontal and vertical gutter space, etc., as follows:

```
<IMG DYNSRC="waycool.mov" ALIGN=right HSPACE=12>
```

The <img dynsrc> tag can also take a number of specialized attributes for controlling video display:

controls
> Adds playback controls for the video.

dynsrc=*url*
> Provides the URL for the video file to be displayed on the page.

loop=*value*
> Sets the number of times to play the video. It can be a number value or set to infinite.

start=fileopen, mouseover
> Specifies when to play the video. By default, it begins playing as soon as it's downloaded (fileopen). You can set it to start when the mouse pointer is over the movie area (mouseover). If you combine them (separated by a comma), the movie plays once when it's downloaded, then again every time the user mouses over it.

For Further Reading

The following titles provide information on developing video for the Web:

e-Video: Producing Internet Video as Broadband Technologies Converge (with CD-ROM), H. Peter Alesso (Addison Wesley Professional, 2000).

QuickTime for the Web: A Hands-On Guide for Webmasters, Site Designers, and HTML Authors, Apple Computer, Inc. (Morgan Kaufmann, 2000).

Web Developer.com® Guide to Streaming Multimedia, Jose Alvear (John Wiley & Sons, 1998).

Inside Windows Media : Learn to Combine Video, Audio, and Still Images to Create Streaming Media, Microsoft Windows Media Technologies Team, Microsoft Corporation (Que, 1999).

Video

CHAPTER 26

Flash and Shockwave

Flash is a ground-breaking multimedia format developed by Macromedia. Flash gives you the ability to create full-screen animation, interactive graphics, and integrated audio clips, all at remarkably small file sizes. Its magic lies in the fact that it is a vector-based format (rather than bitmap), resulting in extremely compact files well suited for web delivery. Vector graphics define objects with mathematical formulas that require far less data than describing each individual pixel of a bitmap image.

Flash began its life as FutureSplash, an animated vector technology by a company named FutureWave. Macromedia acquired FutureSplash in 1997 and developed it into the robust multimedia tool it is today.

Flash movies (*.swf*) are created using Macromedia's Flash authoring tool. Flash (the application) includes tools for illustration, animation, interaction sequencing, sound editing, and a scripting engine. Flash 5, the latest version as of this writing, offers an improved interface and advanced scripting capabilities (ActionScript), making Flash one of the most versatile and powerful formats for web multimedia. For more information (and to download a demo copy), visit Macromedia's site at *http://www.flash.com*.

Shockwave for Director is another multimedia format from Macromedia that allows rich CD-ROM-like multimedia interfaces created in Director to be published on the Web. Director is a powerful tool for synchronizing video, animation, and sound into a complex interactive presentation. While Director Shockwave movies are much smaller than their Director counterparts, they tend to be much larger than Flash movies and are therefore not as well suited for web delivery. In its favor, Shockwave movies can take advantage of the sophisticated Lingo scripting language for complicated interactions (such as games) and presentations. They can also contain QuickTime movies, MIDI audio, and other formats that Flash doesn't support.

This chapter looks at both of these multimedia formats, but it focuses on Flash primarily because it is the most popular and appropriate format for the Web.

Using Flash on Web Pages

Flash movies can be placed *on* a web page, or they can be used *as* a web page. Moreover, with the advanced scripting capabilities introduced in Flash 5, the uses for Flash movies are limited only by imagination. Some possibilities include:

Splash page animation
Interactive navigation toolbars
Animated ad banners
Interactive and zoomable maps
Interactive games
Complex applications (such as shopping), tied into a database on the server
Interactive forms
A whole web site interface, taking the place of traditional HTML pages
Cartoons
Music videos
A "jukebox" interface for playing MP3 files

While Flash introduces a number of significant improvements over what can be accomplished using just HTML, there are a few drawbacks to using Flash as well. Let's look at the pros and cons of using Flash on a site.

Advantages

Many aspects of the Flash file format make it ideal for adding interactive content to web pages:

- **File sizes are small**. As mentioned earlier, Flash's vector format means small files and quick downloads.

- **It is scalable**. Flash images and animations can be resized with no loss of detail, making it easy to fill the whole browser window with a Flash interface without adding to the file size. Flash can be used to create static images, such as maps, where zooming in to view the image in finer detail is desirable.

- **Image quality is high**. Real-time anti-aliasing smooths the edges of graphics and text, regardless of the display size. Users can zoom in on vector graphics with no loss of image quality.

- **It uses streaming technology**. Flash files start playing quickly and continue to play as they download, so they can be pseudo-streamed from an HTTP server. In addition, RealNetworks' RealPlayer 8 can play Flash 3 and 4 files if they have been properly configured for true streaming. RealPlayer 6 and 7 can only play Flash 2. In all cases, the audio track must be contained in a separate RealAudio file (Flash 5 makes it easy to create both files). Flash content can also be contained in QuickTime 5 files and streamed from a QuickTime server.

- **It uses integrated sound**. Flash is a good way to bring background sound and user-triggered sound effects to a web site. RealFlash (described later in the chapter) enables Flash animation to be synchronized with high-quality streaming audio.

- **The Flash format is well supported.** The Flash player required to play Flash files is available for Windows and Mac OS platforms. The Flash player comes installed on Windows machines with Windows 98 or ME. Netscape Navigator 4.06+ and Internet Explorer 5+ contain the Flash player. The Flash format is also natively supported by WebTV. Alternatively, Flash content can be played via ActiveX controls (for IE on Windows) or with the Flash Player Java Edition (on any Java-enabled browser). Macromedia estimates that 95% or more of users are able to view Flash content. (See "Plug-in player required" under Disadvantages for the darker side of Flash support.)

- **It is scriptable.** Flash uses the ActionScript scripting language for controlling Flash behaviors. ActionScript is discussed in the next section of this chapter.

  In addition, you can use JavaScript commands from the HTML file to control a Flash element on a page. The reverse is true as well; by using FSCommands in the Flash movie, you can activate JavaScript commands from within the Flash file to control web page elements. FSCommands are not supported on the Macintosh platform in any browser.

- **It has an open format.** Macromedia has made the Flash file format publicly available, which means that other software developers can build Flash support into their applications. One of the first is Adobe's LiveMotion (a tool for creating interactive buttons and animated objects), which saves its files in Flash format to be played by the Flash player.

Disadvantages

And on the downside . . .

- **A plug-in player is required.** Standard Flash files require the Flash player to be installed on the user's machine. Although this may seem like a small hurdle, particularly since the Shockwave and Flash players are some of the most popular and universally available plug-ins, the words "plug-in required" are enough to make many clients say "no way" without a second thought.

  To make matters more confusing, there are now five versions of Flash movies with their respective players available, so it is still an issue making sure your users have the very latest player version if you are using the very latest Flash features.

  To its credit, Macromedia has anticipated such resistance and has responded with some strategies. First, the Publish feature in Flash 4 and higher (previously the Aftershock utility) makes it easy to generate code that detects the specific player version.

  Additionally, there are alternatives. Flash Player Java Edition enables Flash files to play on any Java-enabled browser. The Flash authoring tool also allows you to export your animation as an animated GIF, although you may need to optimize it in a dedicated GIF animation utility.

- **Content is lost on nongraphical browsers.** Using Flash movies for document headlines and navigation introduces the same problems as using static graphics in place of text. People who cannot view your Flash animation (or even an alternative GIF image) will not be able to read your content. alt text helps, but is limited. In addition, information in a Flash movie cannot be indexed or searched.

- **It always starts on the initial page of the movie.** Users cannot link to a certain page or scene within a Flash movie. Links can lead users only to the first page of the Flash movie.

- **Unix support is limited.** Although there is a Netscape plug-in available for Linux Red Hat 6 and higher and Solaris, other Unix users are out of luck when it comes to viewing Flash files. The Flash Player Java Edition is one solution to this problem. There is no Unix version of the Flash authoring tool.

- **Printing may be problematic.** There may be problems printing Flash content, particularly from a Netscape browser on a Mac.

- **Expensive authoring software is required.** You currently need Macromedia's Flash software to create Flash files. Flash 5 costs $399 ($149 to upgrade from a previous version) as of this writing.

Flash Power Tools

You can do some pretty nifty things with Flash using its built-in features right out of the box. For many users, this is plenty. But Flash isn't just about animation and sound. Using its advanced scripting features and add-on software, Flash movies can be programmed for complex interactive functionality and even serve as the front end for dynamically generated content.

ActionScript

Flash 5 uses the robust ActionScript scripting language for adding behaviors and advanced interactivity to Flash movies. ActionScript is an object-oriented language based on a version of JavaScript (the ECMA-262 spec, for those who need to know), so although it shares characteristics with the JavaScript we know and love, the two are not 100% compatible.

ActionScript, which was introduced in Flash 4, evolved into a much more powerful and useful tool in Flash 5. Not only is it responsible for controlling basic playback and user-triggered behaviors, it also enables Flash to integrate with XML, HTML, and other parts of the web page. The latest ActionScript version features complex math operations that allow advanced programming functionality, such as 3-D modeling. If you are set on becoming a Flash power-user, you will definitely want to learn ActionScript.

For more information on ActionScript, read *ActionScript: The Definitive Guide* by Colin Moock (O'Reilly, 2001).

Macromedia Generator 2

Macromedia Generator 2 is a development tool and server application that composites, produces, and delivers web graphics on the fly. It is integrated with Flash but is a separate commercial product. The web graphics can be GIFs, JPEGs, PNGs, imagemaps, QuickTime Flash movies, animated GIFs, or other Flash movies. Some uses include automatically updated charts and graphs based on real-time information (such as stock information or sports scores), regularly changing bitmap images (such as weather maps), or personalized content based on user input.

To use Generator 2, you create Generator templates (*.swt*) in Flash that separate the actual visual content on the page from the design structure of the page. The dynamically generated content (such as charts, images, personalized messages) can be switched out and delivered to the Flash player either immediately or at scheduled times.

There are two versions: the Enterprise Edition ($2999) and the Developer Edition ($999). As the price suggests, the Enterprise Edition is a more powerful solution, offering better performance, scalability, and administrative tools. It is appropriate for large corporate sites that serve millions of visitors. The Developer Edition brings the same basic functionality to smaller scale sites. For more information on Generator 2, see the Macromedia site at *http://www.macromedia.com/software/generator/*.

Creating Flash Movies

Full-featured Flash movies are best created using Macromedia's Flash software. Obviously, it is beyond the scope of this book to teach the ins and outs of Flash authoring, so I recommend using the tutorials that come with the software as well as support documents provided by Macromedia (*http://www.macromedia.com/support/flash/*). For an incredibly thorough book of tutorials and reference material, check out *Flash 5 Bible* by Robert Reinhardt and Jon Warren Lentz (Hungry Minds, 2001).

File Formats

The Flash authoring tool saves information about a movie in a *.fla* source file (also called a "Flash document" or "Flash editor document"). The *.fla* file contains all the separate elements that make up the movie and its timeline information in a fully editable format.

When the movie is ready to go on the Web, it must be exported to *.swf* format. The suffix originally stood for "Shockwave Flash," but in the face of confusion with Macromedia's Shockwave for Director format, Macromedia has changed its tune and now translates *.swf* to "Small Web Format."

This new moniker is accurate. In the export process, the information from the original layered *.fla* file is flattened down to one layer and one timeline. The resulting file packs a lot of multimedia punch in a size that is appropriate for the Web.

Flash Interface Basics

As noted earlier, it is beyond the scope of this book to teach Flash. However, it is useful to be generally acquainted with the Flash authoring environment. Figure 26-1 shows the core features of the Flash interface as seen on a Macintosh (the Windows version is nearly the same). The following is a brief introduction to the way Flash handles multimedia content.

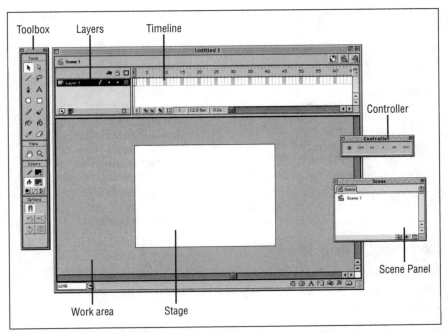

Toolbox   Layers   Timeline

Controller

Scene Panel

Work area   Stage

Figure 26-1: The Flash interface

Stage

The Stage is the area where you compose and preview the movie.

Layers

The elements on a timeline may be stored on separate layers (similar to layers in image editing tools). Layers in Flash control the arrangement of objects from background to foreground, support masking, enable motion and shape tweening, and contain guide elements, frame labels, and actions.

Scenes

Flash movies need only have one scene, but smart developers use scenes to better organize content. Scenes will play in sequential order by default. They may also be scripted to play based on user input (called an Action), like a rollover or a button click.

Timeline

The Timeline is where you control the timing of the animation and assemble the elements from separate layers.

Frames

Like film, Flash movies divide lengths of time into individual frames. A keyframe is a frame in which you define a change in the animation. Static frames reflect no change and merely repeat the content of the prior frame. Animation effects are added by changing content over a series of frames. The most efficient (both in terms of production time and processing power) method for adding animation is *tweening*, in which you create the beginning and end keyframe images and allow Flash to automatically create all the frame "in between."

Library

The Library is where you store all imported items (such as images and audio) and *symbols*, Flash objects that you want to use repeatedly in the same movie (such as a button shape with its various interactive states). When you place a symbol on the Stage, you create an *instance* of that symbol.

Controller

The Controller contains the typical buttons for playing, pausing, and stepping through the frames of a movie when previewing it on the Stage.

Toolbox

The Toolbox contains all the tools for drawing, painting, selecting, viewing, and modifying artwork. Additional tools are available in individual floating panels that can be shown, hidden, or collapsed into a small bar until needed.

Optimizing Flash Movies

There are a number of measures you can take up front to make your *.swf* compress as small as it can. The following are just a few tips:

- Keep your artwork as simple as possible.

- Remove unnecessary points in vector drawings (choose "Optimize" from the Modify menu).

- Limit the number of gradients (choose flat color fills instead).

- Limit the number of fonts and amount of text.

- Use "tweens" and motion guide layers for animation rather than extra keyframes.

- Minimize bitmap usage and avoid setting bitmap images in motion.

- Use symbols and nested symbols whenever possible. However, do not allow symbols to be too large as they can slow down streaming playback.

- Optimize imported media (images, audio) prior to placement in Flash.

- Use MP3 compression for audio whenever possible. It is recommended to save the audio in MP3 before importing, rather than importing raw WAV or AIFF files.

It is a good idea to use Flash's Test Movie or Test Scene functions to check your movie's performance. The Bandwidth Profiler simulates various connection speeds. You can also generate size reports to check the size of media components within the movie (it may reveal elements that could be optimized better).

Configuring the Server

Although no special server software is necessary to serve standard Flash files, you will need to configure your server to recognize a new MIME type. The specific syntax for configuration varies for different servers, so coordinate with your system administrator and see Macromedia's site for further support information. The following information will suit the needs of most servers:

- Type/subtype: `application/x-shockwave-flash`
- File extension for Flash: *.swf*

Adding Flash to a Web Page

Flash movies are generally added to web pages using a combination of the `<object>` and `<embed>` tags with parameters and attributes for controlling display and playback. Both tags are used in order to accommodate the incompatibilities of Internet Explorer and Netscape Navigator. Internet Explorer on Windows uses the `<object>` tag, which enables it to automatically download the ActiveX controls for playing Flash media. Navigator (on Windows, Mac, Linux, and Solaris) and Internet Explorer on the Mac understand the `<embed>` element for Flash placement.

You can either generate the HTML using Flash's Publish feature or write it out by hand. This section takes a look at both methods.

Using Flash Publish Settings

The easiest way to get your SWF files on the Web is to let Flash do the work for you. Flash 4 introduced the "Publish" feature for exporting movies along with automatically-generated HTML for placing it in an HTML document. The built-in Publish function replaces the AfterShock utility used with previous versions of Flash.

The Publish Settings dialog box also allows you to select the export format of the movie (whether it's to be a Flash movie, Generator template, static graphic format, and so on) and control the variables of the export. For now, we'll focus on the HTML settings that are relevant to placing an SWF movie on a page.

The most welcomed feature of the HTML Publish Settings is the collection of pre-formatted templates that generates `<object>` and `<embed>` tags tailored to specific uses. The "Flash Only (Default)" template generates bare minimum code. Other templates generate HTML code with extra functionality, including:

- Plug-in version detection (*Ad 3 Banner, Ad 4 Banner, Ad 5 Banner,* and *Ad Any Banner*)
- Integration with JavaScript (*Flash with FSCommand*)
- Integration with Generator 2 (*Generator Ad Any Banner, Generator Image Output, Generator Only (Default),* and *Generator QuickTime*)
- Creation of a static image for use as an imagemap (*Image Map*)
- Java Player targeting (*Java Player*)
- Display of QuickTime Flash movies (*QuickTime*)

The HTML Publish Settings also allow you to fine-tune various parameters and attributes in the code with simple checkbox and menu options. Upon export, the resulting HTML file can then be brought into an HTML editor or authoring tool for integration with the rest of the page or for additional manual tweaking.

Adding Flash to an HTML Document

To code your page so it is accessible to the maximum number of users, use a combination of the <embed> and <object> tags. Explanations of each of these options follow. Note that technologies change quickly and Macromedia revises their tagging instructions from time to time. Consult the Macromedia support pages (*http://www.macromedia.com/support/director/internet.html*) for updates.

The <embed> tag

The basic <embed> tag is as follows:

```
<EMBED SRC="path/file.swf" WIDTH=x HEIGHT=x
PLUGINSPAGE="http://www.macromedia.com/shockwave/download/index.cgi?P1_
Prod_Version=ShockwaveFlash">
</EMBED>
```

The **width** and **height** values are mandatory and specify the dimensions of the image or movie in pixels. Note that you can also specify the dimensions in percentages (corresponding to the percentage of the browser window the movie fills). The **pluginspage** attribute provides a URL to the page where the user can download the Flash player if it is not found on the user's computer (use the exact URL shown in the example code). It is a recommended attribute, but not mandatory.

There are a number of attributes (some Flash-specific) that can be added within the <embed> tag:

ID=*text or*
NAME=*text*

> This assigns a name to the movie, which is necessary if it is going to be called from a JavaScript or within a form. It is general practice to use the same name as the *.swf* file with the suffix omitted.

QUALITY=low|autolow|autohigh|high|medium|best

> This attribute controls the anti-aliasing quality. autolow starts the animation at low quality (aliased) and switches to high quality (anti-aliased) if the user's computer is fast enough. Conversely, autohigh starts the animation in high quality mode and reverts to normal quality if the computer is too slow. high anti-aliases the animation regardless of computer speed. medium (new in Flash 5) displays more smoothly than low, but not as well as high. best goes further than high by also anti-aliasing all bitmaps. It is the most processor-intensive option.

LOOP=true|false

> Specifies whether the movie plays in a continuous loop. The default is true.

PLAY=true|false

> If play is set to true, the movie will begin playing automatically. A setting of false requires the user to initiate the movie. The default is true.

MENU=true|false

> Right-clicking in Windows or Control-clicking on a Mac on a Flash movie brings up a pop-up menu of playback controls. Setting menu to false reduces the choices in the pop-up right-click menu to "About Flash Player,"

eliminating the playback settings of zoom, quality, play, loop, rewind, forward, back, and print.

`BGCOLOR=#`*`rrggbb`*

Use this setting to override the background color of the Flash movie frame, for instance, to make it match the background color of a web page. The value is a hexadecimal RGB value (see Chapter 16 for an explanation of specifying RGB colors in HTML).

`ALIGN=left|right|top|bottom`

This attribute controls the alignment of the movie in the HTML document, much like the `align` attribute in an image tag (`<img>`). It may not have any effect within a table cell (`<td>`) or a DHTML layer (`<div>` or `<layer>`).

`SCALE=showall|noborder|exactfit`

This is used in conjunction with percentage `width` and `height` values for defining how the animation fits in the player frame. `showall` (the default) fits the movie into the frame while maintaining the image proportion (the frame background may be visible along one or two edges of the movie). `noborder` scales the movie to fill the frame while maintaining the aspect ratio of the movie (one or two edges might get cut off). `exactfit` fits the image into the frame exactly, but may result in image distortion if the scale described and the scale of the movie are inconsistent.

`SALIGN=l|r|t|b`

This attribute positions the movie within the frame and is used in conjunction with the `scale` attribute. The letters `l`, `r`, `t`, `b` correspond to left, right, top, and bottom, respectively. You can use any combination of `l` or `r` with `t` or `b`; for example, `lt` aligns the movie to the top-left corner of the browser window. If the `showall` attribute is selected, the leftover space appears below and to the right of the movie.

`BASE=`*`url`*

Sets the base URL and directory that is used for relative pathnames within the Flash movie.

`swLiveConnect=true|false`

This tag enables Netscape's LiveConnect feature, which allows plug-ins and Java applets to communicate with JavaScript. Set this attribute to `true` when you have FSCommands in your movie; otherwise, it is best set to `false` (the default) because it can cause a delay in display.

The `<object>` tag

The `<object>` tag tells Internet Explorer (3.0 and later) to download and install the particular ActiveX player for Flash files. The following is an example of the basic `<object>` tag:

```
<OBJECT CLASSID="clsid:D27CDB6E-AE6D-11cf-96B8-444553540000"
    CODEBASE="http://download.macromedia.com/pub/shockwave/cabs/flash/
    swflash.cab#version=5,0,0,0" WIDTH=300 HEIGHT=150>
  <PARAM NAME="MOVIE" VALUE="moviename.swf">
</OBJECT>
```

The classid parameter identifies the Flash ActiveX control, and codebase provides the browser with its location for downloading. The value of the classid attribute should appear in your HTML file exactly as it is shown above and applies to all Flash versions. Notice that the codebase attribute points to the Version 5 player. Other player versions and subreleases can be targeted with this method by adjusting the version number. The width and height attributes are required. The first parameter (<param>) establishes the name and location of your Shockwave Flash file.

The same additional controls as outlined for the <embed> tag (quality, loop, play, etc.) can be used with the <object> tag as well. They appear as additional parameters within the <object> tags using the following tag structure:

```
<PARAM NAME="PLAY" VALUE="true">
<PARAM NAME="LOOP" VALUE="false">
<PARAM NAME="SCALE" VALUE="showall">
...
```

Putting it together for all browsers

To make your Flash content available to the maximum number of users, it is recommended that you use both the <embed> and <object> tags. It is important to keep the <embed> tag within the <object> tags so Internet Explorer users don't get two copies of your movie.

 Do not use quotation marks within the <embed> tag when it is placed within an <object> tag. The quotation marks may cause the <object> tag to choke.

The following sample code places an anti-aliased animation on the page that plays and loops automatically:

```
<OBJECT CLASSID="clsid:D27CDB6E-AE6D-11cf-96B8-444553540000"
    CODEBASE="http://download.macromedia.com/pub/shockwave/cabs/flash/
    swflash.cab#version=5,0,0,0" WIDTH=300 HEIGHT=145 NAME="animation">
<PARAM NAME="MOVIE" value="animation.swf">
<PARAM NAME="PLAY" value="true">
<PARAM NAME="LOOP" value="true">
<PARAM NAME="QUALITY" value="autohigh">

    <EMBED SRC=animation.swf WIDTH=300 HEIGHT=145
    PLUGINSPAGE=http://www.macromedia.com/shockwave/download/
    index.cgi?P1_Prod_Version=ShockwaveFlash NAME=animation
    PLAY=true LOOP=true QUALITY=autohigh>
    </EMBED>

</OBJECT>
```

Integrating Flash with Other Technologies

Flash has proven to be such a popular multimedia format for the Web that it can now be integrated with the other web media staples, QuickTime and RealMedia.

Flash and QuickTime

QuickTime is a multitrack container format. Traditionally, this meant tracks for audio and video. In the evolution of QuickTime, support has been added for other tracks such as text, timecode, and (starting with QuickTime 4) Flash content.

To add a Flash track to a QuickTime movie, use the Flash authoring tool and export the file to the "QuickTime Flash" format (*.mov*). The resulting file is a QuickTime movie that can simultaneously play video, audio, and Flash media elements. The QuickTime 4 Player or higher is required to view QuickTime Flash files.

Another option is to export to the traditional "QuickTime Movie" format (also *.mov*). When exporting to QuickTime Movie, the vector Flash information is rasterized and added to the video track of the movie.

QuickTime 4 is only capable of displaying Flash 3 functionality (which means it does not recognize ActionScript commands). The recently released QuickTime 5 supports most of the functions of Flash 4.

As an alternative to using the Flash authoring tool, you can also import an existing *.swf* file into QuickTime Player (or Player Pro) and save it as a QuickTime movie.

Flash and RealPlayer

Flash 5 is capable of exporting Flash files directly to the RealMedia formats required to play in the RealPlayer. This method, called RealFlash, may make sense when publishing Flash content to a site that already relies heavily on the RealNetworks streaming system, such as a radio or news broadcasting site. It is also good for adding short animated movies and simple interactive elements to a page, not for whole site interfaces or highly interactive content like games.

Because the RealPlayer cannot play the audio portion of a Flash file, RealFlash movies are actually made up of three components: a *.swf* movie (stripped of its audio), a RealMedia (*.rm*) file containing the audio track, and a SMIL (*.smil*) document for controlling the synchronization of the playback (SMIL is discussed in more detail in Chapter 27). Flash 5 is capable of exporting all three components (in previous versions, you needed to use the RealMedia authoring tools to create RealFlash).

One of the current limitations of RealFlash is version support. RealServer and RealPlayer 8 can play Flash 3 and 4 files. RealServer 6 and 7 can only read Flash 2 files. You can select the Flash version using the Flash tab in the Publish Settings (in the Flash application) dialog box.

Flash & Shockwave

Flash Resources

If you need a book about Flash, again I recommend *Flash 5 Bible* by Robert Rein-hardt and Jon Warren Lentz (Hungry Minds, 2001). In addition to the many shelves full of other Flash books in your local bookstore, there are a number of resources for Flash online. For information on ActionScript, see *ActionScript: the Definitive Guide* by Colin Moock (O'Reilly, 2001).

- Macromedia's Flash Page: *http://www.macromedia.com/software/flash/*
- Flash Kit: *http://www.flashkit.com*
- Extremeflash.com: *http://www.extremeflash.com*
- Flash Planet: *http://www.flashplanet.com*
- Virtual FX: *http://www.virtual-fx.net*
- Flash Academy: *http://www.enetserve.com/tutorials/*
- Were Here.com: *http://www.were-here.com*
- ActionScripts.Org: *http://www.actionscripts.org*

Shockwave for Director

Macromedia's Director software (which significantly predates the Web) has long been the industry standard for creating multimedia presentations appropriate for CD-ROMs and kiosk displays. Director movies incorporate images, motion, sound, interactive buttons, and even QuickTime movies. In 1996, Macromedia introduced the Shockwave system, which enabled Director movies to be played directly on web pages. While Flash is better suited for the Web, there are some functions that can only be done in Director. Following is a summary of Shockwave's pros and cons.

Advantages

Shockwave has a number of attractive features:

- **It can use Lingo programming.** Because Shockwave can be customized with Lingo programming, it offers functionality—such as the ability to remember user position, keep scores, "know" correct answers, and other games-related functions—that cannot be achieved with Flash. Lingo is a robust scripting environment that offers more control over object properties, list manipula-tion, and a more efficient development environment.
- **It has good compression.** The Shockwave file format offers efficient compres-sion ratios, compressing Director movies to 1/3 to 1/2 of their original size.
- **It has full-featured interactivity.** Shockwave brings full CD-ROM-like interactiv-ity to web pages.
- **It uses streaming technology.** Shockwave movies begin playing very quickly and continue playing as they download so they can be pseudo-streamed from an HTTP server.

- **It has a well supported format.** The Shockwave plug-in is available for Windows and Mac platforms. It is one of the most popular and widely distributed plug-ins.

- **It's scriptable.** Shockwave movies can be controlled by basic JavaScript commands such as `Play()` and `Stop()`. Other JavaScript interactions can be set with Lingo programming within the Shockwave movie.

Disadvantages

And on the downside . . .

- **File sizes are larger.** Despite impressive compression, some Director Shockwave movies (particularly those containing sound and video content) may still be quite large for transferring over network connections. Depending on the nature of the content, Shockwave could be overkill for simple effects (like interactive buttons) that may be more efficiently handled by Flash.

- **A plug-in is required.** Users need to have the Shockwave plug-in installed in order to view your Director movies. The Shockwave plug-in is not as widely distributed as Flash (as of this writing, Macromedia estimates Shockwave to be installed on 60% of the Web user base). Many clients still see this as a prohibitive disadvantage.

- **There is a larger plug-in footprint.** The plug-in required for playing Shockwave files is about 1MB in size and requires more system resources to run.

- **It requires an expensive authoring tool.** In order to create Shockwave movies, you need Macromedia Director, which costs approximately $995 as of this writing.

- **It's difficult to author.** Director, with its Lingo programming language, has a steep learning curve. However, with behaviors (prewritten Lingo scripts that come with Director), it's fairly easy for beginners to jump in and accomplish some sophisticated stuff within a short period of time.

- **It's a proprietary format.** Shockwave movies are in a propriety format that can only be authored using Macromedia's Director program.

Creating Shockwave Movies

Shockwave movies (which use the suffix *.dcr*) must be created using Macromedia Director. Director is a powerful multimedia authoring environment. Although learning the basics of the software itself is not too daunting, to make Director movies do the really cool interactive stuff, you must learn Lingo, Director's proprietary programming language. Lingo, although simple by programming standards, can still take a long time to master, which is why many designers hire Director and Lingo specialists.

That said, a lesson in Director and Lingo is beyond the scope of this book. If you're interested in learning Director, I recommend you spend time with the manual and other available tutorial books. Also, be sure to take advantage of the excellent support material and resources on the Macromedia web site. Pay special attention to tips for optimizing file size and preparing files for streaming.

Once you've created a movie in Director, you must save it in Shockwave format to make it play over the Web. In Director 8.5 (the current version as of this writing), use the Publish command (listed under the File menu) to save your completed movie to Shockwave format. By default, when you publish a movie, Director automatically creates a *.dcr* file and an HTML document that contains all the code necessary for displaying the Shockwave movie. Additional export settings (such as generating code for plug-in detection) are available on the Publish Settings dialog box.

 Director 5 used the Afterburner Xtra to save a movie in Shockwave format. The ability to save directly to *.dcr* format was built into Director as of Version 6, making Afterburner obsolete.

Configuring the Server

Although you don't need special server software to handle Shockwave files, the server must be configured to recognize the new MIME type. The specific syntax for configuration varies for different servers, so coordinate with your system administrator. The following provides the standard necessary elements:

- Type/subtype: `application/x-director`
- File extensions for Director Shockwave: *.dcr* (also *.dir* and *.dxr*)

Adding Shockwave Movies to a Web Page

Like Flash, Director Shockwave files are added to an HTML document with the `<embed>` or `<object>` tags. Internet Explorer for Windows uses the `<object>` tag, which enables them to automatically download the ActiveX controls for playing Shockwave media. Netscape Navigator for Windows and all Mac browsers recognize the `<embed>` tag. To code your page so it is accessible to the maximum number of users, use a combination of the `<embed>` and `<object>` tags.

The easiest way to place a Shockwave movie in an HTML document is to rely on Director's Publish feature to generate the code for you. The following sample code shows the minimal code for placing the *.dcr* file on the page and redirecting the browser to missing plug-ins or ActiveX controls

```
<OBJECT CLASSID="clsid:166B1BCA-3F9C-11CF-8075-444553540000"
    CODEBASE="http://download.macromedia.com/pub/shockwave/cabs/
    director/sw.cab#version=8,0,0,0"
    ID=mymovie WIDTH=640 HEIGHT=480>
<PARAM NAME=src VALUE="mymovie.dcr">

    <EMBED SRC="$MO" WIDTH=$WI HEIGHT=$HE TYPE="application/x-director"
    PLUGINSPAGE="http://www.macromedia.com/shockwave/download/"></EMBED>

</OBJECT>
```

The `width` and `height` values are mandatory and specify the dimensions of the movie in pixels. Note that the values for `classid`, `codebase`, and `pluginspage` must be copied exactly as shown above in order to work correctly.

Within the Publish Settings dialog box, there are a number attributes and parameters settings for controlling the display of control buttons with the movie, how the movie scales in the browser, and dozens of other functions. A complete list of the parameters (and attributes) are listed on the Macromedia web site at *http://www.macromedia.com/support/director/how/shock/objembed.html*.

Director Online Resources

There are a number of useful sites on the web regarding Director and Shockwave for Director.

http://www.macromedia.com/software/director/
  Macromedia's Director product page

http://www.macromedia.com/support/director/internet.html
  Macromedia's Shockwave Support Pages

http://www.shockwave.com
  Shockwave.com (a showcase of Shockwave and Flash media)

http://www.mcli.dist.maricopa.edu/director/
  Director Web

http://www.director-online.com
  Director Online

http://www.updatestage.com
  UpdateStage

Flash & Shockwave

CHAPTER 27

Introduction to SMIL

SMIL (Synchronized Multimedia Integration Language, pronounced "smile") is a markup language (like HTML) for combining audio, video, text, animation, and graphics in a precise, synchronized fashion. A SMIL file instructs the client to retrieve media elements that reside on the server as standalone files. Those separate elements are then assembled and played by the SMIL player. The advantages of SMIL include the ability to:

- Integrate media elements in a time-based presentation
- Reuse media elements in multiple presentations
- Allow users to choose the media tracks they prefer, for example, based on connection speed or language preferences
- Add hyperlinks in a time-based presentation

SMIL is good for simple multimedia presentations, such as audio slideshows and videos with scrolling captions. However, it is not a substitute for the rich, high-impact interactivity offered by Flash or Shockwave.

The SMIL 1.0 recommendation, released in June of 1998, is one of the first XML-based DTDs proposed by the W3C (for an explanation of XML, see Chapter 30). As of this writing, SMIL 2.0, which greatly expands upon the functionality established in the initial specification, is on the verge of becoming a formal recommendation. The SMIL 2.0 specification is broken down into function-specific modules which can potentially be used with other XML languages. One proposed use, XHTML and SMIL, would allow time-based behaviors to be added to HTML elements without the use of a scripting language.

This chapter provides an introduction to how SMIL works and the elements used to control the timing and display of multimedia presentations.

How SMIL Works

SMIL uses tags to control the layout and timeline of a multimedia presentation. It is fairly intuitive, so the best way to get a quick understanding of SMIL is to look at a simple example. The following SMIL code creates a 15-second-long narrated slide-show, in which an audio track plays as a series of three images display in sequence.

```
<par dur="15s">
<audio src="audio_file.mp3" begin="0s">
    <seq>
        <img src="image_1.jpg" begin="0s">
        <img src="image_2.jpg" begin="5s">
        <img src="image_3.jpg" begin="10s">
    </seq>
</par>
```

Looking at the code, it is easy to pick out the audio and image elements. Each points to a separate media file on the server.

All elements contained within the `<par>` element are played in parallel (at the same time); therefore, the audio will continue playing as the images are displayed. The image elements are contained in the `<seq>` element, which means they will be played one after another (in sequence). The `begin` attribute gives timing instructions for when each element should be displayed. In our example, the images will display in slideshow fashion every five seconds.

SMIL Players

There are a number of SMIL players already available:

RealNetworks RealPlayer 8
SMIL's most visible proponent is RealNetworks, who adopted SMIL early on as the file format for synchronizing their G2 streaming media presentations. See *http://www.real.com*.

Apple QuickTime 4.1 (and higher)
The QuickTime player can display SMIL documents containing the full range of QuickTime-supported media formats. See *http://www.apple.com/quicktime/*.

Oratrix GRiNS (SMIL 1.0) and GRiNS for SMIL 2.0
Oratrix creates a full line of SMIL players and authoring tools that are available for Windows, Mac, and Unix systems. See *http://www.oratrix.com/GRiNS/index.html*.

Internet Explorer 5.5 (Windows)
Microsoft has been working on its own multimedia language called HTML+TIME. However, Internet Explorer 5.5 also supports some of the modules from the SMIL 2.0 specification. See *http://msdn.microsoft.com/downloads/*.

For a complete and updated list of SMIL players, check the W3C SMIL page at *http://www.w3.org/AudioVideo/*. Keep in mind that although all media types are supported by the SMIL specification theoretically, in reality, specific SMIL players are limited to the media file formats they already support.

SMIL

SMIL Authoring Tools

While it is certainly possible to write SMIL documents by hand, it is far easier to use an application that generates the code for you, particularly for presentations with complicated timelines. Applications that support SMIL authoring include:

RealNetworks RealProducer Pro
> Powerful tools for building SMIL presentations, including proprietary RealNetworks markup languages, RealPix and RealText, which control the streaming display of images and text, respectively. See *http://www.realnetworks.com*.

RealNetworks RealSlideshow
> This free authoring tool enables consumers to compose quick slideshows. See *http://www.realnetworks.com*.

Oratrix GRiNS Authoring Suite
> Oratrix offers a variety of SMIL authoring tools for creating general SMIL 1.0 or SMIL 2.0 documents, SMIL for RealSystem G2 (both professional and "lite" versions), and SMIL for QuickTime 4.1. They are available for Windows, Mac, and Linux (SMIL 1.0 is available for Unix). See *http://www.oratrix.com/GRiNS/index.html*.

Macromedia Dreamweaver
> Dreamweaver supports SMIL authoring via extensions developed by RealNetworks. They are available for download at the Macromedia Exchange site listed here (search for SMIL or look under Rich Media). See *http://www.macromedia.com/exchange/dreamweaver/*.

Writing SMIL

Explaining every element, attribute, and behavior within the SMIL 2.0 specification is beyond the scope of this chapter; however, what follows is a thorough introduction to the basic structures and components of SMIL.

Well-Formed Code

SMIL is an XML-based language, which means that all of its code needs to be "well formed" according to the rules of XML (see Chapter 30). When writing SMIL (or any XML application), follow these rules:

- Tags are case-sensitive. For the most part, single-word elements and attributes are in all lowercase (e.g., <region>, <audio>, <switch>). Multiple-word elements and attributes use mixed case, also called camel case (e.g. systemLanguage, <priorityClass>, borderColor). It is important to stick to the capitalization structures in the specification.

- All attribute values must be contained in double quotation marks.

- All tags must be closed. For container tags, the closing tag must be present (e.g., <tagname>...</tagname>). Empty tags (standalone elements that don't have closing tags, such as <img> and <br> in HTML) are closed by the addition of a slash at the end of the tag (e.g., <emptytag />).

- Nested elements must not overlap (e.g., <switch><par></par></switch>, not <switch><par></switch></par>).

Document Structure

Like HTML documents, SMIL documents are made up of a head element and body element. The head element contains information about the document, including layout instructions (using the <layout>, <meta>, and <metadata> elements). The body of the document contains the actual media object elements and timeline instructions regarding the sequence in which they appear.

It is generally a good idea to begin with a DOCTYPE declaration (see Chapter 9 for more about DOCTYPE declarations). The skeletal structure for an SMIL 1.0 document is as follows:

```
<!DOCTYPE smil PUBLIC "-//W3C//DTD SMIL 1.0//EN" "http://www.w3c.org/TR/
REC-smil/SMIL10.dtd">
<smil>
   <head>
   ...layout and meta information goes here
   </head>

   <body>
   ...media elements and timing instructions go here
   </body>
</smil>
```

The SMIL 2.0 DTD is broken into 11 separate module-specific DTDs, along with two driver DTDs that hold the modules together. The following DOCTYPE declaration for an SMIL 2.0 documents points to the basic language profile driver:

```
<!DOCTYPE smil PUBLIC "-//W3C//DTD SMIL 2.0//EN"
   "http://www.w3.org/2001/SMIL20/WD/SMIL20.dtd">
```

Controlling Layout

The layout of a SMIL presentation is defined in the <layout> element, which always goes in the <head> of the document. Within <layout>, you can specify the size of the main presentation window (<root-layout>) and establish any number of separate display regions (<region>) within that window. Here's an example:

```
<smil>
<head>
  <layout>
    <root-layout width="400" height="400" />
    <region id="video1" width="320" height="240" top="40" left="40"/>
    <region id="caption" width="320" height="60" top="300" left="40"/>
  </layout>
</head>
```

The layout of this SMIL example sets up a root layout that is 400 pixels square in which the presentation will be displayed. Within the root layout, there are two regions (one labeled video1, the other labeled caption) that will contain actual media elements. Figure 27-1 shows the resulting presentation layout.

The SMIL 2.0 specification includes a multiple-window layout module which allows you to define multiple display spaces (called top level windows) instead of just a single root layout area. Similar to frames in HTML, it allows for media to

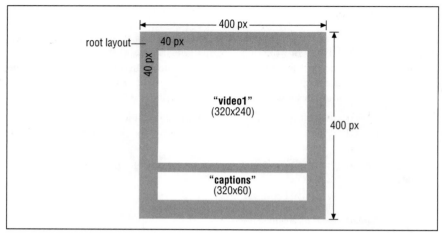

Figure 27-1: A simple SMIL presentation layout

remain in view in one window (such as a table of contents), while swapping out the contents of another. Each top level window (as defined by the `<toplayout>` element placed in the `<layout>` tag) can contain multiple regions.

Media Elements

There are seven basic media objects that can be placed in a SMIL presentation: audio, video, images, text, streaming text, animation, and a generic media placement element for other media types. The following samples show the minimal code for adding media elements to the document:

```
<audio src="pathname/soundtrack.ra" />
<video src="pathname/movie.mov" />
<img src="pathname/illustration.gif" />
<text src="pathname/caption.txt" />
<textstream src="pathname/marquee.txt" />
<animation src="pathname/animation.gif" />
<ref src="pathname/special.rt" />
```

The `audio`, `video`, and `img` (image) objects are fairly self-explanatory; they should be produced appropriately for web delivery and saved in an appropriate file format. `text` adds a static text block to the page, while `textstream` scrolls the text like a marquee.

The `animation` element can be used for animated GIFs (see Chapter 23 for more information on creating them) or animated vector graphics.

 The SMIL 2.0 specification includes a complex animation module for adding motion and change over time to vector graphics and even HTML elements. The animation module of the specification defines the syntax and behavior of the `<animate>` element, which should not be confused with the basic `<animation>` media object mentioned previously.

The `ref` element is a generic placeholder tag for referring to any other type of media. For instance, RealNetworks uses the `ref` element to add its proprietary RealPix documents (a markup language for defining the presentation and behavior of streaming images) to a SMIL file, as shown in this example:

```
<ref src="rtsp://realserver.company.com/pix/ads.rp"/>
```

Putting an element in its place

To place a media object in a particular region (as defined in the `<layout>` of the document), simply call the region by name within the media element tag using the `region` attribute as shown in this example:

```
<smil>
<head>
  <layout>
    <root-layout width="400" height="400" />
    <region id="video1" width="320" height="240" top="40" left="40"/>
    <region id="caption" width="320" height="80" top="320" left="40"/>
  </layout>
</head>

<body>
<par>
    <video src="pathname/movie.mov" region="video1" />
    <textstream src="pathname/marquee.txt" region="caption" />
</par>
</body>
</smil>
```

Timing the Presentation

The SMIL specification provides a number of methods for controlling the timing and synchronization of the presentation. Each presentation is considered to have a timeline along which the playback of various media is referenced.

Time containers

Media elements are placed in special time container elements (`<par>`, `<seq>`, and `<excl>`) that define how the media should be played. The `<par>` element (short for "parallel") defines a group of elements that play at the same time. The `<seq>` element defines a sequence of elements that play one after another, in the order in which they appear in the SMIL document.

When media elements are placed in the `<excl>` time container (short for "exclusive"), only one of those media elements can play at any given time.

Time control attributes

SMIL defines a number of attributes for indicating the specific timing of media elements and groups of elements (defined by time containers). Let's take another look at the narrated slideshow sample from the beginning of this chapter:

```
<par dur="15s">
<audio src="audio_file.mp3" begin="0s" id="audio_1" />
```

```
<seq>
    <img src="image_1.jpg" begin="0s" />
    <img src="image_2.jpg" begin="5s" />
    <img src="image_3.jpg" begin="10s" />
</seq>
</par>
```

The dur attribute of in the <par> element specifies that the display of the elements in that group will have a duration of 15 seconds. The dur (duration) attribute can also be applied to specific media element tags. Some media, like audio and video, have implicit durations. Others, like text and images, require you to specify a duration. If you want an image to stay on throughout the presentation, set the value of dur to indefinite.

The media elements (<audio> and <img>) contain the begin attribute, which specifies at what point in the timeline the display or playback should begin. There is also an end attribute (not shown) for specifying the end time of the media element.

It is helpful to sketch out the intended timeline for a presentation to help plan the timing elements. The simple timeline for our narrated slideshow is illustrated in Figure 27-2.

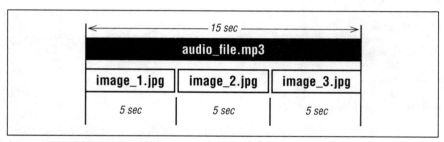

Figure 27-2: The timeline for our simple SMIL slideshow example

Relative timing

There are several ways to control the beginning and end of the playback of a media element. In our example, all time measurements are relative to the beginning of the timeline. Timing may also be based on the begin or end point of another media element (for example, the second image could have been specified to begin playing five seconds after the audio begins as follows:

```
<img src="image_2.jpg" begin="audio_1.begin+5s" />
```

In addition, you can base playback on user input using event names commonly used in HTML and CSS, such as click, dblclick, onMouseOver, and so on. In the following example, a video stops playing when a user clicks on an image of a "Stop" button:

```
<par>
<img src="stop.gif" dur="indefinite" id="stop_button" />
<video src="myvideo.rm" dur="1min" end="stop_button.click" />
</par>
```

Controlling Content Display

The `<switch>` element allows an author to list a number of media options, of which only the first acceptable option gets played; the remaining options are ignored. A media element is deemed "acceptable" when it passes specified test criteria. An example will make this clear.

In the following code, the player will play one of the listed audio files based on the user's connection speed (bit rate) to the Internet. The `systemBitrate` attribute performs a test of the user's connection speed, measured in bits per second. If the bit rate of the user's connection matches the `systemBitrate` value, it plays that media element. If not, it goes on to the next one until it finds one that matches the specified speed. Only one media in a `<switch>` element can be played.

```
<switch>
<audio src="song-cd_quality.ra" systemBitrate="128000" />
<audio src="song-good_quality.ra" systemBitrate="56000" />
<audio src="song-low_quality.ra" systemBitrate="9600" />
</switch>
```

Because the player uses the first media element in the list that passes the test criteria, you should list the options from most desirable to least desirable.

In the SMIL 1.0 specification, test criteria were hyphenated (e.g., `system-bitrate` and `system-screen-size`). This was deprecated by the SMIL 2.0 specification in favor of camel case attributes to be consistent with other developing standards. The following is a list of the predefined test attributes defined in SMIL 2.0.

`systemAudioDesc=on|off`
> *New in SMIL 2.0.* Specifies whether or not closed audio descriptions should be played. Closed audio aids sight-impaired users to understand video content the same way closed captioning supplements audio for the hearing impaired.

`systemBitrate=number` *(bits per second)*
> Sets a target bit rate at which the media may be displayed.

`systemCaptions=on|off`
> Specifies whether a text caption appears in conjunction with an audio file.

`systemComponent=text`
> *New in SMIL 2.0.* Tests for the various components of the SMIL player, for example, whether it supports JavaScript.

`systemCPU=cpu-code`
> *New in SMIL 2.0.* Tests for the type of CPU on the user's machine (for example, X86 or PPC).

`systemLanguage=two-letter language code`
> Tests the user's language preference so the proper language file can be served. See Chapter 7 for a list of two-letter language codes.

`systemOperatingSystem=defined operating system abbreviation`
> *New in SMIL 2.0.* Tests for the user's operating system. Example values include `win9x`, `winnt`, `macos`, `beos`, `linux`, `unixware`, etc.

SMIL

`systemOverdubOrSubtitle=overdub|subtitle`
> Specifies whether overdub or subtitles are rendered. The SMIL 1.0 version, `system-overdub-or-captions`, has been deprecated.

`systemRequired=xml namespace prefix`
> Compares the name of the XML namespace to those that are supported by the SMIL player.

`systemScreenDepth=number` *(monitor color bit depth)*
> Tests the number of colors the user's monitor is capable of displaying. Typical values are 1, 4, 8, 16, 24, and 32.

`systemScreenSize=heightXwidth`
> Tests the size of the user's screen so customized content can be displayed to fit the available space. Typical values are `640X480`, `800X600`, and `1024X768`.

For Further Reading

For a thorough explanation of all SMIL elements and their supported attributes and values, make your way through the W3C's SMIL 2.0 specification located at *http://www.w3.org/TR/smil20/cover.html*. This chapter should give you a good head start toward understanding the specifics of the system.

Books

As of this writing, the only book dedicated to covering the SMIL 1.0 and 2.0 specification is *SMIL for Dummies* by Heather Williamson (IDG Books, 2001).

There is a chapter on developing SMIL presentations in *Designing Web Audio* by Josh Beggs and Dylan Thede (O'Reilly, 2001).

SMIL as it relates to QuickTime is covered in a chapter in *QuickTime for the Web* by Apple Computer Inc. (Academic Press, 2000).

Online Resources

There are a number of useful online resources for learning more about SMIL.

W3C SMIL Home Page
> Go right to the source for a good starting place for research or to keep up to date on the latest developments. See *http://www.w3.org/AudioVideo/*.

RealNetworks Developer Site
> RealNetworks has been very active in developing and supporting SMIL applications. The site includes tutorials for creating SMIL presentations for RealSystem. See *http://www.realnetworks.com/devzone/index.html*.

JustSMIL Home (now part of Streaming Media World)
> This is a great site containing tutorials, product reviews, news, tips, and other useful SMIL information. See *http://smw.internet.com/smil/smilhome.html*.

PART V

Advanced Technologies

CHAPTER 28

Introduction to JavaScript

JavaScript is a client-side scripting language that adds interactivity to web pages and lets designers control various aspects of the browser itself. With JavaScript, you can do such things as display additional information about links, create mouse rollover effects, change the contents of pages based on certain conditions, randomly display content on a page, load content in new browser windows and frames, and (with some help from CSS) move elements around on the page.

A scripting language is somewhere between a markup language, like HTML, and a full-blown programming language, like Java. With JavaScript, you can add extra functionality to your web site using short snippets of scripting code that has a syntax that's fairly easy to understand.

This chapter includes material and code by Nick Heinle and Bill Peña, authors of *Designing with JavaScript* (O'Reilly). For a more advanced JavaScript reference, see *JavaScript: The Definitive Guide* by David Flanagan (O'Reilly). Also note that for simple functionality, you may not need to write your own JavaScript at all; software like Macromedia's Dreamweaver can do the coding for you, with built-in behaviors you can drop in like HTML objects. But as with HTML, if you are going to use JavaScript, you should be familiar with the basics of the language, whether you are using a WYSIWYG editor or not.

JavaScript History

JavaScript was first introduced by Netscape in Navigator 2.0, as a simple scripting language that could be embedded directly in web pages. Since then, JavaScript has evolved through five versions and is now codified in a standard. Note that the name of the language, JavaScript, is only coincidentally related to the Java programming language. Although JavaScript and Java share some similarity in syntax, you don't need to know anything about Java to learn JavaScript.

JavaScript has evolved from Version 1.0 in Navigator 2.0 to Version 1.5 in Netscape 6. Microsoft's name for its version of JavaScript is Jscript, and, for the most part, Jscript mirrors JavaScript's functionality, but also varies from version to version. At the time of this writing, the most widely supported version is 1.2, which is the basis of both Netscape's and Microsoft's 4.0 browser implementations. If you have a script that is written for an older version, say JavaScript 1.1, it will work fine with all of the newer versions. However, if you use features in a later version, say Java-Script 1.5, older browsers will not understand your scripts. Later, you'll learn how to use JavaScript to detect what browser is displaying your page, so you can customize your scripts to be backwards-compatible.

JavaScript (and Jscript) have also been standardized as ECMAScript (ECMA-262). Technically, JavaScript 1.5 is an implementation of the third version of the ECMA-Script standard. Currently, both Netscape 6 and IE 5.5 support this standard version of JavaScript very well, and hopefully they will continue to agree in their support.

JavaScript Basics

JavaScript code is usually placed directly in an HTML document. The code can go in either the head or the body, and there can be numerous scripts in a single HTML document. Here's the syntax:

```
<SCRIPT LANGUAGE="JavaScript">
<!--
script goes here
//-->
</SCRIPT>
```

The <script> tags define the boundaries of the script and set the scripting language to JavaScript. The language attribute is necessary to distinguish Java-Script from other scripting languages, like VBScript, that can also be embedded in web pages. Finally, HTML comments surround the script to hide the code from really old browsers that don't understand the <script> tag. Otherwise, those browsers would just display the code like preformatted text, which isn't very pretty.

Functions

There are two parts to most JavaScript applications: the functions that tell the browser what to do, and actual uses of these functions. Let's take the example of a simple web page that displays a linked document in a second window:

```
<HTML>
<HEAD>
<SCRIPT LANGUAGE="JavaScript">
<!--
function openWin(URL) {
    aWindow = window.open(URL,"composerwindow","toolbar=no,width=350,
height=400,status=no,scrollbars=yes,resize=no,menubar=no");
}
```

```
//-->
</SCRIPT>
</HEAD>

<BODY>
<P><A HREF="javascript:openWin('mozart.html');">Mozart</A></P>
<P><A HREF="javascript:openWin('beethoven.html');">Beethoven</A></P>
<P><A HREF="javascript:openWin('wagner.html');">Wagner</A></P>
</BODY>
</HTML>
```

The JavaScript inside the `<script>` tags defines a function, called `openWin()`, that tells the browser what to do when the function is called. Now look at the body of the document. The `openWin()` function is being called from the anchor tags. Let's take a look at one of those lines:

```
<A HREF="javascript:openWin('mozart.html');">Mozart</A>
```

The line starts off as a normal `<a href>` tag. But the value of `href` is not a standard URL; it's a call to a JavaScript function. The word `javascript:` tells the browser that the link contains JavaScript code. In this case, that code is a call to the `openWin()` function, which was defined up in the head of the document. Since the JavaScript call is in a link, the function is run when the user clicks on the link (the word "Mozart"). The content in parentheses—`mozart.html`—specifies a value that is passed to the `openWin()` function. We'll see what passing is all about when we look at the function. The rest of the line is a standard link—the hypertext and the closing anchor tag.

Now let's look at the `openWin()` function:

```
function openWin(URL) {
    aWindow = window.open(URL,"composerwindow","toolbar=no,width=350,
height=400,status=no,scrollbars=yes,resize=no,menubar=no");
}
```

The first line of code declares a new function with the name `openWin()`; this declaration is simply a way of giving a name to a set of instructions for the browser. The set of parentheses indicates that the function takes *arguments*, and the names of the arguments are listed inside the parentheses. Arguments are information that must be given to a function when it is called; the function uses this information to perform its job. In this example, the `openWin()` function takes one argument, a URL, and uses the URL to open a new window that displays the page at that location.

After the function declaration comes an opening curly bracket ({). You'll see the closing curly bracket (}) on the last line. Everything between these curly brackets is the code that is run each time the function is called.

The two lines of code are actually one line that runs longer than the printable area of this page. The line starts by creating a new *variable*. A variable is just a name that is associated with a piece of information. In this case, we're putting the result of some window-opening code into the variable called `aWindow`. The window-opening code returns information about the window it opened, so if we wanted to do something else to the window later, like close it, we could use aWindow to refer to that specific window. More commonly, variables are used to store information about the current state of the page or the user environment, such as the browser being used or the user's name.

The window-opening code calls the window.open() function, which is a predefined function that is built into JavaScript. It provides a standard way to open a new window and lets you specify a bunch of information about the window to be opened. There are three arguments for window.open(): the URL of the document to be displayed in the window, the name of the window, and the characteristics of the window. Note that when we call window.open(), we're not specifying an actual URL, but instead using the URL argument that is passed into the openWin() function. Thus, when we specify the URL *mozart.html* in the anchor tag, that URL gets passed first to the openWin() function and then to the window.open() function, which results in that document being displayed in the new window.

The second argument to window.open(), "composerwindow", is a string that indicates the name of the new window. A string is simply a collection of characters surrounded by single or double quotes. The final argument is another string that specifies the characteristics of the window: the window's size is 350 by 400; it has scrollbars but no tool bar, status bar, or menu bar; and it cannot be resized by the user. Note that no spaces or carriage returns are permitted inside the string for this final argument.

Now that you understand all the code here, let's review what happens when the user clicks on the links. When a user clicks the Mozart link, the openWin() code runs, passing the URL *mozart.html* to the function window.open(), which opens a new 350×400 window that displays the document at that URL. When the user clicks the Beethoven link, the same function runs, but the code passes the *beethoven.html* URL to the function, and that document is displayed in the window.

Event Handlers

In the previous example, the JavaScript function was triggered when the user clicked on an ordinary link. JavaScript code can also be triggered by more subtle user actions, such as moving the mouse over an element on the page (commonly called a "rollover"), or by browser actions, such as the loading of a page. These actions are called *events*. In JavaScript, you tie specific functionality to events with *event handlers*. An event handler simply watches for a predefined event and executes some code when it occurs. This response to user action is the foundation of interactivity.

In the following example, the onMouseOver event handler triggers a function called turnOn() when the user passes the mouse over the image on the page:

```
<img src="button_off.gif" onMouseOver="turnOn();">
```

The turnOn() function gives the browser instructions to swap out the *button_off. gif* image with another one. This kind of code is the basis of the rollover buttons that are so popular on the Web today. Rollover scripts are discussed in detail in the "Sample Scripts" section of this chapter.

Table 28-1 contains a complete list of event handlers recognized by the different versions of JavaScript.

Table 28-1: JavaScript event handlers

Event handler	Supported by
onAbort	Images (1.1)
onBlur, onFocus	Text input elements (all versions); windows, all form elements (1.1)
onChange	Select menus, text input elements (all versions)
onClick	Button elements, links (all versions)
onDblClick	Entire document, images, links, button elements (1.2)
onError	Images, windows (1.1)
onKeyDown, onKeyPress, onKeyUp	Entire document, images, links, text input elements (1.2)
onLoad, onUnload	Windows (all versions); images (1.1)
onMouseDown, onMouseUp	Entire document, links, images, button elements (1.2)
onMouseOver, onMouseOut	Links, images, layers (1.2)
onReset, onSubmit	Form elements (1.1)

Sample Scripts

How about some useful scripts to get you started? This section offers several scripts you can copy into your web pages.

Status Line Messages

Probably the simplest JavaScript you can add to your site is a message that appears in the status bar (the bar at the bottom that shows URLs or says "Document: Done"). You can use this bar to display a message or extra information when the user places the mouse over a link. To do this, simply add a little JavaScript to a standard anchor tag. You don't even need to write a function or use the `<script>` tag. Browsers that aren't JavaScript-compatible simply ignore the code. Here's how you do it:

```
<A HREF="mozart.com" onMouseOver="window.status='A study of
Mozart's operas'; return true;">Mozart</A>
```

This code displays the text "A study of Mozart's operas" when the user puts the cursor over the Mozart link. This is accomplished using the `onMouseOver` event handler. When the user puts the cursor over the Mozart link, the `window.status` variable, which controls the contents of the status bar, is set to the string specified in single quotes. The `return true;` bit is just some magic required to keep the browser from doing its normal job of writing the URL in the status bar. Without it, the user would never see your status bar message, as it would immediately be overwritten by the URL. To use this code on your site, just replace the text between the single quotes (and the URL and content, of course).

Opening a New Window

We already looked at the code for opening a new window earlier in this chapter, so we'll just take a quick look here at the code that needs to be replaced to use this script on your site. The code again:

```
<HTML>
<HEAD>
<SCRIPT LANGUAGE="JavaScript">
<!--
function openWin(URL) {
    aWindow=window.open(URL,"composerwindow","toolbar=no,width=350,
height=400,status=no,scrollbars=yes,resize=no,menubar=no");
}
//-->
</SCRIPT>
</HEAD>
<BODY>
<P><A HREF="javascript:openWin('mozart.html');">Mozart</A></P>
<P><A HREF="javascript:openWin('wagner.html');">Wagner</A></P>
<P><A HREF="javascript:openWin('beethoven.html');">Beethoven</A>
</P>
</BODY>
</HTML>
```

The code in bold indicates the parts you should alter for your site. Give the new window a name, if you wish, by replacing the text composerwindow. Specify the settings for the window by changing the values of toolbar, status, scrollbars, resize, and menubar from no to yes (or vice versa). Set the width and height appropriately. Remember not to put any spaces or carriage returns in this code.

Note that you can hardwire the function by replacing the text URL in the openWin() function with a specific URL, such as "mozart.html". If you do this, you simply call the function without passing the URL to the function, as follows:

```
<A HREF="javascript:openWin();">Mozart</A></P>
```

Of course, if you are familiar with HTML, you know that you can display a link in a separate window with the target attribute of the <a> tag. The advantage of using JavaScript instead is that you have control over the characteristics of the new window, like its dimensions.

Managing Frames

Another popular job for JavaScript is loading content into frames, particularly loading several different frames with one click. Here is the code for a function that changes the contents of both a toolbar frame and a main frame with a single click. This code assumes that the toolbar frame has been named `toolbar` and the main frame has been named `main`:

```
function changePages (toolbarURL, mainURL) {
    parent.toolbar.location.href=toolbarURL;
    parent.main.location.href=mainURL;
}
```

The actual anchor tag looks like this:

```
<A HREF="javascript:changePages('toolbar_document2.html', 'main_
document2.html');">Change Pages</A>
```

If you use the frame names `toolbar` and `main`, you can use this code as is; just change the URLs you pass to the `changePages()` function. If you change the frame names, for example, to `left` and `right`, you need to change the function as follows:

```
function changePages (leftURL, rightURL) {
    parent.left.location.href=leftURL;
    parent.right.location.href=rightURL;
}
```

Image Rollovers

While browsing the Web, you've probably encountered images that change when you pass your mouse pointer over them. This effect, commonly called a "rollover," is created using JavaScript code that swaps out one graphic for another when the `onMouseOver` event handler is called for the image. Rollovers are popular because they provide a strong visual cue that the graphic is clickable, plus they're just fun!

To begin, you need to make two versions of each rollover graphic: one in an "on" state and one in an "off" state. Buttons in the "on" state typically feature brighter colors, a glow, or some other visual indication of being active. You can also swap in a completely different image if that suits your purpose. The only requirement is that the graphics have exactly the same pixel dimensions, or one will be resized and distorted.

In this section, we'll look at two rollover methods. The first is a simple rollover in which passing the mouse over the graphic changes that graphic. The second example uses a single `onMouseOver` event handler to swap out two images at the same time.

Simple rollovers

Example 28-1 creates a simple image swap when the cursor is over each image. We'll begin by listing the script in its entirety; then we'll take a look at the individual components.

Example 28-1: Simple JavaScript rollover code

```
<HTML>
<HEAD><TITLE>Two Rollover Images</TITLE>
<SCRIPT LANGUAGE = "JavaScript">
<!--
if (document.images) {       A

    // "On" images       B
    img1on = new Image();
    img1on.src = "image1on.gif";
    img2on = new Image();
    img2on.src = "image2on.gif";

    // "Off" images       C
    img1off = new Image();
    img1off.src = "image1off.gif";
    img2off = new Image();
    img2off.src = "image2off.gif";
}

function imgOn(imgName) {       D
    if (document.images) {
        document.images[imgName].src = eval(imgName + "on.src");
    }
}

function imgOff(imgName) {       E
    if (document.images) {
        document.images[imgName].src = eval(imgName + "off.src");
    }
}

//-->
</SCRIPT>
</HEAD>

<BODY>
<A HREF="page1.html"       F
    onMouseOver="imgOn('img1')"       G
    onMouseOut="imgOff('img1')">       H
<IMG NAME="img1" BORDER=0 HEIGHT=20 WIDTH=125 SRC="image1off.gif"></A>

<A HREF="page2.html"
    onMouseOver="imgOn('img2')"
    onMouseOut="imgOff('img2')">
<IMG NAME="img2" BORDER=0 HEIGHT=20 WIDTH=125 SRC="image2off.gif"></A>
</BODY>
</HTML>
```

Ⓐ This line detects whether the user's browser supports the `images` object, which is a prerequisite for image rollovers to work. All the functions in this script are contingent on the browser recognizing the `images` object. If it is not recognized, the browser will not display the rollover effects.

Ⓑ The next four lines handle the "on" graphics for the two images. The code creates an Image object for each graphic and preloads it into memory. To use this code for your own site, you simply need to change the filenames for the images (shown in bold). Don't change any of the other code, though, because the specific variables used here (`img1on`, `img2on`) are critical to the operation of this script.

Ⓒ This section handles the "off" graphics for the two images, again by creating an Image object for each one and preloading it into memory. For your own site, just change the filenames for the images (shown in bold), but don't change any of the other code.

Ⓓ The `imgOn()` function is what activates the rollover. When the user moves the mouse over an image, the `onMouseOver` event handler passes the image name to this function. The function adds the "on" suffix to the name and sources in the appropriate "on" GIF file. None of the code in this function needs to be changed for use on your own site.

Ⓔ The `imgOff()` function returns the graphic to its "off" state. When the mouse passes back out of the image, the `onMouseOut` event handler sends the image name to this function, which attaches the "off" suffix and sources in the appropriate "off" graphic. Again, you don't need to change anything in this function to use rollovers on your own site.

Ⓕ This is the HTML for one of the rollover images within the `<body>` of the document. There are actually two things happening here. First, the image is assigned a name within the `<img>` tag. JavaScript uses this name to refer to this particular graphic slot, so don't change the value of the `name` attribute when using this code for your own site. You do need to change is the `src` attribute to point to the right graphics file, and be sure to set the `width` and `height` attributes appropriately. Second, the calls to the `imgOn()` and `imgOff()` JavaScript functions are set up using the `onMouseOver` and `onMouseOut` event handlers. These need to go within the anchor `<a>` tag. The only thing you need to change in the `<a>` tag is the `href` attribute, to point to the appropriate page for your site.

Ⓖ This line sets up the `onMouseOver` event handler for this rollover. It says to call the `imgOn()` function when the mouse is over the graphic, passing the image name to that function. Nothing in this line needs to be changed to use this script for your own site.

Ⓗ This line sets up the `onMouseOut` event handler for this rollover. It says to call the `imgOut()` function when the mouse leaves the area of the graphic, passing the image name to that function. Again, nothing here needs to be changed for use on your own site.

Example 28-1 uses two image rollovers. If you need more rollovers for your web page, simply follow the naming scheme for adding more "on" and "off" graphics. Note that the graphics filename does not need to be exactly the same as the image object name, as is done in this example. For example, here's the code you'd need to add in the head of the document for a third button:

```
img3on = new Image();
img3on.src = "lighton.gif";

img3off = new Image();
img3off.src = "lightoff.gif";
```

Then, in the body, you'd have the following HTML:

```
<A HREF="brightlights.html"
   onMouseOver="imgOn('img3')"
   onMouseOut="imgOff('img3')">
<IMG NAME="img3" BORDER=0 HEIGHT=20 WIDTH=125 SRC="lightoff.gif"></A>
```

Changing two images at once

You can also use a single onMouseOver event handler to change two graphics on the page simultaneously. In this example, there are images that link to the "jukebox" and "videos" sections of a site. When the user moves the mouse over either image, JavaScript turns that image "on" and also displays an informational graphic in a third image area that has been named holder.

Most of the code for multiple rollovers is the same as the single rollover example in Example 28-1, but with a few additions to establish and display the additional graphic (in this case, the information graphic). Example 28-2 shows the multiple rollover code; an explanation of the additions follows the script.

Example 28-2: JavaScript code for multiple rollovers

```
<HTML>
<HEAD>
<TITLE>Multiple Rollovers</TITLE>
<SCRIPT LANGUAGE = "JavaScript">
<!--
if (document.images) {

    // "On" images
    img1on = new Image();
    img1on.src = "jukeboxon.gif";
    img2on = new Image();
    img2on.src = "videoson.gif";

    // "Off" images
    img1off = new Image();
    img1off.src = "jukeboxoff.gif";     // Inactive Images
    img2off = new Image();
    img2off.src = "videosoff.gif";
```

Example 28-2: JavaScript code for multiple rollovers (continued)

```
        // Information images     ❹
        img1info = new Image();
        img1info.src = "jukeboxinfo.gif";
        img2info = new Image();
        img2info.src = "videosinfo.gif";
}

// Function to activate images
function imgOn(imgName) {
    if (document.images) {
        document.images[imgName].src = eval(imgName + "on.src");
        document.images["holder"].src = eval(imgName + "info.src");     ❺
    }
}

// Function to deactivate images
function imgOff(imgName) {
    if (document.images) {
        document.images[imgName].src = eval(imgName + "off.src");
        document.images["holder"].src = "clear.gif";     ❻
    }
}

//-->
</SCRIPT>
</HEAD>

<BODY>
<!-- First rollover -->
<A HREF="jukebox.html"
    onMouseOver="imgOn('img1')"
    onMouseOut="imgOff('img1')">
<IMG NAME="img1" BORDER=0 HEIGHT=24 WIDTH=100 SRC="jukeboxoff.gif"></A>

<!-- Second rollover -->
<A HREF="videos.html"
    onMouseOver="imgOn('img2')"
    onMouseOut="imgOff('img2')">
<IMG NAME="img2" BORDER=0 HEIGHT=24 WIDTH=100 SRC="videosoff.gif"></A>

<!-- Additional image area -->
<IMG NAME="holder" HEIGHT=100 WIDTH=100 SRC="clear.gif">     ❼
</BODY>
</HTML>
```

❹   These four lines handle the information graphics for each of the previous "on"
    and "off" graphics. The code creates an Image object for each graphic and
    preloads it into memory.

❺   The `imgOn()` function for activating the rollover now includes an additional
    line that changes the `holder` graphic to one of the informational graphics.

ⓒ Similarly, the `imgOff()` function now contains a line that returns the `holder` graphic back to its "off" state (displaying *clear.gif*).

ⓓ This `<img>` tag named `holder` is where the information graphics are displayed. It contains a graphic called *clear.gif* when neither button is activated.

As with the simple rollover script, to use this script for your own site, all you need to change are the graphics filenames and URLs.

Handling Multiple Browsers

Unlike CGI scripts, which run on the server and don't require any particular intelligence on the part of the browser, JavaScript code is completely dependent on browser support. If you put a script on your page, browsers that don't understand JavaScript won't know what to do with it. As I mentioned earlier, these browsers will interpret the code as straight text, and the result is rather unpleasant.

It's even more unpleasant, however, when your code isn't completely understood by a JavaScript-aware browser. As we've already discussed, different browsers, and different versions of the same browser, support different versions of JavaScript. A poorly written script can generate error messages or even crash a user's browser, which discourages return visits. Fortunately, JavaScript provides ways to target the browsers that understand specific JavaScript elements.

Checking for Browsers

If you have a script that you know works in Netscape 6 and IE 5.5 but doesn't work in older browsers, you may want to check browser versions and serve your script to users of the browsers in which it works, but not to users of older browsers. Using the techniques shown in this section, you can serve different scripts to different browsers. This means you can write different scripts for people using the latest browser versions and for users of the Version 4.0 browsers, for example. And you can also have an HTML-only option for browsers that don't support JavaScript (or have it turned off).

The first step is to check the browser's name and version number and assign that information to variables. The following code puts the name of the browser in a variable called `browserName` and the version number in a variable called `browserVersion`. Depending on the name and number in these variables, the variable `browser` is assigned a value corresponding to the appropriate browser. Thus, if the browser is Netscape 6, `browser` is set to `nn6`; if the browser is IE 4, `browser` is set to `ie4`. After the browser identity has been assigned to this variable, you can use `if/else` statements to ensure that only the correct browser tries to run any browser-specific code:

```
<HTML>
<HEAD>
<SCRIPT LANGUAGE = "JavaScript">
<!--
// Check browser name and number and assign info to variable
browserName = navigator.appName;
```

```
browserVersion = parseInt(navigator.appVersion);

if (browserName == "Netscape" && browserVersion == 5)
    browser = "nn6";
else if (browserName == "Netscape" && browserVersion == 4)
    browser= "nn4";
else if (browserName == "Netscape" && browserVersion == 3)
    browser = "nn3";
else if (browserName == "Microsoft Internet Explorer" &&
         browserVersion == 4 &&
         navigator.appVersion.indexOf("MSIE 5.5") != -1)
    browser = "ie55";
else if (browserName == "Microsoft Internet Explorer" &&
         browserVersion == 4 &&
         navigator.appVersion.indexOf("MSIE 5.0") != -1)
    browser = "ie5";
else if (browserName == "Microsoft Internet Explorer"
         && browserVersion == 4)
    browser = "ie4";

// Handle browser-specific code
if (browser == "nn6" || browser == "ie55" || browser == "ie5") {
    // Latest JavaScript code goes here
}

else if (browser == "nn4") {
    // Netscape Navigator 4 specific code goes here
}

else if (browser == "ie4") {
    // Internet Explorer 4 specific code goes here
}
//-->
</SCRIPT>
</HEAD>
<BODY>
<!-- Standard HTML code goes here -->
</BODY>
</HTML>
```

In this code, the first if statement checks to see if the browser is Netscape 6, IE 5, or IE 5.5. If the user is running one of these browsers, the JavaScript code in that if statement is executed. If the browser is not Netscape 6, IE 5, or IE 5.5, the code checks for IE 4 or Navigator 4 and runs the appropriate code in either case. If the user is running an even older browser, no script is run. In any case, the body of the HTML document is displayed normally.

There are a lot of nuances to browser detection. Fortunately, there are a number of different browser detection scripts available on the Web, so you don't have to create your own. You can find a very thorough one, along with a helpful discussion of its use, at *http://www.mozilla.org/docs/web-developer/sniffer/browser_type. html.*

Browser Compatibility

As I noted earlier, varying levels of JavaScript support have been built into browsers since Netscape Navigator 2.0. Table 28-2 shows the version of JavaScript supported by the various versions of Internet Explorer and Netscape Navigator on different platforms. You can use this table to plan your site's browser support and update your browser detection scripts.

Table 28-2: JavaScript support in various browsers

Platform	Browser	JavaScript version
Windows	MS IE 5.5	1.5 (ECMA 3)
Windows	MS IE 5.0	1.3 (ECMA 2)
Windows	MS IE 4.0	1.2 (ECMA 1)
Windows	MS IE 3.0	1.0
Windows	MS IE 2.0	Not supported
Windows	NN 6	1.5 (ECMA 3)
Windows	NN 4.7/4.5	1.3 (ECMA 2)
Windows	NN 4.0	1.2
Windows	NN 3.0	1.1
Windows	NN 2.0	1.0
Mac	MS IE 5.0	1.3 (ECMA 2)
Mac	MS IE 4.0	1.2 (ECMA 1)
Mac	MS IE 3.0	1.0
Mac	NN 6	1.5 (ECMA 3)
Mac	NN 4.7/4.5	1.3 (ECMA 2)
Mac	NN 4.0	1.2
Mac	NN 3.0	1.1
Mac	NN 2.0	1.0
Unix/Linux	NN 6	1.5 (ECMA 3)
Unix/Linux	NN 4.7/4.5	1.3 (ECMA 2)
Unix/Linux	NN 4.0	1.2
Unix/Linux	NN 3.0	1.1
Unix/Linux	NN 2.0	1.0

CHAPTER 29

Introduction to DHTML

HTML is based on thinking of a web page like a printed page: a document that is rendered once and that is static once rendered. The idea behind Dynamic HTML (DHTML), however, is to make every element of a page interactively controllable, before, during, and after the page is rendered. This means you can make things move, appear and disappear, overlap, change styles, and interact with the user to your heart's content. Through DHTML, users get a more engaging and interactive web experience without constant calls to a web server or the overhead of loading new pages, plug-ins, or large applets.

DHTML is not a language itself, but rather a combination of:

- HTML 4.0 (or XHTML 1.0)

- JavaScript—the Web's standard scripting language

- Cascading Style Sheets (CSS)—styles dictated outside a document's content

- Document Object Model (DOM)—a means of accessing a document's individual elements

Since the first edition of this book, Dynamic HTML has developed into a stable standard that is well supported by both Netscape 6 and Internet Explorer 5.5.

Netscape Navigator 4.0 and IE 4.0 supported earlier, proprietary versions of DHTML, and they differed greatly in their support for CSS and dynamically positioned elements. The differences between what these two browser versions called DHTML has created a million migraines among web developers. Accounting for the inconsistencies required creating two separate web pages or jumping through browser-detection hoops to give all users the same experience.

Fortunately, with the latest browsers, there are significantly fewer headaches involved with DHTML. In this chapter, we'll be concentrating on using the W3C and ECMA standards supported by the latest browsers, but we'll briefly cover the earlier versions of DHTML later in this chapter.

Using DHTML

Like most web technologies, DHTML comes with its share of pros and cons. DHTML's reliance on a variety of standards makes it difficult to generalize, so you should decide on a case by case basis whether or not to use DHTML. The following are the major factors to consider when considering using DHTML on your site.

Advantages to Using DHTML

Using DHTML has the following advantages:

- **File sizes are small.** DHTML files are small compared to other interactive media like Flash or Shockwave (see Chapter 26), so they download more quickly.

- **It's supported by both major browser manufacturers.** Both Microsoft and Netscape currently support DHTML in some shape or form.

- **DHTML is a standard.** The World Wide Web Consortium (W3C) has released specifications for DOM 0, 1, and 2, and CSS 1 and 2 (see the web site at *http://www.w3c.org* for more information). These specifications lay the groundwork for DHTML.

- **No plug-ins, ActiveX controls, or Java is necessary.** A visitor to your site needs only a recent web browser to take advantage of your DHTML. This puts fewer requirements on your audience because they don't need to download special software to view your site.

- **There are fewer calls to the server.** Since you can change and move elements after a page is loaded, you don't need to create separate pages just to change styles or display a menu. This saves you time in building pages, and it saves users time because each request to the server takes time and bogs down the browsing experience.

Disadvantages

But keep in mind these disadvantages:

- **Only new browsers support DHTML.** Only recent browsers like Netscape 6, IE 5.5, and Opera 5 support standards-based DHTML. Many people are still using older versions of these browsers, however, so web designers using DHTML must accommodate these older browsers or sacrifice a significant portion of their audience.

- **Netscape and Microsoft have different DHTML implementations.** Different implementations, especially in the 4.0 browsers, can make creating a DHTML document tedious and complicated.

- **DHTML creation has a steep learning curve.** Because DHTML requires at least partial knowledge of many different web technologies (HTML, JavaScript, CSS, and DOM), it takes some learning and practice before you begin creating DHTML content. DHTML tools can go a long way towards eliminating this problem.

How DHTML Works

As I mentioned earlier, DHTML is a combination of HTML, Cascading Style Sheets, JavaScript, and the Document Object Model. Example 29-1 illustrates how these elements work together. The web page shown here uses simple DHTML to change the style of links to be red and underlined when the mouse is rolled over them. You can use this basic format to tie CSS styles to common events like onMouseOver or OnClick, so you can change the styles of most elements on the fly.

Example 29-1: Rollover style changes using DHTML

```
<html>    🅐
<head>
<title>Rollover Style Changes</title>

<style>    🅑
<!--
a { text-decoration: none; }
-->
</style>

<script>    🅒
<!--
function turnOn(currentLink) {
    currentLink.style.color = "#990000";    🅓
    currentLink.style.textDecoration = "underline";
}

function turnOff(currentLink) {
    currentLink.style.color = "#0000FF";
    currentLink.style.textDecoration = "none";
}
//-->
</script>
</head>

<body bgcolor="#FFFFFF">
<a href="#home"    🅔
    onMouseOver="turnOn(this);" onMouseOut="turnOff(this);">Home</a>
<a href="#contact"
    onMouseOver="turnOn(this);" onMouseOut="turnOff(this);">Contact</a>
<a href="#links"
    onMouseOver="turnOn(this);" onMouseOut="turnOff(this);">Links</a>
</body>
</html>
```

🅐 This page is an HTML file, so it starts with normal <html> and <head> HTML tags.

🅑 In the <head>, we have a CSS style sheet, defined using the <style> tag, that removes any text decorations from all the links in the document. In this case, the point is to remove the default underlines from links.

❸ Inside the `<script>` tag, there are two JavaScript functions, `turnOn()` and `turnOff()`, that change the style of a link when the user moves the mouse over and back out of the link. When the mouse enter a link, the text is underlined and turned red. When the mouse exits, these effects are removed.

❹ The script uses the DOM to reference the link's `style` attribute and change the `color` and `textDecoration` properties, which are the DOM equivalents of the CSS properties `color` and `text-decoration`.

❺ In this `<a>` tag, the `onMouseOver` and `onMouseOut` event handlers are used to set up the calls to `turnOn()` and `turnOff()`.

The Document Object Model

The Document Object Model exposes every element of an HTML page to a scripting language, such as JavaScript. Early iterations of the DOM, now called DOM Level 0 and retained for backwards compatibility, gave scripts access to only some objects on a page, including forms, frames, and images. DOM Level 1 and DOM Level 2, however, allow you to access and change almost any part of an HTML (or XHTML) document, so you can modify, add, or remove attributes or even entire elements. (For more information on the DOM specifications, see *http:// www.w3.org/DOM/.*)

In JavaScript parlance, each element of the page is an *object*. The DOM begins with a base object called the document object, which refers to the HTML page itself and everything in it. All the elements contained within the HTML page, such as headings, paragraphs, images, forms, and links, are represented by separate objects. These objects branch off from the document object, like branches from a tree trunk, to form a hierarchy of elements.

To do something such as changing the appearance of a particular element in an HTML document, you first have to reference the object that corresponds to that element. Let's start with a simple example, where we want to reference a particular image in an HTML document. Using JavaScript, the general form of the reference is:

```
document.images["image_name"]
```

Say we have HTML code that looks like this:

```
<IMG SRC="start.gif" NAME="start">
```

To refer to this image, we can use the following JavaScript:

```
document.images["start"]
```

Images, along with some other common elements, such as forms and links, get special treatment in the DOM, so they can be referenced using this simple syntax. For regular HTML elements, like headings and paragraphs, the technique is a bit different. Consider the following HTML document:

```
<html>
<head>
<title>Sample Document</title>
</head>
```

```
<body>
<h1>An HTML Document</h1>
<p id="simple">This is a simple paragraph.</p>
</body>
</html>
```

To refer to the paragraph element in this document, we can use the following JavaScript:

```
document.getElementById("simple")
```

getElementById() is a *method*, or built-in function, of the document object. It returns the HTML element with the specified id attribute in the document, which in this case is the paragraph we are interested in. The document object also has a number of other methods for accessing HTML elements, such as getElementsByTagName() and getElementsByName().

Just referencing an object isn't particularly interesting, however. What we really want to be able to do is manipulate the object, say by changing its appearance or location. One way to manipulate an object is to change its *properties*, which describe different characteristics of the object. In most cases, these properties actually correspond to attributes of the HTML element represented by the object. For example, an image object has a src property that corresponds to the src attribute of the <img> tag. We used this property to implement image rollovers in Chapter 28.

Table 29-1 lists the DOM objects for some common HTML elements, along with some of their properties.

Table 29-1: DOM objects and their properties

Object	HTML element	Properties
document.body	body	alink, attributes, background, bgcolor, style, text, title, vlink
document.links[]	a	attributes, className, href, id, name, style, tagName, title
document.forms[]	form	action, attributes, elements, id, style, tagName, target, title
document.images[]	img	align, alt, attributes, border, height, hspace, id, isMap, name, src, style, tagName, title, useMap, vspace, width

With DHTML, the style property is by far the most important property. It lets you access all of the CSS properties that apply to a particular element, so you can use it to change things like the color, font family, and font size of an element. For example, here's how we can change the color of our simple paragraph to green:

```
document.getElementById("simple").style.color = "00FF00";
```

Creating Layers

Dynamically positioned objects in DHTML are often referred to as layers, probably because they work like the layers used in many graphics programs, such as Adobe Photoshop. A *layer* is a container for content that can be positioned in the x (horizontal), y (vertical), and z (stacking order) dimensions. A typical layer is created with a `<div>` tag surrounding other HTML elements, as shown in Example 29-2. Special attributes in the `<div>` tag define its behavior. Once you've created a layer, you can show and hide it, animate it, or change its appearance in other ways. (Note that this example simply demonstrates creating a layer, not manipulating it in any way; we'll see examples of that shortly.)

Example 29-2: Defining a Simple Layer

```
<html>
<head>
<style type="text/css">
<!--
.welcome { font-family: Geneva, Arial, Helvetica, san-serif;
          font-size: large;
          font-style: oblique;}
-->
</style>
</head>

<body bgcolor="#FFFFFF" text="#000000">
<div id="Layer1"      Ⓐ
     style="position:absolute;     Ⓑ
           z-index:1;     Ⓒ
           left:100px; top:10px;     Ⓓ
           width:300px; height:60px;     Ⓔ
           background-color: #FFCC00;">     Ⓕ

<p align="center" class="welcome">Welcome To Jen's World!</p>
</div>
</body>
</html>
```

Ⓐ This line specifies an `id` for the `<div>`, so that we can manipulate it later with JavaScript.

Ⓑ With the `style` attribute, we specify a number of CSS properties for the `<div>`. First, we make the layer a positionable object by setting the `position` property. The possible values for `position` are `absolute` and `relative`.

Ⓒ This line sets the `z-index` CSS property, which defines the stacking order of layers. While the x and y coordinates for a layer are defined in pixels, `z-index` simply assigns a number to a layer. If two layers overlap, the layer with the higher `z-index` is placed on top.

Ⓓ The `left` and `top` properties define the number of pixels between the left edge of the layer and the left edge of the browser, and the top edge of the layer with the top edge of the browser, respectively.

Ⓔ This line specifies the `width` and `height` in pixels for the layer.

Ⓕ Finally, we set the `background-color` property for the layer.

Figure 29-1 shows what Example 29-2 looks like in a browser.

Figure 29-1: A simple layer

DHTML Examples

Now that you have a basic understanding of the Document Object Model and know how to create layers, we can look at some useful examples to get you started on your own DHTML sites.

Rollover Style Changes

We already examined this script back in Example 29-1. When the user rolls the mouse over a link, the style of the text is changed to be red and underlined. This is done by manipulating the `style` property of links via the DOM. As we discussed earlier, the `style` property gives access to all of the CSS properties for an element. Using JavaScript, we can change the values of the `color` and `textDecoration` CSS properties when particular events occur. In this case, we use the `onMouseOver` and `onMouseOut` events. Here's the script again, to refresh your memory:

```
<html>
<head>
<title>Rollover Style Changes</title>

<style>
<!--
a { text-decoration: none; }
-->
</style>

<script>
<!--
function turnOn(currentLink) {
    currentLink.style.color = "#990000";
    currentLink.style.textDecoration = "underline";
```

```
    }

    function turnOff(currentLink) {
        currentLink.style.color = "#0000FF";
        currentLink.style.textDecoration = "none";
    }
    //-->
    </script>
    </head>

    <body bgcolor="#FFFFFF">
    <a href="#home"
       onMouseOver="turnOn(this);" onMouseOut="turnOff(this);">Home</a>
    <a href="#contact"
       onMouseOver="turnOn(this);" onMouseOut="turnOff(this);">Contact</a>
    <a href="#links"
       onMouseOver="turnOn(this);" onMouseOut="turnOff(this);">Links</a>
    </body>
    </html>
```

You can adapt this script for your own site by changing the `color` and `textDecoration` values, shown in bold. You can also modify the `turnOn()` and `turnOff()` functions to set additional properties the same way. For example, you can set the background of the links to a light yellow color when rolled over, simply by adding this line to `turnOn()`:

```
    currentLink.style.backgroundColor = "#FFFFCC";
```

And here's the corresponding line for `turnOff()`, to reset the background color when the mouse exits the link:

```
    currentLink.style.backgroundColor = "#FFFFFF";
```

Note that when you set `style` properties using JavaScript, as in this example, you must set them to strings.

There's actually one more thing you need to understand about this example: how the `turnOn()` and `turnOff()` functions know which link to modify. In each `<a>` tag, you'll notice that the link passes `this` as a parameter to the `turnOn()` and `turnOff()` functions. In JavaScript, the word `this` plays a special role, allowing an object (or element) to refer to itself. Our example passes `this` to `turnOn()` and `turnOff()` as a simple way of referencing the object for the current link, so that the function operates on the correct one. Using `this` is really just a shortcut; we also could have accessed the correct link using one of the DOM methods described earlier.

Drop-Down Menus

One of the most common interface elements in desktop applications is the menubar with drop-down menus. You can make the same kind of menus with DHTML by showing and hiding positioned layers, as shown in Figure 29-2. When the user clicks on "Resources" or "Links", a layer with links is displayed below it,

just like a normal menu. When the user double-clicks on the link, the layer is
hidden again.

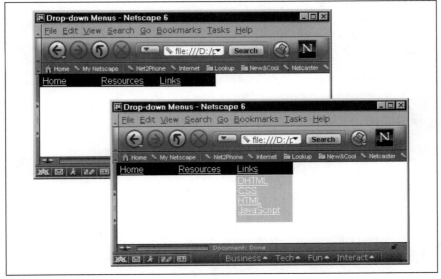

Figure 29-2: A drop-down menu with DHTML

The DHTML code in Example 29-3 creates the menus shown in Figure 29-2. The
JavaScript combines two concepts we've seen before: creating a positioned layer
and manipulating a style via the DOM.

Example 29-3: Drop-down menus with DHTML

```
<html>
<head>
<title>Drop-down Menus</title>

<script language="JavaScript">
<!--
function showLayer(layerid) {
    layer = document.getElementById(layerid);      Ⓐ
    layer.style.visibility = "visible";    Ⓑ
}

function hideLayer(layerid) {    Ⓒ
    layer = document.getElementById(layerid);
    layer.style.visibility = "hidden";
}
//-->
</script>

<style type="text/css">
```

Example 29-3: Drop-down menus with DHTML (continued)

```
<!--
a { font-family: Arial, Helvetica, sans-serif;
    color: #FFFFFF; margin-left: 3px}
-->
</style>
</head>

<body bgcolor="#FFFFFF" text="#000000" topmargin="0" leftmargin="0"
      marginwidth="0" marginheight="0">
<table border="0" bgcolor="#000000" cellspacing="0" cellpadding="2">
  <tr>
    <td width="100"> <a href="#">Home</a></td>

    <td width="100">
      <div id="ResMenu"        ❶
           style="position:absolute; left:110px; top:23px;
                  width:100px; height:62px; z-index:1;
                  background-color:#CCCCCC; layer-background-color:#CCCCCC;
                  visibility:hidden">
        <a href="#">Scripts</a><br>
        <a href="#">Reference</a><br>
        <a href="#">Weblog</a>
      </div>

      <a href="#" onClick="showLayer('ResMenu');"        ❷
         onDblClick="hideLayer('ResMenu');">Resources</a>
    </td>

    <td width="100">
      <div id="LinksMenu"
           style="position:absolute; left:211px; top:23px;
                  width:100px; height:85px; z-index:2;
                  background-color:#CCCCCC; layer-background-color:#CCCCCC;
                  visibility:hidden">
        <a href="#">DHTML</a><br>
        <a href="#">CSS</a><br>
        <a href="#">HTML</a><br>
        <a href="#">JavaScript</a>
      </div>

      <a href="#" onClick="showLayer('LinksMenu');"
         onDblClick="hideLayer('LinksMenu');">Links</a>
    </td>
  </tr>
</table>
</body>
</html>
```

❶ The `showLayer()` function references the layer object for our menu with a document method, `document.getElementById()`, and sets a variable named `layer` to be able to refer to that object again. The ID for the correct layer object is passed into the function as an argument, `layerid`. The showLayer() function is triggered by the onClick event handler for the "Resources" and "Links" links.

ⓑ This line of the function sets the layer's visibility property (through the style property), which is a CSS property that controls the visibility of a layer. When the layer is created, it is hidden, so the showLayer() function sets visibility to "visible" to make the menu appear.

ⓒ The hideLayer() function works just like the showLayer() function, except that it hides the menu by setting visibility to "hidden". The hideLayer() function is triggered by the onDblClick event handler.

ⓓ This <div> tag creates the layer for the "Resources" menu. Note that the layer is given a specific id, so that we can refer to it later. Various CSS properties are set using the style attribute. These properties set the size and position of the layer precisely, so that it appears at the appropriate location for a drop-down menu. The one CSS property we haven't seen yet is visibility; this property is set to hidden so that menu is invisible until the user clicks on the "Resources" link to activate it.

ⓔ This link is created to control the menu. The onClick event handler calls showLayer() to display the menu, and the onDblClick event handler calls hideLayer() to remove it. Each function is passed the argument 'ResMenu', which tells the function which layer to display and hide.

It is pretty easy to adapt this script for your own site: most of the work is in figuring out the layout for your menu links and then determining the exact size and location for each menu layer. In other words, you'll need to adjust the top, left, width, and height properties for the actual content and layout of your page. You can also adjust the various color styles to suit your purposes. The two properties you need to leave as is are position and visibility. Give each menu layer a unique id attribute, and then pass that ID to the showLayer() and hideLayer() functions via the onClick and onDblClick event handlers for your menu link. You don't need to change the showLayer() and hideLayer() functions at all.

Sliding Tabs

Making an object move in DHTML is like making any other style change. All you are doing is changing one of two properties—style.left or style.top—to get an object from one place to another. The illusion of motion happens when you change the object's position incrementally and quickly.

In this example, we're creating a tab on the left-hand side of the browser that is 75 pixels off the left edge of the screen, so that the main content of the tab is not visible. When the user clicks on "show>>", the tab moves right 5 pixels every millisecond until it is completely onscreen, as shown in Figure 29-3. Clicking on the "<<hide" link returns the tab to its original position.

Example 29-4 shows the DHTML code for the sliding tab. As with the drop-down menu, we are creating a positioned layer and manipulating it with the DOM. What's new in this example is the code for moving the layer. Just by changing the style.left property, we've created the illusion of motion.

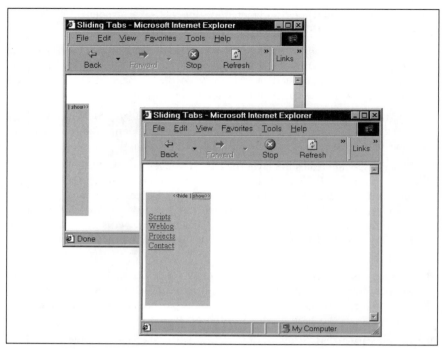

Figure 29-3: A sliding tab with DHTML

Example 29-4: A sliding tab with DHTML

```
<html>
<head>
<title>Sliding Tabs</title>

<style>
<!--
.hideshow { color: #333333; font-size: 9px; font-family: sans-serif;
            text-decoration: none; }
-->
</style>

<script language="JavaScript">
<!--
function showLayer() {
    hiddenLayer = document.getElementById("TabLayer");        Ⓐ
    layerPosition = parseInt(hiddenLayer.style.left);
    if (layerPosition < 0) {
        hiddenLayer.style.left = (layerPosition + 5) + "px";   Ⓑ
        setTimeout("showLayer()", 20);      Ⓒ
    }
}

function hideLayer() {   Ⓓ
    hiddenLayer = document.getElementById("TabLayer");
    hiddenLayer.style.left = "-75" + "px";
}
```

Example 29-4: A sliding tab with DHTML (continued)

```
<html>
//-->
</script>
</head>

<body>
<div id="Layer1"    Ⓔ
    style="position:absolute; left:-75px; top:50px;
            width:115px; height:200px; z-index:1;
            background-color: #CCCCCC; layer-background-color: #CCCCCC;">

  <p align="right" class="hideshow">
    <a href="javascript:hideLayer();" class="hideshow">&lt;&lt;hide</a>    Ⓕ
    <a href="javascript:showLayer();" class="hideshow">show&gt;&gt;</a>    Ⓖ
  </p>

  <p align="left" style="margin-left: 5px;">
    <a href="#">Scripts</a><br>
    <a href="#">Weblog</a><br>
    <a href="#">Projects</a><br>
    <a href="#">Contact</a>
  </p>
</div>
</body>
</html>
```

Ⓐ This line references the layer object for our tab and stores it in the variable named **layer**. Since the **showLayer()** function only needs to work on one layer, we don't get the layer ID as an argument but instead refer specifically to **'TabLayer'** in the call to **getElementById()**.

Ⓑ This line is what actually moves the tab layer. Each time **showLayer()** is called, if the layer isn't in its final position, **style.left** is incremented by 5 (shown in bold), which moves the tab five pixels to the right. If you want to change the distance the layer travels each frame, you can replace this value. A larger value will result in faster movement, a smaller value in slower movement. Note the inclusion of **"px"** here; this specifies the units (pixels) and converts the whole thing to a string. Both are necessary when setting location values in JavaScript.

Ⓒ The **setTimeout()** method is a built-in JavaScript method that lets you create a counter that waits a given number of milliseconds before executing a function. With this method, we can call **showLayer()** repeatedly, where each call moves the layer a few pixels until it is in its final position. Each repetition of the function is equivalent to one frame of animation, so the amount of time **setTimeout()** waits before executing **showLayer()** is, in effect, your frame rate. The second argument to **setTimeout()** (shown in bold) controls how often **showLayer()** is called. We're using a value of 20, which refers to 20 milliseconds. To make the animation go more slowly, increase this value.

Ⓓ The **hideLayer()** function simply moves the tab layer back to its original position, so that the content of the tab is not visible.

E This `<div>` tag creates the layer for the sliding tab. Note that left is set to −75px, which is what pushes the content of the tab out of the visible region of the browser window. Also, because the layer is in fact visible, we don't need to set the `visibility` property.

F The "<<hide" link uses a `javascript:` URL to call the `hideLayer()` function.

G The "show>>" link uses a `javascript:` URL to call the `showLayer()` function.

Browser Detection

All of the DHTML examples we've looked at in this chapter depend on features of the DOM Level 1 and DOM Level 2 standards, which means that they only work in the latest web browsers, Netscape 6 and Internet Explorer 5.5. This means that if you use one of these examples, you must first check for the user's browser type and version, so that you can make sure that the browser supports the script. Each of the example scripts should begin like this:

```
<script language="JavaScript">
var isNN4, isIE4, isDOM;

if (document.getElementById) {
    isDOM = true;
}
else {
    if ( parseInt(navigator.appVersion) == 4) {
        if ( navigator.appName == "Netscape" ) {
            isNN4 = true;
        }
        if ( navigator.appName == "Microsoft Internet Explorer" ) {
            isIE4 = true;
        }
    }
}
</script>
```

This code checks the identity and version of the browser and sets the appropriate variable to `true`: `isDOM` for a standards-compliant version of Navigator or IE, `isNN4` for Netscape Navigator 4, or `isIE4` for IE 4.

Once we have tested the user's browser and set the appropriate variable, we can use that variable to run the right browser-specific code:

```
if (isDOM) {
    // Insert W3C DOM-based DHTML here
}
else if (isIE4) {
    // Insert IE 4 DHTML here
}
else if (isNN4) {
    // Insert Navigator 4 DHTML here
}
```

Layers in the 4.0 Browsers

The DHTML code that we've used to access and manipulate layers works only in the latest web browsers. If you need to support the 4.0 browsers, there are a few things you need to know about their proprietary versions of DHTML.

Netscape introduced a `<layer>` tag in Navigator 4.0 for creating layers, while Microsoft implemented layers with `<div>` tags in Internet Explorer 4.0. As of Netscape 6, Netscape has dropped the `<layer>` tag because it never became a standard, so you can use `<div>` layers in both browsers from now on.

The key thing with DHTML is being able to access the layer objects, so that you can manipulate them. In the Internet Explorer 4.0 DOM, you can access all the layers in a document through the `all` property of the document. A reference to a layer looks like this:

```
document.all.layer_name
```

Thus we would access our sliding tab layer like this:

```
document.all.TabLayer
```

Once you have a reference to a layer in IE 4.0, you can access the CSS properties through the `style` property, just as we've been doing in all of the examples in this chapter:

```
document.all.TabLayer.style.left
```

Unfortunately, with Netscape Navigator 4.0, things aren't quite so simple. You access a Navigator 4.0 `<layer>` like this:

```
document.layer_name
```

So the following code would refer to our sliding tab layer:

```
document.TabLayer
```

In Navigator 4.0, the layer object defines a number of properties and methods that you can use to manipulate the layer. The properties largely correspond to the CSS property names, but you access them directly through the layer object; there is no `style` property:

```
document.TabLayer.left
```

Obviously, this discussion barely scratches the surface of the complexity of developing DHTML for the 4.0 browsers. If you want to learn more, see Danny Goodman's book, *Dynamic HTML: The Definitive Reference* (O'Reilly).

DHTML Tools

Many web designers rely on WYSIWYG tools and editors for creating web pages. These tools make it possible to see the effects of creating and editing immediately. There are a number of DHTML WYSIWYG editors available today that may suit your needs for creating dynamic web pages.

Even with the relatively simple examples we've examined in this chapter, you can see that hand coding DHTML can be complicated and arduous. In addition, the differences between Navigator 4.0 and Internet Explorer 4.0 force web designers to write two additional sets of code for each function, to retain backwards-compatibility. This increases production time and creates code that is difficult to read and maintain.

There are many tools that create DHTML for you behind the scenes. Some of these tools are narrow in focus and provide specific functionality, while others, such as Macromedia Dreamweaver and Adobe GoLive, are full packages with which you can create and maintain whole web sites, as well as write DHTML code.

It is beyond the scope of this book to provide working details of WYSIWIG DHTML tools. Each of these tools has their own pros and cons. Commercial tools with full DHTML support are likely to provide a more robust implementation and better support to users. However, these software packages require a larger investment of time and money. If you want only simple animations or style changes, a shareware tool may be the best way for you to go. Luckily, most web authoring tools are available for free download over the Internet on a trial basis, so you can experiment and choose the one that suits your needs. To learn about available tools, check out the resources listed at the end of this chapter.

WYSIWYG DHTML tools differ greatly in their operation. They have to allow you to view and manipulate layers, styles, scripts, and animation in a graphical way. You can create animations by dragging objects in the editor, thus eliminating the need to write JavaScript that counts pixels and tracks x,y coordinates. Dreamweaver, for instance, features built-in behaviors for rollovers, moving layers, and changing styles. You can also download extensions from Macromedia's web site, most of them created by third-party developers; these add a variety of DHTML behaviors and commands to Dreamweaver.

Advantages

Consider these advantages to using WYSIWYG DHTML tools:

- **There is a shorter learning curve for WYSIWYG editors.** Because DHTML is a combination of HTML, JavaScript, Cascading Style Sheets, and DOM, it has a steep learning curve. An editor hides the complexities of DHTML and allows you to manipulate objects through a timeline or other graphic interface.

- **Editors allow you to create effects more quickly.** An effect that could take hours of coding and then debugging may be created on a WYSIWYG editor in a matter of minutes.

- **Cross-browser implementation is less of a worry.** Browser compatibility is less of an issue with DHTML editors. Most of them create cross-browser DHTML, and most will also tell you which behaviors will work with which browsers.

Disadvantages

There are also some disadvantages, however:

- **WYSIWYG editors are expensive.** Some of these editors can cost hundreds of dollars, which isn't within every developer's budget. Editors can vary greatly in price, so shop around. Luckily, most software companies allow you to try their editor for free so that you can make an educated decision before buying.

- **Editors may not give precise control over your objects.** Not every editor gives you pixel level control over your dynamic objects and pages. Many designs require precise, pixel-level control of dynamic objects. Also, you are viewing your code as your editor chooses to depict it—if bugs do occur in your DHTML pages, they may be more difficult to fix.

- **An editor may not do everything.** By using a WYSIWYG editor, you are removing yourself from your DHTML code by one degree. If you are dependent upon your editor for DHTML effects, new DHTML features cannot be taken advantage of until the company that creates your editor publishes a version that exploits those advancements for you. Most likely they'll charge for the upgrade. Meanwhile, other designers who can write their own DHTML code are able to exploit advancements as soon as they are supported in web browsers.

- **Tools may write unnaturally complex code.** Tools may make some processes more complex than they need to be, for instance, creating custom objects when they're not necessary.

Where to Learn More

This chapter only skimmed the surface of what there is to know about DHTML. The most up-to-date information can be found on the Web. Here are some useful sites:

- CNET Builder.com: *http://builder.cnet.com*

- Webmonkey: *http://www.webmonkey.com*

- Mozilla.org's web developer documentation, including links to all current HTML, CSS, ECMAScript and DOM standards: *http://www.mozilla.org/docs/web-developer/*

- The World Wide Web Consortium's site, for current information on web standards: *http://www.w3c.org*

Netscape and Microsoft are the official sources of documentation for their respective browsers, and these sites are the best place to go for current information and information about support levels and compatibility:

- Netscape: *http://developer.netscape.com*

- Microsoft: *http://msdn.microsoft.com*

CHAPTER 30

Introduction to XML

XML (Extensible Markup Language) is a document encoding or markup standard that has been approved by the World Wide Web Consortium. XML is not so much a language in itself (like HTML), but rather a set of rules for creating other markup languages. It is a *metalanguage* used to define other languages. If this all sounds highfalutin to you, think of it this way: XML provides a way for you to make up your own tags! This is a powerful new tool for exchanging meaningful information.

Consider these two examples, the first using standard HTML markup, the second using a markup language written according to the rules of XML:

```
<p>Bobby Five</p>
<p>4456</p>
<p>111.32</p>

<name>Bobby Five</name>
<accountNumber>4456</accountNumber>
<balance>111.32</balance>
```

The XML file tells a lot more about the information contained in the tags. With meaningful markup tags, elements on the page aren't just headings and paragraphs: they become useful data. So while this information can be displayed on a page, it can just as easily be stored in a database (which is a common use of XML-formatted information). Using XML, various communities—business groups, scientists, trade associations—may now define a markup language to suit their particular needs for information exchange and processing over the Web.

XML can also be used to indicate the structure of specialized information that could not be represented using HTML alone, such as musical notation and mathematical formulas. Chapter 27 illustrates how the XML-based language SMIL is used to assemble multimedia presentations. Chapter 31 discusses how the rules of XML have been applied to the HTML authoring language. We'll look at other examples of XML applications later in this chapter.

Background

The example at the beginning of this chapter highlights the limitations of HTML. HTML was designed specifically for displaying content in a browser, but isn't good for much else. When the creators of the Web needed a markup language that told browsers how to display web content, they used SGML guidelines to create HTML. SGML, Standard Generalized Markup Language, is a comprehensive set of syntax rules for marking up documents and data which has existed since the 1980s. It is the big kahuna of metalanguages! For information on SGML, including its history, see *http://www.oasis-open.org/cover/general.html*.

As the Web matured, it became clear that there was the need for more versatile markup languages. SGML provided a good model, but it was too vast and complex; it had many features that were unnecessary and wouldn't be used in the Web environment. XML is a simplified and reduced form of SGML, tailored just for the needs of sharing information over the Internet. It is powerful enough to describe data, but light enough to travel across the Web. Much of the credit for XML's creation can be attributed to Jon Bosak of Sun Microsystems, Inc., who started the W3C working group responsible for scaling down SGML to its portable, Web-friendly form.

As of this writing, XML is in Version 1.0, which was first issued in February 1998 and revised in October 2000. Various aspects and modules of XML are still in development. For more information and updates on the progress of the standard, see the W3C's site at *http://www.w3.org/XML*.

One of the first things the W3C did once they had XML in place was to apply it to the existing HTML specification. The resulting language is XHTML, which is just HTML rewritten according to the stricter, yet more expandable, rules of XML. For more information on XHTML, see Chapter 31.

How It Works

There are generally two files that are processed by an XML-compliant application to display XML content: the XML document and a style sheet (discussed in this section). In addition, some documents also use a *Document Type Definition* (DTD) that defines each tag allowed in the document along with its attributes and rules for use. The XML client can use the DTD to "decode" the markup and check it for accuracy. DTDs are discussed later in this chapter.

The software that interprets the information in XML documents is called a *parser*. Both Microsoft and Netscape have built XML parsers into the latest versions of their browsers (Internet Explorer 5.5 and higher and Netscape 6).

The XML Document

As we've seen at the beginning of this chapter, an XML document contains marked-up content and looks similar to HTML in that regard. While you may think of a document as containing paragraphs and headings, XML documents can contain a vast variety of content. An XML document might be text-based, like a magazine article, or it could contain only numerical data to be transferred from one database or application to another. An XML document might also contain an abstract structure such as a particular vector graphic shape or a mathematical equation.

It is important to note that an XML document is not limited to one physical file but may be made up of content from multiple files. Markup is used to integrate the contents of different files to form the logical structure of a single XML document.

XML documents are comprised of units called *elements*, which are indicated by tags. These elements may be further described or enhance by *attributes*. These terms should be familiar to you if you have any experience with HTML.

In addition, XML documents may contain *entities*, placeholders for content which you declare once and use throughout the document. We've seen character entities used in HTML (see Chapter 10 and Appendix F), but in XML, entities have a more versatile role.

In XML, entities can be used not only for single characters, but for any string of text, even another chunk of XML markup. Entities provide a useful shortcut for adding frequently used information to a document, such company contact information or a legal boilerplate. Special external entities are what's used to place parts of the XML document that reside in separate files. Entities may be defined in the document itself (*general entities*) or in the DTD for the XML application (*parameter entities*).

Style Sheets and XML

Remember that a markup language only describes the structure of a document; it is not concerned with how it looks. Documents refer to external style sheets that give instructions on how each element should look when displayed in a browser (or other display device).

Like HTML, XML documents can use Cascading Style Sheets (see Chapter 17). A more robust style sheet language called the Extensible Stylesheet Language (XSL) exists for XML documents. The W3C's general rule for which style sheet to use is "Use CSS whenever you can; use XSL whenever you must." XSL creates a large overhead in processing, whereas CSS is fast and simple, making it generally preferable.

XSL is useful when the contents of the XML document need to be "transformed" before final display. Transforming generally refers to the process of converting one XML language to another, such as turning a particular XML language into XHTML on the fly, but it can also be used for transformations as simple as replacing words with other words. An XSLT (Extensible Stylesheet Language for Transformations, a subset of XSL) style sheet works as a translator in the transformation process. XSL is not covered in this chapter; for more information, see the XSL information on the W3C site at *http://www.w3.org/Style/XSL/*.

XML Document Syntax

If you are familiar with HTML, a simple XML document shouldn't be too difficult to understand.

```
<?xml version "1.0" standalone="no"?>
<!DOCTYPE accounts SYSTEM "simple.dtd">
<accounts>
<customer>
    <name>Bobby Five</name>
    <accountNumber>4456</accountNumber>
    <balance>111.32</balance>
</customer>
</accounts>
```

In the first line, the code between the `<?xml` and the `?>` is called an *XML declaration*. This declaration contains special information for the XML processor (the program reading the XML) indicating that this document conforms to Version 1.0 of the XML standard. In addition, the `standalone="no"` attribute informs the program that an outside DTD is needed to correctly interpret the document.

The second line is the `DOCTYPE` declaration. It identifies the *root element* (`accounts` in our example) and the DTD for the document. The root element is the element in the document that contains all other elements. It must be unique, which means it may be used only once in the document. All XML documents *must* have a root element. The root element in HTML and XHTML documents is `html`, since the whole document is contained within `<html>` tags.

The last part of the declaration is a pointer to the DTD itself. The `SYSTEM` identifier points to the DTD resource by location (its URL). In our example, the DTD of the document resides in a separate local file named *simple.dtd*. As an alternative, some declarations use the `PUBLIC` identifier to point to the DTD (or other resource) by a unique name. The advantage to using `PUBLIC` is that it is still valid if the location of the resource changes. Unfortunately, current browsers do not handle `PUBLIC` identifiers well, so it is always good at least to provide a URL as a backup.

Together, the XML and `DOCTYPE` declarations are often referred to as the *document prolog,* which is optional in an XML document. The remainder of the example document contains content tagged according to the elements and rules of the specified DTD.

Well-Formed XML

Browsers often recover from sloppily written or illegal HTML. This is not the case with XML documents. Because XML languages vary, the rules for coding the document need to be followed to the letter in order to ensure proper interpretation by the XML client. When a document follows the XML markup rules, it is said to be *well-formed.*

The primary rules for a well-formed XML document are:

- There may be no white space (character spaces or line returns) before the XML declaration.

- All element attribute values must be in quotation marks (either single or double quotes).

- Tags and attributes are case-sensitive; for example, <par>, <PAR>, and <Par> are considered to be three different tags.

- An element must have both an opening and closing tag, unless it is an empty element.

- If a tag is a standalone empty element, it must contain a closing slash before the end of the tag (for example, <img/>)

- All opening and closing tags must nest correctly and not overlap.

- The document must have a single root element, a unique element that encloses the entire document. The root element may be used only once in the document.

- Isolated markup characters (e.g., <, &, and >) are not allowed in text; use a the equivalent standard character entities instead. Table 30-1 lists the predefined character entities in XML.

Table 30-1: Predefined character entities in XML

Entity	Char	Notes
&	&	Must not be used inside processing instructions
<	<	Use inside attribute values quoted with "
>	>	Use after]] in normal text and inside processing instructions
"	"	
'	'	Use inside attribute values quoted with '

You can check whether the syntax of your XML document is correct using a well-formedness checker (also called a nonvalidating parser). Parsers are built into Netscape 6 and Internet Explorer 5.5. You may also want to check out the list of nonvalidating parsers provided by the Web Developer's Virtual Library at *http://wdvl.com/Software/XML/parsers.html.*

Namespaces

With XML, your document may use tags that come from different "types" of XML documents. For example, you might have an XHTML document that contains some math expressions written using the MathML XML dialect. But in this case, how can you differentiate between an <a> tag coming from XHTML (an anchor) and an <a> tag that might come from MathML (an absolute value)?

The W3C anticipated such "collisions" and responded by creating the *namespace* convention. A namespace is a group of element and attribute names that is unique for each XML dialect. Namespaces take names that look just like URLs (they are not links to actual documents, however) to ensure uniqueness and provide information about the organization that maintains the namespace. When you reference elements and attributes in your document, the browser looks them up in the namespace to find out how they should be used.

Namespaces are declared in an XML document using the **xmlns** attribute. You can establish the namespace for a whole document or an individual element. Typically, the value of the **xmlns** attribute is a reference to the URL-like namespace.

This example establishes the default namespace for the document to be transitional XHTML:

```
<html xmlns="http://www.w3.org/1999/xhtml">
```

If you need to include math markup, you can apply the **xmlns** attribute within the specific tag, so the browser knows to look up the element in the MathML DTD (not XHTML):

```
<div xmlns="http://www.w3.org/1998/Math/MathML">46/100</div>
```

If you plan to refer to a namespace repeatedly within a document, you can declare the namespace and give it a label just once at the beginning of the document. Then refer to it in each tag by placing the label before the tag name, separated by a colon (:). For example:

```
<html xmlns="http://www.w3.org/1999/xhtml"
      xmlns:math="http://www.w3.org/1998/Math/MathML">
```

The full namespace can now be shortened to **math** later in the document. The result is much tidier code (and smaller file sizes!):

```
<math:div>46/100</math:div>
```

Document Type Definition (DTD)

Another important part of XML is the Document Type Definition (DTD), a file associated with SGML and XML documents that defines how markup tags should be interpreted by the application reading the document. A DTD is what turns XML from a metalanguage to a true language designed for a specific task.

A DTD is a text document that contains a set of rules, formally known as "entity, element, and att-list (attribute) declarations," that define an XML markup language. It names new elements and describes the type of data or other elements that an element may contain. It also lists attributes for each element.

A Simple DTD

For example, if you were creating recipes to be accessed over the Web, you might create your own language called RML, or Recipe Markup Language. RML would have tags like `<title>` and `<body>`, but also RML-specific tags such as `<ingredients>`, `<prep-time>`, and `<nutritionalInformation>`.

These tags would be established in a DTD for the new language. The DTD imparts detailed information about what data should be found in each tag. A DTD for Recipe Markup Language might have a line like this:

```
<!ELEMENT ingredients ( li+, text? )>
```

The first line declares an element called **ingredients**. An **ingredients** tag can contain an **li** element and text. The plus sign (+) after **li** indicates that an **ingredients** element will have one or more **li** elements within it. The question mark after **text** shows that text is optional. The Recipe Markup Language DTD would also specify the **li** element:

```
<!ELEMENT li (#PCDATA)>
```

This element contains text only (PCDATA stands for "parsed character data" and is used to indicate text that may contain other tagged elements).

The complete set of rules for declaring entities and elements in a DTD is fairly complex and beyond the scope of this chapter. Refer to one of the sources listed at the end of this chapter for more information.

Valid XML

When an XML document conforms to all the rules established in the DTD, it is said to be *valid*, meaning that all the elements are used correctly.

 A well-formed document is not necessarily valid, but if a document proves to be valid it follows that it is also well-formed.

When your document uses a DTD, you can check it for mistakes using a *validating parser*. The parser checks the document against the DTD for contextual errors, such as missing elements or improper order of elements. Most of the best validating parsers are free. Some common parsers are Xerces from the Apache XML Project (available at *http://xml.apache.org*) and Microsoft MSXML (*http://msdn.microsoft.com/xml/default.asp*). A full list of validating parsers is provided by Web Developer's Virtual Library at *http://wdvl.com/Software/XML/parsers.html*.

When to Use a DTD

DTDs are not required and actually come with a few disadvantages. A DTD is useful when you have specific markup requirements to apply across a large number of documents. A DTD can ensure that certain data fields are present or delivered in a particular format. You may also want to spend the time preparing a DTD if you need to coordinate content from various sources and authors. Having a DTD makes it easier to find mistakes in your code.

The disadvantages to DTDs are that they require time and effort to develop and are inconvenient to maintain (particularly while the XML language is in flux). DTDs slow down processing times and may be too restrictive on the user's end. Another problem with DTDs is that they are not compatible with the namespace convention. Elements and attributes from another namespace won't validate under a DTD unless the DTD explicitly includes them (which defeats the purpose of namespaces in the first place). If you are creating just a few XML documents or if you are using namespaces, a DTD is undesirable.

Examples of XML Technology

With XML's ability to allow customized tagging systems, it's not surprising that it is finding a wide variety of uses. It has already made a big impact on the Internet since its formal introduction in 1998. This section takes a look at just a few of the ways XML is being put to work.

Standard XML Languages

The World Wide Web Consortium monitors standard XML *applications* (languages written according to the rules of XML) that have an impact on how media is presented over the Web, thus changing the Web's capabilities. In fact, virtually all new web-related technologies and languages developed by the W3C follow the rules of XML. This section looks at the more prominent developments.

Synchronized Multimedia Integration Language (SMIL)

SMIL (pronounced "smile") is an XML language for combining audio, video, text, and graphics in a precise, synchronized fashion. It is discussed more thoroughly in Chapter 27.

Scalable Vector Graphics (SVG)

XML has typically been used to define the structure of text elements within a document; however, many groups are working on ways in which it could be used to define graphical information as well. The W3C is developing the Scalable Vector Graphic (SVG) standard. According to the W3C:

> SVG is a language for describing two-dimensional graphics in XML. SVG allows for three types of graphic objects: vector graphic shapes (e.g., paths consisting of straight lines and curves), images and text. Graphical objects can be grouped, styled, transformed and composited into previously rendered objects. Text can be in any XML namespace suitable to the application, which enhances searchability and accessibility of the SVG graphics. The feature set includes nested transformations, clipping paths, alpha masks, filter effects, template objects and extensibility.

The following sample SVG code (taken from the W3C Recommendation) creates an SVG document fragment that contains a red circle with a blue outline (stroke):

```
<?xml version="1.0" standalone="no"?>
<!DOCTYPE svg PUBLIC "-//W3C//DTD SVG 20001102//EN"
"http://www.w3.org/TR/2000/CR-SVG-20001102/DTD/svg-20001102.dtd">
<svg width="12cm" height="4cm">
<desc>Example circle01 - circle expressed in physical units</desc>

<circle cx="6cm" cy="2cm" r="1cm"
        style="fill:red; stroke:blue; stroke-width:0.1cm" />
</svg>
```

The SVG standard provides ways to describe paths, fills, a variety of shapes, special filters, text, and basic animation.

Adobe offers tools for both creating and viewing SVG files. The drawing program Illustrator 9 can now export *.svg* files directly. Adobe's SVG Viewer is a browser plug-in available for Navigator and Internet Explorer 4 and higher for Windows and Macintosh that allows SVG files to display in the browser window.

For more information on SVG, see the W3C pages at *http://www.w3.org/Graphics/ SVG/*.

Mathematical Markup Language (MathML)

MathML is an XML application for describing mathematical notation and capturing both its structure and content. The goal of MathML is to enable mathematics to be served, received, and processed on the World Wide Web, just as HTML has enabled this functionality for text. MathML became a formal W3C Recommendation in February 2001.

Because there is no way to reproduce mathematical equations directly using HTML, authors have resorted to inserting graphical images of equations into the flow of text. This effectively removes the information from the structure of the document. MathML allows the information to remain in the document in a meaningful way. With adequate style sheets, mathematical notation can be formatted for high-quality visual presentation. Several vendors offer applets and plug-ins that allow the display of MathML information in browser windows.

For more information, see the W3C pages at *http://www.w3.org/Math/*.

Resource Description Framework (RDF)

RDF is an XML application used to define the structure of metadata for documents (i.e., data that is useful for indexing, navigating, and searching a site). A formal method for describing the contents of a web site, page, or resource could be useful to automated agents that search the Web for specific information. Metadata could be used in the following ways:

- For resource discovery to provide better search engine capabilities
- In cataloging for describing the content and content relationships available at a particular web site, page, or digital library
- By intelligent software agents to facilitate knowledge sharing and exchange
- In content rating
- In describing collections of pages that represent a single logical "document"
- For digital signatures that allow electronic commerce, collaboration, and other "trust"-based applications

RDF is in the very early stages of development as of this writing. To follow its progress, see *http://www.w3.org/RDF/*.

Other XML Applications

Some XML technologies serve a specific community, as the Chemical Markup Language serves the scientific community, but these technologies are often of limited interest to most publishers. Others are so specific that they serve only a particular intranet of a single business.

XML is poised to become a major player on the Internet. Companies are excited by the technology and have invested large amounts of time and money in its development.

The following are just a few of the ways XML is being implemented today.

Wireless Markup Language (WML)

WML is an XML application for marking up documents to be delivered to handheld devices such as PDAs and cell phones. It is discussed in more detail in Chapter 32.

DocBook

DocBook is a DTD for technical publications and software documentation. DocBook is officially maintained by the DocBook Technical Committee of OASIS, and you can find the official home page located at *http://www.oasis-open.org/docbook/index.html*.

Chemical Markup Language (CML)

CML is used for managing and presenting molecular and technical information over a network. For more information, see *http://www.xml-cml.org*.

Open Financial Exchange (OFX)

OFX is a joint project of Microsoft, Intuit, and Checkfree. It is an XML application for describing financial transactions that take place over the Internet. For more information, see *http://www.ofx.net/ofx/default.asp*.

Simple Object Access Protocol (SOAP)

This technology, developed by Microsoft, DevelopMentor, and Userland Software, uses the ubiquitous support for XML and HTTP to provide a way for applications to talk to each other over the Internet, regardless of platform and through firewalls. For more information, start with this article by Microsoft: *http://www.microsoft.com/mind/0100/soap/soap.asp*. For technical details, see the W3C notes at *http://www.w3.org/TR/2000/NOTE-SOAP-20000508/*.

Where to Learn More

If you are interested in learning more about XML, and if you are a fan of O'Reilly books (as I am), you will want to check out *Learning XML* by Erik T. Ray and *XML in a Nutshell* by Elliotte Rusty Harold and W. Scott Means (both published by O'Reilly in 2001).

The growth and development of XML is well documented online in resources such as the following:

http://www.w3.org

The World Wide Web Consortium's official web site is the best place to go for the latest news on new XML standards and proposals.

http://www.xml.com

XML.com, part of the O'Reilly network, is a clearinghouse of great articles and information on XML.

The following sites have comprehensive information regarding XML:

- The XML FAQ: *http://www.ucc.ie/xml/*
- The XML Cover Pages: *http://www.oasis-open.org/cover/xml.html*
- XML INFO: *http://xmlinfo.com*

CHAPTER 31

XHTML

While the HTML 4.01 specification goes a long way in tidying up HTML, it still suffers from sloppy artifacts of HTML's fast and loose development. Over the years, little was done to make HTML perfectly SGML-compliant. As a result, we have a language with quirky features and browsers that easily forgive basic HTML coding errors.

With the creation of XML (see Chapter 30), the W3C finally had a standard set of rules for defining markup languages. It should come as no surprise that one of the first things they did with their shiny new set of rules is apply them HTML. The resulting XML-ized HTML standard is known as XHTML.

XHTML 1.0 is virtually the same as the HTML 4.01 standard, but more strict. The W3C is aiming eventually to replace HTML with XHTML to keep it in line with the larger family of XML-based markup languages.

This chapter reviews the differences and similarities between HTML 4.0 and XHTML.

XHTML Standards Development

Things are exciting over at the W3C. Now that they have XML on their toolbelts, they seem to be on a roll in rethinking and reshaping document markup. Between January 2000 and June 2001, they have turned out three XHTML Recommendations: XHTML 1.0, XHTML Basic, and XHTML 1.1 (XHTML 1.1 is still "Proposed" as of this writing, but since it's on the verge of approval, I'll count it anyway). This section looks at each one.

XHTML 1.0

The XHTML 1.0 Recommendation (released in January 2000) is really just a reformulation of the HTML 4.01 specification according to the rules of XML. The XHTML 1.0 standard is the focus of this chapter.

Like HTML 4, XHTML 1.0 comes in three varieties—Strict, Transitional, and Frames—each defined by a separate DTD. (For more information on DTDs, see Chapter 30). It is important to specify which version you are using in your document, as modern browsers (IE 5.5+ and Netscape 6) can use this information to turn on "strict" standards-compliant formatting, as opposed to the "quirky" behavior of older, nonstandard HTML. Of course, if you do specify the DTD, then you must stick to it exactly so that your document will be valid (i.e., not breaking any rules defined by the DTD).

You must also make sure to specify the proper namespace declaration for XHTML. This is included in the <html> tag at the start of the document and is discussed later in the section "XHTML Document Declarations."

Strict DTD

This version excludes all deprecated tags and attributes (like <font> and align) to reinforce the separation of document structure from presentation. All style information is delegated to Cascading Style Sheets, which work the same in XHTML as in HTML (see Chapter 17 for more information).

While it is certainly possible to begin constructing web pages and sites according to the Strict DTD, it poses a greater challenge. Because there are still millions of web users with older browsers that don't support style sheets and HTML 4.0, you run the risk of alienating some users (or providing them with only lowest common denominator content). Fortunately, there is evidence that things will get easier in the future. The latest round of major browsers (Internet Explorer 5.5 for Windows, Internet Explorer 5.0 for Macintosh, and Netscape 6 on all platforms) snap into perfect standards-compliance mode when you specify "strict" in the DOCTYPE declaration.

Transitional DTD

The Transitional DTD includes all the deprecated elements in order to cater to the legacy behavior of most browsers. Deprecated tags and elements are permitted but discouraged from use. This DTD provides a way to ease web authors out of their current habits and toward abiding by standards. Most web authors today choose to use the Transitional DTD since it is what works best in most browsers.

Frameset DTD

This specification is exactly the same as the Transitional DTD, except that it includes the elements for creating framed web pages (<frameset>, <frame>, and <noframe>). The Frameset DTD is kept separate because the structure of a framed document (where <frameset> replaces <body>) is fundamentally different from regular HTML documents.

XHTML Basic

The XHTML Basic Recommendation (released in December 2000) is a stripped-down version of XHTML 1.0 aimed at preparing documents for mobile applications such as cell phones or handheld devices. The specification is consistent with the XHTML modularization efforts (discussed next). XHTML Basic contains the minimum elements necessary to be considered an XHTML document, plus images, forms, basic tables, and object support. To read more about it, see the W3C's Recommendation at *http://www.w3.org/TR/2000/REC-xhtml-basic-20001219/*.

XHTML 1.1 (Modular XHTML)

XHTML 1.1 (a proposed recommendation as of this writing) reflects a break-through in the way markup languages are constructed. Instead of one comprehensive set of elements, this specification is broken up into task-specific modules. A module is a set of elements that handle one aspect or type of object in a document. Some modules include the core module, text, forms, tables, images, imagemaps, objects, and frames.

In a world where HTML content is being used on devices as varied as cell phones, desktop computers, refrigerator panels, dashboard consoles, and more, a "one-size-fits-all" content markup language will no longer work. Modularization is the solution to this problem. This recent module approach has a number of benefits:

- Special devices and applications can "mix and match" modules based on their requirements and restraints. For instance, a simple refrigerator console proba-bly doesn't need applet and multimedia support (although, who knows?). With XHTML 1.1, you can create a document that uses only the subset of XHTML that meets your needs.

- It prevents spin-off, device-specific HTML versions. Authors can create their own XML modules, leaving the XHTML standard unscathed.

- It allows "hybrid" documents in which several DTDs are used in combina-tion. For instance, it allows web documents to have SVG (Scalable Vector Graphics) modules or MathML modules mixed in with the XHTML content.

Modularization is the way of the future for markup standards. The SMIL 2.0 specifi-cation is also broken into modules (see Chapter 27), which can then be used with other languages like XHTML. You can read more about the XHTML 1.1 specifica-tion at *http://www.w3.org/TR/xhtml11/*.

Creating XHTML 1.0 Documents

Marking up a document with XHTML is virtually the same as with HTML. Docu-ments are divided into a header and body (except framed documents, which have a frameset area), elements are marked using opening and closing tags, attributes control specific behaviors for those elements, and so on. Therefore, everything you've learned in Part II of this book applies to XHTML as well.

However, because it is an XML application, you need to play by the rigid rules of XML markup. What makes XHTML documents different from HTML 4 documents is that you need to be absolutely sure that your code is well-formed (i.e., exactly follows the syntax rules), you must declare the DTD that the document uses, and you must use the xmlns attribute to indicate the XML namespace. These issues are discussed in the following sections.

Tools

Because XHTML is still an emerging standard, as of this writing, none of the popular commercial web authoring tools generate XHTML standard documents automatically. This situation should change as XHTML is ushered in as the definitive standard, replacing HTML 4.01. In the meantime, Windows and UNIX users can use the W3C's browser and editing tool, Amaya, to generate XHTML documents (see *http://www.w3.org/Amaya/* for more information).

Any tool that is programmed not to rewrite code it doesn't recognize (Macromedia Dreamweaver, Adobe GoLive 4 and higher, and Microsoft FrontPage 2000) should leave your XHTML-formatted tagging alone. There is an extension to Dreamweaver (available for download at *http://www.macromedia.com/exchange/dreamweaver/*; search for XHTML) that will generate the proper document type and namespace declarations.

Another option is to convert existing HTML documents into XHTML. You could use the command-line utility called Tidy, created by David Raggett of the W3C. Tidy cleans up many aspects of an HTML file, including converting it to well-formed XHTML. It is available at *http://www.w3.org/People/Raggett/tidy/*. Microsoft FrontPage 2002 can also convert selected HTML into well-formed XHTML by clicking on "Apply XML Formatting Rules." Microsoft notes, however, that while selected HTML code is converted, it does not convert the HTML page to a complete XML or XHTML document.

Validation

Because XML is so fussy, it is a good idea to run your XHTML documents through a validator to make sure everything is in order. The W3C's HTML validation service (*http://validator.w3.org*) now checks XHTML files for validity.

XHTML Document Declarations

Every XHTML file must begin with declarations that tell the browser which versions of XML and XHTML are used in the document. The browser uses this information to display the document correctly. In Chapter 9 we saw how a DOCTYPE declaration can be added to the beginning of an HTML document. For XHTML, this element is required.

The following is a minimal XHTML document:

```
<?xml version="1.0" encoding="UTF-8"?>
<!DOCTYPE html PUBLIC "-//W3C//DTD XHTML 1.0 Transitional//EN"
        "http://www.w3.org/TR/xhtml1/DTD/xhtml1-transitional.dtd">

<html xmlns="http://www.w3.org/1999/xhtml" xml:lang="en" lang="en">

<head>
<title>Title is required</title>
</head>
```

```
<body>
..content of document...
</body>

</html>
```

Let's look at this sample one element at a time. The document begins with an XML declaration (beginning with <? and ending with ?>) that tells the XML processor that the document uses XML Version 1.0.* The `encoding` attribute specifies the 8-bit Unicode character set (the most common). Be sure that the encoding value matches the character set used in your document (see Chapter 7 for more information on character sets).

The next element is the `DOCTYPE` declaration (the same as we've seen in XML and even regular HTML documents) that references the Transitional DTD, both by a public identifier and via a URL. If your document follows the strict XHTML version, use this declaration:

```
<!DOCTYPE html PUBLIC "-//W3C//DTD XHTML 1.0 Strict//EN"
        "http://www.w3.org/TR/xhtml1/DTD/xhtml1-strict.dtd">
```

And if it is a framed document, use the following:

```
<!DOCTYPE html PUBLIC "-//W3C//DTD XHTML 1.0 Frameset//EN"
        "http://www.w3.org/TR/xhtml1/DTD/xhtml1-frameset.dtd">
```

Finally, there are a few more directions added within the <html> tag for the document. The `xmlns` attribute specifies the primary namespace for the document. A namespace is a unique collection of tags and attributes that can be referenced by the browser. Namespaces are discussed in Chapter 30. More than one namespace may be referenced within a document, for instance, if the document contains other XML applications such as Scalable Vector Graphics (SVG) or MathML.

The `lang` attribute is used to declare that the document language is English, for both the XML and XHTML namespaces.

Well-Formed XHTML

Web browsers are forgiving of sloppy HTML, but XHTML (being an XML application) requires fastidious attention to every detail. These requirements were outlined briefly in the XML chapter (Chapter 30), but we'll go over them in this section as they relate specifically to XHTML.

All-Lowercase Element Names

In XML, all tags and attributes are case-sensitive, which means that <img>, <Img>, and <IMG> are parsed as different elements. In the reformulation of HTML into XHTML, all elements were interpreted to be lowercase. When writing XHTML

---

* Some older browsers (such as Navigator 3) that don't understand XML display the XML declaration text as part of the displayed content. Therefore, if you're sending XHTML documents to these older browsers, you may need to omit this part.

documents (and their associated style sheets), be sure that all tags and attributes are written in lowercase.

If you want to convert the upper- and mixed-case tags in an existing HTML file to well-formed, all-lowercase tags, try the Tidy utility (mentioned previously) or Barebones Software BBEdit (Macintosh only), which can automate the process.

Quoted Attribute Values

XHTML requires that all attribute values be contained in double quotation marks. So where previously it was okay to omit the quotes around single words and numeric values, now you need to be careful that every value is quoted.

End Tags

In HTML, it is okay to omit the end tags for many block elements (such as <p> and <li>) because the browser is smart enough to close a block element when the next one begins. Not so in XHTML. In order to be well-formed, every container element must have its end tag, or it registers as an error and renders the document noncompliant.

Empty Elements

This need for closure extends to empty (standalone) elements as well. So instead of just inserting a line break as <br>, XHTML requires the closing tag as well (
...</br>). Fortunately, you can "close" empty elements simply by adding a slash before the closing bracket, indicating its ending. So in XHTML, a line break can be entered as <br/>.

The notion of closing empty elements can cause some browsers to complain, so to keep your XHTML code safe for current browsers, be sure to add a space before the closing slash (<br />). This allows the closed empty tag to slide right through.

Of course, line break tags aren't the only empty element. Table 31-1 shows all the HTML tags in their acceptable XHTML (transitional DTD) forms.

Table 31-1: Empty tags in XHTML format

<area />	<frame />	<isindex />
<base />	<hr />	<link />
<basefont />	<img />	<meta />
 	<input />	<param />
<col />		

Explicit Attribute Values

In XHTML, every attribute must have an explicit value. There are many attributes in regular HTML that are standalone instructions that take no value, such as noshade and ismap. In XHTML, attributes without values must now use their own names. Therefore, noshade becomes noshade="noshade" and ismap is now ismap="ismap". Table 31-2 lists the attributes which have been given new values in XHTML.

Table 31-2: Explicit attribute values

checked="checked"	disabled="disabled"	noresize="noresize"
compact="compact"	ismap="ismap"	nowrap="nowrap"
declare="declare"	multiple="multiple"	readonly="readonly"
defer="defer"	noshade="noshade"	selected="selected"

Nesting Requirements

It has always been a rule in HTML that tags should be properly nested within one another. The closing tag of a contained element should always appear before the closing tag of the element that contains it. In XHTML, this rule is strictly enforced. So be sure that your elements are nested correctly, like this:

```
<b>I can <i>fly!</i></b>
```

and not overlapping like this:

```
<b>I can <i>fly!</b></i>
```

In addition, XHTML enforces other nesting restrictions that have always been a part of the HTML specification. While XML provides no specific way to indicate which elements may *not* be contained by a given element (this SGML function was dropped in order to make XML more manageable), the XHTML DTD includes a special "Content models for exclusions" note that reinforces the following:

- The <a> tag cannot contain another <a> tag.

- The <pre> tag cannot contain <img>, <object>, <applet>, <big>, <small>, <sub>, <sup>, <font>, or <basefont>.

- The <form> element may not contain other <form> tags.

- The <button> tag cannot contain <a>, <form>, <input>, <select>, <textarea>, <label>, <button>, <iframe>, or <isindex>.

- The <label> tag cannot contain other <label> tags.

Character Entities

XHTML (as a function of XML) is extremely fussy about special characters such as <, >, &, etc. All special characters should be represented in the XHTML document by their character entities instead. Common character entities are listed in Table 10-3, and the complete list appears in Appendix F.

Character entity references should be used in place of characters such as < and & in regular text content, as shown in these exmples.

```
<p> the value of A &lt; B </p>
<p> Laverne &amp; Shirley </p>
```

Places where it was common to use special characters, such as in the title of a document or in an attribute value, it is necessary to use the character entity instead. For instance, the following worked just fine in HTML:

```
<img src="puppets.jpg" alt="Crocco & Lynch"/>
```

But in XHTML, the value must be written like this:

```
<img src="puppets.jpg" alt="Crocco &amp; Lynch"/>
```

Protecting Scripts

It is common practice to enclose scripts and stylesheets in comments (between `<!--` and `-->`). Unfortunately, XML software thinks of comments as unimportant information and may simply remove the comments from a document before processing it. To avoid this problem, use an XML CDATA section instead. Content enclosed in `<![CDATA[...]]>` is considered simple text characters and is not parsed as potential document elements. For example:

```
<script language="JavaScript">
<![CDATA[
...JavaScript here...
]]>
</script>
```

The problem with this method is backwards compatibility. HTML browsers ignore the contents of the XML CDATA tag, while XML browsers ignore the contents of comment-enclosed scripts and style sheets. So you can't please everyone! One workaround is to put your scripts and styles in separate files and reference them in the document with appropriate external links.

id and name Attributes

And finally, while the name attribute is used in HTML to identify elements such as document fragments, frames, and images so they can be referenced elsewhere in the document, XHTML prefers the equivalent (and standards-compliant) id attribute. The name attribute has been deprecated in the HTML 4.0 specification for the elements that once used it. Now that most browsers are HTML 4.0–compliant, you can begin making the transition by using id where you might have used name (or use them both at the same time with the same value).

Try It Out

XHTML is destined to be the future of document markup, but that doesn't mean you need to wait to try it out. By following the previous rules and tips for well-formed documents, you can begin creating XHTML documents that will work on current browsers. The latest batch of standards-compliant browsers know what to do if you declare which XHTML DTD you've used at the opening of your document. The majority of existing browsers know what to do with pages written according to the Transitional DTD.

The downside is that XHTML can be tedious and painful to create since every tag must be in perfect order. Hopefully, the current web authoring tools will catch up and begin making it easy to generate well-formed XHTML in upcoming versions. Until that day, be patient, use a validator, and know that writing standards-compliant code will be worth the added effort in the long term. With the trend toward XML-based information systems, your XML-compliant content will be ready to play along.

CHAPTER 32

WAP and WML

Both mobile devices and the Internet have exploded into widespread use in the past few years, so it stands to reason that the two would be combined. One technology for delivering information to wireless devices (primarily mobile phones, but also pagers and personal digital assistants) is WAP, the Wireless Application Protocol. WAP is a collection of protocols and specifications that work together to give mobile phones access to Internet-like information.

One part of the WAP standard is the Wireless Markup Language (WML), which is used to create wireless applications just as HTML is used to create web pages. WML is an application of XML, meaning that it is defined in a document type definition, or DTD (for more information on XML, see Chapter 30).

The goal of WAP is not to port existing web sites onto mobile phones, because the small screen size and limited bandwidth make that impractical. Rather, it is a system for creating special applications tailored to handheld devices. That is why you often see the phrase "Internet-like information" used in regards to WAP. WAP is good for delivering short, pithy bits of data, such as stock prices, sports scores, movie times, and so on. It is not useful for the complex documents with visual layouts that have made the World Wide Web what it is today.

Many traditional web designers feel pressure to keep up with the Web as it extends into the world of wireless devices. The truth is that unless you make a career shift into wireless application development, it is unlikely that you will be required to design specifically for handheld devices. Still, it is helpful to be familiar with the basics of what is going on in the wireless space.

This chapter begins with a brief introduction to WAP and application development. The second half focuses on WML and how it works, including a summary of the elements and attributes in the current WML specification.

About WAP

As I just mentioned, WAP is not a single entity, but rather a list of protocols and specifications. It is being developed under the guidance of the Wireless Application Protocol Forum, originally founded by wireless industry leaders Nokia, Motorola, Ericsson, and Unwired Planet (which evolved into Phone.com and is currently Openwave). The WAP Forum web site (*http://www.wapforum.org*) is a good resource for the current state of wireless communications, including the complete WAP specification documents.

The Wireless Environment

WAP addresses the special limitations and requirements of mobile phones and similar devices. The distinguishing characteristics are:

* Small screen size. Only a small amount of information can be displayed at once.

* Limited processing power.

* Lack of a full keyboard, making it awkward for the user to enter information. There are some handheld devices that feature a full keyboard, but they are the exception.

* Slow connection speeds. Currently, wireless connection speeds are around 9600 bits per second.

* Costly access. Users are generally paying by the minute or the kilobyte to use a wireless application. It is important to allow them to access information quickly.

All of these factors guide the development of WAP technology and the design process of WAP application developers.

How WAP Works

A WAP application is formatted using WML and WMLScript, the scripting language for adding interactivity to wireless applications. These files can be served from an ordinary HTTP (web) server.

WAP-enabled devices communicate with the web server through a *WAP gateway* (Figure 32-1). The gateway acts as an intermediary between the Internet and the mobile network, converting WAP requests into HTTP requests. A wireless device (such as a mobile phone) requests information via the airwaves to the gateway. The gateway uses the Internet via HTTP to request and receive a WML document from the web server.

Upon arriving at the gateway, the document gets *compiled* into WAP Binary XML (WBXML) before it is sent to the phone. The compilation process reduces the file size by replacing tags with specific single-character codes, and removing comments and extra white space. Once the document has been compiled, it is returned via the airwaves to the mobile phone.

Alternatives to WAP

While WAP is gaining worldwide support, it is not the only system out there for delivering information to wireless devices. Before WAP, pages were delivered using HTTP connections and a mobile-friendly markup language called HDML (see the sidebar "About HDML" later in this chapter). Many phones still support standard HTML content.

iMode (created by NTT DoCoMo, *http://www.nttdocomo.com*) is another wireless communication system that has taken off like wildfire in Japan. iMode phones typically have full-color displays that are capable of displaying graphical layouts and even games. iMode documents are created using a subset of HTML elements (see *http://www.nttdocomo.com/i/tag/index.html* for a complete list).

Many people see the current version of WAP as an interim solution that will eventually be replaced by IPv6 on the protocol side and XML on the markup side. Of course, in the telecom world, once an interim solution gets out in the market, it can have a surprisingly long life, so WAP as it stands today is likely to be around for a while.

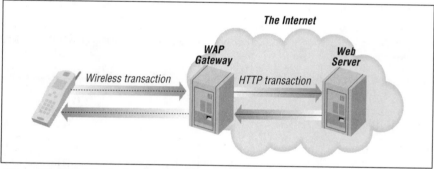

Figure 32-1: Mobile devices access web servers through a gateway

WAP gateways are normally owned by wireless service providers, so you don't need your own gateway to provide WAP applications (unless you're a bank or some similar institution of means). You can serve your content from a regular, properly configured web server. The WAP gateway will find your information as any other web client would.

Serving WAP Content

In order to serve the documents necessary for a WAP application, you need to configure the server to recognize a few new MIME (file) types, listed in Table 32-1. MIME types are explained in Chapter 4. Follow the instructions for your particular server for installing new file types.

Table 32-1: WAP-related MIME types

Description	MIME type	Extension
WML file	`text/vnd.wap.wml`	.wml
Compiled WML file	`application/vnd.wap.wmlc`	.wmlc
WMLScript file	`text/vnd.wap.wmlscript`	.wmls
Compiled WMLScript file	`application/vnd.wap.wmlscriptc`	.wmlsc
Wireless Bitmap Image	`image/vnd.wap.wbmp`	.wbmp

Creating WAP Applications

Before diving into the specifics of the WML specification, let's look at some of the general issues and processes of creating WAP content:

A New Model

If you are accustomed to designing pages for the Web, you will need to adjust (and reduce) your thinking for handheld devices. Due to the limitations in screen size, processing power, and connection speed, normal information-rich web pages are not feasible. In fact, it is useful to abandon the notion of "documents" (information that is displayed and read) and think in terms of "applications" (based on choices and user interaction). WAP applications are typically made up of screenfuls of minimal text and lists of options. Information and interaction design is king as there is virtually no graphic design to be done.

Another difference is that unlike the Web, where it is desirable to entice a visitor to linger at your site as long as possible, a successful WAP application can be measured by how quickly the user can find information or make a transaction and get out.

WAP Browsers

Mobile devices use special browsing software, sometimes referred to as "micro-browsers" due to their size and capacity, to request and display information from a network. As on the Web, not all WAP browsers are created equal. Older devices with outdated browsers are still in circulation, and what works on one device may not work on another at all.

Add to that the fact that the WML specification allows for a range of interpretations of elements and functions, so even browsers that are 100% WML-compliant may have significant differences in their implementation of the standard.

Most WAP-enabled devices use the recently renamed Openwave Mobile Browser (formerly called UP.Browser) developed by Openwave (at one time called Unwired Planet, thus "UP"). For a list of devices that use Openwave browsers and their respective versions, see the Openwave Mobile Browser Phone Reference at *http://developer.phone.com/resources/phones.html*.

Not surprisingly, Microsoft has thrown its hat into the wireless ring with its browser, Microsoft Mobile Explorer for cell phones. MME is a dual-mode browser, supporting both WML and HTML content. The list of devices that use MME is

WAP & WML

growing. For more information on MME, see *http://www.microsoft.com/mobile/phones/mme/default.asp*.

Handheld Devices

There are hundreds of mobile devices on the market. Unfortunately, there is no standard hardware configuration, so it is difficult to anticipate just how your application will look and work when it reaches the end user. The following are some device variables WAP developers contend with:

Screen Size

Screen size varies from one device to another. To give you a ballpark idea, many phone display areas are 95 to 120 pixels wide and 50 to 65 pixels high. Newer phones and PDAs may have larger screens (approximately 300×100 pixels).

Screen resolution is difficult to pin down. To make matters more interesting, the Nokia 7110 phone has pixels that are taller than they are wide (by a ratio of 1.25:1), which can stretch out graphical images.

Text

Because WAP content is primarily text-based, it may be more meaningful to measure screen space in terms of number of characters displayed. In general, mobile browsers can display only 3 to 6 lines of text at a time with 12 to 20 characters per line.

Text may be displayed as either monospace, where all characters are the same width, or proportional, where characters are varying widths. This can make it difficult to anticipate how many characters will fall on a line.

Color depth

The vast majority of mobile devices (particularly in the United States, which lags two years behind the rest of the world in mobile technology) have 1-bit black and white LCD displays. As processor power improves, expect to see grayscale and 8-bit color displays become available in the next few years, as they already are in Japan.

Softkeys

Handheld devices typically feature *softkeys*, buttons that can be programmed for application-specific functionality. How many keys are available, where they are placed, and how they get assigned to actions in the code varies from device to device. Some softkeys are just rendered graphically in the display area. This makes it difficult to anticipate how users will access and navigate through an application.

Size Limitations

Each *.wml* document (called a "deck") within a WAP application has a maximum permitted size of 1400 bytes, although most web developers aim to keep the file size below 500 bytes to improve performance. This size limit refers to *compiled* decks. Your working documents may be a bit larger, so keep an eye on the compiled size of your file as indicated in the emulator or other development tool.

If your deck is larger than 1400 bytes, you must split it logically into separate files.

WAP Emulators

WAP application developers generally use WAP emulators to test their documents. An emulator (or "simulator") is a program that runs on your computer that shows you how your document will appear and function on a wireless device. It alleviates the need to buy a half-dozen cell phones to test your designs.

One of the nifty things about emulators is that they look just like the real thing (see Figure 32-2)—you can even use the buttons to navigate the way you would on a real phone. Unfortunately, emulators do not always *behave* exactly like the real thing. Expect some discrepancies in text layout and even basic functionality, so be sure to test on real devices before going live to avoid surprises.

Figure 32-2: The Openwave Simulator WAP emulator program

The following are some popular WML emulators and their respective sites for downloading. The Openwave Simulator is the most popular due to the widespread use of the Openwave Mobile Browser and its predecessor, the UP.Browser. All of these programs are Windows-only, so Mac and Unix users are out of luck.

Openwave Simulator (previously UP.Simulator)
   http://developer.phone.com/download/

Microsoft Mobile Explorer Emulator
   http://www.microsoft.com/mobile/phones/mme/default.asp

Nokia Toolkit
   http://forum.nokia.com

Ericsson WapIDE SDK
   http://www.ericsson.com/developerszone/

Motorola Mobile ADK
   http://developers.motorola.com/developers/wap/index.html

 The Opera browser Version 5 features experimental support for WAP and WML. While it is not a substitute for a full emulator, it may be useful for testing your WML code or just viewing other WAP applications. For more information, go to the Opera web site at *http://www.opera.com.*

As alternative to a full emulation program, you can view WML pages using one of the web-based emulators at Wapemulator.com (*http://www.wapemulator.com*) or Gelon.net (*http://www.gelon.net*). These emulators are limited in their functionality and accuracy, but they give you a good general idea and allow you to view WAP applications from the comfort of your desktop computer.

About HDML

Before the WAP Forum hashed out the WAP and WML specifications, mobile devices received documents formatted in HDML (Handheld Device Markup Language). WML, which is XML-based and more robust, officially replaces HDML, but HDML will be around as long as the older phones and gadgets that rely on it still linger. HDML is made up of a subset of HTML and a few extra tags appropriate to navigating with mobile devices.

The HDML specification only got as far as "submission" status at the W3C before it was succeeded by the new and improved WML. The proposed HDML specification is available at *http://www.w3.org/TR/NOTE-Submission-HDML-spec.html*. To serve HDML files, the server must be configured for the MIME type `text/x-hdml` and the *.hdml* suffix.

For an overview of HDML, see the Webmonkey article "Intro to HDML," located at *http://hotwired.lycos.com/webmonkey/99/48/index3a.html*.

If you already have HDML applications and would like to update them to WAP/WML, thorough documentation for making the conversion is available at *http://developer.phone.com/technotes/hdml2wml/index.html*.

Introduction to WML

At last we arrive at the nitty-gritty of wireless applications—WML. This section should give you a flavor of how WML works, but it falls far short of a complete education. For more information, refer to one of the complete resources listed at the end of this chapter. The complete set of WML elements and attributes is summarized in the following section.

Document Structure

Because of the unique viewing environment on handheld devices, the whole notion of the "page" and page-based design as they are thought of in HTML is abandoned. WML applications use a "card" metaphor instead. An application is made up of one or more *decks* (.*wml* documents), each containing some number of *cards* (WML elements defined within a document). A card contains a limited amount of information, equal to just a few screenfuls where a screen holds only three to six lines of text.

Because WML is an application of XML (see Chapter 30), WML documents need to be both *valid* (using WML elements properly according to the DTD) and *well-formed* (abiding by the stringent rules of XML markup syntax).

The following is a very simple WML document called *jenskitchen.wml*. It is a "deck" containing two "cards."

```
<?xml version="1.0"?>
<!DOCTYPE wml PUBLIC "-//WAPFORUM//DTD WML 1.2//EN"
                    "http://www.wapforum.org/DTD/wml_1.2.xml">
<wml>
    <card id="intro">
        <p>Welcome to Jen's Cookbook Nook</p>
    </card>

    <card id="book1">
        <p>101 Things to Do with Wild Mushrooms</p>
        <p>Jennifer Niederst</p>
        <p>Price: $19.95</p>
    </card>
</wml>
```

Looking at this example piece by piece, we see that it begins with the standard XML and DOCTYPE declarations (for more information on XML document prologs, see Chapter 30). The <wml> element defines a WML deck; every WML document opens and closes with <wml> tags, and there can be only one set per document.

Decks may contain one or many cards. Our sample deck contains two cards, defined by the aptly named <card> element. Cards can contain a variety of elements, but their contents must always be placed within paragraph (<p>) tags. Because WML is an XML application, each paragraph element must have a closing </p> tag (this is different from HTML, in which the paragraph element can be left unclosed). Note that each card is given a name using the id attribute so it can be referred to later.

Formatting Text

According to the WML specification, all text (in fact, all content elements) must be contained in paragraphs (<p> tags). The <p> element has two attributes: align and mode. `align` works just like text alignment in HTML. The mode attribute can be set to `wrap` or `nowrap`. Text wraps by default, but you can set it to `nowrap` to keep a paragraph on one line. Be warned, however, that while some devices can scroll to the right, others can't, so text set to `nowrap` may be inaccessible to some users. Both alignment and the mode settings may be ignored by some browsers, so be sure your information still works without them.

Line breaks are added within text using the `<br/>` tag. Because WML follows XML syntax, it is necessary to include the slash at the end of the tag to make it a self-closing element.

The specification also includes elements for adding inline styles to text, including:

`<b>`	Bold
`<big>`	Slightly bigger than surrounding text
`<em>`	Emphasized (bold or italic)
`<i>`	Italic
`<small>`	Slightly smaller than surrounding text
`<strong>`	Strong text (bold, italic, or bold italic)
`<u>`	Underlined

Unfortunately, there is no guarantee that a device will display text in the tagged style. Some devices ignore style information entirely, so it is best not to rely on styles for meaning.

Adding Links

Just as on the Web, linking from one page to another is an integral part of using WAP applications. WML uses the familiar anchor (`<a>`) element for creating simple links. In the following example, I've created a link from one card to another by calling the card by name in the anchor tag. This is similar to creating a link to a named anchor in HTML. When a user selects the linked text, the second card loads in the browser window.

```
<wml>
    <card id="intro">
        <p>Welcome to Jen's Cookbook Nook<br/>
        <a href="#book1">Check out our featured book!</a>
        </p>
    </card>

    <card id="book1">
        <p>101 Things to Do with Wild Mushrooms</p>
        <p>Jennifer Niederst</p>
        <p>Price: $19.95</p>
    </card>
</wml>
```

The `<a>` element only allows you to link to other specific cards or decks. The WML specification provides a more versatile tool for navigating between cards: the `<anchor>` element. The anchor element can be used to link to a specific card or a card for which you may not know the location ahead of time, such as the previous card or a card chosen based on user input (via a set variable). The `<anchor>` tag acts as a container for two other WML elements, <go> and <prev>, which give it its functionality.

The following example uses the <anchor> tag with the <go> element to create a simple link (it functions exactly the same as the link in the previous example).

```
<anchor>
    Check out our featured book!
    <go href="#book1" />
</anchor>
```

The <anchor> element can also be used to create a custom "Back" button by using the <prev> element as shown in this example.

```
<anchor>
    Go back!
    <prev/>
</anchor>
```

Images

Although WAP applications are primarily text, it is possible to add simple images to a card (see Figure 32-3). In order for an image to be displayed in a WAP application, it must be in the specially optimized Wireless Bitmap (WBMP) format. WBMP files are 1-bit graphics capable of displaying only black and white pixels. It is recommended that you keep any graphic image as small as possible. No graphic should exceed 150 pixels square. Be aware that some microbrowsers do not support graphics at all, so always provide alternative text.

Figure 32-3: Examples of WMBP graphics in a WAP application

Images are added to the document with the <img/> element. Make sure that it is placed within <p> tags, as shown in this example:

```
<card>
<p><img src="logo.wbmp" alt="Cookbook Logo"></p>
</card>
```

Some mobile devices have stored in their memory a library of small images that can be placed in the WML document using the localsrc attribute in the image tag. The advantage of local images is that they reduce the amount of data that needs to be transferred from the server, so they display more quickly than external WBMP files. It is a good idea also to provide a pointer to an external graphic in case local images are not supported. The following example requests a generic credit card icon from the local image library and specifies an alternative *.wbmp* file. The `alt` text will display on devices that do not support graphics at all.

```
<img localsrc="creditcard" src="card.wbmp" alt="credit card symbol">
```

A complete list of library images and their names is available at *http://developer.phone.com/htmldoc/41/wmlref/taglist.html#575099.*

Creating WBMP Graphics

There are few tools available that can create WBMP files at this time. However, you can download the free UnWired plug-in from RCP Distributed Systems that enables you to create WBMP files in Adobe Photoshop 5 and higher and JASC Paint Shop Pro (or any graphics package that supports plug-ins). It is available at *http://www.rcp.co.uk/distributed/downloads/.*

There is also a Java utility called *pic_2_wbmp* that converts existing BMP files to WBMP format. It is available at *http://www.gingco.de/wap/.*

Tables

WML uses the same basic elements as HTML for creating tables. The table itself is defined with `<table>` tags. A table contains some number of rows (`<tr>`), and each row contains some number of table data cells (`<td>`) that contain the content. Unlike HTML tables, you can explicitly define the number of columns in a WML table using the `columns` attribute in the `<table>` tag. Text alignment is set for each column at the table level (see the tag summary later in this chapter for alignment syntax).

The following sample code creates a table with three columns; the content in the first column is aligned left, and the content in the remaining two columns is aligned right. The result is shown in Figure 32-4.

```
<table columns="3" align="LRR">
<tr>
    <td>Month</td>
    <td>Min</td>
    <td>Max</td>
</tr>
<tr>
    <td>Feb</td>
    <td>4</td>
    <td>41</td>
</tr>
<tr>
    <td>Mar</td>
    <td>25</td>
    <td>62</td>
<tr>
</table>
```

Figure 32-4: WML table in emulator

Tables should be used with caution in WML applications. It is easy for tables to grow too wide to display on the screen, so that users without the ability to scroll horizontally miss information. Some devices may ignore tables altogether, just displaying the cell contents in a list, in the order they appear in the source document. If you do choose to use tables, keep the number of columns and cell content to a minimum, make sure the information makes sense as it appears in the file, and be sure to test the table thoroughly on a number of devices.

Programming Softkeys

Mobile phones and other handheld devices usually feature softkeys, buttons that can be programmed to function however you like (see Figure 32-5). Most often, softkeys are physical buttons on the device, but they may also be rendered graphically in the display area. Because softkey implementation varies considerably from device to device, count on users having varied experiences of your application.

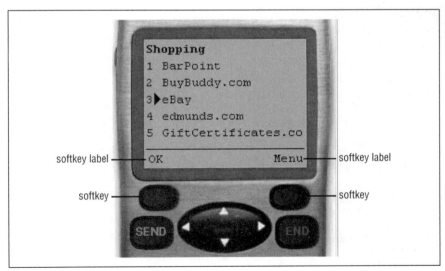

Figure 32-5: Softkey examples on the Openwave Simulator

Softkeys are good for functions and links that don't necessarily have a place in the text flow, such as a Back button or a link to a menu of options that serve the whole application. Actions are assigned to softkeys via the `<do>` element. This element has one required attribute, `type`, that specifies the sort of action being defined. There are seven values for the `type` attribute:

accept	Okay or confirm information
prev	Go to the previously viewed card (like a Back button)
help	Request help
reset	Clear the state (variables) for the card or deck
options	Select from a list of choices
delete	Delete an item
unknown or "" *(empty)*	A generic action

The `<do>` element uses the `label` attribute to specify the text that is assigned to the button. It is recommended that label values be limited to approximately six characters or fewer for best cross-device performance.

Softkey programming is a rich topic that is beyond the scope of this brief WML overview, so we will look only at some simple examples. The first example uses the `<do>` element to create a softkey "Back" button. How the task is assigned to a button is left up to the individual device, so it is for the most part out of the designer's control. Note that because tasks are not part of the content flow, they do not need to be put within paragraph tags.

```
<do type="prev" label="Back">
    <prev/>
</do>
```

Another common action assigned to softkeys is a link to another document or card, as shown in this example.

```
<do type="accept" label="List">
    <go href="list.wml"/>
</do>
```

To add multiple tasks to a card, use the `options` task type. Options may appear on the browser as a pop-up menu of choices or as a link to a separate page with a list of links. The way it is implemented is up to the user's device. This example adds three functions to the page: a link to a search page, a link to a list, and a Back button.

```
<do type="options" label="Search">
    <go href="search.wml"/>
</do>
<do type="options" label="List">
    <go href="list.wml"/>
</do>
<do type="options" label="Back">
    <prev/>
</do>
```

Interactivity

An application is nothing without interactivity. The WML specification provides several elements for the collection of user input and dynamic content generation based on that input. Like HTML, WML contains basic form elements: `<input>` for placing a text input field in the application, `<select>` for defining a list of `<option>`s, and `<fieldset>` for grouping form content into logical sections.

The `<setvar>` element is used to set a *variable*, a mechanism for temporarily storing a bit of information such as user input, a URL, or any text information. In this example, variables containing information about the book (an abbreviation of the title and its price) are set when the user clicks on the "Purchase this book" link. This information is stored and used later in the application, perhaps in a list of selected items.

```
<card id="book1" title="101 Mushrooms">
<p><b>101 Things to Do with Wild Mushrooms</b></p>
<p>Written by Jennifer Niederst<br/>
    Price: $19.95<br/>
    This book will save your dinner parties.
    <anchor>
        Purchase this book!
        <go href="purchase.wml">
            <setvar name="B" value="101Mushrooms"/>
            <setvar name="P" value="19.95"/>
        </go>
    </anchor>
</p>
</card>
```

WMLScript is the client-side scripting language that gives WML applications true functionality. WMLScript is beyond the scope of this chapter, but if you are serious about building mobile applications, it is recommended that you add WMLScript to your repertoire. Unfortunately, it is only supported in the latest WAP-enabled browsers (Version 4 and higher), but it will be an important tool in WAP development in the coming years. Resources for WMLScript are listed at the end of the chapter.

WML Elements and Attributes

The following is a brief summary of the elements and attributes in the WML 1.2 Specification (the latest version as of this writing). Because it is new, not all browsers support the entire specification, so be sure to test your applications.

There are a few core attributes that can be used in nearly every element:

`xml:lang`
Specifies the language for the element.

`id`
Give the item a name that can be referred to later.

`class`
Specifies a class name for the element (so they can be grouped).

\<a\>

```
<a>...</a>
```

Specifies a link to another resource (a specific card or another *.wml* document).

Attributes

```
href=url
```
 Required. Location of the resource.

```
title=text
```
 A brief text description of the link.

```
accesskey=keypad key
```
 Assigns a keypad key to the link.

\<access\>

```
<access/>
```

Specifies a domain name. Only documents (decks) originating from that domain name can access the current document. The \<access\> element is contained within \<head\> tags.

Attributes

```
domain=domain name
```
 The domain that can access the card.

```
path=pathname
```
 Sets a path within the domain.

\<anchor\>

```
<anchor>...</anchor>
```

Specifies a generic link to another resource. It can be used in conjunction with the \<go\> and \<prev\> elements.

Attributes

```
title=text
```
 A brief text description of the link.

```
accesskey=keypad key
```
 Assigns a keypad key to the link.

\<b\>

```
<b>...</b>
```

Specifies bold text.

\<big\>

```
<big>...</big>
```

Specifies text that is slightly larger than the default text.

\<br\>

```
<br/>
```

Indicates a line break within the flow of text.

\<card\>

```
<card>...</card>
```

The unit within the WML document that displays in the device. Cards are logical divisions of the application's functionality.

Attributes

`title=text`
> A brief text description of the card. This may or may not be displayed by the device.

`newcontext=true|false`
> When set to `true`, this attribute reinitializes the state of the browser, clearing the navigational history and any stored variables.

`ordered=true|false`
> Indicates how the card content is organized. A value of `true` indicates the card is part of a group of elements that are handled in sequence; `false` indicates there is no natural order.

\<do\>

```
<do>...</do>
```

Describes an action within the current card, generally assigned to a softkey on the device. The action is indicated by the elements \<go\>, \<prev\>, \<noop\>, or \<refresh\> within the \<do\> element.

Attributes

`type=accept|prev|help|reset|options|delete|unknown` (*or* " ")
> *Required.* Describes the intended use for \<do\> element so the device can decide how to implement it.

`label`
> Specifies a text label for the button or function.

`optional=true|false`
> When set to `true`, the browser can ignore the element. The default is `false` (the element must not be ignored).

`name`
> Gives the element a name.

\<em\>

```
<em>...</em>
```

Specifies emphasized text (display is browser-dependent).

\<fieldset>

`<fieldset>...</fieldset>`

Defines logical sections within content. It is currently poorly supported.

Attributes

`title=text`
> A brief text description of the section.

\<go>

`<go/>`

Specifies a task that navigates to a resource (like a link). The **xml:lang** attribute is not allowed in this element.

Attributes

`href=url`
> *Required.* Specifies the destination URL.

`sendreferer=true|false`
> The default is **false**. When set to **true**, the browser needs to specify the location of the deck containing this task in the request to the server.

`method=get|post`
> The HTTP request method (for form data). It must be either of the values **get** or **post**. The default is **get**.

`enctype=encoding`
> The content type of the form. The default is **application/x-www-form-urlencoded**.

`accept-charset=charset list`
> A list of character encodings used to process the form data.

\<head>

`<head>...</head>`

Specifies an optional header for the document.

\<i>

`<i>...</i>`

Specifies italic text.

\<img>

`<img/>`

Inserts an image into the content flow.

Attributes

`src=url`
> *Required.* The location of the image to be displayed.

`alt=text`

    Provides alternative text to be displayed if the image is missing.

`localsrc=local image name`

    Specifies a predefined icon from the built-in icon library.

`align=top|middle|bottom`

    Defines how the image is displayed relative to the surrounding text baseline.

`vspace=number`

    Holds a specified number of pixels clear above and below the image.

`hspace=number`

    Holds a specified number of pixels space to the left and right of the image.

`height=number`

    Specifies the height of the image in pixels.

`width=number`

    Specifies the width of the image in pixels.

<input>

`<input/>`

Adds a text-entry field to the document.

Attributes

`name=text`

    Required. The name of the variable that stores the user input.

`type=text|password`

    Sets the type of text entry. The default `text` allows normal text entry; `password` hides the entered text from view by displaying stars or dots.

`value=value`

    Provides a default value that displays when the element is loaded.

`format=format`

    Specifies a format for the entered text to restrict text entry to specific alphanumeric patterns (such as dates or credit card numbers).

`emptyok`

    Indicates that it is okay to leave the field empty.

`size=number`

    The width, in characters, of the text entry field.

`maxlength=number`

    Maximum length of the entered text (in characters).

`tabindex=number`

    Sets the order in which the form elements are tabbed through.

`title=text`

    Specifies a description of the text entry screen; the description may or may not be displayed by the browser.

`accesskey=keypad key`

    Assigns a keypad key to the field for quick access.

\<meta\>

`<meta/>`

Provides information about the document; it is placed within the \<head\> element.

Attributes

`http-equiv=name`
> Specifies the HTTP header name.

`name=name`
> Specifies a name for the meta information.

`forua=true|false`
> Specifies whether the meta data is intended for the user agent (the browser). If set to `false`, it must be removed before it reaches the browser.

`content=text`
> *Required.* Specifies the property value.

`scheme=text`
> Used to interpret the data value.

\<noop\>

`<noop/>`

Specifies that nothing should be done. Can disable functionality in the browser.

\<onevent\>

`<onevent/>`

Triggers an action based on a specified event.

Attributes

`type=onenterbackward|onenterforward|ontimer`
> *Required.* Specifies the type of event that will trigger the task contained within the \<onevent\> element tags. The `onenterbackward` value specifies navigation through the browser's history; `onenterforward` specifies any navigation (except the back function); `ontimer` executes the action on timer expiration.

\<option\>

`<option>...</option>`

Specifies one selection within a \<select\> list.

Attributes

`value=value`
> Provides an optional variable for the selection, for example, to store an abbreviated version of the full selection name.

`title=text`
> Gives the selection a name.

`onpick=card id`
> Specifies the id of a card to navigate to when the option is selected.

<optgroup>

<optgroup>...</optgroup>

Deliminates groups of <option>s within a <select> list.

Attributes

title=*text*
> Gives the submenu a title.

<p>

<p>...</p>

Specifies a paragraph of text.

Attributes

align=left|center|right
> Positions the text horizontally in the display.

mode=wrap|nowrap
> Specifies the wrapping mode for the paragraph. nowrap causes the text to display on one line and may require horizontal scrolling.

<postfield>

<postfield/>

Specifies name-value pairs to send to the server.

Attributes

name=*text*
> *Required.* Specifies the name for the pair.

value=*value*
> *Required.* Specifies the variable (value) for the pair.

<prev>

<prev>...</prev> *or* <prev/>

Instructs the browser to go back in its history stack to the previously viewed card. The standard attribute xml:lang is not permitted in this element.

<refresh>

<refresh>...</refresh>

Specifies a refresh task, which updates the browser context (clears history and stored variables).

<select>

`<select>...<select>`

Indicates a list of options in a form. The `<select>` element contains some number of `<option>` elements and may also contain `<optgroup>`s.

Attributes

`title=text`
> Specifies a title, which the browser may or may not display.

`name=text`
> The name of the variable (the value is assigned when the user selects an option).

`value=value`
> Allows a default value to be specified.

`iname=value`
> Specifies a variable whose value will be the index value of the chosen option.

`ivalue=index number`
> Specifies a default selection using the default option's index number.

`multiple=true|false`
> Determines whether multiple options may be selected from the list. The default is false (only one selection permitted).

`tabindex=number`
> Sets the order the select object appears as user tab through the fields.

<setvar>

`<setvar/>`

Specifies the name-value pair for a variable. If a variable already exists, it is overwritten. The `<setvar>` element may only be used within `<refresh>` and `<go>` tags.

Attributes

`name=name`
> *Required.* Specifies the name of the variable.

`value=number`
> *Required.* Specifies the value of the variable.

<small>

`<small>...</small>`

Specifies that enclosed text should be slightly smaller than the default text size.

<strong>

`<strong>...</strong>`

Indicates strongly emphasized text. How it is rendered is device-dependent.

`<table>`

`<table>...</table>`

Indicates the beginning and end of a table.

Attributes

`title=text`
> Specifies the table's title, which the browser may or may not display.

`align=alignment code`
> Specifies the horizontal alignment of cell content for the table. The value is a string of the characters L, C, and R (representing left, center, and right, respectively), one for each column in the table. So a table with four columns might be aligned using `align="RLRC"`.

`columns=number`
> *Required.* Specifies the number of columns in the table. This is a departure from table syntax in HTML.

`<td>`

`<td>...</td>`

Defines an individual cell in a table. The contents of the cell are placed within `<td>` container tags.

`<template>`

`<template>...</template>`

Specifies a template for all the cards in the deck, including `<do>` elements for softkey behaviors.

`<timer>`

`<timer/>`

Sets a timer that can be used to trigger events when it expires.

Attributes

`name=name`
> The name of the timer referenced by the event handler.

`value=value`
> *Required.* Sets the length of time in tenths of seconds.

`<tr>`

`<tr>...</tr>`

Indicates a row within a table. Its contents are some number of `<td>` elements (table cells). The `xml:lang` attribute is not associated with this element.

`<u>`

`<u>...</u>`

Specifies underlined text.

`<wml>`

`<wml>...</wml>`

Indicates the beginning and end of a deck. It is the root element of a WML document (deck).

WAP and WML Resources

I found *Beginning WAP, WML, & WMLScript* by Wei Meng Lee, Soo Mee Foo, Karli Watson, and Ted Wugofski (Wrox Press, 2000) extremely useful in the writing of this chapter. You may also want to check out *Learning WML and WMLScript: Programming the Wireless Web* by Martin Frost (O'Reilly, 2000).

There are a number of great WAP and WML resources online:

WAP Forum
> *http://www.wapforum.org*
> The official site of the group that develops and guides the WAP standard.

AllNetDevices Wireless FAQ
> *http://www.allnetdevices.com/faq/*
> A great place to start learning the ins and outs of WAP and WML.

Openwave (previously Phone.com and Unwired Planet)
> *http://www.openwave.com*
> Openwave creates browsers and development tools for WAP applications.

Openwave Developer Program
> *http://developer.phone.com*
> Openwave's Developer site provides comprehensive resources for WAP developers. It is a must-see.

W3Schools.com
> *http://www.w3schools.com/wap/*
> *http://www.w3schools.com/wmlscript/*
> The W3Schools site offers hands-on tutorials on both WML and WMLScript.

WMLScript Primer
> *http://www.webreference.com/js/column62/*
> This WebReference.com article is a good starting place for learning about WMLScript.

Gelon.net
> *http://www.gelon.net*
> A WAP portal site that contains links to hundreds of existing WAP applications, organized by category.

PART VI

Appendixes

APPENDIX A

HTML Elements

This appendix contains the master list of HTML tags that appear in this book. It includes all tags and attributes listed in the HTML 4.01 specification plus those that are browser-specific and nonstandard (but well-supported).

A number of attributes in the HTML 4.01 specification are shared by nearly all elements. To save space, they have been abbreviated in this appendix as they are in the specification, as follows:

`%coreattrs` indicates the collection of core HTML attributes according to the 4.0 specification:

`id`
> Assigns a unique identifying name to the element

`class`
> Assigns a classification name to the element

`style`
> Associated style information

`title`
> Advisory title/amplification

`%i18n` stands for "internationalization" (i + 18 characters + n):

`lang`
> specifies the language for the element by its two-character language code

`dir`
> specifies the direction of the element (left to right, or right to left)

`%events` indicates the events used by scripting languages which are applicable to the element:

> `onlick, ondblclick, onmousedown, onmouseup, onmouseover, onmousemove, onmouseout, onkeypress, onkeydown, onkeyup`

535

Tag	Description	Attributes	Chapter
`<a>`	Anchor (link)	accesskey, charset, coords, href, hreflang, name, rel, rev, shape, tabindex, target, type, %coreattrs, %i18n, %events *Events:* onfocus, onblur	11
`<abbr>`	Abbreviation	%coreattrs, %i18n, %events	10
`<acronym>`	Acronym	%coreattrs, %i18n, %events	10
`<address>`	Information about the author	%coreattrs, %i18n, %events	10
`<applet>` *(deprecated)*	Java applet	align, archive, alt, code, codebase, height *(required)*, hspace, name, object, vspace, width *(required)*, %coreattrs	12
`<area>`	Area (in client-side imagemap)	accesskey, alt, coords, href, nohref, shape, tabindex, target, %coreattrs, %i18n, %events *Events:* onfocus, onblur	11
`<b>`	Bold text style	%coreattrs, %i18n, %events	10
`<base>`	Base URL	href, target	10
`<basefont>` *(deprecated)*	Basefont	color, face, id, size *(required)*	10
`<bdo>`	Bidirectional override	%coreattrs, %i18n	7
`<bgsound>` *(IE only)*	Background sound	src *(required)*, loop	24
`<big>`	Big text	%coreattrs, %i18n, %events	10
`<blink>` *(NN only)*	Blink	(none)	10
`<blockquote>`	Blockquote	%coreattrs, %i18n, %events	10
`<body>`	Body	alink, background, bgcolor, link, text, vlink, %coreattrs, %i18n, %events *Events:* onload, unload *IE only:* bgproperties, leftmargin, rightmargin, topmargin, bottommargin *NN only:* marginwidth, marginheight	9
` `	Forced line break	clear, %coreattrs	10

Tag	Description	Attributes	Chapter
`<button>`	Button (form element)	accesskey, disabled, name, tabindex, type, value, %coreattrs, %i18n, %events *Events:* onfocus, onblur	16
`<caption>`	Caption (of a table)	align, %coreattrs, %i18n, %events *Nonstandard:* summary, valign	13
`<center>` *(deprecated)*	Centers contained elements	%coreattrs, %i18n, %events	10
`<cite>`	Citation	%coreattrs, %i18n, %events	10
`<code>`	Code fragment	%coreattrs, %i18n, %events	10
`<col>`	Column (within a table)	align, char, charoff, span, valign, width, %coreattrs, %i18n, %events	13
`<colgroup>`	Column group (within a table)	align, char, charoff, span, valign, width, %coreattrs, %i18n, %events	13
`<comment>` *(IE only)*	Comment	(none)	8
`<dd>`	Definition (part of definition list)	compact, %coreattrs, %i18n, %events	10
`<del>`	Deleted text	cite, datetime, %coreattrs, %i18n, %events	10
`<dfn>`	Defining instance	%coreattrs, %i18n, %events	10
`<dir>` *(deprecated)*	Directory list	compact, %coreattrs, %i18n, %events	10
`<div>`	Division	align, %coreattrs, %i18n, %events	10
`<dl>`	Definition list	compact, %coreattrs, %i18n, %events	10
`<dt>`	Definition term (part of definition list)	%coreattrs, %i18n, %events	10
`<em>`	Emphasized text	%coreattrs, %i18n, %events	10
`<embed>`	Embedded object	align, alt, border, code, codebase, frameborder, height, hidden, hspace, name, palette, pluginspage, pluginurl, src, type, units, vspace, width	12

Tag	Description	Attributes	Chapter
`<fieldset>`	Fieldset (group of form elements)	`%coreattrs`, `%i18n`, `%events`	16
`<font>` *(deprecated)*	Font style	`color`, `face`, `size`, `%coreattrs`, `%i18n`	10
`<form>`	Interactive form	`accept`, `accept-charset`, `action` *(required)*, `enctype`, `method`, `name`, `target`, `%coreattrs`, `%i18n`, `%events` *Events:* `onsubmit`, `onreset`	16
`<frame>`	Frame	`frameborder`, `longdesc`, `marginwidth`, `marginheight`, `name`, `noresize`, `scrolling`, `src`, `%coreattrs` *Nonstandard:* `bordercolor`	14
`<frameset>`	Frameset	`cols`, `rows`, `%coreattrs` *Events:* `onload`, `unload` *Nonstandard:* `border`, `bordercolor`, `frameborder`, `framespacing`	14
`<h1>`...`<h6>`	Headings, level 1 through 6	`align`, `%coreattrs`, `%i18n`, `%events`	10
`<head>`	Head of document	`profile`, `%i18n`	9
`<hr>`	Horizontal rule	`align`, `noshade`, `size`, `width`, `%coreattrs`, `%i18n`, `%events`	12
`<html>`	HTML document	`%i18n`	9
`<i>`	Italic	`%coreattrs`, `%i18n`, `%events`	10
`<iframe>`	Inline frame (floating frame)	`align`, `frameborder`, `height`, `longdesc`, `marginheight`, `marginwidth`, `name`, `scrolling`, `src`, `width`, `%coreattrs`, `%i18n`, `%events` *Nonstandard:* `hspace`, `noresize`, `vspace`	14
`<img>`	Embedded image	`align`, `alt` *(required)*, `border` *(deprecated)*, `height`, `hspace`, `ismap`, `longdesc`, `lowsrc`, `src` *(required)*, `usemap`, `vspace`, `width`, `%coreattrs`, `%i18n`, `%events` *IE only:* `controls`, `dynsrc`, `loop`, `start`	12

Tag	Description	Attributes	Chapter
`<input>`	Input (form control) [Input types: text, password, checkbox, radio, submit, reset, file, hidden, image, button]	accept, accesskey, align, alt, checked, disabled, ismap, maxlength, name, readonly, size, src, tabindex, type, usemap, value, %coreattrs, %i18n, %events *Events:* onfocus, onblur, onselect, onchange	16
`<ins>`	Inserted text	cite, datetime, %coreattrs, %i18n, %events	10
`<isindex>` *(deprecated)*	Searchable index	prompt, %coreattrs, %i18n	16
`<kbd>`	Keyboard text	%coreattrs, %i18n, %events	10
`<label>`	Label (for form elements)	accesskey, for, %coreattrs, %i18n, %events *Events:* onfocus, onblur	16
`<layer>` *(NN 4.x only)*	Creates a layer	above, background, below, bgcolor, clip, height, id, left, name, pagex, pagey, src, top, visibility, width, z-index	29
`<legend>`	Legend (for form fieldsets)	accesskey, align, %coreattrs, %i18n, %events	16
`<li>`	List item	start, type, value, %coreattrs, %i18n, %events	10
`<link>`	Link	charset, href, hreflang, rel, rev, media, target, type, %coreattrs, %i18n, %events	11
`<map>`	Map (client-side imagemap)	name *(required)*, %coreattrs, %i18n, %events	11
`<marquee>` *(IE only)*	Marquee	behavior, bgcolor, direction, height, hspace, loop, scrollamount, scrolldelay, vspace, width	12
`<menu>` *(deprecated)*	Menu list	compact, %coreattrs, %i18n, %events	10
`<meta>`	Meta information	content *(required)*, http-equiv, name, scheme, %i18n	9
`<multicol>` *(NN 4.x only)*	Multi-column formatted text	cols, gutter, width	13

Tag	Description	Attributes	Chapter
`<nobr>` *(nonstandard)*	Prevents line breaks from occurring	(none)	10
`<noembed>` *(nonstandard)*	Alternative content when embedded media cannot be displayed.	(none)	12
`<noframes>`	Content that renders on browsers without frames support	`%coreattrs, %i18n, %events`	14
`<noscript>`	Alternative content for scripts	`%coreattrs, %i18n, %events`	28
`<object>`	Generic embedded object	`align, archive, border, classid, codebase, codetype, data, declare, height, hspace, name, standby, tabindex, type, vspace, width, %coreattrs, %i18n, %events`	12
`<ol>`	Ordered list (numbered)	`compact, start, type, %coreattrs, %i18n, %events`	10
`<optgroup>`	Option group (in a form)	`disabled, label` *(required)*, `%coreattrs, %i18n, %events`	16
`<option>`	Option (in a form)	`disabled, label, selected, value, %coreattrs, %i18n, %events`	16
`<p>`	Paragraph	`align, %coreattrs, %i18n, %events`	10
`<param>`	Parameter (named property value)	`id, name` *(required)*, `value, valuetype, type`	12
`<pre>`	Preformatted text	`width, %coreattrs, %i18n, %events`	10
`<q>`	Short inline quotation	`cite, %coreattrs, %i18n, %events`	10
`<s>` *(deprecated)*	Strikethrough text	`%coreattrs, %i18n, %events`	10
`<samp>`	Sample program output	`%coreattrs, %i18n, %events`	10
`<script>`	Script statement	`charset, defer, event, for, language, src, type` *(required)*	12

Tag	Description	Attributes	Chapter
`<select>`	Selection menu (in a form)	disabled, multiple, name, size, tabindex, %coreattrs, %i18n, %events *Events:* onfocus, onblur, onchange	16
`<small>`	Small text	%coreattrs, %i18n, %events	10
`<spacer>` *(NN only)*	Spacer	align, height, size, type, width	12
`<span>`	Span (generic inline text container)	%coreattrs, %i18n, %events	9
`<strike>` *(deprecated)*	Strikethrough text	%coreattrs, %i18n, %events	10
`<strong>`	Strongly emphasized text	%coreattrs, %i18n, %events	10
`<style>`	Embedded stylesheet	type, media, title, %i18n	17
`<sub>`	Subscript	%coreattrs, %i18n, %events	10
`<sup>`	Superscript	%coreattrs, %i18n, %events	10
`<table>`	Table	align, bgcolor, border, cellpadding, cellspacing, frame, rules, summary, width, %coreattrs, %i18n, %events *Nonstandard:* background, height, hspace, vspace *IE only:* bordercolor, bordercolorlight, bordercolordark	13
`<tbody>`	Table body	align, char, charoff, valign, vspace	13
`<td>`	Table data cell	abbr, align, axis, bgcolor, char charoff, colspan, headers, height, nowrap, rowspan, scope, valign, width, %coreattrs, %i18n, %events *Nonstandard:* background *IE only:* bordercolor, bordercolorlight, bordercolordark	13
`<textarea>`	Multiline text area (in a form)	accesskey, cols *(required)*, disabled, name, readonly, rows *(required)*, tabindex, wrap, %coreattrs, %i18n, %events *Events:* onfocus, onblur, onchange	16

HTML Elements

Tag	Description	Attributes	Chapter
`<tfoot>`	Table foot	`align`, `char`, `charoff`, `valign`, `%coreattrs`, `%i18n`, `%events`	13
`<th>`	Table header cell	`abbr`, `align`, `axis`, `char`, `charoff`, `bgcolor`, `colspan`, `headers`, `height`, `nowrap`, `rowspan`, `scope`, `valign`, `width`, `%coreattrs`, `%i18n`, `%events` *Nonstandard:* `background` *IE only:* `bordercolor`, `bordercolorlight`, `bordercolordark`	13
`<thead>`	Table head	`align`, `char`, `charoff`, `valign`, `%coreattrs`, `%i18n`, `%events`	13
`<title>`	Document title	`%i18n`	9
`<tr>`	Table row	`align`, `char`, `charoff`, `bgcolor`, `valign`, `%coreattrs`, `%i18n`, `%events` *IE only:* `bordercolor`, `bordercolorlight`, `bordercolordark`	13
`<tt>`	Teletype (monospaced) text	`%coreattrs`, `%i18n`, `%events`	10
`<u>` *(deprecated)*	Underlined text	`%coreattrs`, `%i18n`, `%events`	10
`<ul>`	Unordered (bulleted) list	*compact*, `%coreattrs`, `%i18n`, `%events`	10
`<var>`	Variable	`%coreattrs`, `%i18n`, `%events`	10
`<wbr>` *(nonstandard)*	Word break (within a `<nobr>` element)	(none)	10

APPENDIX B

List of Attributes

Most HTML tags rely on attributes to modify their behavior and make them more useful. With so many available tags and attributes, it's easy to forget which tag goes with which attributes. For instance, you may know that you want to set the padding value for a table, but you can't remember which tag takes the `cellpadding` attribute (the answer to this one is `<table>`).

The following table provides an alphabetical list of all attributes as listed in the HTML 4.01 specification. The "Related Elements" column provides a list of tags that can use that attribute. The table also lists:

- Accepted values for each tag

- Whether the attribute is required

- A description of the attribute's use

- Whether the attribute has been deprecated (indicated by a D in the "Depr." column)

Note that some attributes appear more than once in the list. This is due to the fact that they may be used differently or may take different values depending on the tag in which they are used.

Name	Related elements	Values	Depr.	Comment
abbr	TD, TH	*text*		Abbreviated name for table cell
accept-charset	FORM	*list*		List of supported character sets
accept	INPUT, FORM	*MIME types*		List of MIME types for file upload

Name	Related elements	Values	Depr.	Comment
accesskey	A, AREA, BUTTON, INPUT, LABEL, LEGEND, TEXTAREA	single character		Assigns a shortcut key that brings focus to (activates) the element
action (required)	FORM	URL		Location of the CGI form processor on the server
align	CAPTION	top|bottom| left|right	D	Positions caption relative to table
align	APPLET, IFRAME, IMG, INPUT, OBJECT	top|middle| bottom|left| right	D	Vertical or horizontal alignment
align	LEGEND	top|bottom| left|right	D	Positions legend relative to fieldset
align	TABLE	left|center| right	D	Table position relative to window
align	HR	left|center| right	D	Horizontal alignment of rule
align	DIV, H1, H2, H3, H4, H5, H6, P	left|center| right|justify	D	Alignment or justification of block element
align	COL, COLGROUP, TBODY, TD, TFOOT, TH, THEAD, TR	left|center| right|justify| char		Horizontal alignment, character alignment, or justification
alink	BODY	color	D	Color of active (selected) links
alt	APPLET	text	D	Alternative text if the applet cannot be displayed
alt (required)	AREA, IMG	text		Alternative text that describes image if it cannot be displayed
alt	INPUT	text		Alternative text for graphic control if it cannot be displayed
archive	APPLET	list of URLs	D	Comma-separated list of preload resources
archive	OBJECT	list of URLs		Space-separated list of preload resources

Name	Related elements	Values	Depr.	Comment
axis	TD, TH	*text*		Names a group of header cells for hierarchical table structures
background	BODY	*URL*	D	Location of tiling background graphic
bgcolor	TABLE	*color*	D	Background color for entire table
bgcolor	TR	*color*	D	Background color for table row
bgcolor	TD, TH	*color*	D	Background color for table cell
bgcolor	BODY	*color*	D	Document background color
border	IMG, OBJECT	*pixels or %*	D	Width of border around linked images or objects
border	TABLE	*pixels* *(default=1)*		Width of frame around a table
cellpadding	TABLE	*pixels or %* *(default=1)*		Spacing within cells
cellspacing	TABLE	*pixels or %* *(default=2)*		Spacing between cells
char	COL, COLGROUP, TBODY, TD, TFOOT, TH, THEAD, TR	*character*		The character along which elements are aligned, such as a decimal point
charoff	COL, COLGROUP, TBODY, TD, TFOOT, TH, THEAD, TR	*pixels or %*		Distance to first occurrence of the alignment character
charset	A, LINK, SCRIPT	*character set name*		Character encoding of the target resource
checked	INPUT	*(no explicit value)*		Sets the initial state of a radio button or checkbox to checked
cite	BLOCKQUOTE, Q	*url*		Location of source document for the quotation
cite	DEL, INS	*url*		Location of document containing explanation for edit

Name	Related elements	Values	Depr.	Comment
class	*All elements but* BASE, BASEFONT, HEAD, HTML, META, PARAM, SCRIPT, STYLE, TITLE	text		The class (or list of classes) for the element (used with style sheets)
classid	OBJECT	url		URL for the specific implementation
clear	BR	left|all| right|none *(default=none)*	D	Used to start flow of text after objects or images aligned against the margins
code	APPLET	applet file	D	Class name of the code to be executed
codebase	OBJECT	url		Location of object's codebase (syntax varies by object)
codebase	APPLET	url	D	URL from which the code is retrieved
codetype	OBJECT	MIME type		Media type of the code
color	BASEFONT, FONT	color	D	Text color
cols	FRAMESET	list of measurements		List of widths (in pixels, %, or relative * values) for columns in a frameset
cols *(required)*	TEXTAREA	number *(default=1)*		Width of a textarea form element, measured in number of characters
colspan	TD, TH	number *(default=1)*		Number of columns spanned by cell
compact	DIR, DL, MENU, OL, UL	*(no explicit value)*	D	Reduces spacing between items in a list
content *(required)*	META	text		Content of meta information
coords	AREA	x,y coords		List of x,y coordinates used in an imagemap; syntax varies according to a given shape
coords	A	x,y coords		List of x,y coordinates used in a client-side imagemap

Name	Related elements	Values	Depr.	Comment
data	OBJECT	*url*		Location of the data used for the object
datetime	DEL, INS	*ISO date*		Date and time of change in ISO format (YYYY-MM-DDThh:mm:ssTZD)
declare	OBJECT	*(no explicit value)*		Declare but don't instantiate flag
defer	SCRIPT	*(no explicit value)*		UA may defer execution of script
dir	*All elements but* APPLET, BASE, BASEFONT, BDO, BR, FRAME, FRAMESET, HR, IFRAME, PARAM, SCRIPT	ltr|rtl *(default=ltr)*		Specifies direction (left to right or right to left) for text
dir	BDO	ltr|rtl *(default=ltr)*		Direction for overridden text
disabled	BUTTON, INPUT, OPTGROUP, OPTION, SELECT, TEXTAREA	*(no explicit value)*		Makes form control unavailable in a given context
enctype	FORM	*Content-type*		Encoding type; defaults to application/x-www-form-urlencoded
face	BASEFONT, FONT	*font name*	D	Comma-separated list of font names
for	LABEL	*ID value*		Associates the label with a control
frame	TABLE	void|above| below|hsides| lhs|rhs|vsides| box|border		Specifies which parts of the table frame to render
frameborder	FRAME, IFRAME	1|0 *(default=1)*		Turns display of frame border on or off
headers	TD, TH	*ID references*		List of header cell IDs that are related to the cell
height	IFRAME	*pixels or %*		Height of inline frame

Name	*Related elements*	*Values*	*Depr.*	*Comment*
height	IMG, OBJECT	*pixels or %*		Height of image or object (will resize original to match specified size)
height *(required)*	APPLET	*pixels or %*	D	Initial height of applet window
height	TD, TH	*pixels or %*	D	Height for cell
href	A, AREA, LINK	*URL*		Location of target document or resource
href	BASE	*URL*		URL that serves as the base for all links in a document
hreflang	A, LINK	*two-character language code*		Identifies language of target document
hspace	APPLET, IMG, OBJECT	*pixels*	D	Amount of space held clear to the left and right of the element
http-equiv	META	*name*		HTTP response header name
id	*All elements but* BASE, HEAD, HTML, META, SCRIPT, STYLE, TITLE	*ID*		A unique ID name given to an instance of an element in a document
ismap	IMG	*ismap*		Indicates image is a server-side imagemap
label	OPTION	*text*		Defines a logical group of options for use in hierarchical menus
label *(required)*	OPTGROUP	*text*		Defines a logical group of options for use in hierarchical menus
lang	*All elements but* APPLET, BASE, BASEFONT, BR, FRAME, FRAMESET, HR, IFRAME, PARAM, SCRIPT	*two-character language code*		Indicates language used in element
language	SCRIPT	*script language*	D	Predefined script language name

Name	Related elements	Values	Depr.	Comment
link	BODY	*color*	D	Color of links in the document
longdesc	IMG	*URL*		Link to long description of image contents (complements `alt`)
longdesc	FRAME, IFRAME	*URL*		Link to long description (complements `title`)
marginheight	FRAME, IFRAME	*pixels*		Height of top and bottom margins
marginwidth	FRAME, IFRAME	*pixels*		Width of left and right margins
maxlength	INPUT	*number*		Maximum number of characters in a form field
media	STYLE	*comma-separated list of media descriptors*		Element is designed for use with these media
media	LINK	*comma-separated list of media descriptors*		Selects style sheet for rendering these media
method (*required*)	FORM	GET | POST (*default*=GET)		HTTP method used to submit the form
multiple	SELECT	(*no explicit value*)		Allows more than one option to be selected in a menu or scrolling list
name	BUTTON, TEXTAREA, SELECT, INPUT, OBJECT	*text*		Names the parameter to be passed on to the forms processing application
name	APPLET	*text*	D	Allows applets to find each other
name	FRAME, IFRAME	*text*		Names the frame for targeting
name	A	*text*		Creates named anchor (for linking to a specific spot on a page)
name	IMG	*text*		Name of image for reference in scripting
name (*required*)	MAP	*text*		Names a client-side imagemap for reference

Name	Related elements	Values	Depr.	Comment
name (*required*)	PARAM	*text*		Property name
name	META	*text*		Metainformation name
nohref	AREA	*(no explicit value)*		Indicates an area of a client-side imagemap that has no associated link
noresize	FRAME	*(no explicit value)*		When present, prevents users from resizing frames
noshade	HR	*(no explicit value)*	D	Turns off 3-D rendering of horizontal rules
nowrap	TD, TH	*(no explicit value)*	D	Suppresses word wrap
object	APPLET	*resource name*	D	Serialized applet file
onblur	A, AREA, BUTTON, INPUT, LABEL, SELECT, TEXTAREA	*script*		When focus is removed from an element
onchange	INPUT, SELECT, TEXTAREA	*script*		When element value changes
onclick	*All elements but* APPLET, BASE, BASEFONT, BDO, BR, FONT, FRAME, FRAMESET, HEAD, HTML, IFRAME, ISINDEX, META, PARAM, SCRIPT, STYLE, TITLE	*script*		When a pointer button is clicked
ondblclick	*All elements but* APPLET, BASE, BASEFONT, BDO, BR, FONT, FRAME, FRAMESET, HEAD, HTML, IFRAME, ISINDEX, META, PARAM, SCRIPT, STYLE, TITLE	*script*		When a pointer button is double-clicked

Name	Related elements	Values	Depr.	Comment
onfocus	A, AREA, BUTTON, INPUT, LABEL, SELECT, TEXTAREA	*script*		When focus is applied to an element
onkeydown	*All elements but* APPLET, BASE, BASEFONT, BDO, BR, FONT, FRAME, FRAMESET, HEAD, HTML, IFRAME, ISINDEX, META, PARAM, SCRIPT, STYLE, TITLE	*script*		When a key is pressed down
onkeypress	*All elements but* APPLET, BASE, BASEFONT, BDO, BR, FONT, FRAME, FRAMESET, HEAD, HTML, IFRAME, ISINDEX, META, PARAM, SCRIPT, STYLE, TITLE	*script*		When a key is pressed and released
onkeyup	*All elements but* APPLET, BASE, BASEFONT, BDO, BR, FONT, FRAME, FRAMESET, HEAD, HTML, IFRAME, ISINDEX, META, PARAM, SCRIPT, STYLE, TITLE	*script*		When a key is released
onload	FRAMESET	*script*		When all the frames have been loaded
onload	BODY	*script*		When the document has been loaded

Name	Related elements	Values	Depr.	Comment
onmousedown	*All elements but* APPLET, BASE, BASEFONT, BDO, BR, FONT, FRAME, FRAMESET, HEAD, HTML, IFRAME, ISINDEX, META, PARAM, SCRIPT, STYLE, TITLE	*script*		When a pointer button is pressed down
onmousemove	*All elements but* APPLET, BASE, BASEFONT, BDO, BR, FONT, FRAME, FRAMESET, HEAD, HTML, IFRAME, ISINDEX, META, PARAM, SCRIPT, STYLE, TITLE	*script*		When a pointer is moved within the element
onmouseout	*All elements but* APPLET, BASE, BASEFONT, BDO, BR, FONT, FRAME, FRAMESET, HEAD, HTML, IFRAME, ISINDEX, META, PARAM, SCRIPT, STYLE, TITLE	*script*		When a pointer is moved out of the element's space
onmouseover	*All elements but* APPLET, BASE, BASEFONT, BDO, BR, FONT, FRAME, FRAMESET, HEAD, HTML, IFRAME, ISINDEX, META, PARAM, SCRIPT, STYLE, TITLE	*script*		When a pointer was moved onto the element's space

Name	Related elements	Values	Depr.	Comment
onmouseup	*All elements but* APPLET, BASE, BASEFONT, BDO, BR, FONT, FRAME, FRAMESET, HEAD, HTML, IFRAME, ISINDEX, META, PARAM, SCRIPT, STYLE, TITLE	*script*		When a pointer button is released
onreset	FORM	*script*		When the form is reset
onselect	INPUT, TEXTAREA	*script*		When some text is selected
onsubmit	FORM	*script*		When the form is submitted
onunload	FRAMESET	*script*		When all the frames have been removed
onunload	BODY	*script*		When the document has been removed
profile	HEAD	*URL*		A metadata profile (dictionary)
prompt	ISINDEX	*text*	D	Initial message in an isindex search field
readonly	TEXTAREA, INPUT	*(no explicit value)*		Prevents editing of initial value in a form text field (textarea, text password)
rel	A, LINK	*link types*		Comma-separated list of forward link types
rev	A, LINK	*link types*		Comma-separated list of reverse link types
rows	FRAMESET	*list of measurements*		Comma-separated list of heights for the rows of a frameset (in pixels, %, or relative * values)
rows *(required)*	TEXTAREA	*number*		The number of visible rows in a textarea field
rowspan	TD, TH	*number (default=1)*		The number of rows spanned by cell

Name	Related elements	Values	Depr.	Comment
rules	TABLE	none|groups| rows|cols|all		Specifies where rules are rendered between rows and columns of a table
scheme	META	*text*		Scheme to be used in interpreting the content (varies by context)
scope	TD, TH	row|col| rowgroup| colgroup		Set of data cells for which the current header cell provides header information
scrolling	FRAME, IFRAME	yes|no|auto *(default=auto)*		Indicates when a scrollbar should appear
selected	OPTION	selected		Defines initial state of an option as selected
shape *(required)*	AREA	*shape*		Shape description (rect, circ, poly) used for interpretation of coordinates (for use in client-side imagemaps)
shape	A	*shape*		For use with client-side imagemaps
size	HR	*pixels*	D	Specifies thickness of horizontal rule
size	FONT	*number*	D	Font size: absolute (1–7) or relative (+1, –1, etc.)
size	INPUT	*number*		Specific to each type of field
size *(required)*	BASEFONT	*number*	D	Base font size for FONT elements (absolute or relative size notation)
size	SELECT	*number*		Number of visible rows in scrolling list
span	COL	*number* *(default=1)*		COL attributes affect N columns
span	COLGROUP	*number* *(default=1)*		Number of columns in group
src	SCRIPT	*url*		URL for an external script
src	INPUT	*url*		URL for image used as a form button

Name	Related elements	Values	Depr.	Comment
src	FRAME, IFRAME	*url*		Source of frame content
src *(required)*	IMG	*url*		URL of image file
standby	OBJECT	*text*		Message to show while loading
start	OL	*number*	D	The number an ordered list should begin counting from
style	*All elements but* BASE, BASEFONT, HEAD, HTML, META, PARAM, SCRIPT, STYLE, TITLE	*style syntax*		Associated style info
summary	TABLE	*text*		Provides description of table contents for nonvisual browsers
tabindex	A, AREA, BUTTON, INPUT, OBJECT, SELECT, TEXTAREA	*number*		Position in tabbing order
target	A, AREA, BASE, FORM, LINK	*window name*		Targets the window or frame to load the target document. The predefined target names are _blank, _self, _parent, _top
text	BODY	*color*	D	Document text color
title	STYLE	*text*		Title for the style
title	*All elements but* BASE, BASEFONT, HEAD, HTML, META, PARAM, STYLE, TITLE	*text*		Specifies an advisory title that may be rendered specially by nonvisual browsers
type	A, LINK	*MIME type*		Advisory content type
type	OBJECT	*MIME type*		Content type for data
type	PARAM	*MIME type*		Content type for value when valuetype=ref

Name	Related elements	Values	Depr.	Comment
type *(required)*	SCRIPT	*MIME type*		Content type of script language
type *(required)*	STYLE	*MIME*		Content type of style language (defaults to text/css)
type *(required)*	INPUT	text|password| checkbox| radio|submit| reset|file| hidden|image *(default=text)*		The kind of widget that is needed
type	LI	disc|square| circle *or* 1|A|a|I|i *(default=disc)*	D	The bullet style or numbering scheme for a list item (depending on context)
type	OL	1|A|a|I|i *(default=1)*	D	Numbering style
type	UL	disc|square| circle *(default=disc)*	D	Bullet style
type *(required)*	BUTTON	button|submit| reset *(default=submit)*		For use as form button
usemap	IMG, INPUT, OBJECT	*url*		A fragment identifier that points to the map element for a client-side imagmap
valign	COL, COLGROUP, TBODY, TD, TFOOT, TH, THEAD, TR	top|middle| bottom| baseline *(default=middle)*		Vertical alignment in cells
value	OPTION	*alphanumeric text*		The value of the option when selected; defaults to content of the option container
value	PARAM	*alphanumeric*		Property value
value	INPUT, BUTTON	*value*		Value of input element, which is passed on to the forms processing program
value	LI	*number*	D	Resets sequence number
valuetype	PARAM	data|ref| object		How to interpret value

Name	Related elements	Values	Depr.	Comment
version	HTML	*url*	D	Link to DTD for the document
vlink	BODY	*color*	D	Color of visited links
vspace	APPLET, IMG, OBJECT	*pixels*	D	Amount of space held clear above and below an element
width	HR	*pixels or %*	D	Length of horizontal rule
width	IFRAME	*pixels or %*		Frame width
width	IMG, OBJECT	*pixels or %*		Size of image or object; browser resizes elements to match specified values
width	TABLE	*pixels or %*		Table width
width (required)	APPLET	*pixels or %*	D	Initial width of applet
width	COL	*pixels, %, or ***		Column width specification
width	COLGROUP	*pixels, %, or ***		Default width for enclosed COLs
width	TD, TH	*pixels or %*	D	Width for cell
width	PRE	*number*	D	Specifies maximum width for preformatted text

APPENDIX C

Deprecated Tags

The World Wide Web Consortium (W3C) is the organization responsible for setting the HTML standard. The W3C takes HTML advancements into consideration when compiling the new standards. Many once-proprietary tags have been rolled into the standard and eventually find universal browser support. Others fall by the wayside.

As HTML advances and improved methods such as Cascading Style Sheets emerge, older tags are put to rest by the W3C. The HTML 4.01 Recommendation has classified a number of HTML tags and individual attributes as "deprecated." The W3C defines a deprecated element as one . . .

> . . . that has been outdated by newer constructs. Deprecated elements are defined in the reference manual in appropriate locations, but are clearly marked as deprecated. Deprecated elements may become obsolete in future versions of HTML.
>
> User agents [browsers] should continue to support deprecated elements for reasons of backward compatibility. Definitions of elements and attributes clearly indicate which are deprecated.
>
> This specification includes examples that illustrate how to avoid using deprecated elements. In most cases these depend on user agent support for style sheets. In general, authors should use style sheets to achieve stylistic and formatting effects rather than HTML presentational attributes. HTML presentational attributes have been deprecated when style sheet alternatives exist.

The tables in this appendix list the elements and attributes that have been deprecated in the HTML 4.01 specification. Substitute tags or methods are listed when provided by the W3C.

Deprecated Elements

The following elements have been deprecated in the HTML 4.01 specification.

Element	Description	Recommendation
`<applet>`	Inserts applet	`<object>`
`<basefont>`	Sets font styles for subsequent text	Style sheets (`color`, `font-size`, `font-family`, `font`, etc.)
`<center>`	Centers elements on the page	`<DIV align=center>`
`<dir>`	Directory list	`<ul>`
`<font>`	Applies font styles	Style sheets (`color`, `font-size`, `font-family`, `font`, etc.)
`<isindex>`	Adds search field	`<form>` and CGI programming
`<menu>`	Menu item list	`<ul>`
`<s>`	Strikethrough text	Style sheets (`text-decoration`)
`<strike>`	Strikethrough text	Style sheets (`text-decoration`)
`<u>`	Underlined text	Style sheets (`text-decoration`)

Deprecated Attributes

The following attributes have been deprecated in the HTML 4.01 specification:

Name	Related Elements	Comment	Replacement Tag
`align`	CAPTION	Horizontal alignment of table caption	style sheet controls
`align`	APPLET, IFRAME, IMG, INPUT, OBJECT	Vertical or horizontal alignment of element	style sheet controls
`align`	LEGEND	Aligns legend relative to its fieldset	style sheet controls
`align`	TABLE	Table position relative to window	style sheet controls
`align`	HR	Horizontal alignment of rule	style sheet controls

Name	Related Elements	Comment	Replacement Tag
align	DIV, H1, H2, H3, H4, H5, H6, P	Horizontal alignment of these block elements	style sheet controls
alink	BODY	Color of selected links	style sheet controls
alt	APPLET	Short description	<OBJECT>
archive	APPLET	Comma-separated archive list	<OBJECT>
background	BODY	Tiling background graphic	style sheet controls
bgcolor	TABLE	Background color for cells	style sheet controls
bgcolor	TR	Background color for row	style sheet controls
bgcolor	TD, TH	Cell background color	style sheet controls
bgcolor	BODY	Document background color	style sheet controls
border	IMG, OBJECT	Link border width around an image	style sheet controls
clear	BR	Control of text flow	style sheet controls
code	APPLET	Applet class file	<OBJECT>
codebase	APPLET	Optional base URI for applet	<OBJECT>
color	BASEFONT, FONT	Text color	style sheet controls
compact	DIR, MENU	Displays lists with reduced spacing	<UL>
compact	DL, OL, UL	Displays lists with reduced spacing	style sheet controls
face	BASEFONT, FONT	Comma-separated list of font names	style sheet controls
height	APPLET	Initial height	<OBJECT>
height	TD, TH	Height for cell	
hspace	APPLET, IMG, OBJECT	Horizontal gutter	style sheet controls
language	SCRIPT	Predefined script language name	

Name	Related Elements	Comment	Replacement Tag
link	BODY	Color of links	style sheet controls
name	APPLET	Allows applets to find each other	<OBJECT>
noshade	HR	Displays rule without 3-D shading	style sheet controls
nowrap	TD, TH	Suppresses word wrap	style sheet controls
object	APPLET	Serialized applet file	<OBJECT>
prompt	ISINDEX	Prompt message	<FORM>
size	HR	Thickness of horizontal rule	style sheet controls
size	FONT	Font size (based on default)	style sheet controls
size	BASEFONT	Base font size for FONT elements	style sheet controls
start	OL	Starting sequence number	style sheet controls
text	BODY	Document text color	style sheet controls
type	LI	List item style	style sheet controls
type	OL	Numbering style	style sheet controls
type	UL	Bullet style	style sheet controls
value	LI	Reset sequence number	style sheet controls
version	HTML	Constant	
vlink	BODY	Color of visited links	style sheet controls
vspace	APPLET, IMG, OBJECT	Vertical gutter	style sheet controls
width	HR	Length of horizontal rule	style sheet controls
width	APPLET	Initial width	<OBJECT>
width	TD, TH	Width for cell	
width	PRE	Character length for preformatted text	

APPENDIX D

Proprietary Tags

Although the vast majority of tags work for both major browsers, Netscape and Microsoft have developed sets of proprietary tags that work only in their respective browsers to gain an edge over the competition. Fortunately, this practice has come to an end (or at least slowed down) now that the browser companies have vowed to comply with standards, but we are still left with a legacy of tags that only work on one browser or another.

Dealing with browser differences is the major cause of headaches for web developers. The tables in this appendix list the available HTML tags that are still supported only in either Netscape Navigator or Internet Explorer.

Microsoft Internet Explorer Proprietary Tags

The following tags and attributes are supported only by Internet Explorer:

HTML tag or attribute	Description

`<basefont>`
　`color=color`
　`face=font face`
	Sets the color and/or font of the entire document when placed in the `<head>` or for subsequent text when placed in the flow of the body text

`<bgsound>`	Inserts an audio file that plays in the background
`<body>` 　`bgproperties=value`	Determines whether background image scrolls with the background

`<body>`
　`leftmargin=n`
　`rightmargin=n`
	Sets the margin between the browser window and the contents of the page

`<caption>` 　`valign=position`	Sets vertical alignment of table caption

HTML tag or attribute	Description
<comment>	Inserts a comment in the HTML source that does not display in the browser (same as <!-- and -->)
<form> target=*name*	Specifies a target window or frame for the output of a form
<frameset> framespacing=*n*	Sets the amount of space between frames
<img> dynsrc=*url* controls loop=*n* start=*action*	Uses the image tag to place video or audio clips
<marquee>	Places scrolling marquee text on the page
<table> bordercolor=*color* bordercolordark=*color* bordercolorlight=*color*	Sets colors for 3-D table borders in the <table>, <td>, <th>, and <tr> tags
<table> frame=value	Controls the display of the outer borders of a table in the <table> tag

Netscape Navigator Proprietary Tags

The following tags are supported only by Netscape Navigator:

HTML tag	Description
<blink>	Causes text to blink on and off
<ilayer>	Inline layer; allows you to offset content from its natural position on the page
<keygen>	Facilitates generation of key material and submission of the public key as part of an HTML form (for privacy and encryption)
<layer>	Creates layers so that elements can be placed on top of each other (useful with DHTML)
<multicol>	Produces a multicolumn format
<nolayer>	Alternative text for layers; browsers that do not support <layer> and <ilayer> display what's between these tags
<server>	Specifies a server-side JavaScript application
<spacer>	Holds a specified amount of empty space (used for alignment of elements on the page and to hold table cells open to specific widths)

APPENDIX E

CSS Support Chart

Browser compatibility—or lack thereof—is the biggest obstacle to adoption of CSS. This appendix provides a comprehensivev guide to how the browsers have implemented support for CSS1. Check this master list to get a rough idea of how well a given property and its values are supported.

This appendix uses the following key:

✓   Supported

✗   Not supported

P   Partial support (some values are supported, some aren't)

B   Buggy support (anything from mangled display to browser crashes)

Q   Quirky support (browser may not act as expected)

This list and the notes that follow are current as of January 2001. For the latest information, please visit *http://style.webreview.com*.

		Windows 95								Macintosh				
	Property or Value	*N4*	*N6*	*IE3*	*IE4*	*IE5*	*IE55*	*O3*	*O4*	*N4*	*N6*	*IE3*	*IE4*	*IE5*
1.1	Containment in HTML	P	✓	P	Q	Q	Q	✓	✓	P	✓	B	✓	✓
	LINK	✓	✓	✓	✓	✓	✓	✓	✓	✓	✓	B	✓	✓
	\<STYLE\>...\</STYLE\>	✓	✓	✓	✓	✓	✓	✓	✓	✓	✓	✓	✓	✓
	@import	✗	✓	✗	Q	Q	Q	✓	✓	✗	✓	✗	✓	✓
	\<x STYLE="dec;"\>	B	✓	✓	✓	✓	✓	✓	✓	B	✓	✓	✗	✓
1.2	Grouping	✓	✓	✗	✓	✓	✓	✓	✓	✓	✓	✓	✓	✓
	x, y, z {dec;}	✓	✓	✗	✓	✓	✓	✓	✓	✓	✓	✓	✓	✓
1.3	Inheritance	B	✓	P	✓	✓	✓	✓	✓	B	✓	B	✓	✓
	(inherited values)	B	✓	P	✓	✓	✓	✓	✓	B	✓	B	✓	✓
1.4	Class selector	✓	✓	B	Q	Q	Q	✓	✓	✓	✓	B	✓	✓
	.class	✓	✓	B	Q	Q	Q	✓	✓	✓	✓	B	✓	✓

	Property or Value	\[Windows 95\] N4	N6	IE3	IE4	IE5	IE55	O3	O4	\[Macintosh\] N4	N6	IE3	IE4	IE5
1.5	ID selector	B	✓	B	B	B	B	✓	✓	B	✓	B	B	✓
	#ID	B	✓	B	B	B	B	B	✓	B	✓	B	B	✓
1.6	Contextual selectors	✓	✓	✓	✓	✓	✓	✓	✓	B	✓	P	✓	✓
	x y z {dec;}	✓	✓	✓	✓	✓	✓	✓	✓	B	✓	P	✓	✓
1.7	Comments	✓	✓	B	✓	✓	✓	✓	✓	✓	✓	✓	✓	✓
	/* comment */	✓	✓	B	✓	✓	✓	✓	✓	✓	✓	✓	✓	✓
2.1	anchor	P	✓	✗	✓	✓	✓	P	P	P	✓	B	✓	✓
	A:link	✓	✓	✗	✓	✓	✓	✓	✓	✓	✓	B	✓	✓
	A:active	B	✓	✗	✓	✓	✓	✗	✗	✗	✓	✗	✓	✓
	A:visited	B	✓	✗	✓	✓	✓	✓	✓	✗	✓	B	✓	✓
2.3	first-line	✗	✓	✗	✗	✗	✓	✓	✓	✗	✓	B	✗	✓
	:first-line	✗	✓	✗	✗	✗	✓	✓	✓	✗	✓	B	✗	✓
2.4	first-letter	✗	✓	✗	✗	✗	✓	✓	✓	✗	✓	B	✗	✓
	:first-letter	✗	✓	✗	✗	✗	✓	✓	✓	✗	✓	B	✗	✓
3.1	important	✗	✓	✗	✓	✓	✓	✓	✓	✗	✓	✓	✓	✓
	!important	✗	✓	✗	✓	✓	✓	✓	✓	✓	✓	✓	✓	✓
3.2	Cascading Order	B	✓	P	✓	✓	✓	✓	✓	B	✓	P	✓	✓
	Weight sorting	B	✓	✓	✓	✓	✓	✓	✓	B	✓	✓	✓	✓
	Origin sorting	B	✓	✓	✓	✓	✓	✓	✓	B	✓	B	✓	✓
	Specificity sorting	B	✓	P	✓	✓	✓	✓	✓	B	✓	B	✓	✓
	Order sorting	B	✓	✓	✓	✓	✓	✓	✓	B	✓	✓	✓	✓
5.2.2	font-family	✓	✓	P	✓	✓	✓	✓	✓	✓	✓	P	✓	✓
	<family-name>	✓	✓	✓	✓	✓	✓	✓	✓	✓	✓	P	✓	✓
	<generic-family>	P	✓	P	✓	✓	✓	✓	✓	✓	✓	P	✓	✓
	serif	✓	✓	✓	✓	✓	✓	✓	✓	✓	✓	✓	✓	✓
	sans-serif	✓	✓	✓	✓	✓	✓	✓	✓	✓	✓	✗	✓	✓
	cursive	✗	✓	B	✓	✓	✓	✓	✓	✓	✓	✗	✓	✓
	fantasy	✗	✓	B	✓	✓	✓	✓	✓	✓	✓	✗	✓	✓
	monospace	✓	✓	✓	✓	✓	✓	✓	✓	✓	✓	✓	✓	✓
5.2.3	font-style	P	✓	P	✓	✓	✓	✓	✓	P	✓	P	✓	✓
	normal	✓	✓	✓	✓	✓	✓	✓	✓	✓	✓	✗	✓	✓
	italic	✓	✓	✗	✓	✓	✓	✓	✓	✓	✓	✓	✓	✓
	oblique	✗	✓	✗	✓	✓	✓	✓	✓	✗	✓	✗	✓	✓
5.2.4	font-variant	✗	✓	✗	Q	Q	Q	✓	✓	✗	✓	✗	Q	✓
	normal	✗	✓	✗	✓	✓	✓	✓	✓	✗	✓	✗	✓	✓
	small-caps	✗	✓	✗	Q	Q	Q	✓	✓	✗	✓	✗	Q	✓
5.2.5	font-weight	P	✓	P	✓	✓	✓	✓	✓	P	✓	P	✓	✓
	normal	✓	✓	✗	✓	✓	✓	✓	✓	✓	✓	✗	✓	✓
	bold	✓	✓	✓	✓	✓	✓	✓	✓	✓	✓	✓	✓	✓
	bolder	✓	✓	✓	✓	✓	✓	✓	✓	✗	✓	✗	✓	✓
	lighter	✗	✓	✓	✓	✓	✓	✓	✓	✗	✓	✗	✓	✓
	100–900	✓	✓	✗	✓	✓	✓	✓	✓	✓	✓	✗	✓	✓

	Property or Value	Windows 95								Macintosh				
		N4	N6	IE3	IE4	IE5	IE55	O3	O4	N4	N6	IE3	IE4	IE5
5.2.6	font-size	✓	✓	P	P	P	P	✓	✓	✓	✓	P	Q	✓
	\<absolute-size>	✓	✓	✓	Q	Q	Q	✓	✓	✓	✓	B	Q	✓
	xx-small – xx-large	✓	✓	✓	Q	Q	Q	✓	✓	✓	✓	B	Q	✓
	\<relative-size>	✓	✓	✓	✓	✓	B	✓	✓	✓	✓	✗	✓	✓
	larger	✓	✓	✓	✓	✓	B	✓	✓	✓	✓	✗	✓	✓
	smaller	✓	✓	✓	✓	✓	B	✓	✓	✓	✓	✗	✓	✓
	\<length>	✓	✓	P	✓	✓	✓	✓	✓	✓	✓	B	✓	✓
	\<percentage>	✓	✓	✓	✓	✓	✓	✓	✓	✓	✓	P	✓	✓
5.2.7	font	P	✓	P	P	P	✓	✓	✓	P	✓	P	Q	✓
	\<font-family>	P	✓	✓	✓	✓	✓	✓	✓	✓	✓	P	✓	✓
	\<font-style>	P	✓	P	✓	✓	✓	✓	✓	✓	✓	P	✓	✓
	\<font-variant>	✗	✓	✗	Q	Q	Q	✓	✓	✗	✓	✗	Q	✓
	\<font-weight>	P	✓	✓	✓	✓	✓	✓	✓	✓	✓	✗	✓	✓
	\<font-size>	✓	✓	B	Q	Q	P	✓	✓	✓	✓	B	✓	✓
	\<line-height>	B	✓	✓	✓	✓	✓	✓	✓	B	✓	B	✓	✓
5.3.1	color	✓	✓	✓	✓	✓	✓	✓	✓	✓	✓	✓	✓	✓
	\<color>	✓	✓	✓	✓	✓	✓	✓	✓	✓	✓	✓	✓	✓
5.3.2	background-color	B	✓	P	✓	✓	✓	✓	✓	B	✓	✗	✓	✓
	\<color>	B	✓	B	✓	✓	✓	✓	✓	B	✓	✗	✓	✓
	transparent	B	✓	✗	✓	✓	✓	✓	B	B	✓	✗	✓	✓
5.3.3	background-image	✓	✓	✗	✓	✓	✓	✓	✓	✓	✓	✗	✓	✓
	\<url>	✓	✓	✗	✓	✓	✓	✓	✓	✓	✓	✗	✓	✓
	none	✓	✓	✗	✓	✓	✓	✓	✓	✓	✓	✗	✓	✓
5.3.4	background-repeat	P	✓	✗	P	✓	✓	✓	✓	B	✓	✗	✓	✓
	repeat	✓	✓	✗	B	✓	✓	✓	✓	✓	✓	✗	✓	✓
	repeat-x	P	✓	✗	B	✓	✓	✓	✓	P	✓	✗	✓	✓
	repeat-y	P	✓	✗	B	✓	✓	✓	✓	P	✓	✗	✓	✓
	no-repeat	✓	✓	✗	✓	✓	✓	✓	✓	✓	✓	✗	✓	✓
5.3.5	background-attachment	✗	✓	✗	✓	✓	✓	✗	✓	✗	✓	✗	✓	✓
	scroll	✗	✓	✗	✓	✓	✓	✗	✓	✗	✓	✗	✓	✓
	fixed	✗	✓	✗	✓	✓	✓	✗	✓	✗	✓	✗	✓	✓
5.3.6	background-position	✗	✓	✗	✓	✓	✓	✓	✓	✗	✓	✗	✓	✓
	\<percentage>	✗	✓	✗	✓	✓	✓	✓	✓	✗	✓	✗	✓	✓
	\<length>	✗	✓	✗	✓	✓	✓	✓	✓	✗	✓	✗	✓	✓
	top	✗	✓	✗	✓	✓	✓	✓	✓	✗	✓	✗	✓	✓
	center	✗	✓	✗	✓	✓	✓	✓	✓	✗	✓	✗	✓	✓
	bottom	✗	✓	✗	✓	✓	✓	✓	✓	✗	✓	✗	✓	✓
	left	✗	✓	✗	✓	✓	✓	✓	✓	✗	✓	✗	✓	✓
	right	✗	✓	✗	✓	✓	✓	✓	✓	✗	✓	✗	✓	✓
5.3.7	background	P	✓	P	P	✓	✓	P	P	P	✓	P	✓	✓
	\<background-color>	B	✓	P	✓	✓	✓	✓	✓	P	✓	P	✓	✓
	\<background-image>	P	✓	✓	✓	✓	✓	✓	✓	P	✓	✓	✓	✓
	\<background-repeat>	P	✓	B	B	✓	✓	✓	✓	P	✓	B	✓	✓

Property or Value	Windows 95 N4	N6	IE3	IE4	IE5	IE55	O3	O4	Macintosh N4	N6	IE3	IE4	IE5
<background-attachment>	✗	✓	✗	✓	✓	✓	✗	✓	✗	✓	✓	✓	✓
<background-position>	✗	✓	✗	✓	✓	✓	✓	✓	✗	✓	P	✓	✓
5.4.1 word-spacing	✗	✓	✗	✗	✗	✗	✓	✓	✗	✓	✗	✓	✓
normal	✗	✓	✗	✗	✗	✗	✓	✓	✗	✓	✗	✓	✓
<length>	✗	✓	✗	✗	✗	✗	✓	✓	✗	✓	✗	✓	✓
5.4.2 letter-spacing	✗	✓	✗	✓	✓	✓	✓	✓	✗	✓	✗	✓	✓
normal	✗	✓	✗	✓	✓	✓	✓	✓	✗	✓	✗	✓	✓
<length>	✗	✓	✗	✓	✓	✓	✓	✓	✗	✓	✗	✓	✓
5.4.3 text-decoration	B	B	B	B	B	B	B	B	B	B	B	B	P
none	Q	✓	✗	✓	✓	✓	✓	✓	Q	✓	✓	Q	✓
underline	Q	✓	B	✓	✓	✓	✓	✓	Q	✓	B	Q	✓
overline	✗	✓	✗	✓	✓	✓	✓	✓	✗	✓	✗	✓	✓
line-through	✓	✓	✓	✓	✓	✓	✓	✓	✓	✓	✓	✓	✓
blink	✓	✓	✗	✗	✗	✗	✗	✓	✓	✓	✗	✗	✗
5.4.4 vertical-align	✗	✓	✗	P	P	P	P	✓	✗	✓	✗	P	✓
baseline	✗	✓	✗	✓	✓	✓	✓	✓	✗	✓	✗	✓	✓
sub	✗	✓	✗	✓	✓	✓	✓	✓	✗	✓	✗	✓	✓
super	✗	✓	✗	✓	✓	✓	✓	✓	✗	✓	✗	✓	✓
top	✗	✓	✗	✗	✗	✓	B	✓	✗	✓	✗	✓	✓
text-top	✗	✓	✗	✗	✗	✓	✗	✓	✗	✓	✗	✓	✓
middle	✗	✓	✗	B	✗	✓	B	✓	✗	✓	✗	✓	✓
bottom	✗	✓	✗	✗	✗	✓	B	✓	✗	✓	✗	B	✓
text-bottom	✗	✓	✗	✗	✗	✓	✗	✓	✗	✓	✗	B	✓
<percentage>	✗	✓	✗	✗	✗	✗	✓	✓	✗	✓	✗	B	✓
5.4.5 text-transform	✓	✓	✗	✓	✓	✓	P	✓	✓	✓	✗	✓	✓
capitalize	✓	✓	✗	✓	✓	✓	✓	✓	✓	✓	✗	✓	✓
uppercase	✓	✓	✗	✓	✓	✓	B	✓	✓	✓	✗	✓	✓
lowercase	✓	✓	✗	✓	✓	✓	✓	✓	✓	✓	✗	✓	✓
none	✓	✓	✗	✓	✓	✓	✓	✓	✓	✓	✗	✓	✓
5.4.6 text-align	✓	✓	P	✓	✓	✓	✓	✓	P	✓	P	P	✓
left	✓	✓	✓	✓	✓	✓	✓	✓	✓	✓	✓	✓	✓
right	✓	✓	✓	✓	✓	✓	✓	✓	✓	✓	✓	✓	✓
center	✓	✓	✓	✓	✓	✓	✓	✓	✓	✓	✓	✓	✓
justify	B	✓	✗	✓	✓	✓	✓	✓	B	✓	✗	✗	✓
5.4.7 text-indent	✓	✓	✓	✓	✓	✓	✓	✓	✓	✓	✓	✓	✓
<length>	✓	✓	✓	✓	✓	✓	✓	✓	✓	✓	✓	✓	✓
<percentage>	✓	✓	✓	✓	✓	✓	✓	✓	✓	✓	✓	✓	✓
5.4.8 line-height	P	✓	P	✓	✓	✓	Q	✓	P	✓	P	✓	✓
normal	✓	✓	✓	✓	✓	✓	✓	✓	✓	✓	✓	✓	✓
<number>	P	✓	✗	✓	✓	✓	✓	✓	P	✓	B	✓	✓
<length>	B	✓	✓	✓	✓	✓	✓	✓	B	✓	B	✓	✓
<percentage>	P	✓	✓	✓	✓	✓	✓	✓	P	✓	B	✓	✓

	Property or Value	Windows 95								Macintosh				
		N4	N6	IE3	IE4	IE5	IE55	O3	O4	N4	N6	IE3	IE4	IE5
5.5.01	margin-top	P	✓	B	P	P	✓	✓	✓	P	✓	B	P	✓
	<length>	P	✓	B	P	P	✓	✓	✓	P	✓	B	P	✓
	<percentage>	P	✓	✓	P	P	✓	✓	✓	P	✓	B	P	✓
	auto	P	✓	✓	P	P	✓	✓	✓	P	✓	B	P	✓
5.5.02	margin-right	B	B	P	P	P	Q	✓	B	B	B	P	P	✓
	<length>	B	✓	✓	P	P	✓	✓	✓	B	✓	✓	P	✓
	<percentage>	B	✓	✗	P	P	✓	✓	✓	B	✓	✓	P	✓
	auto	✗	✓	✗	✗	✗	✓	✓	✓	✗	✓	✗	P	✓
5.5.03	margin-bottom	✗	✓	✓	P	P	✓	✓	✓	✗	✓	✗	P	✓
	<length>	✗	✓	✗	P	P	✓	✓	✓	✗	✓	✗	P	✓
	<percentage>	✗	✓	✗	P	P	✓	✓	✓	✗	✓	✗	P	✓
	auto	✗	✓	✗	P	P	✓	✓	✓	✗	✓	✗	P	✓
5.5.04	margin-left	B	✓	P	P	P	✓	✓	B	B	✓	P	P	✓
	<length>	B	✓	✓	P	P	✓	✓	✓	✓	✓	✓	P	✓
	<percentage>	B	✓	✓	P	P	✓	✓	✓	B	✓	✓	P	✓
	auto	✗	✓	✗	✗	✗	✓	✓	✓	B	✓	✗	P	✓
5.5.05	margin	B	B	B	P	P	✓	✓	B	B	B	B	P	✓
	<length>	B	✓	B	P	P	✓	✓	✓	B	✓	B	P	✓
	<percentage>	B	✓	✓	P	P	✓	✓	✓	B	✓	B	P	✓
	auto	✗	✓	✓	P	P	✓	✓	✓	✗	✓	B	P	✓
5.5.06	padding-top	B	✓	✗	P	P	Q	✓	✓	B	✓	✗	P	✓
	<length>	B	✓	✗	P	P	✓	✓	✓	B	✓	✗	P	✓
	<percentage>	B	✓	✗	P	P	✓	✓	✓	B	✓	✗	P	✓
5.5.07	padding-right	B	✓	✗	P	P	Q	✓	✓	B	✓	✗	P	✓
	<length>	B	✓	✗	P	P	✓	✓	✓	B	✓	✗	P	✓
	<percentage>	B	✓	✗	P	P	✓	✓	✓	B	✓	✗	P	✓
5.5.08	padding-bottom	B	✓	✗	P	P	✓	✓	✓	B	✓	✗	P	✓
	<length>	B	✓	✗	P	P	✓	✓	✓	B	✓	✗	P	✓
	<percentage>	B	✓	✗	P	P	✓	✓	✓	B	✓	✗	P	✓
5.5.09	padding-left	B	✓	✗	P	P	✓	✓	✓	B	✓	✗	P	✓
	<length>	B	✓	✗	P	P	✓	✓	✓	B	✓	✗	P	✓
	<percentage>	B	✓	✗	P	P	✓	✓	✓	B	✓	✗	P	✓
5.5.10	padding	B	✓	✗	P	P	Q	B	✓	B	✓	✗	P	✓
	<length>	B	✓	✗	P	P	✓	B	✓	B	✓	✗	P	✓
	<percentage>	B	✓	✗	P	P	✓	B	✓	B	✓	✗	P	✓
5.5.11	border-top-width	B	✓	✗	P	P	✓	✓	✓	B	✓	✗	P	✓
	thin	✓	✓	✗	P	P	✓	✓	✓	✓	✓	✗	P	✓
	medium	✓	✓	✗	P	P	✓	✓	✓	✓	✓	✗	P	✓
	thick	✓	✓	✗	P	P	✓	✓	✓	✓	✓	✗	P	✓
	<length>	✓	✓	✗	P	P	✓	✓	✓	✓	✓	✗	P	✓
5.5.12	border-right-width	B	✓	✗	P	P	✓	✓	✓	B	✓	✗	P	✓
	thin	✓	✓	✗	P	P	✓	✓	✓	✓	✓	✗	P	✓

Property or Value	Windows 95								Macintosh				
	N4	N6	IE3	IE4	IE5	IE55	O3	O4	N4	N6	IE3	IE4	IE5
medium	✓	✓	✗	P	P	✓	✓	✓	✓	✓	✗	P	✓
thick	✓	✓	✗	P	P	✓	✓	✓	✓	✓	✗	P	✓
<length>	✓	✓	✗	P	P	✓	✓	✓	✓	✓	✗	P	✓
5.5.13 border-bottom-width	B	✓	✗	P	P	✓	✓	✓	B	✓	✗	P	✓
thin	B	✓	✗	P	P	✓	✓	✓	B	✓	✗	P	✓
medium	B	✓	✗	P	P	✓	✓	✓	B	✓	✗	P	✓
thick	B	✓	✗	P	P	✓	✓	✓	B	✓	✗	P	✓
<length>	B	✓	✗	P	P	✓	✓	✓	B	✓	✗	P	✓
5.5.14 border-left-width	B	✓	✗	P	P	✓	✓	✓	B	✓	✗	P	✓
thin	✓	✓	✗	P	P	✓	✓	✓	✓	✓	✗	P	✓
medium	✓	✓	✗	P	P	✓	✓	✓	✓	✓	✗	P	✓
thick	✓	✓	✗	P	P	✓	✓	✓	✓	✓	✗	P	✓
<length>	✓	✓	✗	P	P	✓	✓	✓	✓	✓	✗	P	✓
5.5.15 border-width	B	✓	✗	P	P	✓	✓	✓	B	✓	✗	P	✓
thin	✓	✓	✗	P	P	✓	✓	✓	✓	✓	✗	P	✓
medium	✓	✓	✗	P	P	✓	✓	✓	✓	✓	✗	P	✓
thick	✓	✓	✗	P	P	✓	✓	✓	✓	✓	✗	P	✓
<length>	✓	✓	✗	P	P	✓	✓	✓	✓	✓	✗	P	✓
5.5.16 border-color	P	✓	✗	✓	✓	✓	✓	✓	P	✓	✗	✓	✓
<color>	P	✓	✗	✓	✓	✓	✓	✓	P	✓	✗	✓	✓
5.5.17 border-style	P	✓	✗	P	P	✓	✓	✓	P	✓	✗	✓	✓
none	✓	✓	✗	✓	✓	✓	✓	✓	✓	✓	✗	✓	✓
dotted	✗	✓	✗	✗	✗	✓	✓	✓	✗	✓	✗	✓	✓
dashed	✗	✓	✗	✗	✗	✓	✓	✓	✗	✓	✗	✓	✓
solid	✓	✓	✗	✓	✓	✓	✓	✓	✓	✓	✗	✓	✓
double	✓	✓	✗	✓	✓	✓	✓	✓	✓	✓	✗	✓	✓
groove	✓	✓	✗	✓	✓	✓	✓	✓	✓	✓	✗	✓	✓
ridge	✓	✓	✗	✓	✓	✓	✓	✓	✓	✓	✗	✓	✓
inset	✓	✓	✗	✓	✓	✓	✓	✓	✓	✓	✗	✓	✓
outset	✓	✓	✗	✓	✓	✓	✓	✓	✓	✓	✗	✓	✓
5.5.18 border-top	✗	✓	✗	P	P	✓	✓	✓	✗	✓	✗	P	✓
<border-top-width>	✗	✓	✗	P	P	✓	✓	✓	✗	✓	✗	P	✓
<border-style>	✗	✓	✗	P	P	✓	✓	✓	✗	✓	✗	P	✓
<color>	✗	✓	✗	P	P	✓	✓	✓	✗	✓	✗	P	✓
5.5.19 border-right	✗	✓	✗	P	P	✓	✓	✓	✗	✓	✗	P	✓
<border-right-width>	✗	✓	✗	P	P	✓	✓	✓	✗	✓	✗	P	✓
<border-style>	✗	✓	✗	P	P	✓	✓	✓	✗	✓	✗	P	✓
<color>	✗	✓	✗	P	P	✓	✓	✓	✗	✓	✗	P	✓
5.5.20 border-bottom	✗	✓	✗	P	P	✓	✓	✓	✗	✓	✗	P	✓
<border-bottom-width>	✗	✓	✗	P	P	✓	✓	✓	✗	✓	✗	P	✓
<border-style>	✗	✓	✗	P	P	✓	✓	✓	✗	✓	✗	P	✓
<color>	✗	✓	✗	P	P	✓	✓	✓	✗	✓	✗	P	✓

	Property or Value	Windows 95								Macintosh				
		N4	N6	IE3	IE4	IE5	IE55	O3	O4	N4	N6	IE3	IE4	IE5
5.5.21	border-left	✗	✓	✗	P	P	✓	P	✓	✗	✓	✗	P	✓
	<border-left-width>	✗	✓	✗	P	P	✓	P	✓	✗	✓	✗	P	✓
	<border-style>	✗	✓	✗	P	P	✓	P	✓	✗	✓	✗	P	✓
	<color>	✗	✓	✗	P	P	✓	P	✓	✗	✓	✗	P	✓
5.5.22	border	P	✓	✗	P	P	✓	P	✓	P	✓	✗	P	✓
	<border-width>	B	✓	✗	P	P	✓	P	✓	B	✓	✗	P	✓
	<border-style>	P	✓	✗	P	P	✓	P	✓	P	✓	✗	P	✓
	<color>	✓	✓	✗	P	P	✓	P	✓	✓	✓	✗	P	✓
5.5.23	width	P	✓	✗	P	P	✓	Q	✓	P	✓	✗	✓	✓
	<length>	P	✓	✗	P	P	✓	Q	✓	P	✓	✗	✓	✓
	<percentage>	P	✓	✗	P	P	✓	Q	✓	P	✓	✗	✓	✓
	auto	P	✓	✗	P	P	✓	Q	✓	P	✓	✗	✓	✓
5.5.24	height	✗	✓	✗	✓	✓	✓	✓	✓	✗	✓	✗	✓	✓
	<length>	✗	✓	✗	✓	✓	✓	✓	✓	✗	✓	✗	✓	✓
	auto	✗	✓	✗	✓	✓	✓	✓	✓	✗	✓	✗	✓	✓
5.5.25	float	P	✓	✗	P	P	Q	B	Q	P	✓	✗	B	Q
	left	B	✓	✗	B	B	✓	✓	✓	B	✓	✗	✓	✓
	right	B	✓	✗	B	B	✓	✓	✓	B	✓	✗	✓	✓
	none	✓	✓	✗	✓	✓	✓	✓	✓	✓	✓	✗	✓	✓
5.5.26	clear	P	✓	✗	P	P	✓	B	✓	P	✓	✗	✓	✓
	none	✓	✓	✓	✓	✓	✓	✓	✓	✓	✓	✓	✓	✓
	left	B	✓	✗	B	B	✓	✗	✓	B	✓	✗	✓	✓
	right	B	✓	✗	B	B	✓	✓	✓	B	✓	✗	✓	✓
	both	✓	✓	✗	✓	✓	✓	✓	✓	✓	✓	✗	✓	✓
5.6.1	display	P	✓	✗	P	P	P	P	✓	P	✓	✗	P	✓
	block	B	✓	✗	✗	✓	✓	✓	✓	B	✓	✗	P	✓
	inline	✗	✓	✗	✗	✓	✓	B	✓	✗	✓	✗	✗	✓
	list-item	B	✓	✗	✗	✗	✗	✗	✓	P	✓	✗	P	✓
	none	✓	✓	✗	✓	✓	✓	✓	✓	✓	✓	✗	✓	✓
5.6.2	white-space	P	✓	✗	✗	✗	P	✗	✓	P	✓	✗	✗	✓
	normal	✓	✓	✗	✗	✗	✓	✗	✓	✓	✓	✗	✗	✓
	pre	✓	✓	✗	✗	✗	✗	✗	✓	✓	✓	✗	✗	✓
	nowrap	✗	✓	✗	✗	✗	✓	✗	✓	✗	✓	✗	✗	✓
5.6.3	list-style-type	✓	✓	✗	✓	✓	✓	✓	✓	P	✓	✗	✓	✓
	disc	✓	✓	✗	✓	✓	✓	✓	✓	✓	✓	✗	✓	✓
	circle	✓	✓	✗	✓	✓	✓	✓	✓	✓	✓	✗	✓	✓
	square	✓	✓	✗	✓	✓	✓	✓	✓	✓	✓	✗	✓	✓
	decimal	✓	✓	✗	✓	✓	✓	✓	✓	✓	✓	✗	✓	✓
	lower-roman	✓	✓	✗	✓	✓	✓	✓	✓	✓	✓	✗	✓	✓
	upper-roman	✓	✓	✗	✓	✓	✓	✓	✓	✓	✓	✗	✓	✓
	lower-alpha	✓	✓	✗	✓	✓	✓	✓	✓	✓	✓	✗	✓	✓
	upper-alpha	✓	✓	✗	✓	✓	✓	✓	✓	✓	✓	✗	✓	✓
	none	✓	✓	✗	✓	✓	✓	✓	✓	B	✓	✗	✓	✓

	Property or Value	Windows 95								Macintosh				
		N4	N6	IE3	IE4	IE5	IE55	O3	O4	N4	N6	IE3	IE4	IE5
5.6.4	list-style-image	X	✓	X	✓	✓	✓	✓	✓	X	✓	X	✓	✓
	<url>	X	✓	X	✓	✓	✓	✓	✓	X	✓	X	✓	✓
	none	X	✓	X	✓	✓	✓	✓	✓	X	✓	X	✓	✓
5.6.5	list-style-position	X	✓	X	✓	✓	✓	✓	✓	X	✓	X	✓	✓
	inside	X	✓	X	✓	✓	✓	✓	✓	X	✓	X	Q	✓
	outside	X	✓	X	✓	✓	✓	✓	✓	X	✓	X	✓	✓
5.6.6	list-style	P	✓	X	P	✓	✓	✓	✓	P	✓	X	P	✓
	<keyword>	✓	✓	X	✓	✓	✓	✓	✓	P	✓	X	✓	✓
	<position>	X	✓	X	Q	Q	✓	✓	✓	X	✓	X	Q	✓
	<url>	X	✓	X	✓	✓	✓	✓	✓	X	✓	X	✓	✓
6.1	Length Units	P	✓	P	✓	✓	✓	✓	✓	✓	✓	B	✓	✓
	em	✓	✓	X	✓	✓	✓	✓	✓	✓	✓	✓	✓	✓
	ex	Q	✓	X	Q	Q	✓	Q	✓	Q	✓	Q	Q	✓
	px	✓	✓	✓	✓	✓	✓	✓	✓	✓	✓	✓	✓	✓
	in	✓	✓	✓	✓	✓	✓	✓	✓	✓	✓	✓	✓	✓
	cm	✓	✓	✓	✓	✓	✓	✓	✓	✓	✓	✓	✓	✓
	mm	✓	✓	✓	✓	✓	✓	✓	✓	✓	✓	✓	✓	✓
	pt	✓	✓	✓	✓	✓	✓	✓	✓	✓	✓	✓	✓	✓
	pc	✓	✓	✓	✓	✓	✓	✓	✓	✓	✓	✓	✓	✓
6.2	Percentage Units	✓	✓	✓	✓	✓	✓	✓	✓	✓	✓	✓	✓	✓
	<percentage>	✓	✓	✓	✓	✓	✓	✓	✓	✓	✓	✓	✓	✓
6.3	Color Units	P	✓	P	✓	✓	✓	✓	✓	P	✓	P	✓	✓
	#000	✓	✓	✓	✓	✓	✓	✓	✓	✓	✓	B	✓	✓
	#000000	✓	✓	✓	✓	✓	✓	✓	✓	✓	✓	B	✓	✓
	(RRR,GGG,BBB)	✓	✓	X	✓	✓	✓	✓	✓	✓	✓	X	✓	✓
	(R%,G%,B%)	✓	✓	X	✓	✓	✓	✓	✓	✓	✓	X	✓	✓
	<keyword>	B	✓	✓	✓	✓	✓	✓	✓	B	✓	✓	✓	✓
6.4	URLs	B	✓	✓	✓	✓	✓	✓	✓	B	✓	B	✓	✓
	<url>	B	✓	✓	✓	✓	✓	✓	✓	B	✓	B	✓	✓

Notes

1.1 Containment in HTML @import

WinIE4+ imports files even when the @import statement is at the end of the document style sheet. This is technically in violation of the CSS1 specification, although obviously not a major failing; thus the Q rating.

1.1 Containment in HTML <x STYLE="dec;">

Navigator 4 has particular trouble with list-items, which is most of the reason for the B.

1.3 Inheritance

Navigator 4's inheritance is unstable at best, and fatally flawed at worst. It would take too long to list all occurrences, but particularly troublesome areas include tables and lists.

1.4 Class selector

WinIE4/5 allows class names to begin with digits; this isn't permitted under CSS1.

1.5 ID selector

WinIE4/5 allows ID names to begin with digits; this isn't permitted under CSS1. All browsers apply the style for a given ID to more than one instance of that ID in an HTML document, which isn't permitted. This is properly an error-checking problem and not a failing of the CSS implementations, but it's significant enough to warrant the ratings shown.

2.3 `:first-line`

IE3 incorrectly applies `:first-line` styles to the entire element.

2.4 `:first-letter`

IE3 incorrectly applies `:first-letter` styles to the entire element.

3.2 Cascading Order

There are simply far too many instances of NN4 problems to list here. If writing in support of NN4, make your style sheets as simple and as independent of cascading order as possible.

5.2.2 `font-family cursive`

Despite a preferences setting for cursive fonts, Opera doesn't seem to apply the preference, but instead substitutes another font.

5.2.4 `font-variant small-caps`

IE4/5 approximates the `small-caps` style by making all such text uppercase. While this can be justified under the CSS1 specification, visually, it doesn't render the text in small caps.

5.2.6 `font-size xx-small` through `xx-large`

WinIE4/5/55 and MacIE4/5 all set the default `font-size` value to `small` instead of `medium`. (The exception is IE5/Mac when it's in strict rendering mode.) Thus, declaring an absolute font size (such as `font-size: medium`) almost certainly will lead to different size fonts in Navigator and Explorer. While this isn't incorrect under the specification, it's confusing to many people.

5.3.2 `background-color <color>`

Nav4 doesn't apply the background color to the entire content box and padding, just to the text in the element. This can be worked around by declaring a zero-width border.

5.3.2 `background-color transparent`

Nav4 insists on applying this value to the parent of an element, not the element itself. This can lead to "holes" in the parent element's background.

Opera 4 has a bug that shows up only when a background has been repeated, and the rest of the background of the element is transparent (either by default or when explicitly declared). Scrolling the element offscreen and then bringing it back can cause "holes" to be punched through the repeated images of ancestor elements, thus creating visual anomalies.

5.3.4 `background-repeat repeat`
WinIE4 repeats only down and to the right. The correct behavior is for the background image to be tiled in both vertical directions for `repeat-y`, and both horizontal for `repeat-x`. Nav4 gets this property correct on a technicality: since it doesn't support `background-position`, there's no way to know whether or not it will tile in all four directions if given the chance, or instead emulate WinIE4's behavior. Opera 3.6, MacIE4.5 and WinIE5 all behave correctly.

5.3.4 `background-repeat repeat-x`
WinIE4 only repeats to the right, instead of both left and right.

5.3.4 `background-repeat repeat-y`
WinIE4 only repeats down, instead of both up and down.

5.4.3 `text-decoration none`
According to the specification, if an element is decorated, but one of its children isn't, the parent's effect is still visible on the child; in a certain sense, it "shines through." Thus, if a paragraph is underlined, but a STRONG element within it is set to have no underlining, the paragraph underline still spans the STRONG element. This also means that the underlining of child elements should be the same color as the parent element, unless the child element has also been set to be underlined.

In practice, however, setting an inline element to none turns off all decorations, regardless of the parent's decoration. The only exceptions are Opera and IE5/Mac, which implement this part of the specification correctly. Unfortunately, Opera 4 and Netscape 6 don't span inline images with the text decoration of a parent element. In addition, Netscape 6 appears not to use a parent element's decoration, but instead replicates it onto child elements, which is subtly wrong.

5.4.3 `text-decoration blink`
Since this value isn't required under CSS1, only Navigator supports it (surprise).

5.4.5 `text-transform uppercase`
Opera 3.6 uppercases the first letter in each inline element within a word, which (according to the CSS1 Test Suite) it shouldn't do.

5.4.6 `text-align justify`
In Nav4, this value has a tendency to break down in tables but generally works in other circumstances.

5.4.8 `line-height`
Opera 3.6 applies background colors to the space between lines, as opposed to just the text itself, when the background is set for an inline element within the text. (See the CSS1 Test Suite for more details.)

5.4.8 `line-height <length>`
Nav4 incorrectly permits negative values for this property.

5.5.01 `margin-top`

All margin properties seem to be problematic, or else completely unsupported, on inline elements; see `margin` for details.

5.5.02 `margin-right`

All margin properties seem to be problematic, or else completely unsupported, on inline elements; see `margin` for details. Opera 4 sometimes applies right margins to all the boxes of an inline element, not just the last one. This seems to come and go somewhat randomly, but it's common enough to be easily noticeable.

5.5.03 `margin-bottom`

All margin properties seem to be problematic, or else completely unsupported, on inline elements; see `margin` for details.

5.5.04 `margin-left`

All margin properties seem to be problematic, or else completely unsupported, on inline elements; see `margin` for details. Opera 4 sometimes applies left margins to all the boxes of an inline element, not just the first one. This seems to come and go somewhat randomly, but it's common enough to be easily noticeable.

5.5.05 `margin`

`margin` is fairly well supported on block-level elements in most browsers, with the notable exception of NN4.x. `margin` on inline elements is fully supported in IE5/Mac, IE55/Win, NN6, and Opera 4/5. `margin` should never be used on inline elements in NN4.x, which has severe and page-mangling bugs.

Opera 4's problems with correctly applying right and left margins to inline elements seems to get worse with `margin`.

5.5.06 `padding-top`

All padding properties seem to be problematic, or else completely unsupported, on inline elements; see `padding` for details.

5.5.07 `padding-right`

All padding properties seem to be problematic, or else completely unsupported, on inline elements; see `padding` for details.

5.5.08 `padding-bottom`

All padding properties seem to be problematic, or else completely unsupported, on inline elements; see `padding` for details.

5.5.09 `padding-left`

All padding properties seem to be problematic, or else completely unsupported, on inline elements; see `padding` for details.

5.5.10 `padding`

`padding` is fairly well supported on block-level elements in most browsers, with the notable exception of NN4.x. `padding` on inline elements is fully supported in IE5/Mac, NN6, and Opera 4/5. `padding` should never be used on inline elements in NN4.x, which has severe and page-mangling bugs. Opera 3.6 honors negative padding values, which are illegal, but since you shouldn't use negative padding values, this is an easily avoided problem.

5.5.11 border-top-width

Navigator creates visible borders even when no border-style is set and doesn't set borders on all sides when a style is set. Things get really ugly when borders are applied to inline styles. IE4 and IE5 correctly handle borders on block-level elements but ignore them for inlines.

5.5.12 border-right-width

Navigator 4.x creates visible borders even when no border-style is set and doesn't set borders on all sides when a style is set. Things get really ugly when borders are applied to inline styles. IE4 and IE5 correctly handle borders on block-level elements but ignore them for inlines.

5.5.13 border-bottom-width

Navigator 4.x creates visible borders even when no border-style is set and doesn't set borders on all sides when a style is set. Things get really ugly when borders are applied to inline styles. IE4 and IE5/Win correctly handle borders on block-level elements but ignore them for inlines.

5.5.14 border-left-width

Navigator creates visible borders even when no border-style is set and doesn't set borders on all sides when a style is set. Things get really ugly when borders are applied to inline styles. IE4 and IE5 correctly handle borders on block-level elements but ignore them for inlines.

5.5.15 border-width

Navigator creates visible borders even when no border-style is set and doesn't set borders on all sides when a style is set. Things get really ugly when borders are applied to inline styles. IE4 and IE5 correctly handle borders on block-level elements but ignore them for inlines.

5.5.18 border-top

Opera 3 doesn't apply border styles to table elements, which is the reason for the P rating. IE4 and IE5 don't apply borders to inline elements.

5.5.19 border-right

Opera 3 doesn't apply border styles to table elements, which is the reason for the P rating. IE4 and IE5 don't apply borders to inline elements.

5.5.20 border-bottom

Opera 3 doesn't apply border styles to table elements, which is the reason for the P rating. IE4 and IE5/Win don't apply borders to inline elements, which is the reason for those P ratings.

5.5.21 border-left

Opera 3 doesn't apply border styles to table elements, which is the reason for the P rating. IE4 and IE5 don't apply borders to inline elements.

5.5.22 border

Opera 3 doesn't apply border styles to table elements, which is the reason for the P rating. IE4 and Win/IE5 don't apply borders to inline elements, which is the reason for those P ratings.

5.5.23 width

Navigator 4.x applies width in an inconsistent fashion but appears to honor it on most simple text elements and images. WinIE4/5 applies it to images and tables but ignores it for most text elements such as P and headings. Opera 3.6, weirdly, seems to set the width of images to 100%, but this is largely an illusion, since minimizing the window and then maximizing it again reveals correctly sized images.

5.5.25 float

float is one of the most complicated and hardest-to-implement aspects of the entire specification. Basic floating is generally supported by all browsers, especially on images, but when the specification is closely tested, or the document structure becomes complicated, floating most often happens incorrectly or not at all. The floating of text elements is especially inconsistent, although IE5 and Opera have cleaned up their act to a large degree, leaving WinIE4 and Nav4 the major transgressors in this respect. Authors should use float with some care and thoroughly test any pages employing it.

Opera 4 seems to place floated elements a little bit off from where the ideal place would seem to be, but in general, its support is extremely robust and can generally be counted on.

5.5.26 clear

Like float, clear isn't a simple thing to support. There is typically basic support, but as things get more complicated, browser behavior tends to break down. You should thoroughly test your pages when using this property.

5.6.1 display inline

Opera 3.6 almost gets inline right, but seems to honor the occasional carriage return as though it were a <BR> element, instead of plain whitespace.

5.6.3 list-style-type none

MacNav4 displays question marks for bullets when using this value.

5.6.5 list-style-position inside

The positioning and formatting of list-items when set to this value are a bit odd under MacIE4.

6.1 Length Units ex

All supporting browsers appear to calculate ex as one-half em. This is arguably a reasonable approximation, but it's technically incorrect.

6.3 Color Units <keyword>

Navigator generates a color for any apparent keyword. For example, color: invalidValue yields a dark blue, and 'color: inherit') (a valid declaration under CSS2) comes out as a vaguely nauseous green.

6.4 URLs <url>

Navigator determines relative URLs in a style sheet with respect to the location of the HTML document, not with respect to the location of the style sheet itself.

The material in this appendix has been taken from the *CSS Pocket Reference* by Eric A. Meyer (O'Reilly).

APPENDIX F

Character Entities

Characters not found in the normal alphanumeric character set, such as © or &, must be specified in HTML using *character entities*. Character entities can be defined by name (*&name;*) or by numeric value (*&#nnn;*).

The first part of this appendix presents the standard HTML character entities. The second part presents newly added entities in the HTML 4.0 specification that are not as well supported.

Standard Character Entities

The following table contains the defined standard, proposed, and several nonstandard, bvut generally supported, character entities for HTML. Not all 256 characters in the ISO character set appear in the table. Missing ones are not recognized by the browser as either named or numeric entities.

Entities for which the version conformance column is blank are part of the HTML 2.0 and later standards and will work with nearly all available browsers. Characters whose version column contains "4.0" are part of the HTML 4.0 specification only. As of this writing, they are supported by versions 4.0 and higher of Netscape Navigator and Internet Explorer. An "N" in the conformance column indicates that the character is a nonstandard entity. Use them with caution as results may vary by platform.

Number	Name	Symbol	Description	Version
				Horizontal tab	

			Line feed	

			Carriage return	
 			Space	
!		!	Exclamation point	
"	"	"	Quotation mark	

Number	Name	Symbol	Description	Version
#		#	Hash mark	
$		$	Dollar symbol	
%		%	Percent symbol	
&	&	&	Ampersand	
'		'	Apostrophe (single quote)	
(		(	Left parenthesis	
)		)	Right parenthesis	
*		*	Asterisk	
+		+	Plus sign	
,		,	Comma	
-		-	Hyphen	
.		.	Period	
/		/	Slash	
0– 9		0-9	Digits 0–9	
:		:	Colon	
;		;	Semicolon	
<	<	<	Less than	
=		=	Equals sign	
>	>	>	Greater than	
?		?	Question mark	
@		@	Commercial at sign	
A– Z		A–Z	Letters A–Z	
[		[	Left square bracket	
\		\	Backslash	
]		]	Right square bracket	
^		^	Caret	
_		_	Underscore	
`		`	Grave accent (no letter)	
a– z		a-z	Letters a–z	
{		{	Left curly brace	
|		|	Vertical bar	
}		}	Right curly brace	
~		~	Tilde	
‚		‚	Low left single quote	N
ƒ		ƒ	Small f with hook	N
„		„	Low left double quote	N
…		…	Ellipsis	N
†		†	Dagger	N
‡		‡	Double dagger	N
ˆ		^	Circumflex	N
‰		‰	Per mille (per thousand)	N

Number	Name	Symbol	Description	Version
Š		Š	Capital S, caron	N
‹		<	Less-than sign	N
Œ		Œ	Capital OE ligature	N
‘		'	Left single curly quote	N
’		'	Right single curly quote	N
“		"	Left double curly quote	N
”		"	Right double curly quote	N
•		•	Bullet	N
–		–	En dash	N
—		—	Em dash	N
˜		~	Tilde	N
™		™	Trademark	N
š		š	Small s, caron	N
›		>	Greater-than sign	N
œ		œ	Lowercase oe ligature	N
Ÿ		Ÿ	Capital Y, umlaut	N
			Nonbreaking space	4.0
¡	¡	¡	Inverted exclamation mark	4.0
¢	¢	¢	Cent sign	4.0
£	£	£	Pound symbol	4.0
¤	¤	¤	General currency symbol	4.0
¥	¥	¥	Yen symbol	4.0
¦	¦	¦	Broken vertical bar	4.0
§	§	§	Section sign	4.0
¨	¨	¨	Umlaut	4.0
©	©	©	Copyright	4.0
ª	ª	ª	Feminine ordinal	4.0
«	«	«	Left angle quote	4.0
¬	¬	¬	Not sign	4.0
­	­	–	Soft hyphen	4.0
®	®	®	Registered trademark	4.0
¯	¯	¯	Macron accent	4.0
°	°	°	Degree sign	4.0
±	±	±	Plus or minus	4.0
²	²	2	Superscript 2	4.0
³	³	3	Superscript 3	4.0
´	´	´	Acute accent (no letter)	4.0
µ	µ	µ	Micron (Greek mu)	4.0
¶	¶	¶	Paragraph sign	4.0
·	·	·	Middle dot	4.0
¸	¸	¸	Cedilla	4.0
¹	¹	1	Superscript 1	4.0
º	º	º	Masculine ordinal	4.0

Number	Name	Symbol	Description	Version
»	»	»	Right angle quote	4.0
¼	¼	$1/4$	Fraction one-fourth	4.0
½	½	$1/2$	Fraction one-half	4.0
¾	¾	$3/4$	Fraction three-fourths	4.0
¿	¿	¿	Inverted question mark	4.0
À	À	À	Capital A, grave accent	
Á	Á	Á	Capital A, acute accent	
Â	Â	Â	Capital A, circumflex accent	
Ã	Ã	Ã	Capital A, tilde accent	
Ä	Ä	Ä	Capital A, umlaut	
Å	Å	Å	Capital A, ring	
Æ	Æ	Æ	Capital AE ligature	
Ç	Ç	Ç	Capital C, cedilla	
È	È	È	Capital E, grave accent	
É	É	É	Capital E, acute accent	
Ê	Ê	Ê	Capital E, circumflex accent	
Ë	Ë	Ë	Capital E, umlaut	
Ì	Ì	Ì	Capital I, grave accent	
Í	Í	Í	Capital I, acute accent	
Î	Î	Î	Capital I, circumflex accent	
Ï	Ï	Ï	Capital I, umlaut	
Ð	Ð	Ð	Capital eth, Icelandic	
Ñ	Ñ	Ñ	Capital N, tilde	
Ò	Ò	Ò	Capital O, grave accent	
Ó	Ó	Ó	Capital O, acute accent	
Ô	Ô	Ô	Capital O, circumflex accent	
Õ	Õ	Õ	Capital O, tilde accent	
Ö	Ö	Ö	Capital O, umlaut	
×	×	×	Multiplication sign	4.0
Ø	Ø	Ø	Capital O, slash	
Ù	Ù	Ù	Capital U, grave accent	
Ú	Ú	Ú	Capital U, acute accent	
Û	Û	Û	Capital U, circumflex	
Ü	Ü	Ü	Capital U, umlaut	
Ý	Ý	Ý	Capital Y, acute accent	
Þ	Þ	Þ	Capital Thorn, Icelandic	
ß	ß	ß	Small sz ligature, German	
à	à	à	Small a, grave accent	
á	á	á	Small a, acute accent	
â	â	â	Small a, circumflex accent	
ã	ã	ã	Small a, tilde	
ä	ä	ä	Small a, umlaut	
å	å	å	Small a, ring	

Number	Name	Symbol	Description	Version
æ	æ	æ	Small ae ligature	
ç	ç	ç	Small c, cedilla	
è	è	è	Small e, grave accent	
é	é	é	Small e, acute accent	
ê	ê	ê	Small e, circumflex accent	
ë	ë	ë	Small e, umlaut accent	
ì	ì	ì	Small i, grave accent	
í	í	í	Small i, acute accent	
î	î	î	Small i, circumflex accent	
ï	ï	ï	Small i, umlaut	
ð	ð	∂	Small eth, Icelandic	
ñ	ñ	ñ	Small n, tilde	
ò	ò	ò	Small o, grave accent	
ó	ó	ó	Small o, acute accent	
ô	ô	ô	Small o, circumflex accent	
õ	õ	õ	Small o, tilde	
ö	ö	ö	Small o, umlaut	
÷	÷	÷	Division sign	4.0
ø	ø	ø	Small o, slash	
ù	ù	ù	Small u, grave accent	
ú	ú	ú	Small u, acute accent	
û	û	û	Small u, circumflex accent	
ü	ü	ü	Small u, umlaut	
ý	ý	ý	Small y, acute accent	
þ	þ	þ	Small thorn, Icelandic	
ÿ	ÿ	ÿ	Small y, umlaut	

Extended HTML 4.01 Entities

The HTML 4.01 specification introduces a wide variety of new character entities for rendering foreign languages, mathematical material, and other symbols. Their support is limited to the latest browser versions (IE 5.5 and NN 6, although NN4.x supports the Latin Extended-A set).

Latin Extended-A

Number	Name	Symbol	Description	Version
Œ	Œ	Œ	Capital ligature OE	4.0
œ	œ	œ	Small ligature oe	4.0
Š	Š	Š	Capital S, caron	4.0
š	š	š	Small s, caron	4.0
&#376	Ÿ	Ÿ	Capital Y, umlaut	4.0

Latin Extended-B

Number	Name	Symbol	Description	Version
ƒ	ƒ	*f*	Small f with hook	4.0

Spacing Modifier Letters

Number	Name	Symbol	Description	Version
ˆ	ˆ	^	Circumflex accent	4.0
˜	˜	~	Tilde	4.0

Greek

Number	Name	Symbol	Description	Version
Α	Α	A	Greek capital alpha	4.0
Β	Β	B	Greek capital beta	4.0
Γ	Γ	Γ	Greek capital gamma	4.0
Δ	Δ	Δ	Greek capital delta	4.0
Ε	Ε	E	Greek capital epsilon	4.0
Ζ	Ζ	Z	Greek capital zeta	4.0
&#919	Η	H	Greek capital eta	4.0
Θ	Θ	Θ	Greek capital theta	4.0
Ι	Ι	I	Greek capital iota	4.0
Κ	Κ	K	Greek capital kappa	4.0
Λ	Λ	Λ	Greek capital lambda	4.0
Μ	Μ	M	Greek capital mu	4.0
Ν	Ν	N	Greek capital nu	4.0
Ξ	Ξ	Ξ	Greek capital xi	4.0
Ο	Ο	O	Greek capital omicron	4.0
Π	Π	Π	Greek capital pi	4.0
Ρ	Ρ	P	Greek capital rho	4.0
Σ	Σ	Σ	Greek captial sigma	4.0
Τ	Τ	T	Greek capital tau	4.0
Υ	Υ	Y	Greek capital upsilon	4.0
Φ	Φ	Φ	Greek capital phi	4.0
Χ	Χ	X	Greek capital chi	4.0
Ψ	Ψ	Ψ	Greek capital psi	4.0
Ω	Ω	Ω	Greek small omega	4.0
α	α	α	Greek small alpha	4.0
β	β	β	Greek small beta	4.0
γ	γ	γ	Greek small gamma	4.0
δ	δ	δ	Greek small delta	4.0
ε	ε	ε	Greek small epsilon	4.0

Number	Name	Symbol	Description	Version
ζ	ζ	ζ	Greek small zeta	4.0
η	η	η	Greek small eta	4.0
θ	θ	θ	Greek small theta	4.0
ι	ι	ι	Greek small iota	4.0
κ	κ	κ	Greek small kappa	4.0
λ	λ	λ	Greek small lambda	4.0
μ	μ	μ	Greek small mu	4.0
ν	ν	ν	Greek small nu	4.0
ξ	ξ	ξ	Greek small xi	4.0
ο	ο	o	Greek small omicron	4.0
π	π	π	Greek small pi	4.0
ρ	ρ	ρ	Greek small rho	4.0
ς	ς	ς	Greek small letter final sigma	4.0
σ	σ	σ	Greek small sigma	4.0
τ	τ	τ	Greek small tau	4.0
υ	υ	υ	Greek small upsilon	4.0
φ	φ	φ	Greek small phi	4.0
χ	χ	χ	Greek small chi	4.0
ψ	ψ	ψ	Greek small psi	4.0
ω	ω	ω	Greek small omega	4.0
ϑ	ϑ	ϑ	Greek small theta symbol	4.0
ϒ	ϒ	ϒ	Greek upsilon with hook	4.0
ϖ	ϖ	ϖ	Greek pi symbol	4.0

General Punctuation

Number	Name	Symbol	Description	Version
			En space	4.0
			Em space	4.0
			Thin space	4.0
‌	‌	Non-printing	Zero-width non-joiner	4.0
‍	‍	Non-printing	Zero-width joiner	4.0
‎	‎	Non-printing	Left-to-right mark	4.0
‏	‏	Non-printing	Right-to-left mark	4.0
–	–	–	En dash	4.0
—	—	—	Em dash	4.0
‘	‘	'	Left single quotation mark	4.0
’	’	'	Right single quotation mark	4.0
‚	‚	,	Single low-9 quotation mark	4.0

Number	Name	Symbol	Description	Version
“	“	"	Left double quotation mark	4.0
”	”	"	Right double quotation mark	4.0
„	„	„	Double low-9 quotation mark	4.0
†	†	†	Dagger	4.0
‡	‡	‡	Double dagger	4.0
•	•	•	Bullet	4.0
…	&hellep;	…	Ellipses	4.0
‰	‰	‰	Per mille symbol (per thousand)	4.0
′	′	′	Prime, minutes, feet	4.0
″	″	″	Double prime, seconds, inches	4.0
‹	‹	‹	Single left angle quotation (nonstandard)	4.0
›	›	›	Single right angle quotation (nonstandard)	4.0
‾	‾	‾	Overline	4.0
⁄	⁄	/	Fraction slash	4.0
€	€	€	Euro symbol	4.0

Letter-like Symbols

Number	Name	Symbol	Description	Version
℘	℘	℘	Script capital P, power set	4.0
ℑ	ℑ	ℑ	Blackletter capital I, imaginary part	4.0
ℜ	ℜ	ℜ	Blackletter capital R, real part	4.0
™	™	™	Trademark sign	4.0
ℵ	ℵ	ℵ	Alef symbol, or first transfinite cardinal	4.0

Arrows

Number	Name	Symbol	Description	Version
←	←	←	Left arrow	4.0
↑	↑	↑	Up arrow	4.0
→	→	→	Right arrow	4.0
↓	↓	↓	Down arrow	4.0
↔	↔	↔	Left-right arrow	4.0
↵	↵	↵	Down arrow with corner leftwards	4.0
⇐	⇐	⇐	Leftwards double arrow	4.0
⇑	⇑	⇑	Upwards double arrow	4.0
⇒	⇒	⇒	Rightwards double arrow	4.0
⇓	⇓	⇓	Downwards double arrow	4.0
⇔	⇔	⇔	Left-right double arrow	4.0

Mathematical Operators

Number	Name	Symbol	Description	Version
∀	∀	∀	For all	4.0
∂	∂	∂	Partial differential	4.0
∃	∃	∃	There exists	4.0
∅	∅	∅	Empty set, null set, diameter	4.0
∇	∇	∇	Nabla, backward difference	4.0
∈	∈	∈	Element of	4.0
&#8713	∉	∉	Not an element of	4.0
∋	∋	∋	Contains as a member	4.0
∏	∏	∏	N-ary product, product sign	4.0
∑	∑	∑	N-ary summation	4.0
−	−	−	Minus sign	4.0
∗	∗	*	Asterisk operator	4.0
√	√	√	Square root, radical sign	4.0
∝	∝	∝	Proportional	4.0
∞	∞	∞	Infinity symbol	4.0
∠	∠	∠	Angle	4.0
∧	∧	∧	Logical and, wedge	4.0
∨	∨	∨	Logical or, vee	4.0
∩	∩	∩	Intersection, cap	4.0
∪	∪	∪	Union, cup	4.0
∫	∫	∫	Integral	4.0
∴	∴	∴	Therefore	4.0
∼	∼	~	Tilde operator, varies with, similar to	4.0
≅	≅	≅	Approximately equal to	4.0
≈	≈	≈	Almost equal to, asymptotic to	4.0
≠	≠	≠	Not equal to	4.0
≡	≡	≡	Identical to	4.0
≤	≤	≤	Less than or equal to	4.0
≥	≥	≥	Greater than or equal to	4.0
⊂	⊂	⊂	Subset of	4.0
⊃	⊃	⊃	Superset of	4.0
⊄	⊄	⊄	Not a subset of	4.0
⊆	&sube	⊆	Subset of or equal to	4.0
⊇	&supe	⊇	Superset of or equal to	4.0
⊕	⊕	⊕	Circled plus, direct sum	4.0
⊗	⊗	⊗	Circled times, vector product	4.0
⊥	⊥	⊥	Up tack, orthogonal to, perpendicular	4.0
⋅	⋅	·	Dot operator	4.0

Miscellaneous Technical Symbols

Number	Name	Symbol	Description	Version
⌈	⌈	⌈	Left ceiling	4.0
⌉	⌉	⌉	Right ceiling	4.0
⌊	⌊	⌊	Left floor	4.0
⌋	⌋	⌋	Right floor	4.0
〈	⟨	⟨	Left-pointing angle bracket	4.0
〉	⟩	⟩	Right-pointing angle bracket	4.0

Geometric Shapes

Number	Name	Symbol	Description	Version
◊	◊	◊	Lozenge	4.0

Miscellaneous Symbols

Number	Name	Symbol	Description	Version
♠	♠	♠	Black spade suit	4.0
♣	&clubs	♣	Black club suit	4.0
♥	♥	♥	Black heart suit	4.0
♦	&diams	♦	Black diamond suit	4.0

Glossary

μ-*LAW*

(Pronounced "myew-lah") UNIX standard audio file format.

accessibility

Refers to making web pages available and readable to all users, including those with disabilities such as sight or hearing impairments.

AIFF

Audio Interchange File Format. Standard audio format originally developed for the Macintosh, which is now supported on PCs as well. It is one of the formats commonly used for distributing audio on the Web.

alpha channel

In graphics, an extra channel for storing information about an image. The alpha channel works like a mask that applies properties (such as transparency) to the pixels in the image. Other channels typically include color value information—as in the red, green, and blue channels of an RGB image.

alpha-channel transparency

The method of transparency used by 24-bit PNGs, which use an additional (alpha) channel to store variable levels of transparency (up to 256) for each pixel in the image.

animated gif

A GIF89a that contains multiple frames and a "control block" for controlling the animation timing and display.

applet

A self-contained mini-executable program, such as one written in the Java programming language.

ASCII files

Files that are comprised of alphanumeric characters. Some FTP programs refer to ASCII files as "text" files.

ASP

Active Server Pages. The part of Microsoft's Internet Information Server software that allows server-side scripting for the creation of dynamically generated web pages and database functions. Web pages created with ASP commonly have the suffix *.asp*.

audio bit depth

The number of bits used to define the resolution of the amplitude (or volume) of a digital audio waveform—the more bits, the more accurate the rendering of the original audio source and the larger the resulting audio file. Some common bit depths are 8-bit (which sounds thin or tinny, like a telephone signal) and 16-bit, which is required to describe music of CD quality.

AVI

Audio/Video Interleaved. A digital video format developed by Microsoft in which audio and video information are interleaved in every frame for smoother playback.

binary files

Files made up of compiled data (ones and zeros), such as executable programs, graphic images, movies, etc. Some programs refer to the binary mode as "raw data" or "image data."

CGI

Common Gateway Interface. The mechanism for communication between the web server and other programs (CGI scripts) running on the server.

character entities

Strings of characters used to specify characters not found in the normal alphanumeric character set in HTML documents.

character set

An organization of characters—units of a written language system—in which each character is assigned a specific number.

client

A software application that extracts services from a server somewhere on the network. A web browser is a client that renders and displays documents on remote servers.

CLUT

Color Look Up Table. A list of colors and associated index numbers used to render eight-bit images.

CMYK

Cyan-Magenta-Yellow-Black. The four ink colors used in process printing. Not appropriate for generating web graphics. (RGB is the color mode for web graphics.)

codec

Compression/decompression algorithms applied to media files.

CSS

Cascading Style Sheets. An addition to HMTL for controlling presentation of a document, including color, typography, alignment of text and images, etc.

CSS-P

CSS with positioning. Refers to a proposal for adding positioning capabilities with style sheets. The CSS-P proposal has since been rolled into the CSS2 Specification.

data fork

The portion of a Macintosh file that contains the actual data of the document. See also *resource fork*.

data rate

In video, the rate at which data must be transferred in order for the video to play smoothly without interruption. The data rate (also called "bit rate") for a movie is measured in kilobytes per second (K/s or KB/s). It can be calculated by dividing the size of the file (in K) by the length of the movie (in seconds).

deprecated

In the HTML 4.0 Specification, a label identifying an HTML tag or attribute as "outdated" and discouraged from use in favor of newer constructs (often style sheet controls).

DHTML

Dynamic HTML. An integration of JavaScript, Cascading Style Sheets, and the Document Object Model. With DHTML, content can move across the screen or respond to user inputs.

dithering

The approximation of a color by mixing pixels of similar colors that are available in the image palette. The result of dithering is a random dot pattern or noise in the image.

Document Object Model (DOM)

The browser's internal hierarchical organization of the elements in a document. The existence of a DOM makes page elements available for manipulation via scripting or style sheets. Netscape Navigator's and Microsoft Internet Explorer's DOMs differ significantly.

dpi

Dots per inch. In graphics, this is the measurement of the resolution of a printed image. It is commonly (although incorrectly) used to refer to the screen resolution of web graphics, which is technically measured in ppi (pixels per inch). See also *ppi*.

DTD

Document Type Definition. A file associated with an SGML or XML document that defines how the tags should be interpreted and displayed by the application reading the document.

encoding

The process of converting an analog source (such as an analog audio signal) into digital format. An encoder is the software that does the converting.

frame rate

In video, frames per second; used as a measure of video quality.

FTP

File Transfer Protocol. A protocol for moving files over the Internet from one computer to another. FTP is a client/server system: one machine must be running an FTP server, the other an FTP client.

gamma

Refers to the overall brightness of a computer monitor's display. In technical terms, it is a numerical adjustment for the nonlinear relationship of voltage to light intensity.

GIF

Graphic Interchange Format. Common file format of web graphic images. GIF is a palette-based, 8-bit format that compresses images with the lossless LZW compression scheme. GIF is most appropriate for images with areas of flat color and sharp contrast. See also *LZW compression.*

HDML

Handheld Device Markup Language. A specialized set of HTML tags for creating documents to be displayed on handheld devices such as mobile phones. It has been replaced by WML. See also *WML.*

hexadecimal

A base-16 numbering system consisting of the characters 0, 1, 2, 3, 4, 5, 6, 7, 8, 9, A, B, C, D, E, and F, where A through F represent the decimal values 10 through 15. It is used in HTML for specifying RGB color values.

HTML

Hypertext Markup Language. The format of web documents.

HTTP

Hypertext Transfer Protocol. The protocol that defines how web pages and media are requested and transferred between servers and browsers.

i18n

The W3C abbreviation for "Internationalization" ("i", 18 letters, then "n"), relating to efforts to make the Web accessible in all languages.

imagemap

A single image that contains multiple hypertext links.

indexed color

In graphics, a system for rendering colors in 8-bit images. Indexed color files, such as GIFs, contain an index (also called a palette or color lookup table) of colors and associated index numbers, which is used to render color in the image.

Java

A cross-platform, object-oriented programming language developed by Sun Microsystems. It can be used to create whole applications; however, its primary contribution to the Web has been in the form of Java applets, self-contained, mini-executable programs.

JavaScript

A client-side scripting language developed by Netscape that adds interactivity and conditional behavior to web pages. It has little in common with Java.

JPEG

A lossy compression algorithm developed by the Joint Photographic Experts Group. It is used by files in the JFIF format, which are commonly referred to as "JPEG files." JPEG is most efficient at compressing images with gradations in tone and no sharp edge contrasts. Photographic images are typically best saved in JPEG format.

key frames

In video, master frames placed throughout a video against which the following frames are compared (for use with temporal, or interframe, compression).

Linux

A version of Unix designed to run on PCs.

lossy compression

A method for reducing file size in which some data (usually indiscernible to human perception) is deleted in order to achieve a higher compression rate.

lossless compression

A method for reducing the size of a file without loss of data; in lossless compression, redundant information is removed.

LZW compression

Short for Lempel-Zev-Welch, the names of the inventors. A lossless compression scheme that takes advantage of repetition in data streams (such as a row of pixels of identical color). It is the compression scheme used by graphic files in the GIF format.

MathML

Math Markup Language. An XML application for describing mathematical notation and capturing its structure and content.

MIDI

Musical Instrument Digital Interface. This audio format uses numerical commands to describe the pitch and endurance of notes that are "played" by available digital instrument sounds.

MIME types

Multimedia Internet Mail Extensions. A protocol that defines a number of content types and subtypes and allows programs like web browsers, newsreaders, and email clients to recognize different kinds of files and deal with them appropriately. The MIME type specifies what media a file is, such as an image, audio, or video, and the subtype identifies the precise file format.

MP3

Audio file format (MPEG I, Level-III) capable of high levels of compression with little discernible loss of quality. It has become the standard for sharing audio files over the Internet.

MPEG

A family of multimedia standards created by the Motion Picture Experts Group, commonly used to refer to audio and video files saved using one of the MPEG compression schemes.

namespace

A uniquely named group of element and attribute names. XML documents refer to namespaces in order to prevent confusion between competing DTD tag names.

palette

A table in an 8-bit indexed color file (such as GIF) that provides color information for the pixels in the image. See also *CLUT.*

PDF

Portable Document Format. A file format developed by Adobe Systems used for capturing formatted page layouts for distribution. PDF documents, when viewed with the required Adobe Acrobat Reader, will appear exactly as they were intended.

PHP

Hypertext Preprocessor. An open source, server-side tool for creating dynamically generated web pages (similar to Microsoft's ASP).

PNG

Portable Network Format. A versatile graphics file format that features support for both 8-bit (PNG8) indexed images and 24-bit images (PNG24). PNGs also feature variable transparency levels, automatic color correction controls, and a lossless yet highly efficient compression scheme.

ppi

Pixels per inch. The measurement of the resolution of a screen image.

QuickTime

A system extension that makes it possible to view audio and video information on a computer. It was originally developed for the Macintosh but is now available for Windows machines as well, and has been adopted as the video standard by the ISO in their development of MPEG-4. The term also refers to the file format.

RDF

Resource Description Framework. An XML application used to define the structure of metadata for documents, i.e., data that is useful for indexing, navigating, and searching a site.

RMF

Rich Music Format. A proprietary audio format used by the Beatnik system.

resource fork

Extra code added in the Macintosh file format, used for storing icons, previews, and file type information. This information should be stripped out when sending the file to a non-Macintosh server. See also *data fork.*

RGB color

A color system that describes colors based on combinations of red, green, and blue light.

rollover

The act of passing the mouse pointer over an element's space, or the events triggered by that action (such as a changing graphic or pop-up message, sometimes called rollover events).

sampling rate

In a digital audio file, the number of samples taken per second.

server

A networked computer that provides some kind of service or information.

Server Side Includes (SSI)

Special placeholders in an HTML document that the server is to replace with actual data just before sending the final document to the browser. Extended SSI (XSSI) (part of Apache 1.2 and higher) provides more advanced command functions, including conditional behaviors.

SGML

Standard Generalized Markup Language. A metalanguage that provides a comprehensive set of syntax rules for marking up the structure of documents and data. HTML is a subset of SGML.

Shockwave

Proprietary technology from Macromedia, Inc., for the web delivery of multimedia content.

SMIL

Synchronized Multimedia Integration Language, an XML-based language for creating multimedia, time-based presentation. SMIL combines audio, video, text, animation, and graphics in a precise, synchronized fashion.

spatial compression

In video, spatial compression is applied to each individual frame of the video, using compression schemes commonly used on still images (also called "intraframe" compression).

spatial frequency

Refers to the concentration of detail in an image. For example, an image of a blue sky would be considered to have low frequency. A detailed image, such as a close-up of blades of grass, has high frequency.

SVG

Standardized Vector Graphics. A language for defining two-dimensional vector graphics in XML.

telnet

An internet protocol for logging into and using a remote system on the Internet. Telnet is a client/server system that requires a telnet server running on one computer and a telnet client on the other.

temporal compression

In video, temporal compression takes place over a series of frames, deleting information that is repeated between frames (also called "interframe" compression).

Unix

A multiuser, multitasking operating system developed by Bell Laboratories. It also provides programs for editing text, sending email, preparing tables, performing calculations, and many other specialized functions that normally require separate applications programs.

Glossary

valid code

In an XML application, code that properly uses the elements and attributes as specified in a Document Type Definition (DTD).

W3C

The World Wide Web Consortium. A consortium of many companies and organizations that "exists to develop common standards for the evolution of the World Wide Web." It is run by a joint effort between the Laboratory for Computer Science at the Massachusetts Institute of Technology and CERN, the European Particle Physics Laboratory, where the WWW was first developed.

WAI

Web Accessibility Initiative. The committee at the World Wide Web Consortium (W3C) that ensures that web technologies are accessible to users with disabilities.

WAP

Wireless Application Protocol. A collection of standards and specifications for delivering Internet-like information to wireless devices such as mobile phones, pagers, PDAs, etc.

WAVE

Waveform Audio File Format. This format was developed for the PC but is now supported on Macintosh as well.

Web Palette

The set of 216 colors that will not dither or shift when viewed with browsers on 8-bit monitors.

well-formed code

Code that abides by the strict syntax rules of XML.

WML

Wireless Markup Language. An XML-based language for creating applications for wireless devices. It is part of the Wireless Application Protocol (WAP).

XHTML

A reworking of the HTML 4.0 Specification to abide by the rules and syntax of XML.

XML

Extensible Markup Language. A new standard for marking up documents and data. XML is based on SGML, but with a reduced feature set that is more appropriate for distribution via the Web. XML allows authors to create customized tag sets to provide functionality not available with HTML.

XSL

Extensible Style Language. A system for controlling the presentation of complex XML documents and structured data.

XSSI

Extended SSI. See *Server Side Includes.*

Index

We'd like to hear your suggestions for improving our indexes. Send email to *index@oreilly.com*.

applets on web pages, 52, 185–188
applications (XML), 499
archive attribute, 544
<area> tag, 95, 147, 154–160, 536
   image maps and, 173
ASCII mode, transferring files, 57
.asf (Windows Media) files, 420, 427
ASP (Active Server Pages), 52
asterisk (*) for relative frameset sizes, 238
at-rules (CSS2), 323
attributes, 95, 543–557
   bulleted lists, 134
   deprecated, 559–561
   <div> and <span> tags, 130
   <embed> tag, 442
   fonts, 131
   <frame> tag, 231
   href (see href attribute)
   id and name, 509
   <img> tag, 165, 167
   ordered (numbered) lists, 135
   SMIL, 455, 457
   <table> tag, 191
   text elements, centering with, 140
   WML, 523–532
   XHTML quoted values, 507
audio, 401–421
   adding to HTML documents, 401–421
   background, 418
   choosing formats for, 417
   encoding, 402
   Flash files and, 435
   optimizing for download, 406
   providing transcripts/descriptions, 77
   tools, 405
   (see also accessibility)
aural media type, connecting style sheets
     and HTML, 66
author value (<meta name>), 114
authoring tools, 13
Auto option (FTP utilities), 58
automatic list numbering in CSS2 for
     multilingualism, 86
autoplay attribute (<embed>), 432
AVI (.avi) file format, 428
axis attribute (<td> and <th>), 196, 545

B

<b> (bold) tag, 96, 118, 129, 536
   WML, 524
background
   audio, 418
   colors, 313
      Flash movies, 443
      GIF animation, 396
      tables, 209

images/patterns, 313
   positioning and scrolling, 314
   tiling, 110
style sheet properties, 313
background-attachment property
     (CSS), 314
background attribute, 545
   <body> tag, 104, 110
   <table> tag, 192
   <td> and <th> tags, 194
   <tr> tag, 197
background-color property (CSS), 313
background-image property (CSS), 313
background-position property (CSS), 314
background property (CSS), 314
background-repeat property (CSS), 313
Bare Bones Software, Inc., 100
base attribute (<embed>), 443
<base> tag, 95, 103, 108, 536
   framed documents and, 243
<basefont> tag, 95, 117, 536
baseline height, text, 304
baseline value
   align, 176
   valign, 207, 218
BBEdit (Bare Bones Software, Inc.) HTML
     editor, 100
<bdo> tag, 85, 536
Beatnik, using .rmf files, 416
behavior attribute (<marquee>), 169
bgcolor attribute, 545
   <body> tag, 104, 109
   <embed> tag, 443
   <marquee> tag, 169
   <table> tag, 192, 209, 222
   <td> and <th> tags, 195, 209
   <tr> tag, 197, 209
bgproperties attribute (<body>), 104
<bgsound> tag, 418, 536
Bias (Peak), 405
bi-directional override, 85
<big> tag, 119, 129, 536
   WML, 524
binary mode, transferring files, 57
   WAP, 511
bit depth, 352
   audio files, 402, 406
   GIF files, 342
      animation, 395
   JPEG images, 356
   PNG images, 368
   video clips, 423
Bitstream (font designers), 36
black and white, designing for, 27
   (see also grayscale)
_blank target (<a>), 154, 243

C

caching images, 179

capitalization and small caps in style sheets, 302, 306

<caption> tags, 189, 199, 293, 537

captions for graphics, 77

cards (WML element), 517, 525

cascading style sheets (CSS), 289–326
  accessibility features (CSS2), 78
  conflict resolution, 295
  CSS2 features, 320–324
    at-rules, 323
  fixed page width, 24
  language features for, 86
  positioning with, 307–312, 316–320
  for printouts, 65–68
  properties, 292, 301–316
    background, 313
    box properties, 307–312
    classification, 315
    CSS2, 322
    type-related, 301–307
  selectors, 292, 296–299, 321
  values for rules, 292, 299–301
  XML and, 494
  XSL vs., 501

case-sensitivity
  of HTML, 94
  of XML and XHTML, 506

C/C++ language for CGI scripting, 275

cellpadding attribute (<table>), 192, 208, 212, 545

cells (tables), 194, 199–200
  aligning text in, 206
  collapsing in Netscape Navigator, 214
  coloring, 209
  controlling, 200
  fonts, 218
  size of, 208
  (see also tables)

cellspacing attribute (<table>), 192, 208, 212

cellular telephones, 28

<center> tag, 123, 140, 537

CERN servers, 50

cgi attribute (exec command), 333

CGI (Common Gateway Interface) scripts, 51, 275–279
  environment variables for, 336
  server-side imagemaps, 154, 158
  (see also forms)

cgi-bin directory, 52

changePages( ) (JavaScript example), 248

channels, audio, 403, 406

char attribute, 545
  <col> tag, 190

<colgroup> tag, 191

<tbody> tag, 194, 196

character entities, 508
  references, 144
  XML, 496

character sets
  internationalization and, 81–83
  specifying character encoding, 83

charoff attribute, 545
  <col> tag, 190
  <colgroup> tag, 191
  <tbody> tag, 194, 196

charset attribute, 545
  <a> tag, 146

checkboxes on forms, 255, 264

checked attribute, 545
  <input type=checkbox> tag, 255
  <input type=radio> tag, 257

Chemical Markup Language (CML), 501

Cinepak codec (Radius), 424

circle attribute, 134

cite attribute, 545

<cite> (citation) tag, 119, 129, 537

class attribute, 130, 298, 535, 546

.class files, 186

CLASS selectors (style sheets), 298

classid attribute, 170, 444, 546

classification style sheet properties, 315

clear attribute (<br>), 178, 546

clear property (CSS), 312

clickable imagemaps, 147, 154–160, 173
  multipart images in tables, 226
  text alternatives for, 77, 160

client-pull, meta tags for, 112

clients, defined, 49
  (see also browsers)

client-side imagemaps, 147, 154, 156–158, 173
  multipart images in tables, 226
  text alternatives, 77, 160

CLUTs (color look-up tables), 42, 381

cmd attribute (exec command), 333

CML (Chemical Markup Language), 501

CMYK mode, 46

code attribute, 546
  <applet> tag, 165, 188
  <embed> tag, 166

<code> tag, 119, 129, 537

codebase attribute, 546
  <applet> tag, 165, 188
  <embed> tag, 166
  <object> tag, 170, 183, 444

codecs, video, 424

codetype attribute (<object>), 170

<col> tag, 95, 190, 202, 537

<colgroup> tag, 191, 202, 537

spatial frequency, image, 357
spatial (intraframe) compression, 424
speech displays (see accessibility)
speed
    audio sampling rate, 402, 406
    GIF animation, 392
    video data/frame rates, 423
    (see also performance)
square attribute, 134
src attribute, 554
    <embed> tag, 166, 184, 431
    <frame> tag, 232, 243
    <iframe> tag, 234
    <img> tag, 168, 174
    <input type=image> tag, 256, 266
SSI (Server Side Includes), 327–336
    commands for, 329
    environment variables, 331, 335
    extended (XSSI), 331
    servers and, 329
stacking order, 319
Stage in Flash, 439
standalone tags, 95
Standard Generalized Markup Language
        (SGML), 92, 493
standards for the Internet, 15
standby attribute (<object>), 171, 555
start attribute, 135, 555
    for <img> tag, 169, 433
static positioning, 319
statistics, for browser usage, 7
status bar text, 153
Steinberg, 405
streaming
    audio, 407–416
    video, 430
strict document type declaration, 107
<strike> tag, 122, 130, 541
strike-through, 305
    <s> tag, 121, 540
<strong> tag, 122, 129, 541
    WML, 530
structural HTML tags, 103–114
    misusing, 77
style attribute, 293, 535, 555
style sheets, 289–326
    accessibility features (CSS2), 78
    conflict resolution, 295
    CSS2 features, 320–324
    fixed page width, 24
    link color specifications, 152
    positioning with, 307–312, 316–320
    properties, 292, 301–316
        background, 313
        box, 307–312
        classification, 315
        CSS2, 322

type-related, 301–307
selectors, 292, 296–299, 321
values for rules, 292, 299–301
XML and, 494
XSL vs., 501
<style> tag, 109, 293, 541
    @import function, 295
    style sheets, connecting, 66
<sub> (subscript) tag, 122
submit buttons on forms, 258, 265
subwindows (see frames)
suffixes, filename, 56, 59
summary attribute, 555
    <table> tag, 193
<sub> (subscript) tag, 130, 541
<sup> (superscript) tag, 122, 130, 541
swatches (Photoshop), 42
.swf files (Flash movies), 73, 434, 438
<switch> element, 457
swLiveConnect attribute, 443
.swt files, creating Generator
        templates, 438
Synchronized Multimedia Integration
        Language (see SMIL)
syntax of HTML tags, 95
    style, guidelines for, 98
Syntrillium, 405
System Palette, 38, 383
    for GIF animation, 395

T

tabindex attribute, 146, 270, 555
<table> tag, 191–193, 199, 541
    forms alignment with, 273
    WML, 531
tables, 22, 189–230
    accessibility issues, 78
    deleting whitespace in, 212–214
    fonts and, 218
    formatting appearance, 204–210
    forms
        aligning, 273
        elements in, 211
    multipart images in, 198, 225–230
    sizing, 207, 223
    structure of, 199–203
    templates for, 220–225
    text styles in, 210
    tips and tricks, 218–219
    troubleshooting, 210–218
    ways to use, 198–199
    WML, 520
tags (HTML), 91, 94–96, 535–542
    containers, 94
    deprecated, 558–561
    indents in text, creating with, 142
    lists, 124–126

About the Author

Jennifer Niederst was one of the first designers for the Web. As the designer of O'Reilly's Global Network Navigator (GNN), the first commercial web site, she has been designing for the Web since 1993. Since then, she has been working almost exclusively on the Web, first as Creative Director of Songline Studios (a subsidiary of O'Reilly) where she designed the original interface for WebReview (*webreview.com*) and as a freelance designer and consultant since 1996. In addition to this Nutshell book, Jennifer has also written *Learning Web Design* (O'Reilly, 2001) and *HTML Pocket Reference* (O'Reilly, 1999). She has taught Web design at the Massachusetts College of Art and the Interactive Factory in Boston, MA, and has spoken at major design and Internet events including the GRAFILL conference (Geilo, Norway), Seybold Seminars, South by Southwest (SXSW) Interactive, and the W3C International Expo. In addition to designing, Jennifer enjoys cooking, travel, indie-rock, and making stuff. You can visit her site at *http://www.littlechair.com/.*

Colophon

Our look is the result of reader comments, our own experimentation, and feedback from distribution channels. Distinctive covers complement our distinctive approach to technical topics, breathing personality and life into potentially dry subjects.

The animal appearing on the cover of *Web Design in a Nutshell* is a least weasel (*Mustela nivalis*). There are 67 species of weasel, including the mink, ermine, ferret, otter, and skunk. Weasels, who are characterized by long, slender bodies and short legs, are found on all continents except Antarctica and Australia, and in a vast variety of habitats.

The least weasel is the smallest of the 67 species of weasel. Weighing in at approximately two ounces and measuring less than ten inches long, the least weasel is the smallest carnivore on Earth. They are found throughout the world, in northern climates. In warm weather this weasel's coat is brown, with a white underside. In winter it turns completely white. Thanks to its camouflage abilities and its speed and agility, the least weasel is rarely caught.

The diet of the least weasel is made up primarily of voles and mice, which, because of the weasels' high metabolism, they hunt constantly. One family of these little weasels can consume thousands of rodents each year, making them important in controlling pest populations. Because it is so small, the least weasel can follow mice into their burrows and eat them there. Like other weasels, they will occasionally then make their victim's home their own, lining it with the fur of the former resident when preparing to nest. Least weasels can produce two litters a year, with three to five young per litter.

Emily Quill was the production editor, and Leanne Soylemez was the copyeditor for *Web Design in a Nutshell, Second Edition.* Ellie Cutler and Jane Ellin provided quality control. Joe Wizda wrote the index.

Edie Freedman designed the cover of this book, using an original illustration by Lorrie LeJeune. Emma Colby produced the cover layout with QuarkXPress 4.1 using Adobe's ITC Garamond font.

Melanie Wang designed the interior layout based on a series design by Nancy Priest. Anne-Marie Vaduva implemented the design in FrameMaker 5.5.6 using tools created by Mike Sierra. The text and heading fonts are ITC Garamond Light and Garamond Book. The illustrations that appear in the book were produced by Robert Romano and Jessamyn Read using Macromedia FreeHand 9 and Adobe Photoshop 6. This colophon was written by Clairemarie Fisher O'Leary.

Whenever possible, our books use a durable and flexible lay-flat binding. If the page count exceeds this binding's limit, perfect binding is used.